PRAISE FOR

WESTWARD I GO FREE

Anyone interested in Henry David Thoreau, and especially those of us who mourn for the book he might have written about his late-in-life journey to the Midwest, will be grateful for *Westward I Go Free*. Meticulously researched, brimming with energy and wit, it admirably fills an omission that previous biographies have been content to skip over.

> — Jerry Dennis, author of
> *The Living Great Lakes: Searching for the Heart of the Inland Seas*

Since Thoreau never wrote or lectured about the many wonderful people and scenes he encountered, this excursion's exposure has been limited for a century and a half. Now scholar Corinne H. Smith has illuminated his 'Journey West.' In her superbly written and researched book, she takes us to the places where Thoreau went and describes them, then and now. In addition, she enriches each segment of their trip with her own 'Thoreauvian adventure,' which reveals fascinating connections with Thoreau and others. ... Corinne Smith's insightful, moving, and inspiring account of Thoreau's 'Journey West' is a great pleasure to read and a most significant contribution to our understanding of the author of *Walden*.

> — J. Parker Huber, author of
> *A Wanderer All My Days: John Muir in New England*

Tracing Henry David Thoreau's longest, last, and least-known journey from his home in Concord, Massachusetts to Minnesota, Corinne H. Smith has woven a complex tapestry of history, biography and acute observation that would delight the sage of Walden Pond. In joining Thoreau's 1861 trip to her contemporary travels on the same route, Smith becomes a true 'deep traveler:' not a tourist merely, but an explorer. Along the way, readers will not only get to know Thoreau and his young companion, Horace Mann, but such diverse characters as U.S. Grant, John Muir, Frank Lloyd Wright and a 20th-century Canadian artist bearing the first name Thoreau. ... Packed with facts and astute perceptions, this is a book Thoreau would have eagerly devoured.

> —David K. Leff, author of
> *Deep Travel: In Thoreau's Wake on the Concord and Merrimack*

WESTWARD I GO FREE:

TRACING THOREAU'S LAST JOURNEY

"The most innovative titles and imaginative ideas being published about Thoreau and his influences and contemporaries."

GREEN FRIGATE BOOKS PRESENTS:

—*The Modern Concord Colloquium*—

Profitably Soaked: Thoreau's Engagement with Water—Robert L. France

Uncommon Cents: Thoreau and the Nature of Business—Robert M. Abbott

A Wanderer All My Days: John Muir in New England—J. Parker Huber

Westward I Go Free: Tracing Thoreau's Last Journey—Corinne Hosfeld Smith

Thoreau And The Aquatic Cats of Concord: A Love Story—Mina M. Chat

Deep Immersion: The Experience of Water—Robert L. France

WESTWARD I GO FREE:

TRACING THOREAU'S LAST JOURNEY

CORINNE HOSFELD SMITH

with a foreword by
LAURA DASSOW WALLS

GREEN FRIGATE BOOKS
WINNIPEG MANITOBA
SHEFFIELD, VERMONT
2012

ISBN 978-1-927043-30-1

Library of Congress Control Number: 2012936615

Westward I Go Free: Tracing Thoreau's Last Journey
Corinne Hosfeld Smith

First Edition
Copyright 2012 Corinne Hosfeld Smith

A Flâneur/Peripatetic Production

Green Frigate Books
www.greenfrigatebooks.com
Winnipeg, Manitoba and Sheffield, Vermont

Distributed by River North Editions (Independent Publishers Group)

1. Biography   2. Nature

Portions of this text appeared in two previously published articles:

"What a Difference a Year Can Make: Henry David Thoreau and the Grand Pleasure Excursion of 1861." *Minnesota's Heritage #4, July 2011*, pp.76-89.

"To Be or Not to Be ... Henry." *Thoreau Society Bulletin #272, Fall 2010*.

Printed in Canada
Printing this book on recycled paper saved: 365 trees, 156,419 gallons of water, 62,932 kwh electricity, 17,209 lbs solid waste and 33,547 lbs of greenhouse gasses.

For Ed.

Eastward I go only by force; but **westward I go free**. Thither no business leads me. It is hard for me to believe that I shall find fair landscapes or sufficient wildness and freedom behind the eastern horizon. I am not excited by the prospect of a walk thither; but I believe that the forest which I see in the western horizon stretches uninterruptedly toward the setting sun, and there are no towns nor cities in it of enough consequence to disturb me. Let me live where I will, on this side is the city, on that the wilderness, and ever I am leaving the city more and more, and withdrawing into the wilderness. I should not lay so much stress on this fact, if I did not believe that something like this is the prevailing tendency of my countrymen. I must walk toward Oregon, and not toward Europe. And that way the nation is moving, and I may say that mankind progress from east to west. ... We go eastward to realize history and study the works of art and literature, retracing the steps of the race; we go westward as into the future, with a spirit of enterprise and adventure.

—Henry David Thoreau, *Walking*

CONTENTS

NOTE FROM THE PUBLISHER

Green Frigate Books derives its very name and company motto from an Emily Dickinson quotation linking landscapes of external travel to mindscapes of internal contemplation. Our new scholarly series Flâneur/Peripatetic Productions is designed to particularly explore the realms of deep travel through the disciplines of literary criticism, biography, history, psychogeography, and ecopsychology.

ABOUT THE AUTHOR

Corinne Hosfeld Smith has been a librarian for more than thirty years. Today she serves on the staff of the Mondor-Eagen Library at Anna Maria College, Paxton, Massachusetts. Throughout her life, she has written personal essays and poetry and her book reviews have appeared in the *Historical Journal of Massachusetts, Library Media Connection, Library Journal, The Book Report, The Video Rating Guide for Libraries*, on Rambles.net, and on Amazon.com, where she is a top ranked reviewer. She became a Thoreau fan after reading "Civil Disobedience" and *Walden* in high school in the 1970s. A native of Lancaster, Pennsylvania, Corinne now lives an hour west of Walden Pond. *Westward I Go Free* is her first published book.

FOREWORD

Laura Dassow Walls

One of the challenges in telling the story of Thoreau's life is knowing how to end it. After the double climax of the years spent living at Walden Pond, followed by the years spent writing *Walden*, there seems a certain falling off. Of course even after *Walden* was published in 1854, Thoreau's days continued to be full of incident: daily walks, excursions to Maine and to Cape Cod, meetings with Walt Whitman and John Brown, lectures which were germinating into such rich and ripened essays as "Wild Apples" and "Autumnal Tints." But as his friend Emerson wrote in his essay "Experience," "The years teach much which the days never know." As Thoreau's post-*Walden* days were accumulating into years, just what were those years teaching? Who was Thoreau becoming? What was his next great project, his second great act? We will never know, for the New England scourge of tuberculosis caught up with him before the seeds of his days could flower and mature into the fruits of the years. Thoreau died at 44, barely into middle age.

As Corinne Hosfeld Smith tells us, in the spring of 1861, when faced with the chance to travel and the likelihood that this excursion would be his last, Thoreau's choice was to travel west and see for himself the storied lands of the upper Mississippi. In a way, this apparent departure was really a return to Thoreau's most productive roots: he had grown up in a family that loved to take long walks into the country, and he had begun his first published essay, "Natural History of Massachusetts," by extolling the health to be found in nature. To find that health meant venturing out-of-doors to learn what was in the wind, "what is transpiring from summer to winter in the Carolinas, and the Great Pine Forest, and the Valley of the Mohawk" (*Excursions* 4). From then on, the excursion became his favorite literary form, and the more Thoreau read in the literature of exploration, the more he found his own distinctive voice. Walking became a form of thinking, which took shape as writing—he once remarked that the length of his walks marked the length of his journal entries—and in his second essay, "A Walk to Wachusett," he wrote that "The landscape lies far and fair within, and the deepest thinker is the farthest travelled" (31).

Travelling far, but then returning: the excursion is a literary form that moves in circles, using the near to understand the far, and the far to unsettle the familiar. The traveler, for Thoreau, comes home again, bearing the

gift of renewal. Each day's walk thus became a pocket epic, a Homeric journey, Odysseus encountering wonders abroad and returning to weave them
into stories told to family and friends around the hearth. Or a day's walk
became a scientific expedition: as Thoreau's own knowledge of natural science grew, he was drawn to the narratives of explorers such as Charles
Darwin and Alexander von Humboldt, for whom the least detail of the
places they visited spoke of nature's great global patterns. Thoreau chal-
lenged himself to become the traveler who never left home, the dweller in
perpetual motion who saw each familiar thing with the acute senses and
global wisdom of the scientist abroad. Thus in his daily walks and boating
jaunts he "travelled a good deal in Concord," as he joked in *Walden(4)*, but
to further unsettle the familiar sights of home, he also took off to farther
places: up the Concord and Merrimack Rivers with his brother John; to the
Maine woods, where he encountered a wildness so deep and arresting that
thereafter even his own body seemed strange; to Cape Cod's bleak broad
sandy beaches, where the relentless waves convinced him that the ocean was
a wilderness that reached even into the heart of the city; to French Canada,
where he struggled with strange customs and a language he could barely
speak, moving him to think about the way different nations name a nature
that becomes itself different in the naming. Each of these excursions
became an essay or a book: *A Week on the Concord and Merrimack Rivers; The
Maine Woods; Cape Cod;* "A Yankee in Canada." Even *Walden* was written as
an excursion to a new and foreign realm just a mile away—no more, but no
less—from home and neighbors.

In his essay "Walking," Thoreau meditates not on any one excursion, but
on the form itself: walking becomes the path to find the "wild," both within and without, and the way to restore oneself and one's world to health: "in
Wildness," he famously wrote, "is the preservation of the world" (*Excursions*
202). Here he aligns walking as a philosophy of living with the compass
points of the planet, and his compass always pointed west. As early as
March 1838, just after graduating from Harvard, he had proposed to his
brother John that they decamp "for the West" and seek their fortunes: "Go
I must at all events. . . . It is high season to start. The canals are now open,
and travelling comparatively cheap. . . . There's nothing like trying"
(*Correspondence* 24). John's poor health frustrated this resolution, but four
years later, after John's death, the western wanderlust was still there: Henry
ventured with another walking companion, Margaret Fuller's brother
Richard, "to scale the blue wall which bound the *western* horizon," and walk
to the top of Wachusett (31). The impulse becomes generalized in

"Walking," where Thoreau tells us that the proper direction for the kind of walking he desires is never eastward to Boston or Europe, but westward to Oregon: "I must walk toward Oregon, and not toward Europe. And that way the nation is moving, and I may say that mankind progress from east to west" (196).

It sounds as though Thoreau is echoing the words of his friend Horace Greeley, who had famously advised ambitious young New Englanders to "Go West": but he actually resisted Greeley's advice. The mature Thoreau wanted an *excursion*, rather than a migration. As a spiritual exercise, walking "west" could be done from any place on the globe, perhaps particularly from "the east": westering was a state of mind, not simply a place to go. So all his life he kept his base camp home in Concord—but it speaks volumes that when he did realize how little time he had left, he finally took the journey he'd been preparing for all his life, his journey west. Perhaps it would save him—after all, while the cure for tuberculosis was unknown, the treatment was vigorous outdoor exercise and a change of scene, and he had always prescribed a good outdoor jaunt as the best way to restore one's mental and physical health. He couldn't have been certain, when he started out, of what we know, that this journey would be his last. In a very real sense he would never have the chance to complete it: he came home to Concord, to be sure, but what his last excursion meant, what he learned and thought and saw, and what he would have said to those gathered around the hearth to hear about it—all that remained unsaid. Every other journey had been completed at home, by the act of writing, as he expanded his spare field notes into far-reaching, searching prose. But this journey, which should have been the most important of all, was arrested mid-flight by mortality. In a very real sense Thoreau the writer is still travelling west, for while he may have returned bodily to Concord, to settle his affairs and meet his fate, his writerly self never made it home: in spirit he is journeying westward still.

As Corinne H. Smith shows, the ironies of Thoreau's journey west were many: First and most pressing was the historical accident that a journey taken to connect east and west should involve him so utterly in the war that was dividing north and south. Everywhere he and Horace Mann travelled they saw reminders—soldiers mustering, factories firing up, headlines haunting the newspapers and even deflecting them northward on their return. The Civil War followed them even into Canada, where they discovered that Canadians, fearing that the War between the States would escalate into a war between the nations, were arming against an invasion from the south. Second was the tragic fact, visible only in retrospect, that a journey taken to restore Thoreau's health ended instead with his turn toward death, and a journey that helped launch the career of his traveling companion Horace Mann—on track to become one of the nation's most notable natural scientists—may have contributed to his own tragically early death. Third is the sad realization that this was, in fact, the journey that should have ignited Thoreau's second act. It should have given us, as Ms. Smith says, his *magnum opus*, a book worthy to stand beside *Walden*. Furthermore, this was a book that we needed to have—one to balance *Walden*'s inner circle of meditation and self-making with what Smith calls the "great circle" of exploration and nation-making.

All biographies of Thoreau must somehow face the deep disappointment that his career was cut off in mid-flight. His journey to Minnesota becomes a sort of scapegoat: at best a drain on his uncertain health and a distraction from his proper work, and at worst, perhaps the final blow. Perhaps if he had rested at home instead of exhausting himself abroad, he would have recovered. On top of the fear that this journey may have hastened Thoreau's death is that bitter postscript that it may also have cut off the life of Horace Mann. Thus biographers have read into this journey their own sorrow: Walter Harding gives it just a few paragraphs and ends by calling it "a tragic failure" that left Thoreau more ill than when he left home. The traveling Thoreau's natural history studies were "perfunctory," his contact with Indians "too staged to be satisfactory"—even Thoreau's joy at finding his long-sought wild apple was blasted. In the end he held "only a withered blossom, an all-too-appropriate symbol of the whole trip" (450). Robert Richardson echoes Harding's disappointment: "The trip was a tragic failure in most respects. It was difficult, and Thoreau derived no real benefit from it." He came home in worse health than when he started; his notes are disappointing; only in his botanizing did he show "signs of energy and method" (386-87). The arc of achievement that any biographer seeks for their subject seems to be undermined by this failed journey west, and this perception has left a bitter residue in the telling. If the meaning of a life is culminated by the character of its end, to have Thoreau's life end thus seems to reflect back on, even subtly undermine, all that went before—or at least all those years following the publication of *Walden*: "years of decay and disappointment," worried J. Lyndon Shanley. Why would anyone, ever, want to revisit the scene of this tragedy, make us relive its painful steps?

Why? Because they have caught hold of Thoreau's own spirit, and come to see this journey not in our light but in his own. This is what Corinne Smith has done: her determination to retrace Thoreau's last journey on the

ground and over several years, rather than in the abstract via a few perfunctory paragraphs, meant reliving it fully in Thoreau's own exuberant spirit,
the spirit that saw the setting sun as a morning, not an evening, star.
Thoreau acknowledged that to face westward is also to face the sunset, day's
end. But this end marks a beginning as well. At the close of "Walking," he
dwells on an image of the setting sun "gilding the withered grass and
leaves": "So we saunter toward the Holy Land; till one day the sun shall
shine more brightly then ever he has done, shall perchance shine into our
minds and hearts, and light up our whole lives with a great awakening light,
so warm and serene and golden as on a bank-side in Autumn" (222). As
with so many of his late works, this essay, too, turns out to be about death
and the succession that follows. As for us, who still live: Thoreau implores
his readers "to improve our opportunities then before the evil days come,"
days in which all the surface of God's earth will be fenced and forbidden
with No Trespassing signs (195). As Corinne's travel directions make clear,
that day is long since upon us: the open territory over which Henry and
Horace traveled is occluded with buildings, riven with guardrails, staked out
with private property signs. All this tells us that in a very real sense we are
all, today, "west" of Walden. Demographically, of course, in that the
nation's westward expansion guaranteed that most of us must travel eastward to make our pilgrimages to Walden Pond; but also temporally, in that
Thoreau foresaw his descendants coming of age in sunset times, the "evil
days," when we would inherit a diminished earth.

But Thoreau's point was that he, too, lived in that sunset light from the
west: he documented the ways in which his own inheritance was already
compromised, even by the mid-nineteenth century, and suggested why this
is the condition of modern life. We imagine his Walden Pond to have been
pristine and pure whereas ours is in need of repair; but Thoreau observed
that Walden's shores had been mostly logged off, its hillsides were scored
with the trails of many generations who came before, and its land was
pocked with the cellar holes of decayed houses—one of which was, soon
enough, his own. But these facts did not dampen but inspired his faith in the
future. In 1859, Thoreau replanted the site where his cabin had stood with
new pine seedlings, repairing the damage he had done, and his writings look
ahead with hope toward readers who would know that the lesson of wisdom was not despair but deliberation. By applying this teaching to her own
quest, Corinne has restored the arc of Thoreau's life to wholeness.

Corinne's retracing of Henry and Horace's journey west gives us what
Eric J. Sandeen calls a "linear landscape," one that, being longer than wide,

must be experienced in time, whose twists and bends, "enticing the eye of the observer onward," turn space into a story narrated in time, step by step, a story whose own twists and turns unfold a deeper tale of history on the land (296). This was Thoreau's excursion form, which plays out the interrelatedness of "narrative, motion, and discovery" (306): at their best, linear landscapes "encourage epiphanies, one after the other" (296). In tracing Thoreau's linear landscape from New England to the Great Lakes country and back, Corinne does not relive someone else's journey so much as allow that journey to prompt the serendipities of her own, a *lived* journey that shows us how chance and history twine together on the land. Her "wrinkle in time"—her time, Thoreau's time, always twinned and present together in a double vision—opens up even the flattest and dullest of landscapes into a rich, dense layering of history and change, lives touched and lives lost, places transformed into new identities that still, like palimpsests, reveal the past to anyone prepared to look. Corinne's journey is in this sense a truly Thoreauvian "sauntering of the eye," an intentional walk that nevertheless keeps alert to the surprises that can't be seen head on, but only by looking with what Thoreau calls "the side of the eye."

Isn't this how we all came to Thoreau? By the side of the eye? The only real way to find him is to chance upon him; those who become lifelong readers of Thoreau are those who stayed open to the chance, who allowed themselves to be deflected on their journey, as Smith was, as Thoreau was, by the lifelines that cross our own and open unexpectedly into new vistas, swerve us into unplanned pathways—like the one that started Corinne on her own journey to rediscover Thoreau in the upper Midwest. The enemy is not time, for time and mortality are the only medium we have in which life can take on meaning. The enemy, rather, is hurry: in our haste not to lose time we pass by all the things and connections that Corinne pauses to notice. Thoreau suggested that "Nothing can be more useful to man than determination not to be hurried," for hurry saps our ability to saunter, to permit ourselves to be dis-placed, hence to see anew. By making her own determination not to be hurried, Corinne discovers her great circle route, a world where all things are made of stories. That she slowed down, and listened, and then, like Thoreau, returned to the hearthside to tell us all she saw means that her own book is a sort of linear *Walden*: a guide to our own journey west, and more, an encouragement to embark on our own, Thoreauvian, excursions.

NOTES

My quotations from Thoreau are drawn from the Princeton University Press editions of *Walden* (edited by J. Lyndon Shanley and published in 1971), *Excursions* (edited by Joseph J. Moldenhauer and published in 2007), and Walter Harding and Carl Bode's edition of *The Correspondence of Henry David Thoreau*, published in 1958 by New York University Press. I also quote from the two standard biographies of Thoreau, Walter Harding's *The Days of Henry Thoreau*, first published in 1965 and available in a reprint edition through Dover Publications of New York City; and Robert D. Richardson, Jr.'s, *Henry David Thoreau: A Life of the Mind*, the first stop for anyone interested in Thoreau, which was published in 1986 by the University of California Press in Berkeley, California. My discussion of "linear landscape" is taken from Eric J. Sandeen's meditation on Aurora, Colorado's High Line Canal, which has been turned into an 84-mile path; his essay "Walking the High Line" may be found in the collection entitled *Public Space and the Ideology of Place in American Culture*, edited by Miles Orvell and Jeffrey L. Meikle and published by Amsterdam's Rodopi Press in 2009. My thanks to Corinne for letting me be one of the first readers of her book, and to Dale Schwie for inviting me to the Minneapolis Thoreau Society meeting in October 2007, where I gave a talk on Thoreau and Darwin after hearing Corinne and Dale speak on the topic of Thoreau's last journey. My first reaction was that future biographers of Henry David Thoreau finally had a better way to tell the conclusion of his life story. My own desire to write a biography of Thoreau dates from that moment, and my life since has not been the same: thus are our lives composed of swerves and deflections!

Laura Dassow Walls is the William P. and Hazel B. White Professor of English at the University of Notre Dame. She is the author of a number of books including *Seeing New Worlds: Henry David Thoreau and Nineeenth Century Natural Science*.

PREFACE

"I didn't know that Henry David Thoreau went to Minnesota. Why would he have gone there?"

That's the reaction I usually get whenever I mention to someone that I have studied the two-month journey that led Thoreau and his young traveling companion Horace Mann, Jr., from Massachusetts to Minnesota and back in 1861. I am no longer surprised by the startled reply. After all, I had been a devoted Thoreauvian for more than twenty years before I had learned of this trip myself. Why is it such a big secret? Why don't traditional biographical sketches devote more than one sentence—or at the most, one paragraph—to this expedition?

First of all, we think of Henry Thoreau as being the quintessential New Englander. He is most known for his two-year stay at Walden Pond (1845-1847) and for the publication of the book *Walden; or, Life in the Woods* in 1854. Thoreau spent most of his life in his native town of Concord, Massachusetts. He liked to hike to and around the major mountains of New England: Wachusett, Monadnock, Washington, and Greylock. Longer journeys took him to Staten Island, Cape Cod, Maine, Vermont, and parts of eastern Canada. He visited friends and spoke at lecture halls throughout eastern and central Massachusetts, but those occasions were always on his own terms. Thoreau usually turned down offers to go farther away and tended not to stray too far from home and family. "I have travelled a good deal in Concord," he explained. What he found there was enough to keep him occupied for most of his days.

Secondly, little information has heretofore been available about this trip. Thoreau jotted down a few notes about the landscape, the people, and the plants and the animals he encountered. Seventeen-year-old Horace Mann, Jr., wrote letters home to his mother, describing the duo's activities and reporting on the health of his older companion. Neither man published a formal book about the experience. Without that kind of lasting promotion, the journey has faded from public view. A few twentieth-century scholars have written general articles about it, focusing primarily on the month spent in Minnesota. A slim volume containing the texts of both Thoreau's notes and Mann's letters was published by The Thoreau Society in 1962. But unlike Thoreau's trips to Cape Cod and to Maine, no one to date has traced the path of this particular journey. No one has produced a guidebook to share it with others. Perhaps the route was seen as too long and too difficult.

Perhaps it was not considered as distinctively Thoreauvian because it used railroads and steamboats to get from one point to another, instead of hiking boots or paddles. Perhaps this trip has been unjustly regarded as being unimportant to the fields of literary and environmental history.

Perhaps the experience was most often glossed over because it was ultimately seen as a great tragedy. Henry Thoreau was suffering from consumption, now known as tuberculosis. This excursion was presumably undertaken to restore his health. But after he had spent a month on the road and a month in Minnesota, Thoreau returned to Concord with little, if any, improvement in his condition. He died less than a year later. Horace Mann, Jr., went on to study at Harvard, do additional travel, and conduct botanical research. He died of consumption at the age of 24. This trip does not have a "happily ever after" ending for either man.

Then there's the problem of the name. Some authors refer to this time period in his life as merely "Thoreau's trip to Minnesota." Others call it "The Journey West," based on one line written at the bottom of one page of Thoreau's field notebook. But neither title acknowledges the thousands of miles, the myriad cities and towns, or the marvelous natural features that lie between Massachusetts and Minnesota and along the route that the two men followed. Who would expect to find a plant inventory from Niagara Falls in a report called "The Journey West?" What Canadian would think that "Thoreau's trip to Minnesota" would have included three train rides through present-day Ontario? And what role did Horace Mann, Jr., play in this endeavor? How can we be sure to credit his involvement as well? Even a twenty-first-century marketing expert might find it a challenge to come up with a better, more memorable and more accurate title. For now, we can just continue to refer to it as the Journey West.

Retracing this 1861 excursion was a project that I worked on in varying degrees from 1997 to 2009. It combined four of my passions: reading, research, nature, and travel. I was already an ardent practitioner of long-distance driving. I eventually drove thousands of miles, mirroring the route as closely as was possible by car. I could not simply take the train, because some of the lines Thoreau and Mann took now carry only freight loads, not passengers. Some tracks are gone completely, having been ripped up long ago due to disuse. Only the grassy straight-aways remain to show where the rails once led. And while I did not steam up the Mississippi and Minnesota Rivers, and did not sail across Lake Michigan or Lake Huron, I did take the time to study those bodies of water intently from their shorelines. I could easily imagine seeing the boats that used to troll those waters.

Page thirty of Henry Thoreau's field notebook contains the title, "Notes on the journey West." But that line does not match the handwriting found in the rest of the book. Researchers now believe that the title was written by Thoreau's sister Sophia sometime after he returned to Concord. (*Reproduced from the original manuscript in The Huntington Library, San Marino, California*)

Over the years, section by section, I followed the path of the Journey West. And I did it entirely on my own: without a traveling companion, without a GPS device, and (except when concerned friends forced theirs onto me) without a cell phone. A good car, a classic rock station on the radio, and many gallons of home-brewed iced tea. That was everything I needed to follow in Thoreau and Mann's footsteps.

When I wasn't riding, I was reading. I amassed dozens of books, articles, and brochures about all of the sites along the route. I scrutinized maps from atlases old and new, examining them for the crosshatch lines of railroad tracks. I read 1861 newspapers on microfilm. I used the resources of a multitude of libraries and historical societies, and I sent and received countless e-mail messages from people along the route. My conclusion after such "deep travel," as author David K. Leff has aptly named this kind of work, was that the Journey West was indeed a miraculous piece of history. It deserves more attention than it has been previously given. We have been remiss in overlooking it. Henry Thoreau and Horace Mann, Jr.; accomplished something important here. It is time to remedy this situation.

This book is the result of my work. It combines biography, history, geography, science, and literature, with travel guide. This is not the volume either man would have written, nor is it meant to be. It first provides basic biographical information about Henry Thoreau and Horace Mann, Jr., then the original route of the Journey West is divided into nineteen travel chapters. Each chapter begins with what the men saw and what they did in that particular section of their journey. Included is any pertinent historical information, as well as developments that the two men might not have known about. Next, the same region is brought up to date with descriptions of the changes that have taken place since the time of the 1861 visit. General directions are also provided for those who might want to follow the route themselves today. (Maps can be found at the affiliated website http://www.thoreausjourneywest.com.)

Each chapter includes my own contemporary "Thoreauvian adventure" related to that part of the journey. Since Henry and Horace passed through these areas rather anonymously and did not leave any traces behind, I have done my best to find a connection to the men (and especially to Thoreau) in each place. I will admit that the ties are sometimes rather tenuous, if not altogether tangential. Yet they are there.

Once I began to write about my experiences, I discovered that I was revealing more of my own background and my own thoughts and feelings than I had originally anticipated. I made every attempt to keep the spotlight on Henry Thoreau and Horace Mann, Jr. I have chosen to write my personal adventures near the end of each chapter for good reason. Any reader who would rather not share the journey with me can easily skip those parts. They will miss some interesting disclosures but the choice is theirs.

Scholars may scoff at the casual approach I have brought to my subject matter. I believe that spending years on the road, "with" these two men, gives me the right to address them by their first names. Besides, the phrase "Henry and Horace" has a wonderful, intimate cadence to it. I don't think they would mind such familiarity, especially when I have done my best to complete one of their unfinished projects.

I admit that my exploration has given short shrift to the biggest cities along the route. In my defense, I must say that I'm a child of 1960's suburbia who was taught that cities were places to avoid. We entered the nearest one (Lancaster, Pennsylvania: 1960 population, 61,055) only to meet dentist appointments, to buy school clothes, to shop at the Central Farmers' Market, and to go to the movies. By the time I was old enough to drive, an immense shopping mall had been built between our house and the city. Consequently, I never learned how to parallel park. I believe that today's cities understand this about me. I can navigate through any of them quite confidently and successfully but with one paralyzing fear: not being able to find a place for the car. As I circle block after block in search of a parking garage, I can hear the guffaws of the metropolitan gods booming in my ears. "What do you think you're doing, you silly girl? You'll never get a space. Go back to the country where you belong!" So forgive me, fellow traveler. If you want to explore the sights and scenes of Detroit, Chicago, St. Paul, Milwaukee, Toronto, and Boston, you'll have to do it on your own. You will notice that I tackled Worcester and Minneapolis only in the company of knowledgeable natives.

You will also notice that the narrative contains much speculation. There are many instances of "perhaps" and "maybe." Neither Thoreau nor Mann revealed the full story of each portion of the journey. Even after careful research and exact path-following, there are some things we just cannot know. In those cases, I suggest a number of reasonable possibilities. Future researchers may want to use those tidbits as jumping off points for further digging. I wish them the best.

Anyone seeking a pure version of the contents of Henry Thoreau's Minnesota field notebook should visit the web site of the Thoreau Institute at Walden Woods. At http://www.walden.org, you will find my annotated transcription of every one of his notebook pages. The book in your hands is a more casual narrative of the same basic information, greatly enhanced with historical documentation and my own experiences at various sites along the way. It also serves as a how-to guidebook for others who want to make the trip.

For a century and a half, friends and fans of Henry David Thoreau have heard a little bit about "The Journey West" and have wanted to learn the rest of the story. With publication of this book, here is that information.

The Travelers and their Route

*Perhaps it is easier to live a true and natural life while travelling,
—as one can move about less awkwardly than he can stand still.*
—*Thoreau's Journal*, January 11, 1852

At least half a dozen people waited for the westbound train at the Concord depot on that drizzly May afternoon. One full-bearded gentleman sat alone. His stuffed carpet bag and unopened umbrella lay beside him. With nothing else to do to while away the minutes, he looked up at the sky and studied the misty gray clouds streaming to the north. He thought of the good wishes his mother and sister had just given him, back at the house. He considered the miles that lay ahead. Then he was jarred by a sudden cough, which he stifled with the convenient cloth he had crumpled in his right hand. In his left, he held a map and a ticket. As he wiped his mouth dry, he barely glanced at the newspaper someone had abandoned on the bench. He had no need to read of war.

Standing a few feet away was a young man dressed for travel. He was in constant motion, shifting his weight from one foot to the other: too eager to stand still or to sit down. His face was flushed, either from excitement or embarrassment. His mother—for who else could she be?—bustled around him, smoothing imagined creases from his suit, chattering last-minute reminders. She was of the generation who saw these railroads built, and she was still a little afraid of them. He would write letters every day, wouldn't he? She had to know he was safe. Two teen-aged boys stood closer to the rails, laughing and pretending to push each other onto the tracks. It was all in good fun, and neither heard the woman's half-hearted scolding. She turned her eyes back to her oldest son and was not surprised when tears started. Who knew when she would see him again?

A distant rumble grew ever louder, and a line of sooty smoke appeared beneath the clouds. Every face turned to the left to catch the first glimpse of the oncoming locomotive. The bearded gentleman reached for his carpet bag and eased himself up. The mother grabbed the two younger boys and pulled them back, one on each side of her, until they protested and squirmed away. When the first whistle blew, young Horace jumped at the sound. Henry grimaced a kind smile. The great black mass of steam and machinery chugged in alongside them and came to a full stop. Good-byes could barely be heard above the din. After an exchange of hugs and promises, the two men pulled themselves up the steep steps. The young man got a station-side window seat; the gentleman followed his lead and slid into the seat behind him. The mother and boys waved as the train pulled out of Concord and headed for Groton Junction. They stood and watched until they could no longer see the last car, until the curve in the tracks led the man-made thunder away. Then they turned and walked home.

Henry and Horace were on their way West.

David Henry Thoreau was born on July 12, 1817, in Concord, Massachusetts, and was the third child of four for John and Cynthia (Dunbar) Thoreau. A quiet man, Mr. Thoreau took on the family pencil-making business and turned it into a successful endeavor. He was married to someone who was his exact opposite. Mrs. Thoreau was outspoken and had a dynamic personality. She was a member of such organizations as the Concord Female Charitable Society, the Bible Society, and the Concord Women's Anti-Slavery Society. Whenever she saw an injustice, she was quick to speak her mind. She also took in boarders to help ends meet for the household. Aunts on both the Thoreau and Dunbar sides often came to call as well. The home was a lively one.

Henry (as he was called) and his brother John were schooled at the Concord Academy and additionally enjoyed exploring the outdoors on their own. Education beyond grade school was an expensive option and one not often open to modest middle-class families like the Thoreaus. They could send only one boy to Harvard College, fifteen miles to the east. Since Henry was the better scholar, he would be the one to go. His sister Helen and brother John taught school in order to help fund Henry's education. He entered the college in 1833, and was an average student who did not take the chance to distinguish himself. He did not excel, but neither did he make trouble or rabble-rouse. Through his Harvard studies Henry learned of an entire world that existed beyond Concord: a world of diverse and valuable philosophies and writings. When he graduated in 1837, however, he probably did not attend the commencement ceremony. He missed hearing one of the featured speakers, Ralph Waldo Emerson.

Thoreau went back to Concord and spent time doing what later generations would describe as "trying to find himself." He had already read

Emerson's first book, *Nature.* The opening sentence must have grabbed his attention: "To go into solitude, a man needs to retire as much from his chamber as from society." Another line jumped off the page and presented itself to Thoreau as a credo for a new belief system: "The happiest man is he who learns from nature the lesson of worship." Those words and their author would prove to have a tremendous impact on young Henry.

Lecturer, writer, and former Boston minister Ralph Waldo Emerson had moved to Concord in 1834. It didn't take long for him to meet Henry Thoreau and for the men to realize they were kindred spirits. Based within this rural farming community, they were two intellectuals who could talk to each other and could discuss philosophy, literature, and nature. Because Emerson was fourteen years older than Thoreau, he may have taken on the role of surrogate father; or, at the very least, an eager mentor and friend. It was he who encouraged the younger man to write every day. Henry's first

An ambrotype taken of Henry David Thoreau a little more than a month after he returned to Concord in 1861. (*Courtesy Concord Free Public Library*)

journal entry is dated October 22, 1837, and it consists entirely of a record-ed conversation: "'What are you doing now?' he asked. 'Do you keep a jour-nal?' So I make my first entry today." Thoreau would continue to record his thoughts and observations in his notebooks until the last year of his life.

Encouraging a commitment to writing was not the only influence Emerson had on his young friend. The older man was an advocate of a philosophical and literary movement based on the theories of Immanuel Kant and Georg W. F. Hegel in Germany. Called Transcendentalism, it was picked up by German writer Johann Wolfgang von Goethe and by British authors Samuel Taylor Coleridge and Thomas Carlyle. It made its way to America in the 1830s and drew a following among Emerson's circle of friends. The name came from the idea that "there was a body of knowledge innate within man and that this knowledge transcended the senses." Transcendentalists were seen as a threat to society because they did not respect government, labor, the products of labor, or organized religion. When he spoke at Thoreau's graduation ceremony, Emerson preached Transcendentalism (without using the term) when he told the students that "the ancient precept, 'Know thyself,' and the modern precept, 'Study Nature,' become at last one maxim." Such topics often came up in Emerson's informal parlor discussions among people like Bronson Alcott, Orestes Brownson, Margaret Fuller, Theodore Parker, Elizabeth Peabody, and Jones Very. Henry Thoreau was one of the few who not only talked about Transcendentalism, he took it to heart. He lived it.

Yet he needed to find a job. Men with college degrees typically became doc-tors, lawyers, ministers, or teachers. John and Helen Thoreau were successful teachers without the benefit of having attended Harvard. Education seemed like a good choice for Henry, too. He was hired by the town of Concord to start at the Center School in the fall for an annual salary of $500, making him its highest paid teacher. He lasted just two weeks in the position. When a school committee member visited the classroom to see how the new teacher was doing, he was distressed to find that the students were noisy. (And it's no wonder: how could one person have been expected to manage more than 50 children in such a small space, let alone *teach* them?) The official demanded that Henry use corporal punishment to take control of the room. Thoreau immediately complied by choosing a few surprised pupils at random and tak-ing the ferule to their outstretched hands. Then he promptly resigned. If he had to answer to an intruding authority on a daily basis, the job was not for him. So much for conformity and following society's conventions.

If the townspeople thought Thoreau was strange for giving up a decent job over such a trivial matter, they were even more amazed to hear about his next unusual and independent act. He changed his name. Up to that point he was known as David Henry Thoreau. His family members called him Henry, however, probably to distinguish him from an uncle named David. Now Henry switched the order of his two given names. He did not bother to go through any formal legal procedures to do so; he merely inverted the names on his own. He was Henry David Thoreau for the rest of his life.

After he took on work in his family's pencil-making business, Henry wrote letters to his best friend and older brother John, then teaching fifty miles south in Taunton, Massachusetts. Within the pages of their correspondence, the duo weighed the possibility of teaching somewhere together. Where could they embark on such a venture? In March 1838, Henry thought he had a plan:

> I have a proposal to make. Suppose by the time you are released, we should start in company for the West and there either establish a school jointly, or procure ourselves separate situations. ... Go *I* must at all events. ... I wish you would write soon about this. It is high season to start. The canals are now open, and travelling comparatively cheap. I think I can borrow the cash in this town. There's nothing like trying.

But the brothers Thoreau never made a trip west. Possible teaching prospects in Virginia and Maine arose, got in the way, and ultimately disappeared. In the meantime, an opportunity opened at the Concord Academy, the private school both men had attended as children. Henry began teaching there on his own; and a semester later his brother came home to join him. As a team, they ran an innovative program that included field trips around town and the surrounding landscape. No governing committee members got in their way. They taught at the Academy for almost three years before John's symptoms of consumption forced them to retire from education in April 1841.

Two years prior to their retirement, Henry and John had made a vacation expedition on the Concord and Merrimack Rivers in a boat they had built themselves. The two-week trip in 1839 took them north to the White Mountains of central New Hampshire. Against the background of their sailing and hiking adventure must have lingered an unspoken tension: both brothers were in love with and were attempting to court the same woman. Ellen Sewall was the older sister of Edmund Sewall, a Concord Academy student. For more than a year, one or the other of the Thoreaus visited with or wrote to Ellen in an attempt to win her favor. Each one eventually, separately, proposed marriage. But Ellen's father was a conservative man who did not want his daughter to make a commitment to a Transcendentalist. She reluctantly turned down both men and instead married Unitarian minister Joseph Osgood in 1844. Henry never pursued another romantic relationship. He grew to focus his passions on his writing and outdoor explorations. Years later he remarked in his journal, "How rarely a man's love for nature becomes a ruling principle with him, like a youth's affection for a maiden, but more enduring! All nature is my bride." This was a plausible explanation for not caving to any societal pressure to marry.

John Thoreau never got another chance at love. On New Year's Day 1842, he accidentally cut his finger with a razor. The wound did not heal and tetanus quickly set in. John developed lockjaw and endured painful spasms and delirium until he died on January 11, 1842. He had been suffering with consumption for several years. But such a sudden and violent death was a shock to his family, especially to his brother. Henry experienced psychosomatic symptoms of lockjaw himself, further worrying those around him for weeks. Yet another tragedy struck when five-year-old Waldo Emerson died of scarlet fever on January 27. Thoreau and Emerson shared their family losses together, and in their grief, grew closer as friends.

Henry began to follow further in Emerson's footsteps by lecturing at the Concord Lyceum and by writing pieces for magazines like *The Dial*, the new Transcendentalist periodical. Such work wasn't enough to supply a regular salary, however. The idea surfaced that perhaps a more successful literary life could be found in New York City. Judge William Emerson, brother of Ralph Waldo, lived on Staten Island and was in need of a tutor for his sons. Henry accepted his offer of employment and arrived at "The Snuggery," the Emerson home, in May 1843. When he was not busy with the children, he took time to explore the island and even ventured across the bay and into other parts of the city. In his quest to make publishing inroads, he met key individuals of the day in Henry James and Horace Greeley. Newspaperman Greeley agreed to act as Thoreau's agent and would eventually promote his articles in *The New York Tribune*. This connection was the best outcome of the metropolitan experiment. Henry grew homesick and returned to Concord for good in December 1843.

One person to welcome him back was his friend William Ellery Channing. Known to some as "the Younger" to distinguish him from the Unitarian minister uncle with whom he shared the name, Ellery was four months younger than Thoreau. Another Emerson protégé, he was considered to be one of the more eccentric Transcendentalists. He left Harvard after attending classes for only a few months, and then later moved to the Midwest for a while to farm and to write. By the time Thoreau returned from New York, Ellery had married Ellen Fuller, the sister of Margaret Fuller, and had moved to Concord. The Channings eventually had five children together; but due to Ellery's irregular income from his books of poetry and his tendency to wander off for periods of time, the marriage did not last. His "principal occupation soon turned out to be walking companion for Henry Thoreau—not, as Henry had been at some pains to make clear, a paying proposition." On longer expeditions, Channing proved to be habitually unreliable, either remaining indecisive or failing to meet Thoreau at designated places and times. Still, the two men grew closer to each other than they did to their mentor Emerson or to anyone else. Each tolerated the idiosyncrasies of the other. They were friends for twenty years.

In spite of finding companionship with Channing, Thoreau still missed his brother John. He hoped to honor him by writing a book about their trip on the Concord and Merrimack Rivers, six years earlier. To do that, he needed time and a place to write. Emerson had just purchased some land at Walden Pond, and he offered Henry the opportunity to get away from the Concord town center. Henry spent a little more than $28 to assemble a small wood frame house on a rise above one of the pond's coves. He moved into it on July 4, 1845. This was his personal independence day, eight days shy of his 28th birthday. There he spent two years, two months, and two days adhering to his own schedule of writing in the mornings and observing nature in the afternoons. He may have lived a self-imposed solitary confinement, but his home away from home was not a remote hermitage. It was positioned along a well-worn road, and travelers often passed by his house. Curious visitors from town came out to see Henry. In return, he walked the mile and a half into Concord to visit his parents and the Emersons and to run various errands.

He was on such a mission one day when constable Sam Staples stopped him and raised questions about non-payment of taxes. Thoreau had ignored the Massachusetts poll tax for several years. Staples offered to pay the bill for him, thinking that perhaps the young man could not afford it. But for Henry, it was a matter of principle, not finances. This particular tax had seemingly no purpose and was an example of unfair government intrusion upon the individual. When he refused to pay it once again, Staples followed the letter of the law. He locked Thoreau up. Word of his arrest quickly spread around town. Soon an unidentified person came to the jail and delivered a package containing the tax payment. Popular belief maintains that Aunt Maria Thoreau was the benefactor. When Staples released Thoreau the following morning, the temporary prisoner was livid. He had hoped to make an example of himself and to call attention to the unjust policies of state and local government. He was reluctant to leave the cell. Staples apologetically told him he had to go.

Out of this frustrating experience came a lecture called "Relation of Individual to State." If Henry could not express himself with a remarkable physical act, he could at least write and talk about his intention. He read the speech twice at the Concord Lyceum in 1848. Now the townspeople could hear why he felt that he had to take a stand. "I think that we should be men first, and subjects afterward," he said. Individuals had to obey the "higher laws" of their own common sense and instincts, even if those ran counter to regulations imposed by a governing entity. "The only obligation which I have a right to assume, is to do at any time what I think right," he continued. "Action from principle, the perception and the performance of right, changes things and relations; it is essentially revolutionary." That last word deliberately played upon the history of his hometown: the site where the first significant shots were exchanged between the Colonials and the British regulars to begin the American Revolution in 1775.

Thoreau's words were well received but made scarcely a ripple in the literary or political circles of the day. A year later, Elizabeth Peabody published the lecture as "Resistance to Civil Government" in a single-issue periodical called *Aesthetic Papers*. The essay would later be renamed "Civil Disobedience" when it was released in a compilation volume after Thoreau's death. It did not achieve widespread recognition until many years later, when Mahatma Gandhi and Martin Luther King, Jr., both read it and were influenced by its promotion of nonviolent opposition.

By the time Thoreau gave that lecture, he had been back in Concord for some months. He left the woods and his Walden Pond house in September 1847, "for as good a reason as I went there. Perhaps it seemed to me that I had several more lives to live, and could not spare any more time for that one." The two-year respite had been fruitful. He strengthened his relationship with nature. He finished several essays, drafted his book manuscript, and assembled a lecture about his Walden residency called "A History of Myself." His self-imposed exile of sorts turned out to have been time well spent.

One thousand copies of *A Week on the Concord and Merrimack Rivers* were printed at Thoreau's expense in 1849. The book was reviewed in a variety of periodicals, but even Horace Greeley's front-page article in *The New York*

Tribune did not present an overwhelmingly positive review. Thus did Henry suffer the fate of many a first-time author: thrill and relief at having a title in print, but disappointment and discouragement when it failed to take the world by storm. Four years later, when the publisher wanted to get rid of the unsold stock, Thoreau agreed to take the remainders: all 706 copies. He made light of the situation as he noted in his journal that the volumes were

> something more substantial than fame, as my back knows, which has borne them up two flights of stairs to a place similar to that to which they trace their origin. Of the remaining two hundred and ninety and odd, seventy-five were given away, the rest sold. I have now a library of nearly nine hundred volumes, over seven hundred of which I wrote myself. ... Nevertheless, in spite of this result, sitting beside the inert mass of my works, I take up my pen to-night to record what thought or experience I may have had, with as much satisfaction as ever. Indeed, I believe that this result is more inspiring and better for me than if a thousand had bought my wares. It affects my privacy less and leaves me freer.

Leave it to Henry to put a positive spin on a less than successful venture. He could find satisfaction, if not happiness, in his obscurity.

Yet he already had at least one devoted fan. Harrison Gray Otis Blake of Worcester was one of the individuals who had been given a free copy of *A Week*. A year older than Thoreau, Blake (1818-1898) was a Harvard graduate who began his career in the ministry and then switched to teaching. He exchanged letters with Emerson and was invited to his parlor discussions, where he once met Henry in passing. In 1848, he was so impressed with a Thoreau essay in *The Dial* that he sat down and wrote a letter to its author. The two men began a correspondence and a friendship that would last thirteen years. They enjoyed holding philosophical conversations on paper and in person. Concord and Worcester were only two hours apart by railroad, and the two men visited each other regularly. Thoreau gave at least nine lectures in Worcester, sometimes staying overnight with Blake or with another colleague in that city, tailor Theo Brown. As a traveling companion, Blake proved to be a bit more reliable than Channing. He accompanied Thoreau on walks to two of New England's heights, Mount Wachusett and Mount Monadnock. There they could continue their intellectual ruminations on even higher ground.

Though he did not stray too far from Concord, Thoreau did occasionally travel to points in the Northeast to speak or to make natural explorations.

Emerson was far fonder of being on the lecture circuit than was Henry. While his mentor traveled around the country to speak, Thoreau limited himself mostly to the New England coastline. He lectured in towns from Plymouth to Portland, from Worcester to Waterbury, and once even went as far south as Philadelphia to speak. His natural excursions led him to the wilderness of interior Maine and to the sand dunes of Cape Cod. He fed his fascination with mountains by hiking on and around Wachusett, Monadnock, Greylock, Katahdin, the White Mountains, and the Catskills. Channing and Thoreau traveled together as far north as the city of Quebec and as far west as the Catskills, but Henry was never more than a few days away from his hometown.

He was led farther afield by reading travel narratives. These accounts took him to a variety of places around the world that he never planned on seeing for himself. "I have travelled a good deal in Concord," he claimed. From the comfort of his own sitting room he could indeed journey to the Arctic with Sir George Beck, to Africa with Clapperton and Livingston, to South America with Charles Darwin, and upon the high seas with Richard Henry Dana, Jr. He was especially intrigued by early descriptions of North America and its natives, the Indians. Henry took notes from each volume he read, gathering quotes about the indigenous people in a special set of note-books. Like so many others of his time, Thoreau was intrigued by the pos-sibilities of the "Go West, Young Man" mantra popularized by Indiana edi-tor John Soule and Horace Greeley. "Go *I* must," he had written to John, years before. And yet, inexplicably, he remained in New England.

Henry continued to find other occupations for his time. He stayed with the Emersons while Waldo was away, becoming the temporary man of the house and its caretaker. He worked in the Thoreau pencil factory, improv-ing the quality of the product and devising the thickness grading system still in use today. He taught himself surveying, a job that he performed for indi-viduals and for the town of Concord and one that could keep him outdoors. He gave lectures about his experience at the pond as well as his excursions to Maine and to Cape Cod. Most often, Thoreau spent his days observing nature, writing in his journal, and putting the finishing touches on his sec-ond book manuscript. The latter proved to be tough going and a more dif-ficult process than the first book had entailed.

Walden; or, Life in the Woods was finally published by Ticknor & Fields in August 1854. To simplify the recounting of his experience, Thoreau con-densed his two-year hiatus into a unified year that led from summer to spring. Evident throughout was his devotion to the natural world and his choice to live close to nature. "I would rather sit in the open air, for no dust gathers on the grass, unless where man has broken ground. ... I would rather sit on a pumpkin and have it all to myself than be crowded on a velvet cushion." He described the process of building his house and addressed his attempt to raise a cash crop, "making the earth say beans instead of grass," an effort he abandoned in his second year at the pond. Working as an environmentalist and ecologist before those terms were coined, Thoreau crusaded for saving the undeveloped areas of industrial New England: "Our village life would stagnate if it were not for the unexplored forests and meadows which surround it. We need the tonic of wildness ... We can never have enough of nature."

Indeed, he could already see the effects that industrialization had on the behaviors and attitudes of the people around him. He shared his opinions with his readers. "The mass of men lead lives of quiet desperation. What is called resignation is confirmed desperation." "Let not to get a living be thy trade, but thy sport." "Why should we live with such hurry and waste of life? We are determined to be starved before we are hungry." "To be awake is to be alive. I have never yet met a man who was quite awake." Maintaining one's individuality amidst the conforming pressures of society was necessary, in his mind. "Not till we are lost, in other words not till we have lost the world, do we begin to find ourselves, and realize where we are and the infinite extent of our relations." "Why should we be in such desperate haste to succeed and in such desperate enterprises? If a man does not keep pace with his companions, perhaps it is because he hears a different drummer. Let him step to the music which he hears, however measured or far away." No one knew better than Thoreau that "the mass of men" frowned upon those who ran counter to the accepted system of nineteenth-century society.

Optimistically, his residency at Walden Pond proved that "to maintain one's self on this earth is not a hardship but a pastime, if we will live simply and wisely..." His Spartan manner of living was described, not as a moral blueprint for others to follow, but simply one approach taken by one man at one particular time: "I desire that there may be as many different persons in the world as possible; but I would have each one be very careful to find out and pursue his own way, and not his father's or his mother's or his neighbor's instead." An ultimate realization awaits those who follow their own paths: "I learned this, at least, by my experiment: that if one advances confidently in the direction of his dreams, and endeavors to live the life which he has imagined, he will meet with a success unexpected in common hours." Pursue your own personal goals. Do not permit individuals or circumstances to damper your desires and expectations. Those were and still are valuable words to read and to live by, for anyone involved in any project or at any stage of life.

This time, two thousand copies of his book were printed; and this time, the reviews were much more favorable. Greeley promoted the release a month early by running excerpts in the *Tribune*. Thoreau's friends read the book and accepted it enthusiastically. In 1855, copies of the book were even sent to England, where author George Eliot promoted it in the *Westminster Review*. Though not a bestseller, the first run of *Walden* sold out by 1859. Thoreau tried to convince Ticknor & Fields that a second printing would be worthwhile. The publishing company chose to wait until mid-1862 to issue another shipment. By that time, *Walden's* author could no longer witness its release; but the title has not been out of print since that time.

As his excitement over his second book died down, Henry's life resumed a certain pace of deliberation. He climbed Mount Monadnock, toured New Hampshire's White Mountains, and traveled to Cape Ann in northeastern Massachusetts. He conducted land surveys and measured the course of the Concord River for the town. As his father's health began to falter, Thoreau took on more responsibility for the pencil making business, going as far as New York City to negotiate a deal for black lead. He became the man of the house when his father, John Thoreau, died at the age of 71 on February 3, 1859. Even before that month was over, Henry found himself lecturing again, this time about the beauty of New England's fall foliage. His continued interest in the phenomena of the natural world did not mean he was unaware of the current events swirling around him. Soon enough he would use both pen and podium to again react to the politics of the day.

When written years earlier, his "Resistance to Civil Government" essay began with the Thomas Jefferson maxim which states, "That government is best which governs least." Thoreau took the notion one step further, remarking "That government is best which governs not at all." That particular thought could have been uppermost in his mind throughout the decade of the 1850s. Two political actions especially disturbed him. The first was the 1850 Fugitive Slave Law, which required runaway slaves to be caught and returned to their owners. Outraged by that measure, Northern abolitionists were finally stirred to action after the highly publicized arrest of former slave Anthony Burns in Boston in 1854. Thoreau responded to the incident with "Slavery in Massachusetts," a lecture he read in Framingham on the Fourth of July. He was critical of both state and federal authorities. "The effect of a good government is to make life more valuable,—of a bad one, to make it less valuable," he said. "A government which deliberately enacts injustice, and persists in it, will at length ever become the laughing-stock of the world."

The second piece of troubling legislation was the Kansas-Nebraska Act, which allowed new settlers to decide upon the issue of slavery in both of those western territories. Northerners with abolitionist leanings sent groups west to make sure those states would be inhabited with anti-slavery residents. Connecticut native John Brown was the key radical in this Free State movement, taking his sons to Kansas and participating in the bloodiest fighting in the region. A group of New England men known as the Secret Six began to fund and equip Brown: first for his prairie raids, then to back his plan to attack the armory in Harpers Ferry, Virginia, in October 1859. That final mission went horribly wrong; Brown's men were overcome, and their leader was sentenced to death. The Secret Six were then hunted down for questioning.

Henry Thoreau championed John Brown's anti-slavery activities. He had met Brown when the man came to Massachusetts to gather money and supplies from his supporters, and Henry found him to be a passionate believer in the cause. Reacting to the news from Harpers Ferry, Thoreau wrote "A Plea for Captain John Brown," which he read to audiences in Concord, Boston, and Worcester that fall. In it he portrayed Brown as a hero, while admonishing the authorities and his fellow citizens for not seeing the man in this light. "He had the courage to face his country herself, when she was in the wrong," he said. "No man in America has ever stood up so persistently and effectively for the dignity of human nature, knowing himself for a man, and the equal of any and all governments. In that sense he was the most American of us all." While taking measure of Brown's mission and the tactics he used, the pacifist in Thoreau came to realize something about himself: "I do not wish to kill nor to be killed, but I can foresee circumstances in which both these things would be by me unavoidable." Even violent means, he conceded, might be necessary to achieve a moral goal.

When John Brown was executed on December 2, 1859, Thoreau was one of the speakers at the memorial service held in the Concord town hall. Six months later, on July 4, 1860, his essay "The Last Days of John Brown" appeared in the abolitionist publication *Liberator*, as well as in the ceremonial program for the John Brown Memorial Celebration held at Brown's home in North Elba, New York. Thoreau once again described a hero:

> I never hear of any particularly brave and earnest man, but my

first thought is of John Brown, and what relation he may be to him. I meet him at every turn. He is more alive than ever he was. He has earned immortality. He is not confined to North Elba nor to Kansas. He is no longer working in secret. He works in public, and in the clearest light that shines on this land.

Henry admitted that he had been so engrossed in Brown's activities that he had temporarily abandoned his prime passion. "I commonly attend more to nature than to man, but any affecting human event may blind our eyes to natural objects. I was so absorbed in him as to be surprised whenever I detected the routine of the natural world surviving still, or met persons going about their affairs indifferent." How could this tragic event not impact every living being?

Nevertheless, the world still rotated on its axis. The sun rose and set. Days came and went. Henry spent time measuring the temperature of the waters of local rivers. He studied the pines and oaks and developed his own theories about plant succession. But as he tramped the fields and woodlands surrounding Concord, and as he attended to his surveying and botanical work, the tensions growing in his homeland must have caused him to pause and contemplate the future. What was the country coming to?

Horace Mann, Jr., was born in Boston on February 25, 1844, and was the oldest of the three sons of Horace and Mary (Peabody) Mann. Though the elder Horace served at various times in the legislature at both the state and federal levels, he was best known for his work on behalf of students and teachers. During his eleven years as the secretary to the Massachusetts board of education, he proposed the creation of state teacher-training institutes called "normal schools." His reports and reforms resulted in improving the American public education system and empowering town officials with the authority to support and monitor their schools. For this work, he was held in high esteem. "It is proposed to place Mr. Mann's portrait in all the school rooms of the Commonwealth, and four of our schools have already done this," wrote school superintendent Bronson Alcott in the 1860 Concord town report. The name Horace Mann still graces many school buildings and even lends its moniker to an insurance company for teachers. A statue honors him in Boston.

Horace Mann, Jr., as a teenager. (*Courtesy Concord Free Public Library*)

Mary Mann maintained the family home in West Newton, Massachusetts, and, along with her husband, provided much of her sons' early schooling. Although young Horace was a bit slow in learning to write, he was only five when he began to study Latin. He and his brother George also became comfortable speaking German with one of the household servants. The boys read their father's letters and used maps to follow his journeys whenever he traveled on behalf of his political and educational initiatives. When the whole family had a chance to spend time in Washington, D.C., the boys benefited by seeing exhibits at the new Smithsonian Institution. The Manns emphasized the hands-on study of nature and also of machines. Today we would call this home schooling venture an example of experiential learning or constructivism. By all accounts, it was a nurturing, encouraging household.

Young Horace was a serious, sometimes nervous youth who would rather read or do quiet scientific study than play sports. Childhood diseases seemed to have a greater effect on him than they did on others his age. He was sensitive to loud noises and on several occasions complained about the raucous ruckus made by his two younger brothers at play. He craved order and routine. He appears to have been a visual learner, gaining a better grasp of a concept by seeing and by doing than by classroom instruction. In that respect, Horace thrived in the freedom of his home environment and might have done otherwise if he had been sent to public school every day. What an ironic situation, given his father's preeminence within the realm of education.

In 1853, Mr. Mann was offered the professional opportunity of his lifetime: to build a new college from scratch and to become its first president. Antioch College was to be coeducational and non-sectarian, a place where Mann could implement his educational reforms in a fresh venue. That September, the family moved to Yellow Springs, Ohio, just east of Dayton, and Mann threw himself into his work. His son Horace was still too young to enroll in the college, but the boy's interest in the sciences continued to grow. He had brought "a trunkful of minerals" with him from the East, and in time he began to read academic textbooks. Two chemistry professors befriended him and invited Horace to assist in class demonstrations. He often knew more about the principles of chemistry than their students did. It was an honor for him to be held in such high esteem by men he considered to be experts.

In addition to his love of the sciences, Horace held a keen interest in exploration. He was familiar with the popular travel narratives that were in vogue at the time, and he wished he could follow along with them and be an explorer on a scientific mission. He also developed a talent for drawing and map-making. His opportunities to travel himself had been limited to those following his father's work. After Antioch's first graduation in 1857, Mr. Mann took his family on a well deserved vacation to Mackinac Island in northern Michigan. Little did young Horace know that he would revisit the area four years later and would have a chance then for further exploration.

After he finished his first year of college level classes at Antioch in the summer of 1859, Horace was sent back to Massachusetts. Reports vary regarding this decision. Dr. Samuel Gridley Howe, an old friend of the family, had presumably invited Horace to visit the Howe household, for what would be the boy's first lengthy trip on his own. Mr. Mann's enthusiastic reply said that "Horace has been pining to visit mechanics' and artisans' shops and see the process by which things are made ... and I am afraid we accepted your invitation more for his benefit than for yours." One of Horace's friends later claimed that the choice was meant to restore his health after a period of intensive study. In any case, he traveled east and spent several weeks in the Boston home of Samuel Gridley and Julia Ward Howe.

Eighteen fifty-nine was a busy year for the Howes. While Dr. Howe had a good reputation for his philanthropy and for his work with the Perkins Institution for the Blind, it was not common knowledge at the time that he was also one of the Secret Six, the group of financiers and supporters of John Brown's anti-slavery activities. In fact, Brown himself had visited the Howe home on May 9, 1859, and his son John Jr. would do the same in mid-August, several weeks after Horace Mann's departure. All was in preparation for the futile effort that would eventually culminate in the Harpers Ferry disaster in October. Were Horace's parents aware of Howe's involvement in John Brown's mission? Would they have knowingly permitted their son to be so close to a potentially dangerous situation? Even if the answer had been yes, this would not be the last time the Manns would be involved with a member of the Secret Six.

Back in Yellow Springs, Mr. Mann finished a stressful financial year for Antioch but gave a hearty commencement address. "Be ashamed to die until you have won some victory for mankind," he advised his students. That month he sent his wife Mary back east to check on their son Horace and to visit her relatives. The trip was well-timed, for southwestern Ohio was experiencing a drought with excessive heat that summer, and typhoid fever was prevalent in the area. The younger Manns, George and Benjy, had suffered from it and were on their way to recovery. Their father fell ill but refused to send for his wife or for a doctor. By the time Mary returned to Ohio and to her husband's side, he was beyond help. Young Horace and his aunt Elizabeth Peabody traveled as fast as they could from Boston but were too late. Famed educator Horace Mann died of typhoid fever on August 2, 1859, at the age of 63.

Mary Mann had been supportive of her husband's professional choices but had never felt comfortable in Ohio. She took this opportunity to move the family back to her home state. Her sister Sophia and brother-in-law Nathaniel Hawthorne were in Europe, and they agreed to let her rent The Wayside, their home down the street from the Alcott residence in Concord. When the Hawthornes returned in July 1860, Mary bought a house on Sudbury Road to take care of her small brood: her three sons and her older sister Elizabeth. She enrolled the boys in Frank Sanborn's private school. With her sister, she started a school for youngsters based on the kindergarten concept then popular in Germany. Sanborn became enough of a friend that when he had to flee authorities for his own participation in

Secret Six actions, he spent a night hiding with the Manns at The Wayside.

Horace continued his studies with Sanborn. He was also botanizing on his own and exploring the nature of Concord. "He got a job helping an old gentleman arrange a collection of ferns, for he was intensely interested in natural science." Perhaps that unidentified man helped or encouraged him that year to produce a 32-page publication, *A Catalogue of the Phaenogamous and Acrogenous Plants Contained in Gray's Manual of the Botany of the Northern United States*. Even today, not many sixteen year olds study flowering plants, ferns, and mosses; much less publish formal lists of them. In this respect, Horace was following in his mother's footsteps. Mary Peabody first published *The Flower Children* in 1841, and it was revised at least once during her lifetime. Her 179-page book introduced children to botany by featuring a young girl who met talking flowers in her garden.

Eventually Horace Mann, Jr., was led to Henry Thoreau's door. Horace began to bring specimens to the Concord native, which was something many of the town's young people did. Thoreau first mentioned the budding naturalist in a journal entry dated October 6, 1860. "Horace Mann tells me that he saw a painted turtle in this town eating a unio [river mussel], in our river, in the shell, it evidently having just caught and opened it. He has been collecting shells in Ohio recently, and was obliged to wade at least knee-deep into the streams for mussels, the hogs, which run at large there, having got them all in the shallower water." During the next two weeks, Horace brought Henry the skeletons of a blue heron and an osprey, showed off the body of an American bittern, then later reported on the contents of that bird's stomach. Analyzing what animals ate lent clues to their haunts and eating habits.

As the calendar turned to another year, Horace was busier than ever and was quick to share his finds with Thoreau. The young man reported that he had seen a large number of musk turtles and had collected a number of them to send to Harvard scientist Louis Agassiz. Horace killed a bullfrog that had swallowed a snake. He brought along the stomach contents from a crow, a bittern, and a black duck. He showed off the bodies of a screech owl, two thrushes, a bufflehead duck, a merlin, two pewees, a white-throated sparrow, and a myrtle warbler. While it was a common practice in those days to kill animals in order to study them, Thoreau by now had grown out of that habit. He wrote,

> This haste to kill a bird or quadruped and make a skeleton of
> it, which many young men and some old ones exhibit, reminds

me of the fable of the man who killed the hen that laid the
golden eggs, and so got no more gold. It is a perfectly parallel
case. Such is the knowledge which you may get from the
anatomy as compared with the knowledge you get from the
living creature.

If he lectured Horace along those lines, perhaps he also discounted the boy's
actions as a combination of his youth, exuberance, and scientific inclinations.

The year was 1861, and people had more to think about than the fate of
a few dead animals prepared for someone's personal museum. The southern states were seceding. After a battle at Fort Sumter in South Carolina,
President Lincoln asked for 75,000 volunteers to sign up to help fend off
the "insurrection." Northerners were convinced that the impending war
with the South would end quickly. "Peace in Ninety Days!" was their cry, and
men signed up for three-month military stints of service. Thoreau took his
own personal stand toward the news: avoidance.

> As for my prospective reader, I hope that he ignores Fort
> Sumpter [sic], & Old Abe, & all that, for that is just the most
> fatal and indeed the only fatal, weapon you can direct against
> evil ever; for as long as you know of it, you are *particeps crimin-
> is*. ... I do not so much regret the present condition of things
> in this country (provided I regret it at all) as I do that I ever
> heard of it. ... Blessed are they who never read a newspaper,
> for they shall see Nature, and through her, God.

On the other hand, young Horace "wanted to join the Massachusetts
Volunteers and had to be told that he must spend at least a summer in
Brattleboro [Vermont, with relatives] getting over his cough before he
would be strong enough to be of use." Here, the personalities of these two
men were being unveiled: the nonconformist versus the joiner. Or perhaps
it was merely experience versus youth.

If Horace was coughing that spring, he wasn't the only one. Henry
Thoreau still suffered from a cold that he had caught from Bronson Alcott
the previous December. His condition was eventually diagnosed as bronchitis. On May 3, he wrote to his friend Harrison Gray Otis Blake in Worcester:

> The Doctor accordingly tells me that I must 'clear out' to the
> West Indies, or elsewhere, he does not seem to care much
> where. But I decide against the West Indies, on account of
> their muggy heat in the summer, & the S. of Europe, on ac of
> the expense of time & money, and have at last concluded that

it will be most expedient for me to try the air of Minnesota, say somewhere about St Paul. I am only waiting to be well enough to start—hope to get off within a week or 10 days.

Since Blake had accompanied Thoreau on several previous trips, Henry requested his presence on this longer journey.

Consumption, now known as tuberculosis or TB, was "responsible for one out of every five deaths" in the United States between the years 1800 and 1870. The annual town reports for Concord, Massachusetts, list it as the leading cause of resident deaths in all but one of the years spanning from 1850-1861. Named because "the body was literally consumed by the disease," it was so prevalent that most people could recognize the symptoms: "a hollow cough, an emaciated body, night sweats, and daily intermittent fevers." Today we know that TB is contagious and spreads from individuals who are already infected. But in the mid-1800s, the "popular and medical conception was that consumption was hereditary: those whose parents or siblings had contracted it were predisposed to the disease; and it haunted some families for generations, like a deadly curse." Henry Thoreau's father, paternal grandfather, and sister Helen most likely had died from it. His brother John also exhibited the symptoms of consumption before he died of lockjaw.

In those days, doctors recommended treatments that counteracted what they considered "irritants." Consumption appeared to strike people who traditionally worked inside buildings: lawyers, teachers, and ministers. (Being in close contact with infected persons was not yet seen as part of the problem.) Therefore, part of the remedy was to exercise outdoors. Sufferers were also told to have a mild and non-stimulating diet and to get away from any climate with cold, wet, and windy weather. Of those three considerations, physicians were most adamant about the choice of climate, for they believed "that individuals could halt [the disease's] progress and prolong their lives if they traveled to warmer, in medical terms, less irritating, settings." Though tropical locations like the West Indies were often suggested, the invalids themselves were told "to select the destination and devise the regimen most suitable for their particular constitutions." In other words, heal thyself.

Thoreau already had a Spartan diet. By today's standards, he would be considered a vegetarian. He already spent much of his time outdoors. The only logical remedy left to try then, was travel. Henry aimed for Minnesota. He had at least three reasons for choosing that rather unlikely spot. First of all, visitors to Minnesota were publicizing the region's bracing, restorative climate in reports to Eastern newspapers. The territory had become a state just three years earlier. Naturally, its authorities wanted to attract as many tourists as possible in the hopes that some visitors would eventually opt for relocation and residency. Since railroad lines now led to the banks of the Mississippi River and steamboat companies had regular schedules both upstream and down, it was easier than ever to get to Minnesota. Why not see the sights and improve your health at the same time?

A second justification for making this particular trip was that Thoreau already had a contact person in Minnesota. He appears to have planned this trip according to the pattern he followed during his three Maine excursions. Back then, he began his outings in Bangor, where his cousin Rebecca Billings Thatcher lived with her husband, George A. Thatcher. They could provide a home away from home: a place to start from, and later, a place to return to. George found wilderness guides for Thoreau and/or accompanied him on his treks into the interior forest and around Mount Katahdin. A local resident who was also a relative proved to be an invaluable resource to an out-of-town traveler. The arrangement worked well.

George's brother, Samuel Thatcher, Jr., had moved from Maine to St. Anthony, Minnesota, in 1851. There he established himself as a successful merchant while the community was just getting settled. Word was that Samuel's own respiratory ailment had cleared up after he relocated to the Midwest. Perhaps Samuel, his wife Elizabeth and their children could entertain Henry while the Massachusetts naturalist had a chance to explore the landscape of the Upper Mississippi watershed. The Thatchers were not blood relatives but they would certainly have knowledge of the region. A plan was put into place; Samuel Thatcher was to be Thoreau's host and possible guide for the duration of his stay.

No matter what was Henry Thoreau's real basis for this Journey West, the excursion would give him permission to cross half of the country and to see places he had only read about or had heard about from friends. Here at last was his validated opportunity to "Go West." He might never get another.

After deciding upon his destination, Henry had to pick someone to travel with him. In the tradition of any invalid embarking on a trip, he could not make this excursion on his own. What if the illness escalated and the worst were to happen on the road? It was best to have a friend at hand who would be able to take care of everything and could contact the folks back home. Henry extended an invitation to H. G. O. Blake, who later replied that he could not go. Henry then appealed to his best friend Ellery Channing, but he never gave a definitive answer, one way or the other. With his options growing narrower and time being of the essence, Thoreau somehow landed upon the idea of pitching the offer to Horace Mann, Jr. The two may not have known each other well, and together they would seem an unlikely pair, but the young, exuberant naturalist-in-training already had some traveling experience. He was energetic, held Henry in high esteem, and had the spirit of the explorer in him. He would have to do.

Another requirement for the consumptive on the move was to "arrange an itinerary that maximized the opportunity to meet friends and relatives" along the way. Though Thoreau undoubtedly had some ideas along those lines, it was Emerson who provided him with written contact information. "My dear Thoreau," he wrote,

> I give you a little list of names of good men whom you may chance to see on your road. If you come into the neighborhood of any of them, I pray you to hand this note to them, by way of introduction, praying them, from me, not to let you pass by, without salutation, and any aid and comfort they can administer to an invalid traveler, one so dear and valued by me and all good Americans. Yours faithfully, R.W. Emerson.

Even Waldo was worried about Henry's well-being and the wisdom of making the trip. Unfortunately, that list has not survived the passage of time. We'll never know if Thoreau consulted it, left it behind, lost it, or deliberately discarded it.

Of course, the duo would not be entering uncharted territory or going where no man had gone before. It was not 1804, and they were not Lewis and Clark. Tourist pamphlets listed railroad schedules and a few of the major sights to see. Henry's friends Emerson, Channing, and Margaret Fuller had made Midwestern journeys themselves and had reported on them. Horace had accompanied his family on a vacation to Michigan. Horace's father had ridden along some of the same train routes on his business trips, as had Emerson, during his lecture tours. Thoreau and Mann had undoubtedly heard personal stories about the places they would soon see for themselves. Both were fans of travel narratives, and Henry had read about life on the prairies and plains. The "Go West" motto of the mid-1800s had been heeded by many, especially by New England farmers who were tired of plowing rocky soil for a living. The two men would see a few of them on this trip.

Considering the journey in terms of a similar one today is almost like comparing apples and oranges. The route and the landscape may be similar, but the methods and circumstances are vastly different.

Today individuals traveling between Boston and St. Anthony/Minneapolis have a variety of options. They can spend several hours on an airplane or several days in a car, bus, or train. Henry and Horace's choices were limited: they used trains to cross land and steamboats to sail on water. While steam travel had been possible for 50 years, railroads were relatively new by comparison. Each line was still run by a private local enterprise. During the course of their trip, Henry and Horace used a total of sixteen railroad lines, five boats, and three ferries. Fortunately by 1861, most of those services cooperated with one another by coordinating departure and arrival times and by honoring excursion "through tickets." Planning ahead was important. In bigger cities, each railroad line still had its own station. "Union stations," central outlets that could serve customers using multiple railroad lines, would not be built until later in the century. In the meantime, travelers who needed to change lines had to walk, run, or take a short carriage ride from one station to another in order to catch the next train. The situation can be likened to using two separate airline terminals at the opposite edges of a large metropolitan airport. Henry and Horace usually avoided that problem by staying overnight in city hotels and resuming their travels the following morning.

Railroad authorities were the ones who finally set time standards across the continent. Nineteenth-century travelers had to know the correct time and had to arrive promptly or they would miss their trains. Thoreau observed this phenomenon with sarcasm in the "Sounds" chapter of *Walden* in 1854:

> The startings and arrivals of the cars are now the epochs in the village day. They go and come with such regularity and precision, and their whistle can be heard so far, that the farmers set their clocks by them, and thus one well-conducted institution regulates a whole country. Have not men improved somewhat in punctuality since the railroad was invented? Do they not talk and think faster in the depot than they did in the stage-office? There is something electrifying in the atmosphere of the former place. ... To do things "railroad fashion"

is now the byword ... Men are advertised that at a certain hour
and minute these bolts will be shot toward particular points of
the compass; yet it interferes with no men's business, and the
children go to school on the other track. We live the steadier
for it. We are all educated thus to be sons of [William] Tell.

The country would not be divided into its first rudimentary time zones until
1883. Prior to that, standards were based on the number of degrees east or
west any main depot was from Washington, D.C. The differences were measured in minutes, not full hours. If it was noon in Washington, then it was
12:24 p.m. in Boston and 12:14 p.m. in Albany. This method sounds cumber-
some to us now. Timetables were published in travel guidebooks, along with
notes that advised riders which city clock had dominion over an entire railroad line. For instance, the New York Central Railroad's standard was the
clock in the "Depot at Albany, which is 21 minutes faster than Buffalo time,"
even though the line spanned the entire width of the Empire State and
served both cities. Pocket watches must have been a necessity for a successful trip in the early days of rail.

Money could also pose a problem. Nineteenth-century travelers either had
to take enough gold to last the whole journey, or they had to have contacts
in major cities to get more. They also had to use currency that would be
accepted wherever they traveled, as no federal banking system existed. Banks
were regulated at the state and local levels. Because the country was additionally at war, any Northern bank that had based its worth on Southern invest-
ments was in serious trouble. "So disordered was the condition of banks
throughout the country that, after consulting a bank list, a man was liable at
any moment to find that the various issues in his wallet were worth less than
half their face value." By the time Henry and Horace were ready to leave
Concord, "Bankers were so uncertain about the value of state currency that
... they were discriminating against bills of some Illinois and Wisconsin
banks." Our travelers discovered this fact for themselves when they stopped
in Chicago and Milwaukee. By comparison, we in the twenty-first century
may be spoiled by the convenience of our personal checks, credit or debit
cards, teller drive-through windows and 24-hour ATMs. We take a lot for
granted: including the security and value of the money in our pockets.

Henry kept a running list of his travel expenses. If his figures are accurate, then he spent less than $90 for round-trip transportation and less than
$30 for lodging. Those amounts are laughable to us today; but remember
that sixteen years earlier, he built his house at Walden Pond for twenty-eight
dollars and change.

Compared to today's luggage-wheeling tourist, Henry Thoreau traveled light. He included the following items on a personal checklist: carpet bag, umbrella, half thick coat, waist coat [vest], thin coat, best pants, flannel shirt, three shirts, five to six bosoms [dickies], three pairs of socks, one pair of drawers, smoke cap, slippers, two neckerchiefs, ribbon, buttons, towel, soap, clothes brush, trochees [lozenges], medicine, cotton batting, five to seven handkerchiefs, dipper and bottle, Botany [field guide], seven-inch plant book [for pressing plant specimens], blot paper, writing paper, envelopes, twine, cards, pencils, scissors, tape, compass, microscope, spy glass, and insect boxes. In his pockets he intended to carry two handkerchiefs, shoestrings, pins, needles, thread, stamps, matches, a jackknife, a watch, a guidebook, a U.S. map, a notebook, letters [of introduction], his ticket, and his money. He began the trip with $78.10 in his left pocket, $60 in his right, and $40 tucked inside, for a total travel budget of $178.10. An extra note says that he sent the smoke cap home, and he may have asked for one or two more pairs of drawers to be sent to him in return.

With a few exceptions, young Horace Mann, Jr., was probably outfitted in much the same fashion. He also had an ink bottle and pen and plenty of stationery to write his letters home. He was supposed to peruse his Greek textbook along the way. He carried gold coins in his vest pocket. He also took ammunition along with his gun, which he used to kill birds and other small animals for scientific study. Carrying a jackknife and a gun, Henry and Horace would be searched, detained, and interrogated at any major airport today. At American train stations in 1861, no one gave them a second glance.

In addition to their clothing, toiletries, and naturalist paraphernalia, the duo may have carried a small food supply. Club cars were not yet standard components of long-distance trains. Although they stopped at dozens of towns along the tracks, very few lines allowed enough time for riders to disembark, eat, and relax before continuing their journeys. On Thoreau's expense list, he entered only a few meal and bread purchases, representing a little more than one dollar for food for the entire trip. Henry fished while the men were in Minnesota, and Horace noted at one point that they ate fish almost every night. Even after adding occasional free dinners with local hosts, and assuming that hotels provided meals as part of their fees, the two men must have eaten sparingly. Henry was used to living in that manner. He was also used to making forays into the wild equipped with bags filled with boiled corned beef, hard bread, homemade bread, "a little moist and rich plum cake," sugar, tea, and two or three lemons. He might have taken a few such snacks with him during this more civilized but much longer excursion.

Think of the magnitude of this trip! Henry and Horace passed through ten U.S. states and one present-day Canadian province. They crossed the major rivers of the East: the Connecticut, the Hudson, the Niagara, the Detroit, the Rock, the Wisconsin, the St. Lawrence, and the Merrimack. They sailed on the Mississippi and the Minnesota rivers. They saw the churning waters and mists of Niagara Falls. They rode alongside the famed Erie Canal. They became intimate with three of the five Great Lakes by sailing on Lake Michigan and Lake Huron, as well as by riding the rails along the Lake Ontario shoreline. They were practically within spitting distance of Lake Erie and Lake Superior when they were at Niagara Falls and Mackinac Island. They saw all manner of varying landforms and flora and fauna. The pair stayed in cities that were in their infancy stage, on their way to becoming major metropolitan areas: Worcester, Albany, Detroit, Chicago, St. Paul, Milwaukee, and Toronto. They rode past three state lunatic asylums (Worcester, Utica, Kalamazoo) and three sites that would be named state land-grant universities the following year (University of Minnesota, University of Wisconsin-Madison, University of Vermont). They passed four Shaker communities (Harvard and Hancock in Massachusetts; Enfield and Canterbury in New Hampshire) that were already experiencing membership decline. They accompanied government officials on a river excursion to pay annuities to the Dakota Indians at the Lower Sioux Agency in Redwood, Minnesota. What an itinerary to follow! What sights to see! And all of it was accomplished during the uncertain opening months of the Civil War. Soldiers mustered in Concord before Thoreau and Mann left home.

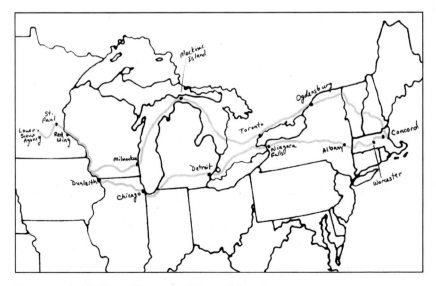

The route taken by Henry Thoreau and Horace Mann, Jr.

In fact, the bodies of the first Massachusetts war dead—three soldiers who had been killed in Baltimore—had arrived with much fanfare in Boston by train on May 1. Once Henry and Horace were en route in mid-May, they saw groups of volunteers training or leaving for battle as they rode through town after town. Perhaps taking in such scenes and reading the news in the papers was enough to force the duo to find the most northern route possible for their return trip to New England. Even though all of the reported skirmishes to that point had taken place in the South, no one knew where the fighting would lead next.

The trip was also accomplished in spite of the tedium of sickness. The main goal was to improve Henry Thoreau's health. His desire to get better must have superseded the state of his own physical condition. In general, whenever individuals are ill, their last consideration would be to undertake a long journey with someone they barely know, to a place they have never been before, and then a month later, take an even longer route home. Young Horace always reported optimistically on his own health and that of "Mr. Thoreau." But we will never know if he was telling the truth. He may have been merely telling his mother what she wanted to hear. After all, Horace's own health had never been robust. The two men may have ended up taking care of one another.

On Friday, May 10, 1861, Ralph Waldo Emerson asked his daughter Ellen to take a map to Henry Thoreau's house. She delivered it and was astonished to discover that her father's friend planned to set out for Minnesota the following day. She immediately invited him to the Emerson house for a send-off supper that evening. He accepted the offer. That night she reported that the "dinner talk was 1/2 Nat. Hist. and 1/2 politics." Emerson was focused on the war effort, for he had just taken it upon himself to arrange for 30 muskets to be delivered to the soldiers drilling in Concord, as his son Edward was in that group. Regarding Thoreau's upcoming trip, Emerson said the idea was "all a mistake." He even suggested at the last minute that Thoreau "should buy Mr. Minot's piece [of land] today." Although the friendship between the two men had been strained for several years, the mentor was still concerned about his once favorite disciple and wished that he would finally settle down before it was too late. Henry ignored the advice.

The morning of Saturday, May 11, began typically enough for Thoreau.

A boy brought him a salamander to identify. He was unfamiliar with the species so, in an ironic role reversal, he sent it to Horace. That afternoon, they caught the train. Two "bachelors of nature" embarked on a Journey West by rail and by water, almost 57 years to the day after Lewis and Clark had begun their own historic venture. Henry scribbled a few notes and wrote at least one letter to a friend while Horace wrote letters home. Those pieces of evidence are all they left behind to document the events of their two-month trip. Neither man had a chance to write a formal essay, report or book about his experiences and observations. We can learn much more about their journey by studying the histories of the time and the places, and by following the paths they took. Westward Ho!

NOTES

This narrative will often quote directly from the field notebook that Henry Thoreau kept during the course of his trip. The text is quoted from those pages, courtesy of The Huntington Library in San Marino, California, which holds the original. The letters of Horace Mann, Jr., are quoted from *Thoreau's Minnesota Journey: Two Documents; Thoreau's Notes on His Journey West and The Letters of Horace Mann, Jr.* (Ed. by Walter Harding. Geneseo, N.Y.: Thoreau Society, 1962).

The definition of Transcendentalism that I most like and used here appears on page 62 of Walter Harding's *The Days of Henry Thoreau: A Biography* (New York: Dover Publications, 1982). The quote about William Ellery Channing being Thoreau's "walking companion" came from page 247 of Perry Miller's *The American Transcendentalists: Their Prose and Poetry* (Garden City, N.Y.: Doubleday, 1957).

Quotes from Emerson's writings and speeches are taken from *The Portable Emerson* (New ed. Edited by Carl Bode. New York: Penguin Books, 1981). All quotes from Thoreau's published works were found as printed in *The Portable Thoreau* (Ed. by Carl Bode. New York: Penguin Books, 1977).

Thoreau's "Go *I* must" letter to his brother John is dated March 17, 1838, and can be found on page 24 of *The Correspondence of Henry David Thoreau* (Walter Harding and Carl Bode, eds. New York: New York University Press, 1958). His remark about newspaper readers being participants in crime comes from a letter sent to Parker Pillsbury and dated April 10, 1861, found on page 611. His letter to Blake mentioning his decision to go to Minnesota is dated May 3, 1861, and is on pages 615-616. Thoreau's food list for hikers was sent to a Worcester minister in a letter dated July 15, 1861, found on pages 623-624. Emerson's note with his list of contacts appears on page 616.

"All nature is my bride" appears in Thoreau's *Journal* entry of April 23, 1857. "I have now a library of nearly nine hundred volumes" comes from the *Journal* entry of October 28, 1853. The naturalist encounters of Horace Mann, Jr., and Henry Thoreau are documented in his *Journal* entries from October 9-16, 1860, and from January 11-May 4, 1861. Thoreau's admonition about killing animals for study is in the entry dated October 9, 1860.

Bronson Alcott's school report that mentions Horace Mann is part of the *Concord Town Report*, dated March 5, 1860-March 4, 1861, page 40.

Biographical information about Horace Mann, Jr., came from several sources, including Louise Hall Tharp's *Until Victory: Horace Mann and Mary Peabody* (Boston: Little, Brown, 1953), Tharp's *The Peabody Sisters of Salem* (Boston: Little, Brown, 1950), and "A Sketch of the Life of the Late Horace Mann, by a Friend and Associate" (in *Bulletin of the Essex Institute*, February 1869, vol. 1, no. 2, p. 28). The "trunkful of minerals" quote is from page 3 of Robert L. Straker's *Horace Mann 1844-1868* (Cornell University, 1956), a manuscript housed at the Concord Free Public Library. Mr. Mann's reply to Samuel Gridley Howe appears on page 309 of *Until Victory*. Details about the Howes' involvement with John Brown's activities can best be found in Edward J. Renehan, Jr.'s *The Secret Six: The True Tale of the Men Who Conspired with John Brown* (New York: Crown Publishers, 1995, p. 183-191). Mr. Mann's "Until victory" speech was found on page 245 of *The Peabody Sisters of Salem*. The quotes about Horace being involved with a Concord fern collection and wanting to go off to war can be found on pages 290-291 of the same book. Worthwhile reading and browsing is Mary Peabody Mann's *The Flower People* (New and rev. ed. Boston: J. R. Osgood and Company, 1875), also at the Concord Free Public Library.

Information about consumption / tuberculosis was gratefully gleaned from Sheila M. Rothman's *Living in the Shadow of Death: Tuberculosis and the Social Experience of Illness in American History* (New York: HarperCollins, 1994). Quotes I have used here appear on her pages 2, 4, 7, 14, 18, 19, 23, 32, and 33. Anyone who is interested in nineteenth-century life in America should read Rothman's book. If Henry Thoreau and Horace Mann had been female, they would have had to work through the disease as best as they could, presumably with household help from another woman. Travel was recommended as a cure only to men, especially to those who could afford it.

An invaluable source for information about the early days of the railroad is Alvin F. Harlow's *Steelways of New England* (New York: Creative Age Press, 1946). The time tables described here were found in *Dinsmore's Railroad and Steam Navigation Guide for the United States, Canada, Etc.: November 1861.* (New York: Dinsmore & Co., 1861). The quote about the diminishing worth of money came from page 129 of Bessie Louise Pierce's *A History of Chicago: Volume H, From Town to City, 1848-1871* (New York: Alfred A. Knopf, 1940).

Ellen Emerson's description of the going-away dinner is located in *The Letters of Ellen Tucker Emerson* (Ed. by E. W. Gregg. Kent, Ohio: The Kent State University Press, 1982, p. 250).

Travel Chapter 1

Saturday, May 11, 1861
Concord to Worcester
via the Fitchburg Railroad and the Worcester & Nashua Railroad

Expenses: Fare from Concord to Worcester, $1.50.

Set out for Minnesota via Worcester.

—Thoreau's Journal, May 11, 1861

The first leg of every journey covers familiar territory. The landscape that Henry Thoreau and Horace Mann, Jr., rode through on that first afternoon was one that Henry had seen many times. The two men caught the westbound Fitchburg Railroad cars in the late afternoon and disembarked at Groton Junction, now known as Ayer. There they boarded a southbound Worcester & Nashua Railroad train and arrived in Worcester at around 7 p.m. The 43-mile ride from Concord took a little less than two hours.

At the time of the trip, Henry lived with his mother Cynthia and sister Sophia in a large house on Main Street in Concord. The train station was only about a block away. When Nathaniel Hawthorne and his family came back from Europe, Mary Mann and her three boys had to give up their tenancy at The Wayside on Lexington Road. They moved into their own place on Sudbury Road, just a few minutes' walk from the station and from the home of the Thoreaus.

This beginning stretch may have been a lark for young Horace. But once they were underway, Henry had no need to jot down the scenes he saw from the train window; he could have sketched them from memory. Soon after leaving the Concord station, the train steamed past the Damon Mill in Westvale, now known as West Concord. Thoreau might have thought back to several unseasonably warm days in May 1859, when he surveyed that mill site for Edward Damon. Henry and his assistants had been besieged by swarms of gnats that flew into their eyes and mouths. Now two years later, the factory workers were busy manufacturing cloth for uniforms to outfit Union Army soldiers. The war was already affecting life in Concord.

South Acton was the first stop. Henry had passed through that station many times; and on at least one occasion he had approached it with horse and wagon. Immediately after John Brown was executed in Virginia in December 1859, one of Brown's men escaped to Massachusetts and needed help getting to Canada. Frank Sanborn asked Thoreau to drive Francis Jackson Merriam to the South Acton railroad station to avoid his capture by authorities. Henry did so without knowing the true identity of his passenger. He merely thought the man insane, as he babbled incessantly during the ride. Merriam in turn assumed that his driver was really Ralph Waldo Emerson. Still, Henry was successful in sending Merriam on his way and thus played a small but active part in the Harpers Ferry aftermath. If he had been found out, he would have been arrested. Again.

The West Acton station could stir fond memories. Just seven months earlier, Thoreau had taken the train to West Acton and then walked to Henderson Inches's Woods in Boxborough. There he found that the sawmill owner had an old woodlot consisting of "an endless maze of gray oak trunks and boughs stretching far around. The great mass of individual trunks" was "very impressive." Henry visited Inches Woods twice that

Today the former Inches Woods in Boxborough barely resembles an old-growth forest and sawmill site. (*Courtesy Alan B. Rohwer*)

November, and he took notes on the circumferences of trunks and the processes of natural succession between pines and oaks. The experience caused him afterward to rave about the virtues of this local property:

> How little we insist on truly grand and beautiful natural features! How many have ever heard of the Boxboro oak woods? How many have ever explored them? I have lived so long in this neighborhood and but just heard of this noble forest,— probably as fine an oak wood as there is in New England, only eight miles west of me. ... That grand old oak wood is just the most remarkable and memorable thing in Boxboro, and yet if there is a history of this town written anywhere, the history or even mention of this is probably altogether omitted, while that of the first (and may be last) parish is enlarged on. ... Seeing this, I can realize how this country appeared when it was discovered. Such were the oak woods which the Indian threaded hereabouts.

Soon enough he would see oaks dominating another habitat: the Midwestern prairies. He would see Native Americans out there, too. But as he rode in a car rattling through east-central Massachusetts, Thoreau had no knowledge of those sights to come.

Approaching the Groton Junction station, the cars came within a mile of the Shaker community of Harvard, Massachusetts. The Shaker sect was an offshoot of the Quaker religion in England and was brought to America when

The farmhouse at Fruitlands, where the Bronson Alcott family and others hoped to create an agricultural and spiritual utopia in 1843.

leader Mother Ann Lee organized a community in eastern New York in 1774. The Harvard site was created in 1791; but by 1861, the settlement was experiencing the population decline felt by many Shaker enclaves. This situation was bound to happen since Shakers did not marry, had no children, and grew in numbers only through conversion. According to census records, the Harvard community peaked at 178 members in 1850. When Henry and Horace's train passed through the area, about one hundred Believers lived there.

After changing trains, the travelers soon traced the western edge of the former Fruitlands property. Here Bronson Alcott and his family had attempted to establish a utopia in 1843. Henry and Horace probably caught a glimpse of the old farmhouse as they rode south toward Worcester. They could then turn their gaze to the west and see Mount Wachusett, one of Henry's favorite mountains. In July 1842, he had made a four-day Concord-Wachusett walk with Richard Fuller, the brother of Margaret Fuller, editor of *The Dial.* From that experience, Thoreau penned his first excursion essay, "A Walk to Wachusett." It was published in *The Boston Miscellany of Fashion and Literature* in January 1843. In 1854, he returned to the top of the mountain, this time by taking the train to Westminster and walking the rest of the way. "With a glass you can see vessels in Boston Harbor from the summit," he wrote. Rising to 2,006 feet above sea level, Wachusett was in turn a landmark that New Englanders could see on the horizon from many vantage points.

Soon the brick buildings of the town of Clinton appeared. Thoreau had toured the Bigelow mills when he lectured in that town on January 1, 1851. The next day he wrote, "Saw at Clinton last night a room at the gingham-mills which covers one and seven-eighths acres and contains 578 looms, not to speak of spindles, both throttle and mule. The rooms all together cover three acres." He described the manufacturing process, obviously impressed. "I am struck by the fact that no work has been shirked when a piece of cloth is produced. Every thread has been counted in the finest web; it has not been matted together. The operator has succeeded only by patience, perseverance, and fidelity." Even the simplest fabric had a story behind it.

But that particular trip had been made in winter, and Thoreau must have encountered some traveling problems or delays at the time. The blowing snow favored one railroad over the other: the north-south Worcester & Nashua line versus the east-west Fitchburg line. Henry wrote, "The direction in which a railroad runs, though intersecting another at right angles, may cause that one will be blocked up with snow and the other be comparatively open even for great distances, depending on the direction of prevailing winds and valleys. There are the Fitchburg and Nashua & Worcester." Ten years later, on a day in May, no one had to worry about those kinds of conditions. The air was rainy and the temperature was only in the 50s. Flowers were blooming, leaves were unfolding, and the world was returning to various shades of green.

Henry Thoreau and Horace Mann, Jr., reached Worcester just before dusk and were greeted by Harrison Gray Otis Blake and perhaps even mutual friend Theo Brown. The travelers had made arrangements to stay with one man or the other. That evening was no doubt filled with good conversation or quiet camaraderie. Perhaps no one mentioned that it might very well be Thoreau's last visit to Worcester. It was.

Today's traveler will see a variety of changes along this route. The old Fitchburg Railroad line is now part of the MBTA, metropolitan Boston's rail and bus system. The commute between Concord and Ayer takes about fifteen minutes. However, you cannot continue by train from Ayer to Worcester because that particular track now accommodates only freight traffic. And once you arrive in Worcester, your gaze may settle upon the beautiful restored twin-towered Union Station that currently offers both bus and rail connections. That wonderful, huge building is a main feature of Washington Square and was built in 1911. Henry and Horace would have arrived at the Worcester & Nashua train station that was located near Foster Street in downtown Worcester. It is no longer standing. The railroad tracks themselves have been diverted several blocks east.

Cloth is no longer manufactured in West Concord, nor is gingham made in Clinton.

Harvard's Shaker community disbanded in 1918. In its place sits a residential development named Shaker Village, with the Shaker Hills Golf Course not far away. However, local Shaker history lives on at the museum property of Fruitlands, where visitors can also tour the Alcott farmhouse. There they can see a display of Henry Thoreau's desk and samples of his rock collection, even though the man himself never visited the Alcott's utopian community.

The descendant trees of Inches Woods can still be seen in Boxborough. The original parcel is generally outlined today by the rectangle formed by Burroughs Road, Liberty Square Road, Depot Road, and Middle Road. That quadrant is bisected by MA Route 111. Today a number of private homes are located there, as are the Sargent Memorial Library and the Blanchard Memorial School. In 1995, an Eagle Scout project placed a plaque on a large rock to tell the story:

Henderson Inches Woods

> Henderson Inches operated a sawmill on this site circa 1806-1865. The mill was used to clear his large oak woods which extended east and west of this location. The mill foundation, millrace and dam are visible before you.
>
> Henry David Thoreau visited and described the remains of Inches Woods in 1860. The last of the woods was cut as part of the Civil War effort.

To see this marker for yourself, you should travel along MA Route 111 and turn north on Liberty Square Road. Look for Guggins Brook along the west side of the road between the entrance driveway for Liberty House and Guggins Lane. You will have to park somewhere and walk off the road a few feet to see the plaque on the rock and to scrutinize the stone mill foundations.

New England is far more wooded today than it was in Thoreau's time. He used to be able to see Mount Wachusett from any height around Concord. With many more trees covering the central Massachusetts landscape these days, that is somewhat trickier to do, but not impossible. Skiing, hiking, and bicycling are now key sports on and around Wachusett. And those who ride, climb, or drive to the top of the mountain can still look east and can in the distance see Boston—now identified by the hazy silhouettes of its tallest buildings, and not by the ship masts in the harbor.

The most dramatic change along this route was the creation of the Wachusett Reservoir. The center of West Boylston that Henry and Horace passed through is now partially submerged. In 1905, the south branch of the Nashua River was dammed at Clinton to form a reservoir that could provide water to Boston and eastern Massachusetts. Parts of Boylston, Clinton, and West Boylston were flooded as a result. The Worcester & Nashua tracks were realigned. The Bigelow mill buildings in Clinton were spared; but others downriver were taken in the transformation. The Old Stone Church is the only structure that remains, and it is almost wholly surrounded by water. Residents and businessmen had no recourse but to comply with the state's orders at the time. The authorities undertook a similar but much larger project at the western edge of Worcester County in the

1930s, when four towns were entirely eliminated. The rest of the state has always had to defer to Boston's need for water.

Emerson said that "No truer American existed than Thoreau." What better place to search for Henry's spirit than in a typical American holiday setting?

A line of casual thunderstorms rolled through central Massachusetts on July 1, 2004. The quick rain could not wash away all of the humidity, and the sky was still gauzy white well into the late afternoon hours. The sun was a mere bright splotch in the midst of the haze, but the moist air did not stop a line of vehicles from descending upon the Fruitlands property in the town of Harvard. Visitors paid a per-car fee, parked in the field, loaded up with armfuls of folding chairs and coolers, and then headed for the hillside below the tea room. The Concord Band would soon regale the audience with patriotic melodies to celebrate Independence Day. Thoreau's hometown musicians would perform a few yards away from his 1861 rail route.

On select evenings throughout the summer, this grassy hillside becomes a natural amphitheater for all to enjoy. Framed by forest on three sides, it provides visitors with one of the finest views in the state: that of Mount Wachusett to the west. It is the perfect backdrop for musical entertainment. The Concord Band has been performing at Fruitlands since 1986.

On this particular evening, adults tapped their feet to the familiar songs of John Philip Sousa, Irving Berlin, and George M. Cohan. They dined on homemade sandwiches and casseroles or wine and cheese while they listened. Children invented games along the outskirts of the crowd, chasing each other or dancing to the music. The shadows grew long and a red rubber-ball sun popped out for a few minutes. It slowly disappeared behind the hills.

Even before the Concord Band struck its first chord, the Fruitlands property had connections to Henry Thoreau. His rock collection is on display in the farmhouse. His friends the Alcotts had lived there. The train tracks to the west are the ones he always rode along to visit Worcester. Mount Wachusett is one of his choicest landmarks. But an additional connection to both Thoreau and Horace Mann, Jr., arose this night as the band offered up "The Battle Hymn of the Republic."

The tune had been known as "John Brown's Body" after the abolitionist's execution in 1859. When Samuel Gridley Howe and his wife, Julia Ward Howe, visited Union troops in Virginia in November 1861, they heard the soldiers and their visitors sing that song. Julia was already a published poet. For some reason, she couldn't get that tune out of her head. She was inspired during the night to create new lyrics to the melody, replacing all of the references to John Brown. The next morning she woke up and wrote down the words we know today. In February 1862, her lyrics were printed on the first page of the *Atlantic Monthly*, and the song soon became a popular war tune. It is still considered to be a patriotic American classic.

The Howes had been good friends with the Mann family. Samuel and the elder Horace were long-time correspondents and were close both professionally and personally. Horace and Mary Mann accompanied the Howes on a double honeymoon and educational tour of Europe in 1843. Young Horace was conceived during the months-long trip abroad. As a teen, he was visiting with the Howes in Massachusetts when his father took ill in Ohio. Dr. Howe was a member of the Secret Six, the men who financially supported John Brown. While Horace was staying with the Howes, Thoreau himself was meeting John Brown and becoming a passionate admirer and supporter of that man's cause: the elimination of slavery.

A series of friendships and abolitionist threads tied our Journey West travelers to the landscape they passed through on that rainy day in May, and returned to us again on a steamy, music-filled day in July.

WHEN YOU GO: The quickest way to follow Thoreau and Mann's rail path by car is to begin in Concord with MA Route 2 West. This road passes over the former Fitchburg Railroad tracks twice: just west of its intersection with MA Route 62 at mile 121.6; and before the I-495 interchange at mile 113.8, where westbound drivers and passengers can glance over the bridge and see the Littleton station below the north side of the highway. You get a good view of Mount Wachusett to the southwest at mile 108. By continuing west on MA Route 2, you will also pass over the former Worcester & Nashua Railroad line between the Harvard and Devens exits at mile 107.9, just before the Oxbow National Wildlife Refuge property. Fruitlands is not far away and is located to the south of the highway.

Take I-190 South at Leominster. As you approach the city of Worcester, look to the east for a string of large electrical poles. They mark the existing freight rail line that mirrors the old Worcester & Nashua track. You will pass over the rails after the Gold Star Boulevard exit, just as I-190 begins to join I-290. The power lines will be hanging above you. Southbound passengers can take a good but quick view down the tracks and into the city of Worcester. Drivers need instead to pay attention to the traffic because they must stay in the right-hand lane to follow I-290 West. Take the MA Route 9 West exit, and follow the signs for MA Route 9 West. Once you turn right onto Highland Street, you will be in the neighborhood of the homes of Thoreau's friends, H.G.O. Blake and Theo Brown. More details about those sites will appear in the next chapter.

To instead follow the rails more closely from Concord to Worcester, use MA Route 2

West, but take the Littleton exit. When you drive north on Taylor Street, you will cross the tracks once. Join MA Route 2A west in Littleton. Cross the tracks again and drive west to Ayer. If you are a true rail fan, you might want to visit the downtown area and absorb its transportation history. Otherwise, just east of downtown Ayer, take MA Route 110 West. In Harvard, you should make a slight detour and visit the Fruitlands Museums property. Not only does it have connections with Henry Thoreau and Horace Mann, Jr., but it also provides an excellent view of Mount Wachusett. The former Worcester & Nashua tracks lie just beyond the farmhouse.

Continue south on MA Route 100, knowing that the tracks are to your west. In Clinton, you will ride quite close to the tracks. Look for the large power line poles that accompany the tracks. In West Boylston, use MA State Route 140 south for a short time, crossing the tracks once. Then take MA Route 12 south, catching glimpses of the silver poles to your east. You will cross the tracks again and will drive alongside them for a time before reaching downtown Worcester. Divert to the I-290 West highway and take the MA Route 9 West exit. Follow MA Route 9 West onto Highland Street and the neighborhood of the homes of Thoreau's friends, H.G.O. Blake and Theo Brown, as mentioned in the directions above.

FOR MORE INFORMATION

Central Massachusetts Convention and Visitors Bureau, 30 Elm Street, Second Floor Worcester, MA 01609. Phone (508) 755-7400. www.centralmass.org or www.worcester.org.

Concord Band, Post Office Box 302, Concord, MA 01742. Phone (978) 897-9969. www.concordband.org.

Freedom's Way Heritage Area, 94 Jackson Road, Devens, MA 01434. Phone (978) 772-3654. www.freedomsway.org.

Fruitlands Museums, 102 Prospect Hill Road, Harvard, MA 01451. Phone (978) 456-3924. www.fruitlands.org.

Johnny Appleseed Trail of North Central Massachusetts, 860 South Street, Fitchburg, MA 01420. Phone (978) 534-2829. www.appleseed.org.

Massachusetts Bay Transportation Authority, 10 Park Plaza, Suite 3910, Boston, MA 02116 www.mbta.com.

Wachusett Mountain State Reservation, Mountain Road, Princeton, MA 01541. phone (978) 464-2987. www.mass.gov/dcr/parks/central/wach.htm.

RECOMMENDED READING

Thoreau's essay "A Walk to Wachusett," which was first printed posthumously in the book *Excursions* (Ticknor and Fields, 1863). Today it can be found online and also in such compilation volumes as *Thoreau's Collected Essays and Poems* (Library of America, 2001). Also, Louisa May Alcott's essay "Transcendental Wild Oats," which details her family's time at Fruitlands. The text can be found online.

NOTES ON THIS CHAPTER

The last residence of the Thoreau family is now called the Thoreau-Alcott House or "the yellow house" and is at 255 Main Street in Concord. Louisa May Alcott's sister Anna eventually bought the home in 1877. The house the Manns lived in is a large grey-blue building at 67

Sudbury Road. Both are now private homes, so please respect the properties and their owners.

The history of the Damon Mill of West Concord can be found in Renee Garrelick's *Clothier of the Assabet: The Mill and Town of Edward Carver Damon* (2nd ed., [Concord, Mass.]: 1988.) Thoreau's personal ferrying of Francis Jackson Merriam to South Acton is detailed on pages 421-22 of Walter Harding's classic biography, *The Days of Henry Thoreau* (New York: Dover Publications, 1982). American Shaker census statistics, maps and many more cultural insights are available in Priscilla J. Brewer's *Shaker Communities, Shaker Lives* (Hanover, N.H.: University Press of New England, 1986). An interesting account of the creation of the Wachusett Reservoir is found in Nancy Sheehan's article "By a Dam Site: Wachusett Flooding Spared Area Industrial Blight," from the Worcester *Sunday Telegram*, August 22, 2004, beginning on page B1.

In a few instances, I have quoted directly from Thoreau's *Journal*. The passage about the view from the top of Mount Wachusett is dated October 19, 1854. The observations about the blowing snow and the Bigelow mills in Clinton are found in the entry for January 2, 1851. The notes about the Inches Woods in Boxborough are dated November 9-10, 1860. Alan B. Rohwer, chair of the Boxborough Historical Commission, has done work in tracing Thoreau's examinations of Inches Woods. You can see his research online at http://www.multimgmt.com/BHSociety/Thoreauvisits.htm and in the article "Walking Boxborough's Woods with Henry David Thoreau" by Glynis Hamel (*Common Ground*, Spring 2008, p. 2), found at http://www.bctrust.org/Newsletters/NewsletterSpring2008.pdf.

Emerson's famous "No truer American" phrase came in his eulogy for Thoreau, the text of which can be found online or in such publications as *The Portable Emerson* (Carl Bode, ed. New York: Penguin Books, 1981, p. 578). The origins of Julia Ward Howe's lyrics are chronicled in Florence Howe Hall's *The Story of the Battle Hymn of the Republic* (New York: Harper & Brothers, 1916, pp. 50-53). The connection of the Howes and the Manns can be read in Louise Hall Tharp's *The Peabody Sisters of Salem* (Boston: Little, Brown and Company, 1950, pp. 170-171).

Travel Chapter 2

Sunday, May 12, 1861
In Worcester

Expenses: none listed.

Sunday. In Worcester. Rode to east side of Quinsigamond Pond with Blake and Brown and a dry humorist, a gentleman who has been a sportsman and was well acquainted with dogs.

—*Thoreau's Journal, May 12, 1861*

Worcester, Mass. ...it is the seat of the State Lunatic Asylum, also of the American Antiquarian Society, founded in 1812. Population, 24,963.

—*Railroad Gazetteer of the United States, Canada, Etc., 1861*

What better way to begin a long journey than by spending a day of leisure with good friends?

Henry Thoreau and Horace Mann, Jr., stayed overnight in the home of one of Henry's friends. Harrison Gray Otis Blake lived at 3 Bowdoin Street, and just a block away was Theophilus Brown at 10 Chestnut Street. Worcester was a regular stop for Thoreau whenever he traveled southwest by train to Connecticut or to New York. He visited this city on at least a dozen occasions and gave at least nine public lectures there. Young Horace may have previously visited the city as well; but he was probably not as familiar with the Worcester area as was Thoreau. It was nearly Henry's second home.

Lake Quinsigamond, once called Long Pond, lies about three miles due east of Blake and Brown's homes on Court Hill. It forms a natural boundary between Worcester and Shrewsbury. Like New York's Finger Lakes, Quinsigamond has glacial origins and, for the most part, is both narrow and deep. Building a bridge over it proved to be a tricky task in the early 1800s. For many years, a floating bridge connected the two sides. It eventually could not support the heavy loads regularly required of it. As a result, that structure was removed or dismantled sometime in 1861, when construction began on an earthen causeway. That might explain why the travelers "rode around parallel" to the lake. By then, the floating bridge may have been either deemed unsafe or was in the process of being replaced.

And so they rode, presumably a party of five: Blake, Brown, the unknown dog-owner with the dry humor, Henry Thoreau and Horace Mann, Jr. It was certainly not out of the ordinary for the older friends to make such a trip to the lake. They had visited it together on at least four previous occasions. Normally, they walked to it. On only one of those lake trips did they go by carriage. That was on June 17, 1856, when Henry's sister Sophia was also in town. She and her brother rode "round a part of Quinsigamond Pond into Shrewsbury" with Blake and Brown. The decision to take the carriage at this time might have been due to the chilly rain that fell sometime during the day, or it might have been a way for Thoreau's best friends to make the trip easier for him, given the delicate state of his health.Nevertheless, whenever the men were not being regaled with canine tales from the unidentified comrade, they might have pointed out a few memorable places to Horace. The north end of the lake was where they held a private early morning picnic three years earlier. They saw ice skaters at one section in February 1859. By passing through Quinsigamond Village on the southeast side of Worcester, they could see the large Washburn wire factory that Mr. Washburn himself squired Henry around in 1855. To Horace, the sights and sites would have been new, while the rest of the men were traveling down memory lane, one last time.

Worcester's Main Street, as depicted in the 1840s by artist John Warner Barber and engraver S. E. Brown. Old South Church can be seen on the right, facing the old City Hall. A newer and much larger City Hall now stands on this block.

In 1861, there were no roads that paralleled or shadowed the Quinsigamond shoreline. Even by riding, the trip thus may have taken the group the better part of the day to accomplish. They may have taken Plantation Street to Lincoln Street to cross the north end of the water; then headed east into Shrewsbury center and south to the town's South Village. Another road could lead them across the southern end of the lake and onto Grafton Street, which would take them back into downtown Worcester. Or maybe they did some impromptu four-wheeled bushwhacking to more closely follow the water's edge. In any case, this was the only type of journey that H.G.O. Blake could now make with his friend Henry. He had turned down the offer to go west. Surely everyone riding in that carriage knew the silent truth. Not only was this excursion to Minnesota something Thoreau had to unde, it was probably his last chance to do so. And soon enough, the next morning, Henry and Horace would resume their advance toward America's prairie land.

Harrison Gray Otis Blake and Thoreau had both studied at Harvard College in the 1830s. Though their years there overlapped, it wasn't until

A later version of one of the Maxham daguerreotypes from Worcester, photographed and printed by Herbert Wendell Gleason in 1906. (*Courtesy of the Walden Woods Project*)

Ralph Waldo Emerson introduced them to each other in the 1840s that their friendship began to take hold. Blake by then was an Emerson disciple. He had evidently been captivated by the "Divinity School Address" that Emerson gave at Harvard's graduation ceremony in 1838. The words of the former minister resonated with the young man. After only one year of work in a New Hampshire pulpit, Blake decided to quit the ministry, the profession he had trained for, just as Emerson had. Harry became a teacher instead and took a position with a private girls' school in Worcester. He wrote letters to Emerson and visited him in Concord on occasion. But upon re-reading an essay Thoreau wrote in an issue of *The Dial*, Blake was inspired to write to Henry as well. Thus began a steady stream of correspondence and a friendship that lasted thirteen years, until Thoreau's death.

Over the course of that time, Henry sent at least 49 letters to H.G.O. Blake. Receiving such pieces of mail from Thoreau was a treat for his Worcester friend. He would spread the word around town and would assemble a group in his living room to listen as Thoreau's latest missive was read aloud. One of the people often present was Theophilus Brown (1811-1879), a man who made his living as a tailor; but one whom frequent sources describe as being "the wit of Worcester" and an accomplished letter writer himself. Theo Brown did not correspond personally with Henry Thoreau, however, for that was Harry Blake's specialty. Thoreau communicated with Brown and other Worcesterites through Blake.

With Blake and Brown as the nucleus, additional members of the local Thoreauvian clique circled around, came and went. One of them was Thomas Wentworth Higginson (1823-1911), who for several years lived close by at 16 Harvard Street. Higginson is now best known both as numbering among John Brown's Secret Six supporters and as the person who befriended Emily Dickinson and published her first anthology of poetry. He came to Worcester in 1852 to become the pastor of the Free Church on Front Street. Higginson spent ten years in the city before leaving for voluntary duty during the Civil War. He led the country's first all-Black regiment.

Other participants in this literary salon included Dr. Seth Rogers (1823-1893), a "practitioner of hydropathy" who offered the water cure in his local facility; David Atwood Wasson (1822-1887), a minister, writer and sometime Concord resident; Henry Harmon Chamberlin (1813-1899), a local businessman; Edward Everett Hale (1822-1909), a minister and writer; Martha Howland LeBaron (1829-1888), an activist and writer; and the Reverend Horace James (1818-1875), pastor of the Old South Church on the Worcester Common. Whenever Henry Thoreau came to Worcester to lecture, these individuals were likely to be in the audience. Thoreau is even said to have spoken in the more intimate setting of Blake's drawing room or parlor on February 22 and 23, 1859.

But Thoreau's friendship with the Worcester folks extended well beyond the leaves of stationery and beyond any city limits. H.G.O. Blake and Theo Brown became Thoreau's occasional traveling companions. This was an honor that was not bestowed lightly. The Worcesterites had read *Walden*. They had seen the paragraph in the "Solitude" chapter that began: "I find it wholesome to be alone the greater part of the time. To be in company, even with the best, is soon wearisome and dissipating. I love to be alone. I never found the companion that was so companionable as solitude." So it may have come as a slight surprise in April 1857, when Henry included an invitation in a letter to Blake: "Come & be Concord, as I have been Worcestered." After almost a decade of exchanging correspondence and being a regular guest in his friends' homes, the Transcendentalist was finally ready to show off his own hometown.

Thoreau had been prompted to write that pun in part because he had just missed a visit from Blake. His friend had stopped by unannounced while Thoreau was spending two weeks with Daniel Ricketson in New Bedford, Massachusetts. But it turned out to be Theo Brown and Dr. Seth Rogers who first responded to the call to Concord. On the Fourth of July, the three men paddled up the Assabet River together. While Henry was a fan of rivers and waterways, he was an even stronger admirer of New England's mountains and hills. It wasn't long before he included his Worcester friends in that passion. The following summer, Blake and Thoreau rode by rail to Troy, New Hampshire, and then walked to Mount Monadnock. A month later, Thoreau met both Blake and Brown at Tuckerman Ravine on the south side of Mount Washington. They spent four days together exploring the White Mountains of northern New Hampshire.

Those men must have passed the Thoreauvian test of companionship and compatibility. Months later, Henry confided in his journal:

> I know of but one or two persons with whom I can afford to walk. With most the walk degenerates into a mere vigorous use of your legs, ludicrously purposeless, while you are discussing some mighty argument, each one having his say, spoiling each other's day, worrying one another with conversation, hustling one another with our conversation. I know of no use in the walking part in this case, except that we may seem to be

getting on together toward some goal; but of course we keep our original distance all the way. Jumping every wall and ditch with vigor in the vain hope of shaking your companion off. Trying to kill two birds with one stone, though they sit at opposite points of [the] compass, to see nature and do the honors to one who does not.

Who knows who or what incident might have prompted such a diatribe? Scholars can offer up a few suspects: Emerson, Ellery Channing, even Bronson Alcott. Since Henry didn't name names, the guilty parties remain anonymous. However, he must not have felt that way about Blake and Brown. They visited him again in April 1859, and the trio spent one morning paddling down the Concord River to the bridge in Carlisle and back. Companions are rather inescapable within the confines of a rowboat. The Worcester men shared Henry's love of nature. They seemed to always be out and about, whenever they were together.

As Thoreau's health was in serious question during the spring of 1861, H.G.O. Blake and Theo Brown walked from Worcester to Concord to check up on their long-time friend. The 40-mile journey took them two days. According to a letter Thoreau wrote to Daniel Ricketson shortly afterward, the three men "had a solid talk ... for a day & a half—though my pipes were not in good order—& they went their way again." Bronson Alcott noted the arrival of Blake and Brown in his journal. As was his wont, he applied his philosophical insight to their appearance:

> These men have something of the disciple's faith in their master's thoughts, and come sometimes on pilgrimage to Concord for an interview with him. This confidence in persons, this love of the mind, enthusiasm for a great man's thoughts, is a promising trait in anyone, a disposition always graceful to witness, and is far too rarely seen in our times of personal indifference, if not of confessed unbelief in Persons and Ideas. I know of nothing more creditable to Thoreau than this thoughtful regard and constancy by which he has held for years some of the best persons of his time. They are not many, to be sure, but do credit alike to him and themselves.

Thoreau may have sensed this dedication as well. The knowledge may have prompted him to ask Harry Blake to accompany him on his projected three-month Journey West. This he did in his last-known letter to his best friend in Worcester, dated May 3, 1861. There Thoreau revealed his goal to go to Minnesota and his need to find someone to go along with him:

... I have just now decided to let you know of my intentions, thinking it barely possible that you might like to make a part or the whole of this journey, at the same time, & that perhaps your own health may be such as to be benefited by it. Pray let me know, if such a statement offers any temptations to you.

All we know is that Blake, using some method of communication, said no. And after one last visit to the lake, he sent his old friend on his way west, with a much younger and newer friend by his side.

"It's the end of an era," said Worcester native and former Thoreau Society President Edmund A. Schofield, Jr. He and I looked at the four-story building known as Harrington Corner. Strategically positioned at Main and Front Streets in downtown Worcester, it stands very close to City Hall. And on this warm, blue-sky September afternoon in 2009, its entire exterior was covered in scaffolding and green gauze tenting.

"From 1852, and up until a few days ago, there had always been a photographic studio located in that building," Ed continued. "But Mary Melikian had to move out last week. Her new place is a few doors down, on Front Street."

I was suspicious. "They're not going to tear it *down*, are they?"

"Oh, no, no, no. The people who own the donut business on the first floor bought the whole building. I've heard that they're going to renovate it, both inside and out."

We were both quiet, thinking. Above the din of continuous traffic, we could hear the whirl of power tools of the construction workers, even from where we stood in front of City Hall. We both knew the significance of Harrington Corner. To devoted followers of Henry Thoreau, the site is nearly a shrine. In the mid-1850s, 16 Harrington Corner, with its entrance on Main Street, was the location of Benjamin D. Maxham's Daguerrean Palace. And it was here in June 1856, that Thoreau sat for his image to be duplicated via daguerreotype. He had three copies made. Each one cost fifty cents. The first two went to Blake and Brown. They might have even been present for the sitting.

The third was sent to fan-by-mail Calvin H. Greene of Rochester, Michigan. Mr. Greene had evidently been wonder-struck by reading Thoreau's *Walden*, and he began corresponding with the author. In a letter that did not survive, he asked Thoreau for a photograph so that he could see his new idol in person. Henry did not have one at the ready. "You may rely on it that you have the best of me in my books, and that I am not worth seeing personally—the stuttering, blundering clod-hopper that I am," he initially answered. But his extended stay in Worcester that June gave him time and opportunity to have such a thing created. He sent the third print to Greene with a bill for fifty cents and an apologetic explanation: "While in Worcester this week I obtained the accompanying daguerreotype—which my friends think is pretty good—though better looking than I." This print has become the most familiar portrait we have of Henry David Thoreau.

On this day in 2009, I followed Ed on his personal "Thoreau in Worcester" walking tour. No one was better qualified. Ed had been a Thoreauvian for more than fifty years. He had done more original research on both Worcester and on Thoreau than anyone I knew: certainly more than anyone else still breathing on the planet. He loved his hometown, "the second largest city in New England, when Providence doesn't cheat on the census," he proudly boasted. Curious, I looked up the statistics later. In the year 2000 census, the Rhode Island capital won that contest by the narrowest of margins, 173,618 to 172,648. I decided not to ask Ed about the 970 bodies that made the difference. I had a feeling he would have a theory about them.

We had just walked down from Court Hill after paying homage to the home sites of Blake and Brown. Neither house remains. Ed maintained that the city should name a nearby grass median with a sycamore tree "Transcendental Park" and put a bench on it. I liked the idea but held my tongue. I could not think of a reason why anyone would choose to sit in the middle of a complex of colliding streets. Still, it would make a nice memorial to Thoreau's Worcester friends, especially since they had much to do with his later popularity.

While we can still walk where Henry and Harry and Theo walked, it's getting more difficult to visit the same buildings they did. Harrington Corner is a pleasant exception, which may be why we felt a connection to it. Many of the others have been torn down and replaced. Take for instance the current City Hall, since it is a good starting point for this downtown tour. It was built in 1898. So we should erase it from view and put in its place a much smaller City Hall on the southeast corner of Main and Front, at about where the George Frisbie Hoar statue currently sits. Next to it sat the Old South Church, with its front door facing City Hall. That was what this side of the Common looked like when Thoreau gave lectures at Worcester's City Hall on April 20, 1849, and on January 4, 1855. On the first occasion, his first-ever speech in Worcester, he spoke on "Economy;" and for the second, he offered his "What Shall It Profit" speech. Neither one was overwhelmingly well received by the general public, according to reports in the newspapers.

We took a closer look at that statue next to the present-day City Hall. George Frisbie Hoar (1826-1904) was noted in stone to have been a "Lawyer—Scholar—Orator—Statesman." A list of his accomplishments followed. Hoar amassed a long history of public service, serving both Worcester and Massachusetts as a state Representative and later, as a U.S. Senator. He was also born in Concord, where he was first a classmate of and then a student of Henry Thoreau. In his autobiography, Hoar recalled with a certain fondness his friendship with the man:

> I went to school with him when I was a little boy and he was a big one. Afterward I was a scholar in his school. ... We used to call him Trainer Thoreau, because the boys called the soldiers the "trainers," and he had a long, measured stride and an erect carriage which made him seem something like a soldier, although he was short and rather ungainly in figure. ... He knew the rare forest birds and all the ways of birds and wild animals. ... He had the most wonderful good fortune. We used to say that if anything happened in the deep woods which only came about once in a hundred years, Henry Thoreau would be sure to be on the spot at the time and know the whole story. ... I retained his friendship to his death. I have taken many a long walk with him. I used to go down to see him in the winter days in my vacations in his hut near Walden. He was capital company. He was a capital guide in the wood. He liked to take out the boys in his boat. He was fond of discoursing. I do not think he was vain. But he liked to do his thinking out loud, and expected that you should be an auditor rather than a companion.

Hoar's statue was crafted by Daniel Chester French, another Concordian and the sculptor responsible for the Minuteman statue at Concord's North Bridge as well as the large image of Abraham Lincoln in his Memorial in Washington, D.C. Additional Concord connections continued to surface in Worcester.

Resuming Ed's tour, we crossed Main Street right there, at City Hall. From that vantage point, we got a good look at Harrington Corner at 427 Main Street. We headed north along Main. The tailor shop of William, Albert, and Theo Brown was once located at the corner of Main and Pearl. It was now the Slater Building, housing a variety of offices at 390 Main. The

Warren Block used to be located behind Brown's store, along Pearl Street. That was at one time the site of H.G.O. Blake's School Parlors. Here Henry Thoreau gave his "Walking, or the Wild" lecture on May 31, 1851.

The next western cross street with Main was Elm. The parsonage for the Old South Church was once located about halfway down that first block of Elm, on the right-hand side. Rev. Horace James lived there when Henry Thoreau visited his home on June 17, 1856. He stopped there to see the minister's reptile collection, but there were amphibians, too: frogs, toads, salamanders. Some of them were in bottles filled with alcohol; others were still alive in separate containers. Rev. James had a few snakes, a turtle shell with someone's initials carved into it, and even a few stuffed birds. It must have been quite a display for a private naturalist to have assembled.

We continued north on Main, and looked at the Commerce Building at 340 Main. This was where Brinley Hall once stood. It was a brick building, three stories tall, that was built in the 1830s, and then demolished in 1895. A lecture hall was located on the top floor. The historic signs on the outside walls told us that Brinley Hall was the site of the first National Woman's Rights Convention in 1850. The Massachusetts Teachers Association was founded here in 1845. What we didn't read was that Henry Thoreau gave three public speeches here. On April 27, 1849, he presented "Life in the Woods." Six days later, on May 3rd, he gave his "White Beans and Walden Pond" lecture. Then on February 13, 1857, he reprised "Walking, or the Wild," the talk he gave six years earlier in Blake's School Parlors. This time, he would have had a larger venue and a wider audience.

We crossed Main Street again and walked down Foster Street. Our target was the building marked as 11 Foster Street. It was now physically attached to the bank at 365 Main Street. In Thoreau's day, there was a Universalist church instead of a bank at that address; and The Bank Block, as it was then called, was a free-standing structure behind it. That was the location of the Natural History Society rooms that Thoreau visited on June 16, 17, and 19 in 1856. Along with Harrington Corner, this was one of the few sites on this tour that has not been torn down.

Unlike Rev. James's private collection, the displays of the Natural History Society were managed by an organization. Thomas Wentworth Higginson was one of its principle founding members (as were Edward Everett Hale and George Frisbie Hoar), and he donated a number of plant species to the cause. These were among the items that Thoreau saw and mentioned in his journal in 1856. It must have been a place that fascinated him, for he dropped in on it three times in four days. All of the collections of the

Natural History Society were now housed at the EcoTarium, which was located on Harrington Way, closer to Lake Quinsigamond than to the downtown area. The interior of 11 Foster Street now consisted of a variety of offices.

Ed and I walked around the corner to the rear of 11 Foster Street, which faced the one-block-long Norwich Street. The plaque attached to the building announced the location of the first railway station in Worcester. We turned around to stare at the building at 19 Foster Street, now housing the Worcester campus of the Massachusetts College of Pharmacy and Health Sciences. That structure did not exist in Thoreau's day. Instead, that was the site of the depot that served the Worcester and Nashua railroad line. That's where Henry arrived from Concord, whenever he took the train to visit this city. That's where Henry and Horace pulled into when they stopped here, on their way to Minnesota. It is *not* the station they left from, however. In the early days of the railroad, each line had its tracks and its own station; and the depot for the Western Railroad was several blocks away. The tracks that ran through this part of town are gone, having been diverted a block or two east of here long, long ago.

The two of us went back to Main Street and headed north again. We stopped at Mechanics Hall at 321 Main Street. This was the site of Henry Thoreau's biggest triumph in Worcester: his lecture titled "The Character and Actions of Capt. John Brown" on November 3, 1859. He had already given this impassioned speech in Concord and in Boston just days earlier. Harry Blake was able to make the arrangements for Thoreau to speak in the Washburn Hall portion of the building, on the second floor. An announcement in that day's *Worcester Daily Spy* read in part:

> ...as Mr. Thoreau never deals in common places,—as he considers John Brown a hero,—and as he has been so moved by the Harper's Ferry affair, as to feel compelled to leave his customary seclusion in order to address the public, what he has to say is likely to be worth hearing.

Admission was ten cents. Bronson Alcott later noted in his journal that Henry's speech "was received here by our Concord folks with great favor, and he won praise for it also at Worcester." Henry was in essence eulogizing a condemned man. John Brown was hanged less than a month later, on December 2, 1859.

Mechanics Hall was built in 1857 to accommodate the Worcester County Mechanics Association. It stood three stories tall. The first floor, at street level, consisted of shops that opened to Main Street. Washburn Hall was located on the second floor. Wire industrialist Ichabod Washburn, perhaps the very man who gave Thoreau a tour of his factory, donated $25,000 toward the construction costs. The lectern that Thoreau spoke from is still part of the facility. The Great Hall was on the third floor. The entire building was renovated and restored during the latter part of the twentieth century. It is on the National Register of Historic Places. The list of speakers and performers who have appeared here throughout the years reads like an impressive Who's Who of the best and most recognizable names and faces in the arts and in society at large. The halls are still used for concerts and lectures today.

Ed and I crossed Main Street and continued to head north. Though we walked several blocks without seeing any major Thoreauvian landmarks, he could not help but point out other notable sites in Worcester history. The Central Exchange Building at 311 Main Street—not that exact structure, but the one that preceded it on that spot—housed the post office for the neighborhood. Here Thomas Wentworth Higginson picked up that first letter Emily Dickinson sent to him, asking him for some advice on writing poetry. The large brick building we passed at 156 Main Street was the first brick building to be erected in town, in 1831. It was the country's longest-running hardware store as well. The First Unitarian Church at 90 Main Street was one of the first Unitarian churches in the country. H.G.O. Blake attended services here. Nearly every inch of every street in Worcester seemed to have some kind of historical significance.

As a matter of fact, if you paid attention and read all of the plaques along Worcester's Main Street, you would discover that this city had almost as many connections to the American Revolution as Concord did. A sidewalk marker in front of the current City Hall reads: "Here July 14, 1776, the Declaration of Independence was first publicly read in New England by Isaiah Thomas from the Western porch of the meeting-house later known as the Old South Church." Ed explained to me that the rider who was carrying the document from Philadelphia to Boston had stopped in Worcester, and local publisher Thomas wanted to know what he was up to. When he learned that the man had the new Declaration with him, Thomas decided to read it aloud to the residents of Worcester. He made history by doing so.

We encountered a few more markers along Main Street. General Henry Knox came through here with the cannon he captured at Fort Ticonderoga during the winter of 1777-1778. George Washington himself passed along this road on his way to Cambridge to assume command of the Continental troops. Had it not been for its distance from Boston and the obstacle caused by Lake Quinsigamond, the British regulars might very well have marched on Worcester instead of Concord and Lexington on April 19, 1775. The "shot heard 'round the world" could have been fired here. Worcester was an important stop on a vital travel route.

In terms of Henry Thoreau and how we think of him today, the city of Worcester has also had a distinguished legacy. It went well beyond what we had seen in our walking tour this day. Harrison Gray Otis Blake inherited all of Thoreau's notebooks and journals when Sophia Thoreau died in 1876. He began to take the journal contents public by reading selections aloud at Bronson Alcott's School of Philosophy sessions in Concord in 1879. The positive reaction he received encouraged him toward more formal publication. Blake culled seasonal remarks from Henry's jottings and assembled them into four volumes: *Early Spring in Massachusetts* (1881), *Summer* (1884), *Winter* (1888), and *Autumn* (1892). These books served to publicize Thoreau's words and to reach an audience not yet familiar with the author of *Walden.*

From Blake the original manuscripts passed on to Elias Harlow Russell (1836-1917), principal of the Worcester State Normal School (now Worcester State University). Thoreau had once met Russell at H.G.O. Blake's house. Russell began negotiations with Houghton Mifflin to publish the entire run of Thoreau's *Journal.* The project eventually came to fruition in 1906, when the bulk of Henry Thoreau's work was published in a twenty-volume set by Houghton Mifflin. That release laid the groundwork for other fans and followers to come, all working to further Thoreau's popularity and reputation. We might not have any of these resources today, if it were not for the efforts of these two Worcester men.

Ed and I discussed these familiar facts as we ambled through the downtown area. He pointed east to the large DCU Center arena a few blocks away. He told me that the first concert to benefit the Walden Woods Project was held there too, in April 1990, back when the building was called the Worcester Centrum. So even in a more contemporary time, Worcester played a role in preserving something vital to Henry David Thoreau and to present-day Thoreauvians.

We reached the intersection of Main with Highland Street and the last stop on our "Thoreau in Worcester" tour. To our left was the large courthouse building, recently replaced by the newer and even bigger one that had been on our right just minutes before. And there was another statue, this time of General Charles Devens (1820-1891) on his horse. Devens practiced law in Worcester; but he also served with an infantry unit in the Civil War, and he was Rutherford B. Hayes' Attorney General. His was another Daniel Chester French sculpture, so we found yet another Concord connection.

But before the sculpture was cast and was moved here from its original starting point down the block, there was a building that sat at this corner. It was the home of the American Antiquarian Society. Henry Thoreau visited this library on January 4, 1855, while he was in town to lecture. "It is richer in pamphlets and newspapers than Harvard," he wrote in his journal. And he would know, since he regularly used the resources of the Harvard library, even as an alumnus. In 1912, the AAS moved to its current home at 185 Salisbury Street. The facility maintains an even more massive collection today, with the specific focus of American history through the Civil War and Reconstruction periods.

We trudged uphill along Highland Street, returning full circle to the car we had left at the Salisbury Mansion parking lot. I was slowing down, even panting. At age 70, Ed was still going strong. He spoke about how E. Harlow Russell taught at one of the Salisbury Mansion buildings, and I have to admit that I was barely listening. We had just spent the better part of two hours walking the streets of downtown Worcester, seesawing across the centuries, and comparing buildings merely drawn on maps to their contemporary counterparts. For much of that time we had chatted, speculated, debated, and even argued over the numerous activities of Thoreau and Mann and Blake and Brown and countless others who frequented these neighborhoods 150 years beforehand. I could not speak for Ed, but I now understood what it was like to be thoroughly Worcestered.

WHEN YOU GO: If you try to recreate today what must have been a slow-paced carriage ride from Harry Blake's house to Lake Quinsigamond, you will be faced with a number of challenges. The first one lies in figuring out exactly where Blake's house was. It's no longer standing. Even his address of 3 Bowdoin Street is nonexistent. In the space of time between Thoreau's and ours, the streets of Worcester have changed: moderately so, west of Main Street; more dramatically so to the east of it. Even if you hold an old city map in one hand and a new one in the other, you'll have to spend a good long while deciphering what was where and how it corresponds with what you see today. You will need to be alert for traffic at the same time.

For your first approach to the site of Blake's home, it is better to be on foot and not behind the wheel, maneuvering a vehicle. A good place to park is in the metered lot at the historic Salisbury Mansion at 40 Highland Street, which is also MA Route 9. Cross at the light and walk south along Harvard Street. Walk past its intersection with Dix Street. Stop at the next intersection, with John Street, and look around. You'll be able to see that Bowdoin Street lies a block beyond John, to the west. You'll also see a maze of lanes before you. They resemble not a proper New England rotary, but a Gordian knot of perplexing pavements that lead seemingly hither and yon. They allow northbound one-way traffic on both Harvard and Chestnut Streets to change direction and cross over to Linden Street, which runs one-way southbound. The spot is formally called Morris Square (and you might even be able to spy the tiny sign that labels it so). In 1861, there was no need for such an enterprise of civil engineering. But in the twentieth century, the residential blocks on either side of that portion of Bowdoin Street were sacrificed in order to accommodate motorists. H.G.O. Blake's former house was in the way and was torn down.

But you might be able to imagine where it was and what it looked like. It was a simple frame building, probably painted white. It stood two and a half stories tall, with several chimneys rising above the gabled roof. Enough property lay behind it to ensure that Thoreau could see and hear the birds in the trees of Blake's yard. The house was perched in one of two places: either on the grassy median that now contains a small sycamore tree and the remnants of a stone foundation, or in the yard just south of that median, adjacent to a large white building. Harry Blake lived in a location that was certainly in the thick of things at the time, just one block west of Worcester's Main Street. Unfortunately, that position led to its ultimate demise.

It's a bit easier to find the site where Theo Brown and his family lived, about a block south. Tragically, the end result is the same. Like the home of his friend Blake, Brown's house at the northeast corner of Chestnut and Sudbury is gone, in this instance replaced by a parking lot rimmed with a spiked wrought-iron railing. Sadly enough, whenever I have driven past it, the space has always been devoid of cars. It's as if the property has been cordoned off merely as a monument to macadam. Surely leaving one city-sized house there would not have interfered with local commerce.

Nevertheless, you can pick that general area of Worcester's Court Hill as a starting point for your jaunt to Lake Quinsigamond. Head for MA Route 9, and turn right (east) on that road. You may then be technically driving on Highland Street, but it will soon become Belmont Street. Go through the congestion of Lincoln Square and head uphill. Cross over I-290 and be prepared for the road to narrow from four lanes to two. At the top of the long hill, give a nod to Bell Pond on the right, where Thoreau encountered ice fishermen on February 23, 1859. No high-rises lined the beach then. On the other side of the street is an entrance to Green Hill Park. That property includes the "Hermitage Woods" that Thoreau and his sister Sophia and their aunts visited on June 14, 1856. You might still be able to find descendants of the buckthorn bushes that Henry saw and documented in his journal on that day.

From that point Route 9 continues generally downhill toward the lake and gets wider along the way. At its intersection with Lake Avenue, you have a choice to make. You can continue east and cross the lake at the exact spot where the floating bridge existed in Thoreau's time. The town of Shrewsbury lies on the other side, with shopping and dining opportunities galore. Or, you can turn south on Lake Avenue in order to hang out at the Lake Park portion of Quinsigamond State Park. This site can offer a somewhat quiet respite from the city and the traffic, and it offers nice views of the water. Or, you can turn north on Lake Avenue to visit Regatta Point, the other portion of the state park. That's where the local rowing teams launch and train, using the length and narrowness of the former glacial river to their ultimate arm-numbing advantage.

If you've reached that intersection without having come to a clear decision, the drivers behind and beside your car may quickly make up your mind for you. Never fear! Armed with either a good map or a good nose for navigation, you can still do what Henry, Horace and their companions did on that day: ride parallel to the lake. "I think that not only the channel, but one or both banks of every river should be a public highway, for a river is not useful merely to float on," Thoreau once wrote. Back in 1861, he and his friends had no such roads to ride along in order to admire the glistening waters of Quinsigamond, as contemporary travelers do.

No matter what lane you find yourself in, or what road you have been forced to take, you should be able to eventually return to Lake Avenue in Worcester or to Quinsigmond Avenue in Shrewsbury. These roads generally parallel the lake to the west and east, respectively. You can skirt the north end of the lake with Lincoln Street and the south end with U.S. Route 20. Don't expect to have an unobstructed view of the lake for the duration of the trip, however. And be prepared for Worcester and Shrewsbury to reveal their distinct personalities: the industrial city versus the upscale suburban community. The block-like businesses and work-er homes lie on the west side; the cottages and McMansions on the east. None of them were here in 1861. We can go where Thoreau has gone, but we can never see exactly what he saw. At least his dream of a shoreline roadway is realized here, though probably not quite in the form he would have envisioned.

Even the busiest of drivers, those who are merely passing through the Worcester area and are headed for other destinations, can catch a tiny glimpse of this bit of "Thoreau Country" from I-290. The northernmost end of Lake Quinsigamond lies just west of exit 22, at about mile marker 10. Look for the water and, in three seasons, the practicing teams of rowboats. You can tell your passengers with confidence that Henry David Thoreau once ate a lakeside breakfast in that neighborhood.

FOR MORE INFORMATION

Central Massachusetts Convention and Visitors Bureau, 30 Worcester Center Boulevard, Worcester, MA 01608. Phone (800) 231-7557. www.centralmass.org or www.worcester.org.

Mechanics Hall, 321 Main Street, Worcester, MA 01608. Phone (508) 752-5608. www.mechanicshall.org.

Quinsigamond State Park, 10 North Lake Avenue, Worcester, MA 01605. Phone (508) 755-6880. www.mass.gov/dcr/parks/central/quin.htm.

Salisbury Mansion, 40 Highland Street, Worcester, MA 01609. Phone (508) 753-8278. www.worcesterhistory.org/mansion.html.

RECOMMENDED READING

Letters to a Spiritual Seeker (Henry David Thoreau, ed. by Bradley P. Dean, W.W. Norton: 2004), which provides the text and details of 50 pieces of existing correspondence between Thoreau and his Worcester friend, Harrison Gray Otis Blake.

NOTES ON THIS CHAPTER

Insights into the lives of H.G.O. Blake, Theo Brown, and the other locals are offered in two long articles penned by Ruth Hallingby Frost: "Thoreau's Worcester Associations: His Intimate Friends" and "Thoreau's Other Friends and Acquaintances in Worcester." Some of that material was published in *Nature Outlook* magazine. Frost's original manuscript is on file with the American Antiquarian Society. Also helpful in establishing the relationship between Thoreau and Blake is Brad Dean's book, *Letters to a Spiritual Seeker* (New York: W.W. Norton: 2004), as well as the usual biographies, including Walter Harding's *The Days of Henry Thoreau: A Biography* (New York: Dover Publications, 1982). Details about the Maxham daguerreotype was based on those sources as well.

A detailed chronology of Thoreau's lecturing activities once appeared on the Thoreau Institute web site at http://www.walden.org, and is slated to be reposted. That invaluable resource was drawn from work done by Bradley P. Dean and Ronald Wesley Hoag which first appeared in the 1995 and 1996 issues of *Studies in the American Renaissance*, edited by Joel Myerson.

Entries in Thoreau's *Journal* that pertain to visiting Worcester or traveling with Worcester friends can be found under the following dates: June 3, 1851; January 4-5, 1855; June 12-19, 1856; February 12-15, 1857; July 4, 1857; May 23, 1858; February 22-25, 1859; May 11-12, 1861. The diatribe about walking with or without a companion appears on November 8, 1858. The quote about rivers and public highways comes from page 236 of *Wild Fruits: Thoreau's Rediscovered Last Manuscript* (Bradley P. Dean, ed., New York: W.W. Norton, 2000). Correspondence between Thoreau and Calvin H. Greene is included in *The Correspondence of Henry David Thoreau* (Walter Harding and Carl Bode, eds., New York: New York University Press, 1958). The letter to Daniel Ricketson that mentioned Blake and Brown's walk to Concord was dated March 22, 1861. Bronson Alcott's journal entry about the same was dated March 1, 1861. George Frisbie Hoar wrote about Thoreau on pages 70-72 of his *Autobiography of Seventy Years* (New York: C. Scribner's Sons, 1903).

The 1971 reprints of the two 1870 F.W. Beers atlases, *Atlas of the City of Worcester, Worcester County, Massachusetts* and *Atlas of Worcester County, Massachusetts* lent a hand in determining the positions of roads.

The floating bridge that spanned Lake Quinsigamond in the mid-1800s was replaced by an earthen causeway that limited sailing and effectively cut the lake into two parts. The best description of the various bridges that have existed at that spot is in Albert B. Southwick's essay "Getting Across the Lake" in *Once-Told Tales of Worcester County* (Worcester: Telegram & Gazette, 1985). I found additional documentation in town reports that reported that the causeway work was begun in the fall of 1861, and that the finished product opened in June 1862. But the floating bridge would have had to have been removed first, before any dirt and gravel was brought in. I have been unable to determine for certain what the state of the bridge was in May 1861. It may have remained in place; it may have been gone by the time of Henry and Horace's visit.

H.G.O. Blake lived at 3 Bowdoin Street when Thoreau corresponded with him and visited with him. But in later years, Blake moved to other locations in the neighborhood: to the houses currently standing at 69 West Street and at 46 William Street. He died in the latter in 1898.

Ed Schofield and I actually walked this "Thoreau in Worcester" tour twice, several years apart. What appears here is an amalgam of the two, though the Harrington Corner renovation occurred in the fall of 2009. Ed often included two more tidbits/stops on this tour. One was that whenever H.G.O. Blake traveled away from Worcester in the days when he owned Henry Thoreau's manuscripts, they were stored in Antiquarian Hall, formerly located at the current site of the General Devens statue. The other was that the new courthouse on Main Street contains H.G.O. Blake's will, which bequeaths Thoreau's manuscripts to E. Harlow Russell. I am in eternal debt to Ed for sharing his knowledge with me.

Travel Chapter 3

Monday, May 13, 1861
Worcester to Albany
via the Western Railroad

Expenses: Through-ticket from Worcester to Chicago, $25.25.
At Springfield, 6 cents. At Albany, .50 + $2.00.

The latter part of the day rainy. The hills come near the railroad between Westfield and Chester Village. Thereafter in Massachusetts they may be as high or higher, but are somewhat further off. The leafing is decidedly more advanced in western Massachusetts than in eastern. Apple trees are greenish. Red elder-berry is apparently just beginning to bloom. Put up at the Delavan House. Not so good as costly.

—Thoreau's Journal, May 13, 1861

We see things much greener here than at home. Our room overlooks the railroad and also the Hudson river.

—Horace Mann Jr.'s letter of May 13, 1861

H.G.O. Blake probably drove Henry Thoreau and Horace Mann by carriage to the depot of the Western Railroad in downtown Worcester, just east of Washington Square, in order to catch the 9 a.m. train that Monday. The station was little more than a dozen blocks from Blake's home; but if Henry was not feeling up to the walk, it was best to ride the distance. After goodbyes and good wishes, the two travelers continued on their Journey West. Now they headed into less familiar territory. They would not see a familiar face again until they reached Chicago.

Massachusetts and New York residents were at odds long before any caustic Red Sox-Yankees rivalry forced baseball fans to choose between the two. As the colonies grew and the United States was formed, both Boston and New York City wanted to become the commercial center of the country. New England had an early advantage with its flourishing maritime industry operating out of Salem, New Bedford, and Cape Cod, as well as from Boston harbor. A true economic leader would not only have to attract international coastal trade, but also accommodate interior exchange. On that playing field, New York took the lead in 1825, when it opened the Erie Canal and created a link between the Great Lakes and the Hudson River valley. Boston was suddenly a runner-up in the competition. Its 27-mile-long Middlesex Canal to New Hampshire paled in comparison to New York's cross-state accomplishment. That is, until men began financing and building railroads.

The 1830s saw a flurry of activity in the field of transportation. Private railroad companies were established, stocks were issued, locomotives were designed, and tracks were laid. The Boston and Worcester Railway connected those two cities on July 4, 1835. But its directors were already looking west, speculating on reaching Springfield and crossing the Berkshire Mountains into New York State. There they hoped to link with an existing railroad line that could take riders all the way to the Hudson River.

By 1836, surveyors and engineers William H. Swift, William Gibbs McNeill, and George Washington Whistler were scrambling about the hills and valleys of western Massachusetts, searching for the best path the Western Railroad Corporation could carve through that dynamic landscape. The directors wanted to save money by laying only a single track. Major Whistler, by then the chief engineer of the project, instead insisted that all of the supporting infrastructures be wide enough to accommodate two tracks in order to plan for the future.

Once the engineers' report was filed, work began on various sections. The Worcester to Springfield span opened on October 1, 1839. Two years later, in December 1841, and with the temporary use of several miles of track on the Hudson & Berkshire line, the Western Railroad became a reality. Travelers could now successfully take the train from Boston to Greenbush, N.Y., where a ferry would carry them across the Hudson River to Albany. A grand celebration ensued, as railroad administrators and Boston officials rode west and were received and entertained by Teunis Van Vechten, the mayor of Albany, and by the governor of New York, William H. Seward. The editor of the *Utica* (N.Y.) *Daily News* wrote, "We have hitherto been strangers to the people of Boston and they to us. ... But the Capitals of the Bay and the Empire State now lie cheek by jowl. ... Boston will be our sister depot." What a slap in the face for the folks down in New York City! For seven or eight years, they had been talking about creating a New York & Albany Railroad. Their mere words had yet to lay a single rail. The men of Boston and Massachusetts had beaten the New Yorkers to their own capital city.

The effort had not been without its challenges. Along the Western's 155-mile length, only seven miles passed over relatively level land. The engineers' route led the rail bed along the swampy Quaboag River, and many times over the Westfield River and its winding West Branch. In between lay the wide Connecticut River, which required the construction of a seven-span wooden bridge at Springfield. And then there was the Berkshire Range, which led the tracks up to a height of 1,456 feet above sea level. When it was completed in 1841, the Western Railroad of western Massachusetts was the longest and most expensive railroad project undertaken by a single American corporation to that date.

Major Whistler hired veteran contractor and Scottish stonemason Alexander Birnie to design and build more than two dozen bridges, culverts, and walls along the line. Included were ten keystone arch bridges that would carry the railroad high above the curvaceous Westfield River. Assembled of local stone and without the use of mortar, the arches represented a labor-intensive, costly addition to the project. But wooden bridges placed in such remote outposts would have been difficult to reach for routine maintenance. The stone arches, it was hoped, would stand for some time on their own.

When Henry Thoreau and Horace Mann rode the length of the Western on May 13, 1861, parts of the stretch already held two tracks instead of the original one. Major Whistler's prophesy had quickly come true. In 1847, work was begun to expand the entire line to a double track.

Less than half an hour after leaving Worcester, Henry and Horace passed just two miles north of the birthplace of Clara Barton (1822-1912) in North Oxford. Barton had moved away from the tiny white house many years earlier, and had been working for the U.S. Patent Office in Washington, D.C., since 1854. As the two men rode close to her home, Barton was already attending to war casualties who were making their way to the nation's capital. It would be another year before the War Department officially allowed her to take her nursing practice directly into the field of battle.

Onward our travelers rode: through Charlton, Spencer, and the Brookfields. In West Brookfield, they passed two miles south of the childhood home of women's rights and antislavery leader Lucy Stone (1818-1893). The outbreak of the war had given her a break from speaking engagements, and she had returned to her farm in Montclair, New Jersey. Stone occasionally followed the same lecture circuit and spoke in some of the same venues that Thoreau did. In fact, the two had shared the platform at the Massachusetts Anti-Slavery Society rally in Framingham on July 4, 1854. A frenzied gathering in the wake of former slave Anthony Burns' recent arrest in Boston, the festivities featured additional speeches by William Lloyd Garrison, Moncure Conway, Sojourner Truth, Wendell Phillips, and Stephen Foster. It was then that Henry Thoreau took the stage and issued the searing words of his "Slavery in Massachusetts" lecture. "A government which deliberately enacts injustice, and persists, in it," he insisted, "will at length ever become the laughing-stock of the world." At the Warren-Palmer town line, the train crossed the Quaboag River via a stone arch bridge that the passengers benefited from but could not see for themselves.

At about 11:30 a.m., the train pulled into the Western station in Springfield, a city of 15,000 residents. Riders were given 45 minutes to walk about, stretch their legs, and perhaps catch a bite to eat before the locomotive would start pulling them through the Berkshires. Thoreau's expense account indicates that he spent six cents in Springfield. What did he buy? Issues of the *Springfield Republican*, the local newspaper that his friend Frank Sanborn contributed to as a correspondent, cost just two cents each. Perhaps instead he bought a lunchtime snack to make do until he and Horace had dinner in Albany. No other clue exists.

Three quarters of an hour did not provide much time to stroll around the small but bustling city. Henry Vose, one of Thoreau's Harvard classmates, had practiced law here for many years, and Thoreau corresponded with him on at least one occasion. But in 1859, Vose had been selected judge of the Massachusetts Superior Court and had accordingly moved to Boston. We do not know of any other connections Henry and Horace might have fostered in Springfield.

Having no friends to visit, they may have taken the opportunity to walk up State Street and observe the activity at the large complex of brick buildings just a few blocks south of the station. That was the busy Springfield Armory, a military arsenal that had been in operation since the Revolutionary War. Now 350 men were currently assembling rifle muskets at the production rate of 1500 per month. Thirty thousand Springfield rifles had recently been sent to arm units in New York and Pennsylvania. The frenzy at the armory was a reminder that the country was indeed at war.

If the travelers caught part of the Armory operation, Henry Thoreau at least would have been reminded of the poem written about the place by Henry Wadsworth Longfellow (1807-1882). It had become quite popular when it was first published, sixteen years earlier. With "The Arsenal at Springfield," Thoreau's former Harvard professor took a strong anti-war stand. Here's how the twelve-stanza verse began, as its author looked upon the long rows of finished rifles standing upright, barrel by barrel and stock by stock:

This is the Arsenal. From floor to ceiling,
   Like a huge organ, rise the burnished arms;
But from their silent pipes no anthem pealing
   Startles the villages with strange alarms.

Ah! what a sound will rise, how wild and dreary,
   When the death-angel touches those swift keys!
What loud lament and dismal Miserere
   Will mingle with their awful symphonies!

I hear even now the infinite fierce chorus,
   The cries of agony, the endless groan,
Which, through the ages that have gone before us,
   In long reverberations reach our own.

If the action at the Armory didn't hold the men's interest, they could have walked to a storefront on Main Street where a new business had just opened. It was an indoor shooting gallery. "Patriotic Union men" were invited inside to take pot shots with live ammunition at a posted image of Jefferson Davis, the President of the Confederacy. The initial promotion in the *Springfield Republican* did not state what the price of admission might be for such entertainment. But young Horace did have his own shotgun with him.

When their train ride resumed, the cars crossed over the Connecticut River and began not only an ascent into the mountains, but also a game of leapfrog with the Westfield River. Both Henry and Horace noted here that the leaves were a bit fuller and the landscape a bit greener than what they had witnessed in Concord just two days earlier. These observations seem backward, for they were headed into the interior and into mountains that were technically in the next hardiness zone. Back home, the effects of the still-cool water of the Atlantic along the Massachusetts coast could have accounted for the difference. The Berkshires were also more wooded than the farmland of Middlesex County, so they might have appeared naturally greener. And the state had just had a rainy week, receiving more than two inches in the previous seven days. In any event: Spring was springing, and Henry and Horace were documenting the season's advance as they rode high above the cascading Westfield waters, courtesy of Whistler and Birnie's stone arch bridges.

Perhaps as they passed through the mountain towns of Chester, Becket, and Hinsdale, Henry Thoreau looked out a west-facing window and had a chance to recall his previous excursion to the Berkshires. He had been 27 years old when he left Concord on foot for a solo journey in the summer of 1844. He first hiked to Mount Monadnock in New Hampshire, where he camped at the summit. Then he continued southwest through the valleys of the Connecticut and Deerfield Rivers to the town of North Adams and to Massachusetts' highest peak at 3,491 feet, Mount Greylock. He knew it as "Saddle-back Mountain." An energetic but far from accomplished climber, Thoreau painstakingly made his way up its steep sides without benefit of guide or path. When he reached the top, he could see the buildings of Williams College in Williamstown, five miles to the northwest. Though he himself had attended the oldest and most prestigious educational institution in the state (if not the country), Henry admired both the sight and the site:

> It would really be no small advantage if every college were thus located at the base of a mountain, as good at least as one well-endowed professorship. It were as well to be educated in the shadow of a mountain as in more classical shades. Some will remember, no doubt, not only that they went to the college, but that they went to the mountain. Every visit to its summit would, as it were, generalize the particular information gained below, and subject it to more catholic tests.

No stranger to the mountains of New England, Thoreau had already walked to Wachusett in central Massachusetts and had climbed Mount Washington in northern New Hampshire by the time he scaled Greylock. Still, the view from such heights never failed to impress him. After spending what must have been an uncomfortable and chilly night sleeping on the ground, covered only with discarded wooden boards as makeshift blankets, Thoreau awoke to a magical sight. "All around beneath me was spread for a hundred miles on every side, as far as the eye could reach, an undulating country of clouds, answering in the varied swell of its surface to the terrestrial world it veiled. It was such a country as we might see in dreams, with all the delights of paradise." To the southwest, he had already caught a glimpse of his goal for this trip: "the summits of new and yet higher mountains, the Catskills, by which I might hope to climb to heaven again...." He set his compass for Pontoosuc Lake to the south and made his way down the mountain.

Back then, the plan was for his new friend Ellery Channing to meet him at the railroad station in Pittsfield. There the two men intended to board a westbound Western train, proceed to the Hudson River, then sail south and spend some time exploring those elusive mountains. By the time he joined Channing, Henry had been camping out for more than a week. He looked and smelled as if he had slept in his clothes; as he certainly had. He was so disheveled that later that day, a fellow passenger on the excursion boat mistook him for a deckhand.

Yes, perhaps that memory brought a faint smile to Thoreau's face as they pulled into Pittsfield in the middle of the afternoon on that May day. Perhaps he shared the tale with Horace, so his young companion could be amused as well.

Two miles south of the Pittsfield station lay Arrowhead, the home of fellow writer Herman Melville (1819-1891). One of the windows in Melville's second-floor study offered a clear view of Mount Greylock in the distance. Its dark silhouette against a blue sky reminded him of the whales he had seen during his South Seas travels. He was thus inspired to write *Moby-Dick; Or, The Whale* in that very room in the early 1850s. Melville still owned the Arrowhead property in 1861, but he is likely to have been living in New York City on the day that Henry and Horace rode past it.

After leaving Pittsfield, the train next stopped at the Shaker community of Hancock. Hancock's Shaker village had been created in 1783, and it was the third oldest such settlement in the country. Residents called their utopia "The City of Peace." In the 1830s, it had served more than 330 followers of Mother Ann Lee. But by 1861, it was experiencing the population decline felt by all Shaker enclaves. When Henry and Horace's train passed by, about 170 Believers remained. They were still known for the crops they raised— especially medicinal herbs and vegetables—as well as for their expertise in the crafts of woodworking, basketry, and broom making. They still operated their dairy business from the distinctive round stone barn that had been specifically designed for efficiency in milking cows. The rail travelers might have been able to see the barn's unusual profile from the Hancock station. Perhaps a Believer or two had gotten on or off the train.

Because Thoreau had ridden this portion once before, he probably was not surprised when the train passed through a tunnel in Deane Hill, right at the state border, after three o'clock. They emerged into the rolling landscape of eastern New York State, and clattered through the towns of Canaan, Chatham, Kinderhook, and Schodack. They rode within four miles of Lindenwald, the home of President Martin Van Buren (1782-1862). The eighth U.S. President was probably home that day; but it is unlikely that either Henry or Horace would have cared to stop, make introductions, and visit for a while. Horace had not yet been born when Van Buren served his term (1837-1841). The New Yorker's stint in office was not necessarily cause for celebration or even polite conversation, and his name would not have appeared on Emerson's list.

Soon after Van Buren was sworn in, the nation fell into The Panic of 1837, the first economic depression experienced in this country. Then came the forced removal of the Cherokee Indians as they were marched from the southern states to Oklahoma along the "Trail of Tears." When rumors first began to circulate about the proposed ousting of the Indians from their homeland, Ralph Waldo Emerson wrote a scathing letter to Van Buren, demanding to know if the talk was true. If the President had any knowledge or involvement in that project, Emerson was quick to exact judgment. "You, sir, will bring down that renowned chair in which you sit into infamy if your seal is set to this instrument of perfidy; and the name of this nation, hitherto the sweet omen of religion and liberty, will stink to the world." Emerson's warning and indictment neither postponed nor prevented the evacuation.

Now in ill health at the age of 78 in 1861, Van Buren nevertheless was following the news from the South. He strongly supported Lincoln's call for volunteers. After all, he had taken an antislavery stance regarding the annexing of Texas while he was in office. A committee of concerned Kinderhook residents had recently called on the former President at Lindenwald to ask for his advice in assembling a local war effort. Feeling that he could not personally participate in such a venture, Van Buren however "authorized the committee to give his unqualified support for the meeting." He also heartily encouraged New York state politicians to back Lincoln and the federal government's initiatives to restore the Union. It would be his last public pronouncement.

The Western railroad deposited Henry Thoreau and Horace Mann at the Greenbush station just before 5 p.m. From that point, the men took a ferry across the Hudson to Albany, a thriving city of 75,000. The 1861 railroad gazetteer (the nineteenth-century equivalent of a Triple-A guide) advertised New York's capital as "the entrepot of the commerce of the northern section of the Mississippi Valley and of the Lakes with the seaboard. Its manufactures are varied and extensive; it is also one of the largest markets for lumber in the United States." What the promoters failed to mention was the proliferation of slaughterhouses in the city and the fact that the livestock business was then more important to the local economy than was lumber. Cattle drives were still common. But with no bridge to link the commercial district with the railroad line, the beasts either had to swim for the opposite shore or walk across the (hopefully) frozen river in winter. Many never made it to dry land. It was a one-way trip for them, in any case.

Evidently cows were not the only quadrupeds familiar to Albanians. Until 1854, residents had been free to throw their garbage in the streets, where roaming pigs cleaned up the mess. When officials finally took charge to end this nasty habit, they first had to round up the 15,000 well-fed waste management specialists. One can only imagine what that task entailed. Suffice it to say that by the time Henry and Horace reached the western shore of the Hudson, the place had been cleaned up considerably.

The Delavan House was the biggest and best hotel in town. Built in 1845, the five-story building took up an entire city block at Broadway and Steuben Street, and could serve up to 400 guests. Proprietor Theophilus Roessle attracted customers with ads that promised "all the Modern Improvements and Conveniences for the Accommodation of the Traveling Public." Any and every dignitary who stopped in the city stayed there. State legislators made it their headquarters. Notable guests over the years included P.T. Barnum, Charles Dickens, and William Marcy "Boss" Tweed. On February 18, 1861, President-elect Abraham Lincoln rode through Albany on his way from Illinois to Washington for his March 4 inauguration. When he arrived at the Delavan, the halls were "crowded to suffocation," even though most of the city had voted against him. As Lincoln rested in his comfortable hotel room that night, a young actor named John Wilkes Booth was performing in the play *The Apostate* across town at the Gayety Theater. Booth was staying at Stanwix Hall on Broadway, just three blocks from the Delavan. No one knows if the two men bumped into each other or even made accidental eye contact that day.

Three months later, it was Henry Thoreau and Horace Mann who checked into the Delavan House. At two dollars a night, it was one of the more expensive hotels the two would encounter on their trip. Henry's caustic journal remark that the establishment was "not so good as costly" was a

The Delavan House (1845-1894) of Albany, New York.

bit premature. Less lavish lodgings lay ahead for the travelers in the months
to come. What Henry spent an additional fifty cents on is unknown. The
ferry trip might have been included in the Western Railroad's fare. And dinner should have been part of the Delavan's package.

The old Western Railroad line still exists in its entirety, though it has undergone numerous name and ownership changes. Devoted rail fans know it best
as the Boston & Albany. Over the years, it has also been part of the systems
of the New York Central, the Penn Central, and Conrail. Both Amtrak passenger trains and CSX freights still use it; and yes, travelers can still ride via
rail, from Worcester to Albany, if they wish. Actually, their destination will
technically be Rensselaer, as the Albany-Rensselaer station is located on the
eastern side of the Hudson. The trip takes four and a half hours if the train
is on schedule and includes just two stops: Springfield and Pittsfield. In 1912,
part of the original rail bed in the Berkshires was straightened to make the
line more practical. Otherwise, what one might experience today comes close
to what Henry and Horace did, discounting the advancements and changes
that have resulted from the passage of time.

The Western Railroad station in Worcester is gone, however. It would be
lodged underneath I-290 if it were still standing today. Anyone boarding a
train in Worcester must use the Union Station in Washington Square. Built
in the French Renaissance style in 1911, the building is distinguished by the
white domed towers that rise above the highway and form part of the
unique skyline of the city. After rail traffic diminished in the late twentieth
century, the station was closed, abandoned, and left to sit idle for more than
twenty years. An initiative to refurbish it to its original splendor began in the
late 1990s, and it finally reopened in July 2000. Now known as "The
Beautiful Portal to the Heart of the Commonwealth," the Union Station
includes a Grand Hall that is available for events and receptions. The structure itself is a stunning site inside and out, and is an interesting destination
for visitors even if they are not among the travelers boarding a train or a bus.

The homes of Clara Barton, Herman Melville, and Martin Van Buren
have been restored and are open for public tours. Lucy Stone's family farm
property is owned and protected by Massachusetts' Trustees of
Reservations, which acquired it in the early 2000s. Sadly, the original Stone
family farmhouse was lost to fire in 1950. All that remains on the acreage is

the cellar hole of the home and the barn foundation. Plans are underway to make the site an educational and inspirational experience for future visitors.

Because of dense forest between the road and the water, the stone-arch Whistler bridge that carries trains over the Quaboag River at the Warren-Palmer line is best seen from MA Route 67 after a light snow has fallen. Private property surrounds it. Nearby Palmer now bills itself as the "Town of the Seven Railroads;" and its public library houses a railroad research center. Palmer's 1884 Union Station, which was designed by Henry Hobson Richardson, has been restored and is now a railroad-themed restaurant. Trains running between Worcester and Springfield buzz by it several times a day.

One of the Keystone Arches that remains standing today but serves only hikers, not trains.

Though they officially closed for business in 1968, many of the old brick armory buildings still stand at the corner of State and Federal Streets in Springfield. Part of the original complex now constitutes the Springfield Armory National Historic Site, a museum which is open to visitors. The buildings on the south side of Federal Street house several businesses and a technology center. But the majority of the structures now represent the home of the Springfield Technical Community College, established in 1967. Though the institution has added a few newer structures over the years, many of the buildings still date to armory days and have been restored.

The Hancock Shakers disbanded in 1960. A portion of their property with its original buildings, including the distinctive round stone barn, is well maintained and is now a popular tourist attraction. The Shaker Museum and Library is located just over the state border in Chatham, New York. While its current site contains representative collections of Shaker history and craftsmanship, officials there are currently working to include restoration of the original settlement at Mount Lebanon, N.Y. The only active Shaker community left in the U.S. is located in Sabbathday Lake, Maine.

More than 12,500 acres are now protected as the Mount Greylock State Reservation, the first state park created in the Commonwealth (1898). Having climbed Greylock himself, Thoreau might be interested in hearing that present-day scientists "have compared the transition in forest vegetation zones from base to summit as if walking from Pennsylvania to northern Maine in one day." The Appalachian Trail (AT) winds through the Berkshires of western Massachusetts and includes a hike up Greylock. The pathway crosses the old Western railroad line in the town of Dalton.

A bridge across the Hudson River at Albany was finally erected in 1866: the same year, coincidentally, that the local livestock market hit its peak. That was when "a thousand carloads of cattle arrived weekly" at the slaughterhouses. One assumes that some gains were made simply by the fact that fewer animals were lost to the current of the Hudson.

Sometime after 8 p.m. on December 30, 1894, someone was too casual about tossing a lit cigar, cigarette, or match into an elevator shaft at the Delavan House. The entire hotel was soon ablaze. About 100 guests were on the premises, and many were eating in the dining room. Included were politicians Hamilton Fish and George R. Malby, who were both campaigning for the post of Speaker of the State Assembly. Firemen responded as quickly as was feasible; but flames were already igniting windows on the fifth floor when help and water arrived. In the meantime, men and women escaped as best as they could on their own, even if it meant jumping out of windows into the street or onto the snow banks below. Neighboring buildings were thankfully protected from flying embers by a thick covering of recent snow on their roofs. But the prestigious Delavan was a goner, a mere shell in what seemed like moments. Several of its walls fell before midnight.

When morning came and the smoke began to clear, the finger pointing began. Why hadn't the firemen arrived in time? Why hadn't enough water been available to quench the flames? A debate even developed over the responsibility of combing the rubble for further casualties. The police reportedly said that it was "not their duty to look after the dead." Firemen were still training water onto the steaming ashes the next day, but a clerk with the Fire Commissioner's office denied further involvement by his men, stating that it was up to "the owners of the property to dig the bodies out if there were any." Certainly one of the current proprietors couldn't take charge of such an undertaking: he was recuperating from the pneumonia he had caught from exposure during the night of the crisis. And though Albany employed four coroners at the time, their duties were described as being "of a general nature, and not being confined to any one section" of the city. "None of them [had] shown any disposition to move in the matter yet." Unfortunately, many of the Delavan's servants lived on the top floor, and they had the slimmest chance of getting out of the building in time. The eventual death count from the fire was seventeen. All but one of the victims had been a hotel employee.

The ruins of the Delavan sat on that downtown block for several years before the decision was made to build a Union Station in its place. The rest of the structure was razed; and workers still found buried human remains there: three, even five years after the conflagration. Finally in 1900, downtown Albany was connected with multiple rail lines and an actual station to accommodate them. Travelers no longer had to disembark in Rensselaer (formerly, Greenbush) and somehow cross the river to reach the capital. The station served the city until it was shut down on December 29, 1968. Like the facility in Worcester, it too was abandoned and languished in deterioration for decades until it was restored and reopened—but as a bank, not as a railroad center. Those who now visit Albany via rail will experience the same situation that Henry and Horace faced. They will have to leave the train at the Albany-Rensselaer station on the east side of the river and find a way to cross the Hudson. These days, the trip is made via bus or taxi. U.S. Route 20 is nearby and leads into the city. Swimming or walking on the ice is seldom required.

The most distinctive features along this section of Henry and Horace's trip remain the Whistler bridges. And it is by that name that they are known, even though they were in fact assembled by Alexander Birnie (1803-1858). After successfully building a bridge over the Passaic River in New Jersey, the stonemason worked for several railroad lines in New England, including the Boston & Providence and the Providence & Stonington. In the early 1840s he moved his family from the Berkshires to Hastings on Hudson, N.Y., and lived there quite peacefully for more than twenty years. Ironically, he was in the midst of creating an artificial fish pond on his expansive property when he was accidentally killed while blasting rock for the project.

The accomplishments of George Washington Whistler (1800-1849) with the Western Railroad were widely celebrated, and his work soon caught the attention of the Russians. Czar Nicholas I asked him to become the "consulting engineer for the projected railroad between St. Petersburg and Moscow." By 1842, Whistler was on the other side of the globe, overseeing the construction of a line that would open for traffic at the end of the decade. Nicholas was so impressed that he awarded Whistler the Order of St. Anne in 1847. But the American was not fated to witness the completion of his Russian project. He caught Asiatic cholera and died in St. Petersburg. His body was brought back to Stonington, Connecticut, for burial. To New Englanders, this man may be remembered for his railroading expertise and the commissioning of the stone arch bridges. To the rest of the world, he might better be referred to as "Whistler's Father." For it was his artist son James Abbott McNeill Whistler (1834-1903) who gained fame for his *Arrangement in Grey and Black*, a painting of his mother sitting in a rocking chair.

Of the ten original stone arch bridges, only five have survived to the twenty-first century. Two are still used many times daily by trains that weigh 40 times more than the locomotives they were built for. The rest were abandoned by the railroad when the tracks were evened out in 1912. At least three were destroyed in 1927, when the effects of a hurricane caused a series of upstream dams to fail. The resulting wall of water was powerful enough to wipe out not only some solid stonework, but also a fair amount of the towns of Becket and Chester. Today the Keystone Arch Bridges Trail, created by the Friends of the Keystone Arches, provides access to the remaining bridges. This pathway offers spectacular views not only of Birnie's handiwork, but also of the landscape deemed the most remote and road-less tract in Massachusetts. The Westfield River has been named a Wild and Scenic River. Present-day explorers may want to survey the bridges by canoeing or kayaking beneath them. Caution should be taken on the water, however, because whitewater conditions can develop without warning.

These days the struggle for supremacy in the Northeast is fought each year on the hardwood, on the ice, and on the gridiron. Super Bowls XLII and XLVI (which both pitted the New York Giants against the New England Patriots) notwithstanding: by far the most critical and intense battles for the title occur each summer at Fenway Park and at Yankee Stadium. To today's public, a division pennant or a World Series trophy means much more than a pair of railroad tracks leading from Boston to Albany, especially if the prize comes at the expense and humiliation of that other team and that other city. Who says history doesn't repeat itself?

As usual Henry Thoreau and Horace Mann, Jr., left behind no physical trace of having traveled from Worcester to Albany on the Western Railroad in

1861. But I assigned myself the task of looking for something along the way that represented the Thoreauvian life or philosophy; something that would mystically invoke the spirits of the two men; or something that might have gotten their nods of approval. To do so, I decided to visit the small hill town of Chester, Massachusetts on June 5, 2004.

"Chester on Track" is an annual event that celebrates not only the history of a town but also the railroad line that runs through it. Begun in 1992, the single-day fair in this tiny settlement (pop. 1337) features a parade, food stands, vendors, craft stands, and tours of local sites. It also offers one of the best opportunities to hike along the Keystone Arch Bridges Trail and to see those Whistler bridges in person. The festivities are centered on Chester's Main Street, which turns off U.S. 20 and leads right to the railroad tracks.

On this day, I headed for the rails and for the old railway station perched beyond them. The depot is said to date to 1840; and if that is true, then it was indeed one of the stops for Henry and Horace's train in 1861. When additional tracks were laid in Chester and up the mountain, the station itself ended up sitting in the middle of the rails. In January 1990, the building was moved to the east side. Now it is a museum that features railroad history. To reach it you have to walk or drive under the existing tracks first. Once you step inside, you feel as though you've gone back in time. The memorabilia on display here represents each of the railway companies that came through Chester over the years. The property also includes rail cars that you (or your children) can climb into and imagine you are steaming on to Pittsfield.

Tables and booths for the craft fair vendors were set up next to the station. I walked from one to the next, looking for something appropriate. One local craftsman sold hand-carved walking sticks. "Grown by Nature, Finished by Dave" read David McClaflin's business card. Henry might have nodded in appreciation at that notion. I tucked Dave's information into my notebook. So far, so good. The station was vintage, and Thoreau was known to use a walking stick on occasion. I decided to look for further inspiration at the home of the Chester Historical Society.

"The old cell is downstairs," said Fay Piergiovanni, an Historical Society member. I tip-toed tentatively down the wooden steps, walked around the furnace, and followed the one-note drone of an active dehumidifier. An iron gate marked this place for what it once was: a jail. Upstairs, the first floor held historical displays that showed what life was like here when the local emery industry was in full swing. It was a bright and fascinating collage of old photos and personal possessions, but the ground floor with its natural stone walls was minimalist, bare and damp. The cell was ironically about the size of Thoreau's house at Walden Pond. Two old cots rested inside. It called to mind that one night when Henry stayed in the jail in Concord—perhaps under conditions similar to these—for refusing to pay the state poll tax. It was a thought-provoking place: one that was a relief to turn away from, to walk back up the steps and into a brighter and livelier atmosphere with people and conversation.

But for me, it was the sight of the stone arches themselves that best evoked the image of the past. I drove to the remote parking area and followed a paper map. The path curved gently through the woods and led to a riverbank where the West Branch of the Westfield River rushed to keep its appointment with the Connecticut. The natural setting was breathtaking. I looked to the left and was almost startled to see a huge double arch stone bridge spanning the water. To suddenly see something man-made in this quiet place was jarring, yet somehow perfect.

I continued along the trail and was soon able to walk right where the Western Railroad tracks used to be: where Henry and Horace's train passed, so long ago. After a while, I realized that I had been hearing a low rumble in the background. It was getting louder. A train inched its way up the mountain from West Springfield. Standing on the former rail bed, I could look across the river and see several locomotives pulling boxcars and trailers up the line. Who can explain that thrill we still get when we see and hear a train coming? Back here in the woods with no other human intrusion, the brilliant colors of a contemporary train should have looked even starker to my eyes. But they didn't. It was merely a trip back to a simpler time. The design of the engines had changed, and a winking amber light now took the place of a caboose. But when I waved, the engineer lifted a hand in return, and my heart jumped just a little.

"Chester on Track" now takes place annually on a Saturday in May. The Chester Foundation runs and organizes the event. If you go then, you can enjoy the fun and good food available during the festival. But at any time at all, you can hike the old rail bed. You'll be able to witness for yourself the Keystone Arches and will be surrounded by the gorgeous Berkshire scenery. At the same time, you can admire the ingenuity of George Washington Whistler and his colleagues. Way back when, they crafted a transportation line that was such an unrealistic proposition in their day that folks called it a "Railroad to the Moon."

WHEN YOU GO: Today the most practical way to drive from Worcester to Albany is via I-290 and I-90 (the latter known alternately as the MassPike and the New York State Thruway). The eight hours the trip took in 1861 has been divided in half, due to the fast and straight highway system and the freedom to drive by 34 towns without stopping. Riders on the MassPike pass over the railroad tracks twice: first at the Brimfield-Palmer line, on the bridge that crosses the Quaboag River; and later at the Montgomery-Russell line, as the Westfield River flows underneath. The rails come close to the north side of the road upon entering New York and may be seen in winter. A bridge in Chatham carries trains back over the highway. And when I-90 splits from the Thruway east of Albany, the tracks mirror those lanes that lead northwest to the city. The rails stay between that bypass and the river until they reach Rensselaer.

Path-followers who want a closer look and a more accurate tracing of the route taken by Thoreau and Mann should be able to do so with the aid of a good road atlas that features topographical maps. Cobbling together an itinerary that includes MA Route 9, MA Route 67, U.S. 20, MA Route 8, NY Route 295, U.S. 9, and NY Route 9J will make a good start. The tracks are best seen in East Brookfield and Brookfield along MA Route 9; in Warren and West Warren along MA Route 67; along U.S. 20, generally from Palmer to Chester; along MA Route 8 from Becket to Pittsfield; and along NY Route 295 from Canaan to Chatham. A driving excursion that shadows the rails exactly would be an exhausting one and would require a good navigator, either human or electronic, especially in New York state. It would also take much longer than eight hours.

FOR MORE INFORMATION

Albany County Convention and Visitors Bureau, 25 Quackenbush Square, Albany, NY 12207. Phone (800) 258-3582. www.albany.org

Amtrak, http://www.amtrak.com

Arrowhead, 780 Holmes Road, Pittsfield, MA 01201. Phone (413) 442-1793. www.mobydick.org

Berkshire Visitors Bureau, Berkshire Common, Plaza Level, Pittsfield, MA 01201. Phone (413) 443-9186 or (800) 237-5747. www.berkshires.org

Chester Railway Station, 10 Prospect Street, Chester, MA 01011. Phone (413) 354-7878. www.chesterrailwaystation.org

Clara Barton Birthplace Museum, 68 Clara Barton Road, North Oxford, MA 01537-0356. Phone (508) 987-5375. www.clarabartonbirthplace.org

Friends of the Keystone Arches, P.O. Box 276, Huntington, MA 01050. keystonearches.org

Greater Springfield Convention and Visitors Bureau, 1441 Main Street, Springfield, MA 01115. Phone (800) 723-1548 or (413) 787-1548. www.valleyvisitor.com

Hancock Shaker Village, Route 20, Pittsfield, MA 01201. Phone (800) 817-1137. www.hancockshakervillage.org

Lucy Stone Home Site, West Brookfield, MA 01585. Phone (413) 532-1631. www.thetrustees.org/pages/1613_lucy_stone_home_site.cfm

Martin Van Buren National Historic Site, 1013 Old Post Road, Kinderhook, NY 12106.
Phone (518) 758-9689. www.nps.gov/mava/Main.htm

Quaboag Valley Chamber of Commerce, 3 Converse Street, Suite 103,
Palmer, MA 01069. Phone (413) 283-2418. www.quaboag.com

Shaker Museum and Library, 88 Shaker Museum Road, Old Chatham, NY 12136.
Phone (518) 794-9100. www.shakermuseumandlibrary.org.

Springfield Armory National Historic Site, Federal Street, Springfield, MA. Phone (413)
734-8551. www.nps.gov/spar

RECOMMENDED READING

Thoreau's "Tuesday" chapter in *A Week on the Concord and Merrimack Rivers*, in which he
describes his 1844 visit to the Berkshires and the Catskills.

NOTES ON THIS CHAPTER

The early days of the railroad make for fascinating reading. Here I started with Alvin F.
Harlow's classic work, *Steelways of New England* (New York: Creative Age Press, Inc., 1946).
The *Utica Daily News* reporter's words are quoted on page 132 of that work. Ronald Dale
Kerr's *The Rail Lines of Southern New England: A Handbook of Railroad History* (Pepperell,
Mass.: Branch Line Press, 1995) provides information about every railroad company and line
that ever existed in the area, including Massachusetts. Statistics specific to laying track in the
Berkshires and building the Keystone Arches were gleaned from the Friends of the Keystone
Arches' web site at http://keystonearches.org/history and from personal correspondence
with Friends President Dave Pierce.

Clara Barton's story is told in a variety of sources. I found a nice rendering of the basics
in *Very Sincerely Yours, Clara: Selected Correspondence of Clara Barton, Founder of the American
Red Cross, from the Clara Barton Birthplace Museum Collection* (North Oxford, Mass.: The
Barton Center for Diabetes Education, Inc., 2003).

Good biographies of Lucy Stone include Andrea Moore Kerr's *Lucy Stone: Speaking Out
for Equality* (New Brunswick, N.J.: Rutgers University Press, 1992) and Joelle Million's *The
Woman's Voice, Woman's Place: Lucy Stone and the Birth of the Woman's Rights Movement*
(Westport, Conn.: Praeger, 2003). Details about the anti-slavery speeches heard in
Framingham are delineated in Sandy Petrulionis' book, *To Set This World Right: The
Antislavery Movement in Thoreau's Concord* (Ithaca: Cornell University Press, 2006), pages 102-
104.

The text of Thoreau's "Slavery in Massachusetts" lecture was taken from the version that
appears in *The Essays of Henry David Thoreau* (Lewis Hyde, ed. New York: North Point
Press, 2002). His comments about Williams College and the need for a college's proximity to
a mountain are found in *A Week on the Concord and Merrimack Rivers*, in the ninth paragraph
of the "Tuesday" chapter. The quotes about the view from the top of the mountain follow
soon afterward. Details about his hike on Greylock begin on page 54 of William Howarth's
Thoreau in the Mountains: Writings by Henry David Thoreau (New York: Farrar, Straus, Giroux,
1982). Ellery Channing himself comments on the state of Henry's appearance on page 34 of
his biography, *Thoreau, the Poet-Naturalist, with Memorial Verses* (Frank Sanborn, ed. New
York: Biblio and Tannen, 1966 reprint of the 1902 edition).

The production rate of the Springfield Armory at the time was listed in the *Massachusetts
Weekly Spy* on May 1, 1861. Longfellow's "The Arsenal at Springfield" was originally included in the 1845 publication, *The Belfry of Bruges and Other Poems*. The full text of the poem

can be found online and in most compilations of his work. The announcement of the new shooting gallery in Springfield was found in the May 17, 1861, issue of the *Springfield Republican*, which I accessed at the American Antiquarian Society in Worcester, Mass.

Details of the Hancock Shakers were gleaned from Priscilla J. Brewer's book, *Shaker Communities, Shaker Lives.* The "Life at the Village" page of the Hancock Shaker Village web site was also useful (http://www.hancockshakervillage.org).

The text of Ralph Waldo Emerson's letter to President Martin Van Buren can be found in *Emerson's Antislavery Writings* (Len Gougeon and Joel Myerson, eds. New Haven: Yale University Press, 1995). Martin Van Buren's 1861 activities are found in John Niven's *Martin Van Buren: The Romantic Age of American Politics* (New York: Oxford University Press, 1983).

The quote about Albany being an "entrepot of commerce" comes from the July 1861 edition of the *Railroad Gazetteer of the United States, Canada, Etc.* The fascinating history of Albany can be discovered in a number of books. I got the tidbits about the cattle, the pigs, and the timing of Lincoln and Booth's visits from William Kennedy's *O Albany! Improbable City of Political Wizards, Fearless Ethnics, Spectacular Aristocrats, Splendid Nobodies, and Underrated Scoundrels* (New York: The Viking Press, 1983). Additional information, including the particulars of the railroad station transformation, were found in Paul Grondahl's *Major Erastus Corning: Albany Icon, Albany Enigma* (Albany: Washington Park Press, 1997). The ad copy for the Delavan Hotel appears in *The Albany Directory for the Year 1861: Containing a General Directory of the Citizens, a Business Directory, a Record of the City Government, Its Institutions, etc. etc.* (Albany: Adams, Sampson & Co., 1861).

The fate of Albany's Delavan House can be read in painstaking and horrific detail in the accounts that appeared in *The New York Times* at around the time of the fire. They include "The Delavan House Victims: Albany City Authorities Refuse to Recover the Bodies from the Ruins" (January 2, 1895); "The Delavan House Victims: The Mayor Orders a Search of the Ruins: All the Albany Hotels Are to Be Inspected" (January 3, 1895); and "Two Bodies Are Recovered: One of the Delavan House Victims Identified: Little Progress Being Made in the Investigation" (January 8, 1895). I accessed these articles electronically via the ProQuest Historical Newspapers database.

Information about the vegetation on Mount Greylock was obtained from the web site for the park, under the direction of the Massachusetts Department of Conservation and Recreation: http://www.mass.gov/dcr/parks/mtGreylock/nature.htm.

A biography of stonemason Alexander Birnie appears in volume two of the *History of the Connecticut Valley in Massachusetts, with illustrations and biographical sketches of some of its prominent men and pioneers* (Philadelphia: Louis H. Everts, 1879). The quote about the Czar and George Washington Whistler is from Whistler's entry in volume 20 of the *Dictionary of American Biography* (New York: C. Scribner's Sons, 1958). More details about his life can be found in Albert Parry's biography, *Whistler's Father* (Indianapolis: The Bobbs-Merrill Company, 1939).

Travel Chapter 4

Tuesday, May 14, 1861
Albany to Suspension Bridge
via the New York Central Railroad
and the Rochester, Lockport & Niagara Division of
the New York Central Railroad

Expenses: At New York Central House, $1.50.

Albany to Schenectady a level pitch pine plain with also white pine, white birch, and shad-bush in bloom, with hills at last. No houses; only two or three huts on the edge of woods without any road. These were the last pitch pines that I saw on my westward journey.

—Thoreau's Journal, May 14, 1861

We arrived at the Suspension Bridge last night at about half past eight, and stopped over night at the New York Central House.

—Horace Mann, Jr.'s letter, May 15, 1861

Now the men were finally entering new territory. Henry and Horace could take in new sights and see changes in the landscape as they rattled through these upstate towns. Of course, their explorations were limited to their views from the car windows. Nevertheless, they sat and watched the state of New York go by.

The New York Central left Albany at 8:30 a.m. It would take twelve hours to reach the western edge of the state. But just north of the capital city, Thoreau was already making an attempt to botanize from the train. His brief notes were meant to be memory joggers for a later time, when he could call up the images he had seen and write more extensively about them. Unfortunately in this case, he never had a chance to do so.

But a man can see only so much in an ever-advancing window-framed world. That's why Thoreau's notes more often describe the landscape at large, rather than specific trees or plants. His knowledge of the terrain from this point on was based solely on the facts he had gleaned from reading travel narratives, consulting his railroad guidebook, and listening to friends who had already made the trip.

North of Albany, Henry saw a "P. pine plain," a large tract of pitch pines that were distinctive from the rest of the scenery. This inland Pine Barrens was formed by the same kinds of glacial forces that had created Walden Pond and the surrounding sandy soil of Walden Woods. If he had had a chance to study the place, he would have recognized the similarities. Perhaps even with a quick glance, he did.

The route of the New York Central was one that other entities had already followed. With the Adirondack Mountains to the north and the Catskills to the south, the easiest path was the one in the middle, carved out by the Mohawk River. And so from Schenectady to Utica, the railroad tracks traveled along its banks. As the locomotive pulled the men upstream and west, the Mohawk itself flowed east toward the Hudson. So did the waters of the Erie Canal, which had also been placed in that tight valley. Three lines of transportation operated independently but cooperatively, in close quarters, for nearly eighty miles.

The train stopped at the station in Syracuse for twenty minutes, probably to take on wood and water for the locomotive. The travelers had a chance to get out and walk around a bit before continuing their trek west. That could be when Henry and Horace saw firsthand the "large city like streets" of Syracuse, with its population of 30,000. But a twenty-minute layover was hardly enough time to do much exploring. The major industry of the city was its expansive salt works, which lay a number of blocks northwest of the station, at the southern edge of Onondaga Lake. With his interest in the mechanics and processes of factories like the ones in Westvale and Clinton and Worcester, Thoreau may have wished for more time to learn about this business of salt.

Four years earlier, a correspondent for *The New York Times* did just that:

> [T]he prosperity of Syracuse is attributable, first and foremost, to a wonderful gift of God—obtained with little trouble, and absorbed by a never-failing demand—the SALT SPRINGS.
> …

> For fifty years past both supply and demand have marched with mighty strides, until, at this present time, no less than *one million five hundred thousand* barrels are annually made and sold.
> …

At present, about 200 acres are covered over with "works." The best brine is procured from wells 200 to 300 feet deep. It is raised by means of force pumps, worked by water wheels, which are themselves turned by the waste water from the Canal, and forced up into immense tanks, or reservoirs, which are placed at such elevation as to carry up a supply of water in the pipes to a considerable distance.

There are two methods of manufacturing the salt. One by solar evaporation, the other by the application of artificial heat; the first being considered most profitable. For this process pans are built, twelve feet wide, a number of rods long, and six inches in depth. The brine is let into the first pan direct from the reservoir. It stands here a certain time, until the matters held in mechanical suspension, the dirt, small stones, &c., are deposited. It is then drawn by siphons into the second pan.

And it was these large evaporation pans that Henry and Horace could see for themselves just after the train pulled out of the Syracuse station. The tracks led them close to the vats and to the lake; and then moved on to Weedsport and points west.

Henry noticed the swampland that was prevalent in central New York. Known for his love of such habitats, he may have ached to examine the wetlands in person. "Would it not be a luxury to stand up to one's chin in some retired swamp for a whole summer's day, scenting the sweet-fern and bilberry blows, and lulled by the minstrelsy of gnats and mosquitoes?" he once wrote. "I enter a swamp as a sacred place, a *sanctum sanctorum*. There is the strength, the marrow, of Nature." Well, the residents of this region probably would not have agreed with him. Some of those mosquitoes could be laced with the "Genesee fever" that sickened and killed hundreds of people. At the time, however, no one suspected that the tiny insects transmitted the disease. It was merely thought that the swamp itself had a supernatural power that could endanger unwary human beings.

It was the Genesee River that Henry saw in Rochester: that "interesting River & falls dividing it." The train crossed the river and over one of the four falls, making a much more impressive sight than Thoreau had time to give pen to. His friend Nathaniel Hawthorne was a bit more descriptive after he passed through Rochester in 1832:

The Genessee [sic] has contributed so bountifully to their canals and mill-dams, that it approaches the precipice with diminished pomp, and rushes over it in foamy stream of various widths, leaving a broad face of the rock insulated and unwashed, between the two main branches of the falling river. Still it was an impressive sight, to one who had not seen Niagara.

And indeed, when Henry got a glimpse of the Genesee version, he had yet to see the falls at Niagara. Rochester—"Flour City"—used the rushing water to power its flour mills.

The city was then the home of Frederick Douglass (1818-1895), the former slave turned writer, lecturer, and abolitionist. In the early 1840s, Douglass had made regular visits to Concord to attend meetings of the Middlesex County Anti-Slavery Society. He spoke there on a number of occasions and may have even boarded with the Thoreaus. It was Douglass who had first been scheduled to speak on the subject of John Brown at Boston's Tremont Temple on November 1, 1859. When he became unable to attend the program, Henry Thoreau stepped in as a capable substitute, on Ralph Waldo Emerson's recommendation. He delivered the "Capt. John Brown" speech that he had given two days earlier in Concord. On November 3, he reprised it in Mechanics Hall in Worcester.

The name of Frederick Douglass may have appeared on Emerson's list of contacts. Douglass was very likely in Rochester on May 14, but he was far too busy to entertain visitors. The war had given him much work to do. The opening page of his most recent issue of *Douglass' Monthly* carried the slogan "Freedom for all, or chains for all," accompanied by images of an American eagle and the Stars and Stripes. And with an essay called "How to End the War," Douglass proposed not only the immediate freeing of the slaves, but also a plan for recruiting them into troops to fight on the Union side. In mid-May he may have already been working on the speech he would give in Rochester on June 10, called "The American Apocalypse." He quickly took to the lecture circuit that summer and fall, continuing to take his impassioned message to cities throughout the Northeast and Midwest. Henry and Horace were on the road at the same time, trying their best to avoid the war, as well as talk of it.

Another Rochester reformer had worked with diligence that spring. Susan Brownell Anthony (1820-1906) had planned for a National Woman's Rights Convention to take place in New York in May. After the inaugural event was held in Worcester's Brinley Hall in 1850, the activists had adhered to a regular schedule. Similar conventions had been held annually in ten of the next eleven years in selected cities across the Northeast, but that was before Fort Sumter had been fired upon. Now the war and its anti-slavery focus had taken center stage, even among the proto-feminists. Susan's colleagues pleaded with her to cancel the convention. She reluctantly did so. While she was by that time gaining in fame, Susan B. Anthony would not have been a likely entry on Emerson's contacts list.

Henry Thoreau and Horace Mann, Jr., arrived at the village of Suspension Bridge, N.Y., at about 8:30 p.m. The community was small, consisting of only a few blocks of houses and several hotels conveniently located next to the railroad tracks. The two men chose to stay at the New York Central House, a frame hotel that had been built in 1854. Nearby was the gorge of the Niagara River and the famed double-decker Suspension Bridge that spanned it. Canada West lay on the other side.

Tomorrow it would finally be time to see Niagara Falls.

Thoreau did not mention the Erie Canal in his jottings. Young Horace did not write home about it. But the travelers had no doubt seen "Clinton's Ditch" from the train. It shadowed their route all the way to Lockport, where it angled south to reach Buffalo. They couldn't help but notice it: to spot merely the top halves of boats as they sailed by, seemingly upon a grassy sea. Or to watch a plodding mule dragging a thick tow line. Perhaps those sights were too obvious to write about. Surely a number of folks thought that the canal was already out of style by 1861. It was considered old technology.

Work on the Erie Canal began in Rome, N.Y., on July 4, 1817, just eight days before Henry Thoreau was born. The 363-mile-long channel was dug in eight stages that took eight years of hard labor and more than seven million dollars to complete. It was politician DeWitt Clinton's dream come to fruition after years of talk and proposals. When the westernmost portion was finally finished, it was time for the grandest of celebrations to announce the achievement.

At 10 a.m. on October 26, 1825, a flotilla of officials that included Governor Clinton pushed off from Buffalo. Their destination was the island of Manhattan, 425 miles away. They would use the new canal to flow east to the state capital of Albany, and then ride over the waters of the Hudson River to head south from there. But the planners had wanted to somehow get the word to New York City that the group was on its way. It would be more than twenty years before inventors would discover a way to send a telegram to the city. The idea of a service provided by a fleet of Pony Express riders was 35 years away, and was not practical through the central

New York swampland. The men had to do some creative thinking and impromptu communication problem solving.

So they devised a "cannon telegraph." Cannons from the War of 1812 were found and distributed equidistant along the length of the channel, with each operator positioned within earshot of the next. When Clinton and his companions began their voyage, the nearest gunner fired his charge. Miles away, the next gunner heard it and did the same. It took just 80 minutes for the folks in Manhattan to get the message via this string of artillery. They immediately sent back a reply in the same fashion.

A canal boat waits for passengers at the present-day Erie Canal Village in Rome, New York.

By comparison, the watercraft toting its human cargo took nine days to reach Manhattan. And so on November 4, 1825, casks of Lake Erie water were poured into the Atlantic Ocean to symbolize the "wedding of the waters." The New Yorkers thought they had really made a difference. And at the time, they had. They had launched a commerce line that could transport people and goods in both directions, all the way from the Midwest to the East Coast. Residents in the interior could now dine on fresh oysters that sailed in from Long Island.

The coming of The Iron Horse over the course of the next two decades changed American reliance on the canal systems for long-distance transportation. By the time Henry and Horace rode next to the man-made waterway, it was being used solely for freight. Passengers preferred the speed and timeliness that the railroads could offer. The territory that had taken Clinton and his minions more than a week to traverse could now be crossed in just hours. And yet the canal was then in its second permutation. It had in recent years been the scene of an extensive enlargement project: one that expanded the original channel from 40 feet wide and four feet deep to 70 feet wide and seven feet deep. With the additional room, freight barges could pass one another easily. Larger boats could be used and shipping times would be faster, with fewer delays due to waits in long lines. In spite of those improvements, it was only a matter of time before much of the freight traffic on the canal shifted to the nearby rails.

The tracks of the old New York Central Railroad are fairly easy to find and follow today. Amtrak still runs passenger trains from Albany to Rochester along that route. The line from Rochester to what was then the village of Suspension Bridge now handles just freight cars.

You won't find "Suspension Bridge" on a present-day map, though. The old settlement was officially absorbed into the rest of Niagara Falls, and the bridge that lent its name to that community is gone as well. Another one called the Whirlpool Rapids Bridge stands in its place. More information on that structure will surface in the next chapter. The original New York Central House was destroyed by fire on May 28, 1871, a little more than ten years after Henry and Horace roomed there.

The Erie Canal went through one more reconfiguration during the opening decades of the twentieth century. This time, existing rivers like the Mohawk were employed to the advantage and the use of potential canal traffic. Today both recreational watercraft and freight shipments can still use this combination of natural and man-made channels, called the New York Barge Canal, to cross the expanse of New York State.

The canal's legacy has grown well beyond its initial utilitarian role. Historic canal sites can be found in many of the towns located along the original route. The New York State Canalway Trail System has used or has added to the old flat towpaths in order to accommodate hikers and bicyclists. A New York State Canalway Water Trail is also planned, complete with campsites positioned at fifteen-mile intervals, so that recreational paddlers can benefit as well. Someday you will be able to walk, pedal, or paddle the 500-plus miles from New York City to Buffalo, simply by following the Hudson River and the path of the old Erie Canal. "Clinton's Ditch" is still on the map and continues to prove its usefulness, 185 years after that first "wedding of the waters."

While the canal and the railroad brought business and prosperity to many of the towns, only a few netted significant growth. Syracuse and Rochester were the winners among the lot, with Rome and Utica coming in at the next tier. Although each one of these cities has seen major businesses thrive and then die or move away, a fair percentage of the population has chosen to stick around to create new possibilities. A majority of New York State's residents still live along the Thruway corridor though, thankfully, not in a continuous suburban sprawl. Plenty of wide open spaces of farmland and forest can be enjoyed as you travel from one side of the state to the other, no matter which method of conveyance you use.

The old New York Central railroad line still crosses the Genesee River near the High Falls in Rochester. (*Courtesy GCheatle*)

It has been almost a century since Syracuse (population 145,170) was supported by its salt industry. Vats filled with evaporating brine no longer lie at that southeastern edge of Onondaga Lake. Today the region is better known as a center for computer and technology businesses, as well as the home of Syracuse University, founded in 1870. Fans of the Orange swarm in to cheer their teams on to victory and to further the economy of Onondaga County.

Three of the original four waterfalls of the Genesee River can still be seen in the city of Rochester. The "High Falls" that Thoreau and Mann rode over make an impressive sight. The 96-foot drop is a must-photograph opportunity from the Pont de Rennes pedestrian bridge. That vantage point allows you to witness and absorb the dynamic geology of the landscape.

You'll be able to later compare those rock layers with the stratifications seen in the Niagara Gorge and other points west.

Frederick Douglass and Susan B. Anthony are both buried in Rochester's Mount Hope Cemetery, which is a beautiful and peaceful property to visit at any time of the year. Highland Park bills itself as "The Lilac Capital of the World;" and during the lilac festival held in the second half of May, it would be difficult to argue with that title. With the decline of the flour industry in the late 1800s and so many public parks in place instead, Rochester has been transformed into "Flower City."

Two special habitats that Thoreau noted can still be seen today. That "pitch pine plain" is now partially protected as the Albany Pine Bush Preserve. It is tinier now than it was when Henry caught a glimpse of it, due to the stress of development and encroaching suburbia. But at least it has gained attention for its uniqueness, beauty, and diversity of wildlife. The state legislature created the Albany Pine Bush Preserve Commission in 1988, "to protect and manage the unique and endangered natural communities and species of the Albany Pine Bush for ecological, recreational and educational benefits." The pine bush is a natural home for the Karner blue butterfly and the Inland barrens buckmoth, two rare insect species. It's too bad Henry Thoreau didn't have a chance to explore this ecosystem firsthand.

One of those large swampy regions in the center of the state is now the site of the Montezuma National Wildlife Refuge. This property came under protection in 1938, and it covers more than seven thousand acres. It is just a small portion of the greater Montezuma Wetlands Complex that comprises about 50,000 acres. Plans appear to be underway to protect as much of this vital wildlife resource as is feasible.

"Low bridge, everybody down / Low bridge, for we're comin' to a town." The melody and lyrics made me regress to the 1960s. Once or twice a week, one of the Mennonite or Brethren women who taught at Farmdale Elementary School would wheel an upright piano into our classroom. While the teacher played, we would learn and sing the old American folk songs spelled out in our slim music books. "The Erie Canal" was one of them. My memory conjured up a tiny drawing of a canal boat and a mule on a towpath in the top corner of the page.

But those days were long, long gone. It was 2008, and I was perched on top of a canal boat, gliding effortlessly along a portion of the old Erie Canal. The tour guide had an autoharp with her—another blast from the past—and she was leading us in song. Even if we hadn't thought of them or sung them in decades, the words and the tune launched automatically out of our mouths. Now the "low bridge" warning made sense. The boat sat high in the water. When you sat on the upper deck, you had to pay attention and duck down so that you didn't get clocked on the noggin by a bridge abutment passing overhead. Didn't that kind of thing happen to the bad guys on the silver screen, whenever they chased the hero along on the top of a moving train? Maybe the Hollywood scriptwriters got the idea from canal boats and bridges. Or maybe from the folksong learned in elementary school.

It was National Trails Day, the first Saturday in June. In spite of Henry and Horace's silence on the subject, I decided to conduct my own personal exploration of the historic Erie Canal. My first stop was the Erie Canal Village just west of Rome, N.Y. Canal sites abound across the breadth of New York State. Many of them host Canalway Trail Celebrations this first weekend. I chose the one closest to where the first channel was dug. As soon as I arrived, I boarded the red white and blue canal boat with a few other visitors. A young woman served as our tour guide, and she shared with us the history of the three versions of the Erie Canal as we moved quietly over the water. Then we sang the famous song and a few other popular old tunes.

On this day, we were powered not by a mule named Sal, but by two muscular horses pulling two men perched on a two-wheeled sulky. A thick yellow tow rope was attached to the carriage chassis; and as the horses walked along the shore, the rope alternately grew taut then lax, as the wooden craft itself gained a few feet of speed. The ride was not quite what I expected. It was steady and slow, oh so very slow. I could not imagine traveling from Buffalo to Albany at that pace. Any number of adjectives came to mind: old-fashioned, countrified, rural, rustic, pastoral, bucolic. But as we inched along, I realized that none of those words went quite far enough in describing the serenity of the scene. We passed the cars in the parking lot; then woods and wild habitats began to edge both banks of the channel. I could easily imagine that we had discovered a way to return to that simpler age of the early 1800s. It was nice to visit that time period, if just for a little while. All too soon, the horses helped us turn the boat around, and we floated back to the landing.

I walked through the various 1840s-era buildings and exhibits found on the property. I learned more about the canal, but also about the making of cheese and of the history of the horse-drawn vehicle. Henry Thoreau and

Horace Mann would not have seen this little community from the nearby railroad track. This is a reconstructed site from the twentieth century, assembled with period buildings that originated elsewhere and were moved here for historical preservation. Apart from my fellow visitors in contemporary garb, the place appeared to be frozen in time. But I could not dawdle: I had another site to see.

I drove west toward Syracuse and exited at the town of Canastota. My target was the Canastota Canal Town Museum on Canal Street. The online descriptions of its treasures had enticed me, and I arranged my trip schedule around its limited hours of operation. I was already entranced when I parked down the block from the museum. The old canal lay right next to the street (hence the name). Just two blocks south was the old New York Central railroad line. Henry and Horace's train stopped at the depot there in the early afternoon of May 14, 1861. I felt history in the air.

To say the Canastota Canal Town Museum was chockfull of that history would be to diminish the wealth of information and artifacts on display there. Every inch of wall space, every corner of every room, every curio cabinet crammed into that tiny building was a celebration of Canastota, its past and its people. It didn't take me long to understand that what I had seen earlier in the day was a generalized approach to the canal way of life. Here in front of me now were the visual results of what the canal traffic had meant to one particular town. Here, yes, were details about the canal and the industries it brought to the area. There was so much more to take in that I had trouble seeing it all. A person could easily spend hours here and be astonished by revelations at every turn. From cut glass and microscopes to the lives of Italian Americans and to Amelia Earhart showing up at the opening of the local airport—this museum was a proud representation of the heritage and the personalities of its town. I thought to myself that this place was the quintessential example of a local museum. The folks who had done the research and the people who ran the Canastota Canal Town Museum were a part of a good and decent effort. Other towns could take note and follow their format.

I was still thinking about the displays in that museum the next day on my drive back to Massachusetts. That's when I decided to do one more canal-related activity: take a ride with the Erie Canal Cruises. This time, Captain Jerry Gertz and his contemporary tour boat *Lil' Diamond II* led us east down the Mohawk River and the New York Barge Canal. We passed under the New York Thruway and went through a lock that lowered our vessel to the river's next level. While the short trip was a vastly different experience from the one offered by an historic canal boat towed by horses, the outing was an interesting one. The captain explained that a number of present-day canal users were participating in a "Great Circle Cruise." If you had your own yacht and six or seven months to spend on the water, you could sail along the continent's east coast from Florida to New York, use the Hudson River and Erie Canal to reach the Great Lakes and Mississippi River watershed, and then sail down to the Gulf of Mexico and around again. It's a "5,600-mile circumnavigation of the eastern half of the United States," according to Captain Jerry's web site. The independent explorer in me found the idea to be an intriguing one. But I'm a land animal at heart. Just cruising over a few miles of the Mohawk River and the current canal in a tour boat was adventure enough.

I learned at least one important lesson this weekend: that the Erie Canal is something that *is*, not something that *was*. Back in that music class in elementary school, we thought we were singing about ancient history: about an archaic method of transportation that came and went; about a man-made feature that no longer existed in any form; about a system that had merely consisted of boats and draft animals. Central New Yorkers know better. They are lucky to have this resource at hand, both with its historical aspects and its new recreational ones. I was almost jealous that I didn't live closer to it. "For you'll always know your neighbor / You'll always know your pal / If you've ever navigated on the Erie Canal."

WHEN YOU GO: Today the fastest and most direct way to get from Albany to Niagara Falls is via the New York Thruway (I-90). At times you'll see markers designating the road as being part of the Erie Canalway National Heritage Corridor. Between Schenectady and Utica, the highway shares the valley with the Mohawk River, the canal, and the railroad line. The two waterways will be your closest companions. The rails might be more difficult to see, especially in the full-leaf seasons of summer and fall, because they lie on the opposite bank of the river for much of that stretch. At Herkimer the road crosses the river, canal, and tracks and gives you a good view of all of them. Just past Utica, the roadway passes over them all again, and the rails veer north. Near Oneida they pass underneath the road again. Finally, west of Weedsport, the tracks make one more appearance under I-90. And then they are gone, tracing a more northern route.

When you reach the Buffalo area, you should follow I-290 to arc north of the city. At that point, you have two main choices for reaching Niagara Falls. You can continue north with I-190, which leads across Grand Island. This highway includes two sets of relatively high and narrow bridges over the Niagara River. While they offer interesting near-aerial views of both the waterway and the distant falls, they can mean a few minutes of dicey driving for the squeamish amongst us. The alternative is to exit onto U.S. 62, Niagara Falls Boulevard, which stays on the mainland but is a slower and longer route. Your peace of mind is a consideration when making your decision.

Henry and Horace's actual path via the New York Central can be more closely followed by car by using smaller state roads: NY Route 5 from Albany to Elbridge and NY Route 31 from Elbridge and Jordan to Niagara Falls. This route plays hopscotch with the rails and takes you through many of the towns and cities that the men passed through. Be prepared for this trip to take a long time, however. The state of New York is wider in reality than it appears on the map, especially when you are using the two-lane roads less traveled.

Of course, a more accurate re-enactment would be to board an Amtrak train in Schenectady or at the Albany-Rensselaer station in Rensselaer and ride the rails to Rochester. You can even take the train from Rochester to Niagara Falls—but that current route takes a southern spin and does not follow the old New York Central tracks. Only freight loads now use the old auxiliary line from Rochester to Niagara Falls. You could rent a car in Rochester and drive along NY Route 31 west to follow the original tracks the rest of the way. Don't jump into an open boxcar, just to stay true to historical integrity.

FOR MORE INFORMATION

Albany Pine Bush Preserve. 195 New Karner Rd, Albany, NY 12203.
   Phone (518) 456-0655. www.albanypinebush.org

Amtrak. Phone (800) 872-7245. www.amtrak.com

Canastota Canal Town Museum, 122 Canal Street, Canastota, NY 13032.
   Phone: 315-697-5002. www.canastota.com/organization.asp?key=43

Erie Canal Cruises, 800 Mohawk Street, Herkimer, NY 13350. Phone 315-717-0350.
   eriecanalcruises.com

Erie Canal Village, 5789 New London Road, Rome, NY 13440. Phone (888) 374-3226.
   www.eriecanalvillage.net

Friends of the Montezuma Wetlands Complex, c/o Montezuma NWR, 3395 US Route 20
   Seneca Falls, NY 13148. www.friendsofmontezuma.org/

Greater Rochester Visitors Association, 45 East Avenue, Rochester, NY 14604.
   Phone (800) 677-7282. www.visitrochester.com

Montezuma National Wildlife Refuge, 3395 US Route 20 East, Seneca Falls, NY 13148.
   Phone (315) 568-5987. www.fws.gov/r5mnwr/

New York State Canal Corporation, 200 Southern Blvd., P.O. Box 189, Albany, NY
   12201-0189. Phone (518) 436-2700 or (800) 422-6254.
   www.nyscanals.gov/index.html

Susan B. Anthony House, 17 Madison Street, Rochester, NY 14608.
   Phone (585) 235-6124. www.susanbanthonyhouse.org

Syracuse Convention and Visitors Bureau, 572 South Salina Street, Syracuse, NY 13202.
   Phone (800) 234-4SYR. www.visitsyracuse.org

RECOMMENDED READING

"Sketches from Memory: The Canal Boat," a short essay by Nathaniel Hawthorne, found in *Mosses from an Old Manse*. Hawthorne had a chance to see the area from the water instead of the rails. The Hawthorne essay called "Rochester" can be found online at www.history.rochester.edu/canal/bib/hawthorne/roch.htm.

NOTES ON THIS CHAPTER

I continue to be intrigued by the history of the Erie Canal. I consulted many books and found the following to be the most useful for my purposes here: George E. Condon's *Stars in the Water: The Story of the Erie Canal* (Garden City, N.Y.: Doubleday & Co., 1974), which contains the most amusing and detailed rendition of the "cannon telegraph" story; Ronald E. Shaw's *Erie Water West: A History of the Erie Canal, 1792-1854* (Lexington: University of Kentucky Press, 1966); Carol Sheriff's *The Artificial River: The Erie Canal and the Paradox of Progress, 1817-1862* (New York: Hill and Wang, 1996); and Debbie Daino Stack and Ronald S. Marquisee's *The Erie Canal* (Manlius, N.Y.: Media Artists Inc., 2002).

For information about Frederick Douglass and his work in Rochester, I looked at a number of reference works as well as Philip S. Foner's *Frederick Douglass: A Biography* (New York: The Citadel Press, 1964) and William S. McFeely's *Frederick Douglass* (New York: W.W. Norton, 1991). Sandy Petrulionis' wonderful book *To Set This World Right: The Antislavery Movement in Thoreau's Concord* (Ithaca: Cornell University Press, 2006), helped to define the connection between Douglass and Thoreau. No other Thoreau biography does so.

I searched a variety of sources in an attempt to track down Susan B. Anthony's activities in May 1861. The book that helped the most was the one that accompanied the documentary film by Ken Burns and Paul Barnes, *Not for Ourselves Alone: The Story of Elizabeth Cady Stanton and Susan B. Anthony, an Illustrated History* (by Geoffrey C. Ward. New York: Alfred A. Knopf, 1999).

The New York Times article about Syracuse is dated September 1, 1857, and is titled "Syracuse: Its Salt Works—Methods of Manufacture—Wealth of the City—Hotels, etc." and is signed merely by the-correspondent's initials, H.S.O. The text can be found online at http://query.nytimes.com/mem/archive-free/pdf?_r=1&res=9405E5DC163CEE34BC4953DFBE66838C649FDE. Librarian Kimberly Kleinhans from the Onondaga County Public Library helped me determine the location of the New York Central railroad station and the salt vats in Syracuse in 1861. Longtime friend George Cheatle was kind enough to drive me around Rochester to take photos of buildings and waterfalls.

Details about the rock formations of western New York can be found in *Roadside Geology of New York* by Bradford B. Van Driver (Missoula, Mont.: Mountain Press Publishing Company, 1985.)

I am grateful to Neil Yetwin of Schenectady for pointing out to me the existence of the Albany Pine Bush Preserve. You can learn more about it from the preserve web site or from the colorful guidebook by Jeffrey K. Barnes, *Natural History of the Albany Pine Bush: Albany and Schenectady Counties, New York, including a field guide and trail map* (Albany: New York State Museum, 2003).

Thoreau's first quote about his love of swamps is found in his *Journal* entry for June 16, 1840. The second, in which he calls swamps his "sanctum sanctorum," comes from the essay "Walking." Nathaniel Hawthorne's quote about the Genesee River and its waterfalls is from his essay "Rochester," first published in *New-England Magazine* in December 1835. The text can be found online.

Travel Chapter 5

Wednesday, May 15, through Sunday, May 19, 1861
Niagara Falls, Goat Island and environs

Expenses: To Niagara Falls, 4 cents.
At Niagara Falls, paper, 5 cents.
To Goat Island, 25 cents.
Trochees (2), 50 cents.
To Suspension Br[idge] & back & over Br[idge], 33 cents.
At Niagara Falls, $5.00.
Paper & bread, 15 cents.
To Bridge & paper, 9 cents.

This morning at 10 minutes of eight we came up here, two miles in the cars, and went around to find a boarding place; we went to ever[y] house but one in the town I believe and at last took a room at the American House where we are now for one dollar a day. Mr. Thoreau seems to feel better all ready, and I think that he will get better before long. I have seen the falls though I have not been to look at them yet, and I hear them roaring now all the time. I am very well. I do not know of any more to say now but I will write again in a day or two and tell you what I have seen.

—Horace Mann, Jr.'s letter of May 15, 1861

To Niagara Falls. p.m. to Goat Island. Sight of rapids, from Brid[g]e like sea off Cape Cod. Most imposing sight as yet. The great ap[parent] height of the waves tumbling over the successive ledges at a distance, while the water view is broad & boundless in that direction as if you were looking out to sea, you are so low. Yet the distances are very deceptive. The most distant billow was scarcely more than 1/4 a mile off, though it appeared 2 miles or more. Many ducks constantly floating a little way down the rapids, then flying back & alighting again. Water falling ap[parently] broken into length of 4 or 6 or more feet. Masses of ice under edge of cliff.

—Thoreau's field notebook

Henry Thoreau and Horace Mann, Jr., had traveled 500 miles by train, by the time they reached the community of Suspension Bridge. And except for spending that one day in Worcester, they hadn't had a chance to study any of the passing countryside. Five days at Niagara Falls would be a welcome respite from the rails. And it marked the first opportunity for the two naturalists to do some serious botanizing.

Western New York was experiencing the same kind of cold and wet spring that the two men had seen in eastern Massachusetts. Some parts of Niagara County even got a light frost on Friday night, May 17. *A Niagara Falls Gazette* writer lamented:

> The last month of Spring is nearly gone, yet we have had very little warm weather. We have seldom known such a backward season. Frequent rains and continued cold weather have delayed farmers so that but a small proportion of work, appropriate to the season, has been done. ... Fruit trees of all kinds, except the peach, give promise of great abundance. Only some of the more forward kinds are yet in full bloom.

Conditions might have been less than optimal for making natural observations. But Henry and Horace would have to see what they could find, once they left the hotel.

The cool air may have aggravated Thoreau's symptoms of consumption or given him a sore throat. He bought two boxes of troches, a popular throat lozenge. Newspapers of the day carried advertisements for Brown's Bronchial Troches, which could cure "cough, cold, hoarseness, Influenza, any Irritation, or Soreness of the Throat, relieve the Hacking Cough in Consumption, Bronchitis, Asthma, and Catarrh" and could "give strength in the voice of public speakers and singers." Among the testimonials listed in the ads was a nod from the Rev. Henry Ward Beecher: "Have proved extremely serviceable for hoarseness." Hopefully they helped to relieve Henry Thoreau's discomfort as well, at least temporarily.

Just one year earlier, Thoreau had exchanged several letters with two men in this part of the country. Both Charles M. Morse of Rochester and Benjamin H. Austin, Jr., of Buffalo expressed an interest in having Henry Thoreau come to their cities to lecture on "scientific subjects." Replies were sent to both requests that indicated the author's preference to speak on "such as you might infer from reading my books." If acceptable, those selections would instead "be transcendental" in nature. Evidently that clarification did not match the correspondents' requirements. Thoreau did not lecture in

New York State in 1860, or at all. The next May, he was visiting the area for the very first time, with no speaking engagements to clutter up his schedule.

More than forty years after Thoreau and Mann's journey, one historian insisted that Henry's old friend Ellery Channing had planned to meet the two men in Niagara Falls in May 1861. That was the reason they stayed in the area for five days, the author maintained: they were waiting for Ellery. But the travelers didn't need an excuse like that one to stick around the Falls. There were enough sights to see and plants to document to hold their attention for several days. And if Channing had said he would meet the duo there, well, Thoreau at least knew in his heart the likelihood of that happening. Ellery was not the most reliable traveling companion. The bottom line is that Henry and Horace spent five days exploring the area around Niagara Falls, on their own.

THE AMERICAN HOTEL

> This is quite a town—with numerous hotels & stores—pave streets & &c.—I imagine the falls will soon be surrounded by a city.
>
> —*Thoreau's field notebook*

Horace wrote to his mother that the men had traversed the town, looking for a possible place to stay. There was a good reason why they were initially having problems finding accommodations. It was May 15, the opening day of the tourist season. If they had arrived any earlier, the two would have been met with locked doors and no rooms at all. Had Mr. Thoreau done some homework and planned for that opening day arrival? Or did the circumstance turn out to be a chance accident? In either case, the full houses meant that Henry and Horace were not the only visitors at Niagara Falls that week.

The American Hotel was located at the southeast corner of Falls and Second Streets. Right across the street was the railroad depot, where trains ran either to the village of Suspension Bridge or to Buffalo. The Niagara River and the bridge to Goat Island were three or four blocks away. The building dated to the 1850s and had been previously known as the Clarendon Hotel. Under that name, it had been advertised as having many sought-after features:

> This Hotel has peculiar advantages over any other hotel in this village; it is located directly opposite the Railroad Depot and [is] one of the best managed hotels in the United States. It is a large, commodious stone building, and just near enough for

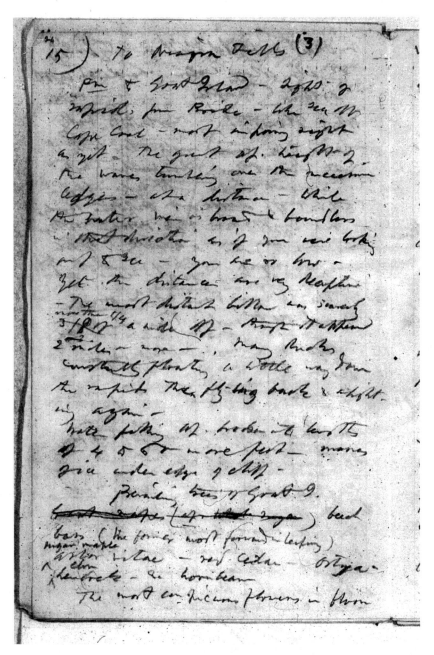

Page 24 of Thoreau's field notebook, which marks the beginning of his Niagara notes. "To Niagara Falls, PM to Goat Island – sight of rapids from Bride [miswriting of "bridge," or Bridal Veil falls?] like sea off Cape Cod – most imposing sight as yet – The great ap. height of the waves tumbling over the recessive ledges – at a distance – while the water view is broad & boundless in that direction as if you were looking out to sea – you are so low." *(Reproduced from the original manuscript in The Huntington Library, San Marino, California)*

a pleasant walk or ride to the Falls, being a distance of about 30 rods. We would recommend any person or parties who contemplate visiting the Falls, to call at the above mentioned hotel. The proprietors are pleasant, affable and agreeable; having the greatest care for the comfort of their guests. The house is new and of modern structure, rooms neat and clean and in short all seem to be calculated for the comfort and convenience of the traveling public. A porter is always in readiness at the Depot to convey baggage to the hotel free of charge.

The name of the facility had been changed to "American Hotel" early in 1859. At the cost of one dollar a day, it was more in line with Thoreau's budget than the two-dollar-a-night Delavan House in Albany.

FRIENDS AND THE FALLS

Horace Mann asked me if I did not hear the sound of the falls as we went—from the Depot to the Hotel last night—but I had not—though certainly it was loud enough. I had probably mistaken it for a train coming or a locomotive letting off steam of which we hear so much at home. It sounds hardly as loud this morning though now only ⅓ of a mile off—As I sit in my chamber is as if I were surrounded by many factories in full blast

—Thoreau's field notebook

Thoreau and Mann were familiar with the phenomenon of the falls. Henry might have heard about them personally from Margaret Fuller, Nathaniel Hawthorne, Ralph Waldo Emerson, or even Theodore Parker, as each one had visited the area years earlier. Horace might have heard about them from one of his relatives or one of his parents' friends. Now they would get to see the rushing water themselves.

Nathaniel Hawthorne had included the Niagara Falls area on the tour he made of the northeastern United States in 1832. He found himself simultaneously attracted to and repelled by the cataract. When he arrived in town, he had his bags taken to his room and ate a leisurely dinner before finally sauntering over to see the waterfalls. He spent time on Goat Island and its bridges and even walked down the slippery steps to the base of the cliff; all the while trying to ascertain the site's effect on his senses. He had gotten soaked by its water, and yet he wondered:

Were my long desires fulfilled? And had I seen Niagara? Oh, that I had never heard of Niagara till I beheld it! Blessed were the wanderers of old, who heard its deep roar, sounding through the woods, as the summons to an unknown wonder, and approached its awful brink, in all the freshness of native feeling. Had its own mysterious voice been the first to warn me of its existence, then, indeed, I might have knelt down and worshipped. But I had come thither, haunted with a vision of foam and fury, and dizzy cliffs, and an ocean tumbling down out of the sky—a scene, in short, which nature had too much good taste and calm simplicity to realize. My mind had struggled to adapt these false conceptions to the reality, and finding the effort vain, a wretched sense of disappointment weighed me down. ...

Gradually, and after much contemplation, I came to know, by my own feelings, that Niagara is indeed a wonder of the world, and not the less wonderful, because time and thought must be employed in comprehending it. Casting aside all pre-conceived notions, and preparation to be dire-struck or delighted, the beholder must stand beside it in the simplicity of his heart, suffering the mighty scene to work its own impression. Night after night, I dreamed of it, and was gladdened every morning by the consciousness of a growing capacity to enjoy it.

Had all of its previous visitors done the rest of us a great disservice? Did their descriptions cause our imaginations to work with such fervor that the pictures in our heads were far more dramatic than the ones before our eyes? Hawthorne sat on Table Rock, an outcropping on the Canadian side, for hours of contemplation before leaving the area. He revealed later through his writing that he was much affected by the sight of the falls. After a lengthy intimacy with the water, Hawthorne found a way to make the place his own, successfully shedding the perspectives of others.

Margaret Fuller experienced a similar set of emotions when she stopped by Niagara Falls on her way to the American Midwest in 1843. "Happy were the first discoverers of Niagara, those who could come unawares upon this view and upon that, whose feelings were entirely their own," she wrote. She too had known what to expect of the falls: or at least, she *thought* she knew.

When I first came I felt nothing but a quiet satisfaction. I found that drawings, the panorama, &c. had given me a clear notion of the position and proportions of all objects here; I knew where to look for everything, and everything looked as

I thought it would. ... For the magnificence, the sublimity ... I was prepared by descriptions and by paintings. When I arrived in sight of them I merely felt, "ah, yes, here is the fall, just as I have seen it in picture." ... At last, slowly and thoughtfully I walked down to the bridge leading to Goat Island, and when I stood upon this frail support, and saw a quarter of a mile of tumbling, rushing rapids, and heard their everlasting roar, my emotions overpowered me, a choking sensation rose to my throat, a thrill rushed through my veins, "my blood ran rippling to my finger's ends." This was the climax of the effect which the falls produced upon me—neither the American nor the British fall moved me as did these rapids.

This sight was the one Henry Thoreau mentioned in his own notes, with "the waves tumbling over the successive ledges at a distance, while the water view is broad & boundless in that direction as if you were looking out to sea, you are so low." But Thoreau did not record any of the emotions he might have been feeling about any of the various sights of the Niagara Falls area. Perhaps he felt no need to do so in his field notebook. Or perhaps he viewed the scene merely with the eyes of the scientist. At this point in his life, he was more interested in the details than in the inspirations they might evoke.

Instead he wrote (perhaps as the draft of a letter home) about the sound of the rushing water. He equated it with "a locomotive letting off steam" and "factories in full blast." Henry David Thoreau—whom we often consider to be the quintessential naturalist and Transcendentalist—heard in the voice of the largest natural phenomena of the Northeast not the song of nature, but of Man and his instruments of industrialization. How odd, we might think. And yet: when you stand next to the falling water today and close your eyes to the wild and the wet, that's *exactly* what the falls sound like.

Thoreau's pragmatic view of Niagara Falls had been one-upped five years earlier by Abraham Lincoln. In 1856, U.S. Congressman Lincoln returned home to Illinois, from Washington, by way of Niagara Falls. When he was asked what he thought of that large and impressive natural wonder, the future leader of the country responded: "The thing that struck me most forcibly when I saw the Falls was, where in the world did all that water come from?" For him the cataract was a consideration for logic and cause and effect, not for emotion or beauty. It may have had a similar meaning for Thoreau.

BOTANIZING ON GOAT ISLAND

Together or with each man on his own, Thoreau and Mann "botanized," or investigated and studied the plant life on Goat Island for several days. The island was uniquely positioned in the middle of the Niagara River, with the American "Luna" Falls on one side of it and the Canadian "Horseshoe" falls on the other. It was part of a typical northeastern woodland habitat, but one that obviously sustained a more continuously humid atmosphere than did other representative parcels on the mainland. Both Henry and Horace began collecting plant samples here. Thoreau had his plant press with him, as well as his compass, microscope, spy glass, and one or two botany manuals. More than likely he consulted one of his own editions of Asa Gray's *Manual of the Botany of the Northern United States*. Young Horace might have been similarly equipped. He had his shotgun along so that he could "collect" animal specimens. But he probably did not do so until the duo reached Minnesota. Horace was an avid amateur naturalist, though, and he was accompanying a self-taught expert. He must have learned a lot during this two-month excursion. The lessons began at Niagara.

The text of Thoreau's field notebook shows the scientist at work. While on site, he listed the plants he had seen, either by scientific or common name. If he wasn't sure of something, he scribbled a question mark after a name. At times he described one specimen in terms of another: such-and-such a flower looked like a certain species, but with purple petals instead of the expected white ones, for example. Later he went back and checked with published authorities to verify or to further clarify his own identifications. Sometimes he wrote more definitive classifications above or next to his original notes, based on what he learned from books. Or he would cross out an initial entry and replace it with what he thought was the correct one. Or he would specifically confirm that a name was either found or not found "in Gray," referring to Asa Gray's manual. If necessary, more extensive research could be done once he got back home.

Of course, Thoreau and Mann and the other field naturalists of the day were using strictly textual guides. No illustrations were included. Written taxonomic keys described each plant in technical botanical detail. Anyone who wanted to decipher the identity of a specimen had to count its parts, examine leaf placements, confirm its color, measure portions, analyze its natural habitat, and decide if it matched the published entry, often based on a set of words just one paragraph in length. Knowledge of Latin helped. And even by 1861, these botanic manuals were far from complete. Amateur and professional scientists were still busy documenting the natural resources of the United States, and they were generally moving over the continent from east to west. If you found a species where no one else had seen it, you might very well be the first to discover it. Or you might have incorrectly identified the plant. Therein lay the challenge.

During his time on Goat Island, Henry Thoreau documented seeing 28 species: ten trees, two shrubs, and sixteen non-woody flowering plants. He was limited by his time constraints and by the season. In mid-May, the spring wildflowers were in full bloom and the trees were just beginning to show green. The standard, lush flora of summer had yet to appear. His trees were the basswood, beech, elm, hornbeam, arborvitae, hemlock, hop-hornbeam, red cedar, shadbush, and sugar maple. Shrubs were buffalo-berry and pickly gooseberry. Wildflowers and smaller plants included cutleaf grape fern, cutleaf toothwort, downy yellow violet, Dutchman's breeches, field peppergrass, large white trillium, may apples, showy orchis, small-flowered crowfoot or buttercup, spring beauties, stinking Benjamin, white baneberry ("cohush"), white dogtooth violet, spring cress, sand cress, and dwarf ginseng. He appears to have kept some of the flower samples in his plant press for further study.

THE SUSPENSION BRIDGE AND THE CANADIAN SIDE

> 17 Go to Suspension & walk up Canada side—completest view of Falls from that side—Pestered by coach men &c. &c. —Clifton House commands best view of any Pub. House
>
> —*Thoreau's field notebook*

Thoreau and Mann had overnighted in the village of Suspension Bridge when they first reached the Niagara Falls area on Tuesday, May 14. On Friday, May 17, they took the short train ride back north to the bridge. At the time, the famed Suspension Bridge was the only way to cross the river and enter Canada West. With an expense listed at 33 cents for the entire side trip that day, it is difficult to ascertain if the two men hiked the entire length of the bridge as well as the coastline of the Canadian cliffside, or if they hired a carriage for any part of their time on the "other" side.

German American John Augustus Roebling (1806-1869) designed and supervised the building of the structure that lent its name to the nearby community. His first suspension bridge was already successfully spanning the Monongahela River in Pittsburgh when he accepted the contract to build another one over the Niagara River in the early 1850s. By then his factory in

Trenton, New Jersey, was producing all the wire rope he would need for the project. At Niagara, he designed a double-decker bridge to accommodate railway traffic on the upper level, while carriages and pedestrian traffic crossed on the lower level. It opened in 1855, and immediately made an important connection between New York and Canada West, as well as a tie between the New York Central rail line and the Great Western Railway of Canada.

It might seem odd to have locomotives traveling across the top deck, as heavy as they were. But engineers had already learned their lessons from earlier railroad *faux pas*. Years before in the Northeast, rails had been run through existing covered bridges in order to cross small rivers and streams. When those structures kept catching on fire, the builders realized the now-obvious fact: that a locomotive spewing hot ash and cinders could easily and quickly ignite a wooden enclosure. Train engines needed to be out in the open to avoid disaster. That was certainly one reason Roebling's upper deck was devoted to locomotive traffic.

The suspension bridge over the Niagara River was an accessible link between the United States and what was then a self-governing British colony. As such, it was often used by Harriet Tubman and others to accompany runaway Southern slaves to safety. If the toll collector on the lower level was not known to be a sympathizer, the escapees may have had to scamper across the upper level instead, along the railroad tracks. With the churning river far below them, the trip may have caused more than a few hearts to pound a lot faster. But with freedom beckoning on the opposite shore, any temporary discomfort was worth the effort.

Because of its more direct view of the falls, the Canadian community of Niagara Falls has always been more attractive to the tourist trade than the American side. Sure, you could stand right next to the rapids and the cataracts over in New York. But in Canada, you could admire both sets of falls from a short but safe distance, as the never-ending contents of four Great Lakes poured over the ridge, right before your eyes. You need not get wet, if you chose not to. Then again, opportunities for immersion appeared on this side as well.

Thoreau was either parroting his travel guidebook or speaking from personal experience when he noted that the view was best from the Clifton House. Built in 1833, the hotel was known for being the most elegant establishment on the Canadian side. It had been renovated in 1860, a year before Thoreau and Mann's visit. Not only did the facility boast brand-new furnishings throughout its expanse, but it now also had ten bathrooms for guest use. It was certainly the kind of place that Henry Thoreau would have deemed as being "not so good as costly." Yet he may have stood near the Clifton House, just to get that "completest view." That would have been free.

But not everything could be seen for free on the Canadian side. Two innkeepers with hotels near the Horseshoe Falls were then engaged in a bitter rivalry with each other, and both were after every tourist dollar available. It was Thomas Barnett's Table Rock House versus Saul Davis's Table Rock Hotel, and the losers in the battle were often unsuspecting American visitors.

Davis had "arrangements" with local carriage drivers that rewarded them financially for depositing tourists at his hotel doorstep, often against the riders' wishes. Someone from the inn would then entice the visitors to enter the building so that they could get an up-close and personal look at the "boiling springs" or the use of the stairway that led to the base of the falls. Women would be led into one room, men into another, and all were asked to put on oilskins in order to stay dry for the tour. The tourists would be taken down to see the cascading water for a few minutes. When they climbed back up to the hotel, they would be told that the fee for the oilskin rental (and evidently, for getting their clothes back) was five dollars. Most travelers didn't carry that much money with them. Tempers would rise, fights would break out, and the authorities would have to be called in. But most of the Americans were on vacation. They might have been angry, chagrinned, and frustrated; but they didn't want to stay and file charges and appear in court. Nor did they want a pending legal obligation that required their return to Canada. To escape relatively unscathed, they paid as much money as they could, and then they went back home. As a result, this kind of scam went on for years, for the most part unchallenged, in that neighborhood.

Was Henry Thoreau one of their victims? Of his day spent on the Canadian side, he wrote in his notebook, "Pestered by coach men &c. &c." If he had been merely "pestered" by the drivers, why would he have included the then common abbreviation for "et cetera," twice? Isn't that an indication that part of his story has been left out? Perhaps a vital part? Did he mask the real set of events by using that convenient shorthand? Surely he knew what he meant. He knew what happened on the Canadian side of Niagara Falls. A casual reader of his notebook, if one ever came along, would have no clue. The question is: If a stranger came running up to Henry Thoreau and yelled, "You've *got* to see this!" would he have followed the man?

And then there's that line item in his expense account. For most hotel fees, he included the name of the hotel on the same line as the city name. Here, right beneath the charges to go over the Suspension Bridge and back, he wrote "At Niagara Falls—$5.00." Horace told his mother that the two men had booked a room at the American Hotel for one dollar a day. They stayed for five days. We have no way of knowing what fees Horace might have paid for himself and his companion. Is that five dollar item listed on Thoreau's expense account the cost of the hotel: a dollar a day for five days? Or did Henry get scammed by the Canadians for an oilskin rental, as so many other American tourists did back then?

Nevertheless, the two men saw the falls and other sights along the west bank that day. Then they must have spent an uneventful Saturday and Sunday back in their space at the American Hotel. None of the infamous Niagara daredevils were in the area; no one was making an attempt to walk on a rope tied from one country to the other. Thoreau includes some tree circumference measurements in his notes for that time, but not much more. Perhaps after a few days of botanizing and experiencing who knows what across the border, the duo was more than ready to move on.

In Margaret Fuller's narrative of her time at Niagara Falls, she wrote: "We have been here eight days, and I am quite willing to go away. So great a sight soon satisfies, making us content with itself, and with what is less than itself. Our desires, once realized, haunt us again less readily. Having 'lived one day' we would depart, and become worthy to live another." Thoreau echoed that sentiment at the end of *Walden*: "I left the woods for as good a reason as I went there. Perhaps it seemed to me that I had several more lives to live, and could not spare any more time for that one." Niagara Falls was just one stop, it was not their intended destination. Henry Thoreau and Horace Mann had other places to see.

Seven months after Henry and Horace's visit to Niagara Falls, a group of men in the area formed the Buffalo Society of Natural Sciences. The first president of the organization was George W. Clinton, local judge and son of long-time New York Governor and Erie Canal visionary, Dewitt Clinton. Among the society's first objectives was to prepare a catalog of the plants found in and around Buffalo. In early 1864, Judge Clinton released an inaugural twelve-page pamphlet called *Preliminary List of Plants of Buffalo and Its Vicinity* (Buffalo: Young, Lockwood & Co.'s Steam Press, 1864). In his introduction, Clinton qualified the results by explaining that this inventory was a mere beginning and that it was assembled "over two seasons' explorations, and is, necessarily imperfect."

Appearing on Clinton's list are twenty of the 28 species Thoreau documented seeing on Goat Island in 1861. Seven others are at least represented by other individuals within the same botanical families; and slight variations in nomenclature might explain some of those differences. But Thoreau saw at least one tree that Clinton's men didn't: the Eastern hemlock. If Henry Thoreau had had time to publish his findings, the Buffalo men might have been able to include his observations in their own inventory. Their collections and scientific undertakings eventually formed the foundation of the present-day Buffalo Museum of Science.

But even closer to the falls, Thoreau's work on Goat Island went unnoticed. In 1921, Charles Mason Dow, former Commissioner of the State Reservation at Niagara, compiled a comprehensive two-volume resource called *Anthology and Bibliography of Niagara Falls* (Albany: J.B. Lyon Company, 1921). Dow included Falls-related excerpts from seemingly every published travel narrative, botanical study, or scientific observation he could find, dating from 1840 to his own time. He made one now noticeable exception. The 1861 visit by Henry Thoreau and Horace Mann, Jr., was not mentioned at all. Perhaps if Dow had realized that Frank Sanborn's *First and Last Journeys of Thoreau* (Boston: The Bibliophile Society, 1905) included a plant inventory from Goat Island, he might have used the information in his own book. But only 489 copies of Sanborn's set had been released by that exclusive organization. Few people owned or read it. And Thoreau's original field notebook was by then held by a private collector in California. No wonder no one knew of its contents.

The wooden building that served as the kitchen and woodshed of Niagara Falls' American Hotel caught fire in the early morning of January 5, 1863. The flames spread quickly throughout the rest of the hotel complex, and guests and boarders had to save themselves and leave their belongings behind. Owner Ansell Chappell of Brockport soon began to rebuild the establishment. But alas, just nine months later, on September 30, 1863, the unfinished structure burned down again. A new hotel named the Spencer House was put up on the same site, and it opened on April 3, 1867.

But by the beginning of the twenty-first century, that part of downtown Niagara Falls has been completely reconfigured. Old Falls Street runs just between First and Third Streets, with no intersection where Second Street used to be. Without the corner lot as a guide, it is difficult to visualize the former placement of the American Hotel. It could be the site of the Castellani Art Museum at the Falls, which was built in 2004 as a satellite to the gallery located on the Niagara University campus. The old hotel lot could be where the pedestrian walkway is, or instead, the block where The Conference Center Niagara Falls sits. No matter: if it still existed, the American Hotel would now bask in the shadow of the 26-story Seneca Niagara Casino and Hotel at 310 Fourth Street.

Over on the Canadian side, the Clifton House with the "completest view of the falls" burned down in 1898. The hotel was reconstructed in 1906, but it burned down again in 1932. The Oakes Garden Theatre now stands in its place. The problem with the hotel owners, the carriage drivers, and their "pestering" was eventually cleared up in the 1870s, after a new premier in Ontario addressed the situation and launched a criminal investigation. A few years later, the Barnetts went bankrupt and as a result, the Davis establishment had a monopoly on the tourists who ventured to that end of the street. Brash enticement was not necessary on a captive audience.

No current map includes "Suspension Bridge." The community was absorbed into the rest of incorporated Niagara Falls decades after our travelers were there; and no longer is a local post office called by that name. Roebling's creation of engineering is gone as well. The bridge that carried Thoreau and Mann to Canada and beyond lasted until the late 1870s, when demand required its renovation. A new version of the suspension bridge opened in 1886. Yet another structure, this time an arch bridge with no guide-wires, was soon constructed in the same spot as the previous two. It opened in 1897, and it is still in use today, but only to local commuter traffic. It is now known as the Whirlpool Rapids Bridge. It's still a double-decker, with the rail line running along the top and two lanes for passenger cars on the lower level.

John Augustus Roebling went on to design and oversee construction of the Brooklyn Bridge over the East River. But a freak accident during the process left him with a foot injury and a case of tetanus. He died of lockjaw in 1869, and did not live to see his most famous bridge completed.

The Niagara Reservation (as the park was called then) was created in 1885, making it the oldest state park in the United States. The creation of the park was due largely to the work of a group called Free Niagara, who wanted the area to be kept free and open to the public as a natural resource. Central Park designer Frederick Law Olmsted was among the members of Free Niagara.

With so many changes in the man-made features, you might think that the falls themselves would be the only constant when comparing them from the year 1861 and to today. You might think that as nature's features on the landscape, the falls of the Niagara River would be very much like they were when Henry Thoreau and Horace Mann, Jr., visited them. And you would be wrong. On the surface, Thoreau's observations appear to be as true today as they were when he saw them. Dig deeper and you discover the truth. It may very well be that on dear planet Earth, no other piece of nature has been more poked, prodded, tamed, controlled and managed by humans than has Niagara Falls.

It was probably only natural for humans to want to figure out a way to harness the power of the constant and rushing water. "Direct current" plants began to pop up along the gorge. And once electrical engineer Nikola Tesla (1856-1943) invented a motor that ran on coils of alternating current, the Niagara River's fate was sealed. Power plants were built along the waterway. Millions of kilowatt hours of electricity can now be generated and shared by both the United States and Canada. Even the flow of the river itself can be manipulated so that the falls are fuller during the peak days and hours of tourist season. A bigger-than-life statue of Tesla himself sits on Goat Island between the parking lot and the falls, so that every visitor must walk past him and pay tribute to his contribution to the local economy.

But the most egregious affront to Niagara came in 1969, when the American Falls were "dewatered." In other words, they were effectively turned off. A dam was built so that the river water had only the Canadian "Horseshoe" Falls as an outlet. The goal was for geologists and engineers to look at the rock foundation and the accumulation of debris at the bottom of the cliff. Removal or some kind of deconstruction might be deemed necessary or desirable for the health of the cataract. After six months of study, the answer was No. Nature should be left to her own devices. The dam was lifted, the river resumed its course, and the cascade seems to have been operating just as well ever since.

I decided to re-enact Henry and Horace's visit to Niagara Falls and to Goat Island over Memorial Day weekend, 2005. With my schedule, it was chronologically as close as I could get to their mid-May experience.

I drove onto the island, paid the parking fee, and found an empty space to pull into. I arrived early in the morning, but others had already beaten me to the best spaces. I stuffed my notebooks, pens and inspirational Thoreau books into my green backpack, and I flung it over my shoulder as I shut the car door. A few steps away from the car, I saw an informational sign erected by the park service. I was a tourist now, so I stopped to read it. At first glance, it appeared to offer exactly the kind of details that I was after:

Goat Island Flora

Goat Island's plants grow so well because of the continual moisture in the atmosphere and the deep, rich soil. The moisture protects the plants from late spring frosts, and the soil allows for greater root penetration and nutrition.

In the 18th and 19th centuries, the lush beauty of Niagara Falls and the nearby islands attracted many botanists. The Swedish botanist, Peter Kalm, came to the falls in 1750. Although he did not collect any plant specimens from Goat Island (the first bridge to the island was not built until 1817), he observed and recorded them from the mainland.

By 1877, noted botanists Joseph Dalton Hooker and Asa Gray had visited Goat Island. Here, they discovered a greater variety of vegetation growing within a limited space than anywhere else in America east of the Sierras, or in Europe. They also noted the rare beauty of the old forest and the equally rare loveliness of the rock foliage on the gorge wall below the island.

By 1888, David Day, a local botanist, had collected plant specimens on Goat Island. He found Kalm's lobelia and Kalm's St. John's wort, named for specimens found by Kalm near the Canadian flank of the Horseshoe Falls. Day prepared a catalogue for the Niagara Reservation State Park's commissioners. In it he listed the 758 native species and 151 foreign species of flora he was able to identify. He also made an unbelievable discovery. Of the 175 species of trees and shrubs native to Western New York, 140 were on Goat Island!

Goat Island is a wonderful place to view the falls and enjoy the quiet contemplation of nature. As you stroll along the trail in the woods and along the shoreline paths, please remember that all wild plants in the park are protected; they should not be damaged or removed.

This last paragraph struck me as particularly funny. Ever since I had driven onto the island, I had heard and seen a colorful tourist helicopter hovering just overhead. I thought at first that we were under siege. Was I unaware of some conflict at this international border that had occurred in the middle of the night? Or had someone stepped too close to the water and was in need of being rescued? It was an intrusion that grated on my nerves after only a few minutes. Whatever creatures of nature were here must feel similarly bombarded every day.

I again scanned the sign. I whipped out my notebook and wrote down the words. I took photos of it. And I began to get angry. Peter Kalm, Asa Gray, Joseph Dalton Hooker, David Day. What about Henry Thoreau and Horace Mann, Jr.? They received no acknowledgement at all for visiting and botanizing on this site in May 1861. I knew why, of course: neither man had a chance to publish his findings from the trip. And Thoreau's notes are always referred to as "The Journey West" or his "Trip to Minnesota." Who would think that a plant inventory from Niagara Falls could be found in a notebook labeled that way? Then too: Thoreau's documentation of fewer than 30 species didn't come close to those tallied by the more famous scientists of the nineteenth century. So he lost notoriety on several counts. Maybe this is a situation I could remedy. I started walking.

The falls were simply wonderful and mesmerizing. They were loud, too. If not for all the other people taking up space along the railings, I could have stood there and watched the water all day long. It was a challenge to get a decent photo of the falls without catching some other family posed in front of them. Still, I probably spent more time gazing at the water and at the skyline views than the average visitor did. I peered over the rim to see the *Maid of the Mist* and its boatload of ponchoed cargo cruising on the Niagara River, far below. Other fans of immersion surfaced from the Cave of the Winds underneath the falls, still wearing their rain gear. Buses arrived and launched their hordes onto the scene. Children ran along the paved paths, captivated by the sheer power around them. Passels of camera-toting tourists of varying ages and ethnicities moseyed up to the edges and paused for a few minutes to get photographic proof for distant friends and family. Then it was off to lunch, to the gift shop, or to a seemingly safer, man-made attraction. Minutes later, another batch or two appeared to take their place. It was a never-ending interchange of human bodies, all made insignificant by the surrounding environment.

I sauntered along the outer edge of the island on a ribbon of macadam. At the other end were The Three Sisters, tiny outcroppings consisting of mostly rocks and trees. Bridges linked them to each other and to Goat Island. Small shoreline pools between them attracted sea gulls, intent on finding food or creating mischief among their feathered colleagues. You could sit on a crag (as Hawthorne did on Table Rock, long ago) and let the Niagara River rush past you toward the falls. It was more personal than the falls themselves. It was quieter in a way, with fewer people, even though the roar of the water still supplied continuous background noise. And the view up the river looked very much to me as it must have appeared to Thoreau: "The great ap. height of the waves tumbling over the recessive ledges—at a distance—while the water view is broad & boundless in that direction as if you were looking out to sea—you are so low." I wondered if that would be the only place I would "find" him today.

Much of this island park is manicured and tamed nature: with well-mown grass lawns, paved parking lots and roadways, and black squirrels that scour trash-can spillover and bound right up to you to beg for something fresher. What wildness there is has been pushed out to the edges, toward the shore-lines, the falls and the river, where wildness is magnified. I could see the exceptions on my map: two wooded tracts that sat in the middle of the island interior, divided by a driveway. Compared to the open spaces around them, they looked like examples of the proverbial Forest Primeval.

I marched confidently into one of them, even as my Western European ancestry sent a fleeting fear of such places through my nervous system. I stopped for a second to let that feeling dissipate. My eyes needed time to adjust to the change in light anyway. I shivered a bit, too, as the temperature dropped a good ten degrees. Gradually I felt that the aura around me was an overwhelming sense of Rebirth and Green. I could smell it, I could taste it. The trees were just beginning to leaf out. The ground cover looked like a continuous carpet of nondescript vegetation. Any organism assigned to the forest floor had taken advantage of the unblocked sunlight of spring and had grown and blossomed accordingly. It took me a few minutes to see the plants as individuals.

"They're still here!" Had I yelled those words out loud, or were they just in my head? I caught my breath at the sight of what I considered to be old friends: an expanse of may-apples, little pixie umbrellas hovering a foot off the ground. I crouched down to look underneath. Most of their white petals had fallen off, and the apples themselves were getting larger. Nearby was a patch of large white trillium, though those flowers were beginning to wilt and looked singed around the edges. Upon closer inspection, I found that the trillium was interspersed with trout lily, what Thoreau and others called "dog-toothed violet." The miniature, lily-like heads were droopy, but the mottled leaves that remained gave them away. I snapped a few photos in the shadowy wood. These were the typical spring wildflowers of a northeastern forest, yes; but they were also among the species that Thoreau saw here in 1861. They were plants that only nature can grow successfully, not man. Perhaps these were the very descendents of Henry and Horace's observations.

As I tiptoed between and around the greenery, I finally saw my ultimate favorites: Dutchman's breeches. Their delicate, fern-like fronds were visually interesting enough. Then, dangling from their stalks were white blooms resembling poufy pantaloons, hanging upside down to dry on a laundry line. I love them. I took a few close-up photos and then straightened up to merely absorb the space for a while. No one else had followed me into the forest. It was peaceful. And it was easy to imagine two men from long ago stepping through this wood, inspecting every plant, writing down their scientific names, and taking a few samples for a plant press or a personal herbarium. No park service signs would have warned them against this practice back then.

I rejoiced on two counts. First of all, I was happy that this part of the island seemed to be allowed to grow according to its own fashion. Secondly, I was pleased as punch that what Thoreau wrote about in 1861 could still be found here today. I smiled as I returned to the driveway and followed it back to my car.

I have returned to Niagara Falls and Goat Island on several occasions, in varying seasons, since that day I first saw the wildflowers in that interior forest. Each time I make the touristy saunter to the edge of the falls to examine the torrent. I always make a point of reading that sign by the parking lot, the one that *does not* mention Henry and Horace. Someday, I tell myself, people will know. Someday.

WHEN YOU GO: To best visit the Niagara Falls area, I recommend staying in a hotel on the New York side, within walking distance of the cataract. Then you won't have to worry about parking, and you'll get some exercise as well. You can also walk across the Rainbow Bridge (built in 1940-1941) to the Canadian side to get the more complete view of the falls. Don't forget that you will need a passport and another form of identification (like a driver's license) to cross over the bridge and back. The photo opportunities alone are worth the trek.

FOR MORE INFORMATION

NEW YORK

Cave of the Winds Tour, Goat Island, Niagara Falls, NY 14301. Phone (716) 278-1730.

Devil's Hole State Park, Robert Moses Parkway, Niagara Falls, NY 14301. Phone
(716) 278-1762. www.nysparks.com/parks/42/details.aspx

Maid of the Mist Boat Tours, Niagara Falls State Park, Niagara Falls, NY 14303. Phone (716) 284-8897. www.maidofthemist.com

Niagara Falls Reservation State Park and Observation Tower, Prospect Street, Niagara Falls, NY 14303. Phone (716) 278-1770. www.niagarafallsstatepark.com/

Niagara Gorge Discovery Center, 1700 Pine Avenue, Niagara Falls, NY 14301. Phone (716) 278-1070.

Niagara Tourism and Convention Corporation, Phone (800) 338-7890. www.niagarausa.com

ONTARIO

Journey Behind the Falls, Niagara River Parkway, Niagara Falls, ON Canada Phone (905) 354-1551.

Niagara Falls Tourism, 5515 Stanley Avenue, Niagara Falls, ON Canada L2G 3X4. Phone (800) 563-2557. www.niagaratourism.com

The Niagara Parks Commission, Post Office Box 150, Niagara Falls, ON Canada L2E 6T2. Phone (877) 642-7275.

Regional Niagara Tourist Council, 2201 St. David's Road West, Post Office Box 1042, Thorold, ON Canada L2V 4T7. Phone (905) 685-1571.

RECOMMENDED READING

"My Visit to Niagara," a short narrative by Nathaniel Hawthorne, which details his trip there in 1832, when the town on the New York side was still called Manchester. Hawthorne mistakenly calls the Niagara River the St. Lawrence. Found online or in *Tales and Sketches* (The Library of America). Margaret Fuller's view is contained in the first chapter of her *Summer on the Lakes, in 1843* (reprinted by the University of Illinois Press, 1991). That text can also be found online.

NOTES ON THIS CHAPTER

Niagara Falls is a fascinating place and an intriguing, never-ending topic of research. I am heavily indebted to the resources and personnel of the Local History Department of the Niagara Falls Public Library on the New York side. I also used the general collection and research files of the Niagara Falls Public Library of Ontario.

Pierre Berton's book *Niagara: A History of the Falls* (Toronto: McClelland and Stewart, 1992) was one of the first books I read. It provided me with basic information, but also made the hairs on the back of my neck stand up when I reached the part about the hotel owners making arrangements with the carriage drivers to deposit unsuspecting tourists at their doorsteps. That's when I half-remembered something Thoreau wrote. I took another look at his notes and found his comment, "Pestered by coachmen, &c. &c." Then I checked his expense account and found the five-dollar line item. Was Thoreau taken in by scam artists? A researcher lives for such delicious discoveries.

Another vital book is Ginger Strand's *Inventing Niagara: Beauty, Power and Lies* (New York: Simon and Schuster, 2008). If you want to know anything about the area's history, especially regarding the harnessing of the Niagara River's water power, you must read this book. Ms. Strand also mentions Harriet Tubman's use of the Suspension Bridge to accompany former Southern slaves to freedom.

Roadside Geology of New York, by Bradford B. Van Driver (Missoula, Mont.: Mountain Press Publishing Company, 1985) and *Colossal Cataract: The Geologic History of Niagara Falls*, edited by Irving H. Tesmer (Albany: State University of New York Press, 1981), both provided information about how the falls developed.

The article about the cool spring weather appeared in the *Niagara Falls Gazette* on May 22, 1861. The write-up about the American Hotel when it was named the Clarendon appeared in that paper on July 7, 1856.

Horace told his mother that he and Thoreau stayed at the "American House." I could find references only to the "American Hotel" during that time period in Niagara Falls. I assume that they were the same establishment. With all of the name changes that the hotels underwent in the 1800s, I would not be surprised if another one slipped through the cracks of research and documentation. But the location of the American Hotel at Second and Falls Street seems to make sense when compared with Thoreau's notes about how far the falls were from his room.

Nathaniel Hawthorne's impressions of the falls are found in "My Visit to Niagara," in *Tales and Sketches* (The Library of America). Margaret Fuller's view is contained in the first chapter of her *Summer on the Lakes, in 1843* (reprinted by the University of Illinois Press, 1991). Abraham Lincoln's remarks were recorded by his one-time law partner and biographer William H. Herndon in *Herndon's Lincoln: The True Story of a Great Life* (Chicago: William H. Herndon, 1889).

Correspondence to Thoreau from the men of western New York appears on pages 583-585 of *The Correspondence of Henry David Thoreau* (Walter Harding and Carl Bode, eds. New York: New York University Press, 1958).

Frank Sanborn was the first person to attempt to assemble the details of Thoreau and Mann's journey to the Midwest. Sanborn had been friends with Henry Thoreau and had taught young Horace and his two brothers in Concord. In addition to looking at Thoreau's trip notebook, the editor at times called upon personal knowledge to flesh out his narrative. In *First and Last Journeys of Thoreau, Lately Discovered Among His Unpublished Journals and Manuscripts* (Boston: The Bibliophile Society, 1905), Sanborn mentioned in three separate passages that Thoreau expected to meet friend Ellery Channing at Niagara Falls. Channing himself did not bring up the subject in his own published biography of Thoreau, released in 1901. But Sanborn was also a friend (and later, a housemate) to Ellery Channing. Had the man once told Sanborn of his plan to make such a trip, in retrospect? And if so: was he telling the truth?

Sanborn perpetrates this possible myth with further embellishment once again in 1917, in his book *The Life of Henry David Thoreau, Including Many Essays Hitherto Unpublished, and Some Account of His Family and Friends* (New York: Houghton Mifflin, 1917):

> For companion on this latest tour he was to have been accompanied, as on so many before, by Ellery Channing; whose courage, his spirits, or his money gave out at the last, and Channing failed to meet him at Niagara, as he had given Thoreau to understand he might do. His friend was much disappointed, and had to fall back on the companionship of young Horace Mann, a student of natural science, modest and good-natured, but not very conversible, and without the lively wit and Shakespearean versatility of Channing, in which Thoreau delighted and found refreshment.

By the time Sanborn wrote those lines, none of the three men mentioned in this paragraph were alive to support or dispute his words. And he seems unduly harsh in his assessment of the personality of his former student, Horace Mann, Jr., and of the teen's compatibility with that of Henry Thoreau. But Thoreau was prepared for this excursion to be a journey of discovery. He packed his botanic manuals and all of his instruments for studying local flora and fauna. Maybe he did not want to be saddled with a companion with "lively wit and Shakespearean versatility." Maybe he instead preferred that someone would share his interest in the natural world and the detailed documentation of selected parts of it. In that respect, Horace was the better choice; and perhaps, the best choice from Concord.

Any subsequent researcher who has connected Channing with this theoretical meeting in Niagara Falls has cited one of Sanborn's two books as the source. And over the course of the ensuing years, Frank Sanborn's writings have come under fire as being less than reliable. Did Ellery Channing really tell Henry Thoreau he would meet him in Niagara Falls? Maybe the question no longer matters. The facts are these: Henry and Horace spent five days there without Ellery Channing.

Thoreau's twenty plants from Goat Island that matched the list published for the Buffalo Society of Natural Sciences are these: American basswood (*Tilia americana*), American elm (*Ulmus americana*), Eastern arborvitae (*Thuja occidentalis*), Eastern red cedar (*Juniperus virginiana*), Shadbush (*Amelanchier canadensis*), Buffalo-berry (*Shepherdia canadensis*), Prickly gooseberry (*Ribes cynosbati*), Cutleaf grape fern (*Botrychium dissectum*, though the Buffalo men said *Botrychium lunaroides v. dissectum*), Cutleaf toothwort (*Dentaria laciniata*), Downy yellow violet (*Viola pubescens*), Dutchman's breeches (*Dicentra cucullaria*), Large white trillium (*Trillium grandiflorum*), May apple (*Podophyllum peltatum*), Showy orchis (*Orchis spectabilis*), Small-flowered crowfoot or buttercup (*Ranunculus abortivus*), Spring beauty (*Claytonia virginica*), Stinking Benjamin (*Trillium erectum*), White dogtooth violet (*Erythronium albidum*), Spring cress (*Cardamine rhomoidea v. pupurea*), and Sand cress (*Arabis lyrata*).

The seven questionable ones are these:

American beech. Thoreau wrote just "beech." I find it as *Fagus grandifolia*. The Buffalo men listed *Fagus ferruginea*, which some current sources say is "red beech."

American hornbeam. Thoreau wrote just "hornbeam." I find it as *Carpinus caroliniana*. The Buffalo men listed *Carpinus virginiana*. Today that species might be considered the same as *Ostrya virginiana*, Eastern hop-hornbeam. Did Thoreau see both? Or was he inconsistently using "hornbeam" and "Ostrya" to mean the same tree in his notes? That was not his typical *modus operandi*, according to Ray Angelo's *Botanical Index to the Journal of Henry David Thoreau* (Salt Lake City: Gibbs M. Smith, 1984).

Eastern hop-hornbeam (*Ostrya viginiana*, or merely "Ostrya" as Thoreau liked to refer to it). Again: Did he see both? Which one did the Buffalo men see?

Sugar maple. Even Thoreau wasn't quite sure what he had seen at first. He wrote "Great Maple (ap. white sugar)" in his list of Goat Island trees, then crossed out all of those words. (His "white maples" were what we now call silver maples.) Three lines later, he crammed the words "sugar maple" between other entries. Today we use *Acer saccharum* as the sugar maple and *Acer saccharinum* as the silver maple. The Buffalo men listed the existence of *Acer saccharinum* in their region. Perhaps they reverted to the old usage of that *Acer saccharinum* designation, for it had been used to describe sugar maples at an earlier time. So: Did Henry see a sugar maple? Did the Buffalo men see silver maples or sugar maples? Today it is difficult to tell. And today, both species are present.

Field peppergrass. Thoreau listed it as *Lepidium campestre*. The Buffalo men had *Lepidium virginicum* on their list, which is now called Virginia pepperweed.

White baneberry, or "Doll's eyes." Thoreau called it "Cohush." According to Ray Angelo's *Botanical Index*, the equivalent of Thoreau's "cohush" was *Actaea pachypoda*. The Buffalo men list *Actaea spicata* v. *rubra* (a red variety) and *Actaea spicata* v. *alba* (a white variety). The latter might have matched the ones Thoreau saw.

Dwarf ginseng, or as Thoreau wrote, *Aralia trifolia*. The Buffalo men put *Aralia racemosa* (American spikenard), *Aralia hispida* (Bristly sarsaparilla) and *Aralia nudicaulis* (Wild sarsaparilla) on their list.

How the Buffalo men missed seeing the Eastern hemlock (*Tsuga canadensis*) is a mystery. It is a distinctive tree that currently grows in thick stands along the southern shore of Walden Pond. Thoreau surely recognized it.

Travel Chapter 6

Monday, May 20, 1861
Niagara Falls to Detroit
via Great Western Railway of Canada

Expenses: To Bridge & paper, 9 cents.
At Detroit, 50 cents.

20") Niagara Falls to Detroit Canada agreeably diversified i.e. more as compared with N.Y. with a view of L. Ontario quite sea-like—Decidedly more level W of London—& wet but prob. rich—great fens with bullrush (?)& wild fowl S of L. St Clair (of which a long & fine view) on each side the Thames crossing

Saw about Thamesville a small plump bird red head & black-ish or bluish back & wings—with **broad** white on the round-ed wings & tail—Prob. Red-head woodpecker

—Thoreau's field notebook

After spending five days as botanists and tourists at Niagara Falls, Henry Thoreau and Horace Mann, Jr., left the American House and went back north to the village of Suspension Bridge. They crossed the bridge by train this time and headed across Canada West with the Great Western Railway of Canada. They left the New York side at 9:30 a.m., arrived in Windsor a little after 6 p.m., and took a ferry across the Detroit River to Detroit. No bridge spanned the waterway at the time.

Certainly from a traveler's point of view, it made perfect sense to cut across Canada at this point. From Niagara Falls, the best way to reach Chicago was to use the Great Western Railway here and then the Michigan Central Railroad across Michigan. At the time of Henry and Horace's ride, this part of the world was a self-governing British colony. It had been called Upper Canada from 1791-1841, when the Union Act established a single legislature for the entire region north of the United States. (Lower Canada included present-day Quebec.) From 1841 on, this area was called Canada

West. It was only fitting that our western-heading adventurers passed through it.

Merely traversing this part of the colony by train didn't offer any insights into the lives of its residents or the wildlife of its fields and forests, however. A fifteen-minute stop in Hamilton and a ten-minute one in London could not provide any time at all for downtown exploration. Our travelers were once again limited to what they could spy from their passenger car windows. And from Jordan to Hamilton, what Henry Thoreau saw was Lake Ontario, looking very much like a large sea rising from the shoreline. The tracks in Hamilton led right along its edge, almost skimming over the water itself. It was no doubt a mesmerizing sight.

But by looking specifically toward the lake from his seat on the north side of the train, Henry Thoreau completely missed seeing a major geologic feature to the south: the Niagara Escarpment. No one would have called it by that name back then, and it would be years before scientists would understand the forces that created the formation. Had Henry turned around, however, he would have noticed a hill, a continuous ridge that increased in altitude from St. Catharines to Hamilton. It would never reach the height of say, Mount Wachusett, and it might not have seemed like anything special at the time. But the escarpment represented the kind of change in the landscape that Thoreau regularly documented in this trip notebook. And for him to avoid its mention must mean that his eyes were drawn instead to Lake Ontario.

Today geologists tell us that the Niagara Escarpment was formed during the Silurian and Ordovician Periods, some 430-450 million years ago. A shallow sea lay over the land now known as the state of Michigan; and an outer rim of rock developed in a near-perfect arc around it. The scarp begins around Rochester, N.Y., and heads due west to Hamilton, Ontario, becoming more prominent along the way. Then it turns north and makes a large half-circle through central Ontario, proceeding along the Bruce Peninsula, Manitoulin Island, the southern edge of Michigan's Upper Peninsula, and south into Wisconsin through the Door Peninsula. Together with the nearby Onondaga Escarpment, this ridge helped to bring into existence the drama of the falls and the gorge of the Niagara River. But in 1861, no one would have known any of its history. They would have noticed only that this small, skinny mountain served as a backdrop for the lakeside towns and that it resulted in hilly sections of Hamilton. It meant that the railroad had to be laid closer to the shore. Any bigger picture was out of reach of scholarship.

The men continued west. At the town of Woodstock, the Thames River joined the course of the Great Western Railway. It played leapfrog with the tracks through London, Thamesville and Chatham, and then emptied into Lake St. Clair. The train continued through Stony Creek, Belle River, and Tecumseh before coming to the end of the line in Windsor. From there, the railway company offered the services of its ferry, *Union*, to cross the river to Detroit.

If they saw any dark faces at all in the cars or on the passing railway platforms that day, perhaps Thoreau and Mann would have understood that they had been riding through the very region that was a destination for escaped American slaves. Harriet Tubman was known to have escorted individuals across the suspension bridge at Niagara Falls. Those people had to end up somewhere. A fair number made their way to the area of Elgin County, Canada West: where they could own their own homes and farms, and could live with their families and friends in freedom.

While Henry and Horace were crossing Canada West that day, a nineteenth-century version of a Homeland Security investigation was being launched back home in Massachusetts. Deputy marshals representing the U.S. government were walking into the main telegraph offices and seizing all of the original handwritten message requests from the previous six months. "This movement is to detect the probable correspondence of traitors, and ascertain who they are," reported the *Springfield Republican*. The stacks of papers were taken to an office in Boston where they were scrutinized, specifically for missives sent to destinations south of the Mason-Dixon line. Similar raids took place in other Northeastern cities. Within days, some persons of interest were identified by this effort. The War Between the States was only in its second month, and already the search was underway for participants in espionage.

After Henry Thoreau's first excursion to Canada in 1850, he wrote: "I do not suppose that I have seen all British America ... I wished to go a little way behind that word Canadense, of which naturalists make such frequent use; and I should like still right well to make a longer excursion on foot through the wilder parts of Canada." Unfortunately, that kind of exploration would have to wait for another day.

It is not known where the two men spent the night. Thoreau's ledger shows that he spent fifty cents in Detroit. And in his notes for the next day, he wrote: "The one dollar houses in Detroit are the Garrison & the Franklin H." The Garrison House was located at 65-69 Jefferson Avenue; the Franklin House was at 68 Bates Street. Both were close enough to the ferry and to the Michigan Central station that our travelers could have stayed in either one. Did Henry and Horace split the cost of a room that night? Or did they have a less-than-acceptable experience at an even cheaper establishment? Was Thoreau's note thus meant to be a memory-jogger for the journey home, so as not to repeat a past mistake? We simply do not know.

When Canada became a Dominion in 1867, it was immediately divided into four provinces: Ontario, Quebec, Nova Scotia and New Brunswick. Today it covers the entire top of the North American continent with ten provinces and three territories. All of the cities and towns that Thoreau and Mann passed through that day have since gained greatly in population, especially those settlements clustered between Niagara Falls and Hamilton. Those who study human geography can probably present a myriad of reasons for this region's growth: its proximity to New York State; its proximity to Toronto; its position between Lakes Erie and Ontario and thus historically good transportation routes. Or maybe it's just because these communities make good places to live. A lot of people like it there.

The Niagara Escarpment in Ontario is now seen as an anchor for a national system of conservation and an initiative for preserving open space. More than one hundred parks are either already in place or are proposed for sites on or near the remarkable ridge. The Bruce Trail, named after James Bruce, the 8th Earl of Elgin (1811-1863), follows the scarp from Niagara Falls to Tobermory at the tip of the Bruce Peninsula. Hikers can walk the trail in sections or can make their way from one end to the other: all 500 miles of it.

One of Henry and Horace's friends, Dr. Samuel Gridley Howe, came to this part of Canada West in 1863. He was specifically interested in the living conditions of the former American slaves. His observations would later become a report for the Commission on the Canadian Negroes and forwarded to the U.S. Secretary of War, Edwin McMasters Stanton. The Americans were already predicting what the ramifications would be if/when four million slaves were suddenly given emancipation. Howe's comments became part of the Congressional debate on the Fourteenth Amendment.

The first bridge connecting Windsor and Detroit was built in 1929, and the following year saw a transportation tunnel dug between the two cities as well. This kind of engineering technology made the Detroit River ferries obsolete. But long before that time, the *Union* had retired from ferry service. It burned at Sarnia on the St. Clair River.

It hardly matters which hotel Thoreau and Mann stayed at in Detroit: the Garrison House, the Franklin house, or an unnamed hostelry. That part of downtown Detroit looks nothing like what it did in 1861. Interstate 75 and other modern additions have seen to that.

During the last week of September 2007, I drove across southern Ontario from Niagara Falls to Detroit. I had at least three reasons for the trip. The first was to follow the 1861 route of Henry Thoreau and Horace Mann, Jr., naturally. The second was to fulfill my speaking duty at a Thoreau conference in Minneapolis. And the third was to make a stop in Grimsby, Ontario, to see a new Thoreauvian friend.

Greg Smith came from Grimsby to Concord, Massachusetts, earlier in the year. I gave him a tour around the town and around Walden Pond, and we had some good discussions about Thoreau that day. Now Greg was about to return the favor by showing me the site of the old Great Western station in his hometown. Henry and Horace's train rolled past there on that long-ago day in May.

I maneuvered through the highway maze around St. Catharines and successfully exited at Grimsby. I turned south and almost immediately saw the old station. The building had found new life as a pottery and antiques store. I pulled into the parking lot, where Greg and his friend James W. Bond were waiting for me. We chatted a bit, then took our time walking in and around the store. Greg found an old photo of the 1850s station, and we compared it with what we saw in front of us. The railroad tracks had been moved over the years, but the structure of the station building was certainly the same. I loved the before-and-after aspect of the two images. This outing was fun enough for me.

But the two men surprised me by driving me to another site. We headed up the ridge behind the downtown area and were soon in the Beamer Memorial Conservation Area. We climbed out of the car and sauntered down one of the trails to a lookout point. Greg and James told me the details about the Niagara Escarpment along the way. When we came out of the woods, I saw what they meant. We were on top of the scarp, high enough to see the mists rising from Niagara Falls, 30 miles to the east. We could look down on the business district of Grimsby. Through the haze of the humid fall day, we saw the skyscrapers of Toronto to the north, 30 or 40 miles away, on the other side of Lake Ontario. I was shocked. I had made the same mistake that Thoreau did. On the drive in, I had concentrated so completely on the highway and on my views of the lake that I completely missed seeing this ridge. It was noticeable enough when you knew it was here. What is it about Lake Ontario that steals our attention away from the rest of the natural world? Its blue-ness? The fact that it indeed looks like an expansive sea? Or is it because it's just so darn big?

It was at that point that I understood that Henry Thoreau had been sitting on the north side of the train. If he had seen this ridge, he would have mentioned it in his notebook. And because he had not written about it, I had not been focusing on it, either. More than that, I had known nothing of the scarp until Greg and James showed it to me, leading me to question my own ability as a deep traveler.

Two years later, on September 30, 2009, I happened to be driving this same route again, but just from Niagara Falls to Woodstock. This time I tried to ignore the view of Lake Ontario. I kept glancing to the south whenever the traffic would allow. I was rewarded by seeing the Niagara Escarpment grow ever taller, the farther I drove. If two Canadian friends had not taken me to the top of that ridge to walk around and to see the surrounding landscape, that geological formation might still be invisible to me today.

WHEN YOU GO: The most expedient way of crossing southern Ontario here is to begin in Niagara Falls and to watch for the signs for the Queen Elizabeth Way (QEW). Follow the QEW west toward Hamilton and Toronto, even though you won't be going as far as Toronto during this segment of the trip. At Hamilton, change to Highway 403 West. At Woodstock, Highway 403 West leads right into Highway 401 West. Travel the length of this route to Windsor. There you will find directions for a bridge to cross the Detroit River and into the city of Detroit.

Be prepared for a lot of traffic, lane changes, and exits from Niagara Falls to Brantford. This part of Ontario has grown into a near-continuous metropolitan area that leads into Toronto.

If you keep your eye on the southern horizon from time to time, you can see what Thoreau did not: the advancement of the Niagara Escarpment. You can catch it from the QEW. In the beginning, it appears just as a forested ridge to your left. When a high concrete curve carries you above the landscape, you can get a great view of Lake Ontario—but remember also to glance the other way, to see the scarp. The ridge grows taller and much more noticeable by the Grimsby exit. It might get lost from your line of sight in metropolitan Hamilton. But on Route 403 just west of Hamilton, you will have a chance to get up close and personal with it. You'll see the "Entering the Niagara Escarpment" sign. You will drive next to it for a few miles, and then through it, and then poof! The ridge turns north. The rest of the ride to Windsor does not include another physical landmark of such dynamic proportions.

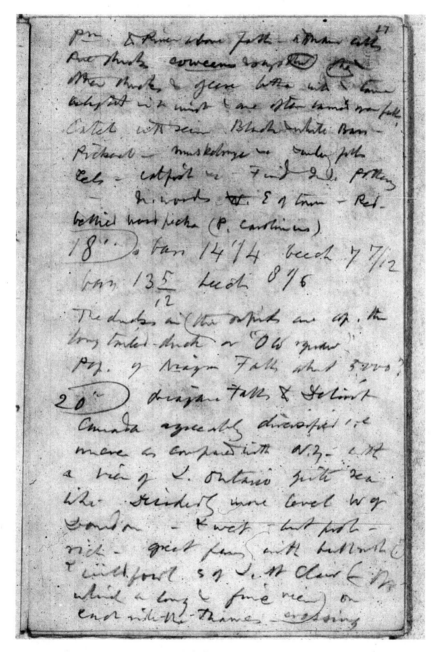

Page 27 of Thoreau's field notebook, which notes the men's May 20th crossing from "Niagara Falls to Detroit. Canada agreeably diversified i.e. more as compared with N.Y. with a view of L. Ontario quite sea-like – Decidedly more level W of London -- & wet but prob. rich – great fens with bullrush (?) & wild fowl S. of L. St. Clair (of which a long & fine view) on each side the Thames crossing" (*Reproduced from the original manuscript in The Huntington Library, San Marino, California*)

Because of the congestion, it might be a difficult task to leave the highways behind and follow the railroad tracks themselves from Niagara Falls to Hamilton. Armed with a good road
map or a back-road atlas, you may be able to find your way around. I can recommend exit-
ing the QEW after St. Catharines, then finding a main street running west but south of the
highway, one that can lead you into Route 8 in Hamilton. When you leave Hamilton, use
Route 5 from Dundas to Paris, Route 5 from Paris to Woodstock, and Route 2 west from
Woodstock to Windsor. You will be able to watch the Thames River change positions with
the rails during that last section as well. Have your camera ready.

Of course, you can re-enact Henry and Horace's journey even more closely by riding along
with VIA Rail Canada. You can take the train from Niagara Falls to Aldershot, which lies just
north of Hamilton on Burlington Bay. Then switch to the line that leads across southern
Ontario to Windsor. Both segments generally follow the old Great Western track.

FOR MORE INFORMATION

Beamer Memorial Conservation Area, Ridge Road, Grimsby, ON Canada L3M 4E7.
www.npca.ca/conservation-areas/beamer-memorial/default.htm

The Bruce Trail Conservancy, PO Box 857, Hamilton, ON Canada L8N 3N9.
Phone (905) 529-6821. www.brucetrail.org

Buxton Historic Site and Museum, 21975 A.D. Shadd Road, North Buxton, ON Canada
N0P 1Y0. Phone 519-352-4799. www.buxtonmuseum.com

Niagara Escarpment Commission, 232 Guelph Street, Georgetown, ON Canada L7G
4B1. Phone (905) 877-5191. www.escarpment.org

Niagara Peninsula Conservation Authority, 250 Thorold Road, Welland, ON Canada L3C
3W2. Phone (905) 788-3135. www.ncpa.ca

Ontario Ministry of Natural Resources, Ontario Parks, 300 Water Street, 6th Floor, PO
Box 7000, Peterborough, ON Canada K91 8M5. Phone 800-667-1940.
www.mnr.gov.on.ca

Ontario Travel, 1000-201 City Center Drive, Mississauga, ON Canada L58 4E4.
Phone www.ontariotravel.net

Royal Botanical Gardens, 680 Plains Road West, Hamilton/Burlington, ON Canada L7T
4H4. Phone 905-527-1159. www.rbg.ca VIA Rail Canada. www.viarail.ca.

RECOMMENDED READING

Thoreau's essay "Slavery in Massachusetts," since many former slaves relocated to this part
of Canada. The text can be found online and in many Thoreau anthologies.

NOTES ON THIS CHAPTER

Remember: an American needs a passport or an "enhanced" driver's license to enter Canada,
and vice versa.

In addition to *Roadside Geology of New York* by Bradford B. Van Driver (Missoula, Mont.:
Mountain Press Publishing Company, 1985), information about the Niagara Escarpment can
be found in *Colossal Cataract: The Geologic History of Niagara Falls*, edited by Irving H.
Tesmer (Albany: State University of New York Press, 1981)

McGill University has digitized the 1880s atlases representing the counties of Canada. *In Search of Your Canadian Past: The Canadian County Atlas Digital Project* (http://digital.library.mcgill.ca/countyatlas/default.htm) is a marvelous resource to be able to consult.

The story of the invasion of telegraph offices is recounted in the May 22, 1861, issue of the *Springfield Republican*. I saw an original copy at the American Antiquarian Society.

The account of Dr. Samuel Gridley Howe's visit to Canada West can be read at the Buxton Historic Site and Museum web site (http://www.buxtonmuseum.com) and in Victor Ullman's book, *Look to the North Star: A Life of William King* (Boston: Beacon Press, 1969). That biography makes for an excellent read, for Americans and Canadians alike. King made a tremendous impact on the lives of former Southern slaves; yet he does not show up in traditional history books.

The *Union* is mentioned and pictured in William Oxford's *The Ferry Steamers: The Story of the Detroit-Windsor Ferry Boats* (Erin, Ont.: Boston Mills Press, 1992).

Thoreau's quote about Canada appears in the last paragraph of *A Yankee in Canada*, a short travelogue that was first included in a posthumous publication by Ticknor and Fields called *A Yankee in Canada, with Anti-Slavery and Reform Papers* in 1866.

TRAVEL CHAPTER 7

Tuesday, May 21, 1861
Detroit to Chicago
via Michigan Central Railroad

Expenses: Breakfast, &c, 17 cents. [May] 21. Detroit to Chicago. Very level to Ipsylanti [Ypsilanti], then hilly to Ann Arbor, then less hilly to Lake M[ichigan]. All hard wood or no evergreen except some white pine, when we struck Lake Michigan, on the sands from the lake partly & some larch before. Phlox varying from white to bluish & paint[ed] cup; deep scarlet & also yellow ? or was this wall flower? All very very common thro' Michigan & the former, at least, earlier.

—*Thoreau's field notebook*

Henry Thoreau and Horace Mann, Jr., probably boarded a west-bound train of the Michigan Central Railroad in Detroit at 7 a.m. Maybe they ate breakfast first. Maybe they ate on the train.

But they definitely did not make a side trip to the town of Rochester in Avon Township, Oakland County, located about fifteen miles north of Detroit. Thus they passed up the chance to visit with Calvin H. Greene, one of Thoreau's admirers and correspondents. By continuing their journey without such an interruption, Henry was reneging on multiple promises he had made to Greene that he would stop by "if I ever come into your neighborhood." What circumstances might have caused Thoreau to make such a decision?

Calvin H. Greene had first written to Henry David Thoreau after reading and being impressed with the book *Walden* in 1856. It might have been easy for the reader to sense a kinship with the author and with the settings and situations described in the text. The two men had been born in the same year. Both held a variety of manual jobs during their lifetimes, and both were at times called upon to be educators. Rochester, Michigan, and Concord, Massachusetts, were both farming communities located outside of and within moderate reach of major cities. The church was a powerful entity in both towns. In such an environment, it would have been a challenge

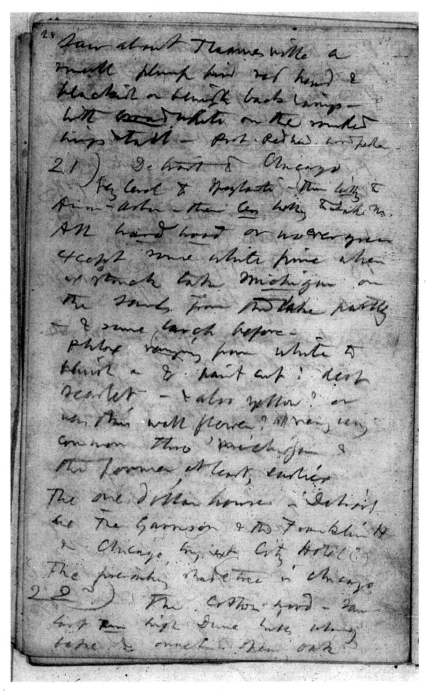

Page 28 of Thoreau's field notebook, which shows the May 21st crossing of Michigan, from "Detroit to Chicago. Very level to Ipsylanti– then hilly to Ann Arbor – then less hilly to Lake M." (*Reproduced from the original manuscript in The Huntington Library, San Marino, California*)

for any young man to privately establish his own belief system independent of the local authorities. To be true to oneself and not to be merely blindly answerable to others was a Thoreauvian concept that Greene could have eagerly embraced. He wrote to Henry in response.

Though Greene's letters have not survived, Thoreau's written replies have. Even with only one side of the dialogue available, we can ascertain what the Michigander must have said or asked. Henry Thoreau's first letter to Greene was polite enough and was dated January 18, 1856. "I am glad to hear that my 'Walden' has interested you—that perchance it holds some truth still as far off as Michigan. I thank you for your note." Greene had also inquired about the availability of Thoreau's first book, *A Week on the Concord and Merrimack Rivers*, since he could not find it locally. Thoreau told him he could buy a copy directly from the author for one dollar and twenty-five cents. He did not mention that he still had hundreds stored upstairs in his attic.

Energized in return, Greene immediately followed with another letter and included money for *A Week*. This time he must have also requested a photographic image of the author. Henry wrote back and said, "You may rely on it that you have the best of me in my books, and that I am not worth seeing personally—the stuttering, blundering clod-hopper that I am." He redirected the conversation back to Greene's turf. "I like the name of your county. May it grow men as sturdy as its trees. Methinks I hear your flute echo amid the oaks. Is not yours too a good place to study theology?"

We do not know if Greene answered that last question in his next letter. But he *did* ask if Thoreau would consider traveling to Rochester to deliver a lecture. At the time (May 1856), Calvin Greene was teaching in the Avon Lyceum, a local private school. He no doubt wanted the author either to speak to his students or in a wider public forum. Thoreau's answer was No:

> I thank you heartily for your kind intentions respecting me. The West has many attractions for me, particularly the lake country & the Indians. Yet I do not foresee what my engagements may be in the fall. I have once or twice come near going West a-lecturing, and perhaps some winter will bring me into your neighborhood, in which case I should probably see you. Yet lecturing has commonly proved so foreign & irksome to me, that I think I could only use it to acquire the means with which to make an independent tour another time.

Five years after writing those words, Henry Thoreau was traveling with Horace Mann, Jr., through Michigan and through Mr. Greene's neighborhood, seemingly incognito.

Thoreau acquiesced to Calvin Greene's request for a portrait. He had three daguerreotype images made in Worcester, Massachusetts. One he sent to Greene in a letter dated June 21, 1856. The long-distance fan was appeased for a while.

A year later, Greene wrote again to re-invite the writer to Rochester. Thoreau seemed by this time to be growing a bit uncomfortable with the correspondent:

> You are right in supposing that I have not been Westward. I am very little of a traveller. ... You will excuse me for not responding more heartily to your notes, since I realize what an interval there always is between the actual & imagined author, & feel that it would not be just for me to appropriate the sympathy and good will of my unseen readers. ... Nevertheless, I should like to meet you, & if I ever come into your neighborhood shall endeavor to do so.

Greene must have offered to be Thoreau's Midwestern cheerleader, in a manner of speaking. Henry countered with another idea. "Cant [sic] you tell the world of *your* life also? Then I shall know you, at least as well as you me." This arrangement was becoming rather one-sided, with one correspondent ever demanding stuff and favors from the other. Perhaps thankfully for Thoreau, the exchange dropped off. Mr. Greene did not write back for two years.

Henry Thoreau gave his impassioned John Brown speech at three Massachusetts sites in 1859. Calvin Greene heard or read about them. He wanted a copy of the speech, and once again he wrote to the author. He included stamps to cover the postage costs. Yet again, Thoreau had to turn him down. Some of the local newspapers had quoted from his lecture, he explained, but none had published the text in its entirety. "I am glad to know that you are interested to see my things, & I wish that I had them in a printed form to send to you. ... I return the stamps which I have not used. ... I shall be glad to see you if I ever come your way." Or maybe not. Those were the last words Henry Thoreau wrote to Calvin Greene.

Thoreau was not averse to exchanging letters with readers or fans. His friendship with Harrison Gray Otis Blake of Worcester had begun in similar fashion. Blake read an essay Thoreau wrote; and he took that opportunity to contact the author for further clarification. Thus began years of correspondence and visits between Concord and Worcester. Blake became a disciple and a valued comrade within Henry Thoreau's tiny social circle.

Why wasn't Calvin Greene given the same opportunity? Any number of arguments could be made. Like Thoreau, H. G. O. Blake was a Harvard graduate (while Greene had attended Oberlin College), and the two had met in person before their correspondence began. They lived within a two-hour train ride of one another. The discussions they engaged in with their pens could be expanded upon in person, and vice versa. The same could be said of friend Daniel Ricketson of New Bedford, Massachusetts. A man from Michigan didn't have that local advantage.

Or maybe Thoreau resolved by then that he had friends enough. Maybe he had gotten a bad vibe from either Greene's tone or his enthusiasm. Maybe the difference was that Blake and Ricketson's letters were intellectually stimulating, brimming with opinions and philosophies, questions and wonderings. All Mr. Greene seemed to want was Thoreau's picture, copies of all of his writings, and his physical presence in Rochester.

Perhaps Henry was familiar with the celebrity sentiment attributed to Horace Mann the elder, young Horace's father: "More will sometimes be demanded of you than is reasonable. Bear it meekly, and exhaust your time and strength in performing your duties, rather than vindicating your rights." The Transcendentalist filled as many of Greene's requests as he was comfortable with at the time.

By this May day in 1861, heading westward across Michigan on the train, Henry Thoreau might have legitimately forgotten about Calvin Greene and those invitations to visit him. He might have remembered them but determined that he and Horace were better served by continuing along their charted path. Or he might have remembered Greene and decided he did not want to foster a further relationship with the man. Maybe he breathed a sigh of relief, thinking that he had dodged a bullet and an unwanted encounter.

Little did Thoreau know that an even more fervent fan awaited him in Chicago.

The Michigan Central pulled Henry and Horace across the width of the state. Soon they passed through Ann Arbor, home of the University of Michigan campus. According to the 1861 railroad gazetteer, the town had 10,000 residents. The university itself enrolled between 500-600 students; hardly enough to fill even one section of a stadium of any size.

Once again, Thoreau made the most of the ride by scrutinizing the passing landscape and botanizing from the car window. It was springtime. Flowers were unfolding. As they rode, Henry Thoreau began to glimpse trees with pink and white blossoms dotting the farmland. What were they? He wasn't sure. The train did not make any lengthy stops on this route.

There were no opportunities to jump out for even a second to explore the countryside, retrieve a specimen, compare it to a botanical manual, and make a definitive identification.

But he might have already been thinking of a possibility: *Malus coronaria,* the crab apple. It didn't grow in New England in Thoreau's lifetime, and he longed to see one. Ten years earlier he outlined in his journal the attributes of various apple species. Wild apple trees and the fruit they produced were some of his favorite sights, smells, and tastes of nature.

> And wilder still there grows elsewhere, I hear, a native and aboriginal crab-apple, *Malus* (as Michaux, or as Emerson has it, *Pyrus) coronaria* in Southern States, and also *angustifolia* in the Middle States; whose young leaves "have a bitter and slightly aromatic taste," (Michaux), whose beautiful flowers perfume the air to a great distance. 'The apples ... are small, green, intensely acid, and very odoriferous. Some farmers make cider of them, which is said to be excellent: they make very fine sweet-meats also, by the addition of a large quantity of sugar" (Michaux). Celebrated for "the beauty of its flowers, and for the sweetness of its perfume." (Michaux).

Thoreau included select descriptions found in the 1819 translation of Francois Andre Michaux's three-volume work, *The North American Sylva.* He had borrowed both the French and the English editions of the reference from the Harvard College library. Obviously the crab apple tree as outlined by Michaux was both beautiful and useful.

· And now Thoreau might finally have a chance to see crab apples in person. How frustrating that the train kept clattering past them!

The Michigan Central line crossed much of the state by heading due west. Once they left Kalamazoo a little after noon, the tracks took a southwest turn. At the town of Niles, the rails straightened out again and headed toward the lake. When the travelers reached New Buffalo in mid-afternoon, they got their first view of Lake Michigan. The railroad line skirted the southern shore into northern Indiana and then crossed the border into Illinois. The train carrying Henry Thoreau and Horace Mann, Jr., reached Chicago at 6 p.m. It deposited them onto Lake Street, in the heart of the city.

Today the former Michigan Central Railroad line still transports both freight and passengers. Much of the state remains noteworthy for its orchards and its fruit production. Ann Arbor has more than ten times as many residents today as it did when Henry and Horace's train passed through it. Enrollment for the three campuses (Ann Arbor, Dearborn, and Flint) of the University of Michigan totals more than 50,000. And on select Saturdays in the fall of the year, more than 110,000 spectators cram into Michigan Stadium to witness the exciting action taking place on that Big Ten gridiron. Many more around the country watch those contests on television and in the comfort of their own living rooms or at neighborhood taverns.

When Calvin Harlow Greene (1817-1898) learned of Thoreau's death in 1862, he must have been both distraught and disappointed. Now he would never have a chance to meet his hero in person. He could write to the man's sister to express his condolences, however. Sophia Thoreau in turn penned a polite response and maintained that her brother had been "the happiest of mortals." She passed along to Greene a rare treasure: a copy of a crayon drawing of Henry rendered by Samuel Worcester Rowse. And to his query regarding the identity of Thoreau's local traveling companion, Sophia told Greene that William Ellery Channing had "most frequently accompanied him in his walks."

A subsequent exchange of letters between Sophia Thoreau and Mr. Greene revealed his reason for asking that slightly unusual question. Evidently Greene's brother in California was in the process of either crafting or having a third party carve a unique walking stick, a cane. The two had intended to send it as a gift to Henry Thoreau, the ultimate saunterer. Now that he was gone, the next best recipient would be the person who often walked with him. According to a later editor, "The cane was of manzanita wood, the handle was made from a buffalo horn, and the silver mountings were engraved with appropriate quotations from Thoreau's writings." Even as a symbol of fan devotion, the piece was extravagant. There is no record of the price the Greenes might have paid for such a special order.

Early in March 1863, the beautiful cane arrived in Concord. "It was with mingled feelings of pleasure and pain that I looked on this gift," wrote Sophia, noting that the act itself was "a rare instance of friendship, most worthily bestowed. I handed the cane at once" to Ellery Channing, "who expressed great satisfaction." Perhaps knowing correctly that Ellery would never fully convey the proper gratitude of the moment, Sophia expressed her own thanks to Greene. "Allow me to thank you for this token; it would have been fully appreciated by my departed brother." Those were the most comforting words a long-distance devotee could hear; and the consideration that lay behind them was almost as good as being there in person. Which of course was the obvious next step.

The first week of September 1863, found Calvin H. Greene renting a room at the Middlesex Hotel in Concord, Massachusetts. He spent days visiting the spots that any Thoreauvian pilgrim, from that point forward, would make a point to see: Walden Pond, the site of Thoreau's house along its shore, the remains of his beanfield, his grave in the town's New Burying Ground, the Assabet and Concord rivers, and Brister's Spring. "I have doubtless crossed and recrossed the dear, absent man's path so many times in this morning's trip!" he wrote in his diary. He walked to the Revolutionary War monument on the shore of the Concord River, behind the Old Manse. Along the way, he passed the green in the center of town, which was filled with soldiers in the midst of drill, still intending to join in the ongoing fight with the South. He met and talked with Bronson Alcott, Ellery Channing, Ralph Waldo Emerson, Frank Sanborn and a number of other residents who had known Henry Thoreau. He stopped at the Mann house and chatted with Mary Peabody Mann, her sister Elizabeth Palmer Peabody, and even young Horace, now nineteen years old. "Found the young man greatly interested in Botany," Greene noted. He met Henry's two maiden aunts and was welcomed into the Thoreau household by Sophia and her mother, Cynthia Thoreau. They insisted that he board with them for the rest of his stay. So he did.

Those days could only have been an enchanting (albeit bittersweet) experience for the fan from Michigan. Was it enough to see his hero's favorite places, to see the pages of *Walden* come alive, to walk where Thoreau had walked, and to talk to his friends and relatives? Yes and no. While the memory of the trip would surely linger with him forever, it could not hurt to take a physical memento back home so that those thoughts could be visually prodded every once in a while. Calvin Greene took at least two. He learned that the remnants of Thoreau's Walden house had been moved to a farm near Estabrook Woods. He headed there. "Took a memento, a broken shingle, as a fitting emblem," he wrote. And imagine his astonishment when Sophia and Cynthia Thoreau urged him to also take home a book from Henry's personal library! Mr. Greene chose a volume that Thoreau had used while at Harvard: *A Classical Dictionary*, by John Lempriere. "D. H. Thoreau" was inscribed on the flyleaf. The young man had not yet changed his name when his hands first touched those pages.

Ten years after his return to Michigan, Calvin Greene was still thinking of the Thoreaus. He sent Sophia a book of poetry, and she responded again with kind words. "I hope you may see our village again: its charms increase from year to year." Well, you didn't have to ask a Thoreauvian twice to visit Concord. Sophia planted the idea for a return trip with Mr. Greene. It did not take him long to make a decision.

In late August 1874, he was back at the Middlesex Hotel. He saw the changes that eleven years had brought. The town green was empty of soldiers; but in their place was a new granite Civil War monument. "*Now* only some of their *names* are on record *there*. Such is life!" he wrote. Just a block away was the New Burying Ground; but the Thoreau plot had been moved up the road to Sleepy Hollow Cemetery. He paid his respects to Henry there, as well as to Cynthia Thoreau, who now joined her husband and three of her four children. Greene walked with Ellery Channing to the farmhouse that Thoreau had been born in, located on Virginia Road. He met with Bronson Alcott and with Frank Sanborn. But Sophia Thoreau had moved to Maine. The Manns were gone, too. Time had moved all things forward.

Again he found solace by journeying to the special places. Brister's Spring was one of them. "As it had become a sacred fountain, I lay down and deliberately drank seven swallows of its cool, clear water to the memory of its absent poet." And then there was the piece of land where Thoreau had lived deliberately for more than two years.

> Arose this morning about Four o'clock and started for a last visit to Walden Pond. I shall probably not see it again. Here I sit with my back against a little pine sapling, now growing on the site where once stood the hut. A few feet in front of me is a small but gradually increasing pile of stones to which every friend of Thoreau is expected to add his unit. I brought one up from the pond as my contribution and pencilled on it the word 'Bethel.' I also set out near by a plant of 'Life-everlasting' that I had found while on the way here.

Finished with his duties, the pilgrim made his way back to Michigan.

Calvin Greene could be considered to have led a rather fulfilling life for a literary fan. He had corresponded and had meaningful exchanges with his favorite author. He never got to meet the man in person; but he did have a chance to talk with his close friends and family members. He had indeed walked where the man had walked and had seen much that Thoreau had seen. Mr. Greene could not have asked for more, really. And it all came about because he had had the courage to write to Thoreau and to ask him for a copy of his portrait. It was just as Mr. Emerson wrote: "Once you make a decision, the universe conspires to make it happen."

Around the time that Henry Thoreau and Horace Mann, Jr., traveled across the state of Michigan in 1861, Dr. Samuel Arthur Jones (1834-1912) was in the process of getting several degrees in homoeopathic medicine from colleges in Philadelphia and St. Louis. His parents were Welsh, and he had been born in England. In 1842, the family immigrated to central New York. As a young man, Jones studied medicine and served as a Union army doctor during the Civil War. Afterward he practiced in several cities on the East Coast. In 1875, he moved to Ann Arbor to become the first dean of the University of Michigan Homoeopathic Medical College. It was a post that he held for just a few years. But it was the initial impetus for Jones to settle and stay in Ann Arbor.

Dr. Jones set up a private medical practice in town in the early 1880s. That was when he began to study the writings of Thomas Carlyle. Those readings led him to the works of the American Transcendentalists and to Henry David Thoreau. He too fell under the spell of the man of *Walden*. Jones absorbed everything written by and about the man. By 1889, Jones himself was writing and publishing essays and delivering lectures in Ann Arbor about Thoreau. Yet, as a driven and obstinate man, he wanted to know and do even more. He dismissed the then-popular assessments of Thoreau as being a hermit, a stoic, and merely an imitator of Emerson. "Dr. Jones came to believe that the current interpretations of Thoreau were inadequate or unfair, and he set out, late in 1889, to set the record straight," according to one report. In order to do that, he had to contact other individuals who had access to primary-source information about Thoreau and about Concord, Massachusetts.

Thus developed over time a web of correspondents and correspondence. Included were a few of Henry's friends and acquaintances: Daniel Ricketson, H. G. O. Blake, Frank Sanborn, and Edward Emerson, son of Ralph Waldo Emerson. Alfred "Fred" Winslow Hosmer was a store owner and an amateur photographer who lived in Concord. Henry S. Salt lived in England and was one of Thoreau's first biographers. Letters practically flew from Dr. Jones's desk between and among these men over the course of more than a decade. This was indeed the time to uncover the real truths, for the people who had known Thoreau were still alive to share their stories. That would not always be the case. All these first Thoreau scholars had to do was to find them and to ask the right questions.

Like the fan from Rochester, Dr. Jones felt the need to make the trip to Concord. He did so in August 1890, where he met and talked with residents and a few of his correspondents about Thoreau. Jones was convinced "that Thoreau's importance would in future be greater even than that of Emerson." But some details needed to be cleared up first. Had Henry's house at Walden Pond been used as a station on the Underground Railroad? (No.) Who had paid the poll tax so that Henry could be released from jail? (Probably his Aunt Maria Thoreau.) Who was the woman that both Henry and his brother John had loved and courted? (Ellen Sewall, by this time married to the Rev. Joseph Osgood.) Dr. Jones and his fellow researchers also aimed to document all of the existing portraits taken of Thoreau. They wanted to redeem the seemingly unfair character sketches of Thoreau's parents, as they had been presented in a negative light in an early biography by Frank Sanborn. Above all, the men wanted to uncover and preserve as many of Thoreau's letters as possible.

Calvin Greene was 80 years old when Dr. Jones "discovered" him living just sixty miles away from Ann Arbor, as the crow flies. The letters Henry Thoreau wrote to Greene back in the 1850s had been published in Frank Sanborn's *Familiar Letters of Henry David Thoreau* (Boston: Houghton, Mifflin, 1894). Jones read them in that volume. He was shocked to learn that a Michigan man had actually corresponded with Thoreau. And he was still alive! Jones immediately wrote to Greene and made arrangements to visit with him in Rochester.

The two men met in early May 1897. They must have had a lively discussion on the subject of their shared affection/obsession. Greene gave Dr. Jones copies of the six letters he had received from Thoreau. He also gave him the three letters sent by Sophia Thoreau and a few other items, including his copy of the Maxham daguerreotype. Jones was noticeably overwhelmed when he told his pen pals of his experience. "He is worthy of the letters that Thoreau sent him. I could gladly lick the dust off his shoes. He is old and poor, but great God what a MAN!!"

> [M]y visit to Mr. Greene has enabled me to be born again. I am taking lessons from Thoreau's Michigan correspondent, and I am going to place all my Thoreau relics into the library of the University of Michigan. The authorities are even now preparing the glass case that will retain them. ... Mr. Greene's making me the depository of all his treasures *before* he dies, set me to thinking that it would not do to keep these relics as mere curiosities in my own house; no, I must put them where they can *enthuse* many a young heart. The library is a fire-proof building, and so the letters, books and all will be safe.

A tradition of collecting "Thoreauviana" had begun: in Michigan, of all places.

Dr. Jones developed a lecture around Calvin Greene's correspondence and diary entries. He delivered it at the University of Michigan and in Pontiac. After being briefly delayed by illness, Jones set about compiling the material into a publishable format. He consulted with Calvin Greene by letter in order to do so. Unfortunately, Dr. Jones was overzealous and could be both pompous and stubborn. Greene did not feel that he was being portrayed accurately in the manuscript. A year after their seemingly glorious meeting in Rochester, Jones told someone:

> I send just a line to convey bad news, namely, the insufferable egotism and self-conceit of Thoreau's Michigan correspondent have obliged me to throw up the projected edition of the Letters. … [H]e has found so much fault that I am disgusted, and have dropped him and his conceit. He has been sulking for some time, but his last two letters are such that only his years keep me from answering them as they deserve. … [W]hile I have done him every honor consistent with the truth, and had kept my own name wholly out of sight in the whole book—he has as good as slapped me in the face. … He is so whimsical that I shall see that he never gets hold of the Thoreau relics again. I have a paper that will hold him, and they shall go where they [are] promised—to the UNIVERSI-TY.

So much for the ability of the spirit of Henry David Thoreau to bring people together.

Nevertheless, Samuel Arthur Jones's *Some Unpublished Letters of Henry D. and Sophia E. Thoreau: A Chapter in the History of a Still-Born Book* was released in 1899. Calvin Greene passed away while the book was still in the publisher's hands, so he did not live to see it become a reality. It's just as well. The book was really his own memoir, but his name was never mentioned in the text. Jones referred to Greene only as Thoreau's "Western correspondent." The doctor kept his own name out of it, referring to himself only as the "editor" or "ex-professor" throughout the pages. And he disguised someone else's identity as well, although contemporary scholars have found his code easy enough to crack. Dr. Jones was truthful in his portrayals of Henry and Sophia Thoreau in the book. That may well have been his focus all along.

Dr. Jones produced a number of additional pamphlets and limited-edition books surrounding Thoreau topics. Among his legacy were the ongoing compilations and updates of a comprehensive Thoreau bibliography: lists of books and articles that described, mentioned or paid homage to anything related to Thoreau. This tradition continues even today in the issues of the *Thoreau Society Bulletin*, the quarterly newsletter of that organization.

Truly, Dr. Samuel Arthur Jones and his correspondents did good work. They laid the foundation for future Thoreau scholarship, both in approach and substance. And if some of their exchanges ended up in passionate disagreements and strained relationships, well, that tendency too has been passed down through the years. Emotions still run high among Thoreau devotees and scholars today.

Henry Thoreau may have thought he had very little to do with one particular man in Michigan. But it turned out that two men in Michigan ended up having a *lot* to do with *him*.

In August 2008, I was like those two travelers of old. I passed through Michigan on my way to Minnesota. I had my own wheels, though, so I was not limited to the path of the railroad bed. I was in control of my own destiny. And I was on the trail of the two Michigan men who helped to popularize and create the image we hold today of Henry Thoreau.

My first stop was Rochester, Michigan. Henry and Horace didn't make it here. But I was curious about Calvin Greene, and I wanted to "find" him. I spent some research time in area libraries, digging into their history books. Unfortunately, Mr. Greene had not been a mover and a shaker in the community. He was mentioned in just a few reference book entries in his occasional role as an educator. Avid Thoreauvians from all over the world would recognize his name as the person who stirred Thoreau to sit for that daguerreotype session in Worcester. But here in his hometown, most people wouldn't know him from Adam. It was all a matter of perspective.

The lone exception was a small portrait tacked onto the wall of the local history room at the Rochester Hills Public Library. I almost missed it. It was a faded reproduction of that famous portrait of Thoreau. Underneath it was an explanation in decades-old text, typewritten on a yellowed sheet of paper:

> Commissioned by mail in 1856 by Rochester resident Calvin
> H. Greene (1817-1898), an early admirer of Thoreau's, and
> taken in Worcester, Massachusetts, this portrait, known as the
> Maxham Daguerreotype, was the first photographic likeness
> ever taken of Thoreau. After passing from Greene's posses-

sion, the photograph changed hands several times before finally being donated, in 1972, to the National Portrait Gallery, Washington, D.C., where the original now resides.

The typist evidently had been unaware that Henry Thoreau had had three images taken that day, and that he passed the other two on to his friends, Blake and Brown. It was another example of personal perspective. But at least Mr. Greene was acknowledged in a tiny way in this town.

I then drove a few miles east, through the winding roads and meticulous landscapes of substantial subdivisions and golf courses. I paid my respects to the Greene family at their final resting place in the small Washington Center Cemetery in rural Macomb. The modest tower monument was engraved with the names of his parents, his maternal grandmother, and either a brother or a cousin. Calvin Greene's name was listed here too, and it was only later that I learned that he and his wife had actually been buried at another cemetery. "Pioneers of 1822," the stone proclaimed. The Greenes had been among the first settlers in the area and were proud enough to announce it for all time. The marker stood at a tilt, a victim of the natural collision of four-season weather with hillside soil. I hoped that someone would be around to push it back up again whenever gravity finally won out. Pioneers still deserved to be honored.

I overnighted in a nearby hotel. The next morning I was off to the University of Michigan. This time I wanted to find something that epitomized the contribution of Dr. Samuel Arthur Jones to the Thoreauvian cause.

I had done my homework and had already searched the library's online catalog. Dr. Jones's extensive collection of Thomas Carlyle research had been deposited with the university after his death, and that information temporarily distracted me. I waded through all kinds of entries, looking for something special. I saw that Michigan owned Jones's copies of the four volumes of Thoreau's *Journal* that H. G. O. Blake compiled and edited from 1881-1892. I clicked from one record to another: *Summer, Autumn, Winter,* and *Early Spring in Massachusetts.* When I studied the last screen, I was intrigued by the special notes that were added by a thoughtful archivist.

> Autographed presentation copy from H. G. O. Blake to Samuel A. Jones. (Note on t.-p.) Manuscript notes throughout text and on fly-leaf at end. Note: Introduction signed: H. G. O. Blake.

What a find! A book that offered a connection to both Dr. Jones and Harrison Gray Otis Blake, back in Worcester! The volume became my target resource. It was shelved in the special collections room of the Hatcher Graduate Library.

Since the fall semester had not yet started, the streets near the campus in Ann Arbor were almost deserted. Finding a place to park was a piece of cake. I followed the campus map downloaded from the university web site and walked through the archway of East Hall and into the Diag. I knew where I was. I had seen this place on television a number of times. I was suddenly filled with such awe that my first inclination was to whisper, "I'm at *Michigan*, Mom!"

I surprised myself. I rarely talked to my mother. I thought of her most often under two specific circumstances. The first was whenever I heard the national anthem. Mom had been a stickler for tradition and accuracy. She had sung in church choirs all her life; she knew how the famous melody was supposed to go. To her, the deciding factor for a correct performance of "The Star-Spangled Banner" lay entirely in the word "banner." Only the second syllable was supposed to move across two tones. If the singer had the audacity to slur up on "ban," my mother would immediately shake her head and "tsk, tsk, tsk" for the rest of the song. Individual interpretation was neither permitted nor encouraged on that sacred piece of music.

The other time I thought of her was whenever I watched college football on TV. Mom had taught me the rules of the game. My father gave me the music: the ability to play an instrument that I could carry, and the impetus to spend four years in high school and four years in college marching up and down that one hundred yard grid with others dressed just like me. But it was Mom who taught me what the actual game was all about: four downs, the line of scrimmage, running backs, wide receivers, an off-side motion versus an illegal procedure. Every Sunday in season, we watched two NFL games on television. We latched on early to the old AFL and the new AFC and adopted the Kansas City Chiefs as our team. After I enrolled at a college in western Pennsylvania, we joined the throngs of Pittsburgh Steelers fans in the middle of their fabulous four-time Super Bowl winning run.

On the autumn Saturdays of my childhood, we settled in for big-time college football. We watched all of the rivalries: Pitt and Penn State; Michigan and Ohio State; Army and Navy: North Carolina and North Carolina State; Nebraska and Oklahoma; UCLA and USC. My father had a degree from Lehigh, and Mom was a graduate of the University of Pennsylvania. But the contests of the Engineers and the Quakers were rarely broadcast. For some reason, Mom liked Michigan. I had visions of someday traveling to the other edge of the country and parading through Pasadena with a Trojan helmet on my head and a cardinal and gold cape flung around my shoulders. Mom and I would often pick opposing teams to support, just to antagonize each other. We cheered loudly together against Notre Dame, every time. We knew all of the fight songs by heart and sang them loudly when "our" teams scored. Sometimes dancing around the living room with the cat was involved. My father escaped to the basement to practice his music.

To realize that I was actually standing on the University of Michigan Diag took me unexpectedly right back to my mother. I could feel an invisible block-lettered "M" hanging over me in maize and blue. I could imagine the distinctive design of the players' helmets. I started humming "Hail to the Victors" to myself as I slowly marched in step to the graduate library.

I needed to shift my focus as I opened the door and inhaled the distinctive library air. I was not here for football. I was here to do research related to Henry David Thoreau. I took a combination of stairs and elevators to reach the seventh floor.

This was not my first experience with academic archives. In my travels, I had done research in numerous public libraries along the way. Back home, I spent time in several of Harvard University's libraries as well as those of the Five Colleges in the Amherst area. I knew the general routine. Don't bring extra items with you; you'll just have to leave them at the door. Only pencils are allowed. Nowadays a laptop is welcomed; but sometimes the case must be checked into a locker first. I had left my computer in the trunk of my car and carried just a legal pad: old-fashioned technology. Because I thought it might prove useful, I had brought along my copy of the second edition of *Early Spring in Massachusetts*, published in 1893. It too was back in the car. I didn't want to have it confused with the first edition I was about to see.

I signed in and made my request. The dark green volume that was delivered to me looked exactly like the one I owned. It was in good condition for being more than a century old. The pages were not frail or crumbling at their edges. Still, I sifted through them carefully. Many had handwritten notes scribbled in pencil in the margins. But the real treasures appeared at the beginning of the book. After a few moments of staring and synthesizing, I understood what I had in front of me. Some might consider it an amazing piece of Thoreauviana.

This copy of *Early Spring in Massachusetts* had originally belonged to Harrison Gray Otis Blake of Worcester. Blake had inherited all of Thoreau's notebooks, and he edited them into four volumes consisting of seasonal entries with appeal to a wide audience. *Early Spring* came out in 1881. Blake used this copy of the first edition to point out numerous errors in the text. His notes in the margins told what corrections and changes needed to be made to the original manuscript whenever a revised edition was undertaken. Most of them were minor matters of punctuation, spelling, paragraph spacing, and the like. But there were *a lot* of them; many more than I could copy onto my pad in the space of several hours. He may have done some odd editing when it came to lifting Thoreau's words from the old notebooks. But Blake was obviously a perfectionist when it came to seeing how those passages were finally offered to the public. Just for these notes alone, this book was an interesting artifact.

Marks on and around the title page told a portion of the rest of the story. Blake wrote his name at the top, followed by "Received from Houghton Mifflin & Co., Feb 24th, 1881." In a different and fresher ink, those words were followed by "Presented to Samuel A. Jones, Sept 4, 1890." At first I thought that Blake had given this book to Dr. Jones in person as some grand gesture of friendship. But no. Later I discovered that Blake mailed this volume to Jones, just a few weeks after they had met in person in Worcester. The good doctor had gone through his own copy of *Early Spring* and had found errors that *he* thought should be corrected in a second edition. He sent his marked-up book to Blake. Blake in turn sent this volume to Jones, showing that he had found the same mistakes as well as a number of others. In the letter that once upon a time, but no longer, accompanied this volume, Blake wrote:

> I found your package here on my return frm. a short excursion, & during the few days between that excursion & another, occupied myself considerably with copying what I wished to, frm. my vol. into the one you sent. It did not seem worth while to be sending books backwards & forwards much over such a long distance; besides I do not care for another copy of the earlier edition. Some of the errata I found corrected in the vol. you sent, wh. of course saved some copying. I have indicated such corrections by a c or cd. in the vol. I send.

I had seen those instances of "c" and "cd" and wondered what they referred to. From Blake's letter, it sounded as if he had added his notes to Dr. Jones's book and sent that same volume back to Ann Arbor. But only one man's handwriting appeared throughout the book. And Blake's note at the top of the title page meant that the book truly once belonged to him. It was a bit of a conundrum in that respect. But what was not at all difficult to understand was what Dr. Jones afterward did with this book, and what his correspondence and friendship with H. G. O. Blake had meant to him personally in the end.

When Blake died in 1898, mutual friend Alfred W. Hosmer sent Dr. Jones a copy of the obituary that had been printed in the *Boston Advertiser*. Jones pasted Blake's notice into this copy of *Early Spring in Massachusetts*, on the flyleaf before the title page. Underneath the clipping he wrote:

> Slip preserved in memoriam April 22nd, 1898. Thus doth this world grow poorer for me.
>
> *Samuel A. Jones*

They might have lived more than 700 miles apart. They might have had different backgrounds and different ways of considering the life and work of Henry Thoreau. And although Jones seems to have antagonized Blake almost as much as he did Calvin Greene, even he knew what was lost when one of Thoreau's friends passed on. Both of these men had done their best to convey their knowledge and adoration of Thoreau to the rest of the world. Who knows what literary history would be changed if they had not?

The clock struck noon as I walked out of the library. The campus carillon was chiming from across the way. Its selection was "Amazing Grace." We had sung that hymn at my mother's funeral, fifteen years ago. I guess that was her way of telling me that she had heard my earlier whisper. She knew where I was and what I was doing. She might even approve. I smiled, looked up at the sky and said, "Thanks, Mom." Then I turned away from the Diag and strolled through the brick archway, back to my car.

Later in a hotel room in northern Illinois, I spread my notes out on the king-sized bed and picked up my second edition of *Early Spring in Massachusetts*. I turned the pages and checked my own penciled scribblings, looking back and forth for what seemed like an eternity. It didn't take too long for me to come to a conclusion. Each and every one of the errors Blake and Jones found in the first edition had been magically corrected in the second.

WHEN YOU GO: Today you can use Amtrak and ride the rails to most faithfully trace Henry and Horace's journey across Michigan. By car, the fastest route is to take I-94 from Detroit to Chicago. Use Exit 66 and a variety of back country roads if you want to get a closer look at the railroad tracks in the western portion of Michigan. Be sure to stop at the

Indiana Dunes National Lakeshore to get the dynamic beach experience. If the weather is good, you'll see the outline of the Chicago skyline in the distance, seemingly floating above the water.

FOR MORE INFORMATION

Amtrak, www.amtrak.com.

Illinois Bureau of Tourism, 100 West Randolph Street, Suite 3-400, Chicago, IL 60601. Phone (800) 406-6418. www.enjoyillinois.com.

Indiana Dunes National Lakeshore, 1100 N. Mineral Springs Road, Porter, IN 46304. Phone (219) 926-7561. www.nps.gov/INDU/index.htm

Indiana Office of Tourism Development, One North Capitol, Suite 600, Indianapolis, IN 46204-2288. Phone (800) 289-6646. www.visitindiana.com.

Kalamazoo Nature Center, 7000 North Westnedge Avenue, Kalamazoo, MI 49009. Phone (269) 381-1574. www.naturecenter.org.

Travel Michigan, Michigan Economic Development Corporation, 300 North Washington Square, Lansing, MI 48913. Phone (800) 644-2489. www.michigan.org.

University of Michigan, www.umich.edu.

Ypsilanti Historical Museum and Archives, 220 North Huron Street, Ypsilanti, MI 48197. Phone (734) 482-4990. www.ypsilantihistoricalsociety.org.

RECOMMENDED READING

Thoreau's essay "Wild Apples," which includes the mention of his Midwestern crab-apple investigation. This is the only published account of any portion of the Journey West that Thoreau had a chance to write. It was printed posthumously. The text can be found online. A nice anthology that includes it is William Rossi's *Wild Apples and Other Natural History Essays* (Athens, Ga.: University of Georgia Press, 2002).

NOTES ON THIS CHAPTER

The text of the letters that Thoreau sent to Calvin H. Greene appear in *The Correspondence of Henry David Thoreau* (Walter Harding and Carl Bode, eds. New York: New York University Press, 1958). The letters are dated January 18, 1856; February 10, 1856; May 31, 1856; June 21, 1856; July 8, 1857; and November 24, 1859.

The excerpt from Thoreau's Journal that describes crab apple trees is from the entry dated May 23, 1851. The full citation of "Michaux" is Francois Andre Michaux's *The North American Sylva, Or A Description of the Forest Trees, of the United States, Canada, and Nova Scotia. Considered particularly with respect to their use in the Arts and their introduction into Commerce; To Which Is Added A Description Of The Most Useful Of The European Forest Trees. Illustrated by 150 Coloured Engravings* (Paris: C. d'Hautel, 1819). The crab apple entry appears on pages 67-69 of volume two. Thoreau faithfully recorded the exact wording. The title page Americanizes the compiler's name to F. Andrew Michaux. And the Emerson he referred to was not Ralph Waldo, but instead George Barrell Emerson (1797-1881), a Harvard man who organized the Boston Society of Natural History and worked for the state's Zoological and Botanical Survey. Thoreau owned an edition of Emerson's book, *A Report on the Trees and Shrubs Growing Naturally in the Forests of Massachusetts* (Boston: Dutton and Wentworth,

1846). Emerson included apple species in his *Pyrus* chapter.

Calvin Greene's correspondence with Sophia Thoreau appears in Samuel Arthur Jones' *Some Unpublished Letters of Henry D. and Sophia E. Thoreau: A Chapter in the History of a Still-Born Book* (Jamaica, N.Y.: Marion Press, 1899). His diary entries regarding his visits to Concord are included in the last portion of the book.

Along with that work, further keys to understanding the circumstances surrounding Dr. Samuel Arthur Jones and Calvin Greene are found in *Toward the Making of Thoreau's Modern Reputation: Selected Correspondence of S. A. Jones, A. W. Hosmer, H. S. Salt, H. G. O. Blake, and D. Ricketson* (Fritz Oehlschlaeger and George Hendrick, eds. Urbana, Ill.: University of Illinois Press, 1979). This book makes for fascinating and amusing reading. The quote about Dr. Jones' eagerness "to set the record straight" appears on page five. His supposition that "Thoreau's importance would in future be greater even than that of Emerson" appears on page 29 and is relayed from Jones' own book, *Thoreau and His Biographers*. Also quoted here is Jones' letter to Hosmer dated May 29, 1897; Jones' letter to Hosmer dated June 11, 1897; Jones' letter to Hosmer dated May 17, 1898; Blake's letter to Jones dated September 4, 1890; and Jones' letter to Hosmer dated April 23, 1898.

And what became of the three copies of the famous Maxham daguerreotype? Calvin Greene's copy still resides at the National Portrait Gallery of the Smithsonian Institution. The one that Thoreau had given to H. G. O. Blake is now part of The Henry W. and Albert A. Berg Collection of English and American Literature at the New York Public Library. (An Alfred Winslow Hosmer photograph of Blake's copy is held at the Concord Free Public Library in Concord, Massachusetts.) Theo Brown's copy of the daguerreotype is on file with The Thoreau Society collections at the Thoreau Institute, Walden Woods Project, in Lincoln, Massachusetts. The three images were taken within minutes of each other.

TRAVEL CHAPTER 8

Wednesday, May 22, 1861 in Chicago

Expenses: Map of Minnesota, $1.00.
Envelopes, 10 cents.
At Metropolitan H, $3.00

22) The cottonwood - Saw last PM high Dune hills along lake
& much open oak wood low but old (?) with black trunks but
light foliage—Chicago about 14 ft above lake—sewers or
main drains fall but 2 feet in a mile - Rode down Michigan
Avenue. See the land loom across the lake 60 miles. Ch. built
chiefly of limestone from 40 miles SW. Lake st. the chief business one. Water milky. Fencing on RR in Canada & Michigan
narrow boards - & Virginia fence—no posts & rails. Another
small fenny prairie on Calumet (?) river S of L. Michigan with
that rank dry grass (not bullrush) in it.

—Thoreau's field notebook

Rev. Mr. Collier—173 Randolph 1 to 4 p.m.

—Thoreau's field notebook

I walked around most all day ... and saw considerable of
Chicago. I went to Mr. Clarke's in the afternoon after considerable trouble in finding it and found he had gone out but I
saw his wife. I saw him later in the afternoon in town. I saw
also Mr. Carter, who let me have a check for a $100 which I
got turned into gold. The Chicago banks are having a good
deal of trouble just now and I suppose most of them must fail
so I was very lucky in getting gold, as it is scarce in the city. I
got it of a Mr. Wiley, a kind of a banker, a friend of Mr.
Thoreau's. ... I am very well and Mr. Thoreau is getting along
very well also, excepting a little trouble that the water gives
him in the bowels, though that is of no account.

—Horace Mann Jr.'s letter of May 23, 1861

Henry Thoreau and Horace Mann had been on the road for two days since leaving Niagara Falls. They were eleven days away from home. Chicago was a good place to stop and take stock of their assets and their schedule. It was the largest city (population: 109,420) they would encounter during the Journey West, until they got back to Boston. The weather turned out to be perfect for this "extra" day of exploration in the city.

THE PLACE

Thoreau and Mann had arrived at the Michigan Central depot at Lake Street at 6 p.m. the previous evening. Then they had made their way to the Metropolitan Hotel at the corner of Randolph and Wells Streets, a little more than a dozen blocks away. The Metropolitan was a six-story, 160-room facility that catered to out-of-town businessmen and to railroad travelers. Its proprietor, Mr. B. H. Skinner, was "formerly of Boston;" and the man evidently took great care and pride in his job.

> He has a fondness for seeing everything go right; and it has long since ceased to be a burden to him to administer the affairs of a vast House. His equanimity is never disturbed; he is always happy to see his old friends, and every new guest feels, before they have been in his house twenty-four hours, that they may number him among their acquaintances.

> [The Metropolitan] is free from the rush or confusion of many other places; and while it maintains the celebrity it has so justly won, it will continue to be resorted to by those who think more of luxury and taste than of noise and parade—of perfect cleanliness in everything, than of mere show. ... One dollar and fifty cents per day is the regular charge of the Metropolitan.

The two men from Massachusetts were obviously in good hands.

From what little information they recorded, it seems as though Henry and Horace went their separate ways on this day. The teenager straightened out their finances while his older companion took some time to scrutinize the cityscape. Both men interacted with other people here, perhaps more than they did with one another. This was one of the few places where they would have an opportunity to do so.

Chicago was no doubt buzzing about the war with the southern states, already more than a month old. In fact, Senator Stephen A. Douglas had given a fiery public speech here on May 1st, with the intent of rallying the

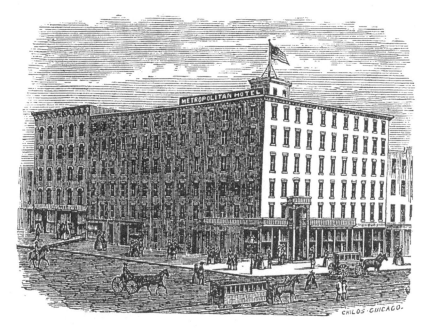

Thoreau and Mann stayed at the Metropolitan Hotel, at the corner of Randolph and Wells Streets. (From Isaac D. Guyer's *History of Chicago: Its Commercial and Manufacturing Interests and Industry*, published by Church, Goodman & Cushing in 1862.)

crowd and drumming up overwhelming support for the Union cause. But very few people had seen him since then. Now, three weeks later, he was said to be still holed up at the Tremont House, four blocks away from Henry and Horace's hotel. Word on the street was that he was quite sick and might even be dying. Local residents were both skeptical and saddened by the news.

Douglas had been a political opponent to Abraham Lincoln in both state and federal elections in recent years. But once Fort Sumter was fired upon, the "Little Giant" became one of the President's strongest allies. After meeting with Lincoln at the White House for almost two hours in April, Douglas embarked on a lecture tour "to insure the loyalty of the Northwest." He spoke in the Ohio River town of Bellaire; in Columbus, Ohio; and in Indianapolis. Then he proceeded to Illinois, where he took the podium at the state capital at Springfield and in Chicago. His was a nationalistic mission. "Every man must be for or against the United States," he told his audiences. "There can be no neutrals in this war, only patriots—or traitors. ... Unite as a band of brothers, and rescue your Government and its capital and your country from the enemies who have been the authors of your calamity." His words were met with cheers and applause.

As soon as he delivered his speech in Chicago, Douglas complained of feeling ill. He and his wife Adele retired to their rooms at the Tremont House. Senator Douglas soon showed the symptoms of inflammatory rheumatism, which had been a recurring disease for him. He developed a high fever that led him into sporadic bouts of delirium. Adele sent for her husband's personal physician to hurry from Washington. The outlook was not an optimistic one.

But the Senator was not the only one having problems at that point. As Horace wrote to his mother, "The Chicago banks are having a good deal of trouble just now and I suppose most of them must fail." His was a succinct and apt assessment of the currency situation in the city. Mr. Wiley could have provided him with the basic details.

Even before the outbreak of the Civil War, the banks had experienced "a good deal of trouble." The federal government had no oversight in the business. "Wildcat banking" was prevalent. The term referred to the fact that private bankers often did not operate with standard or ethical practices. Just a few years earlier, the Bank of Chicago had such close ties with a group of Spiritualists that at least one of them was working behind the counter. This "medium" called upon her ethereal and mystical powers to determine which depositors would be permitted to cash in their notes and which ones would be shuffled out the door, empty handed. A court order eventually closed down that institution.

But by 1861, a more concrete problem had arisen. According to historical accounts, most of the "currency of the Illinois banks was backed in considerable part by securities of southern states on deposit with the auditor." "Georgia notes" had been among the most prevalent bills in circulation in Chicago. And as soon as the battle lines were drawn between North and South, local financiers were cut off from their southern assets. Residents had no easy way of determining whether the banks they had been using were still solvent. Instances of counterfeiting increased, too. "A good deal of trouble" seems more likely to have escalated into "sheer chaos." The travelers from Massachusetts were indeed lucky to have connections to insiders who could find them ready cash.

While Horace was straightening out their financial situation, Henry had an opportunity to jot down some quick notes about the vegetation and the scenery. He probably learned that the name "Chicago" was said to originate from a Native American word meaning either "wild onion" or "stinking onion." That designation was not meant to be a compliment. The lakeshore had once been a wet forest, and it was still a bit swampy and aromatic in places. Thoreau had probably seen that "fenny prairie" around the Calumet River, well south of the city, as they rode into Chicago on the train the night before. And the oaks he saw were indeed one of the prevailing tree species of the Midwestern prairies.

But what most Easterners noticed upon reaching this metropolis was how low the horizon was here. Lake Michigan was flat. The layout of the city next to it was level, and so was the land stretching beyond it. It was a settlement of buildings without a background. Anyone who was used to living with even slightly dynamic terrain would experience a sense of sudden otherworldliness when first facing this site. If Thoreau and Mann had ridden across northern Ohio and Indiana, they would have gotten this feeling hundreds of miles earlier in their journey. Rattling over the southern half of Michigan wasn't quite as disconcerting. Here the two men might have felt exactly what other New Englanders felt, including Margaret Fuller, when she passed through Chicago in 1843.

Margaret wrote:

At first, the prairie seemed to speak of the very desolation of dullness. After sweeping over the vast monotony of the lakes to come to this monotony of land, with all around a limitless horizon,—to walk, and walk, and run, but never climb, oh! it was too dreary for any but a Hollander to bear. How the eye greeted the approach of a sail, or the smoke of a steamboat; it seemed that any thing so animated must come from a better land, where mountains gave religion to the scene.

So too was it common for visitors to look to the east and across Lake Michigan to see—or to *imagine* to see—the coastlines of Indiana and Michigan on the other side. Was that really land over there, or merely a mirage? It depended on how much humidity hovered in the atmosphere, and how many heat waves trembled above the lake. Eastern eyes searched for any landmark at all, for comfort's sake. Whether or not Thoreau saw "the land loom across the lake 60 miles" that day is a matter of conjecture. He did have his trusty spyglass with him, however.

THE PEOPLE

Here Mr. Emerson's list of contacts may have proven useful to Henry and Horace. The travelers needed spending money, and knowing a Chicago banker was crucial. Benjamin B. Wiley might have been included on Emerson's list. William Hull Clarke's name may have appeared there as well. And one of those men may have even taken Mr. Thoreau on a carriage ride down Michigan Avenue, to witness in action one of the major streets of commerce in Chicago. Unfortunately, the "Mr. Carter" that Horace saw remains unidentifiable.

BENJAMIN B. WILEY

Like H.G.O. Blake of Worcester and Calvin H. Greene of Michigan, Benjamin B. Wiley had first written to Henry Thoreau after being favorably impressed with the Concordian's writings. At the time of his first letter in 1856, Wiley was working as a banker in Providence, Rhode Island, about 60 miles south of Concord. He was about sixteen years younger than Thoreau. He was an intelligent and thoughtful admirer; and he asked a number of philosophical questions in his polite correspondence. Through his ruminations and queries, it appears as though Wiley was a youth in search of a spiritual mentor. When Henry replied with a few lengthy responses of his own, perhaps Wiley thought that he had indeed discovered his literary life coach.

"B. B." Wiley soon made a pilgrimage to Concord to meet Thoreau in person. Though no detailed account of their encounter survives, Wiley hints in later letters that he, at least, thought the meeting went well. He also stopped in Worcester to see H.G.O. Blake and Theo Brown. But several months later, Wiley relocated to Chicago and took a job at a banking firm there. As with many young people who take such risks, he wasn't sure at first of the wisdom of the move. And at that point in his life, he was a reluctant businessman at best, as he confided to his Concord correspondent.

> I am here at the wish of others as well as the result of my own reasoning but I will not become a common business drudge for all the wealth of Chicago. Instead of a trader I am going to be a man. I believe a divine life can be nourished even in this Western Shrine of Mammon. ... Were I more gifted I would now leave trade forever and be your Plato. I freely admit to you that this kind of life is not what pleases me.

What *did* please Mr. Wiley was the amount of leisure time he had to walk around the city and along the nearby shore of Lake Michigan. The flatness of the horizon took a bit of getting used to, however. "Everything being level I have nothing on the land to meet my New England bred eyes," he wrote.

Without a landscape to interest him, he instead turned to the sky. He studied the clouds billowing over the lake and searched their forms for intriguing images. When he once saw in them "a vast bird with outstretched wings holding her course towards the East," he decided that the sight represented his "own desire of progress towards the source of … inward illumination."

But the low horizon line was not the only thing a newcomer to Chicago had to face. Wiley told Thoreau:

> The Lake water is carried over the city for drinking &c. It is almost always discolored by storms. That which comes moderately clear I fancy I can render white by beating with my hands and if allowed to stand, a sediment of lime is deposited. It makes some trouble with strangers' digestive organs and I am not entirely accustomed to it. If you have at your tongue's end a description of your own way to make a filter, I should probably put it in practice & should appreciate your kindness.

At the time, Henry responded in the negative, saying that he had never had a need for such a device. If the words of young Horace's letter to his mother from Chicago are to be believed, then perhaps Thoreau had forgotten B.B. Wiley's warning about drinking the water, when he visited the city himself a few years later. This would explain the "little trouble … in the bowels," as Horace reported.

Wiley was also the first (and perhaps, even the only) person who had the courage to ask Henry Thoreau for an explanation of one of the most metaphoric passages in the book *Walden*. Unlike the decades' worth of puzzled students and scholars who would come after him, Mr. Wiley had the undue advantage of being able to ask the wordsmith himself for the correct interpretation:

> If it be not unfair to ask an author what he means I would inquire what I am to understand when in your list of employments given in Walden you say "I long ago lost a hound a bay-horse and a turtle-dove." If I transgress let the question pass unnoticed.

Thoreau obviously enjoyed his correspondence with Mr. Wiley enough to know that he was obligated, in some manner, to respond to his long-distance friend's query. So he did:

> How shall we account for our pursuits if they are original? We get the language with which to describe our various lives out of a common mint. If others have their losses, which they are busy repairing, so have I *mine*, & their hound and horse may

perhaps be the symbols of some of them. But also I have lost, or am in danger of losing, a far finer & more etherial treasure, which commonly no loss of which they are conscious will symbolize—this I answer hastily & with some hesitation, according as I now understand my own words.

Had Henry sufficiently answered B. B.'s question? Or had he raised even more? Evidently the description was good enough for Mr. Wiley. The topic did not surface again on paper.

The exchange of thoughtful and philosophical letters between B. B. Wiley and Henry Thoreau came to a quiet end in 1858. But whenever Ralph Waldo Emerson passed through Chicago on his winter lecture tours, he would run into Mr. Wiley and would write home that he had met up with Henry's friend in the city. It is reasonable to assume that Emerson would include B. B. Wiley's name on his list of contacts along the journey route. And although Horace wrote of his financial dealings with Mr. Wiley, Henry did not repeat his old friend's name in his notes. We do not know if the two former correspondents reconnected on that day in Chicago.

WILLIAM HULL CLARKE

Another possible entry on Emerson's list was the name of William Hull Clarke. William was also a New Englander who had relocated to Chicago. His brother, Unitarian minister and Transcendental Club member James Freeman Clarke, was more well known in East Coast religious and literary circles. James had been one of the founders and editors of *The Western Messenger*, a Unitarian magazine published in Cincinnati in the 1830s. Though he had then served a congregation in Louisville, Kentucky, James was now back in the Boston area with his own parish, the Church of the Disciples.

Like his brother James, William too had come west in the 1830s. By the middle of the decade, he and his younger brother Abraham were the owners of one of the first drug stores to be established in Chicago. And when Margaret Fuller came out to explore the Great Lakes region, she did so with William's sister, Sarah Ann Clarke, as her traveling companion. The women made the most of having friendly and familial connections in Chicago, and they spent several days with Sarah's relatives. When they decided to travel inland to see the prairie land of north central Illinois, William became their guide. He squired Margaret and Sarah by wagon as far west as the Rock River before heading back toward Lake Michigan. Margaret wrote that the young man was "equally admirable as marshall and companion, who knew by heart the country and its history, both natural and artificial." The group spent several weeks traversing the interior.

Margaret Fuller and William Clarke had known each other as friends before this excursion. But historical and biographical records suggest that William may have developed or even re-ignited an unrequited crush on Miss Fuller that month, during their days together. One twentieth-century reporter wrote that:

> Mr. Clarke at that time was somewhat discouraged and had begun to lose the elasticity of youth under the burden of his discouragements, but … Margaret's sympathy discovered the depth and delicacy of his character and her unconquerable spirit lifted him to cheerfulness and he received courage which never more forsook him.

If that assessment bears any truth at all, then it may explain William's behavior in later years. Margaret Fuller eventually moved to Italy, where she married Italian marchese Angelo Ossoli and had a son. All three were lost in a shipwreck off the coast of Long Island when they were returning to the United States in 1850. It seems to be more than mere coincidence that William Clarke simultaneously retired from his business and traveled to Italy on his own that year. Did he go there to mourn Margaret? Was he a man in search of solace and closure? And if so: was he able to find them by retracing her footsteps in Europe?

When he came back to the Midwest after his year abroad, William Clarke dedicated himself to the study of engineering. By 1861, he was working as the Assistant Engineer with the Sewer Commissioners of Chicago. He was involved in the process of surveying and laying what would total almost 223 miles of sewer lines throughout the metropolis. He had married Annie Gay, another New Englander, whose love he thought would help him find "the solution to the riddle of life." They had a daughter and two sons.

Horace Mann evidently saw both William and Annie Clarke during his time in the city. Henry Thoreau wrote William Clarke's name and address in his notes, then later crossed out the line. One interpretation might be that he had delegated the Clarke mission solely to Horace. But on another page, he quoted the fact that the "sewers or main drains fall but 2 feet in a mile," immediately followed by the notation that he "Rode down Michigan Avenue." Such intimate information about a city sewer system is hardly a promotion found in tourist guidebooks. Thoreau may very well have learned such details from William Hull Clarke, the local expert on the subject. And since no expense is listed for hiring a carriage, perhaps William was also the one who offered to show Thoreau around the town with his own horse and buggy. Perhaps the two men were even able to exchange a few remarks about their mutual acquaintance, Margaret Fuller, who by then had been gone for more than a decade.

REV. ROBERT COLLYER

William Hull Clarke was a member of a Unitarian group in Chicago that had helped attract the Rev. Robert Collyer to its pulpit in 1859. And it might have been through Clarke that Collyer learned of Henry Thoreau's presence in the city. (If Mr. Emerson included Robert Collyer's name on his list, he did so solely on reputation or on word of mouth. He had not yet met the man in person.) Somehow the minister convinced the author of *Walden* to meet with him at his home for three hours that afternoon. He would turn out to be one of the most ardent fans that Henry Thoreau would ever chance to meet.

Robert Collyer had been born in England; and he had immigrated to America in 1850. He worked as a blacksmith in Pennsylvania while he simultaneously ministered as a lay preacher in the Methodist church. Collyer had been raised to believe that slavery was wrong; and the swelling abolitionist movement in the northern states captivated him when he heard Lucretia Mott lecture on the subject. He was so full of new passion that he tried to transfer that mission to his Methodist congregation. The feeling was not mutual, however; and as a result, he resigned from that church in 1859. He was a man of high emotion who looked for worthy causes. He was immediately drawn in like-mindedness to the Unitarian faith, and he was encouraged to pursue a new opening in Chicago. The Unity Church was born, and Rev. Collyer was called upon to serve it.

Henry Thoreau, on the other hand, was a member of no congregation at all. And as evidenced by his casual dismissal of Calvin Greene in Michigan, he may not have been entirely comfortable in the presence of shameless admirers: especially those who were previously unknown to him. The mystery remains then, why Thoreau would agree to and endure an entire afternoon of conversation with a fiery Unitarian minister who loved every word his companion had heretofore put to paper. But the man lived right down the street from the Metropolitan Hotel. There was seemingly no escape. What was a stereotypical "invalid traveler" to do?

Thoreau sat on the sofa in the Collyer living room, and the two men chatted. According to his host:

[Thoreau's] voice was low, but still sweet in the tones and inflections, though the organs were all in revolt just then and wasting away and he was making for the great tablelands beyond us Westwards, to see if he could not find there a new lease of life. His words also were as distinct and true to the ear as those of a great singer. … He would hesitate for an instance now and then, waiting for the right word, or would pause with a pathetic patience to master the trouble in his chest, but when he was through the sentence was perfect and entire, lacking nothing, and the word was so purely one with the man that when I read his books now and then I do not hear my own voice within my reading but the voice I heard that day.

Neither man recorded in detail what their discussion topics might have been. But they had at least one mutual acquaintance in Moncure Daniel Conway, another Unitarian clergyman who was also an abolitionist. They could have exchanged insights about him. They could have talked about slavery, abolitionism, and John Brown's efforts two years earlier to end the "peculiar institution." Thoreau and Collyer may have also turned to the realm of literature and may have shared the particulars of the books and authors they were currently reading. Robert Collyer had read Emerson, and he appreciated Nathaniel Hawthorne's work. Surely he would have relished speaking with someone who knew those men and lived in the same town as both of them. Then again, if the host sensed that his guest was too tired or too ill to sufficiently sustain his end of the conversation, then the encounter could easily have leaned more toward sermon than dialogue. Poor Henry!

After Thoreau went back to the Metropolitan Hotel for the night, Collyer dashed off a short letter to him. He thanked the author for his visit. He encouraged him to write a travelogue about the Journey West, in the style of his first two books. Collyer offered an attachment (that does not survive) with follow-up information to something that had surfaced in their chat. (It may have referred to the work of the contemporary black poet, James Monroe Whitfield.) The minister also extended an invitation for Thoreau and Mann to stop by Chicago on their way home and to spend more time with him. Henry evidently did not send a messenger back with a reply.

When late June rolled around, and Thoreau and Mann were heading back to Massachusetts, they took a more northern route instead and crossed

Wisconsin by train. They did not return to Illinois or to Chicago. Thus did they successfully dodge another meeting with the Rev. Robert Collyer. But their choice of routes made no difference. By that time, Collyer was working in Washington, D.C. He had temporarily joined the U.S. Sanitary Commission. The war was escalating, and men were getting wounded and killed. Help was needed; and, as usual, Robert Collyer responded. The paths of the minister and the naturalist did not cross again.

Stephen A. Douglas (1813-1861) never left the Tremont House. He died there on June 3rd. By that time, Thoreau and Mann were in Minnesota. Chicago, Washington, and many other Northern cities quickly mourned. Portraits and statuettes of the Senator were draped in black and were displayed in store windows. Chicago hosted a huge funeral, attended by thousands. The tomb of Senator Douglas and a tall monument topped by his statue are now part of a memorial park on East 35th Street in Chicago.

Four months after Thoreau and Mann stayed at the Metropolitan Hotel, the facility expanded with the purchase of the Hotel May, located right next door along Wells Street. Now the establishment boasted 220 bedrooms. It competed with the Tremont House as being one of the best hotels in the city.

In 1863, the establishment of a National Banking System helped to solve the financial problems in Chicago. The year 2009, however, saw the failure of nineteen banks based in Georgia. By comparison, only one institution from Chicago failed during the years from 2000-2009.

After Henry Thoreau died in 1862, his friend B.B. Wiley began exchanging letters with James Martineau, a British philosopher and minister. In Martineau, he seems to have found the kind of spiritual correspondent that he had been looking for. Perhaps he saw this man as a kind of replacement for Thoreau. And perhaps that is why Mr. Wiley relinquished his ownership of all of Thoreau's written replies in 1863. He turned them over to Ralph Waldo Emerson, who then passed them on to Sophia Thoreau, Henry's sister. Even Emerson wondered if B.B. Wiley later regretted giving up the pages that at one time had meant so much to him.

But Wiley did not abandon his Concord and Transcendental connections altogether. For the next nine years, he served as a local agent for Mr. Emerson. Whenever the famous author came through Chicago on his winter lecture tours, it was B.B. Wiley who handled Emerson's appointments, his finances, and his mail. Emerson was grateful for the younger man's service, and often mentioned him in letters to his family members back home. Wiley "attended me like a friendly shadow," Emerson said on one occasion.

He "plainly delights in playing the part of good angel to me," he wrote on another. Emerson had been the lucky beneficiary of a key relationship that had started with his own friend, Henry Thoreau.

And Mr. Wiley was not the only resource that Waldo Emerson found in Chicago. The Rev. Robert Collyer made it his duty to welcome the Concordian—sometimes to the point of insistence—whenever he discovered that the author was in town. Emerson, in turn, would agree to hold some of his lectures either in the Collyer living room or at the Unity Church. He overnighted at the minister's home at least once, although the accommodations at the Tremont House were much more to Emerson's liking. But even those elegant quarters were not safe from Collyer's notice. During one visit, the writer had hardly had enough time to check in before he reported to his family members, "Mr Collyer's card I have already found under my door." For good or for bad, the reverend evidently kept pace with what he considered to be arrivals of importance in his adopted city.

Exactly ten years after Thoreau and Mann passed through Chicago, the American Midwest experienced one of the most severe droughts in memory. By the fall of the year, the region was as dry as dust. Not a drop of rain had fallen in three weeks, and the prairie land was a tinderbox. Local fire departments raced hither and yon to douse every flame. But their responses were hampered by the number of their workers, by their water supplies, and by the horse-drawn equipment that serviced them.

No one knows exactly what happened on the night of Sunday, October 8, 1871. Perhaps a reckless or drunk smoker tossed a glowing match to the floor. Perhaps it was a case of spontaneous combustion within the three-ton load of timothy hay that had just been delivered. Or maybe a cow really did kick over an oil lantern. But one fact is certain: a barn owned by Patrick and Catherine O'Leary caught fire on Chicago's DeKoven Street. A strong and hot wind from the southwest quickly blew the flames north toward the downtown area. Ahead of them lay plenty of fuel: 23,000 metropolitan acres that contained mostly structures made of wood. Human error and even a bit of nonchalance resulted in several miscues and miscommunications to the authorities. Soon the fire was unstoppable. Even with the hasty assistance of incoming crews from surrounding towns, the teams of exhausted firemen had no way to keep up.

The inferno raged for two days, as frantic Chicagoans ran for their very lives. When it was over, one-third of the city was destroyed. Gone up in smoke were 18,000 buildings that totaled almost $200 million in property damage. Gone were the city's chamber of commerce, the post office, the courthouse, the *Tribune* headquarters, and the central train depot. Gone were various banks, schools, theaters, hotels and churches. Gone were the Metropolitan Hotel, the Tremont House, and the Unity Church. The devastation would have been even more complete if Nature herself had not provided her own relief: a drenching rainstorm. Indeed, it could have been worse.

Nevertheless: some 200 to 300 people died in the fire. An astounding 100,000 were suddenly homeless, or "burned out." That second number included Benjamin B. Wiley; Robert and Ann Collyer and their four children; and many of the minister's parishioners, like William and Annie Clarke and their three children. At the height of the melee, an eyewitness spotted the Reverend Collyer on the street, sobbing over the sudden and overwhelming loss of his home, his church, and all of his books and other possessions. Only his wife Ann could hold him and comfort him.

But the good man regained control of his emotions by the time the next Sabbath day arrived. He and his flock met among the ruins of the Unity Church for their Sunday morning service. One reporter noted:

> Accordingly, at a little before noon, the people gathered in the warm and pleasant sunshine in front of the gutted walls of their former house of worship, which stood up grand and terrible amid the surrounding waste of desolation. Shattered stones and beams were all about; a thin vapour of smoke was curling up where the old pulpit had stood; the overturned and broken capital of a Doric column lying before the church door, served the preacher for a platform.

Together the people sang familiar hymns and listened to the appropriate Bible verses that were offered. Then they settled in for Robert Collyer's sermon, his *piece de resistance*. By this time, he was able to provide his listeners with both solace and hope.

> For two or three days after the catastrophe I was stunned; at first I felt as if I had somehow or other got personally injured in the fight with the flames. But after two or three days, I began to wonder what I should say to you when we should come together this morning, and it has all come to me in one word, that the fire makes no difference to me. If you'll stay here, I will, and we'll work together and help each other out of our troubles. ... I don't mean to desert you and the church; I mean to stick by you, and I want you to stick by me. ... We'll find, in the end, that we've done the right thing in holding by

one another, and we'll find that we all have this glorious, liberal Christian faith that has held us up all through, and has not failed us in the darkest moment of our lives.

After the closing hymn, William Hull Clarke stood up. He thanked the Rev. Collyer for his commitment to the congregation. And he proposed that the Unity Church be rebuilt as soon as possible. This measure was immediately met with glee and was approved with "a shout of gladness." Fund-raising efforts for reconstruction began at once.

An artist's rendition of Collyer "preaching on the site of his church" appeared on the cover of *Harper's Weekly* a few weeks later. The image came to represent the resiliency of the residents. Plans for rebuilding the whole city developed quickly. The Chicago Relief Association kicked into gear and divided the area into districts for easier distribution of supplies and necessities. Robert Collyer was named the superintendent of his home area.

When Ralph Waldo Emerson visited the city in late November, he saw firsthand the losses sustained by B.B. Wiley, the Collyers, and the Clarkes. He was both attracted and repulsed by what he saw before him.

> The ruins of the city were very dreary to see,—in some places, picturesque,—as we came into it. From my chamber window I see the form of a sailing ship, all day, & the ruins of an Episcopal stone church, I believe,—& another gothic form, close by.

A new Chicago was to arise from those ashes. Thanks to the diligence of Collyer's parishioners and other donors from around the country, a new Unity Church was erected. It was formally dedicated in December 1873. A new Tremont House reopened in 1874. The Metropolitan Hotel was not rebuilt.

Benjamin B. Wiley (1833?-1903) transitioned from banking into the real estate business. He became a member of the Chicago Mechanics' Institute and also became a Mason. He appears to have attended the Third Unitarian Church, and not the Unity Church. At the mature age of 55, Mr. Wiley married a California journalist and artist named Alice Denison. His British correspondent, James Martineau, was pleased by this surprising news.

> It is never too late to grow wise; and though I must say you have been pretty long about it, I will not doubt that the product is all the nearer to perfection for the duration of its growth. So that it is with confidence as well as good faith that I heartily congratulate both you and Miss D. on the near

prospect of your completing the true conditions of human life. The innocent skepticism of your Chicago friends, to whom you have become a model old bachelor, will only add piquancy to the wonderful change, and put all the rationalists to shame by proving the possibility of instantaneous conversion.

Those sentiments, along with some of the other philosophic replies that B.B. received from James Martineau, were made public in an issue of the *Atlantic Monthly* magazine in 1900.

The letters that Mr. Wiley had received from Henry Thoreau first appeared in *Letters to Various Persons by Henry D. Thoreau,* a volume that Ralph Waldo Emerson edited and released in 1865. It was in those pages that B.B. Wiley had revealed to Henry Thoreau that he intended to become a man upon moving to Chicago. In the end, he had become a *rich* man. In addition to his property holdings in the Midwest, Wiley also owned silver mines in Colorado and gold mines in California. The once reluctant banker from Providence had done all right for himself by choosing to Go West.

William Hull Clarke (1812-1878) spent sixteen years overseeing Chicago's labyrinthine sewer system. He lost his dear wife Annie in 1874, after eighteen years of marriage. Both he and Robert Collyer became founding members of the Chicago Literary Club when it organized that very same year. In April 1878, just six months before his death, William Clarke delivered a lecture to that prestigious group. His topic that day was "Recollections of Some Literary Women Who Have Visited Chicago." His exact text is unrecorded in the club's historic files. But undoubtedly, a key focus of his talk would have been the life and work of his friend and author, Margaret Fuller.

Robert Collyer (1823-1912) left Chicago to take a position with New York City's Church of the Messiah in 1879. It was from that pulpit on January 28, 1883, that he delivered a lecture called "Thoreau." More than two decades had passed since he had met the man in person. He was obviously still a fan, and he still had fond memories of that day when he had spent three hours with one of his favorite writers. He could expound on his subject matter at some length.

A man came to see me in Chicago whom I was very glad and proud to meet. It was Henry Thoreau of Concord, the Diogenes of this new world, the Hermit of Walden Woods. The gentle and loving misanthropist and apostle of individualism so singular and separate that I do not know where to look for his father or his son—the most perfect instance to be found I think of American independence run to seed.

It seems to me now that to see Thoreau as I did that day in Chicago and hear him talk was the one thing needful to me, because he was so simply and entirely the man I had thought of when I read what he had written. There was no lapse, no missing link; the books and the man were one.

But it was not just their sole meeting that Rev. Collyer drew upon for his material. For, like other devoted admirers, the minister had himself made a pilgrimage to Concord, Massachusetts, in the months just after Thoreau's death. It was an unforgettable experience that he still recalled vividly.

I went to Concord not very long after to see his grave and to wander through Walden Woods and sit by the pond, to talk with Mr. Emerson about him to my heart's great content. … That was a day also to be marked with a white stone. Concord and the woods and the talk with the one man in all the world who had known Thoreau best gave permanence to the photograph I had taken of him in the year before and helped to bring out the lights and shadows.

After discussing Henry's life and writings (for many listeners would not have been familiar with them), the minister drew his conclusions about their importance to our society at large.

So I say again and finally that we need such men as Thoreau in every generation, full to the brim and running over with the dissidence of dissent. Men who will take no man's say-so and cut their life by no man's pattern. Men who will neither lead nor be led, but will just live their life in their own way and then report to us what they have found we cannot find, who are content to work in the harness or to train in the regiment.

So we need to have wider spaces between man and man that we may send out and downward great roots and stand fast in our own simple manhood, and Thoreau nobly helps to teach us that secret.

The reaction of Collyer's audience to this speech is unknown. The seventeen-page tribute was eventually included in a volume called *Clear Grit: A Collection of Lectures, Addresses and Poems* (Boston: American Unitarian Association, 1913). When read today, the full sermon is just as full of passion on the printed page as it must have been when heard delivered in person by Robert Collyer. Little did Henry Thoreau know what a lasting impression he made on that singular man of the cloth, just by sitting on his sofa for a few hours on a sunny spring afternoon.

In the fall of 2009, I was finalizing the particulars of this manuscript, figuring out exactly which details to include in each one of the nineteen travel chapters. That's when I realized to my horror that I didn't have a "Thoreauvian adventure" chosen for the Chicago chapter. My aversion to big cities had come back to exact its revenge against me. And at this point, it was too late for me to drive across three or four states to get to the Windy City and create one. What could I do?

With the practiced habit of a dedicated procrastinator, I worked on all of the other chapters first. When only one blank space remained, I unfolded a Chicago street map and stared at it, hoping either to spot a familiar name or to be filled with the light of sudden insight. I had lived for eight years in its northern suburbs, and I had been a member of a few environmental groups while I was in the area. Now I had to put my brain in gear and to think about what we did and where we went back then.

My eyes fell first to the bigger and more well-known lakeshore attractions: Navy Pier, Shedd Aquarium, the Field Museum of Natural History. I shook my head, discounting the traditional tourist sites. They were all good places to visit; but they hardly embodied the spirit of Henry Thoreau. I kept scrutinizing the grid, even though my personal memory of the streets of Chicago was admittedly limited. I was almost convinced that I would not be able to come up with anything appropriate at all. I would have to apologize to the readers for the hole in this chapter.

Then a germ of a memory wiggled into my head. I was once at a meeting at a particular nature center in the city. Not many people had showed up because the weather had been iffy. But the site's origins might indeed have a connection to Thoreau. I opened a few of my desk drawers and sifted through papers and brochures in search of an answer, or at the very least, an old file folder. Sure enough, within a few minutes I landed upon the announcement that I had typed up for the event, ten years earlier. I confirmed my idea with an accompanying newsletter and a quick Internet search. Now the vision of that place was beginning to come back to me.

The property of the North Park Village Nature Center lies well northwest of downtown Chicago, at least eight miles away from where Henry

Thoreau and young Horace Mann spent their day, meeting people and seeing the city. Around the time of their visit, this parcel was a tree nursery owned by Norwegian immigrant Pehr Petersen. He would eventually supply all of the greenery that decorated the grounds of the 1893 World's Fair, as well as many of the first trees that outlined the community's streets and boulevards.

In 1911, city officials bought the former nursery at Peterson and Pulaski Streets in order to create the Chicago Municipal Tuberculosis Sanitarium. Once the facility opened in 1915, it must have been relatively easy to shuffle anyone infected with the disease off to the remote setting, which then lay on the northern edge of the city. Ominous red-brick buildings had been constructed to house a hospital, a dispensary, and lodging and dining halls for the inmates. Smaller cottages could accommodate entire families who were suffering from the disease.

Medical knowledge by then had progressed a bit since Henry Thoreau's day. No longer were doctors recommending travel as a cure for consumption. Now, individuals with TB were removed from the general circle of society and were sent to live in one of these sanitariums, which were then springing up all over the country. Outdoor exercise was still encouraged, however. Many of these places, like the one in Chicago, were surrounded by "a buffer of Nature:" an inspirational wild area that had walking trails winding through it.

After this particular institution closed its doors in the 1970s, its 158-acre property was left alone. One history states that the land at this time "was protected not by any conservation laws but by its haunting history and dark paths." No one wanted to venture onto it, unless they had construction debris they wanted to dispose of in secret.

The following decade brought developers with an eye toward the revenue possibilities offered by such a large, albeit overgrown, tract. A variety of strip malls and condominiums could surely fit on such a space. One proposal even called for construction of a conglomerate called the Green Acres Shopping Center. Outraged citizens and professors at Northeastern Illinois University (a next-door neighbor) took their concerns to Mayor Jane Byrne. She listened.

As a result, an easement was acquired in 1989. It ensured that the land would be protected from development for at least the next 75 years. Staffers from the university began to lead walks and hold classes there. A nature center was established in the former dispensary building, with an addition that doubled its space in 1997. Other red-brick structures were renovated and repurposed as well. Today, the property that once quarantined tuberculosis sufferers offers a wide variety of services, with many that are open to the public. Key among them is the North Park Village Nature Center and its dedicated 46 acres, now considered to be one of the gems of the Chicago Park District.

When I visited this place in December 1999, it was on a gray day, one of pure murk. A bit of sleet and ice had fallen overnight; and the soil that lay underneath wasn't quite ready for winter. The temperature difference created an ominous fog that hovered a few feet off the ground. As I turned into the slightly slippery driveway of the North Park Village Nature Center, all I could see before me was white mist, dark tree shapes, and, looming amongst them, institutional brick buildings that spoke of a different time and a different purpose. I expected to hear the bellow of a foghorn at any second.

Just a handful of people attended our meeting. Those who were there wanted to get our business over and done with and get back home. No one wanted to walk the trails or do any exploring in the bone-cold and clammy air. So I went home feeling rather unfulfilled and disappointed by the experience. And I never had a chance to go back and see the place on a better day.

As I assembled my manuscript in an apartment that sat almost 1000 miles east of Chicago, I knew I could not make a quick return trip in person. Instead, I decided to call the North Park Village Nature Center and talk to its director, Julie Sacco. I suspected that she would be able to explain to me what I missed.

But before I could even pick up the phone, I was excited by the connections I could make between this center and Henry Thoreau. It seemed more than a little coincidental and wonderful that a property with a history tied to tuberculosis—Thoreau's fatal malady—was now focused on nature and the environment. And the fact that the building itself was once the dispensary was terrific, too. The root of the word "dispensary" included a commitment to stewardship, according to my trusty dictionary. It reminded me of a passage from *Walden*:

> Our village life would stagnate if it were not for the unexplored forests and meadows which surround it. We need the tonic of wildness,—to wade sometimes in marshes where the bittern and the meadow-hen lurk, and hear the booming of the snipe; to smell the whispering sedge where only some wilder and more solitary fowl builds her nest, and the mink

crawls with its belly close to the ground. At the same time that we are earnest to explore and learn all things, we require that all things be mysterious and unexplorable, that land and sea be infinitely wild, unsurveyed and unfathomed by us because unfathomable. We can never have enough of nature.

Instead of traditional medicines and first-aid treatment, this site now offered "the tonic of wildness" to thousands of urbanites who sought a respite from city life. The bittern, meadow-hen, snipe, and mink might not be found there; but a variety of wildlife still lived on this land, including deer and coyote. Thoreau never saw those two mammals himself. Eastern Massachusetts was not wild enough for them, back then. But today, parts of Chicago are.

Director Julie Sacco was happy to share over the phone the details of the North Park Village Nature Center. Julie became involved with the center as a volunteer, well before the time of my own visit. She had now been its leader for three years.

We started with the property history and then moved on to more contemporary activities. The Maple Syrup Festival is one of the most popular events offered; and it makes use of the descendants of trees established by Pehr Petersen himself, when he ran his nursery here. The No Child Left Inside initiative creates opportunities for work with local schools. And the summer day camp program is so successful that slots for 220 campers fill up in just the first 90 minutes of registration time. Julie's energy for the center came through the line and nudged into my soul. I grew ever more remorseful for not having gone back when I first had the chance.

The vibrant picture she painted began to remove the fog from that dismal December image that still lingered at the back of my brain. As I looked at a downloaded map of the grounds and listened to Julie's descriptions, I felt the color wash in and animation take over. The burr oaks in the savanna began to leaf out in green. Prairie grasses grew tall and waved with the slightest breeze. Mallards paddled and chattered from open water in the wetlands. Hikers took to the trails. The adults tended to saunter, while the children ran ahead. There was much to see and do.

When I asked Julie what aspect of her job surprised her the most, she thought for a few seconds. Then she said: "How 85,000 annual visitors can have just that many different interpretations and expectations of us. We try to offer as much as possible to as wide an audience as possible and yet keep true to our primary goals of ecological restoration and environmental education." It sounded like a large order, but also one that the North Park

Village Nature Center was aptly filling.

She was most proud of the ongoing ecological restoration of the property. The landscape was continually improving to better accommodate the needs of plants, wildlife, and people. Visitors who returned after a time away were astounded at the positive changes they witnessed by comparison. Julie told me that if I had really explored the place ten years ago, I would be amazed to see the differences in it today. I would be able to gaze upon habitats more indicative of the roots of the region, complete with native plants and animals benefiting from them. She thought I would be favorably impressed.

She didn't have to resort to any high-pressure sales techniques. I was sold. I knew exactly where I would be headed, the next time I found myself in the big city of Chicago. I would know where to find the tonic of wildness.

WHEN YOU GO: With more than two million people living in Chicago and at least another six million housed in the expansive outer suburbs of "Chicagoland," the Windy City and its environs offer little resemblance to the scene that Henry Thoreau and Horace Mann, Jr., witnessed in May 1861.

However, visitors can make a valiant effort to stroll around and walk where those two men walked, which would be in the general vicinity of the present-day Wacker Drive and "The Loop." The Metropolitan Hotel once stood at the southwest corner of Randolph and Wells Streets. Current online maps indicate that a national donut franchise may now be perched at that spot. Robert Collyer and his family lived along Randolph Street as well, probably in the area near today's Daley Civic Center. The Tremont House, the favorite stopover for both Stephen Douglas and Ralph Waldo Emerson, was located at the northwest corner of North Dearborn and West Lake Streets. That parcel is now reported to be a parking lot. The old Hinsdale Street is now called West Chestnut Street; and the house where the William Clarke family lived would have sat near its corner with Franklin Street. That's just north of the Merchandise Mart, where all of the railroad lines come together. That ultra-busy station replaced the old Galena & Chicago Union Railroad depot, which Thoreau and Mann used to leave Chicago on the morning of May 23, 1861. Of course, a walk down Michigan Avenue would be in order as well. But it hardly looks now the way Thoreau saw it back then.

Robert Collyer's Unity Church congregation did not construct its own building until 1867. It stood at 929 North Dearborn Street, across the street from Washington Square Park. It was rebuilt on the same lot in 1873, after the fire destroyed all but the limestone walls of the original. This version of the Unity Church remains standing. Since 1910, it has been known to locals as the Scottish Rite Cathedral. Online reporters say that it is in the process of being sold, and its future remains uncertain.

FOR MORE INFORMATION

Chicago Botanic Garden, 1000 Lake Cook Road, Glencoe, IL 60022. Phone (847) 835-5440. www.chicago-botanic.org.

Chicago History Museum, 1601 North Clark Street, Chicago, IL 60614. Phone (312) 642-4600. www.chicagohistory.org.

Chicago Park District, 425 East McFetridge Drive, Chicago, IL 60605. Phone (312) 742-PLAY. www.chicagoparkdistrict.com.

City Galley in the Historic Water Tower, 806 North Michigan Avenue, Chicago, IL 60611. Phone (312) 742-0808.

Explore Chicago. Phone (877) 244-2246. www.explorechicago.org.

North Park Village Nature Center, 5801 North Pulaski Road, Chicago, IL 60646. Phone (312) 744-5472. www.chicagoparkdistrict.com.

RECOMMENDED READING

Miracle under the Oaks: The Revival of Nature in America by William K. Stevens (New York: Pocket Books, 1995). Read about the recovery of a piece of land in Chicago.

NOTES ON THIS CHAPTER

Descriptions of the Metropolitan Hotel appear in a variety of historical sources, including the one quoted here: Isaac D. Guyer's *History of Chicago: its commercial and manufacturing interests and industry: together with sketches of manufacturers ... with glances at some of the best hotels, also the principal railroads which enter Chicago* (Chicago: Church, Goodman & Cushing, 1862).

Information about Stephen A. Douglas was gleaned from Gerald M. Capers' *Stephen A. Douglas: Defender of the Union* (Boston: Little, Brown and Company, 1959); Robert W. Johannsen's *Stephen A. Douglas* (New York: Oxford University Press, 1973); and George Fort Milton's *The Eve of Conflict: Stephen A. Douglas and the Needless War* (Boston: Houghton Mifflin Company, 1934).

The state of Chicago's banks came from Bessie Louise Pierce's *A History of Chicago. Volume II: From Town to City*, 1848-1871 (New York: Alfred A. Knopf, 1940); and F. Cyril James's *The Growth of Chicago Banks. Volume I: The Formative Years, 1816-1896* (New York: Harper & Brothers Publishers, 1938).

Margaret Fuller's observation about the flatness of the prairie is found in Chapter Two, "The Lakes," of her *Summer on the Lakes*, in 1843. Additional insights into her trip came from Richard V. Carpenter's article, "Margaret Fuller in Illinois." [*Journal of the Illinois State Historical Society* (1908-1984), v. 2, no.4, January 1910, pp.7-22.]

Excerpts of letters exchanged between B. B. Wiley and Henry Thoreau appear in the 1958 *Correspondence* volume and are dated December 21, 1856; April 7, 1857; and April 26, 1857. Thoreau's metaphoric passage in *Walden* is found in the "Economy" chapter: "I long ago lost a hound, a bay horse, and a turtle-dove, and am still on their trail. Many are the travellers [sic] I have spoken concerning them, describing their tracks and what calls they answered to. I have met one or two who had heard the hound, and the tramp of the horse, and even seen the dove disappear behind a cloud, and they seemed as anxious to recover them as if they had lost them themselves." Wiley's correspondence with James Martineau appears in "Some Letters of Martineau" (*Atlantic Monthly*, v. 86, October 1900, pp. 489-499).

Biographical details about William Hull Clarke came from histories of Chicago; the memorial read at the meeting of the Civil Engineers Circle of the Northwest on July 1, 1879; and letters he wrote to his brother, James Freeman Clarke, which are housed with Harvard's Houghton Library. The Chicago Literary Club web site (http://www.chilit.org) lists his contributions to the organization.

Main sources regarding the Reverend Robert Collyer are *Some Memories* (Boston: American Unitarian Association, 1905); *Clear Grit: A Collection of Lectures, Addresses and Poems* (Boston: Beacon Press, 1913); and John Haynes Holmes' *The Life and Letters of Robert Collyer* (2 vols., New York: Dodd Mead and Company, 1917). The text of Collyer's "Thoreau" sermon appears in *Clear Grit* and also online on The Thoreau Reader web site at http://thoreau.eserver.org/Collyer.html. Collyer's thank-you note to Thoreau appears in the 1958 *Correspondence* volume. Emerson noted Collyer's insistence in his letter to Ellen Emerson, dated December 8, 1867.

Wiley, Clarke, and Collyer are occasionally referenced in Ralph Waldo Emerson's journals, notebooks, and letters. Sources include *The Journals and Miscellaneous Notebooks of Ralph Waldo Emerson* (Edited by Ronald A. Bosco and Glen M. Johnson. Cambridge, Mass.: The Belknap Press of Harvard University Press, 1982); and *The Letters of Ralph Waldo Emerson* (Edited by Ralph L. Rusk. New York : Columbia University Press, 1939).

The FDIC's most recent "Failed Bank List" appears online at http://www.fdic.gov/bank/individual/failed/banklist.html.

An overview of the Great Chicago Fire of 1871 is found in Jim Murphy's *The Great Fire* (New York: Scholastic, 1995). Although it is intended for a young adult audience, it serves as a good starting point. Also helpful is Edgar Johnson Goodspeed's *History of the Great Fires in Chicago and the West* (New York: H.S. Goodspeed & Co., 1871). Frank A. Randall's *History of the Development of Building Construction in Chicago* (2nd ed., Urbana, Ill.: United of Illinois Press, 1999) provides exquisite detail about individual structures. Rev. Collyer's reaction to the fire and his subsequent sermon are found in volume two of John Haynes Holmes's *The Life and Letters of Robert Collyer, 1823-1912*. His image on the cover of *Harper's Weekly* can be seen in a variety of online digital collections, including http://www.chicagohs.org/fire/queen/pic0160.html.

Many thanks to Craig Pfannkuche of Memory Trail Research, who was willing, at the last minute, to search for genealogical details about Wiley, Clarke, and Collyer in Chicago.

The story of The North Park Village Nature Center was gleaned from a phone interview with Julie Sacco on April 8, 2010, and "A Pearl Anniversary for a Gem of a Place" (*Urban Naturalist: Quarterly Nature Newsletter of the Chicago Park District*. October-December 2009, pp. 1, 14, 15). Thoreau's "tonic of wildness" quote appears in the "Spring" chapter of *Walden*.

Travel Chapter 9

Thursday, May 23, 1861
from Chicago to Dunleith, Illinois
via the Galena & Chicago Union Railroad and the Illinois Central Railway

Very level 1st 20 miles—then considerably more undulating. Greatest rolling prairie without trees just beyond Winnebago. Last 40 miles in NW of Ill. quite hilly. Mississippi backwater in Galena River 8 miles back. Water high now—flooded thin woods with more open water behind.

Much pink flowered apple like tree (thorn like) thru Illinois which may be the Pyrus coronaria. Distances on prairie deceptive—a stack of wheat straw looks like a hill in the horizon ¼ or ? mile off—it stands out so bold & high. Only one boat up daily from Dunleith by this line—in no case allowed to stop on the way. Small houses—with out barns surrounded & overshadowed by great stacks of wheat straw—it being threshed on the ground. Some wood always visible—but generally not large. The inhabitants remind you of mice nesting in a wheat stack— midst their wealth. Women working in fields quite commonly. Fences of narrow boards. Towns are as it were stations on a RR.

—Thoreau's field notebook

The cars left Chicago, Thursday morning about ten o'clock and we got to Dunleith at 20 minutes after six in the evening and went onto the boat "Itasca" & got our suppers, then I went on shore and got a few minerals out of the bluff and also a few flowers, when I went back to the boat and went to bed.

—Horace Mann Jr.'s letter of May 26, 1861

The train of the Galena & Chicago Union Railroad was scheduled to leave Chicago at 9:15 a.m. that day. If Horace's time keeping was correct, then perhaps the rail crew had experienced a slight delay with the equipment. Just one day of rest in the big city was probably enough for both Massachusetts men. They still had one more state left to cross by rail. They may have been eager to resume their trip.

They were again traveling where other Transcendentalists had gone before. Henry's friend Ellery Channing had lived briefly in northern Illinois more than twenty years earlier. Margaret Fuller had explored this countryside in 1843. In the preceding decade, Ralph Waldo Emerson had visited Chicago and the Prairie State during five of his wintertime lecture tours. The landscapes he saw here during the months of January and February were different from what Henry and Horace would be seeing today, of course. Spring was marching toward summer. The vegetation was turning many shades of green. And those mysterious trees were piquing Henry's interest again, just as they had done throughout central Michigan. What were those white and pink blossoms? Could they possibly belong to a crab apple species that was not native to Massachusetts?

What was Thoreau's impression of America's Midwestern prairie? As he documented from the train window, only the northeastern portion of Illinois was relatively flat. The terrain gradually became more dramatic as the train steamed northwest across it. So much for the notion that this part of the country was simply flat and visually uninteresting.

If he and young Horace had expected to see the mythical, stereotypical prairie—the one where the native grasses grew so tall that they could hide a man on horseback—they might have been disappointed. What they were seeing instead were new towns being laid out by men from back east. What they were most often seeing in the fields were displaced New Englanders. John Deere was making plows in Moline, Illinois. Cyrus McCormick and his brothers were building reapers in Chicago. And farmers who were frustrated by the hard, rocky soils found elsewhere were relocating to the Midwest by the hundreds in order to make a fresh start. This was prime crop planting season in a fertile land.

A Currier & Ives print shows the typical work of the Midwestern wheat farmer.

By half past noon, Thoreau and Mann were pulling into the town of Marengo. They may not have been aware of it, but to the northeast and fewer than ten miles away lay the three parcels of land that Ellery Channing had bought in 1839. He had acquired "more or less" 160 acres (as the deed was worded) in order to take up farming himself. And although the soil was rich and ripe for planting and harvesting, Ellery was not successful in his venture out here. Even if he had been motivated to devote his daily life to the necessary tasks, the fact is that his purchase was problematic from the start. The properties were not adjacent to one another. The largest piece, comprising 80 acres, was five miles away from the other two. One inexperienced agriculturist would certainly have had trouble managing such a situation all by himself, without the neighborliness of any sizable community nearby. It should not be surprising that in less than a year, the Transcendental poet sold his holdings and moved to Cincinnati. He would end up relocating to Concord, Massachusetts, in 1843.

Just after two o'clock, the train stopped in Rockford. But it did not linger here; it merely picked up and dropped off more passengers. Henry Thoreau and Horace Mann had no chance to explore the Rock River, which passed through this city and headed toward the Mississippi, just like them. The two men had already crossed an invisible divide today. It was, literally, a watershed moment. Here every drop of water was following a path to the Gulf of Mexico, and not to the Atlantic Ocean. They could say they were in the West at last.

No railroads had yet led into northern Illinois when Margaret Fuller made her circuit of this same region. She and her companions used horse-drawn carriages to travel westward from Chicago. Even then, they witnessed the impact that the incoming farmers were having on the prairie. Margaret lamented that the settlers' methods would "in the course of twenty, perhaps ten, years, obliterate the natural expression of the country. This is inevitable, fatal," she mused. But she still saw hope in that kind of progress. "We must not complain, but look forward to good result," she wrote.

Margaret fell in love with the Rock River valley. Her small party followed the meandering waterway south from Rockford. Each bend that they encountered seemed to unveil a scene that "was of even a more sumptuous character" than the one they had just left behind. The lush woods and interesting islands and rocky bluffs were a feast for the senses.

> The aspect of this country was to me enchanting, beyond any
> I have ever seen, from its fullness of expression, its bold and

impassioned sweetness. Here the flood of emotion has passed over and marked everywhere its course by a smile. The fragments of rock touch it with a wildness and liberality which give just the needed relief. I should never be tired here, though I have elsewhere seen country of more secret and alluring charms, better calculated to stimulate and suggest. Here the eye and heart are filled.

The eastern riverbank at the town of Oregon offered a tall bluff known as the "Eagle's Nest." Margaret climbed to the top and was so inspired by the beautiful valley view that she penned a lengthy poem on the spot. She imagined the place to be the peak of Mount Olympus, where Zeus (in the form of an eagle) had just deposited the prince Ganymede, who was thus slated to become cupbearer to the gods. Her stanzas were written from the viewpoint of the young boy himself as he wondered when the bird would come back to retrieve him. A fragment of classic Greek mythology had temporarily settled on this ridge overlooking the Rock River. Who but a Transcendentalist would consider crafting such an analogy?

Young Horace Mann may have had his Greek textbook with him, but he and Mr. Thoreau were hardly thinking of legends and gods as their locomotive rattled into Freeport. The town of seven thousand residents marked their only extended stop of the day. Here, the two men had just fifteen minutes to transfer from the Galena & Chicago Union Railroad to the Illinois Central. But it might have been the easiest move they made on the trip. Freeport was one of the few places where two rail lines used the same station. The facility included a woodhouse, a water tank, a restaurant, and a ticket office with waiting rooms. The men might have had to carry their bags to another string of nearby cars. Nevertheless, they had no time to give more than a glance to the community that lay on the other side of the tracks.

If they had ventured along its streets, they would have been able to meet and converse with individuals who had seen history in the making here just three years earlier. Freeport had hosted the second Senatorial debate between Abraham Lincoln and Stephen A. Douglas on the chilly and rainy day of August 27, 1858. Lincoln had spoken for an hour; Douglas, for an hour and a half. Then Lincoln was permitted a half hour to voice a response. In spite of the questionable weather, the crowd numbered between 10,000 and 15,000 people. Even an avowed non-voter like Henry Thoreau might have been intrigued by the bitter ironies represented here. For although Douglas had gone on to win that Senate race after participating in a seven-city debating junket, it was now Mr. Lincoln who was sitting behind the big desk in Washington. Senator Douglas was instead lying on his deathbed at the Tremont Hotel back in Chicago. Even the biggest lives can quickly and dramatically change direction.

The Illinois Central led the travelers through the tiniest of towns: through Eleroy, Lena, Nora, Warren, Apple River, Scales Mound, and Council Hill. Indeed, they were merely "stations on a RR," as Thoreau jotted in his notes. In most instances, roads and property lines had been only recently set out. And the surrounding agricultural landscape included low rolling rises, with bottomland woods that were still flooded from snowmelt and spring rains.

The 1861 edition of the *Railroad Gazetteer of the United States, Canada, Etc.,* described Galena as "the chief town of the Illinois lead country, and the entrepot between Chicago and Minnesota." Settlers and miners had begun arriving here in the 1830s. The town had grown into a thriving community of 10,000 residents. Although it was perched six miles from the biggest river in the country, Galena was still an important port and center of commerce on its own. But in the springtime, the river water often backed up the six miles from the Mississippi into the town. With the Galena River flowing right next to the train tracks, Henry Thoreau could not help but notice how high it was. It could obviously pose a threat to Galena's Main Street district.

The former Illinois Central depot in Galena is now a tourist information center.

When Henry and Horace passed through Galena on the train, the Grant brothers, Orvil and Simpson, were operating a leather goods store on Main Street. A third brother, Ulysses, had recently moved with his wife and four children to Galena from St. Louis. He was a West Point graduate who had participated in the Mexican War. He had since resigned from the military and was helping with the family business. But after Fort Sumter had been fired upon, the men of Galena had gathered to answer President Lincoln's call for volunteers. Ulysses S. Grant was pressed into action. He led the 150 men of the Jo Daviess Guards out of town on April 25, and they had headed for the capital city of Springfield to receive their orders. They had already been gone for a month.

In the "Sounds" chapter of *Walden*, Henry Thoreau had included an original poem that began:

> What's the railroad to me?
> I never go to see
> Where it ends.

On May 23, 1861, and after 1200 miles of traveling, Mr. Thoreau learned exactly where those tracks ended: at the Mississippi River.

Upon reaching the river town of Dunleith, Henry and Horace immediately boarded the waiting steamboat, the *Itasca*. It was after 6 p.m., and dinner might have still been available from the kitchen. But Horace was evidently in a mood for exploration after being cooped up in a rail car all day long. The sandy bluffs north of town beckoned him. He climbed around the rocky rises and brought some samples back to the boat. The travelers' Journey West would now shift from the rails to the mightiest of North American waters. They were getting closer to their destination.

The name of the settlement of Dunleith was changed to East Dubuque in 1877.

The rails of the old Galena & Chicago Union Railroad now carry only freight loads between Chicago and Rockford. Most often they carry new automobiles from the Chrysler assembly plant in Belvidere to points east.

The original Illinois Central line from Freeport to East Dubuque also provides a transportation outlet for freight. But the tracks from Rockford to Freeport have been removed. The rail bed remains and is easy to spot: not only because of its width and general appearance, but also because it provides a base for a series of larger-than-normal electrical poles. The old path can best be seen and studied in the middle of the tiny town of Winnebago, where a dramatic cut makes obvious the absence of the rails. And the pole-laden trail also crosses U.S. 20 at road level as the highway nears Freeport. Drivers can pull over and imagine the old locomotive chugging through this farmland, carrying Thoreau and Mann and other passengers behind it.

Away from the cities, some of the land is still farmed. Chicagoland is pretty much wall-to-wall people, from Lake Michigan to the Fox River valley and beyond. But once the sprawl is left behind, the ride across northern Illinois is a peaceful and bucolic one. The settlements between Freeport and Galena—Lena, Nora, Warren, Apple River, Scales Mound, and Council Hill—are still merely "stations on a railroad." U.S. Route 20 passes well to their south, and so does most of today's traffic. Which may not be a bad thing.

The depot that Henry and Horace's train stopped at in Marengo had been built in 1851. It would be used as both a passenger and a freight station for more than one hundred years. This particular railroad line stopped transporting passengers in the 1950s. Freight operators used the building only into the early 1960s. In 1967, the station was moved four miles down the road to become the visitor center at the Illinois Railway Museum in Union. Some sources claim it to be the oldest train station west of the Appalachian Mountains to be in regular, continuous use. Others claim that the process of moving it disrupted its "continuous" distinction; and that the specialty rides the museum offers at various times of the year are not really "regular." Nevertheless, it is one of the few stations that Thoreau and Mann passed by and that have survived into the twenty-first century. Visitors can witness history when entering that old train station today.

Another opportunity for railroad nostalgia lies to the west, in Galena. Still standing is the Italianate two-story brick station that was built for the Illinois Central in 1857. Thoreau and Mann's train stopped here as well. The building now houses the local Tourist Information Center.

The city of Galena now has fewer than half the number of residents it had in 1861. Instead of lead, it produces artists. And instead of being a commodity entrepot and a transportation center, Galena now serves as a quick and trendy vacation retreat for residents of Chicagoland or Down-State. Whenever someone quips, "Oh, we're going to Galena for the weekend," everyone else in the room sighs wistfully. They wish they too had planned such a getaway. The trip is easy enough to make from just about any

point in the northern half of the Prairie State. And unless a blizzard is rag-
ing with blinding wind-blown snow off the plains, the road conditions in
that area are apt to be favorable in any season. The city has charm, shops,
and historical sites; and it is "away." It fills the boxes on every tourist's
checklist.

If you approach this part of the state in the spring of the year, you will
still see what Thoreau called, "Flooded thin woods with more open water
behind." Many a field turns into a temporary pond—and many a woodlot
becomes a swamp—in the valleys of the Rock River and the Mississippi
River, once the snows of winter melt away. So much water wants to flow
south to the Gulf of Mexico that the regular channels cannot possibly hold
it all.

Flooding is something that the city of Galena has had to deal with since
the Native Americans lived here and since the eastern settlers came to stay.
Just as Thoreau noted, the Mississippi River would back up into the Galena
River, which flowed right next to the downtown business district. The river
would literally run backwards, miles away from its outlet into the mighty
Mississippi. After farmers began plowing and planting on properties in the
surrounding countryside, much of the topsoil they loosened went along for
the ride with the springtime rains. The rivers began to build up with silt.
Floods grew more frequent and more difficult to manage. The worst one
came in late February 1937, when Galena sustained more than $500,000 in
damages and also lost two of its residents. Definitive action needed to be
taken. As a result, today's visitors can see an earthen riverbank levy, as well
as a set of large metal doors that can close off Main Street and its old, original brick buildings. Both offer protection from rising waters, if necessary.
Still, even in mid-summer, the Galena River can appear as if it is either
standing completely motionless or indeed, is flowing backward.

Galena's adopted son, Ulysses S. Grant (1822-1885), was given a hero's
welcome when he returned to the city on August 18, 1865. The grateful residents presented him with a five-year-old brick home in honor of his out-
standing service as a general during the Civil War. But Ulysses and his wife
Julia didn't get a chance to rest here long. In 1867, Grant became the U.S.
Secretary of War. The following year, he was elected President. He spent
two terms in the White House and retired in 1877, when he, Julia and son
Jesse embarked on a world sightseeing tour. They came back to live briefly
in Galena. But in 1880, the Grants relocated to New York City and rented
out their northwestern Illinois home. The former President set about the
task of writing his memoirs and made arrangements for friend Samuel

Clemens to publish them. Though the volumes turned out to be an enormous success, Grant himself didn't live to reap their benefits. He died of cancer just two months after finishing the manuscripts.

Their visits and periods of residency in Galena were intermittent and necessarily sporadic. Tallied all together, the Grants may have spent just two years here over the course of fifteen calendar years. Yet Ulysses S. Grant is still honored in this town. The Grant Home is a state historic site that is open to visitors. Each April, a Ulysses S. Grant birthday celebration is held here. A variety of activities and concerts takes place throughout the year in Grant Park, which lies on the eastern bank of the Galena River. A statue of the man stands guard over the recreational parcel that was named for him. Those who cannot travel to northwestern Illinois can still make contact with the former President fairly easily. A new rendering of his most famous portrait appears on the face of every U.S. fifty-dollar bill.

In January 1997, I was living in Woodstock, Illinois. I belonged to a book discussion group that met at Volo Bog State Natural Recreation Area in Ingleside. We had been given something short to read this month, given the busy-ness of the season. It was an essay by Henry David Thoreau called "Walking." I was excited about the selection. I had not indulged in my appreciation of Thoreau in a good, long while. It would be nice to reconnect with him.

I got hooked on Henry when I was in tenth grade, back in southeastern Pennsylvania, when we read "Civil Disobedience" in English class. Then it was on to *Walden* in twelfth grade, and to all fourteen of his *Journal* volumes when I was in college. I still had my funky 1970s paperback copy of *Walden* with all of my wavering underlines that marked my favorite observations. I still had the sheaf of blue-lined notebook pages that contained all of the vital quotes I had culled from the *Journals* that I had checked out, one by one, over the course of my four years at Clarion State College. I still had five years worth of newsletters from The Thoreau Society, which I had joined soon after taking my first job as a school librarian. And I still had a file of other articles about Thoreau and about Walden Pond, which I had clipped or copied and had stuffed into a desk drawer, whenever they had come my way.

In the back of my mind, I had thought that maybe one day I could write my own version of The Great American Novel and could even feature

Henry Thoreau as a character. I was never sure how that might work. But every once in a while, the idea popped into my head while I was busy with something else, or while I was driving around to visit various historical sites in western Pennsylvania. It was fun to swirl it around for a little bit and to play with it, to think of its possibilities. But I had other obligations. The notion of a novel had to be filed away into a dark corner as well.

And then, Life stepped in. I made choices that took me away from Thoreau, away from my love of nature, and away from my love of travel. The biggest choice gave me a new and simpler last name. Individual interests were put aside for the greater good of a contracted partnership. I let my Thoreau Society membership expire. Somehow it no longer seemed relevant to me.

Eight years later, a mutual and amicable decision put me back on my own. The situation gave me a chance to figure out what I *really* wanted to spend my spare time on. I dedicated myself to Nature and to her causes. I volunteered at a local nature center. I joined several environmental organizations. One of them, the Windstar Foundation, held an annual conference in Aspen, Colorado. I drove to it from my home in central Pennsylvania. It was my first long-distance trip, and it was the first time I had traveled west of Ohio. Some of my co-workers and friends expressed concerns about a single woman driving alone for thousands of miles. But I was fearless. I encountered no problems on the road. And my subsequent success exhilarated me. I drove to Aspen every August for four years.

Once again, Life intervened. I relocated to Chicagoland, seemingly on a whim. By then, I'd already passed though northern Illinois several times, so I wasn't afraid at all of making the move. My cat and I lived for eighteen months with a roommate and two dogs, and we were just too-too close to the city. Once again by mutual agreement, I struck out on my own. The cat and I moved to the rural outskirts that lay northwest of the metropolis. I rededicated myself to nature. I volunteered at Volo Bog in Ingleside and at Tekakwitha Woods Forest Preserve in St. Charles. In addition to my librarian job at a big suburban high school, I also became its environmental club advisor. Interacting with other environmental educators in the area got me thinking that I should make such a commitment more "official." So by 1997, I began to work toward a second master's degree: this time, in Outdoor Teacher Education, through Northern Illinois University.

When I began to read "Walking" in preparation for the discussion group, I was startled to realize that this was new material for me. Somehow I had missed reading this essay during my earlier, decade-long focus on Thoreau. I recognized a few of the oft-quoted sentences. I carefully underlined (with a ruler, this time) all of the key passages that resounded with me. This essay quickly made an impact, just as *Walden* did when I was seventeen years old, and just as his *Journal* volumes did during my undergraduate years. Once again, Thoreau spoke here of nature, of travel, and of the societal constraints that many people seemed to live with and to silently endure.

> Our expeditions are but tours, and come round again at evening to the old hearthside from which we set out. Half the walk is but retracing our steps.

> When sometimes I am reminded that the mechanics and shopkeepers stay in their shops not only all the forenoon, but all the afternoon, too, sitting with crossed legs, so many of them—as if the legs were made to sit upon, and not to stand or walk upon—I think that they deserve some credit for not having all committed suicide long ago.

> Nowadays almost all man's improvements, so called, as the building of houses and the cutting down of the forest and of all large trees, simply deform the landscape, and make it more and more tame and cheap.

> In short, all good things are wild and free.

> I know that something akin to the migratory instinct in birds and quadrupeds ... affects both nations and individuals, either perennially or from time to time.

> Eastward I go only by force; but westward I go free.

> The West of which I speak is but another name for the Wild; and what I have been preparing to say is, that in Wildness is the preservation of the World. Every tree sends its fibers forth in search of the Wild.

As I turned the pages, Henry Thoreau seemed to be speaking directly to me: a native Pennsylvanian who enjoyed driving to Colorado and who had relocated to Illinois. I repeated those magic words to myself: "Eastward I go only by force; but westward I go free." They described the life I had created for myself. "Let me live where I will, on this side is the city, on that the wilderness, and ever I am leaving the city more and more, and withdrawing into the wilderness." Thoreau used Boston and Massachusetts as his reference points, for Boston was due east of Concord. His hometown lay between the city and the wilderness, so to speak. Illinois was set up in exactly the same fashion, with Chicago to the east and everything else to the west. I grew up in a similar place, with Philadelphia and its suburbs sitting several hours to my east, and seemingly a whole world stretching away to my west. I had chosen to go to a college in western Pennsylvania, and I had found my first school librarian job there as well. It was only in recent years that I had broken loose from the borders of my home state and did some further exploration on my own, most often to the west. "Westward I go free," indeed!

I was energized by the time I got to the book discussion at Volo Bog's nature center library. A small handful of people gathered around the table. As usual, naturalist Stacy Miller had done meticulous preparation. (And she brought cookies, which were always a vital component of our talks.) She provided some basic information about Thoreau, which I callously set aside as being all too familiar facts. Then she opened up an old issue of *National Geographic* to a double-page spread labeled "Travels of Henry David Thoreau." I was mesmerized. What I saw was new to me.

I recognized most of the orange lines that traced the journeys Thoreau took during his lifetime. They ran to Quebec, to Maine, to Cape Cod, and all over New England. But one path circled the Midwest and looked as though it passed right through our backyards, right over where we were sitting. I read the tiny date: 1861. What was this? Why had I not known of this before? Nobody around the table, including Stacy, knew any of the particulars about that route. It made me wonder. Had Henry Thoreau really come to Illinois, and to our little part of it?

We set those questions aside and had a boisterous discussion about "Walking." Part of the fun in reading Thoreau was in the many ways you could interpret his words. I pointed out a section where he chided—sarcastically and perhaps even chauvinistically—those people who wasted their days with afternoon naps. A possible implication was that stay-at-home females did just that, quite a bit. No one else had read that passage in that way; and of course, every other woman in the room was dutifully indignant. Nevertheless, "Walking" was generally well received by the members of our little group. It immediately became one of my personal favorites.

Over the course of the next five years, I kept myself fairly busy. I worked as a school librarian and volunteered at nature centers. I earned my master's degree from Northern Illinois University. I was even suddenly inspired to write and finish that Great American Novel that had lingered for decades in my brain. It brought Henry Thoreau to contemporary life as a reluctant time traveler. I started to submit it to literary agents, not really knowing what I would ever do if someone actually wanted to publish it.

I continued my long-distance driving tours as well. The conferences in Colorado came to an end; but I found other reasons to hit the road. I made regular trips to New York, Pennsylvania, and Ohio to visit friends and relatives. I added the state magnets of Montana and the two Dakotas to my refrigerator door, where a quirky map of my geographical conquests began to grow. I finally made the ultimate pilgrimage to Concord, Massachusetts, for Christmas 2000. It was just as fascinating a place as I had imagined. I re-joined The Thoreau Society and started attending its Annual Gathering conferences in Concord in 2001. I entrenched myself once again in Henry's camp.

Now that my first book manuscript was behind me, I was itching to take on another project. I had never quite forgotten that map of Thoreau's travels that Stacy showed us, years earlier. I wanted to figure out exactly where he came through Illinois, so I used my librarian connections and started to do some digging. I began with that 1981 *National Geographic* article, written by Professor William Howarth of Princeton University. General Thoreau biographies seemed not to be of much help at all in my effort. The only detailed source I landed upon was a 1962 Thoreau Society booklet that took a transcription of Henry's field notebook and supplemented it with the texts of young Horace's letters. But even that volume didn't provide a clear picture of their route through the Prairie State. I knew they had crossed this territory by train. But which tracks did they use? And did that line still exist today?

I was in the midst of this quandary when Valerie De Prez invited me to dinner. Valerie was the naturalist at Tekakwitha Woods Forest Preserve. We had become friends, and she read my unpublished novel about Thoreau. We talked about it at the dining room table with her husband David and son Colin. I told them about my current difficulties in tracing Thoreau's Journey West through Illinois. Valerie didn't know much about that trip, either, but David said that he had once read an article on the subject. He began to regale me with pieces of information that I had not unearthed myself. I was speechless. I asked him for the details, but he didn't remember all of them. He promised to e-mail the citation to me sometime during the next week.

David was true to his word. But I wondered if he had made a mistake. He told me that he read about Thoreau's Journey West in an article called "John Muir's Yankee Friends and Mentors: The New England Connection" by Edmund A. Schofield. I had my doubts, since the title didn't seem appropriate at all. But I gave it a shot. And when I got the pages from a downstate college through interlibrary loan, I was fascinated by what I saw.

For reasons that will become clearer in a subsequent chapter, Dr. Schofield had traced the whole length of Thoreau and Mann's Journey West. Through his research, I learned that the two men left Chicago on the morning of May 23 on the Galena & Chicago Union Railroad. Just by knowing the name, I located the tracks by consulting both new maps and old atlases. Miraculously enough, I discovered that my commute to school led me over those very tracks four times a day! I felt as though a magnificent secret had been revealed. Henry Thoreau had passed through the city where I worked. I wanted to share this news with the world, or at least, with everyone in northern Illinois.

I found the tracks and the abandoned beds and drove along them multiple times, from Wayne to East Dubuque. I took photos. I created my own map, combined it with a few signature Thoreau quotes, and sent the page as a handout to all of the high school English departments and public libraries along the route. I yelled "Thoreau's train!" to myself whenever I had to wait at one of the railroad crossings for a passing freight. I laughed anytime I was stopped at the tracks in Huntley. Instead of carrying Henry and Horace to the Mississippi River, those freight cars were taking hundreds of new Dodge Neons from Belvidere to new owners and paved driveways in new places. It was hardly "Thoreau's train" any longer.

But even after finding my own personal Thoreau connection in northern Illinois, I discovered that living in the Midwest was starting to wear on me, after an eight-year run. I was a native Pennsylvanian. I was an East Coast person at heart. I had met good people here and I had a good job. I had done and seen some marvelous things. But it was time for me to move back east. Tornado watches and warnings scared the stuffing out of me. The ever-expanding sprawl of Chicagoland was starting to encroach on my daily commute. I knew that eastern Pennsylvania was getting to be the same way. So in my job search, I decided to target rural New York state and Massachusetts. After a few interviews and visits, I was offered a public library director's position in late December 2002. By mid-January 2003, my cat and I were living in the middle of Massachusetts, just 90 minutes away from Walden Pond.

At a librarian workshop in Shrewsbury in May 2003, I sat next to Nick Langhart from the Boylston Public Library. We introduced ourselves to each other and we chit-chatted during one of the breaks. I soon learned that he was originally from Ohio. We started comparing notes as non-natives to the

Bay State. He asked what drew me to Massachusetts. I replied that I had wanted to relocate from Illinois, and that I had gotten a job here. But in a lower voice and as a kind of aside, I added, "I'm also a fan of Henry David Thoreau." I didn't know why I said it that way, like an apology, or even an admission to a sordid crime. But I figured Nick would understand such an infatuation, since we were in a literary profession and we were sitting only about an hour away from Concord. He did.

"Oh, then you know Ed Schofield," he said.

I felt my mouth drop open. It took more than a few seconds for me to be able to find my voice and respond. "No, I don't *know* him," I said. "I know *of* him. I read an article that he once wrote about Thoreau." I could not possibly tell Nick what Ed's information had meant and what it had started for me. If I started rambling about the Journey West and the train tracks in Illinois, we could easily be here for the rest of the week.

It turned out that Ed then worked at Tower Hill Botanic Garden, which was right down the street from the Boylston library. As Nick told me more about his associations with Ed, I was really only halfway listening. To think that the researcher who had inspired me was here in the area! My mind was spinning. When the presenter called our eyes back to the front of the classroom, I could hardly hear her. It was all I could do to stay in my chair. Moving to Massachusetts had obviously been the right thing to do.

Even though I was excited about the prospect, I didn't want to rush into contacting Ed. I had a fair amount of work to do in my new job. It took me nine months to summon up the courage to leave a message for Ed Schofield at Tower Hill.

Thoreau people are funny. When two of them meet, they can talk for hours. And hours and hours and hours. Finding someone who shares your Thoreauvian interest can be an exhilarating experience, for there is then no need for further explanations. I was already familiar with this phenomenon. I was therefore not surprised when Ed and I ended up speaking for hours over the phone, on several occasions. The first time we met in person, Ed and I spent seven hours talking. I shared with him all of the research I had done on Thoreau's Journey West, using the information in his article as a foundation. During one of our meetings, I showed him my photos and my handouts that covered the Illinois section of Henry and Horace's route.

Ed seemed to be impressed. "You know, no one's ever done the entire Journey West. Someone should. And someone should write about it and publicize it. The subject matter deserves it. Henry David Thoreau deserves it."

"Why don't *you* do it, Ed?" I asked. "You've already done some of the legwork as research for that article, the one that got me following the train tracks across Illinois."

"No, I never had any intention of going any further with it," he said. "And at this point, I have other projects in mind. I have many more articles I want to write. Dozens, actually."

He made me think. "Well, I've already done the Illinois part," I began. "And now that I live in Massachusetts, I can probably do the section that runs through here." I continued to think out loud. "The tail end of the trip, the trail through Vermont and New Hampshire, would be easy enough to follow as well. It's not very far away." I gave it a few more seconds of thought. "I have friends in western New York, and I visit them every once in a while. So it wouldn't take too much effort to trace that part of the path, either." That was where I stopped.

"But why do it piecemeal?" Ed asked. He paused; and then he came up with a zinger. "I think if you're going to trace any part of the Journey West, you ought to do it *all*."

I immediately flashed back to the time that Stacy showed us that *National Geographic* map, seven years earlier. In my mind, I could see the orange line that marked Thoreau and Mann's route through ten states and through Ontario. Much it of lay along interstates that I had already followed during my own travels. How much more time would it take to follow those roads again and just add the extra places I hadn't yet seen? How much behind-the-scenes research would I have to do to fill in all of the historical cracks left by Henry and Horace with their spotty reporting? I didn't know how I could fit it all in and still maintain a full-time job with supervisory responsibilities. But it sure might be fun to try.

I came back to the present moment, and I looked up at Ed. "OK. I'll do it." And by uttering those five quick syllables, I altered the course of my own life forever.

Over the next couple of years, it took me a few job changes before I landed upon one that supported me and still gave me time to write and to travel. I asked the ultimate in performance of two durable automobiles that could manage not only my lengthy planned trips, but also the occasional whim of driving hundreds of miles just to see a certain scene or to do a bit of vital research. And when I was not traveling, I was reading about all of the places that sat along the route. The more I learned, the more fascinated I became with this two-month adventure taken by two interesting men, a century and a half ago. The world did indeed need to know these details.

For me, the Journey West did not begin in Massachusetts or in Minnesota.

I joined the trek on the Illinois prairie, smack-dab in the middle of it all. And while Henry Thoreau and Horace Mann certainly had a lot to do with my participation in it, a number of contemporary guides initially pointed me in the right direction as well: Stacy Miller, Valerie De Prez, David De Prez, Nick Langhart, and Ed Schofield. Without the leadership of their seemingly chance remarks and acts, I might never have taken on this wonderful project. Thank you, everyone.

WHEN YOU GO: This portion of Thoreau and Mann's Journey West route provides some of the best and the closest access to the railroad tracks they rode over in 1861. Travelers just have to extract themselves from the non-stop suburbia of Chicagoland first. That's a task that takes a good, long while.

The tracks run directly west from Chicago to West Chicago and lie between IL Route 64 (North Avenue) and IL Route 38 (Roosevelt Road). Take either road west. Turn north on IL Route 59. When you reach Army Trail Road, turn left (west). As you drive through the exclusive suburb of Wayne, you will cross the single pair of rails, looking old and unused and slightly shabby in comparison to the McMansions now surrounding them. Turn right (north) on IL Route 25. The rails of the old Galena & Chicago Union Railroad will use a bridge to pass over you (just after you drive over another set of rails belonging to a different line, so don't be confused). Follow IL Route 25 north into Elgin and watch for signs to lead you to U.S. 20 West. You will immediately cross the Fox River. If you have a chance to take a quick glance at downtown Elgin below and to your right, you will see the railroad tracks following the western bank of the river.

U.S. 20 will carry you the rest of the way across northern Illinois. The tracks are easily seen from Marengo to Rockford, where they often lie next to the roadway. Stop at the Illinois Railway Museum in Union, and sit in the station building to reminisce. Once you go through or around Rockford, you should keep an eye out for the large poles that mark the abandoned railroad grade. If you have a detailed map, you might be able to follow the dotted line that marks the former rail path. You will also be able to more closely trace the old Illinois Central tracks between Lena, Council Hill and all of the little towns along the way.

If you choose to stay on U.S. 20, be sure to pull over and climb up the steps of the Long Hollow Tower on the hilltop just west of Elizabeth. On a clear day, you can see three states from the top of that structure: Illinois, Wisconsin, and, in the haze across the river, Iowa. The view confirms what Henry Thoreau saw and noted: that this part of the Prairie State is far from flat. It consists of an undulating, rolling prairie land that turns into a hilly landscape by this juncture of the journey. Thoreau didn't even have to leave the train to figure that out.

Devoted admirers of the Transcendentalists may also want to make a short side trip to the town of Oregon, Illinois. At Lowden State Park, you can stand at the exact spot where Margaret Fuller was inspired to pen her poem, "Ganymede to his Eagle." From Rockford, take IL Route 2 south to Oregon. When you reach the main street (IL Route 64), turn left (east) and cross the Rock River. Once on the eastern bank, turn left (north) onto River Road. Lowden State Park will appear on your left in about a mile. Drive in, find a place to park, and walk to the river overlook. You may have to share it with an immense concrete sculpture of Black Hawk, but he probably won't mind. He is forever gazing west. Like the view from the top of Long Hollow Tower, the vista offered here verifies the truths that Illinois is not just a prairie, and it is not entirely flat. This diversion to Oregon will add at least an hour to your schedule. It could last much longer if you take full advantage of the chance to admire the scenery or to grab a bite to eat.

If speed is your watchword and you merely want to cross the state as quickly as possible, then begin by taking I-90 from Chicago to Rockford. You'll cross the Journey West railroad tracks just once along this stretch of the interstate: near mile marker 28.5, between the exits for Randall Road and Route 47. The rails will be headed north to Gilberts. Before you reach Rockford, take the exit for U.S. 20 west. Thereafter, you must be content to follow a road slightly less traveled. Watch for speed limit changes at the edges of each town.

FOR MORE INFORMATION

Galena / Jo Daviess County Convention & Visitors Bureau, 101 Bouthillier Street, Galena, IL 61036. Phone (877) 464-2536. www.galena.org.

Illinois Bureau of Tourism, 100 West Randolph Street, Suite 3-400, Chicago, IL 60601. Phone (800) 406-6418. www.enjoyillinois.com.

Illinois Railway Museum, PO Box 427, 7000 Olson Road, Union, IL 60180. Phone (800) BIG-RAIL. www.irm.org.

Lowden State Park, 1411 North River Road, Oregon, IL 61061. Phone (815) 732-6828. dnr.state.il.us/Lands/Landmgt/Parks/R1/LOWDENSP.HTM.

Northern Illinois Tourism Development Office, 200 South State Street, Belvidere, IL 61008. Phone (815) 547-3740. www.visitnorthernillinois.com.

Stephenson County Historical Society, 1440 South Carroll Avenue, Freeport, IL 61032. Phone (815) 232-8419. www.stephcohs.org.

Tekakwitha Woods Forest Preserve and Nature Center, 35W076 Villa Maria Road, St. Charles, IL 60174. Phone (847) 741-8350. www.kaneforest.com/tekakwitha/natureCenter.aspx.

Ulysses S. Grant Home, (500 Bouthillier Street) Galena State Historical Sites, PO Box 333, Galena, IL 61036. Phone (815) 777-3319. www.granthome.com.

RECOMMENDED READING

The "Sounds" chapter of *Walden*, which focuses mainly on the intrusion of the Fitchburg Railroad line on the pond environment and on Henry Thoreau's sensibilities. "Chapter 3" of Margaret Fuller's *Summer on the Lakes, 1843*, which includes the text of the poem that was inspired by the view of the Rock River valley. Although it will be recommended again further along the route, you may also want to read Thoreau's inspirational essay, "Walking."

NOTES ON THIS CHAPTER

Basic information about William Ellery Channing's 1839-1840 land experiment in northern Illinois can be found in the two biographies of him: Robert N. Hudspeth's *Ellery Channing* (New York: Twayne Publishers, 1973), and Frederick T. McGill, Jr.'s *Channing of Concord: A*

Life of William Ellery Channing II (New Brunswick, N.J.: Rutgers University Press, 1967).

I am indebted to Craig Pfannkuche at Memory Trail Research, Inc., for researching the Channing deed for me. According to the deed, the purchase was made on November 9, 1839, but wasn't officially filed until March 28, 1840. The separate parcels were of 80 acres, 55 acres, and 25 acres. Today the 80-acre property lies on the northwest corner of the intersection of Dunham Road and Menge Road, just west of U.S. Route 14 in Woodstock. It sits not far from the headquarters of the McHenry County Conservation District. The other two properties lie on either side of Lamb Road, off IL Route 120 at Woodstock. The Chicago and Northwestern railroad line passes through one of them. If Ellery Channing had been able to hold on to his land a little longer, he might have been able to cash in on a sale to a rail company.

Margaret Fuller wrote about her Midwestern journey in *Summer on the Lakes, 1843*. The quotes here came from Chapter 3.

Sources abound regarding the 1858 Lincoln-Douglas debates in Illinois. One eye-opener is Allen C. Guelzo's *Lincoln and Douglas: The Debates that Defined America* (New York: Simon & Schuster, 2008).

Cheryl Gleason of the Freeport Public Library provided key information about the railroad station that served both the Galena & Chicago Union and the Illinois Central.

An overview of Galena's problem with flooding appears in Jane Holland's article, "What is the story behind the big green floodgates on Main Street?" (*The Galenian* 21: 1, Spring/Summer 2001, pp. 14-19).

General information about Ulysses S. Grant and his family was gleaned from a variety of reference sources, including the history and chronology posted on the Grant Home web site, http://www.granthome.com. H. Scott Wolfe of the Galena Public Library District confirmed for me via fax (dated June 19, 2002) that Grant and Thoreau's paths did not cross on May 23, 1861. A terrific book about two fascinating men can be found in Mark Perry's *Grant and Twain: The Story of an American Friendship* (New York: Random House Trade Paperbacks, 2004). It is said that the Grants arrived in Galena on the *Itasca* in April 1860. So although Thoreau and Mann didn't get to see or meet the Grants, they at least traveled by the same steamboat.

The three references noted during my own search for Journey West answers are, in full:

William Howarth's "Thoreau: Following the Tracks of a Different Man." *National Geographic* 159 (March 1981): 349-387.

Walter Harding's *Thoreau's Minnesota Journey: Two Documents: Thoreau's Notes on the Journey West and The Letters of Horace Mann, Jr.* Geneseo, N.Y.: The Thoreau Society [Thoreau Society Booklet No. Sixteen], 1962.

Schofield, Edmund A. "John Muir's Yankee Friends and Mentors: The New England Connection." *Pacific Historian* 29 (1985): 65-93.

"Life" happens to us all. Stacy Miller is now married and is Stacy Iwanicki. She is still the Natural Resources (Education) Coordinator at Volo Bog State Natural Area in Ingleside, Illinois. Valerie and David De Prez have since divorced; and Valerie (now Valerie Blaine) is still the Nature Programs Manager for the Kane County Forest Preserve District in St. Charles, Illinois. She also writes a regular nature-oriented column for a suburban newspaper, the Arlington Heights *Daily Herald*. David teaches biology on Chicagoland's North Shore. Nick Langhart is now the director of the Forbush Memorial Library in Westminster, Massachusetts. Ed Schofield retired from Tower Hill Botanic Garden several years after I first met him. As usual, he kept himself busy with projects in both Concord and Worcester.

My first novel manuscript, *Watching Henry*, remains unpublished.

Travel Chapter 10

Friday, May 24, through Sunday, May 26, 1861
Dunleith, Illinois, to St. Paul, Minnesota
via the Mississippi River and the steamship Itasca

Expenses: Ticket to St. Paul, $11.50.
Apples, 5 cents.

The boat left Dunleith about 8:30 in the morning and went over to Dubuque across the river, and got under way about 9 o'clock in the morning. We got to Pra[i]rie du Chien about 5 p.m. and had to wait till 8 p.m. for the cars which were late; in the morning we stopped at Brownsville, the first town on the river in Minnesota, about five o'clock, and at about four in the afternoon we entered Lake Pepin, arrived at Red Wing at about 7:30 p.m. and a litt[l]e while after they left there we went to bed.

—Horace Mann Jr.'s Letter, May 26, 1861

Up river. River say 60 rds wide—or ¾ to 1 mile between bluffs—broad flooded low intervals covered with willows in bloom (20 feet high rather slender) & prob. other kinds—& elms & white maple & cottonwood. —now boatable between the trees & prob. many ducks there. Bluffs say 150 to 200 ft. high. Rarely room for a village at base of cliffs. ….

—Thoreau's field notebook

Henry Thoreau and Horace Mann, Jr., had spent the night on the steamboat *Itasca*, a side-wheel packet that had been built four years earlier in Cincinnati. It was docked at Dunleith, Illinois. On the morning of May 24, it began its journey along the Mississippi River. Though the travelers' ultimate destination was the settlement of St. Paul, Minnesota, their first stop was just across the water: Dubuque, Iowa.

Dubuque was a bustling river town of 13,000 residents. Included among them was a young family that would later prove important to the Transcendentalists of Concord, Massachusetts. Austin Adams (1826-1890) and his wife, Mary Newbury Adams (1837-1901), had been educated back East, had married and had moved to the area in the late 1850s. Mr. Adams' law practice was already doing well; and Mrs. Adams was no doubt attending to the needs of three-year-old Annabel and six-months-old Eugene. On this day in 1861, they probably would not have found any reason to be down at the riverside, watching the *Itasca*. And Henry and Horace did not know the Adams family. Both men were instead studying the river and the high sandstone banks on either side of it. Such dynamic bluffs were uncommon back in their native New England.

Thoreau and Mann steamed up the Mississippi River on the *Itasca (Courtesy of the Minnesota History Society)*

Were the Concord men initially disappointed at this view of the Mississippi? At this particular spot, the water stretched only about a quarter of a mile between Illinois and Iowa. It hardly looked "mighty." It could just as easily have been the Hudson or the Connecticut River from this vantage point. Only the yellowish bluffs revealed its Midwestern origins and identity.

In 1861, steamboats like the *Itasca* were still chugging up and down the Upper Mississippi valley. Once the war began in earnest however, President Lincoln closed the lower portion of the river to both traffic and trade. That proclamation caused a young riverboat pilot named Samuel Clemens to leave the river for good and to return to his home in Missouri. Soon he would embark on his own western journey and a brand-new career in journalism.

Henry Thoreau never met Mr. Clemens, but he might have admired the kind of life the man had been living. Thoreau once mused:

The river is by far the most attractive highway, and those boatmen who have spent twenty or twenty-five years on it, must have had a much fairer, more wild and memorable experience than the dusty and jarring one of the teamster, who has driven, during the same time, on the roads which run parallel with the stream.

For the next few days, he and Horace would have an opportunity to *be* those boatmen and to travel on that famous and "attractive highway."

Henry had done his homework. He was an avid reader of travel narratives. He had read accounts of historic journeys that had been made throughout the American Midwest. He scrutinized maps; and as a surveyor, he crafted his own. He no doubt knew that the Mississippi would grow wider as the boat steamed north. Near Red Wing, Minnesota, it was broad enough to be given a bigger name: Lake Pepin. Once, as he perused a map of this part of the country, he speculated:

> How deceptive these maps of western rivers! Methought they were scattered according to the fancy of the map-maker,—were dry channels at best,—but it turns out that the Missouri at Nebraska City is three times as wide as the Mississippi at Burlington, and Grasshopper Creek, perhaps, will turn out to be as big as the Thames or the Hudson.

Living as he did in a town where two rivers flowed together to form a third, Thoreau was enchanted early on with even the *concept* of such a feature:

> For the first time it occurred to me this afternoon what a piece of wonder a river is. A huge volume of matter ceaselessly rolling through the fields and meadows of this substantial earth—making haste from the high places, by stable dwellings of men and Egyptian pyramids; to its restless reservoir—One would think that, by a very natural impulse, the dwellers upon the headwaters of the Mississippi and the Amazon, would follow in the trail of their waters to see the end of the matter.

During this trip, however, he and young Horace would see neither the mouth nor the headwaters of the Mississippi River. But they would follow its course for more than 300 miles. Along the way, they could admire slices of Iowa, Wisconsin, and Minnesota from the deck of the *Itasca*. Ironically enough, the steamboat was named for the very lake where the water originated.

Even though this was Henry Thoreau's first personal excursion on the river, he may have recognized some of the scenery. Twelve years earlier in a hall in Boston, he had witnessed a "moving panorama" of this very valley. Painter Samuel B. Stockwell had depicted the details of the Mississippi shoreline on a long canvas that was steadily unrolled before the audience. The effect was such that it seemed as though the viewers themselves were floating along the river. Stockwell's "Panorama of the Mississippi" led them from the Gulf of Mexico and New Orleans all the way to the Falls of St. Anthony in Minnesota, and then back downstream. A live narrator explained the features of the passing scenery to the audience; and it took two or three hours to see the entire performance. Newspaper reviewers could not promote the exhibit enough.

> Stockwell's Panorama has been "rendered with a truthfulness and fidelity one could hardly anticipate in a painting of such great extent. The river is seen under various aspects, by moonlight, at sunrise, sunset, during storms and in fogs and with the most picturesque effect, whilst the monotony of the continuous stream is broken by innumerable steamboats, rafts, flatboats and canoes."

> It "has been pronounced by thousands who have witnessed it— most of whom are familiar with the scenery—as the most gigantic, correct and beautiful work of the kind ever presented to the public."

> "No one can sit and view a single section of this work without being impressed with the fact of its fidelity to nature."

Thoreau himself took some time to write about Stockwell's rendition. He contrasted the landscape with a similar demonstration he had attended a few months earlier: one based in Europe and painted by Bostonian Benjamin Champney.

> Some months ago I went to see a panorama of the Rhine. It was like a dream of the Middle Ages. I floated down its historic stream in something more than imagination, under bridges built by the Romans, and repaired by later heroes, past cities and castles whose very names were music to my ears, and each of which was the subject of a legend. There were Ehrenbreitstein and Rolandseck and Coblentz, which I knew only in history. They were ruins that interested me chiefly. There seemed to come up from its waters and its vine-clad hills and valleys a hushed music as of Crusaders departing for

the Holy Land. I floated along under the spell of enchantment, as if I had been transported to an heroic age, and breathed an atmosphere of chivalry.

Soon after, I went to see a panorama of the Mississippi, and as I worked my way up the river in the light of today, and saw the steamboats wooding up, counted the rising cities, gazed on the fresh ruins of Nauvoo, beheld the Indians moving west across the stream, and, as before I had looked up the Moselle, now looked up the Ohio and the Missouri and heard the legends of Dubuque and of Wenona's Cliff [sic]—still thinking more of the future than of the past or present—I saw that this was a Rhine stream of a different kind; that the foundations of castles were yet to be laid, and the famous bridges were yet to be thrown over the river; and I felt that *this was the heroic age itself*, though we know it not, for the hero is commonly the simplest and obscurest of men.

And now here they were, on this working waterway, *docked at Dubuque!* The next day they would see Winona's Cliff in person, on the Minnesota side of the river. They would see Indians, too. With settlements laid out so recently, indeed, no one had yet built any bridges across this part of the Mississippi. Here, the future of America was unfolding, geographically removed from some of the turmoil and unrest found in other parts of the country. And some of those everyday heroes might be found on board the *Itasca* or living in the river towns that it steamed past.

The 300-mile trip upriver lasted almost three days. After leaving Dubuque, the *Itasca* headed north, with Iowa on its port side and Wisconsin at starboard. It reached Prairie du Chien, Wisconsin, at about 5 p.m. on Friday. About twelve hours later and by the light of a full moon, the ship passed Brownsville, Minnesota, and soon afterward, La Crosse, Wisconsin. The travelers entered Lake Pepin at about 4 p.m. on Saturday and by 7:30 p.m., they were at Red Wing, Minnesota. The *Itasca* docked at St. Paul in the wee hours of Sunday morning. Young Horace took that opportunity to write to his mother and to assure her that they had reached one of their main destinations. "The two days we had on the river were the most beautiful days we have had this spring, they were very warm and not a bit of wind till late yesterday afternoon when a little breeze came up and sometime in the night it commenced to rain." According to him, steaming up the Mississippi was one of the best parts of the journey thus far.

Henry Thoreau might have felt the same way. The good weather might have invigorated both his powers of observation and his pen. Or perhaps it was the knowledge that he had finally made his way to The West. He scribbled more notes during these river-bound days than he did on any previous segment of the trip. From a printed guidebook or captain's log, he copied a chart of distances between La Crosse and St. Paul and all of the towns between the two. He noted that Prairie du Chien was deemed "the smartest town on the river," and that it exported "the most wheat of any town bet. St. Paul & St. Louis;" so much so that "great heaps" of the stuff could be found there, "covered at night & all over the ground." And he seemed to be most intrigued by the methods of commerce being conducted all along the waterway.

> Land on the shore often with a plank. Great rafts of boards & shingles 4 or 5 rods wide & 15 or 20 long. Very few small boats. ... Occasionally a little lonely house on a flat or slope— often deserted—banks in primitive condition bet. the towns which is almost everywhere. Load some 9 or 10 cords of wood at a landing—20 men In 10 minutes ... Every town a wharf— with a storage building or several & as many hotels as anything—& commission merchants— "Storage, Forwarding, & Commission" one or all these words on the most prominent new building close to the water side. Perhaps a heap of sacks filled with wheat on the natural quay or levee close by— or about Dubuque & Dunleith a blue stack of pig lead— which is in no danger of being washed away. See where they have dug for lead—in the sides of the bluffs for many miles above Galena—The steamer whistles—then strikes its bell about 6 times funereally & with a pause after the 3d - & you see the whole village making haste to the landing—commonly the raw stony or sandy shore—the postmaster with his bag the passenger & almost every dog & pig in the town— of commonly one narrow street under the bluff— & back yards at angles of about 45° with the horizon. If there is more flat space—bet. the water & the bluff—it is almost sure to be occupied by a flourishing & larger town.

Though Thoreau had commented earlier in his notebook that the steamboat was not scheduled to make stops at the towns, it evidently did make a few. Other boats would have been traversing the channels to do some business as well. And in any case, gang-planks must have been used to reach the shore.

Around Wabasha, Minnesota, the travelers saw "Indians encamped" in the area "with Dacotah shaped wigwams." The settlement could have been the Mdewakanton Sioux band led by Wabasha III. The sight must have mirrored what Thoreau had seen in Stockwell's Mississippi River panorama, years before. This was Henry and Horace's first real glimpse of Native Americans in their own territory—or rather, on what had been, until very recently, their own land. Before they left Minnesota, the Massachusetts men would have an opportunity to get even closer to its native people.

But what commanded the attention of both Henry Thoreau and Horace Mann, Jr., were the sandstone and dolomite bluffs on either side of the river. Horace had investigated them as soon as they reached Dunleith and the Mississippi. After checking in on the *Itasca*, he "went on shore and got a few minerals out of the bluff and also a few flowers," before he returned to the boat and went to bed. While they steamed north, the two men noted the beauty of the bluffs: rising and falling at times, and providing backgrounds to river towns and communities. As the *Itasca* passed by the town of Red Wing (named after the Dakota chief and not directly the blackbird of its marshes), they could not help but notice Barn Bluff, which rose more than 340 feet above the Mississippi. Now, here was something worth exploring! But they did not then have an opportunity to stop and climb it. Perhaps the men made promises to each other to make the time to do so on their return trip.

As he had done from the train windows, Henry Thoreau made an attempt to botanize from the deck of the *Itasca*. From a distance he could identify the kinds of trees that grew along the river banks and atop the bluffs: willows, elms, silver maples, cottonwoods, aspens, ashes, and basswoods. North of La Crosse, the white pines began to grow. And when the steamboat docked at Prairie du Chien, Thoreau was able to scrutinize the area for smaller plants. There he found patches of Pasque flower (*Pulsatilla nuttalliana*), Birdfoot violet (*Viola pedata*) and Hoary puccoon (*Lithospermum canescens*). Travel by such a large and public craft might have been efficient, but it could not offer the personal experience with the water and with nature that a two-man rowboat did. Still, Thoreau might have reinvigorated a belief here that he had documented more than twenty years earlier:

> Rivers are the natural highways of all nations, not only levelling [sic] and removing obstacles from the path of the traveler—quenching his thirst—and bearing him on their bosom, but conducting him through the most interesting scenery of a country most rich in natural phenomena, through the most populous portions of the globe where the animal and vegetable kingdoms attain the greatest perfection.

Since the boat steamed up the river along its deepest channels, away from the shoreline, the species the two men could see most often and more clearly were birds. Thoreau had long before prophesied their presence as well: "Let a man live in any part of the globe and he will hear the same simple spring sounds to cheer him. Along the Nile and the Orinoco and the Mississippi birds of the same genus migrate." True enough, here small ducks caught his eye, as well as kingfishers, crows, jays, white-bellied swallows and passenger pigeons. He even "saw a large hawk or eagle pair ... over the bluffs of the Mississippi." But above all, he saw the typical residents of North American wetlands: "Red wing b. bird the prevailing to Mississippi R." During that third week of May, the red-winged blackbirds were either busy in courtship or in building their nests. The males would have been showing off their red and gold and white shoulder blazes, and the females would have been simultaneously beguiled and outraged. "No two have epaulets equally brilliant," Thoreau once noted. "Some are small and almost white, and others a brilliant vermilion. They are handsomer than the golden robin, methinks."

Perhaps the *Itasca* was not too noisy or too removed to allow its passengers to hear the distinctive song of the red-winged blackbird as they steamed northward. Thoreau noted in his journal several previously enjoyable instances of witnessing "a concert of red-wings." He even made an attempt to translate that warble into written form:

> The strain of the red-wing on the willow spray over the water to-night is liquid, bubbling, watery, almost like a tinkling fountain, in perfect harmony with the meadow. It oozes, trickles, tinkles, bubbles from his throat,—*bob-y-lee-e-e*, and then its shrill, fine whistle.

Where twentieth-century birders would hear "conk-kar-ree," "konk-la-ree," or "o-ka-lay," Thoreau heard "bob-y-lee-e-e." In any case: it would have been a lovely accompaniment that echoed over the river, as Henry and Horace and the rest of their shipmates passed towns, Indian settlements, and islands and marshes, on their way to St. Paul. They reached that outpost of 12,000 residents in the early morning hours on Sunday, May 26, 1861. The Concord men left the *Itasca* at about 6 a.m.

After catching breakfast at the American House, Henry Thoreau and Horace Mann, Jr., set out for St. Anthony. They aimed for the home of merchant Samuel Thatcher, Jr. A native of Maine who had moved to Minnesota in 1851, Mr. Thatcher was to be their host and possible guide for the duration of their stay. The two Concord men had traveled 1300 miles in fifteen days to get this far. Now they were near their goal and the real starting point for their Western adventure. The stagecoach covered those last nine miles in a rainstorm and along muddy roads, hardly providing a glorious welcome for the long-distance travelers. Nevertheless, their spirits might have been boosted by the prospect of meeting new friends and the anticipation of planning a variety of activities and tours in the area.

But when they deposited themselves on the Thatcher doorstep, Henry and Horace were met with an unfortunate surprise. Samuel was suddenly and severely ill. He had sustained life-threatening injuries after being involved in a carriage accident. The man could barely lift a pen to write a letter. His entire household was in disarray, as his wife Elizabeth and grown children were attending to his needs. None of the Thatchers could help the two out-of-town visitors, who were now additionally without a place to stay. Concern surely turned to disappointment and frustration.

Henry Thoreau and young Horace Mann were on their own and a long, long way from home. Now what would they do?

The steamboat *Itasca* continued to make trips along the Mississippi River, during and after the Civil War. The craft was destroyed when it caught fire at Paducah, Kentucky, in 1868.

A railroad bridge connecting the two Dubuques was built across the river in 1869. The "Old High Street Bridge" designed for regular traffic followed in 1887. The current Julien Dubuque Bridge was erected in 1943.

Dubuque, La Crosse, Winona, Wabasha, and Red Wing have all grown into sizable river communities. While Prairie du Chien is still a busy port, the city has fewer residents today than it did when Thoreau and Mann stopped there. The transport of wheat and other grains is no longer the mainstay of its economy.

During the winter of 1870-1871, Bronson Alcott traveled throughout the Midwest on one of his "conversational tours." He spoke to small club gatherings and held conversations in select living rooms. His topics ranged from education and philosophy to the lives and works of the primary authors of Concord: a list which by then included his daughter Louisa. He had a general travel itinerary in mind but made adjustments to his schedule whenever he acted on tips from new associates. It was such an affiliation that led him in mid-December to Dubuque, Iowa, and to the home of Austin and Mary Newbury Adams. His visit there began a friendship that would last a lifetime.

Bronson Alcott later made a friend in Mary Newbury Adams of Dubuque, Iowa. (*Courtesy Special Collections Department / Iowa State University Library*)

By then, four children (ages 5-12) made for a busy household, even with the help of at least one servant. Austin Adams had a thriving law practice in town. He eventually would be headed toward a judgeship with the Iowa Supreme Court. Mary was active in the women's suffrage movement and had begun her own Conversational Club of Dubuque two years earlier. Her sister Frances did similar work in Detroit; and there her husband, John J. Bagley, would soon be elected Governor of Michigan. In this stop along the Mississippi River, Bronson Alcott made some key connections. He did not know that he was also laying the groundwork for establishing his own Concord School of Philosophy later in the decade.

Alcott spent more than two weeks with the Adams family. He remarked in his journal that Mary and Austin were:

> leading influences here and throughout the West. Mrs. Adams is a sister of Mrs. Bagley of Detroit, and *the representative woman of the West.*—a lady of culture and character, reminding me of Marg. Fuller. Herself and husband have drawn around them a circle of highly intelligent and earnest persons whom I met

last evening and held a Conversation, the first of three or four which I am to give here.

On this and a successive trip, Alcott "found their names an open door for me wherever I went in Iowa." He recommended their hospitality to other speakers who were traveling through the area. Mr. Emerson later stopped at the Adams' house during one of his own lecture circuits.

In Mrs. Adams especially, Alcott found a kindred spirit. She was an educated and intelligent woman who was doing the kind of outreach that he admired. She not only reminded him of former *Dial* editor Margaret Fuller, but also of a modern-day Sibyl, an oracle in the ancient Greek and Roman tradition. "I was charmed and instructed by her wit and subtlety of genius," he told a friend. She had devoted her "sisterly attentions" to him while he was in town. After he returned to Concord, he and Mary Adams began to write long letters to one another. "Have a letter from Mrs. Adams of Dubuque," he noted in his journal, "advocating in her Sybilline [sic] manner the importance of Conversations and Clubs as organs of educating the people." In that respect, she was in essence his Midwestern counterpart.

Mary Adams was just as impressed with Mr. Alcott, if not more. He "broke the prejudice of the men, then made them respect—then esteem—then reverence him," she reported to her sister:

> But it is a long time since any one had gone in with me into my ideal life—into my real existence … so long since I had been treated as if my ideals were true[;] treated as if I was what it was possible for me to become[,] that it brought the infinite peace of joy [if] not ecstasy. I have some good friendships too, these aid us to complete ourselves, but this visit was not of a friend but a Christ that removed scales from eyes—put me on my feet.

From Bronson she had gained personal insights as well as the attentions of a life-long correspondent.

It was inevitable that Mary Newbury Adams would in turn travel to Massachusetts to visit with the Alcotts. She did so in June 1872. During her visit, Bronson Alcott accompanied her to the Unitarian picnic being held at the new amusement park at the edge of Walden Pond. The two friends and other attendees also walked to the site where Henry Thoreau had once lived. The house itself was long gone. But Bronson had called upon his friend many times there during his two-year residency. Thoreau had even documented those occasions in *Walden*, referring to his guest as "One of the last of the philosophers." Alcott knew where the tiny building had stood. He showed the plot to the picnickers, probably with a bit of pontificating about the man and his philosophies. What happened next was the beginning of a Thoreauvian legend. Bronson described the scene in his journal:

> Mrs. Adams suggests that visitors to Walden shall bring a small stone for Thoreau's monument and begins the pile by laying stones on the site of his hermitage, which I point out to her. The tribute thus rendered to our friend may, as the years pass, become a pile to his memory. The rude stones were a monument more fitting than the costliest carving of the artist. Henry's fame is sure to brighten with years, and this spot visited by admiring readers of his works.

Thus was the Walden Pond cairn started by a woman from Iowa, in the Gaelic tradition of using such natural tokens to memorialize a landmark.

Certainly Bronson Alcott and other remaining friends of Thoreau publicized this practice. But the pile took on a life of its own, even in those early days. Six years after Mary Adams donated the first stones, her friend Alcott wrote: "Thoreau's Cairn has grown a good deal this summer—every visitor at Walden adding a stone. When will you come and see what you [have] begun so happily for his memory?" Mrs. Adams continued to send her lively letters to Bronson and to his family members, but she did not return to Concord. Still, the cairn continued to grow.

When The Thoreau Society was organized in the early 1940s, its members began to hold annual meetings in Concord. One of the features of these gatherings was a walk to the site of Thoreau's house at Walden Pond. The tale of Bronson Alcott and Mrs. Adams and the origins of the cairn were well documented. By now, many decades later, the pile was rather large. And when a group of Thoreauvians stood at that site on July 4, 1945—precisely one century after Henry Thoreau had taken up residence there—some folks started to compare the placement of the stones with the descriptions of the house site in the book *Walden*. Speculations arose. Had Alcott directed Mary Adams to the right spot? Was the cairn sitting *exactly* where the building had once stood? How would we ever know for sure?

Roland Wells Robbins (1908-1987) was in the crowd that day. The questions intrigued the local resident: so much so, that within a few months he launched an impromptu archaeological dig to determine with certainty the exact position of Thoreau's house. Using the pages of *Walden* as a guide, Robbins probed and dug around the outskirts of the cairn. In late October 1945, he struck man-made plaster. Soon he discovered the chimney foundation for the small structure. After he made some calculations and roped off the rectangular footprint, the results were obvious. "[T]wenty-five per cent of the cairn actually occupied part of the ten by fifteen foot area where Thoreau built his house," he wrote. Bronson Alcott had been correct after all, when he told Mary Adams where to place her stone, back in 1872.

Now that the house site was uncovered, The Thoreau Society installed more permanent granite posts to mark the former corners of the building. The cairn was shifted to one side to accommodate the new display. Visitors continued to bring stones to it, in order to honor Henry David Thoreau. Then, without warning in 1975, workers from Massachusetts' Department of Environmental Management carted the pile away. "This was done primarily because vandals were constantly throwing the rocks around and beyond the site area, which quickly became unsightly," read an official report. "Already short of staff, the man-hours needed to police the area was becoming a problem." And just that quickly, a century-old tradition was wiped away by a blunt and blundering bureaucracy.

Thoreau fans protested. The Commonwealth had not fully understood the emotion and meaning behind the contributions to that "unsightly" heap. Some folks had brought stones from home, marked with personal inscriptions. Now those tributes had been unceremoniously dumped elsewhere. What an insult.

After much deliberation, the state brought the stones back and restored the cairn at the Walden house site on July 17, 1978. Was it really the remnants of the old cairn, or just a pile of random rocks? Perhaps some things are best left to trust and imagination.

Because of her contributions to the suffrage movement and to the organization of local women's clubs, Mary Newbury Adams was honored with induction into the Iowa Women's Hall of Fame in 1981. Fans of Henry Thoreau will remember her for something else altogether: for being the first person to leave a memorial stone at the Walden house site. Every day, visitors to the pond duplicate her random, yet deliberate act. The cairn grows ever wider and taller.

By January 17, 1998, I had been living in northern Illinois for three years. And I had caught newspaper articles about the eagle-watching celebrations that were being held in Mississippi River towns in Iowa and Wisconsin. Until that moment, I had been unaware that eagles wintered along the river and fished in the open water at each dam. I remembered seeing my first bald eagle in the wild as I drove along a ridge above the Mississippi in southeastern Minnesota a few years earlier. Now I understood why I saw it there. I wanted to see more. We had had a decent season already; the several inches of old crusty snow on the ground was refreshed every couple of days. But the roads were clear, and no precipitation was forecast for that day. I decided to make the three- to four-hour drive to northeastern Iowa.

Along the way, I thought about my admiration for raptors in general. My favorites were the red-tailed hawks. I liked to look for them in the trees along the interstates whenever I drove to Pennsylvania or New York. I counted them and kept a little notebook in my car with my dated lists of how many hawks I had seen. I usually spotted at least one during my daily commute to work. After a while, it was easy to pick out the bird's unique profile as it sat on a high branch, watching for any unsuspecting critter below that could make for a quick and tasty lunch. From the front, the hawk looked like a stocky post and almost part of the tree itself. Its light-colored chest distinguished it from that which was wood. From the side, the hawk looked like an upside-down top-heavy pear, with a tiny head and a slip of a tail, as it poised for an instant dive into the drainage ditch. It was in those moments that I was glad to not be a mouse.

Now a big white meadow stretched between the bluffs of East Dubuque and Dubuque. It was the Mississippi, of course. Somewhere underneath all of that snow, the water was still flowing toward New Orleans. When I stopped at a visitor's center, I heard a man from Chicago asking the clerk if a person could walk across the river now. "Well, maybe a *rabbit* could," she replied, with as much seriousness as she could muster. I hid a smile as I grabbed a few brochures and returned to my car. I figured we would later hear on the news, if the guy made an attempt to act on his theory.

I turned north and headed toward the town of Guttenberg, about a 40-mile drive from Dubuque along U.S. 52. With two Ts at the end of that first syllable, the word was *not* pronounced like the name of the old German printer of Bibles. It instead started with "gut," like the slang term for your stomach. Guttenberg attracted wintering eagles because Lock and Dam Number 10 filtered the Mississippi there. North of the dam, the river could be completely snowed over. But the man-made turbulence of the installation assured an open expanse of water just south of it. While fish successfully flowed through the dam, they could become temporarily dazed by the experience. Whenever they floated close to the surface, the eagles flew down to grab them and carry them away. It was an endless all-you-can-eat seafood buffet.

I miscalculated a bit and arrived in Guttenberg a little too late for most of the informational presentations. But I got to see some of the local artwork on display. I walked into the Café Mississippi, where scopes were set up for easy eagle viewing. Everyone else must have had their fill, for I appeared to be the only person who wanted to look through the viewfinders. So I parked myself there for a while over a light lunch.

As I squinted and scanned the sky with one eye, I could hear from across the room a few friends enjoying each other's company, laughing and joking amongst themselves. I didn't pay any attention to their chatter until I heard one of them say, "Oh, now he's just showing off." I couldn't tell if the speaker was referring to someone in their small group, or if he meant the lone bald eagle that had suddenly appeared before me. It was soaring well above us and was turning in slow circles. I duly followed it around and around with the scope. "Majestic" was a word that didn't seem worthy enough to describe what I was seeing. My cheeks were soon wet, and I barely knew how they got that way. There was something about the sight of that bird that struck an emotional chord. It might have done so even without its national symbol status.

I was used to spotting hawks and turkey buzzards during my long-distance drives. When I saw something big flying, my brain flipped through invisible flash cards to make a suitable match. First I judged it by size, which was "bigger than crow." If I saw a brownish body and a red tail, it was obviously my favorite kind of hawk. If the bird was bigger and dark, with its head tucked in while in flight, then it was a vulture or turkey buzzard, known as "T.B." for short. If it was similar in size but suddenly showed off a white head and a white tail, then "oh my God it was an eagle." A primal shiver went through my nervous system.

I watched this eagle for a good long while. I tried to wipe off my face as casually as I could so that the others in the room wouldn't notice. I began to consider the ridiculousness of one person to have been so mesmerized by the sight of just one bird. So I left, satisfied both with lunch and with the vision I saw through the scope. I got back in my car and headed south to Dubuque and to the bridge to Illinois.

Farms and fields lay on either side of the road. Since everything but the road was covered with snow, I seemed to be driving through the quintessential Currier & Ives winterscape. I looked around at Iowa and took my time as I went, much to the disdain of the truck driver riding my back bumper.

Suddenly I saw some dark splotches in a tree, behind a field on my left. I quickly looked for the next crossroad to take, just as my mind said "bigger than hawk." I pulled over into a plowed-off lane with the horn of an eighteen-wheeler ringing in my ears. It sped around me in a flurry of snow and a mixture of dredged-up dirt, sand and gravel. It took a few seconds for the cloud to dissipate. I was okay; so was my car. And so was the truck, which disappeared around the next curve. I probably gave the driver something to complain about later. "Damn tourist," he might have said.

Now I turned my attention to that tree. I got out my binoculars and focused in on it. Three bald eagles were perched on separate branches. Jackpot! I spent the better part of an hour watching them from my car. I was far enough away that the birds didn't care about me at all. I turned off the ignition, then put it back on for heat, then turned it off again when I was warm enough. I laughed out loud when I realized that I was witnessing a life-imitates-art-imitates-life kind of moment. The three of them were sitting so straight and so stiffly that I was immediately reminded of the Muppet character Sam the Eagle. These guys weren't blue, and they didn't have angry black eyebrows. But otherwise, the resemblance was uncanny. Were they siblings? Associates? A pair of parents with one youngster? Or twins attended by either a Mom or a Pop? They all appeared to be about the same size, and all had adult markings. And none of them moved a feather while I studied them from afar. Maybe they were taking afternoon naps, pleasantly full after having feasted at the dam. Eventually I too grew tired; and I had many miles to go before I could sleep. I started up the car again and inched back onto the now empty road, leaving the three eagles to the business of taking care of their own lives. I silently wished them well.

In 1861, Henry Thoreau jotted down in his field notebook that he "Saw a large hawk or eagle pair blackish over the bluffs of the Mississippi." He had his spyglass with him. But he had either been too far away from the birds, or they had been too quick for him. His mind had gotten as far as the size card and didn't have a chance to complete the rest of the identification. Of course, Thoreau and Mann traveled along this river in late spring and early summer. If either one of them saw an eagle, it wasn't because the bird was wintering here. No snow lay on the ground, and the locks and dams did not yet exist. But it was not out of the realm of possibility for Thoreau to have seen either golden eagles or bald eagles in this part of the country. It's too bad he didn't get a closer look.

On occasion, Thoreau had seen a few "white-headed eagles," as he called them, back home in Massachusetts. He seems to have been just as taken with them as I had been, when I watched that lone flier through the scope in Guttenberg.

> Suddenly I look up and see a new bird, probably an eagle, quite above me, laboring with the wind not more than forty rods off. It was the largest bird of the falcon kind I ever saw. I was never so impressed by any flight. She sailed the air, and fell back from time to time like a ship on her beam ends, holding her talons up as if ready for the arrows.

He also appeared to go through the same kind of process I did in making an attempt to determine its species on the fly.

> Saw a large bird sail along over the edge of Wheeler's cranberry meadow just below Fair Haven, which I at first thought a gull, but with my glass found it was a hawk and had a perfectly white head and tail and broad or blackish wings. It sailed and circled along over the low cliff, and the crows dived at it in the field of my glass, and I saw it well, both above and beneath, as it turned, and then it passed off to hover over the Cliffs at a greater height. It was undoubtedly a white-headed eagle. It was to the eye but a large hawk.

A few weeks later, Thoreau remarked that he "Saw my white-headed eagle again, first at the same place, the outlet of Fair Haven Pond." This time he had ample opportunity to watch it soar.

> He was first flying low over the water; then rose gradually and circled westward toward White Pond. Lying on the ground with my glass, I could watch him very easily, and by turns he gave me all possible views of himself. ... He rose very high at last, till I almost lost him in the clouds, circling or rather *looping* along westward, high over river and wood and farm, effectually concealed in the sky. We who live this plodding life here below never know how many eagles fly over us. They are concealed in the empyrean. I think I have got the worth of my glass now that it has revealed to me the white-headed eagle. Now I see him edgewise like a black ripple in the air, his white head still as ever turned to earth, and now he turns his under side to me, and I behold the full breadth of his broad black wings, somewhat ragged at the edges.

Of course, eventually such a sight had Thoreau applying some anthropomorphic philosophies to what he was witnessing.

It lets itself down with its legs somewhat helplessly dangling, as if feeling for something on the bare meadow, and then gradually flies away, soaring and circling higher and higher until lost in the downy clouds. This lofty soaring is at least a grand recreation, as if it were nourishing sublime ideas. I should like to know why it soars higher and higher so, whether its thoughts are really turned to earth, for it seems to be more nobly as well as highly employed than the laborers ditching in the meadow beneath or any others of my fellow-townsmen.

But we will never know for sure what those eagle thoughts are, either when the bird is soaring above us or is sitting in a tree with several of his brethren. We might very well be disappointed if we did. Their notions may not be noble considerations at all, but merely the processes of a predator planning for potential sources of prey. And soaring may just be an aerobic exercise for stretching wings and keeping them in good working order.

Three years after my first visit to Guttenberg, I returned for another eagle watching weekend. I attended a presentation featuring a raptor expert with three live rehabilitated birds: a great-horned owl, a kestrel, and a bald eagle. Seeing such creatures up close did not diminish their ability to awe this human's eyes. They made me want to stay quiet and to get as small as possible: though if I were a mouse, that attitude and technique could very well lead to my own peril.

And this time, when I was on the shoreline at Lock and Dam Number 10, I saw an eagle dip down and grab a fish right out of the Mississippi. With its catch clutched firmly in its talons, it flew to the Wisconsin side of the river and joined fourteen of its feathered fellows in the largest of trees. Yes, this time there were fifteen eagles perched among the branches of one large tree. That beat the three Sams I saw the last time. It was certainly worth the drive to Iowa to see them.

WHEN YOU GO: Today the easiest way to make the northbound trip along the Mississippi River is to drive the designated Great River Road stretches in Wisconsin, Iowa, and Minnesota. Start on either side of the river and look for the distinctive green-and-white signs with the ship's wheel insignia. By following these roads, you will get good views of the waterway and will pass through some of the towns where Thoreau and Mann's steamboat stopped. Occasionally you'll see railroad tracks and freight trains using the same route, passing between your car and the river. Don't be distracted by them. Up until now we were always looking for the rails that the travelers passed over. Now we have to change our focus and imagine instead the sight of the steamboat chugging up the river. If you prefer a closer experience, you might even consider taking one of the riverboat cruises that are available on Lake Pepin or in La Crosse, Wisconsin.

My preference is to drive up the Wisconsin side of the river, using mostly WI Route 35. Cross the Mississippi on one of the bridges at La Crosse, and take U.S. Route 61 in Minnesota, the rest of the way to the Twin Cities. The Iowa side is just as nice; but some of its side roads are not paved. Weather conditions should be considered if you make Iowa your north-bound choice.

FOR MORE INFORMATION

Iowa Great River Road, www.iowagreatriverroad.com.

Minnesota Great River Road, www.mnmississippiriver.com.

National Eagle Center, 50 Pembroke Avenue, Wabasha, MN 55981. Phone (877) 332-4537. www.nationaleaglecenter.net.

Upper Mississippi River National Wildlife and Fish Refuge, 51 East Fourth Street, Winona, MN 55987. Phone (507) 452-4232. www.fws.gov/midwest/UpperMississippiRiver.

Wisconsin Great River Road, www.wigreatriverroad.org.

RECOMMENDED READING

Mark Twain's *Life on the Mississippi*, his memoir of his time as a riverboat pilot. His book *Roughing It* is the story of what he did immediately after leaving the river. Both are available online and in a variety of print editions.

NOTES ON THIS CHAPTER

The Thoreau quote that begins, "The river is by far the most attractive highway," appears in the "Tuesday" chapter of *A Week on the Concord and Merrimack Rivers*. The subsequent passages about rivers come from his journal entries of September 2, 1856, and September 5, 1838. The quotes about Stockwell's panorama are from the essay "Walking." His description of Bronson Alcott is found in the "Former Inhabitants; and Winter Visitors" chapter of *Walden*. "Rivers are the natural highways" is from his journal, marked in the Dover edition as being written between 1842 and 1844. The "birds of the same genus migrate" entry was dated after March 13, 1846. The quotes about red-winged blackbirds come from entries dated May 14, 1853, and April 22, 1852. Those about eagles come from entries dated March 27, 1842; April 8, 1854; April 23, 1854; and March 29, 1858. Most bird quotes were found and gleaned from Helen Cruickshank's *Thoreau On Birds* (New York: McGraw-Hill Book Company, 1964).

The quotes from Horace Mann, Jr., come from his letter dated May 26, 1861.

Details about Stockwell's Mississippi panorama are few, as the painting was sold soon after its Boston performance and was never seen again. Newspaper accounts of the exhibit came from the November 2, 1849 issue of the *Boston Daily Atlas*; and the June 12 and June 19, 1849, issues of the Baltimore *Sun*. These articles were accessed through the America's

Historical Newspapers database and the Boston Public Library web site. Additional supporting documentation was found in John Francis McDermott's book, *The Lost Panoramas of the Mississippi* (Chicago: The University of Chicago Press, 1958) and Joseph Earl Arrington's article, "The Story of Stockwell's Panorama," in *Minnesota History* 33:7 (Autumn 1953), pp. 284-290.

The friendship of Bronson Alcott and Mary Newbury Adams is chronicled in both Alcott's journal and in his correspondence. During their first meeting, the two discovered that they shared a common relative through marriage. Bronson's daughter Anna Alcott had married John Bridge Pratt, who was "a nephew of Alvin Adams wife," according to a letter Mary Adams sent to her sister. Bronson's quotes are found in his journal entry of December 16, 1870; in a letter sent to Charles D. B. Mills on May 28, 1873; in a letter sent to Ellen A. Chandler on January 20, 1871; in a letter to Mary Newbury Adams on January 2, 1871; and in his journal entry for August 9, 1873. Mrs. Adams' description of Bronson Alcott is found in a letter to her sister dated January 3, 1871, published in "Alcott in Iowa: Two Letters of Mary Newbury Adams and Five Letters of A. Bronson Alcott" by Richard L. Herrnstadt in *Studies in the American Renaissance* 9 (1985), pp. 323-331.

Sources of information about Mary Newbury Adams include Benjamin F. Gue's *History of Iowa* (New York: Century History Company, 1903, volume 4); Louise R. Noun's *Strong-Minded Women: The Emergence of the Woman-Suffrage Movement in Iowa* (Cedar Falls, Iowa: The Iowa State University Press, 1969); and *The Biographical Dictionary of Iowa*, found online as part of the University of Iowa Press Digital Editions, at http://digital.lib.uiowa.edu.

The history of the cairn at the Thoreau house site at Walden Pond is available in a variety of sources. Bronson Alcott's journal entry for June 12-13, 1872, includes the description of Mary Newbury Adams' initial idea for the cairn. In the letter he wrote to her on August 21, 1878, he states that the pile "has grown a good deal this summer." The quote from the official report about the cairn's 1975 removal was found in "A History of the Cairn" by James Dawson, *Thoreau Society Bulletin* 232 (Summer 2000). Roland Robbins told of the "twenty-five percent" coverage in his book, *Discovery at Walden* (1947; reprinted in 1999 by the Thoreau Society, Lincoln, Mass.). Summary information was also found in W. Barksdale Maynard's *Walden Pond: A History* (New York: Oxford University Press, 2004).

Samuel Thatcher, Jr. (1805-1861) was the brother of George A. Thatcher of Bangor, Maine. George was married to Thoreau's cousin, Rebecca Billings Thatcher, and had acted as Thoreau's host and guide during his excursions to the Mount Katahdin area. Samuel's injuries are not outlined in detail in Thoreau's notebook or in Horace Mann's letters. But evidence suggests that the carriage accident left him at least partially paralyzed, if not completely incapacitated. He died on August 31, 1861, a month and a half after Henry and Horace returned to Concord. The obituary that appeared in local newspapers reported that Mr. Thatcher had suffered "a prolonged illness which he bore with great fortitude and patience." He was described as a "highly respected and esteemed" man who "ever manifested a deep interest in whatever tended to develop and advance the commercial, moral and social growth of the community in which he resided, as also of his adopted State." It's too bad he didn't have a chance to show Thoreau and Mann around Minnesota.

TRAVEL CHAPTER 11

Sunday, May 26, to Sunday, June 16, 1861
in and around St. Anthony, Minneapolis, and St. Paul, Minnesota
via various modes of transportation

Expenses:

At St. Pauls' (breakfast)	.50
To St. Anthony	.75
Brown paper at St. Anthony	.10
Toll "	.28
Board & washing"	7.50
To Hamilton's (150)	.75
Cheated	. 5
At L. Calhoun	6.00
At St. Anthony	.10
	1.00
To St. Pauls	.75
(At St Pauls (Merchant Hotel)	3.50
paper & bridge	.10
Pectoral	1.00

We are at a house here called the Tremont House, and from the window of my room I can see a little bit of the Falls of St. Anthony, though not enough to know how they look.

… After supper I went up onto the prarie [sic] back of the town and got a few flowers for Mr. Thoreau. He is doing very well now and I think will be a great deal better before long.

—Horace Mann Jr.'s letter of May 26, 1861

Humans can be resourceful and resilient creatures when they are called upon to be so. Henry Thoreau and young Horace Mann had already shown that they could entertain themselves during the days they spent botanizing at Niagara Falls. They had already proven their problem-solving prowess by successfully getting ready cash on the financially-strapped streets of Chicago. Now they faced their biggest challenge to date: devising an itinerary for exploring central Minnesota on their own. How quickly can change come to the plans of man!

ST. ANTHONY AND MINNEAPOLIS (MAY 26 TO JUNE 5)

Before the two men left the Thatcher residence, they were able to acquire some helpful information. Samuel Thatcher could barely write; but he took the time to pen a brief letter of introduction for the visitors to present to Dr. Charles L. Anderson, a local physician. In it, he explained that Thoreau had "come to Minnesota to Clear up his Bronchitis and to Botanize," and that he had "in company with him Mr. Mann son of late Horace Mann." Thatcher noted that "Any attention Shown to my friend Thoreau" would be personally gratifying to him, as he himself was incapacitated. Armed with that piece of paper and the possible recommendation to seek out a hotel located along the riverfront, Henry and Horace left the family members to concentrate on their more urgent duties.

In 1861, the city of St. Anthony was officially six years old and was home to about three thousand residents. Founders and newcomers alike fully expected this frontier town to someday bloom into a metropolis. And why shouldn't it be able to do so? The settlement sat close enough to the Falls of St. Anthony that businesses could benefit from harnessing the natural power of the river. The local lumber industry was already floating logs on the river, as they awaited transformation into consumable wood products. The city streets were filling with mills, shops, churches and people. St. Anthony was on its way up and was destined to become what one reporter predicted would be "the great manufacturing and commercial emporium for the country between Lake Michigan and the Rockies." No wonder Samuel Thatcher had found his way there from Maine a few years earlier.

Several hotels had already been built to serve travelers and to overlook the Mississippi River and the falls. Looming from the crest of a nearby ridge was the six-story Winslow House, a stone edifice that could easily have matched the elegance of Albany's Delavan House and many of the accommodations the men had seen in Chicago. But during the previous four years, the Winslow had attracted primarily a Southern audience. Tourists who steamed all the way up the Mississippi were only too glad to pay for the use of its opulent offerings. Once Mr. Lincoln prohibited through-traffic on the river, the hotel's guest roster dropped off considerably. The Winslow closed.

Five days before Thoreau and Mann reached St. Anthony, workers had begun to remove all of the furniture from what had once been the most expensive hotel in town.

Perhaps as a result, Thoreau and Mann chose to stay at the Tremont House on Main Street, at a rate of 75 cents per day. The Tremont, originally known as the Jarrett House, was a frame structure that had been built in 1856, and had been expanded in 1858. Horace soon ran off to explore the town and the surrounding prairie. Henry wrote at least one letter home, so that his sister Sophia would know of Mr. Thatcher's condition and of their need to change plans. Thoreau himself wasn't sure what their new schedule might entail. "I cannot see where I may be a fort-night hence," he told her. But mail from Massachusetts could still be sent to the Thatcher household, where the two men could easily retrieve it, as needed.

From left to right: The Winslow House, the Upton Block, and the Tremont House (formerly the Jarrett House), in then-St. Anthony in 1858. Photographer: Benjamin Franklin Upton. (*Courtesy of the Minnesota Historical Society*)

Henry and Horace spent their first full day in St. Anthony (Monday, May 27) visiting the closest and most obvious sites they could find on their own. The bridge to Nicollet Island was just a few blocks northwest of their hotel. So off they went to explore the large island in the middle of the Mississippi. It proved to offer a treasure trove of biodiversity. Thoreau used nearly three full pages of his field notebook to document the species they saw that day. Granted, most of these plants were rather commonplace. At ground level were at least three kinds of rock cress, as well as Virginia waterleaf (*Hydrophyllum virginianum*), Blue phlox (*Phlox divaricata*), Nodding chickweed (*Cerastium nutans*), Rock-brake (*Allosorus gracilis*), Violet wood sorrel (*Oxalis violacea*), Common plantain (*Plantago major*), and Shepherd's purse (*Capsella bursa-pastoris*). The Hoary puccoon (*Lithospermum canescens*) with its yellow blossoms was "the showiest flower now," as it had been when the two traveled days before "in Michigan & Illinois."

In the air or around the prickly ash trees (*Zanthoxylum americanum*) were birds like the Killdeer (*Charadrius vociferous*), the Brown thrasher (*Toxostoma rufum*), and the Eastern kingbird (*Tyrannus tyrannus*). The men had heard and seen a Red-headed woodpecker (*Melanerpes erythrocephalus*) drilling into a telegraph pole near the St. Anthony post office. They heard tree frogs (*Hyla*) as they walked along the prairie. Surely exposure to such sights and sounds as these were why the two men had come to the American West.

From the island, the men could see Minneapolis, the community of 5,800 residents, growing just beyond the five-cent toll bridge that led to the opposite shore. Then they could turn back east to gaze upon St. Anthony. They could probably spot the Winslow House and the Tremont House as familiar landmarks, in addition to the sturdy limestone building of the nearby Universalist Society church. Just north of the island, they inspected the floating boom in the water. Horace mentioned this barrier to his mother in a letter and explained that it was designed "to catch logs and keep them from going over the falls." "Look out the meaning of Boom in a dictionary," he advised her. To the south lay the falls, Hennepin Island, and a few smaller outcroppings. These "inaccessible islands … will some time be entirely washed away," speculated Horace, "for they seem to be going slowly now." He was learning to read the landscape as well as his teacher and traveling companion did.

Once the men returned to the mainland, they wandered around the perimeter of St. Anthony and onto the land outside of the city limits. They may have seen prairies being plowed under in Illinois, but here in Minnesota, it was not yet fully succumbing to the hand of man. While walking among the native grasses and wildflowers, they came upon a singular habitat that was new to their New England eyes: "oak openings." Regular fires would clear out the brush of the usual forest understory. The fire-resistant bur oaks were left to stand apart from one another and were able to stretch out their branches. Enough space was left between the trees that a wagon could easily be driven among and through them. "The burr oaks are low & spreading," Henry noted, with "the bark generally darker than a white oak which grows in the woods. They are from 1 to 3 rods apart." This oak-hickory-butternut ecosystem and the savanna's oak openings were unlike the typical northeastern woodland scenery of Massachusetts.

Less than a mile southeast from their hotel sat the campus of the University of Minnesota, which had been created in the previous decade, before the territory was even a state. "Old Main" had been constructed as its first building in 1858, and it was around this structure that Henry and Horace now hiked. The grounds looked nothing like the famous and well-manicured yard at Harvard, Henry's historic alma mater. On this property, the natural habitat had been allowed to intrude. "The Minnesota University here is set in the midst of such an oak opening—& it looks quite artificial," Thoreau wrote. Though he wondered if the trees minded being included as part of an academic arena, he surmised that in the end they would probably "thrive as if nothing had happened" to them. He spoke merely of the oaks, of course, and not of the scholars who sat or studied or sauntered underneath their branches.

Oak openings grace the lawn in front of Old Main at the University of Minnesota in 1888. (*Courtesy of the Minnesota Historical Society*)

DR. CHARLES L. ANDERSON, TOUR GUIDE

On Tuesday, May 28, Henry Thoreau and young Horace Mann used their letter of introduction to seek the services of Dr. Charles L. Anderson as an impromptu tour guide. During the nine days the two were based in St. Anthony, they would spend four of those days in the company of this knowledgeable man.

Charles Lewis Anderson was 33 years old. He was not only a physician but was also an avid amateur scientist. He had been born in Virginia, and had been raised in Indiana. He earned an undergraduate degree from Franklin College and a medical degree from Indiana Asbury University (later renamed DePauw University). He relocated to St. Anthony in 1854, and set up his first medical practice there. He later moved his office to Minneapolis, where he and his wife Meriel now lived with their two small daughters. Dr. Anderson therefore turned out to have valuable connections on both sides of the Mississippi River. During his tenure in the area, he served as the Superintendent of Schools for Hennepin County, which covered the cities of St. Anthony, Minneapolis, and a large tract of land to the north and west. He was vice-president of the Union Medical Society. And in 1861, he also held the office of vice-president for the Minneapolis Athenaeum. The men from Massachusetts were lucky enough to have landed in the lap of a key man in this region.

Over the course of four separate days (May 28, May 29, May 31, and June 3), Dr. Anderson used his own carriage to drive Henry and Horace around Minneapolis and to other sites west of the river. They visited Lake Calhoun and Lake Harriet. They saw the St. Peter's River, also known as the Minnesota River, which emptied into the Mississippi just below Fort Snelling. They played tourist at Minnehaha Falls. Henry Thoreau had been correct in assuming that a local resident would know exactly the kinds of features he would be interested in seeing. He had no way of predicting that such a resource would be found in Charles Anderson instead of in Samuel Thatcher.

During their outings, Dr. Anderson surely regaled his new friends with historical information and supplied them with a few tips about the native plants and animals. Their second day together, Wednesday, May 29, would have provided several opportunities to do so. That was the day the three men rode first to Minnehaha Falls and then proceeded to Fort Snelling.

Minnehaha Creek begins at Lake Minnetonka, west of Minneapolis, and empties into the Mississippi River more than twenty miles later. Not far from its outlet, it makes a dramatic cascade over a bluff to create Minnehaha Falls. The waterfall was originally known as Brown's Falls. Its name was changed soon after Henry Wadsworth Longfellow penned and popularized his epic poem, *The Song of Hiawatha*, in 1855. Longfellow had never visited the area, but he had seen illustrations of Brown's Falls, and he used that setting in his work. He forced his fictional hero Hiawatha to leave the Ojibway lands of Michigan and Wisconsin and to head even farther west to find his wife:

> In the land of the Dacotahs,
> Where the Falls of Minnehaha
> Flash and gleam among the oak-trees,
> Laugh and leap into the valley.
>   There the ancient Arrow-maker
> Made his arrow-heads of sandstone,
> Arrow-heads of chalcedony,
> Arrow-heads of flint and jasper,
> Smoothed and sharpened at the edges,
> Hard and polished, keen and costly,
>   With him dwelt his dark-eyed daughter,
> Wayward as the Minnehaha,
> With her moods of shade and sunshine,
> Eyes that smiled and frowned alternate,
> Feet as rapid as the river,
> Tresses flowing like the water,
> And as musical a laughter:
> And he named her from the river,
> From the water-fall he named her,
> Minnehaha, Laughing Water.

Odds are good that Charles, Henry and/or Horace knew and could recite some portions of Longfellow's lengthy Indian story, if not those specific lines. *The Song of Hiawatha* was the most popular poem of the nineteenth century, having sold 100,000 copies in its first two years of publication. Longfellow had been one of Thoreau's professors at Harvard. Now here they were, standing at *the* Minnehaha Falls, as featured in the literary masterpiece. It certainly could not compare to the waterworks that Henry and Horace had seen at Niagara several weeks earlier, but it was nice enough. And now, it too was famous.

Horace later described Minnehaha Falls to his mother as being "very beautiful." And even though he had an opportunity to let loose his youthful exuberance, he chose to be sensible and grown-up in the company of the two older men. "The water falls about 60 feet and there is a hollow behind it so that you can go there though it is very wet so I did not try it," he said. Instead, he played the role of scientist as he collected fossils and other specimens in the area. The group "staid around there for a while," and then they moved on to the nearby fort.

Northerners expected the War Between the States to last only three months. That's as long as it would take to straighten out those wayward brethren south of the Mason-Dixon line, they thought. Coincidentally, three months is how long Henry David Thoreau had originally planned to be away from his family, his friends, and his hometown of Concord. Was such an itinerary merely an accident, or was it part of a deliberate withdrawal on his part? Was Thoreau hoping to avoid all talk and news of war by being on the road for the presumed duration of the struggle? If so, his tactic was not much of a success. He and Horace could not escape the war. They witnessed evidence of it as they saw units of local men assembling, training, or leaving for battle, in town after town.

The scene at Fort Snelling was no exception. This site had been a government outpost since the 1820s, and was originally set up to defend the country's northwestern frontier. From its perch on a bluff above the confluence of the Mississippi and Minnesota Rivers, Fort Snelling was well poised to both monitor traffic on the water and to encourage trade among the trappers, the settlers, and the Indians. At the same time, its surrounding stone wall offered solid protection for the compound. Henry described it as a "Fort of limestone (tawny or buffish) 10 feet high at the angle of the 2 rivers." Inside were enough barracks to house both enlisted men and officers. Additional structures stored equipment or provided the standard amenities for whatever military community might be based there.

But once Minnesota became a state in 1858, the need for such a facility at that location diminished. The fort was sold. Plans were developed to lay out a residential town on that acreage instead. Fortunately, not much of the physical work had begun on that project. Now the former post was once again bustling with activity, as volunteers gathered there for training before leaving for the South. According to Thoreau's notes, 600 men were currently getting instruction at the post. Three hundred others had already left on their trip downriver that morning. Word had probably not yet reached the West that Union and Confederate forces were at that moment clashing at Aquia Creek in Virginia.

Horace was judgmental in his assessment of the proposed troops. He wrote that he and his companions had seen "a little of the regimental drill at four o'clock; they are all green at it." He may have been comparing them with the neighbors he had seen practicing back home on the Concord town common, a month earlier. And while Horace might at one point have considered joining their cause, perhaps he was now relieved to have another obligation that demanded his attention. To choose otherwise at this moment would be to let down both his mother and Mr. Thoreau. He could do neither.

HORACE'S SHOTGUN AND KEG

In fact, the seventeen-year-old was waging his own kind of battle: that of Man vs. Nature. He had brought along his trusty shotgun in order to "collect" animals during the trip. And now that he and his fellow traveler were planning to stay in one place for an extended period of time, he could attend to this work in earnest.

Henry Thoreau had once followed the same, accepted habit of the day: that of killing animals to study them. John James Audubon had used that very technique in order to create his well-known, beautiful, and accurate renderings of American birds. But once Horace began to bring such broken and lifeless bodies to Thoreau for identification, the naturalist of Concord railed against the practice. At least he did so in the pages of his private journal. Whether or not he lectured Horace in person is not known. Perhaps Henry hoped that the young man would eventually reach a more advanced level of research on his own; and that one day, the behavior of the living creature would prove to be a more valuable study than the mere details of its color and appearance. But for now, Horace was interested only in acquisition; and the more, the better.

On Monday, May 27, Horace made an agreement with a man in St. Anthony. He gleefully wrote to his mother about it:

> I went to a Drug store in town here, and got a five gallon keg into which I had some alcohol put and I put my birds and animals in it. I can leave it at the drug store as long as I please. When I fill it I shall send it home. The gentleman at the drug store is named Charles Crawford and he is a very pleasant young man, and helps me a great deal by allowing my keg to be there as I should have no place to put it if he did not.

Mr. Crawford happened to hail from Massachusetts. He was not only a druggist, but was also a member of the local board of education. Crawford probably recognized and supported the visiting youth's scientific endeavors. Now that Horace had a place to store his bounty, he set out to do some actual collecting. He entered the prairie, armed with his weapon.

Horace did not report all of his conquests to his mother, so the actual number and identification of his specimens remains unknown. But from his brief written references, it is obvious that he had a penchant for aiming at passenger pigeons and rose-breasted grosbeaks. Among the fur-bearers, he snagged several chipmunks and at least one red squirrel. The best find of all was probably the abundance of Thirteen-lined ground squirrels (*Spermophilus tridecemlineatus*) that were indigenous to the plains and prairies. These were new animals to the men from Massachusetts. Dr. Anderson called them "gophers." These creatures were bigger than chipmunks and smaller than groundhogs. As the three men made their way back to St. Anthony from Fort Snelling, young Horace blasted away at regular intervals in order to get "some more birds and gophers." His companions were probably chatting about wildflowers and trees, or speculating about the abilities of the pseudo-soldiers they had seen at the fort.

Henry Thoreau was also intrigued by the gophers. After he saw one in the company of Charles Anderson during their first field trip together, Henry wrote that it made "a queer note like a plover, over his hole." Anderson identified the animal for him and showed him where its burrow was. And before too long, Thoreau was including gopher details in his notebook:

> The tridecemlineatus—Dirty grayish white beneath—above dirty brown with 6 dirty tawny—or clay colored or very light brown lines—alternating with broad (3 times as broad) dark brown lines stripes—the last having an interrupted line of square spots of the same color with the first mentioned—running down their middle—reminding me of the rude pattern of some Indian work—porcupine quills—baskets & pottery—

These were the findings of a scientist who was intent upon the close examination of his subject matter. In spite of his personal opinions, Thoreau had been curious enough about the gopher to want to inspect and handle its body after his friend's shotgun gave him the chance to. He could not resist the temptation for a better look, and his choice was certainly understandable. He had never before seen a Thirteen-lined ground squirrel. They were not native to New England.

Later, after the duo returned home, Henry was able to incorporate the interesting rodents into his "Dispersion of Seeds" report. He described their affinity for the fruit of basswood trees:

> Great quantities of bass nuts are swept down the streams which the trees overhang in August and are carried in freshets still further inland, and they are even blown over the snow and ice to great distances. In Minnesota I have found them in the pouches of the gophers on the prairie.

It would take more than a century for that note to be formally published.

Horace spent more than two and a half weeks filling his keg. He probably gave no thought or consideration to any of the possible consequences of his actions. Who knows how many infants he also condemned to death whenever the adults failed to return to the nest or to the burrow? Those were the days when The West teemed with life, and it seemed to all be there for the taking. The buffalo may have gone away, but the passenger pigeons and the gophers were still around in vast numbers. Horace sent his mother a drawing of himself, shooting a bird out of a tree. "I would have shot a cart load more if my arms had not been so sore from the old gun kicking," he wrote. Surely one keg full of critters, procured by just one man, would not make a dent in any one of those populations.

On Saturday, June 15, Horace sealed the keg and arranged for it to be sent back to Concord. He gave his mother advance instructions for what she and his brother George should do with his plunder.

> I shall send two things, a keg and a box from St. Anthony on Saturday, the keg will contain birds and animals in alcohol and the box a few stones and some clothes which I shall send home to get out of the way, also some of Mr. Thoreau's clothes and on top I shall put the plants which I get here; I wish that you would open the box and take out the plants and put them where they will dry and if you are willing perhaps you had better look them over a little and see that none of them gets moldy. George may take the bung out of the head of the keg and if it is not quite full of alcohol perhaps he had better fill it up but I do not want him to open it.

Horace would have a lot of follow-up processing to do once he got home. He wanted to save the enjoyment of doing that work for himself.

HENRY'S ZEAL FOR LOCAL RESEARCH

Henry Thoreau had acquired a lot of firsthand knowledge about the natural world: about the plants and animals that could be found in his day in the northeastern corner of the United States of America. Here, in the American West, he found many species that were as familiar to him as old friends. Much of the ground-cover greenery here was commonplace. But some discoveries were startlingly new. The oak openings of the prairie and the existence of the Thirteen-lined ground squirrels each brought home the fact to Thoreau that he was not in Concord anymore. Could his scientific background, as extensive as it was, really translate to this region in the middle of the country?

He once worried about this very dilemma and gave voice to it in his journal long before he ever suspected that he would venture this far west:

> A man is worth most to himself and to others, whether as an observer, or poet, or neighbor, or friend, where he is most himself, most contented and at home. There his life is the most intense and he loses the fewest moments. Familiar and surrounding objects are the best symbols and illustrations of his life. If a man who has had deep experiences should endeavor to describe them in a book of travels, it would be to use the language of a wandering tribe instead of a universal language. The poet had made the best roots in his native soil of any man, and is the hardest to transplant. The man who is often thinking that it is better to be somewhere else than where he is excommunicates himself. If a man is rich and strong anywhere, it must be on his native soil. Here I have been these forty years learning the language of these fields that I may the better express myself. If I should travel to the prairies, I should much less understand them, and my past life would serve me but ill to describe them. Many a weed here stands for more of life to me than the big trees of California would if I should go there. We only need travel enough to give our intellects an airing.

Minnesota was now giving Henry's intellect a fair airing. He drew first upon his personal foundation of natural facts. Then he added the authority of the botany manuals that he had brought with him on the journey. Complementing those sources was Dr. Anderson's stockpile of local expertise. The tri-fold combination offered good results.

Every day Thoreau went out, took a look around, and documented what he saw in his field notebook. If he could identify a plant by scientific name, he did so. Only on occasion did he resort to using a common name for any plant. If the species was an unfamiliar one, he described its color and appearance with enough detail that he could look it up later in a reference book at home. And as he so diligently recorded back in Concord, he also noted the status of the plant, if he deemed it important. "In bloom," "in flower," "in fruit," or "not out" were some of his designations. When paired with the dates of observation, his pages could reflect the growing trends throughout the entire route of the Journey West.

Henry recorded the individual birds and plants he saw on Nicollet Island, on Hennepin Island, and at Minnehaha Falls, Lake Calhoun, and Lake Harriet. But being able to fully interpret and appreciate the wider landscape required historical knowledge as well.

Thoreau had already read a variety of travel narratives that covered this part of the country. He had tackled at least four books in Henry Rowe Schoolcraft's six-volume set, *Historical and Statistical Information Respecting the History, Condition, and Prospects of the Indian Tribes of the United States.* This was the work that had inspired Professor Longfellow to invent the story of Hiawatha and Minnehaha. Thoreau had also read Schoolcraft's *Narrative of an Expedition through the Upper Mississippi to Lake Itasca,* almost ten years earlier. He was now covering some of that same ground himself.

Reading the history *of* a place, while *in* that place, would have many advantages. The reader could understand what the authors were referring to. He could see the information on the printed page come to life, just by looking out the nearest window.

For several days now, Henry Thoreau had been reading articles in a periodical called *Transactions of the Wisconsin State Agricultural Society.* He had borrowed the 1852 issue, presumably from Charles Anderson, and had been methodically working his way through the thick volume. Here he read reports describing Wisconsin's plants and animals, and then he jotted down the most interesting findings in his field notebook for future reference. Surely Minnesota's version of nature would be closer to the kind found in Wisconsin than it would be to the natural history of Massachusetts. These were eye-opening treatises for Henry.

According to Horace, Saturday, June 1, began as a cloudy day. His weather forecast might explain why Thoreau's pages for that day consist entirely of passages copied from a variety of published sources. Henry was obviously using either Dr. Anderson's personal library, or he had been given access to the resources of the Minneapolis Athenaeum. The Athenaeum had been organized by a group of local men two years earlier, and its shelves were just beginning to fill. Still, either collection might have had the sources Thoreau used that day, which included several past issues of *The Annals of the Minnesota Historical Society,* the 1860 compendium of *Collections of the Minnesota Historical Society,* and J. W. Bond's book, *Minnesota and Its Resources* (New York: Redfield, 1853). From these authorities, Thoreau quoted facts about the Dakota Indians and the origins of the state.

Especially helpful was an article he found that had been penned by the current Governor of Minnesota, Alexander Ramsey. Ramsey wrote a retrospective that detailed the discoveries of the primary explorers to the region. Thoreau repeated their magical names in his notebook: Pierre Le Sueur, Jonathan Carver, Lewis Cass, Henry Rowe Schoolcraft, Jean Nicollet, John Charles Fremont, Stephen H. Long, William Hypolitus Keating, Zebulon

Montgomery Pike, Claude-Jean Allouez, Louis Hennepin, Jacques Marquette, William Morrison, and George Catlin. He had already read many of their expedition accounts, but not each and every one. Perhaps he intended the register to be a potential library request list. Once he returned to Concord, he could search out the valuable narratives that he had somehow missed. He could fill in the gaps.

The facts from the histories were interesting, and so were the identities of the various species that were encountered on the prairie. But Henry Thoreau was by now intrigued by natural *processes* as well. Nine months earlier, when he had spoken before the Middlesex Agricultural Society, his topic had been "The Succession of Forest Trees." He explained to his audience the intertwining of pines and oaks. Cut one, and the other one will undoubtedly arise, he told them. Nature "is all the while planting the oaks amid the pines without our knowledge;" and when someone chanced to mow down a stand of pines, he would unwittingly "rescue an oak forest." He had seen this theory proven many times across the landscape of New England. No one, until then, had seen fit to document or publicize the phenomenon.

Out here on the prairie, Thoreau now appeared to be captivated by the concept of the oak openings. He mentioned them often in his notebook and tried to grasp their development and significance. "Keep out fire & the oak-openings will grow up," he wrote. "Oak openings with hazel bushes the rule." Both Hazelnut (*Corylus Americana*) and Northern bedstraw (*Galium boreale*) appeared to be "very common in O. openings," he noted. Eventually he saw more connections: "In O. openings—with hazel & willow & aspen—roses & smooth sumacs—& lonicera [Honeysuckle]." It was a much bigger picture than he might have imagined from first glance.

It was during one of his trips to the lakes with Horace and Dr. Anderson that Thoreau had an epiphany regarding Midwestern tree succession. Here there were no pines to interact with the other species. But he could spot a definite trend, as species advanced from the water's edge to the open land beyond. He documented this newly-found progression as: "1st aspen & willow—Then elm & ash—& at last oak." A bold stroke of his pen immediately followed this passage. Was it a stray slip of the hand, or a deliberate exclamation point? If it was the latter, then Thoreau might have been showing his excitement at finally understanding what was going on here. It was not the pine-oak see-saw that he knew so well from back home. Nature had created another pattern to follow, a true path of tree succession. The sequence could be studied even more diligently around the shores of Lake

Calhoun, Lake Harriet and throughout the surrounding plains.

Henry and Horace's forays with Charles Anderson always led them away from the river and St. Anthony and Minneapolis, and almost always took them farther west. This was the region where Thoreau had his revelations about oak openings and about tree succession. Clearly, this was the direction where the best opportunities for botanizing and field research lay. Clearly, this was the area that the two men from Massachusetts now needed to concentrate on. A relocation was in order.

LAKE CALHOUN (JUNE 5 TO JUNE 14)

On Wednesday, June 5, Henry and Horace left the Tremont House in St. Anthony and headed west. They hired a coach to take them four miles southwest of Minneapolis and to the southern edge of Lake Calhoun. According to Thoreau's expense account, the two men must have split the total travel cost of $1.50. Somehow Henry lost five cents in the exchange and felt the need to document that indignity as well.

Late Spring had burst into the warm days of full Summer. Prairie land passed into plains. The communities and commercial interests that lined the banks of the Mississippi River were left behind in favor of the more rural setting of Hennepin County's lake district: Lake Calhoun, Lake Harriet, Lake of the Isles, and Cedar Lake. The possibilities for scientific exploration seemed endless here. And at the daily rate of just 50 cents, the men were saving money at the same time. What a great deal!

A few days later, Horace described the new place to his mother:

> You see by the date of this letter that we are staying at a house on the edge of Lake Calhoun. It is a beautiful sheet of water, perhaps a mile and a half or three quarters the longest way and nearly a mile the other way in breadth; it has an outlet by which it MTT [empties] itself into Lake Harriet, which lies a little ways to the SE of here, and that again MTT into the Minnehaha and goes over the falls. We are staying at the house of a Mrs. Hamilton, a widow, and one of the first settlers near this lake.

Elizabeth Hamilton was an Illinois native, and her husband had been from Kentucky. All of the people Henry and Horace were meeting in Minnesota were from someplace else. These were the true pioneers who were serving to populate and Americanize a brand-new state. How different they were from the firmly entrenched residents of Massachusetts!

With the freedom the open plains gave them, Henry and Horace went their separate ways. Each man could let his own interests and discoveries dictate his daily activities. Horace still carried his shotgun and still took animals at whim. St. Anthony wasn't really that far away from the lake, so he could walk or ride back and could add more specimens to his keg at Crawford's drug store whenever he needed to. But he was collecting plants by now, too. Perhaps Thoreau was exerting some influence in that direction. Henry had brought his own plant press with him, in anticipation of encountering some species unknown to New Englanders. Without a similar device at his convenience, Horace used the best flattening agent he could think of: a bed post. It worked just as well.

Thoreau and Mann had spent nearly a month on the road together. They had shared railroad cars, steamboat cabins, and hotel rooms. By this time they were as familiar with one another as any friends could be. Each was no doubt beginning to adopt some of the mannerisms, speech, and traits of the other. The tendency would have been natural and unconscious. Horace's mother could probably begin to hear Mr. Thoreau's voice in her son's letters:

> The house is surrounded with very thick woods which is full of great big musquitoes [sic], so when you walk in them, particularly near nightfall, they swarm around you in such a cloud that you can hardly see through them. There are also a great many [passenger] pigeons in the woods back of the house, (though I should hardly know them from a musquito here by *size*).

Wasn't equating birds and irritating insects using the same kind of sarcasm and humor that might be found in a passage of *Walden*? What seventeen-year-old would employ such an analogy?

Mr. Thoreau might not have been holding formal classes in the natural sciences for his student body of one, but Horace was learning from his teacher, nonetheless. The young man eagerly passed on his new-found knowledge of the Western environment in his letters.

> The "oak openings" on the praries [sic] consist of small oaks scattered around at some distance (1 to 10 rods) from one another and where the fire has not run for several years the hazel bushes spring up; also little oaks and aspens, and after a little longer basswood trees, which I think are planted by the little spermophili (stripped [sic] squirrels) carrying the nuts from the woods to their holes to eat, and then the brush begins to get thicker and thicker till it is very hard to get through it.

Horace may have been partially parroting his traveling companion, but he was also witnessing the connections between certain plants and certain animals. He understood the same process of succession that had fascinated Thoreau.

As for Henry, he was busy with his own daily observations of plants, trees, and animals. The American Plains were certainly not devoid of wildlife; but they required a different way of looking, in order to spot species and patterns. He continued to be intrigued by the kinds of vegetation that took over after humans left the land alone.

> In a pasture again grown up to hazel—snowberry bush—smooth sumac—viburnum—young oaks &c—(cleared some 6 or 7 years ago) now pretty much as it was then. Of small burr [sic] oaks at wide intervals.

But animals also caught his eye, including a soft-shelled turtle (*Triomyx*) that he spied in or around one of the lakes.

> shell brown spotted with dark brown—with a narrow light brown edge—Very webbed feet - & a peculiar snout 3/16 inch long—head looking much like the short pointed tail–The whole creature very flat—shell about 7 or more inches long depth about 1 ? inches–

We can only hope that Henry left the turtle to enjoy another day. It was much too big to fit into Horace's keg.

In a way, Henry Thoreau seemed to be repeating his past. He had left St. Anthony and Minneapolis and had relocated to the edge of a lake removed from most, but not all, of society. But this time, he had chosen to do so in order to study nature first, and to write about the experience as a result. When he moved to Walden Pond from the town center of Concord sixteen years earlier, his intentions had been reversed. He "went to the woods" not only to "live deliberately," but to have the time and space in which to pen the manuscript for his first book, *A Week on the Concord and Merrimack Rivers*. His natural observations had certainly been an important part of his experience by the pond, but they were secondary to his main task of writing.

And although Lake Calhoun and Lake Harriet may have looked similar to Walden Pond and Flints Pond on a map, they were vastly different in real life. Thoreau measured Concord's Walden and had found it to contain about 61 acres of water. Flints Pond, in neighboring Lincoln, was about twice that size. West of Minneapolis, Lake Harriet held more than 340 acres of water, and Lake Calhoun came in at more than 420 surface acres. These were the biggest inland bodies of water that Henry Thoreau had ever had a chance to live by and explore. Perhaps that fact had also been a key to his decision to move there.

Of course, the habitat was not quite the same as the one surrounding Walden Pond. Walden was nestled into a glacial depression, with gravelly ridges rising from every inch of its shoreline. Lake Calhoun and Lake Harriet mirrored the plains that surrounded them. They were flat. They shimmered in the sun like glittering horizon lines; like mirages amongst a grass-covered desert. Some of the terrain around them did rise and fall into smallish hillocks. Mrs. Hamilton's house was even perched upon one of them. But those slight heights did not impede the grander view that could be enjoyed in every direction.

At the lakes, Horace collected clams and other shells to add to his keg. Henry took a much closer look:

> See a scum on the smooth surface of the lake 3 or 4 feet fromshore—The color of the sand of the shore—like pollen & lint—which I took it to be. Taking some up in my hand I was surprised to find it the sand of the shore—sometimes pretty large grains 1/10 inch diam—but most 1/20 or less some dark brown some white or yellowish—some minute but perfectly regular oval pebbles of white quartz I suppose that the water rises gently lifts up a layer of sand where it is slightly cemented by some glutinous matter for I felt a slight stickiness in my hand after the (gravel or) sand was shaken off.—It was in irregular oblong patches 3 or 4 inches long

Nothing escaped his attention: not even the tiniest remnants of rock that floated, and eventually settled, upon the floor of Lake Calhoun.

Henry Thoreau and young Horace Mann swam in the lakes. They ate fish almost every day, and they drank from the lake. Thoreau had recovered from the intestinal discomfort caused by the water of Chicago. Horace was doing very well, too. The days were warm, and thunderstorms rumbled across the plains at night. Theirs may have been an idyllic life. Perhaps it even seemed as if they had found an Eden out on the edge of the prairie.

They had been staying at Mrs. Hamilton's house for nearly a week when Henry got the urge to complete some unfinished business. Perhaps he was skimming through the pages of his field notebook and happened to land upon some of his earlier trip notes. Or maybe his hostess innocently asked him if he was indeed discovering all of the plants and trees that he intended to find in Minnesota and the Midwest. No matter what triggered it, Henry's attention was turned back to the days when he and Horace were riding across Michigan and Illinois: back to the time when they saw pink and white flowering trees in the distance. Had those been crab apple trees, after all? How could he be sure?

Unfortunately, the calendar had now turned to June 11. Three weeks had passed since the men had crossed those states by train. Three weeks had passed since they had seen those trees in bloom. What were the odds that Henry might be able to locate similar trees, here and now, so much farther north? Surely their flowering days would be nearing their end, or they might be entirely finished altogether. Without the colorful petals as a guide, he would not be able to recognize or identify them.

As soon as Henry decided to resume his search for the elusive crab, he asked the nearest expert he had access to: Elizabeth Hamilton. He later documented the resulting pursuit in his notebook:

> She said the wild apple grew about her premises—her husband 1st saw it on a ridge by the lake shore—They had dug up several & set them out but all died—(The settlers also set out the wild plum & thimble berry &c) So I went & searched in that very unlikely place—but could find nothing like it though Hamilton said there was one there 3 feet higher than the lake—but I brought home a thorn [hawthorn] in bloom instead—& asked if that was it. She then gave me more particular directions - & I searched again faithfully & this time I brought home an Amelanchier as the nearest of kin—doubting if the apple had ever been seen there—but she knew both these plants. Her husband had first discovered it by the fruit—but she had not seen it in bloom here—

Back and forth Henry went. Mrs. Hamilton sent him to various points on her property. He ventured to those places and found other species instead. When he brought those samples home, she would shake her head and would send him out again. To put it bluntly, this technique wasn't bearing any fruit at all. Was no one else in the area able to offer better advice?

Henry Thoreau left the house again, and this time he headed for another residence instead of a tree-filled field. According to his notes, he called on a man named Fitch, and they talked about the crab apple. "Said it was found the same they had in Vermont," wrote Henry. His companion may very well have been the Reverend Jonathan Fitch, a 61-year-old Episcopalian minister who was then assigned as a missionary to that part of Minnesota. Rev. Fitch was a Vermont native. And if he didn't know everything there was to know about botany, at least he knew his fellow lakeside dwellers pretty well. Fitch recommended that Thoreau find Jonathan Grimes, a local miller and farmer. Off Henry went.

Jonathan Taylor Grimes was probably the nearest and best expert when it came to fruit-bearing trees and plants. The Virginian had brought his family to Minnesota in 1855. From his 160-acre farm near Lake Harriet, he did a brisk business in raising and selling fruit to local residents. His flour mill was also about to land a deal with the government to supply provisions to the troops for the duration of the war. Mr. Grimes was both knowledgeable and savvy.

When Thoreau arrived at the Grimes property, he learned that the man he sought was elsewhere, running an errand. One of Grimes's sons started Henry on his search for the crab apple tree on their property:

> The boy showed me some of the trees he had set out this spring but they had all died. having a long tap root & being taken up too late. but then I was convinced by the sight of the just expanding though withered leaf—& plucked a solitary withered flower best to analyze—finally stayed & went in search of it with the father in his pasture—where I found it first myself—quite a cluster of them.

At last, Henry Thoreau had come face to face with the elusive crab apple tree! Was he at all disappointed that the fruit looked more like sprigs of cherries than individual, fist-filling apples? Did he try nibbling one of the tiny green orbs, as he collected his specimens? In any event, he must have considered this treasure hunt to be a scientific success.

After he returned to Concord, Thoreau wrote a narrative about the search. His story was eventually included in an essay titled "Wild Apples."

> I never saw the crab-apple till May, 1861. I had heard of it through Michaux, but more botanists, so far as I know, have not treated it as of any peculiar importance. Thus it was a half-fabulous tree to me. I contemplated a pilgrimage to the "Glades," a portion of Pennsylvania where it was said to grow to perfection. I thought of sending to a nursery for it, but doubted if they had it, or would distinguish it from European varieties. At last I had occasion to go to Minnesota, and on entering Michigan I began to notice from the cars a tree with handsome rose-colored flowers. At first I thought it some variety of thorn; but it was not long before the truth flashed

on me, that this was my long-sought crab-apple. It was the prevailing flowering shrub or tree to be seen from the cars at that season of the year,—about the middle of May. But the cars never stopped before one, and so I was launched on the bosom of the Mississippi without having touched one, experiencing the fate of Tantalus. On arriving at St. Anthony's Falls, I was sorry to be told that I was too far north for the crab-apple. Nevertheless I succeeded in finding it about eight miles west of the Falls; touched it and smelled it, and secured a lingering corymb of flowers for my herbarium. This must have been near its northern limit.

Horticulturalists would agree. The typical crab apple (*Malus coronaria*) had its true origins in East Asia. The shrubby tree is said to have been introduced to North America in 1724. Its natural growing range extended from central and western New York and Pennsylvania, through the Ohio River valley, and north into Michigan and Indiana. It flourished as far south as the Appalachian states, and in Alabama and Arkansas. But it was quite unusual to find it in Minnesota.

Henry later wrote that he had dealt with some people "of southern birth" while visiting Minnesota. He could have been referring to Dr. Charles Anderson and to Jonathan Grimes, who were both from Virginia. Did any of his conversations with them turn to the current troubles with the Southern states? Did those former Southerners try to keep in touch with friends and family members who were left back home? If so, they had just gotten some bad news. The U.S. Post-master General announced that, as of June 1, 1861, mail service was being suspended to any state that had seceded. Envelopes addressed to Southern cities would end up in the Dead Letter bin instead. "Post Offices will be opened in the rebel States as the United States forces advance," read the published report. The Union was expecting victory. Mail delivery would resume accordingly.

But that could take a while. Word came via telegraph that the first sizable battle of the war had taken place at Big Bethel in southeastern Virginia on June 10. By all accounts, the Confederates had won that day. They had sustained just ten casualties and had lost only one soldier. The Northern side tallied eighteen deaths, with another 53 men wounded and five missing. The details seemed to indicate a lot of confusion, especially among the Union troops. Some of their soldiers had been dressed in gray and had thus attracted what would later be called "friendly fire" from Union guns. This report did not instill much confidence in the residents north of the Mason-Dixon line. It looked as if this struggle would take more than three months to resolve after all.

Both Horace and Henry insisted in their letters that they paid no attention to the war news while they traveled. Any previous skirmishes they had heard about may have seemed incidental. But the men could neither avoid nor ignore the talk about what happened at Big Bethel in Virginia. This war was real. Their kinsmen were being killed down South. Perhaps this news was enough to make the two men think about turning around and returning to Concord. They may have even considered taking a more northern route home, just in case.

At the same time, the two men stumbled upon or were shown an advertisement that now appeared in local newspapers. A "Grand Pleasure Excursion" was being planned to visit the Lower Sioux Agency in Redwood, Minnesota. Steamboat passengers would have a chance to see "nearly five thousand Indians," the announcement predicted. Henry and Horace must have agreed that this was an opportunity they could not let pass before they left Minnesota. Since the flotilla was scheduled to leave from a dock in St. Paul on June 17, the men had to head back to the Mississippi River towns in order to join the party. They would have to say goodbye to Mrs. Hamilton and say goodbye to the Lake Calhoun region with its oak openings, its fascinating plants and animals, and its "musquitoes."

ST. ANTHONY AND ST. PAUL (JUNE 14 TO JUNE 17)

Henry Thoreau and young Horace Mann left Mrs. Hamilton's boarding house just after noon on Friday, June 14. They stopped in Minneapolis to meet with Dr. Anderson one last time. Henry asked him for some assistance in identifying a species of blueberry or bilberry. Anderson in turn showed his visitors a rattlesnake he had found on the prairie. Thoreau's notes don't indicate whether the creature was alive or dead. We can probably safely assume it was the latter.

Back home in Concord, Bronson Alcott was calling on the Thoreau household that day to hear the latest news about Henry and Horace. He was gratified to hear that the men were "finding some new plants in those parts" and had been "enjoying the country house and the wild life" around Lake Calhoun. He ruminated in his journal about the ultimate meaning of this trip for Thoreau:

> The West opens a new field for his observations; and to one
> whose everyday walk was an expedition into some unexplored

region of Concord in search of novelties, though his track had been taken yesterday, that wilderness must have surprising attractions. ... I know not to whom that wild country belongs if not to this old explorer, and think it has waited with an Amazonian patience for his arrival ... His visit must have been predestined from the beginning, and this lassitude of these late months only the intimation of his having exhausted these old fields and farms of Concord of the significance they had for him.

Even his friend Bronson understood that Thoreau's journey was not being made merely for health considerations. The naturalist had been long overdue to discover newer, fresher horizons and the "surprising attractions" they held. The fact that Thoreau's letters conveyed "nothing about his health" encouraged the Concordians. They assumed he had experienced "a change for the better."

Henry and Horace proceeded across the river to St. Anthony. Horace retrieved his keg from Mr. Crawford and made arrangements to send it home, along with a box of plant samples that both he and Henry had collected. The two men may have even stayed overnight at St. Anthony once again, based on the entries recorded on Thoreau's expense sheet.

In order to get back to St. Paul, they retraced the steps they had taken when they first reached the region. That meant that they once again boarded a Concord stagecoach of the Minnesota Stage Company to cover those last nine miles between St. Anthony and St. Paul, at a cost of 75 cents for the trip.

By Saturday, June 15, they were back in St. Paul. Henry and Horace checked in to the Merchants Hotel at the corner of Third and Jackson Streets. The oldest hotel in the city, the Merchants had been built originally of tamarack logs in the late 1840s. By now, the structure had been greatly improved, with native stone walls that rose four stories above the street. The hotel offered some of the best accommodations in St. Paul.

But Henry and Horace didn't suddenly become citified. They were far from finished with their botanizing efforts. All along the drive to St. Paul, Thoreau kept an eye on the vegetation that passed by the stagecoach window. The mustards were beginning to bloom. Some of the varieties were unfamiliar to him. He wrote down the details of each one so that he could figure out their identities later.

The two Massachusetts men hadn't had time to see much of St. Paul when they had arrived on the *Itasca* on May 26. Back then, they were too

eager to get to the Thatcher home in St. Anthony. Now they had the whole
weekend to explore while they waited for the *Frank Steele* to leave for
Redwood on Monday.

On Saturday afternoon, they walked across the Wabasha Street toll bridge
that led to the western (but really, southern) shore of the Mississippi River.
They found "a few new plants," according to Horace. He painted a word
picture of the scene for his mother:

> The bridge is a very long one and descending the whole way
> from St. Paul to the other bank, for it commences on a bluff of
> sandstone at St. Paul about 100 ft high and goes down to
> almost the level of the river on the other side. As I said, the city
> of St. Paul is built right along on the edge of a steep sandstone
> bluff, the sandstone being very soft and crumbling, so that the
> bank swallows dig holes in it and build nests and lag eggs in
> them. In some parts of the bank the sandstone is all specked
> with little holes and I should think that there were hundred of
> them, every one or nearly every one inhabited and the young
> swallows would come to the mouth of the hole to be fed.

Fortunately for the swallows, Horace's keg was already sealed and was on its
way back to Concord. Henry acknowledged the birds in his notebook as well.
But he disagreed with his companion's assessment of the consistency of the
sandstone. Thoreau noted that the rock was "so hard you could not make the
hole with your hand, or *would* not." It sounds as though he may have made
an attempt to do so.

On Sunday morning, the two men went to Carver's Cave, located along
the riverside bluffs and east of downtown St. Paul. The site had been named
for Jonathan Carver, one of those early explorers that Governor Ramsey
had listed in his article. Thoreau had read and owned a copy of Carver's
travel narrative and thus should have been familiar with the history of this
spot. According to Carver's account, the cave was quite deep and contained
a number of native carvings in the walls. Here the explorer had addressed
hundreds of Sioux in 1767, and had asked them then to side with Great
Britain's interests in the region, rather than with those of the competing
French. The cave was therefore both an historical and a geological landmark. By 1861, however, its inner rooms must have already been inaccessible. Not being able to climb into it, Thoreau wrote instead about the botan-
icals surrounding the bluff. He found more mustard plants there, as well as
a large specimen of Solomon's seal (*Polygonatum biflorum*).

Although Horace almost always reported that Mr. Thoreau's health was fine, his cough must have returned. The pectoral that he bought in St. Paul was basically a liquid cough medicine. One of the most popular brands was Ayer's Cherry Pectoral, prepared by Dr. J. C. Ayer & Co. of Lowell, Massachusetts. According to its newspaper advertisements, the tonic was intended "For the rapid cure of Coughs, Colds, Influenza, Hoarseness, Croup, Bronchitis, Incipient Consumption, and for the Relief of Consumptive Patients, in advanced stages of the Disease." The company was nothing if not confident in the formula's restorative properties:

> This is a remedy so universally known to surpass any other for the cure of throat and lung complaints, that it is useless here to publish the evidence of its virtues. Its unrivalled excellence for coughs and colds, and its truly wonderful cures of pulmonary disease, have made it known throughout the civilized nations of the earth.

If it was good enough for the rest of the "civilized" world, it would probably work for Henry David Thoreau.

After hiking and sight-seeing around the city of St. Paul for several days, Henry Thoreau and Horace Mann, Jr., were both certainly mentally, if not physically, prepared for their next adventure: steaming up the Minnesota River in order to see the Dakota Indians.

The officials who ran the city of St. Anthony, Minnesota, made every attempt to keep up with the two communities growing on either edge of it. But the competition was too great. In the Spring of 1872, St. Anthony officially merged with its larger neighbor directly across the Mississippi River. Today all of the St. Anthony sites that Thoreau and Mann saw and visited have Minneapolis addresses (if they are still standing). A newer suburb called St. Anthony is located well north of the original city.

Like the much larger waterfalls on the Niagara River, the Falls of St. Anthony have undergone tremendous changes as a result of civilization and man's intervention and need for power. Now a lock and dam system span the Mississippi River at that point.

The Winslow House never again operated as a hotel. In the 1870s, it served as part of Macalester College. A decade later, it became the home of the Minnesota College Hospital. The structure was torn down to make room for the Minneapolis Exposition building in 1887. By then, the

Tremont House was long gone. It was lost to fire in 1873.

The Universalist Society church that stood near the Tremont House was sold to the French Canadian Catholic community in the 1870s. A group with that affiliation has worshiped in it ever since. Today it is known as Our Lady of Lourdes Church. Many additions and renovations have taken place in the building since Thoreau and Mann saw it in 1861. Among the most striking are the substantial bell tower, several tall steeples, and the intricate stained glass windows.

Universalists gathered as a congregation at another site across the river. In 1876, they opened their own Church of the Redeemer at the corner of Eighth Street and Second Avenue. As part of the dedication festivities, the Rev. Robert Collyer of Chicago was invited to participate in the celebration. It would be the first time the minister and Thoreau fan had ever spoken from a pulpit in Minnesota. To the more than one thousand people in attendance, he offered one of the prayers during the service itself. Later, during a more casual proceeding in the afternoon, Collyer, "preached on the predestination of things," according to a local reporter. His lesson "was to see God in everything—good, bad or indifferent." He included no insights from Henry David Thoreau this time, but instead quoted verses by John Greenleaf Whittier. One visitor was moved to publish an honest opinion of the man's delivery:

> Mr. Collyer had very little of the style of the elocutionist, and very little of what is generally accepted as oratorical. The secret of his power is his thought. It is what he says. It is his big heart that attracts people and his freedom from pulpitisms and, we might say, preacherisms.

When yet another minister from Chicago addressed the crowd later that evening, the poor man couldn't match what had been witnessed earlier. His words were "not equal to the occasion, or at all up to the average of the day," said the press. It appears as if the Reverend Robert Collyer had successfully wowed another Western audience.

Since that time, the site and the name of the church have changed over the years. The First Universalist Church is now located at 3400 Dupont Avenue South in Minneapolis. The congregation celebrated its sesquicentennial in 2009. It is proud to be "not only the oldest continuous Unitarian Universalist congregation in Minnesota, but also the largest Universalist church in the United States."

Thoreau was neither the first nor the last naturalist to be intrigued by the wide spacing of the bur oaks on the prairie. Anyone who studies the natural sciences in the Midwest quickly learns about the savanna habitat called "oak openings." Examples of oak openings can still be found on many properties throughout the region.

The University of Minnesota expanded its jurisdiction and now operates additional campuses that are scattered across the state. Three are located in the Twin Cities area: the East Bank campus, the West Bank campus, and the St. Paul campus. The East Bank campus was the original site that Thoreau and Mann were able to walk around when they visited St. Anthony. The Old Main building was destroyed by fire in 1904. But bur oaks do indeed still thrive on the land, "as if nothing had happened." According to a flurry of e-mails from present-day University staff members, including campus landscape architect Tom Ritzer, some of the current trees are certainly old enough to have been standing there in 1861. Another connection to Thoreau's hometown now appears on the campus as well. The statue of Governor John S. Pillsbury, which stands by Burton Hall, was crafted by Concordian Daniel Chester French.

Lake Calhoun, Lake Harriet, and Minnehaha Park are all maintained as public recreation areas by the Minneapolis Park and Recreation Board. That agency also oversees Nicollet Island Park, which is located on the southern end of the island. All four sites are now located within the city limits of Minneapolis.

One or more of the lakes can be seen during the opening and closing credits of the 1970s sitcom, *The Mary Tyler Moore Show*, as Mary strides confidently along a paved walkway. She may very well have been walking in Thoreau and Mann's footsteps. Had Henry David Thoreau in turn tossed his hat into the air on Nicollet Avenue? Probably not. Some of his plant samples would have fallen out of it.

Fort Snelling saw active military duty through the years of World War II. A decade after it closed, the fort was named Minnesota's first National Historic Landmark in 1960. Historic Fort Snelling is now owned by the Minnesota Historical Society. During the summer months, historical interpreters and re-enactors show visitors what life was like for the soldiers stationed at the outpost in the 1820s. The Fort Snelling History Center and nearby Fort Snelling State Park lie adjacent to the property and are worth exploring as well.

The site of Carver's Cave is now contained in Indian Mounds Park in St. Paul. The main portion of the cave was destroyed by the intrusion of an early railroad line and other developments over the years. While some cave remnants remain, the park also includes examples of native mounds built during the Hopewell period, more than two thousand years ago.

The Mississippi River is still spanned by a bridge at St. Paul's Wabasha Street. The current structure is not the original that Henry and Horace walked over in 1861. That one was first replaced around 1899.

Jonathan Taylor Grimes (1818-1903) joined the Minnesota State Horticultural Society, and he continued to be highly regarded as a known authority in his field. He and his wife raised eight children on the farm that Thoreau once visited. The Grimes home in Edina, Minnesota, is listed on the National Register of Historic Places. However, it should be pointed out that the family built and moved into the house *after* Mr. Grimes met Thoreau and showed him the crab apple trees on that property.

When Henry and Horace reached Milwaukee on June 27, the older man took the opportunity to write a thank-you note of sorts to Dr. Anderson of Minneapolis. He used several paragraphs to summarize what he and Horace had seen and done since leaving the Upper Mississippi region. He signed off with a few words of appreciation: "Thanking you for your kindness to an invalid traveller." Dr. Anderson had certainly proven to be a valuable guide and a very good, albeit accidental, acquaintance.

Although we do not have the physical evidence to prove it, that note must not have been the last piece of correspondence that was exchanged between Dr. Anderson and a man from Concord, Massachusetts. How else can we explain the following sequence of events?

Charles L. Anderson left his wife and two daughters behind in Beloit, Wisconsin, on May 13, 1862—less than a year after he said goodbye to Henry and Horace—and began to head southwest. He would send for his family later, when he had a practice established somewhere in Nevada.

Edward W. Emerson, son of Ralph Waldo Emerson of Concord, boarded a west-bound train in Boston on May 12, 1862: six days after the death of Henry David Thoreau, and just three days after his funeral. Young Edward's destination was Omaha, Nebraska, where he was planning to meet Dr. Charles L. Anderson. The duo would then travel together by wagon train to Nevada.

How could Edward Emerson have learned of Dr. Anderson's plans, if not from either Henry or Horace? Perhaps the good doctor had written to invite one of the Minnesota travelers along for a journey even *farther* West. He may have been unaware at the time that Henry himself was unable to travel. And Anderson may not have known of Horace's upcoming commitment to college study. So one of the men, or even both of them, must have mentioned this new western adventure to Edward or to his father. Edward had just spent a less than stellar year at Harvard and was looking for something else to do. Here was a chance to see the whole continent and to travel in the company of both a doctor and a scientist. What young man could pass up such a wonderful opportunity?

Edward Emerson, Dr. Anderson, and a Mr. Rheem met in Nebraska. There they joined a wagon train that took them as far as Salt Lake City. From there they made their way on horseback to Carson City, Nevada. At least the records show that Dr. Anderson reached Carson City on August 29, 1862. Other sources indicate that Edward Emerson arrived in Sacramento, California, on August 31, 1862. The two men must have parted in Carson City. Edward would eventually ride on to San Francisco, sail down to Panama, cross the isthmus, and sail north to New York City. He was back in Concord in early October 1862. By then, he was ready to resume his studies at Harvard.

For the next five years, Charles Lewis Anderson (1827-1910) practiced medicine and botanized in and around Carson City, Nevada. His wife and two daughters joined him there in 1863. Four years later, they all moved to Santa Cruz, California. There, Anderson gained notoriety as a botanist. He often sent plant samples to Dr. Asa Gray at Harvard (and thus perhaps also to Horace Mann, Jr., before 1868). A number of plant species are named for him, including two species of Sierra wildflowers: Anderson's buttercup (*Ranunculus andersonii*) and Desert peach (*Prunus andersonii*). Dr. Anderson was also one of the founders of the Santa Cruz Free City Library. All of the interests and the specialties he had developed in Minnesota came to true fruition in this city on the edge of Monterey Bay and the Pacific Ocean. He lived out the rest of his days there.

Thirteen-lined ground squirrels still live in many of the states that comprise the American Midwest. But Passenger pigeons (*Ectopistes migratorius*) have been extinct since 1914, when the last surviving bird died in a zoo in Cincinnati. Many more marksmen than just Horace Mann, Jr., had been killing the pigeons in large quantities during the nineteenth century. Their demise was not merely the fault of one seventeen-year-old adventurer wielding an old shotgun with a kick.

Thanks to the efforts of nurserymen and hybridizers, Crab apple trees now come in many varieties and can be grown just about anywhere. You can even spy them in a number of yards in Concord, Massachusetts. A small but nice one stands on a front lawn directly across from the main entrance to Sleepy Hollow Cemetery, Thoreau's final resting place. Today, he wouldn't have far to go to see one.

On August 15, 2008, I returned to Minnesota to see the sites that had been closed during my trip here the previous fall. I also needed to take a Henry David Thoreau tour of Minneapolis and to find all of the places that he and young Horace visited. My guides and experts for the day were Minneapolis natives Dale and Kay Schwie. I first met the Schwies at a Thoreau Society Annual Gathering in Concord, Massachusetts. Ever since I started tracing the route of the Journey West, they have been supportive and willing to provide as much help as possible.

We left their home in Richfield and headed north into the city. Dale was driving, and Kay chose to sit in the back. She wanted me to take the passenger seat in order to have unobstructed views of the sights. I was just glad that I didn't have to navigate the highways and city streets myself. I could concentrate instead on what I could see from the front and side windows on this bright and beautiful summer day.

We crossed the Mississippi River, and Dale made a left-hand turn onto a small side street. Our first stop was Our Lady of Lourdes Church at One Lourdes Place. Back in 1861, this was the meeting place for the Universalist Society. We parked and got out of the car to get a closer look. It was a solid, impressive stone building. It had been just a simple block of rock back when Thoreau was in the neighborhood. Now it had a tall steeple flanked by two smaller ones and offered a much more elegant appearance.

The door was propped open for some construction work, and we took the risk of tip-toeing inside ourselves. The interior was peaceful and beautiful: or it would have been, if our ears had not been assaulted by the sound of power tools. Dale walked over to chat with the workers, who were busy with ongoing upgrades and restorations. Kay and I stood in the aisle and looked up at the ceiling and at the beautiful stained-glass windows surrounding us. When we went back outside into the strong sunlight, we were satisfied that we had seen something Thoreau and Mann would have seen. We didn't know if they stepped inside the church. But surely they saw the structure anytime they left their hotel. A plaque on a nearby boulder recited the history of the building. Dale and I both snapped photos of it.

The three of us walked down a set of stairs and around some buildings to reach Main Street. The river was calmly flowing right in front of us. I could not stop gazing at it and at the pretty cityscape of downtown

Minneapolis just beyond it. Then I remembered some of its history. "So, where are the Falls?" I asked Dale.

"Right down there." He pointed downstream, to a spot along the opposite shore that was surrounded by yellow man-made barriers. I squinted, but all I saw was a slight depression in the water. I was disappointed. I didn't expect Niagara, but I figured I would at least see rocks and rushing riffles and maybe a bit of misting rising from the power of the cataract. This sight was too artificial for me. My attention was drawn instead to a log lying in the water, closer to our side. Several Canada geese and a heron were perched on it, sunning themselves. I took photos of them instead of the mechanical busy-ness across the way. They had found serenity in the midst of a metropolis.

We followed a lovely tree-covered path between the street and the river, taking careful note of every one of the St. Anthony Falls Heritage Trail information markers we came across. One of them made the three of us gasp and look across the street. The placard showed an historic image of the Winslow House, the Upton Block, and the Tremont House. According to the accompanying text, the Upton Block was "still standing as part of St. Anthony Main." That was the name of the stone and brick building across the street. We hurried over to see it for ourselves.

St. Anthony Main is "the host to the Minneapolis riverfront district." It's a large complex of shops and offices. We walked inside and sauntered among the storefronts. I reached out to touch one of the old brick walls, presumably from the original Upton Block. Again, I think: Henry and Horace would have seen this very wall. Probably.

The old Tremont House had been located on the corner of Main Street and Pine Street (now known as Second Avenue Southeast). As we popped outside again and scrutinized the footprint of St. Anthony Main, we came to the realization that the "corner" for the Tremont House no longer existed. It was enveloped by St. Anthony Main, so we were as close as we could get to Henry and Horace's hotel. I couldn't speak for Dale and Kay, but I was excited about this discovery. I looked back at the Mississippi and tried to imagine the view from their hotel room in 1861. Had a heron been sitting on a log in the water back then, too?

Within minutes we were driving along the tiny perimeter road of nearby Nicollet Island. I was surprised by the number of homes here. Dale said that the island was quite industrial in the 1950s, and that it once housed a major roofing company. I had had another picture in my mind. I had assumed that Nicollet would offer the same kind of all-encompassing, natural park atmosphere that Goat Island did at Niagara Falls. It did not:

at least not in its entirety. Nicollet happened to be the only residential island along the full length of the Mississippi River. As we passed some lovely and historic (and no doubt pricey) homes, Dale said that his brother went to DeLaSalle High School, which was located here. We soon drove past it. A school on an island! He and Kay discussed the ongoing controversy about whether or not DeLaSalle should be allowed to carve a football field out here. Football on an island! I was amazed at everything I saw and heard.

Then we headed west, past the Minneapolis cityscape and toward Lake Calhoun. I admitted to the Schwies that I had been to this area before. During my first visit to the city eleven years earlier, I deliberately sought out the house that was shown in the opening credits of *The Mary Tyler Moore Show*. I had learned that the fictitious home of Mary, Rhoda, and the Lindstroms (Phyllis, Lars, and Bess) really did exist. I still had photos of it from my last drive through. This time, however, Dale didn't turn down that street in order for me to reminisce. We were supposed to be concentrating on Henry and Horace and the year 1861.

We drove around the shoreline of Lake Calhoun, and then parked and got out to walk around a bit. The lake offered a very wide, very flat view. Trees on adjacent properties created a dark green edging that circled much of the water. This was a peaceful place. A few people fished from a nearby dock. The day had become a hot and lazy one, bordering on downright uncomfortable when standing in the full sunlight. Still, it was wonderful to think that Henry Thoreau and Horace Mann had spent time here, and that they had perhaps hung out exactly where we were standing. It was enough to give a Thoreauvian a few shivers of delight.

One of my favorite quotes from *Walden* came to mind: "Walden is blue at one time and green at another, even from the same point of view. Lying between the earth and the heavens, it partakes of the color of both." Here was Lake Calhoun, a perfect mirror of the cloudless, endless sky of the prairie. The bubbling tree-line created a dark green crust around the rim of this luscious blueberry custard pie stretching out in front of us. The shiny skyscrapers of Minneapolis rose from beyond the far shoreline. Spending eleven days at Lake Calhoun sounded like a good plan to me. Just let me find some shade to sit in, please.

Kay and I followed Dale down the path to a rock with a plaque mounted in it. The marker dated from 1908, and was attributed to the Native Sons of Minnesota:

On the hill above was
erected the
first dwelling
in Minneapolis by
Samuel W. and Gideon H. Pond
Missionaries to the Indians
June 1834

"Thoreau mentions the Pond mission in his notes," said Dale. I nodded, recognizing the name. I knew that the two Pond brothers of Connecticut had established several missions after they traveled out to this region, and that Thoreau had invoked their names on more than one occasion. We discussed that segment of Minnesota's history, as we looked across the street at the "hill above," now heavily loaded with the glittering golden-domed complex of St. Mary's Greek Orthodox Church. It took a good bit of imagination to picture what the old log mission must have looked like and how it must have been positioned upon that height. But the Pond brothers had picked a great location back then.

If we had had the time, I would have loved to walk the whole way around the lake. But we had several more sites to see. And I hadn't brought any sunscreen or an umbrella along with me today.

Dale drove us down to the southern edge of the lake and to the area once owned by the Hamiltons. Now a small row of detached homes sat on the nearby ridge. But I could envision a time before they were built. The old boarding house may have sat close to the water, and the rest of the Hamilton acreage must have stretched out well into the prairie land beyond. Henry could have walked out that way, in search of his crab apple trees and oak openings.

We left the Calhoun Parkway, drove south toward Lake Harriet, and then turned west. We made our way up a hill to find the Jonathan Taylor Grimes house on West 44th Street. The home was now a private residence and an historical landmark. It was a Gothic Revival cottage with sharp roof lines and decorative window shutters. I hopped out of the car and took a few clandestine photos, then got right back in so we could be on our way. The Schwies and I know that the Grimes family built this house in 1869, eight years after Henry Thoreau had met the man of the house. But it was the thought and the slight connection that counted.

Dale, Kay and I stopped for a light lunch at a little deli we passed between the lake and Mr. Grimes's house. As we nibbled upon our sandwiches, the conversation of course focused almost entirely upon Henry and Horace.

This kind of outing was like a merry treasure hunt for us. And those two men from Massachusetts left us fairly good directions for this portion of the Journey West.

After our brief but relaxing respite, we headed east to Minnehaha Park. This place was far more than just the site of Minnehaha Falls. Just about every corner of the park offered a feast for the eyes and the rest of our senses. Several groups were using the recreational facilities for parties this afternoon. We sauntered over to the falls, of course; and eventually we viewed the water from just about every possible angle. The waterfall reminded me of some of the ones we used to see whenever my parents and I vacationed in the Poconos in the 1960s. Click click click went the shutter on my camera.

Kay said that a ledge used to sit behind the falls, and that kids would climb around back there when she was a child. I could see a mark in the rock where it must have perched. I remembered that young Horace mentioned having the same access. But sometime in the intervening decades, the park authorities decided that the ledge presented a potentially dangerous situation, so they removed it. Kay and I shook our heads at how overly protective our society has become.

Dale, on the other hand, was up at the top of the falls. He was mesmerized by the mask sculpture of the Dakota chief, Little Crow. The depiction was haunting. Dale once met the artist here, and he told us again how he watched the man thread the strands of black hair into the piece. We agreed that this was yet another Thoreau connection, since Henry mentioned Little Crow in a letter he wrote after seeing the Dakota Indians at the Lower Sioux Agency in Redwood.

When I questioned Dale about the original ledge behind the falls, he said that he too remembered it well. When he was a boy, he and his friends would ride their bikes to Minnehaha. They would spend hours exploring its woods and its hillsides, and they would clamber around and behind the water. I grew jealous, even though I was not sure I would ever have scaled the old ledge. I also considered myself lucky to have tour guides who were on such intimate terms with this place.

As we walked along the rushing creek above the falls, we spied the sculpture of Hiawatha and Minnehaha that was crafted by Jacob Fjelde in 1911. Hiawatha was shown carrying Minnehaha in his arms, presumably to safety. Native spirits dueled with the image of a white poet from New England. This park simultaneously honored both.

My favorite place here—second to the falls, of course—was a garden overlook, complete with a fountain. In addition to the gorgeous blooms that grew to towering heights here, the site included passages from *The Song of Hiawatha* that had been carved into stone. You could walk around in circles and read portions of the verses as you went. I was quite impressed. I later learned that a replica of Henry Wadsworth Longfellow's home sat somewhere in the park as well. It was almost a shame that Professor Longfellow never got a chance to come here in person. At least his student, Henry Thoreau, did.

It was back into the car for us, as we ventured to Historic Fort Snelling, our final stop on the tour. We checked out the history center and the gift shop first, then walked toward the sturdy bluff-toned walls of the fort. A few wispy clouds had gathered above us. But the sun continued to boldly command this August day.

Back east, a facility like this one would have been protected by a stockade of tall, pointed logs. But this native stone wall was both strong and beautiful. It gleamed nearly white in the strong afternoon light. The soldiers were dressed in a variety of uniforms that were unfamiliar to me. Many wore red jackets with gold braiding and white trousers. When I asked one of them for a time reference, his reply indicated that he and the other men were portraying the early days of the fort, the 1820s. That was a little early for my background; but was fascinating, nevertheless. We sat in on a talk given by one of the interpreters and were rewarded with his concluding performance on the fife. I snapped a photo to share with my own flute-playing father.

The fort had been restored nicely, and we walked around to inspect many of the soldiers' quarters and other buildings. We climbed to the top level of the Round Tower and enjoyed seeing snippets of the Mississippi and Minnesota rivers, merging way below the bluffs. Colonel Snelling's residence sat at the far end of the parade ground and also had great views from its windows. A few highways interrupted each panorama now. But it was easy to see why the fort was created at this location.

After we watched the cannon drill, Dale, Kay and I strolled through one of the buildings and stood out on the back porch, welcoming the shade. As we leaned over the railing and chatted about what we had seen, a groundhog ventured out from the rocks below. Dale and I both quietly raised our cameras and aimed at the chubby guy. Click. And as I was taking his picture, I saw more movement at the edge of the frame. Another creature had come out of the rocks—and it was a thirteen-lined ground squirrel! "Horace didn't get them all!" I whispered to my friends. Kay smiled and laughed softly. I was always heartened to see these little prairie gophers. I managed to capture this one on film before he scurried off to attend to his business. What a great place he has found to live.

We left as the fort was closing. We had had a full day of driving and walking. We had communed with the spirits of Henry Thoreau, Horace Mann and with each other. It was a pleasant weariness that overtook us as we trudged back to the car. If it had made any sense at all in this Midwestern outpost, I would have said that we had been both Concord and Worcestered many times over today.

Of course, the three of us didn't hit *all* of the Thoreau-Mann sites that we could have, in the Twin Cities. We didn't walk around the campus of the University of Minnesota in search of old oak trees. We didn't try to locate the present-day footprints of the American House and the Merchants Hotel in downtown St. Paul. We didn't walk across the Wabasha Street bridge and look back at the capital city, now twenty times larger than it was in 1861. We didn't go to Indian Mounds Park and pretend to see Carver's Cave. But we had had a full day, nevertheless. We would have needed a second one to include St. Paul on our tight schedule. As it was, we could easily have spent several hours at each one of our stops.

In retrospect, I thought we did and saw enough. We walked in Henry and Horace's footsteps in a number of places. We didn't want to exhaust ourselves in the name of re-enactment. Besides: such omissions gave me yet another excuse to return to the Minneapolis-St. Paul area someday. And of course, I would.

Three months after I returned to Massachusetts from Minnesota, my landlord gave me some bad news. He was losing the house to foreclosure. I had only the weeks between Thanksgiving and Christmas to find another apartment and to move. I started looking around; and fairly quickly, I found another house that needed a second-floor tenant. Unbelievably, it was only four or five blocks away from my current place. I struck a deal with the owner, and I soon started loading my car with boxes. I made a few trips every day, all the while cursing the amount of junk I had collected over the course of fifty years.

The weather matched the bleakness of my task. It was that gray time of the year: the days between fall and winter. No snow had fallen yet. But you could tell from the air that it wouldn't be long before the flakes would come. We had already gotten a nasty ice storm that left us without electricity for two days. The New England landscape was painted with only washed-out hues. It was rare to see much color outside now.

I was carrying a box into the house when my new landlord stopped me on the front porch to chat. He gave me a few last instructions on living here. While I listened, I looked out at the yard and at a nearby tree. Even though it had lost its leaves, I could tell that it was neither a maple nor an oak. In fact, it looked kind of scraggly; and small fruit still dangled from its branches. "What kind of tree is that?" I asked, nudging a shoulder toward it.

"That's a crab apple tree," said Bill.

I smiled to myself. Wouldn't Henry be pleased? I had found a home.

WHEN YOU GO: It is not too difficult to find the sites that Henry Thoreau and Horace Mann, Jr., visited in the Twin Cities area. Just having some good maps should do the trick. Of course, it wouldn't hurt to land upon a resident with both street knowledge and a good sense of direction. Don't turn down the opportunity to learn from a local expert. That's the lesson Henry and Horace discovered here.

FOR MORE INFORMATION

Historic Fort Snelling, 200 Tower Avenue, St. Paul, MN 55111. Phone (612) 725-1171. www.mnhs.org/places/sites/hfs.

Indian Mounds Park, 10 Mounds Blvd., St. Paul MN. Phone (651) 632-5111. www.stpaul.gov/facilities.aspx?page=detail&RID=53

Meet Minneapolis, Minneapolis Convention & Visitors Association, 250 Marquette Avenue South, Suite 1300, Minneapolis, MN 55401. Phone (888) 676-MPLS. www.minneapolis.org.

Minneapolis Park & Recreation Board, 2117 West River Road, Minneapolis, MN 55411. Phone (612) 230-6400. www.minneapolisparks.org. [manages Minnehaha Falls Park, Lake Calhoun, and Lake Harriet]

Saint Paul Convention & Visitors Authority, 175 West Kellogg Boulevard, Suite 502, Saint Paul, MN 55102. Phone (800) 627-6101. www.visitsaintpaul.com.

University of Minnesota, www.umn.edu.

RECOMMENDED READING

Henry Wadsworth Longfellow's epic poem, *The Song of Hiawatha*. The text is available online and appears in most Longfellow anthologies. Also consider reading any book by Sigurd F. Olson. *Reflections from the North Country* is a good place to start.

NOTES ON THIS CHAPTER

I owe much to Dale and Kay Schwie of Minneapolis, who not only squired me around their town, but also pointed me in the direction of great sources of information. Dale has always insisted that we focus on Henry Thoreau's health in Minnesota and not on his illness.

Samuel Thatcher's original letter of introduction to Dr. Charles L. Anderson is on file in the Nineteenth-Century American Studies Collection, which is part of the James K. Hosmer

Special Collections Library located at the Minneapolis Central Library. Thoreau's thank-you note to Dr. Anderson remains there as well, and its text was also printed in *The Thoreau Quarterly*, v. 14 no. 3-4, Summer-Fall 1982, pp. 156-159.

Sources of information about the early days of St. Anthony and Minneapolis included Edward A. Bromley's *Minneapolis Portrait of the Past: A Photographic History of the Early Days in Minneapolis* (Minneapolis: Harrison & Smith, 1890); and Lucile M. Kane's *The Falls of St. Anthony: The Waterfall that Built Minneapolis* (St. Paul: Minnesota Historical Society Press, 1987). Helpful articles were: "The Stagecoach Business in Pioneer Minnesota," *Gopher Historian*, v. 22 no. 3, Spring 1968, pp. 1-6; Emily O. Goodridge Grey's "The Black Community in Territorial St. Anthony: A Memoir," *Minnesota History*, v. 49 no. 2, Summer 1984, pp. 42-53; and "Governing a Frontier City: Old St. Anthony, 1855-1872," *Minnesota History*, v. 35 no. 3, September 1956, pp. 117-129. The last one was the source of the quoted prediction about the great future ahead for St. Anthony. Some thought the city could be the next Lowell, Massachusetts.

In September 2009, DeLaSalle High School opened its new sports complex on Nicollet Island.

Thoreau's worry about whether or not his scientific knowledge would apply to the prairies was written in his Journal entry of November 20, 1857. His dealings with people "of southern birth" was noted in his letter to Frank Sanborn, written from Red Wing, Minnesota, on June 25, 1861. The text of his lecture, "The Succession of Forest Trees," is found in a number of published anthologies. I think the essay, "Wild Apples," is best found in the volume edited by William Rossi, *Wild Apples and Other Natural History Essays* (Athens, Ga.: The University of Georgia Press, 2002). "Dispersion of Seeds" and Thoreau's observation of thirteen-lined ground squirrels eating bass nuts did not appear in a publication until the release of *Faith in a Seed*, edited by Bradley P. Dean (Washington, D.C.: Island Press, 1993, p. 80).

For the details of the books that Henry Thoreau read and/or owned, I am indebted to Robert Sattelmeyer's *Thoreau's Reading: A Study in Intellectual History with Bibliographical Catalogue* (Princeton: Princeton University Press, 1988).

Horace Mann, Jr.'s letters for this section were dated May 26, June 1, June 7, June 10, and June 12.

Bronson Alcott's visit to the Thoreau household on June 14, 1861, is detailed in his journal entry for that day, found in *The Journals of Bronson Alcott* (ed. by Odell Shepard. Boston: Little, Brown and Company, 1938, p. 340).

Online census records for 1860 provided some of the dates and origins of Charles L. Anderson, Charles Crawford, Jonathan Fitch, Elizabeth and William Hamilton, and Jonathan Taylor Grimes.

Biographical details about Dr. Charles L. Anderson were found in Olga Reifschneider's *Biographies of Nevada Botanists, 1844-1963* (Reno: University of Nevada Press, 1964); her article titled "Dr. Anderson in Wild & Wooly Carson City," *Nevada Highways and Parks*, v. 26 no. 3, Fall 1966, pp. 16-55; Willis Linn Jepson's "The Botanical Explorers of California—V.: Charles Lewis Anderson," *Madroño: A West American Journal of Botany*, v. 1, 1929, pp. 214-216; and Larry Blakely's online document, "Who's in a Name? People Commemorated in Eastern Sierra plant Names," found at http://www.csupomona.edu/~larryblakely/whoname/who_andr.htm.

Edward Emerson's planned meeting with Dr. Anderson is referenced in Albert J. Von Frank's *An Emerson Chronology* (New York: G.K. Hall, 1994), with pointers toward Ellen Tucker Emerson's *The Life of Lidian Jackson Emerson* (Boston: Twayne Publishers, 1980); and volume one of *The Letters of Ellen Tucker Emerson* (Kent, Ohio: The Kent State University Press, 1982).

Much analysis has been posed about Henry Wadsworth Longfellow and the origins of *The Song of Hiawatha*. Reference works like Gale's *Nineteenth-Century Literary Criticism* offer a plethora of commentary. Two additional focused sources are Helen Carr's "The Myth of Hiawatha," *Literature and History* 12:1 (1986), pp. 58-78; and Chase S. Osborn and Stellanova Osborn's *Schoolcraft–Longfellow–Hiawatha* (Lancaster, Penna.: The Jaques Cattell Press, 1942).

Jonathan Grimes's life touched many of his fellow nurserymen and horticulturalists. Upon his death, they shared their fond memories of the man in the 1903 issues of *The Minnesota Horticulturalist*. The May 23, 1895, issue contained a nice two-page biography of Grimes. In addition, Ruth Thompson offered a succinct retrospective in her column, "Minnesota Memories: Jonathan T. Grimes, Early Settler" *Minneapolis Morning Tribune*, November 3, 1947.

Details about Our Lady of Lourdes Church, Minnehaha Falls, and Fort Snelling were gleaned from personal observation, from brochures picked up on site, and from institutional web sites. David C. Smith's *Parks, Lakes, Trails and So Much More: An Overview of the Histories of MPRB Properties* (Minneapolis Park and Recreation Board, 2008) is a treasuretrove of details about all of the parks in Minneapolis, including Nicollet Island, Minnehaha Park, Lake Calhoun, and Lake Harriet. It is posted on the board web site at http://www.minneapolisparks.org.

Gary Fouty, Gary Johnson, and Tom Ritzer of the University of Minnesota were kind enough to answer my questions about bur oaks on the East Campus. A history consulted was James Gray's *The University of Minnesota: 1851-1951* (Minneapolis: The University of Minnesota Press, 1951).

Dale Schwie gave me the tip about Robert Collyer's participation in Minneapolis' Universalist church opening in 1876. His source was a newspaper article transcript, based on the original report that had been pasted in a ledger book. It resides with the Minnesota Historical Society. Dale and Kay are proud members of First Universalist Church.

An article titled "No More Mails for Dixie's Land" announced the cessation of postal delivery to the Southern states in the Canadian paper, *The London Free Press and Daily Western Advertiser* on June 5, 1861.

Two Thoreauvian natural history mysteries remain. The pages of his field notebook mention a deer on Nicollet Island and an eagle eating a blue jay on an island at Lake Minnetonka. Questions arise about the animal in the first note and the location in the second note. Did Thoreau himself see a deer on Nicollet Island? The issue is up for debate. Most Americans can spot deer in any rural area these days, especially at dawn or at dusk. In Thoreau's time, however, over-farming and loss of habitat made those sightings rather unusual. Evadene Burris Swanson of Minnesota openly questioned Thoreau's note in 1939. "Since deer were probably very rare if still occurring in nature on Nicollet Island in 1861, it is probable that this animal, if alive, was a captive." ("The Manuscript Journal of Thoreau's Last Journey." *Minnesota History* 20 (June 1939): p. 170.)

Thoreau's note about the eagle appears immediately after the words: "Walk westward." The eastern end of Lake Minnetonka is about ten miles due west of Lake Calhoun and Mrs. Hamilton's boarding house. Minneapolis native Dale Schwie doubts that Thoreau would have walked all of the way to the edge of Lake Minnetonka and then come right back. It would have been a challenge at the time, not to mention at least a 20-mile round trip, to boot. According to Thoreau's notes, this westward walk took place on his second day at Lake Calhoun. Why would he venture that far away from a place he had just gotten to? Furthermore, even Thoreau's spyglass would not have provided a decent view of the island nearest to the Minnetonka shoreline. A boat of some kind would have been necessary to get close enough to see such a sight. Since Thoreau scribbled down none of those kinds of details and related no personal impressions of the immensity of Lake Minnetonka, Dale is adamant. "I have no reason to believe he went out there," he says. Perhaps as Thoreau went out walking that day, he met someone coming from the west who related the eagle-eating-jay story. Today that appears to be the only logical explanation for the note. As Thoreauvians are wont to quip in such situations: "Only Henry knows for sure, and he ain't talkin'."

Travel Chapter 12

Monday, June 17 to Saturday, June 22, 1861
from St. Paul to the Lower Sioux Agency at Redwood and back to St. Paul
via the Minnesota River and the steamboat Frank Steele

Expenses: Fare to Redwood & back, $10.00
St. Paul (again), $2.00

After spending some three weeks in and about St. Paul, St. Anthony, and Minneapolis, we made an excursion in a steamer some 300 or more miles up the Minnesota (St. Peter's) River, to Redwood, or the Lower Sioux Agency, in order to see the plains & the Sioux, who were to receive their annual payment there.

—Thoreau's letter to Frank Sanborn, June 25, 1861

I shall keep a kind of Journal of our trip up the Minnesota I think, or I shall try to, for I do not know how well I shall succeed. I am very well and Mr. Thoreau is getting along pretty well. It is a splendid morning and I hope we shall have good weather all the way.

—Horace Mann Jr.'s letter, June 17, 1861

Henry Thoreau and Horace Mann, Jr., had explored the settlement of St. Paul over the weekend. On Monday afternoon, they joined the "Grand Pleasure Excursion to the Sioux Agency." This outing would take them well into the interior of the state. On this short journey, they would accompany the government officials who were responsible for making the annuity payments to the Dakota people. According to the promotions in the local newspapers, two steamboats would be heading up the Minnesota River. The excursion would leave St. Paul at 4 p.m. on Monday. The payments to the Indians would be made on Wednesday and Thursday. Five thousand natives were expected to show up. The trip was proclaimed as one that "promises to be the best that has taken place for a long time." How could the two men from Massachusetts resist the opportunity to join the group?

The riverboat excursion was well promoted in the local newspapers.

Although the French traders and Ojibway had called them "Sioux," the Native Americans who lived in the Upper Great Plains knew themselves as "Dakota," meaning "ally" or "friend." The Mdewakanton band of the Dakota lived along the northernmost portion of the Mississippi River. They established permanent villages here but also used the nearby prairies and plains for hunting and gathering expeditions. Additional Dakota bands populated the lands to the west.

Once Fort Snelling was built and the local lumbering industry began to grow, white settlers began arriving in the region. The U.S. government finally outlined and established the Minnesota Territory in 1849. Two years later, with the Treaty of Traverse des Sioux and the Treaty of Mendota, the Dakota essentially signed away their rights to the southern half of the territory. The parcel totaled almost 24 million acres. Once the Indians were pushed even farther west, people from New England, the East, and the South began to arrive and to set up new towns. In 1858, Minnesota became the 32nd U.S. state, using the same borders it had adopted as a territory.

According to the treaty agreements, four bands of Dakota were assigned to a reservation located in the middle of the state. It straddled the Minnesota River and stretched from the South Dakota line to a site just north of the new German American town of New Ulm. At first, the Indians were permitted to live within ten miles of either side of the river. In 1858, that twenty-mile-wide strip was negotiated down to just the ten-mile belt along the southern shoreline. About six thousand Dakota were supposed to live there.

Two centers had been established to provide basic support services for the Indians. The Lower Sioux Agency at Redwood aided the Mdewakanton and Wahpekute bands. The compound contained enough buildings to resemble a small village. Included was a school, sawmill, several stores, and stables. The Upper Sioux Agency at Yellow Medicine was located farther up the Minnesota River and was designed to serve the Sisseton and Wahpeton bands. Officials and staff members at both agencies aimed to acculturate the Dakota: to encourage them to give up the chase and instead take up the plow. Individuals who cut their hair and wore white men's suits soon became known as "Farmer Indians." Those who had long hair and refused to give up their hunting and fishing privileges were "Blanket Indians." Groups exhibiting both lifestyles could be found in this part of Minnesota in the late 1850s.

The Dakota now had their reservation land and agencies to serve them. The treaties also guaranteed that each member of the tribe would receive an annuity payment each year. The U.S. government put aside more than a million dollars in its Treasury so that it could annually withdraw five percent of the interest to pay the Indians. This financial agreement was scheduled to last for fifty years.

Henry Thoreau had long fostered a fascination with Indians. During the previous twelve years, he kept a separate series of journals designated as "Indian books." In those eleven volumes, he copied key passages from sources he read. These were selections that mentioned America's native peoples or described their traditions in depth. The information came from Thoreau's wide reading choices: from the travel narratives of early American explorers, to works specifically dedicated to the subject matter. One of his main sources was Henry Rowe Schoolcraft's six-volume reference, *Historical and Statistical Information Respecting the History, Condition and Prospects of the Indian Tribes of the United States* (Philadelphia: Lippincott, Grambo, 1851-1857). Whenever he found interesting details about Indians, he wrote them down. Thoreau's intent with this ongoing project is still not known. Was he compiling information for his own personal edification and reference purposes? Did he want to eventually write and publish his own book about Indians? If so, he never got around to it.

Thoreau's personal interactions with Native Americans were limited. He met some individuals back home in eastern Massachusetts, including a few Wampanoags in Middleborough. One of his guides in Maine was Joe Polis, a Penobscot. But these encounters were rare and were generally with select members of the tribes. Now that he and Horace were on a western journey, they could see groups of real Indians in their native environment, or what was left of it. Having an opportunity to actually be among the Dakota was certainly a reason he and his young companion signed on for this excursion.

The Minnesota River begins at Big Stone Lake, a body of water perched on the border of South Dakota and Minnesota. From there the river flows directly southeast to the city of Mankato. Then it makes an abrupt turn to the northeast and toward the Twin Cities. The Minnesota joins the Mississippi River at Minneapolis, where Fort Snelling stands on the point that overlooks the confluence. Formerly known as the St. Peter's River, the Minnesota had its name officially restored to its native designation in 1852, thus matching it with the name of the state it traverses. "Minnesota" is said to mean "sky-tinted water."

The Minnesota River has two distinctive features. The first is its actual path. The river curves through the plains and the prairie, almost to the extreme. Its course on a map resembles a playful, squiggling line: one that takes its good old time reaching its destination. For that reason, its mileage can be difficult to ascertain. The distance between any two towns along the river can be counted with one number by land and a much higher one by water. Steamboat passengers were sometimes frustrated by the circumstances they found themselves experiencing. "The river ... is distressingly crooked," wrote one early reporter. "Sometimes we go 6 to 15 miles to achieve one; and so frequent and aggravated are the ox-bows that we pass every house on four sides at least." Another correspondent had more fun with the situation: "The Minnesota river is always on a bender. Long may she wave!"

The second feature of this river is its dependence upon snowmelt. A hard winter that results in a sizable quantity of snow can bring about springtime floods along the Minnesota. And the more water it holds, the more accommodating it is for the navigation of large water craft. Once steamboat excursions became popular along this river in the 1850s, their captains grew to learn that the earlier they could travel in the season, the better. In good years, river traffic could begin in March and last until the middle of summer. After that point, however, the chances of grounding a boat on a sandbar or an exposed snag grew ever more likely. Passenger and freight transportation via the Minnesota would gradually diminish during those weeks, until it finally had to be curtailed for the rest of the year. Only another winter could replenish the river.

The spring of 1861 had been a wet one. The Minnesota River "opened with a big flood;" and the first steamboat to try her out was the *Albany*, which reached Mankato on the first of April. The *Fanny Harris* and the *Favorite* soon retrieved contingents of soldiers from Fort Ridgely and brought them east so that they could continue down the Mississippi and help to "quell the southern rebellion." The water level of the Minnesota was said then to be so high that the riverboat crews could tell only by the positions of passing towns if their boats were actually following the true river channel. During the next two months, several companies operated boats that steamed up and down the course of the river. The water level began to drop dramatically as time went by, however. One report claimed that the "river had fallen 12 inches" during the week before the Lower Sioux Agency excursion was scheduled to take place. If that statement was even partially true, then this trip could get dicey.

The *Frank Steele* was a side-wheeled steam packet that had been built in Kentucky in 1857. This was the fifth year that the boat had been cruising along the Minnesota, and it was Captain N. B. Hatcher's second year on the waterway. Surely he was aware of the risks of taking a steamboat all the way to Redwood this late in the season. Though the excursion had been widely advertised as a flotilla of two steamboats, someone made the decision to take just the larger boat. Perhaps ticket sales were not as brisk as had been expected. Perhaps Hatcher laid down a ruling before the trip began.

Nevertheless, the *Frank Steele* left St. Paul on Monday afternoon and began to steam up the Minnesota River. Its destination was the Lower Sioux Agency in Redwood, 200 river miles away. On board was a diverse grouping of individuals. Governor Alexander Ramsey and his wife, Anna Earl (Jenks) Ramsey, were the most notable. Additional politicians included Indian agent Thomas J. Galbraith, who was in his first month of work in that position;

From left to right: the steamers *Grey Eagle, Frank Steele, Jeannette Roberts* and *Time and Tide* at the lower levee, St. Paul, in 1859. The *Frank Steele* played host to the 1861 Grand Pleasure Excursion on the Minnesota River. Photographer: William Henry Illingworth. (*Courtesy of the Minnesota Historical Society*)

U.S. District Attorney George A. Nourse; Jared Benson of Anoka, who was then Speaker of the Minnesota House of Representatives; and Alfred B. Brackett, Deputy Sheriff of Ramsey County. Four or five Englishmen—described by one observer as "well-behaved Cockneys"—went along for the ride. About 25 "painfully dirty" volunteers were headed for Fort Ridgely. And 25-30 ladies were also in attendance. In all, the steamboat had around 100 people on it when it shoved off from St. Paul, and it was rather crowded from the beginning. But each time the boat stopped at a town, other people came aboard, and no one left in return. "It is a small boat," wrote young Horace, "so that a great many of [the passengers] have to sleep wherever they can around on chairs, or on the floor, or on trunks, etc."

Thoreau and Mann were lucky enough to have gotten a stateroom. Those spaces were private but small. Everyone had to share communal washing facilities, courtesy of the onboard barber shop. The crew provided three meals a day; but according to one customer, the food was "greasy and badly cooked." Thoreau noted the presence of "a small cannon for salutes, & the money for the Indians (aye, and the gamblers, it was said, who were to bring it back in another boat)." The promoters had also guaranteed live musical entertainment. "The Great Western Band will go up on the *Steele* and all can exercise themselves in dancing on the way, and be amused at the way the Indians do it when they arrive at Redwood." This was billed as a "Grand Pleasure Excursion," after all. With a saloon that took up most of the space on its first floor, the *Frank Steele* must have exuded a real "party-boat" atmosphere.

By 9 p.m., the assembly had reached the town of Shakopee. Twelve hours later, Tuesday morning at 9 a.m., they were at Henderson. It took another twelve hours to reach Mankato. Progress was painfully slow, as Captain Hatcher and his crew steered the steamboat around the curves and made an attempt to avoid numerous snags in the water. Henry Thoreau later wrote an extensive letter to Concordian Frank Sanborn, in which he described the experience.

> This is eminently *the* river of Minnesota, for she shares the Mississippi with Wisconsin, and it is of incalculable value to her. It flows through a very fertile country, destined to be famous for its wheat; but it is a remarkably winding stream, so that Redwood is only half as far from its mouth by land as by water. There was not a straight reach a mile in length as far as we went,—generally you could not see a quarter of a mile of water, & the boat was steadily turning this way or that. At the greater bends, as the Traverse des Sioux, some of the passen-

gers were landed & walked across to be taken in on the other side. Two or three times you could have thrown a stone across the neck of the isthmus while it was from one to three miles around it. It was a very novel kind of navigation to me. The boat was perhaps the largest that had been up so high, & the water was rather low (it had been about 15 feet higher). In making a short turn, we repeatedly and designedly ran square into the steep and soft bank, taking in a cart-load of earth, this being more effectual than the rudder to fetch us about again; or the deeper water was so narrow & close to the shore, that we were obliged to run into & break down at least 50 trees which overhung the water, when we did not cut them off, repeatedly losing a part of our outworks, though the most exposed had been taken in. I could pluck almost any plant on the bank from the boat.

Horace wrote to his mother about the crookedness of the Minnesota River as well. He even timed one of its more intricate maneuvers: "Just after we passed New Ulm there was a great bend and the river came round so as to be about two rods from itself ... It took us seventeen minutes to go round at the rate of about 8 miles an hour."

During the daytime, the heat of summer and its "broiling sun" descended upon the passengers as well. One person went ashore and saw a thermometer that registered "103 degrees in the shade." Someone else put a positive spin on the entire experience: "The favorable weather, and the magnificent country compensated for the difficulty of navigation and made the excursion most delightful." "It is a beautiful day," agreed Horace, but "rather hot in the sun."

Since the river was at times only just wide enough to accommodate the *Frank Steele*, Henry Thoreau was given a wonderful opportunity to botanize from its deck. Traveling on the Minnesota wasn't the same as steaming up the Mississippi. On that wider and mightier river, the *Itasca* hadn't floated close enough to the shoreline to be able to identify much more than the largest trees. Here, trees and bushes were falling *into* the steamboat at the narrowest bends. In addition to the prevalent cottonwoods (which were responsible for many of the snags in the water), he saw elms, black willows, and long-leafed willows. Smaller plants included daisy fleabane, honewort, and larkspur. Both Thoreau and Mann mentioned seeing a large meadow "which was pink with wild roses" somewhere before the town of Henderson. Henry thought the patch was large enough to hold "acres" of blooms.

But it wasn't just the flora that caught Thoreau's attention. Flocks of passenger pigeons flew above and around the boat. He also saw swallows, king-fishers, blue jays, warbling vireos, red-winged blackbirds, blue herons, Wilson thrushes, and rose-breasted grosbeaks. He heard the call of the whippoor-will. Turtle tracks could clearly be seen on the muddy and sandy shores. Sometimes the turtles themselves were sitting in the sun. A few muskrats had built lodges along the periphery. Small, young ducks were still learning how to swim around the clumps of fuzzy down that were dropping from the cot-tonwoods. The Minnesota might consist of "sky-tinted water." But when Henry scooped up a sample of the river, he deemed it to be "clay-colored water, yet pretty clear in a tumbler when settled." Henry treated this mini-trip like a scientific excursion to a new and different world. He took advantage of the situation and documented his observations in his field notebook.

One area that intrigued him was the "Big Woods." As they steamed upriv-er, Thoreau noted that the "big wood" was located near Henderson. On the way back, he wrote that it "may have been from Le Sueur to Belle Plaine." The original 2000-square mile forest known as the "Big Woods" was a sin-gular habitat of south-central Minnesota, and it once stretched from Mankato to Monticello. It was such a different landscape from the prairie and oak openings that early French explorers called it *bois fort* or *bois grand*, which Americans later translated into "Big Woods." At the time of this excursion, most of those trees had not yet been cut. It made for a notewor-thy change of scenery from the deck of the *Frank Steele*.

If Henry and Horace scrutinized the surrounding landscape when the steamboat stopped at the town of Henderson, they might have seen a farm-house or even the farmers themselves standing on top of the bluff on the other side of the river. German immigrants Wilhelm and Sophia Ney had come here in the 1850s, and they bought acreage that overlooked Henderson. Part of the "Big Woods" was on their property.

Though he was certainly busy botanizing, Thoreau didn't ignore his fellow passengers altogether. An "Illinois man" engaged him in conversations about plants and birds. The gentleman is mentioned several times in the notebook. In a few instances, he served as a Midwestern guide and provided Henry with local names for some of the plants they saw on the shore. Thoreau either never learned the man's name, or he chose not to write it down.

The "voyage was nearly half over" when he ran into Joseph May on board. May (1836-1918) was the son of Samuel and Lucretia May and was thus a cousin to Louisa May Alcott and her sisters back in Concord. "It has chanced that about half the men whom I have spoken with in Minnesota, whether travelers or settlers, were from Massachusetts," Thoreau wrote to

Frank Sanborn. He made a special note to tell Sanborn about meeting Joseph May because both men had attended Harvard at about the same time. May was a seasoned traveler himself, having spent some time in Europe. He would soon enroll in the Harvard Divinity School and would follow his father's path to the pulpit. May "had been looking for us at St. Anthony," Thoreau said. The Alcotts must have told their relative of Henry and Horace's original intention of staying with the Thatcher family. It was only by the oddest circumstances then, that Thoreau and May's paths crossed at all.

By early Wednesday evening, the *Frank Steele* reached Fort Ridgely. Horace wrote that the steamboat had "been within 8 miles of it by land a little after noon but on account of the crooks it took us a good while to get there." If at all possible, the Minnesota River was getting narrower and curvier. Captain Hatcher decided to dock here and make a night of it, rather than pass over the last 20-30 miles of this stretch in the dark. The two dozen or so volunteers immediately left the boat for their new temporary residency at the fort, presumably to be trained for war.

A number of the other passengers went ashore as well, merely to tour the facility. Construction on Fort Ridgely had begun just eight years earlier, in 1853. The main purpose of the post was to monitor and maintain the quiet coexistence of the incoming settlers and the Dakota who lived along the river. On this day in 1861, the officer in charge apologized to some of the visitors for the emptiness of the quarters. He explained that the troops who had left for the war in April had taken all of their furnishings with them; so the place was rather bare. Horace climbed up to the fort and noted that the sides closest to the prairie were guarded by "granite garrison houses, two stories high." Another visitor remarked that the ridge that the fort rested upon commanded "a glorious view, almost unlimited, in every direction." As for the outpost itself,

> It is better described as a military station, having none of the ordinary characteristics of a Fort, consisting only of a collection of buildings, rectangularly arranged, the soldiers' barracks, a most comfortable and spacious building, filling the entire northerly side; the storehouse, also stone, and the officers' quarters, these being neat wooden houses, occupying the other three sides. A few large cannon, with two mountain howitzers are still remaining, but there is no attempt at entrenchment.

Having seen enough, the travelers gradually returned to the boat. They went to bed knowing that they would see the natives at the Lower Sioux Agency the next day.

But according to one passenger, it was far from easy to fall asleep that night. Now that the *Frank Steele* was stationary,

> the mosquitoes hitherto kept off by the motion of the boat, make a dead set at us, driving some from their berths to deck and detouring others from seeking theirs. By about two in the morning feeling drowsy enough to defy the troublesome inseckts, we were fairly under way for the land of dreams. But by this time the band is drunk and will play the liveliest tunes overhead to the confusion of slumber till seized by a sudden desire to refresh themselves by a walk in the night air and rejoin the boat some miles ahead they train off and the noise of their instruments dies gratefully away in the distance.

With the musicians finally out of range, this man hoped to find "sleep at last." Then a thunderstorm promptly arrived on the scene, bestowing such a downpour onto the boat that it flooded at least one stateroom. One wonders how many people thought at that point that the "grand pleasure" was leaking out of this particular excursion. And they had yet to see the Indians!

The *Frank Steele* resumed its journey the next morning at first light, at 4 a.m. It reached the sloping riverbank by the agency at Redwood at 9 a.m. One passenger noted that "a number of swarthy young vagabonds in ragged blankets" had run alongside the steamboat for the last few miles. With the craft docked at its ultimate destination, a crew member lit the fuse of the onboard cannon in order to announce to the neighborhood the excursion's arrival. But the cannon had been "fully charged for a loud report," and it "burst when it was fired." The back of the gun, "the breech, weighing about thirty pounds, was thrown into the cabin, passing through a crowd of passengers, breaking the railing, cabin door, &c." Miraculously, no one was injured in the accident. By that time, some of the Dakota had boarded the boat and "at once began to examine everything with the greatest curiosity." There was certainly much to see on a fancy steamboat.

Word was received that the annuity payment would *not* be made today after all. But the agency would be hosting a council meeting at 1 p.m., with a feast and a traditional dance to be presented afterward. Captain Hatcher informed the excursionists that the *Frank Steele* would be staying at Redwood only into the evening hours. Anyone who wanted a ride back to St. Paul would have to return to the boat at the conclusion of the dance.

Henry Thoreau and Horace Mann, Jr., spent the extra time botanizing. They did not go far to get a good start. The steep slope at Redwood contained a variety of plant life. But Thoreau failed to recognize some of the specimens, and neither could he find them in his copy of Asa Gray's botanical manual. He was relegated to making detailed descriptions with the hopes of learning their identities later. His notebook inventory included such entries as "smooth parsnip-smelling plant on prairie;" "yellow composite flower of prairie, going out of bloom, clasping leaves;" and "Hypoxis-like flower, but more slender & 2-flowered only." Evidently no one had yet documented the existence of these wildflowers.

Once they climbed the ridge above the river, Henry and Horace could see most of the domain of the Lower Sioux Agency. Thoreau later wrote:

> Redwood is a mere locality, scarcely an Indian village—where there is a store & some houses have been built for them. We were now fairly on the great plains, and looking south, and after walking that way 3 miles, could see no trees in that horizon. The buffalo was said to be feeding within 25 or 30 miles–

Horace went a little farther in his explorations and brought more plant samples back with him. The two men might easily have been on sensory overload. To not only be walking among the Dakota, but also to be standing on some of the flattest landscape they had ever seen! Which feature commanded their attention more?

Thoreau noted that the Indians he saw looked "hungry, not sleek & round-faced." He had also heard that each chief would earn $100 and each brave would get $20 whenever the annuity payment actually took place. Another passenger counted 40-50 "Farmer Indians" in attendance. "Fifty-five new suits of clothing had been distributed before our arrival, and many are already endeavoring to carry out the desires of our government, though probably with little success." The agency grounds were awash with a variety of individuals and fashion styles: from natives to white politicians; from buckskins to ballroom dress.

At noon or at 1 p.m. (for the reports differ), "a council was held under the north side of the missionary's house." The government officials sat in chairs and spoke from their seats. Other Dakota and visitors stood gathered in small groups on the surrounding grounds. Interpreters were supplied for both sides. The Indians smoked and passed their pipes around to one another during the proceedings. To any statement that was agreeable to them, the Dakota automatically chanted a hearty "Ho!"

The first speaker was Clark W. Thompson, the regional Superintendent of Indian Affairs. He had been visiting the Minnesota River agencies in order to prepare for the annuity payment, and he had met the *Frank Steele* excursion when it arrived. He was still new to the position, having just assumed his duties on May 14, 1861. His St. Paul based office had oversight of a number of tribal arrangements in the northern plains area. He began the meeting by telling the Dakota "that he had been appointed by the Great Father at Washington, to look after their interests, and those of all the Red men of the State. He would try to do it faithfully." He probably did not mention to them that he would first have to clean up the debt and the ignored tasks left by Redwood's outgoing Indian agent, Joseph R. Brown. Another speaker would bring up that matter.

Next came Governor Alexander Ramsey, "saying he was glad to see so many whom he had seen ten years before, when they were under his care." The governor wanted to assure the Indians "that the Great Father has a fort a short distance" from the Lower Sioux Agency; but that "he was sending soldiers, not to harm or menace them, but as a token of respect for their Great Sioux nation, and to protect them against bad white men." In reality, Fort Ridgely was being used those days as a training ground for troops heading south. The Indians were probably aware of that fact.

Newly appointed Indian agent Thomas J. Galbraith wrapped up the governmental speeches. He told the Dakota "that he was sent to look after the interests of this nation only; that he intended to protect them and give them justice, and care for them as a father should care for his children." He too had to play catch up with duties that had been left unfulfilled. One of his first missions was to plant a thousand acres of corn. It was a little late in the season; but the planting nevertheless had to be done so that enough food could be put in storage for the winter months.

The Dakota spokesman of the day was Red Owl, an Mdewakanton from Wabasha's band. He was known to oppose the farming initiative and to support the traditional life to which his people had been accustomed. One excursionist described him as "a dark, sinewy man, of intelligent countenance, in which, singularly enough, might be traced no slight resemblance to Demosthenes." Various reporters commended Red Owl on his abilities as a true "orator." He was "energetic," and he "enunciated earnestly, and gesticulated fiercely and vigorously." At least one bystander wondered at the accuracy of the interpretation, for surely Red Owl's "speech was emasculated of all its native vigor and eloquence." Yet, even if the whites did not get an exact rendering of his words, they got the gist of his salient points. He made quite a number of them.

Given the chance to speak, the Dakota representative made the most of his opportunity. According to one viewer, "His complaints were many and bitter. Said they had been promised all these things before, and had been cheated out of them." The treaties had guaranteed them money, supplies and property; but the Indians never got "more than enough to cover the nakedness of the women and children." The former Redwood agent had rarely been on site, Red Owl claimed, and he had additionally mismanaged finances. Dollars that went toward building a "score of worthless little one story houses" would have been put to better use in the education of his people. Supplies either never made it to the Agency or were not distributed logically and in a timely fashion. He requested "a store-house of their own, where the goods cannot slip through any body's fingers!" Their allocations should not be "scattered about the State, or carted off to another tribe to be returned in small parcels or not at all." Since new government men had just been assigned to see to their needs, Red Owl and his friends may have rightly decided that this council was the perfect time to set the record straight and demand the services that were due to them. When would they be able to do this again, in front of such a large group of witnesses?

At least some of the white visitors were moved by Red Owl's passionate address. Henry Thoreau later wrote that the man had "the advantage in point of truth and earnestness, and therefore of eloquence. ... They were quite dissatisfied with the white man's treatment of them & probably have reason to be so." Another excursionist noted that,

> The speeches consisted of the usual excuses and fair promises on our side, and the ordinary complaints from the Indians, of injustice and fraud, probably, alas! too well founded in fact. There was, to a sympathetic spectator, a touching contrast between the plausible demeanor and language of the white dignitaries, and the simple, untutored earnestness of the savages.

According to the few printed third-party reports, the Dakota were the clear winners of the podium that day.

Henry Thoreau also wrote that "The most prominent chief was named Little Crow." Thoreau did not learn Red Owl's name until he read it in a newspaper article a few days later. Had Thoreau met Little Crow in person at the Lower Sioux Agency? Or had someone else pointed out Little Crow to him? We do not know.

At the conclusion of the council meeting, Governor Ramsey presented the natives with two beef oxen. (The beasts probably made the trip up the river in the hold of the *Frank Steele.*) Thoreau jotted in his notes that one of the oxen was "cut in 5 parts," and a general feast ensued for all in attendance. Thoreau also saw one of the Indians start a fire for his pipe by striking a flint and using the spark to ignite maple wood fragments. Finally, the man from Massachusetts was getting a chance to see for himself the techniques and habits of native culture that he had hitherto only read about.

At about 5 p.m., a group of 30-50 dancers arrived on the scene. Thoreau's notes about this "monkey dance" were brief: "12 musicians on drums & others strike arrows against bows. The dancers blow some flutes—keep good time—move feet & shoulders, one or both—no shirts—5 bands there." As a flute player himself, he might have been most interested in that aspect of the performance.

Another excursionist submitted a lengthier report to a local newspaper and added an editorial review at its conclusion.

> The dancers, mostly young, quickly ranged themselves around a squatting group of older men, who began beating rude drums, with great energy and in a sort of rhythm adapted to the performance. The dance was to be the "monkey dance," a new invention, so said, originating in a dream of some young brave. The monkey was represented by a papoose about as big as one, gaily dressed and held by a good looking squaw. The dancers were dressed in various colored shirts, leather leggin[g]s, mostly, and strange, helmet-shaped caps, of fur and horse hair, with small horns and gaily painted and decorated. The faces of the men when exposed, and the limbs, were brightly painted, the colors being apparently earthy pigments, coarsely laid on. All being ready, ... the dance began. It consisted of nothing but the rudest hoppings about the circle, some times in single line, and sometimes two or more deep, with wild howls and vehement gesticulations and brandishing of the little hoops held in their left hands. On the whole, if at all interesting, it was still more a pitiable, disgusting spectacle. Finally, if there is any sincere interest felt by those concerned with Indian affairs, in elevating the moral and social conditions of these poor childish creatures, all such relics of their barbarism as these dances, should be conscientiously discouraged.

That correspondent voiced the opinions of other excursion members by expressing disappointment at not being able to witness the annuity payment itself. But what the group had seen "gave perhaps as good a spectacle of Indian manners and character as could be enjoyed in so short a visit." The dance lasted about an hour. Afterward most of the visitors made their way back down the slope to the Minnesota River. The steamboat and its impatient crew awaited them.

Captain Hatcher aimed the *Frank Steele* back to Fort Ridgely for the night. Left behind in Redwood were the top government officials and a smattering of people who were determined to see the annuities paid in person. The rest of the passengers evidently celebrated in style, now that they were heading downstream without the biggest celebrities along for the ride. One said that "A delightful evening was spent on deck, listening to music from the Great Western Band, and afterward to a quartette of stringed instruments, besides an excellent solo, 'Sound from Home,' upon the violin." Certainly, this was the kind of music the excursionists were more accustomed to hearing than the native dancing and drumming they had witnessed earlier in the day. Life was quickly returning to normal for them.

The on-board band continued to entertain everyone during the two-day trip back to St. Paul, and not merely with their instruments. Some of the performers launched into an impromptu reenactment of the Lower Sioux Agency proceedings. One of the band members imitated Red Owl. Another one, "by the aid of stuffing under his vest," did a good job of mirroring Governor Ramsey. Others portrayed the rest of the Dakota, "arrayed in moccasins and quilts borrowed from the state-rooms, and armed with their bows and arrows." In this version of the council meeting, the head of the state told the natives that "South Carolina has been set apart to your tribe for a reservation, and you can henceforth occupy it as a perpetual hunting ground." The faux Indians "performed their part to a charm" by chanting "Ugh" after each one of the governor's pronouncements, all to the amusement of the audience. A good time was obviously had by all in attendance.

Neither Henry Thoreau nor Horace Mann mentioned the tableau in their notes or letters, so it is possible that they missed the performance. Thoreau did however witness the show-and-tell of his fellow passengers as they flaunted the trinkets they had purchased at the Agency. Many had paid from fifty cents to several dollars for authentic Indian prayer pipes carved from red quartzite, or pipestone. According to one reporter, the pipes "were almost the only thing [the Dakota] had ready to sell." The unique stone came from quarries along the river and was soft enough to be crafted into intricate designs. They were "cut with singular dexterity, and ... [were] sometimes quite elaborate, imitating quite well, heads of men and horses, even the whole human form, and often cunningly inlaid in arabesques of lead. ... The fine ones were often as much as six or eight inches in length and finely polished." Now that they had passed from Dakota hands into those of the excursionists, the red stone pipes were fated to be among the rows of random artifacts perched upon fireplace mantels or on the shelves of curiosity cabinets.

But none of them would be going back to Concord and into the drawing room of the Thoreau home. Instead, Henry Thoreau had carried away bigger treasures: three pieces of Dakota buckskin clothing decorated with colorful quills and beads. He now owned a dress, a shirt-jacket, and a pair of trousers. His fascination with Indians had obviously led him to somehow acquire these items; but how? Had Thoreau found the buckskins in a free discard pile, after wool and cotton clothing had been distributed to the natives? Had he bartered with one of the Dakota to acquire them? Had he negotiated with a white trader who may have gotten the garb in an exchange with a "Farmer Indian"? Was Thoreau acting out of concern, hoping to financially assist at least one of the Dakota by buying these clothes? Or was he thinking merely of preserving evidence of this Native American culture before it was entirely extinguished? Unfortunately, we do not know his intentions. He left us no answers.

As the *Frank Steele* steamed back to St. Paul, Captain Hatcher faced the same kinds of difficulties that he and his crew had tackled on the way up to Redwood. Thoreau noted that they were somewhere near New Ulm when the boat "Pushed over a tree & disturbed the bats" and simultaneously took in "a cartload of earth." Both Henry and Horace documented a delay when a fog descended over the Minnesota River after the boat had passed Mankato. The next morning, Horace got up to find that they "were stuck fast about two miles north of St. Peters, but we got off in about half an hour." That might have been the same instance that Thoreau wrote of when he told Frank Sanborn:

> We once ran fairly on to a concealed rock, with a shock that aroused all the passengers, & rested there, & the mate went below with a lamp expecting to find a hole, but he did not. Snags & sawyers were so common that I forgot to mention them. The sound of the boat rumbling over one was the ordinary music. However, as long as the boiler did not burst, we knew that no serious accident was likely to happen.

Without further incident and by the light of a full moon, the *Frank Steele* arrived at the St. Paul dock on Saturday night at 9 p.m. The newspaper reports would later commend Captain Hatcher and his crew on a job well done. Henry Thoreau and Horace Mann, Jr., checked back into the Merchants Hotel for the night. The next morning, they would begin making their way home.

The water level of the Minnesota River continued to drop. One report stated that "by the last of June [it] became so low that navigation above the rapids had to be suspended." Those rapids were located near the town of Carver, only 30 miles upriver from Minneapolis. By comparison, the Lower Sioux Agency lay about 170 miles past those rapids. The "Grand Pleasure Excursion" had returned to St. Paul successfully and seemingly, just in time.

According to the report that Superintendent Clark W. Thompson later filed with authorities in Washington, the annuity payment finally took place at the Lower Sioux Agency on Wednesday, June 26. The one at the Upper Agency at Yellow Medicine, 40-50 miles upriver, was held on Tuesday, July 16. Sarah F. Wakefield, a doctor's wife who lived near the Upper Agency, later documented the latter event:

> There were at Yellow Medicine, I believe, four trading houses, where were kept groceries and dry goods for the Indians, cheating the creatures very much. Indians would buy on credit, promising to pay at the time of payment. They have no way of keeping accounts, so the traders have their own way at the time of payment. All the Indians are counted, every person giving his name, each Band by themselves. At the time of payment they are called by name from the window to receive their money (which at the Upper Agency was only nine dollars to each person). As soon as they receive it, the Traders surround them, saying, you owe me so much for flour. Another says you owe so much for sugar, &c., and the Indian gives it all up, never knowing whether it is right or not. Many Indians pay before the payment with furs, still they are caught up by these Traders, and very seldom a man passes away with his money. I saw a poor fellow one day swallow his money. I wondered he did not choke to death, but he said "They will not have mine, for I do not owe them."

What would Thoreau and Mann and the *Frank Steele* passengers have thought if they had been witness to such a scene? The description does not paint a positive picture of any of the parties involved.

The stone warehouse at the Lower Sioux Agency was built in 1861, in response to Red Owl's request during the June ceremony witnessed by Thoreau and Mann. It is the only building remaining from that time.

In October 1861, Indian agent Thomas J. Galbraith reported that the construction of a stone warehouse was almost finished at the Lower Sioux Agency. That portion of Red Owl's demands, voiced at the council in June, had evidently been acted upon. That was the good news. Seen now only in retrospect, the bad news was this: no one knew it at the time, but the week-long delay in the payment of the 1861 annuities was a mere precursor to the series of devastating events soon to take place. And those were the last annuities paid to the Dakota of the Minnesota River valley.

Over the course of the next nine months, tensions developed in central Minnesota. Discontent began to simmer in the relationships between the settlers and the Indians; between the traders and the Indians; between the Indians and U.S. government officials; and among the Dakota themselves, between those who farmed and those who hunted. Disagreements and mis-understandings centered on the basics of life: supplies, food, money, and land ownership. Different people had different ideas and wanted to lead different ways of life. Alas, that kind of diversity was not championed in the

American Midwest in the nineteenth century.

Mother Nature added to the mix by dealing a few bad hands of her own. In the fall of 1861, an infestation of cutworms destroyed the corn crop of the Dakotas. The winter that followed was a cold and hard one that deposited much snow in central Minnesota. The usual spring flooding resulted. Without a previous harvest in storage to rely on, the Dakota were hungry and were struggling to survive even by the summer of 1862. The June annuity payment, which could have helped them, was met with delay upon inexplicable delay. The recipe for certain disaster was brought to a full rolling boil.

With frustrations escalating, a group of four young Dakota killed five white settlers in Acton Township on August 17, 1862. Immediately the Indian community at large knew that consequences would have to follow. A council should be held: but whom could the Indians turn to for advice? Dakota spokesman Red Owl had died a year earlier, just a few months after giving his impassioned speech at the Lower Sioux Agency ceremony. Little Crow seemed to be his most likely successor as a chief and advisor. The frenzied and fight-ready members of the Dakota soldiers' lodge immediately went to see him at his house near Redwood Falls.

Little Crow was straddling a cultural line. He had adopted some of the white man's ways, but he still adhered to traditional Dakota religious beliefs. One of the young Dakota soldiers accused him of being a coward. In response, Little Crow not only denounced him but made an intelligent assessment of the challenges their people were now facing.

> We are only little herds of buffaloes left scattered; the great herds that once covered the prairies are no more. See!—the white men are like the locusts when they fly so thick that the whole sky is a snowstorm. You may kill one—two—ten; yes, as many as the leaves in the forest yonder, and their brothers will not miss them. Kill one—two—ten, and ten times ten will come to kill you. Count your fingers all day long and white men with guns in their hands will come faster than you can count.

To those Dakota who thought that all of the U.S. soldiers were busy enough down in the southern part of the country, Little Crow also had a warning.

> Yes; they fight among themselves—away off. Do you hear the thunder of their big guns? No; it would take you two moons to run down to where they are fighting, and all the way your

path would be among white soldiers as thick as tamaracks in the swamps of the Ojibways. Yes; they fight among themselves, but if you strike at them they will all turn on you and devour you and your women and little children just as the locusts in their time fall on the trees and devour all the leaves in one day. You are fools.

Nevertheless, Little Crow confirmed that he would lead the people and take part in the oncoming battle.

The Dakota attacked the Upper and Lower Sioux Agencies, Fort Ridgely, and the town of New Ulm. Though they did some damage to both life and property, they could not notch a clear win at any of the venues. In the middle of September, an army of one thousand U.S. soldiers led by Colonel Henry H. Sibley finally moved up the Minnesota River valley. A peace party began negotiating with Sibley with regard to captives and their release. Little Crow's prophecy of whites being like locusts appeared to have come true.

After more than a month filled with skirmishes and fights, an estimated 500 whites had been killed. The number of Dakota deaths was more difficult to ascertain, but was probably at least several dozen. Governor Ramsey reacted by stating that the "Sioux Indians of Minnesota must be exterminated or driven forever beyond the borders of the State." In the end, 38 Dakota were publicly hanged at Mankato for their participation in the war. More than 300 were imprisoned nearby. About 1700 Dakota men, women, and children spent a cold week in November marching a 200-mile trail of tears from Redwood to Fort Snelling, where they could be more closely guarded. The rest of the Indians were pushed west and out of Minnesota. The treaties were nullified, the annuities were cancelled, and the reservations and their agencies were disbanded. The Dakota War of 1862 was effectively squelched. The governor got what he wanted.

Henry Thoreau did not live to hear this tragic news from Minnesota. How would he have felt, knowing that the Dakota people he had seen during the "Grand Pleasure Excursion" were now either dead, imprisoned, or exiled? What might his reaction have been when receiving word that the makers and previous owners of the buckskin clothing were gone from the Minnesota River valley? Which side would he have taken? Would he have accepted the Dakota's fate as the natural and necessary conclusion of an indigenous culture that was standing in the way of western civilization? Or would he have been mortified at the murders taking place out on the Plains? We do not know.

In the twentieth and twenty-first centuries, Thoreau scholars and fans have debated his silence on the issue of native rights. After all, Thoreau had been a staunch abolitionist. He had supported and participated in the Underground Railroad. He had believed in John Brown and his design to end the abhorrence of slavery in the South. Why had Thoreau not also campaigned for the rights of Indians, since he was so obviously intrigued by them?

One possible reason could relate to proximity. Back home, he had had only a few interactions and conversations with native people; and those individuals had been practically assimilated into the dominant society. It was only when he went to Minnesota that he got a glimpse of what native life had really become. When he returned to Concord, he had other projects that he needed to work on. He had no time to worry about what was happening elsewhere in the country, especially in a region that lay 1500 miles to the west. But I would like to think that if Henry Thoreau had learned of the fate of the Dakotas, the news would have given him something sizable to contemplate. Perhaps it would have been the catalyst that would have caused him to pick up his pen, step to the front of the lecture hall, or otherwise take arms against that particularly nasty sea of American trouble. How could he have remained unmoved?

In spots where it has not been deliberately straightened, the Minnesota River can be just as winding and twisted today as it was in the past. It can flood with snowmelt in the springtime and can grow shallow and dry with the heat of the summer sun. Individual paddlers are encouraged to explore the scenic waterway by canoe or by kayak. Checking water levels ahead of time is advised. Steamboats of traditional size and weight would still run into problems if they attempted the full trip from St. Paul to Redwood Falls and back, especially after mid-summer.

Some of the settlements that Thoreau and Mann passed by have grown into sizable cities and towns: Shakopee, Chaska, Jordan, Belle Plaine, Henderson, Le Sueur, St. Peter, Mankato, New Ulm, and Redwood Falls. Located at the most abrupt turn in the river, Mankato is now the largest city along the route, with more than 39,000 residents. Henderson still has fewer than a thousand.

Across the river from Henderson, members of the Ney family continued over the years to work their land. The farm passed down through subsequent Ney generations until the 1990s. When Ruth Ney passed away, she bequeathed 360 acres to Le Sueur County for the purpose of creating a wildlife preserve. Another Ney relative donated 80 more acres, and the Wilhelm Ney Memorial Wildlife Game Refuge was formed. Soon afterward, the Ney Environmental Education Foundation was organized as well. Today Le Sueur County officials and a separate board of directors manage the Ney Nature Center on the property. Original farm buildings remain, including the homesteaders' cabin that was built in the mid-1850s. The Ney Nature Center gained public attention when deformed frogs were found in a pond on the site in 1995 and 1996. Its domain includes a fragment of the "Big Woods." Much of the rest of the "Big Woods" has been lost to agricultural or urban development. The largest fragment is preserved in Nerstrand-Big Woods State Park, about 55 miles due south of Minneapolis.

Fort Ridgely was abandoned as a military outpost in 1867. The state purchased the fort itself in 1896, and then acquired the 148 acres surrounding it to establish Fort Ridgely State Park in 1911. A nine hole golf course was opened within the park in 1927. Today the combination historic site and state park occupies 478 acres. Amenities include a variety of hiking trails, a campground, and a newly-renovated golf course. The interior educational exhibits at the fort are open only from Memorial Day to Labor Day; but the grounds are open year round and are available to anyone with recreational or historic pursuits.

All but one of the original buildings of the Lower Sioux Agency were destroyed during the conflict between the United States government and the Dakota people in 1862. The brand-new warehouse was gutted by fire, but its stone walls survived. The structure was eventually purchased by a German immigrant who turned it into a farmhouse. It served as a private residence under various ownerships for almost one hundred years and experienced a number of exterior changes during that time period. In the late 1990s, the Minnesota Historical Society undertook the project of restoring the warehouse to its 1861 condition. Today it is part of the Lower Sioux Agency Historic Site. The property includes a visitor center that offers exhibits and programs, a series of interpretive trails, and footpath access to the former ferry crossing of the Minnesota River. The site is open only from Memorial Day to Labor Day.

In spite of their forced exile from the state of Minnesota, some Dakota gradually returned to the greater Redwood Falls area. Others had remained in the river valley all along because they had maintained loyalty to the U.S. government in 1862. Those "loyalists" had each been given up to 80 acres of land. A reservation was established here through legislative acts in 1888, 1889, and 1890. Now the tribal land of the Lower Sioux Indian Community consists of more than 1700 acres. Many members live on the reservation or within ten miles of it. The tribe now operates a number of businesses, including the Jackpot Junction Casino and Hotel, located just a mile and a half west of the Lower Sioux Agency Historic Site.

The main quarry that served as the source of the red quartzite for the Dakota people is now part of the Pipestone National Monument, located in southwestern Minnesota, near the South Dakota border. There, native craftsmen demonstrate their carving skills to visitors. The stone is still mined on a select basis by those with Native American ancestry. An old quartzite quarry is located in New Ulm. Pieces of the distinctive rock can still be plucked from the Minnesota River shorelines.

Little Crow left Minnesota after the 1862 war. He spent months traveling throughout present-day South Dakota, North Dakota, and Manitoba, meeting with other Dakota and searching for an ideal spot for relocation. In July 1863, Little Crow and his son Wowinape were back in central Minnesota, near the town of Hutchinson. They were picking berries when Little Crow was shot and killed by a white settler. According to one historian, "Wowinape dressed his father in new moccasins for his trip into the afterlife, wrapped his body in a blanket, and departed." But the settlers found the seemingly-abandoned body. Little Crow's killer was given $500 by the state in exchange for the scalp lock. The Indian's skull was donated to the Minnesota Historical Society; and it and his forearms "were put on display in a case in the society's museum." His remains were eventually removed from public eyes during the twentieth century. In 1971, they were turned over to his descendants, who buried him in a private plot in South Dakota. A statue of Little Crow now stands in downtown Hutchinson. An artist's rendition of his face has been installed beside Minnehaha Falls in Minneapolis.

The three pieces of buckskin Dakota clothing that Henry Thoreau brought home from the Lower Sioux Agency excursion are now owned by the Concord Museum in Concord, Massachusetts. A century and a half after their creation, the dress, shirt-jacket, and pair of trousers are hardly in display condition. They remain in storage. Photos of each item can be viewed on the museum's web site.

The owners of the Merchants Hotel in St. Paul continued to make improvements to the facility. Multi-story additions were erected on either side of the original structure. In 1870, the original log building where

Thoreau and Mann stayed was finally torn down, and a four-story stone edifice took its place. For decades, the proprietors of the Merchants Hotel enjoyed their status as being one of the most successful hostelries in the Twin Cities area. The massive complex eventually held 275 rooms, a variety of lounges, a large billiard hall, and a basement barber shop. But by the turn of the century, other and more lavish accommodations began to be available in the area; and in 1921, the Merchants Hotel declared bankruptcy. It was demolished in 1923. Today the Minnesota Telecenter occupies that block between Kellogg (formerly Third Street) and Fourth Street.

A promotional postcard for the Concord Museum shows a variety of Thoreau artifacts, including a pair of Dakota buckskin trousers he acquired during the Lower Sioux Agency excursion. (*Courtesy of Lynn Sugarman*)

On May 31, 1864, the *Frank Steele* was docked at La Crosse, Wisconsin. A government official was on board to supervise the inspection and the testing of the boilers. But he evidently mismanaged the process. Interior pressure built with such force that one of the steel drums burst. The first mate and eight deck hands were dosed with steaming, scalding water. Two men died of their injuries within a few days. Though initial reports stated that the boat would quickly resume a regular schedule, it appears not to have done so. That accident ended the career of the *Frank Steele*, after just seven years of river duty.

In the fall of 2007, I drove from Massachusetts to Minnesota in order to participate in a Thoreau-related program. On Saturday, October 6, I would be attending a symposium called "Henry David Thoreau: His Journey to the Twentieth Century" at the Minneapolis Central Library. Friend and fellow Thoreauvian Dale R. Schwie and I were scheduled to give a tag-team presentation on "Thoreau's 1861 Journey to Minnesota." We would be the opening act for the day, so we had to do a good job. We had just one hour to outline the basics of the Journey West for the audience. We had divided our talk into three parts. I would take Henry and Horace from Concord to the Mississippi River. Then Dale would lead them up to the Twin Cities area and talk about what they saw and did in Minnesota. When he was done, I would get the two men home. We had created a computerized slideshow with appropriate graphics, and we had practiced our scripts together. Both of us had presented the subject in public on previous occasions, as solo speakers. We both knew that the only challenge we faced was fitting everything we wanted to say into that one-hour time slot.

I would not talk about the Lower Sioux Agency excursion this time. Dale would cover it. But I thought I should at least make the drive out to the Agency and to Fort Ridgely before our event. Up to this point, I had only read about both places. And if I intended to follow the entire length of Thoreau and Mann's route, then I would have to make the trip along the Minnesota River someday. I had built extra time into my schedule so that I could visit these sites a few days before I was due to be in Minneapolis.

The trouble is, I already knew that I would have to come back and do it all again. The visitor centers and main exhibits were closed for the season. I decided to go out there anyway, to see what I could see. At least I would be assured of knowing the terrain whenever I got another chance to visit.

The drive along the Minnesota River was interesting and relaxing. The trip took a little longer than I expected; but I hardly needed to set any land-speed records. I was in tourist mode. I had never been to this part of the state, so everything was new and different. I already had a hotel reservation in New Ulm. I had lots of time to explore.

It seemed easiest to stop at Fort Ridgely first. When I pulled into the lot at the park office, it was obvious that the building was closed. Visitors were on their honor to put their entrance fees in the special envelopes and slip them into the box. I filled out all the paperwork, enclosed my dollar bills, and was soon on my way, driving uphill to the actual fort. The lot there was empty as well. I guess I was the only one who wanted to see the place on this cloudy weekday in the middle of autumn. I parked the car and started walking, snapping photos along the way.

This was a western fort, for sure. The grounds were wide and open. I was used to the ones back east: those that had spiky log stockades forming lumpy but solid circles around a group of log cabins. That was my stereotyped image of a fort. After all, that was what I had seen on *F Troop* on TV. Hadn't those guys been stationed somewhere west of the Missouri River? I had watched every episode with glee and admiration. Sometimes I wished I could be Wrangler Jane. On other days, my affections ran to the Lone Ranger or to the Cisco Kid. I was *heavily* into The West and cowboys and Indians stories when I was younger. Maybe that explained my attraction to Thoreau's own Journey West.

My vision of the traditional American fort had first disappeared during a trip I made from Illinois to Wyoming in June 2000. Back then, I was registered to participate in a bird of prey survey at The Nature Conservancy's ranch near Tensleep, a tiny town in north central Wyoming. Along the way, I made a spur of the moment stop at Fort Laramie.

But when I pulled my car onto the site, I was somewhat disappointed. The fort didn't look like what I had envisioned. All I saw were separate block buildings with a lot of space between them, and situated at right angles around a long, rectangular yard. Where was the stockade? How in the world could soldiers defend such a seemingly haphazard arrangement of structures? Anyone who wanted to could just come riding or walking into the compound. I was baffled beyond belief.

One by one, I toured the buildings. When I entered the trading post, I saw that its shelves were outfitted with all kinds of items that would have been available for purchase back in the day. One counter was stacked with furry animal pelts. The man who greeted me was either dressed for the part or was a true historical interpreter. Normally I didn't bother such folks, but he and I were alone. "I have questions," I said. He nodded and told me to ask away. I explained my confusion at the missing wooden stockade to guard against intruders. "What's to prevent anyone from attacking this place, the way it's set up?"

He opened his arms and lifted them as if to reach out and embrace the store. "You're standing in it." He explained that the Native Americans relied on the fort's trading post for food and supplies. It wasn't just for the convenience of the soldiers and the settlers. "Why would they attack it? They'd only be hurting themselves in the long run. They would be eliminating their main source of commerce. Besides, where would we get enough wood here to build a stockade?" He let me think about that. He had a point. We were in the middle of the Great Plains. Often the only trees to be found were a few cottonwoods lining the riverbanks, with their roots eager to access whatever water they could reach. I had been approaching the picture of a fort with eyes from the East, back where we had hardwood forests galore. I felt like a dunce. So much for the historical accuracy of *F Troop*.

That conversation came back to me, now that I was standing at Fort Ridgely. The grounds were similar in layout to those at Fort Laramie, with no wooden stockade. Many of its original buildings were gone, but markers showed where they once stood. I sauntered around the perimeter and read all of the informational placards. I was pleased to learn that the stone storehouse, still standing, had been here in 1861. Horace Mann had come all the way up to this ridge, and he could have seen this same structure. That was good. That made a connection for me. But by the time I made my way back to the flagpole, I was angry. How could I not be, after reading about the horrible travesties that took place in this region in 1862?

I looked south, toward the Minnesota River. I could not see the waterway itself through its natural border of trees. I thought about a steamboat crawling slowly along that shallow, winding river. The cloudy day had suddenly turned a bit chilly, and I zipped up my jacket. That's when I heard the wind. It was the same faint, soft rustling that came from a stand of pine trees swaying in a breeze. But there were no evergreens here, and the blades of dry grass around me were not moving. All of the leaves on the plants were perfectly still. I was getting an eerie sensation, made even more sinister by the knowledge that people had died near here. I could feel goose bumps rising on my arms, underneath my jacket and several layers of clothing. And I realized that I had had that familiar experience under similar circumstances at just one other place.

It had been a little farther along on that same western trip in 2000. I had concluded my duties in Wyoming, and I had decided to return to Illinois by a northern route through Montana, North Dakota, and Minnesota. I deliberately stopped to visit the Little Bighorn Battlefield National Monument. That's where I had heard the wind. I was standing on that grassy hillside, which was littered with named stone markers that showed where each one of the soldiers fell. I heard that pine-needle sigh (or sough), and the only trees in sight were the cottonwoods down at the Little Bighorn River, at least half a mile away. I had read enough about Custer and the fight, and it was a valuable experience to see where it had taken place. But I could not stay there long. The sound of the wind and the feeling it evoked were too much to bear.

Custer's last stand came fourteen years after the Dakota war in Minnesota. But it too was part of the bigger battle waging between the Native Americans and the U.S. government in the 1800s. And by now we know that it did not end well for the Indians.

These thoughts were swirling around in my head as I crossed the Minnesota River to reach the Lower Sioux Agency Historic Site. As at the fort, the visitor center here was closed. Chains were strung across the entrance and exit lanes so that you could not reach the parking lot. I pulled the car far enough into the lane so that it did not extend onto the road. The pavement was sloped, so I was actually stopped at about a forty-five degree angle. I pulled on the emergency brake, just in case. Then I got out and took a few long-distance photos of the center and the stone warehouse on the property. Everything looked interesting. I could not wait to come back and learn more about the place.

I got back in the car, turned the key in the ignition, released the brake, and looked in the mirror to see what was behind me. I saw nothing, absolutely nothing. Just sky. No horizon line at all. "Whoa," I said. I turned my head around to see for myself. Still nothing. It was disconcerting. I even turned the car off and got out to make sure there was a world behind me. There was. I got back in and started it up again. With both feet working the gas and the brake pedals, I eased out onto the road, hoping no other vehicles were coming toward me. It was not a well-traveled stretch, so I made it out okay. I surveyed the surrounding landscape. It was flat and covered with gold and brown fields. It was the prairie and the plains, both at once. Occasional farmhouses circled by trees stood by themselves in the middle of what must have been vast parcels of acreage. I hadn't quite realized how level and remote it all was until I lost the horizon in my mirror.

As I drove toward Redwood Falls, I soon saw the Sioux-owned casino to my right. So close to the historical site? I wondered to myself. Then I remembered that the Little Bighorn in Montana had a casino sitting right beside it as well. I decided not to analyze the sociological, ethnological, or economic aspects of that trend. I visited a convenience store in Redwood Falls, then headed to a hotel room in New Ulm. The next morning I drove back to Minneapolis.

I returned to the Minnesota River valley on August 16, 2008. Dale and Kay Schwie had already squired me around Minneapolis. Now it was time for me to rediscover Fort Ridgely and the Lower Sioux Agency.

Once again, I hit the fort first, just as it was opening for business. I spent time examining the exhibits and chatting with the helpful staff members. I took a few more photos of the storehouse. I knew I should stand and look down toward the river, but I just could not bring myself to do it. I was afraid of that wind sigh, even though this day was full of sunshine with nary a chill in the air. I was distracted instead by some motion in the grass. Soon a small rodent sat up tall and looked around. "They're still here!" I said with excitement, but subdued enough so as not to disturb the critter. Young Horace Mann didn't collect *all* of the thirteen-lined ground squirrels in Minnesota. Some of their descendants still existed. I stalked this one quietly and snapped a few decent photos before he dropped out of sight. When I approached that area, I found no hole or any kind of opening. He had just disappeared into the lawn. At least he had tolerated my presence for a few minutes. I thanked him and wished him well before I headed to the car.

I reached the Lower Sioux Agency by early afternoon. I had a chance to wander through the center before joining one of its interpretive programs for adults. The site was featuring children's activities today; so a number of families were here with young people. They were learning how to play games and to do the kinds of chores that Dakota children would have performed in the 1850s. They painted a merry, vibrant scene. I walked through the stone warehouse, built just after Henry Thoreau and Horace Mann, Jr., were here. Indian agent Thomas J. Galbraith had been immortalized, for his name was embedded in the stonework. The warehouse faced an open area labeled "Government Agency Grounds" on the map. I wondered where the festivities took place in 1861. The speeches and the native dancing may have happened on this spot. I stood in awe, imagining.

The Agency has several walking trails. I followed the one that led to the Minnesota River. Unlike that flat prairie across the street from the entrance, this part of the landscape was forested and dropped down a bluff to meet the water. It would have been the perfect place to do some botanizing. I was soon standing on the shoreline, right at the point where the *Frank Steele* waited, long ago. I could not picture it sitting here now. The water was too shallow, this late in the season. A few of the surrounding cottonwoods were old enough to have been standing here in 1861. Too bad they couldn't tell us the real story about the excursion, and about everything that happened here the following year.

I started picking up every interesting rock I saw. This has been a habit of mine since childhood, and there was no stopping it now. My apartment was cluttered with glass jars full of sand and shells and rocks from all over the country. Eventually I had a small bag filled with new geologic treasures, courtesy of the Minnesota River. With a little imagination, a few of them even looked like ancient artifacts. One was either part of an old clay pot, or a portion of a twentieth-century municipal pipeline that had decayed and broken apart from constant use. A few pebbles were distinctly red, perhaps examples of the quartzite found in the area. Nevertheless, these souvenirs were going home with me. They could sit on my desk and remind me of a place 1500 miles to the west, where Henry David Thoreau met the Dakota people, and where he somehow acquired three pieces of buckskin clothing.

WHEN YOU GO: Re-creating this portion of the journey today is easy enough to do: you just follow the Minnesota River. If you merely take an overland route from St. Paul to Morton, you can drive about 115 miles one way and spend more than two hours doing so. But that would ignore the river altogether, and that's not the point of this trek.

By taking the roads that shadow the Minnesota River shoreline, you will travel about 160 miles over the course of perhaps four hours. That's not quite the 200 miles and several days' worth of steaming slowly upriver that the *Frank Steele* did with its ever-increasing cargo. This trip too will take dedication and will involve the better part of your day, especially if you intend to turn right around and go back without staying overnight somewhere along the way. But you really should spend some time exploring the area.

In general, take U.S. 169 from the greater Minneapolis area south to Mankato. You will cross over the Minnesota River just north of Le Sueur. At Mankato, turn on to U.S. 14, heading west to New Ulm. From that point you can stay on the north side of the river and take MN Route 21 to Fort Ridgely. Or you can drive through New Ulm and use U.S. 14 and MN Route 68 to reach the Lower Sioux Agency. If you have a good road atlas, you can find lanes that more closely parallel the river on this stretch. Not all of them will be paved, however.

While you are in New Ulm, you might want to stop to find an historical marker that mentions the steamboat that Henry Thoreau and Horace Mann, Jr., traveled with. Use MN Route 37, which is New Ulm's 20th South Street. Look for a big rock on the north side of the road, somewhere between the Minnesota River and Broadway. You won't be able to read the plate embedded into the stone from your car, but there are plenty of parking lots on this block. Get out and walk to it. You might even have to bend down to read the text.

On May 7th, 1857, the
steamer *"Frank Steele"*
landed with about 60
or 70 families of set-
tlers from Cincinnati,
at a place a quarter of
a mile directly south-
east from this point.

That trip with its cargo of German Americans must have been one of the first such errands for the *Frank Steele*. Another marker listing even more riverboats can be found along Front Street near the playground. By the way, New Ulm is still known as the most German city in the United States. The percentage of residents who can claim German heritage is higher here than in any other community in the country.

Another stop you should make along this route is along U.S. 169, just north of St. Peter. There you can visit the Treaty Site History Center, which serves as the headquarters of the Nicollet County Historical Society. The Treaty of Traverse des Sioux was signed near here in 1851. The center offers exhibits and information about the treaty and the Dakota people as well as other aspects of the county's history. The adjacent property includes trails to and along the Minnesota River at "the place of crossing," or as the Dakota called it, "Oiyuwege." Some of the "Grand Pleasure Excursion" passengers left the *Frank Steele* to walk around here in 1861. You can follow in their footsteps.

FOR MORE INFORMATION

Fort Ridgely Historic Site, 72404 County Road 30, Fairfax, MN 55332. Phone (507) 426-7888. www.mnhs.org/places/sites/fr.

Friends of the Minnesota Valley, P.O. Box 20697, Bloomington, MN 55420. Phone: (952) 881-9065. www.friendsofmnvalley.org.

Lower Sioux Agency Historic Site, 32469 Redwood County Highway 2, Morton, MN 56270. Phone (507) 697-6321. www.mnhs.org/places/sites/lsa.

Lower Sioux Indian Community, PO Box 308, RR #1, Morton, MN 56070. www.lowersioux.com.

Minnesota River Scenic Byway, New Ulm Convention & Visitors Bureau, 1 North Minnesota Street, New Ulm, MN 56073-1727. Phone (888) 463-9856. www.mnrivervalley.com.

Minnesota Valley National Wildlife Refuge, 3815 American Boulevard East, Bloomington, MN 55425. Phone (952) 854-5900. www.fws.gov/midwest/minnesotavalley.

New Ulm Chamber of Commerce, 1 North Minnesota Street, PO Box 384, New Ulm, MN 56073. (507) 233-4300. www.newulm.com.

Ney Nature Center, PO Box 93, Henderson, MN 56044-0093. Phone (507) 248-3474. neycenter.org.

Pipestone National Monument, 36 Reservation Avenue, Pipestone, MN 56164. Phone (507) 825-5464. www.nps.gov/pipe.

Redwood Area Chamber and Tourism, 200 South Mill Street, Redwood Falls, MN 56283. Phone (507) 637-2828. www.redwoodfalls.org.

Treaty Site History Center, Nicollet County Historical Society, 1851 North Minnesota Avenue, St. Peter, MN 56082. Phone (507) 934-2160. www.nchsmn.org/sites.html

Recommended Reading

Diane Wilson's *Spirit Car: Journey to a Dakota Past* (St. Paul: Borealis Books, 2006). Wilson's search for her own ancestry leads her to the Lower Sioux Agency and the details of the Sioux Wars of 1862. Interested individuals may also want to track down a library or used bookstore copy of Minnie Ellingson Tapping's *Eighty Years at the Gopher Hole: The Saga of a Minnesota Pioneer (1867-1947)* (New York: Exposition Press, 1958). Tapping lived in the Minnesota River valley; and she devotes several pages of this memoir to a fantasy dialogue with river traveler Henry David Thoreau.

Notes on this Chapter

Six primary-source accounts were used to compile the description of the 1861 Lower Sioux Agency excursion via the *Frank Steele*. These were:

Henry Thoreau's jottings in his field notebook.

Henry Thoreau's letter to Frank Sanborn, dated June 25, 1861, as it appears in *The Correspondence of Henry David Thoreau* (Edited by Walter Harding and Carl Bode. New York: New York University Press, 1958, pp. 618-622).

Horace Mann's letters home.

"Local Affairs: A Trip to Redwood, and a Day Among the Indians." *Pioneer and Democrat* (St. Paul, Minn.), (June 28, 1861): 8.

W.A.C. "A Week on the Frontier." *State Atlas* (Minneapolis) (July 3, 1861). Reprinted in *The Thoreau Society Bulletin* 57 (Fall 1956): 1-4.

Arthur Sterry's "A Short Visit to an Indian Reservation" (unpublished manuscript). Excerpts were printed in "By Steamboat to Redwood Agency." With transcription and introduction by Patricia Hampl. *Preview: A Regional Magazine* 9 (March 1975): 13-16.

Some of the authors painted positive pictures and others saw many of the negatives in the experience. It was therefore worthwhile to read them all and make seemingly neutral comparisons. Other than identifying passages specifically written by Thoreau or Mann, I did not credit the other authors in my own text. I did set their comments in quotes.

The 1861 reports of Superintendent Clark W. Thompson and Agent Thomas J. Galbraith are both included in *Report of the Commission of Indian Affairs, Accompanying the Annual Report of the Secretary of the Interior, for the Year 1861*. Neither man mentions the "grand pleasure excursion" attached to the annuity payment ceremony at the Lower Sioux Agency. However, certain details they offer help to clarify the situation. Thompson states that he reached the Upper Sioux Agency on June 16; so obviously, he could not join the excursion party in St. Paul the next day. He also says he "witnessed the payment to the Lower Sioux band on June the 26th." Galbraith describes the progress in the building of the stone warehouse.

Useful in recounting this portion of the journey was Thomas Hughes' *A History of Steamboating on the Minnesota River* (L'Anse, Mich.: Regional History Reprints, [1902]). Helpful as well was Charles Fisk's online resource, "The First 50 Years of Continuous Recorded Weather History in Minnesota (1820-1869)—A Year-by-Year Narrative Account" http://home.att.net/~station_climo/purpose.htm. The Minnesota River was heavily used as part of the Red River oxcart trail linking St. Paul with the Selkirk Settlement (later Winnipeg) in Manitoba (Rhoda Gilman's *Red River Trails 1820-1871: Oxcart Routes Between St. Paul and the Selkirk Settlement*, Minn. Historical Soc. Press, 1979) and has remained an attractive river of travel and adventure (E. Sevareid's *Canoeing with the Cree*, Borealis Books, 2005).

I consulted a wide range of books and references while attempting to create an accurate report of the Dakota Indians, the Lower Sioux Agency, and the events of 1861 and 1862 in central Minnesota. One of my first sources was Kenneth Carley's *The Dakota War of 1862: Minnesota's Other Civil War* (2d ed. St. Paul: Minnesota Historical Society Press, 1976). Gary Clayton Anderson's *Kinsmen of Another Kind: Dakota-White Relations in the Upper Mississippi Valley, 1650-1862* (St. Paul: Minnesota Historical Society Press, 1997) was a book I referred to often. Sarah F. Wakefield's account of the Yellow Medicine annuity payment was originally published in *Six Weeks in the Sioux Tepees* (Shakopee, Minn.: Argus Books, 1864). A new version with supplemental material by June Namias was published by the University of Oklahoma Press in 2002.

Two additional books by Gary Clayton Anderson proved invaluable. *Little Crow: Spokesman for the Sioux* (St. Paul: Minnesota History Society Press, 1986) was the main source of my information about both Little Crow and Red Owl. I used the text of Little Crow's speech as it appears in *Through Dakota Eyes: Narrative Accounts of the Minnesota Indian War of 1862* (Ed. by Gary Clayton Anderson and Alan R. Woolworth. St. Paul: Minnesota Historical Society Press, 1988). Details about Fort Ridgely and the Lower Sioux Agency and their histories were additionally gleaned from on-site promotional brochures and from personal experience.

If you go to the Concord Museum web site (http://www.concordmuseum.org) and click on "Thoreau Collections," you can search for photos and information about the three pieces of Dakota buckskin clothing that Henry Thoreau brought or sent back home. Use "Indian" as a search term.

The best source I found for the history of St. Paul's Merchants Hotel came in Larry Millett's *Lost Twin Cities* (St. Paul: Minnesota Historical Society Press, 1992). Additional old histories of the city confirmed some of the details.

The demise of the *Frank Steele* was reported in issues of the *La Crosse Daily Democrat*, dated May 31, 1864, and June 3, 1864. Many thanks to the staff of the La Crosse Public Library, for locating them for me.

Details of the formation of the Ney Nature Center in Henderson were found in various issues of their newsletter and on their web site (http://neycenter.org).

I was not the first Thoreauvian from the East who made her way out to Fort Ridgely and to the Lower Sioux Agency in central Minnesota. Back in the late 1970s, Mary Sherwood visited the sites and reported on her experiences in "Thoreau's Minnesota Trail in 1978. Part 1." (*Thoreau Journal Quarterly* 10 [October 1978]: 25-34). Part two of Mary's account covered her travels as she followed Thoreau's footsteps in the Twin Cities.

Information about red quartzite was supplied by Dale Schwie and geologist Jon D. Inners.

I believe that Henry Thoreau copied information into his Indian notebooks solely for his own personal use. I do not believe that he ever intended to publish a book about America's indigenous people. Why would he, and how could he have done so? He was a writer of travel narratives, not ethnologies. He did not have enough experience with Indians of any band or tribe to presume to be an expert on any of them. One twelve-hour stint at Redwood was not enough to go on, either. Granted, each of his published works contains observations of the residents of the region in question, often from both the past and the present. It is therefore logical to assume that if Thoreau had had a chance to write a full account of this Journey

West, he would have included a detailed chapter about what he saw at the Lower Sioux Agency. And if he had been assembling such a book during the fall of 1862, he would have incorporated the fate of the Dakota into it. I believe he would have been both saddened and outraged at the news.

TRAVEL CHAPTER 13

Sunday, June 23 to Thursday, June 27, 1861
St. Paul, Minnesota, to Prairie du Chien, Wisconsin
via the Mississippi River and the steamship War Eagle

Expenses: Fare to Red Wing: $2.00
Stamps: .15
At Red Wing: $3.00

The grand feature hereabouts is, of course, the Mississippi River. Too much can hardly be said of its grandeur, & of the beauty of this portion of it—(from Dunleith, and prob. from Rock Island to this place.) St. Paul is a dozen miles below the Falls of St. Anthony, or near the head of uninterrupted navigation on the main stream about 2000 miles from its mouth. There is not a "rip" below that, & the river is almost as wide in the upper as the lower part of its course. Steamers go up to the Sauk Rapids, above the Falls, near a hundred miles farther, & then you are fairly in the pine woods and lumbering country. Thus it flows from the pine to the palm.

—Thoreau's letter to Frank Sanborn, June 25, 1861

We ... started this morning at 9:30 to come down here and arrived a few minutes after 2 p.m. We got a room at the Metropolitan House which is right on the landing and then went up on top of Red-wing bluff which is about a dozen rods off and I can look right at it out of this window. I see three ladies on top of it now. The Bluff is very high, perhaps 400 or 500 feet with a round long top with no trees except near the river side and on that slope. It is about half a mile long and between the cliffs perhaps 30 or 40 rods wide, and runs in a SW and NE direction. ... The Bluff and town are both named from the old Sioux chief Red Wing who was buried on this bluff about ten years ago...it is a mound about two rods in diameter at the base and five feet high with a flat top on about the highest point of the bluff.

—Horace Mann Jr.'s letter of June 23, 1861

On Sunday morning, Henry Thoreau and Horace Mann, Jr., left St. Paul and headed down the Mississippi River to Red Wing, Minnesota. Neither one of them made written note of their mode of transportation; but their timetable corresponds exactly with the steamboat schedule. Since neither traveler mentions the name of a new craft, it is possible that the *Frank Steele* was turning south too, and that they went with it. In any case, it must have been a relief to get back on the wider waterway, with little chance of grounding the boat in the shallows and with no tight curves for the captain to navigate. "Our faces are already set toward home," Thoreau wrote. They would cover just 64 miles of that return trip this time. They stopped to spend a few days at the town of Red Wing.

Perhaps Henry and Horace had been intrigued enough by the nearby landform called Barn Bluff to make a special effort to explore it on their way back down the river. Perhaps Dr. Charles Anderson recommended it as well. Nevertheless, it was a good idea.

At the time of their visit, Red Wing was less than ten years old and registered fewer than 1,300 residents. An even lower number were in town when Thoreau and Mann landed on its shore, for 114 men had left for St. Paul two months earlier, in order to form Company F of the First Minnesota Infantry. Certainly Red Wing had the usual variety of services available to travelers. One of the largest buildings in Red Wing even housed Hamline University, Minnesota's first university. The school was founded in 1854, and was affiliated with the Methodist church. But the first duty Henry and Horace had upon their arrival was to find the post office. Before they had left on the Lower Sioux Agency excursion, they had warned their correspondents to direct all mail to Red Wing. Four letters from Mary Mann were waiting for Horace. Henry had one from his sister Sophia and another from Concord acquaintance Frank Sanborn. Wanting to explore Barn Bluff as quickly as possible, the two men took their letters with them on their climb and read them on the top of the hill, perched high above the Mississippi.

Of all of the rocky rises Thoreau and Mann saw as they steamed up and down the river, Barn Bluff in Red Wing was one of the most unusual and accessible. It had once been an island, back in the era of the glaciers; and it consisted of conspicuous layers of dolomite, sandstone and limestone. It stood 1000 feet above sea level and about 340 feet above the waters of the Mississippi. (Horace's estimations were a tad generous.) Paths led to its flat-top summit, where one of the Dakota chiefs named Red Wing was buried. But this was hardly a bare or barren crag. Vegetation had found purchase in the porous soil lying on and around the bluff. It was yet another interesting site for two botanists to investigate. They spent many hours over the next three days doing so.

Thoreau and Mann stayed at the Metropolitan Hotel for a dollar a day. The two-and-a-half story structure had been built four years earlier, right next to the river and the bluff, at the end of Potter Street. "The stages stopped in front of the Metropolitan Hotel, and the boats landed back of it. When the water was high they put the plank from the boat to the steps of the hotel." Using this establishment as a base, the men had handy access to everything they wanted to see and do.

Barn Bluff loomed behind Red Wing's Metropolitan Hotel (seen at the right edge) in the 1860s. (*Courtesy of the Minnesota Historical Society*)

Based on their writings, both men seemed to be energized by their time in Red Wing. Henry jotted down multiple notes and wrote at least one long letter. Horace replied with some detail to his mother's missives. Both spent time botanizing and documenting their findings. Maybe they were pleased to be able to dally here for a few days, examining this unique place. Maybe their senses were heightened with the knowledge that they would soon be leaving the valley of the Mississippi. This would be their last chance to explore its habitat. Maybe the summer sun and good weather electrified their systems.

Or maybe they were just excited to be heading home.

Horace continued to report that he and Mr. Thoreau were both doing fine. But his companion confided in a letter written in Red Wing that he had "performed this journey in a very dead and alive manner, but nothing has come so near waking me up as the receipt of letters from Concord." The travelers weren't really on their own when they knew that their friends and family members were thinking of them and were wondering how they were doing.

And while they both insisted that they had no time on this trip to read newspapers, Henry Thoreau made at least one exception here. He read an article about the Lower Sioux Agency excursion in a St. Paul newspaper, perhaps pointed out to him by Professor Wilson of Hamline University. The writer noted that about 500 Indians had been in attendance, and that the speaker for the Dakota had been Red Owl. Thoreau might not have known the man's identity before seeing his name in print, after the fact.

But their adventure on the Minnesota River and their encounter with the Dakota were both well behind them. It was the plant world that commanded their attentions here. Young Horace was most excited about finding "*Pulsatilla Nutalliana* in bloom on top" of Barn Bluff. Both men botanized along the riverside and around the other bluffs, too. Thoreau included the following sightings in his comprehensive journey list: American dragonhead (*Dracocephalum parviflorum*), Black-eyed susan (*Rudbeckia hirta*), Creeping vervain (*Verbena bracteosa*), Daisy fleabane (*Erigeron strigosus*), Downy paintbrush (*Castilleja sessiliflora*), False dandelion (*Cynthia virginica*), Green-flowered milkweed (*Acerates viridiflora*), Pale-spike lobelia (*Lobelia spicata*), Peppercress (*Lepidium*), Silverweed (*Potentilla anserina*), and Stiff coreopsis (*Coreopsis palmata*). The Lobelia was "bluer than common," and Peppercress was the "commonest weed." Today residents and experts would recognize these species as being typical wildflowers found on the prairie in the early part of the summer.

According to Horace, Monday was "a very hot day, though there was, as there always is, a strong wind blowing from some quarter or other, which makes the heat much easier to bear." During their morning walk in the blufflands, Henry and Horace "found a good many strawberries growing wild, which we ate." They both took turns swimming in the Mississippi. Theirs must have been an idyllic vacation.

To make up for the four letters he got from his mother, Horace in turn wrote four back to her: one for each day he spent in Red Wing. He described the area and his activities, but he also took the opportunity to answer all of the questions she had posed to him in writing. She was evidently following the war effort much more than he was; and on that topic, he quite innocently told her, "I do not know as I have any-thing to say." He had been busy with other things.

His reaction was much more animated and soaked with adolescent insistence when he defended his reasons for not doing his homework with the Greek textbook he had brought along on the trip.

> I have not had any time lately to study Greek, as I thought it was acting like a fool to travel round and go to new places and not see any of them or get any specimens from them on account of the Greek. And as we have not been stationery [sic] in any one place long, and while we were I wanted to be collecting Animals, Plants and Minerals, I thought I had better let the Greek go, and especially as I knew I could not get into college this fall at any rate and hope that you will not fret about it.

Perhaps Henry Thoreau had said as much to the young man; and Horace was merely parroting the opinions of his older and wiser companion. You've got the rest of your young life to read the classics, Thoreau might have quipped; but you may never again have a chance to explore America's prairielands in person. It was either good advice well taken or a mature declaration on Horace's part.

Tuesday, June 25, began with an early morning thunderstorm. Showers lingered in the area throughout the day. During a break in the weather, Horace took the opportunity again to climb to the top of Barn Bluff. "I went up on top of the bluff to gather some pulsatilla for Uncle Nat," he wrote to his mother. "I gather[ed] a good lot of it, but it commenced to drizzle, and by the time I got home I was pretty damp." A true downpour soon ensued, and the young man spent the rest of the afternoon napping.

Horace actually had *two* uncles named Nat, and they both happened to live in Concord at the time. Nathaniel Cranch Peabody (1811-1881) was the brother of Horace's mother and was a homeopathic physician. Nathaniel Hawthorne (1804-1864), the noted author, was married to Horace's aunt, Sophia Peabody. The "pulsatilla" that Horace collected was pasque flower, now known as *Anemone patens*. In spite of the time of the year, it was still in bloom at the higher elevation of the bluff. Horace obviously recognized the plant as a useful ingredient in homeopathic medicine. We should assume that he collected it for Dr. Peabody to administer to his patients, and not as a kind of literary inspiration for Mr. Hawthorne. Horace might have shipped the pile of plants home from Red Wing to avoid having to carry it in his bags for the rest of the journey.

Henry Thoreau took the opportunity of the rainy day confinement to write a lengthy letter in reply to Frank Sanborn. He also made his way to the Hamline University building in downtown Red Wing. Either by appointment or by happenstance, Henry Thoreau met that day with Horace Brown Wilson, who had joined the faculty in 1858. Wilson was a professor of mathematics, natural science, and civil engineering. Perhaps Dr. Charles Anderson of Minneapolis had suggested that Henry stop in Red Wing to talk with the professor. The two men might have found much to discuss. Wilson was a native of central Maine. He had been a teacher for a number of years. He had even worked as a civil engineer in New Albany, Indiana, before moving to Minnesota in 1858. Thoreau's experience in teaching and with property surveying could have been sources of commonality for conversation. But while Wilson taught in the natural sciences, he seems to have been less interested in them as a personal or professional endeavor. In his later career he was more involved with the business of education and with politics, and not in any field of science.

After they had spent several days exploring Red Wing and Barn Bluff, Henry Thoreau and Horace Mann, Jr., boarded the *War Eagle* in the afternoon of June 26, 1861. It was a reasonably good day for the trip for, as Horace told his mother, "It is quite a cool day in the wind, though the sun is pretty warm." The steamship was a side-wheel packet that had been built in Cincinnati in 1854. Its interior was outfitted for the stylish comfort of its passengers:

> ...the cabins are furnished, with just enough of the gilt work to give them a cheerful appearance. All the modern steamboat improvements have been attached, and the barber shops, wash room &c, are on a liberal scale. ... The carpets, of the finest velvet, are from Shilito & Co.'s; the furniture from S. J. Johns; mirrors from Wiswell's; and the machinery by David Griffey.

This time, the two Massachusetts men intended to leave the boat at Prairie du Chien, Wisconsin, the place that Thoreau had previously referred to as "the smartest town on the river." They had decided not to retrace their westbound route in order to return home.

Henry Thoreau did not generally mention individuals by name in his field notebook, especially those people he met just in passing. But one of the few remarks he made during this part of the journey was: "Mrs. Upham of

Clinton with us—has a cousin Clifton in Bedford." The passage conjures up a typical traveling scene. Fellow passengers tend to introduce themselves to one another in terms of geography, hoping to find common ground and perhaps even a conversation starter. Obviously when Henry or Horace (or both) said that they were from Concord, Massachusetts, this Mrs. Upham exclaimed that she had a cousin who lived in Bedford, the town just northeast of Concord. Where their interaction or discussion led from that point, we are left to ponder.

The *War Eagle* carried Thoreau and Mann from Red Wing to Prairie du Chien. (*Courtesy of the Murphy Library, University of Wisconsin – La Crosse*)

It is quite likely that the woman on the *War Eagle* that day was Margaret Barker Upham (1839-1919). Margaret had been born in Castine, Maine; and when she was still a child, her family relocated to Dixon, Illinois. By the early 1860s, her cousin John Quincy Adams Clifton (1833?-1885) was working as a lumber agent based in Boston, though he may indeed have been living or doing business in Bedford. Margaret's reasons for steaming down the Mississippi that day are unknown. She might have been visiting friends or relatives in the St. Paul or Red Wing area. Her husband might have been called to Fort Snelling in Minneapolis. Certainly if she was heading back to Dixon, she would have planned to leave the steamboat when it stopped at Clinton, Iowa. Then she would be required to take a ferry across the river and ride in a stagecoach for about fifty more miles to get home.

At the time of this trip, Margaret was the wife of Dr. Zalmon McMaster, an army doctor. She was also eight months pregnant with her first child. She may have called herself by her maiden name for a variety of reasons. Perhaps it was out of habit, for she had been married for only two years.

Perhaps she was following suffragist Lucy Stone's landmark example by refusing to take her husband's surname. Perhaps, as one of her descendants suggests, she was not entirely happy in her marriage and was already doing her best to forget about it. Nevertheless, she was already an outspoken and independent woman: traveling long distances under personal circumstances that would have confined lesser mothers-to-be directly to their beds or to some private chambers; and chatting casually with strange men on steamboats. Did she know who Thoreau was then, or did she learn his identity sometime afterward? She did not leave us written proof, either way.

Henry Thoreau and Horace Mann left the *War Eagle* at Prairie du Chien on the morning of June 27, 1861. They never saw or heard from Mrs. Upham again.

Today the city of Red Wing is home to more than 16,000 residents. Outsiders may recognize its famous name for its stoneware industry, which began using local clay for its craft in 1868; and also for its shoe business, which started in 1905. But now the city is also seen as a worthy stop for tourists with wider interests. In 2008, the National Trust for Historic Preservation listed Red Wing as one of its "Dozen Distinctive Destinations." The organization said that the city "perfectly combines an impressive architectural history with an enviable natural environment." That same year, *National Geographic Traveler* magazine named Red Wing one of its "Top Historic Destinations in the World." Evidently Henry Thoreau and young Horace Mann were ahead of their time when they decided to stay here for a few days.

Red Wing is also one of the few sites along this journey route where one can find local documentation stating that Thoreau and Mann came to this place. An historical marker at Barn Bluff reads in part: "Explorers and visitors including Zebulon Pike, Major Stephen H. Long, Henry Schoolcraft, and Henry David Thoreau climbed the bluff and remarked about the beautiful scenic views Barn Bluff offered of the Mississippi valley." Thoreau might have felt honored to be included in such an esteemed listing. And in *A History of the City of Red Wing, Minnesota*, printed in 1933, author Christian A. Rasmussen offered a short but accurate summation of the travelers' time here:

> A visitor of note to Red Wing in 1861 was Henry D. Thoreau, the philosopher of Walden. He came as one of that multitude

of health seekers, accompanied by Horace Mann, a youthful botanist, and son of the famous educator of that time. In his diary, published later, he makes special reference to the grandeur of the scenery hereabouts, the remarkably isolated position of Barn Bluff, and lists a formidable line of botanical specimens he found hereabouts.

Rasmussen might have learned about Frank Sanborn's *First and Last Journeys of Thoreau, Lately Discovered Among His Unpublished Journals and Manuscripts* (Boston: The Bibliophile Society, 1905). At the time of his research, that two-volume set was the only published source of the jottings found in Thoreau's field notebook. Sanborn had created an impromptu narrative from them. But the Red Wing historian might also have heard about the contents of Thoreau's field notebook from Mabel Densmore, a local resident. She had recently typed a page-by-page transcript of the original volume for the science library of the University of Minnesota.

Hamline University was based in Red Wing until 1869, when the school had to close because of financial constraints and low enrollment. It had operated for fifteen years in Red Wing. Its original building was demolished in 1872. When the university finally reopened in 1880, it did so at a new site in St. Paul. It continues to educate young people there today.

From the time of Thoreau's visit until 1908, part of Barn Bluff was quarried for its limestone. When additional destruction was undertaken to improve the nearby railroad line, a citizen protest ensued. It seemed unthinkable that "the old sentinel of the city" could be willfully and "permanently disfigured." "Any man can make a park, but it took God Almighty to make Barn bluff!" remarked Mrs. John H. Rich, voicing the thoughts of many of her fellow townspeople. The digging was halted. In 1910, Barn Bluff became a city-owned park and is thus now protected land. Though trails to its summit had been in existence since the time of the Native Americans, a stairway for easier ascent was constructed in 1929. Today even casual hikers can make the trip to the top and can take in the stunning views of the city, the surrounding landscape, and the Mississippi River valley below.

On November 15, 1869, the community of Red Wing celebrated an addition to its fire department: "a new hose cart, one of those two wheeled affairs, with a reel between for the hose, surmounted by an arch carrying a bell, propelled by being pulled by ropes." To mark the occasion, a fancy ball was held in a downtown hall. The cart was present at the gala; but it had been first taken apart in order to fit through doorways and to make the trip up two flights of stairs. There it was reassembled and placed on the stage as a guest of honor.

And then came word that the Metropolitan Hotel was on fire.

What happened next reads like a script for a slapstick comedy. According to one historian, the new hose cart "was rushed to the door. But it could not be gotten through the door with the wheels on. So they were removed and it was gotten down to the street, the wheels replaced, and the run made to the fire, but the hostelry was burned to the ground." So much for a hearty inauguration of the brand-new fire fighting equipment.

Today the former site of the Metropolitan Hotel is occupied by the mills of Archer Daniels Midland, a company that "transforms crops such as corn, oilseeds, wheat and cocoa into food ingredients, animal feeds, and agriculturally derived fuels and chemicals." It uses the river and the railroad to transport its products.

The *War Eagle* continued to steam up and down the Mississippi River for years, carrying both passengers and cargo. It was docked at the railroad depot at La Crosse on May 14, 1870. While barrels of lamp oil were being loaded onto the steamboat, someone discovered that one of the barrels was leaking. Before the problem could be fixed, the *War Eagle*, an adjacent barge, and several nearby buildings had caught fire. Five people lost their lives. The steamboat sank. But some artifacts from the boat have since then been retrieved. The La Crosse County Historical Society has compiled a detailed exhibit about the *War Eagle* and its fate. Visitors can see it and learn more at the Riverside Museum, located at the north end of Riverside Park in La Crosse.

In 1862, Professor Horace Brown Wilson (1821-1908) enlisted in the Sixth Minnesota Infantry. As the captain of Company F, he not only fought against the Confederates in the South, but also against the Dakota in central Minnesota. Wilson came back to Red Wing after the war and served as the superintendent of schools for Goodhue County. He went on to advance to the post of state superintendent of schools. Later he served four terms as a state senator and one term as a state representative.

Less than a month after having met Henry Thoreau on the *War Eagle*, Margaret Barker Upham McMaster gave birth to a daughter, Marian Lois McMaster, in Eureka, Illinois, just east of Peoria. Zalmon McMaster served as an army doctor during the Civil War but died either during the fight or soon afterward. Margaret moved to Chicago; and in 1868, she married Charles Henry Wright, the city editor of the Chicago *Times*. Together they had a son, Charles Henry Conrad Wright. Little Marian's surname was changed to Wright. After she was widowed for a second time in one decade, Margaret relocated with her children to the East Coast and generally based herself in Cambridge, Massachusetts, and around Harvard College. Her daughter married a Harvard professor; her son graduated from Harvard and eventually taught there as well. Margaret spent many years as a journalist and a supporter of women's suffrage. She had a number of magazine articles to her credit. For a time, she was a European correspondent for *Art Amateur* and other American periodicals.

In 1897, Margaret B. Wright published the travel narrative, *Hired Furnished, Being Certain Economical Housekeeping Adventures in England* (Boston: Roberts Brothers, 1897). The text described the particulars of an extended holiday that she and her son Charles spent together, when they rented cottages and villas mostly in the southern part of England and along the northern coast of France. Now, *this* was the way to travel and to become immersed in another culture, she maintained. Hers was a nineteenth-century precursor to the contemporary "time share" experience.

> Time is money, we are often enough reminded; yet thousands of us have more time than money, time that perhaps cannot better be used than in the place of many dollars otherwise necessary for seeing Europe. … As told in these pages, furnished cottages are abundant all over England, hundreds to be obtained at the prices named. … Established in one of these cottages or villas, living expenses are as much under one's own control as in one's native village or city. … "Hired furnished" has not often been tried by Americans in rural England. Two at least of the small number of those that have tried it [Margaret and her son Charles] enthusiastically recommend the plan to those dreamers who are forever "haunted by the horizon," and for whom imagination gilds and refines into fairer than palaces, temporary homes in a foreign land that only ten or twenty dollars a month may "hire furnished."

Margaret devoted one chapter of the book to her trip to the Island of Jersey, where she and Charles trekked specifically in search of Henry David Thoreau's ancestors and heritage.

> Henry Thoreau was entirely satisfied with his own little corner of life; he never expressed the slightest desire to go to Europe; no thread of pre-natal love and memory stretched though ever so imperceptibly between him and Jersey whence his father's Uncle Peter now and then sent greetings. Curiously remote the Island of Jersey must indeed have seemed to the American Thoreaus because remote from their sympathy and interest. It were as though the insular habit of their ancestors lived in them still, even on a continent.

Margaret had obviously done some research before the trip. She had no doubt read *Walden*. She knew of "Uncle Peter's letters to his niece Elizabeth Thoreau, published in all biographies of her nephew Henry Thoreau." The journalist must have read the two American biographies printed by that time: William Ellery Channing's *Thoreau, the Poet-Naturalist* (1873) and Frank B. Sanborn's *Henry D. Thoreau* (1882). While Channing merely mentioned the Jersey origins of the Thoreaus, Sanborn reprinted the text of some of the letters from "Uncle Peter." He found them in an entry of Thoreau's *Journal* from 1855, when Henry noted that his Aunt Maria had passed the three old letters down to him "for safe-keeping."

So the Wrights knew the proper location and the names to ask for, in order to find Henry Thoreau's only living but distant relatives. After launching an investigation and questioning the locals, they eventually found the target of their search. The duo met and had tea with the granddaughter of Thoreau's great-uncle Peter: "Sophia Thoreau, cousin twice removed to Henry Thoreau of Concord." The Jersey woman seemed slightly amused by the encounter. "I never knew that I had American cousins till we learned it by the Henry Thoreau biographies," she said. Her son echoed that thought and made a reference to the state of his relative's fame—or the lack of it— at the time:

> "Whenever I see Americans," he says, "I ask them about Henry Thoreau." Then he added, quizzically, "They generally answer, 'Henry Thoreau? who was he?'"

Margaret and Charles stopped at the cemetery at the St. Helier's churchyard, expecting to find the graves of Peter and his parents, Philippe and Marie Thoreau. To their dismay, they learned that the remains had been moved decades before, when the nearby road was widened. Gone were the original tombstones and their inscriptions; and no one knew for sure where the Thoreaus themselves had ended up. It must have been a crushing conclusion to the Americans' journey. But at least they had gotten a chance to chat with two living, breathing Thoreaus.

The lingering, underlying question here is: *Why?* Why did Margaret Upham Wright go out of her way to track down contemporary Thoreau descendents? Since she lived less than twenty miles from Concord, it is logical to assume that she had made the traditional Thoreauvian pilgrimage to Walden Pond, to Sleepy Hollow Cemetery, and to the streets of the man's hometown on at least one occasion. How much more devotion did it take to cross the bigger pond to the east and search out the tiny island home of his ancestors? Was it because of her now local Massachusetts connections? Was it because of her family's interactions with Harvard, Henry's own alma mater? Was it merely a literary exercise undertaken by an experienced journalist and her well-educated son? Or might she have felt a familiarity because she herself had once met the man in person?

As voiced by the young Jersey man, the reality was that Henry Thoreau was not yet widely known or diligently read during the late nineteenth century. (Dr. Samuel Arthur Jones' efforts in Michigan, notwithstanding.) It took a concerted effort to find his writings and to find information written about him. Why would Margaret still be thinking enough about Thoreau to want to trace his family tree in person, and more than 30 years after a casual meeting on a steamboat on the Mississippi? What, if anything, happened between Mrs. Upham and Henry Thoreau that day on the river? Unfortunately, neither one of them has left us more than the clues presented above. We will never know for sure what transpired on the deck of the *War Eagle* on that sunny day in June.

On April 16, 2009, I walked into one of the rooms of a renovated brick mill building in Gardner, Massachusetts.

Our local writing group, Women of Words (WOW for short), was collaborating for the third year in a row with the Greater Gardner Artists Association. During that group's art exhibit in April, six of us poets walked through the rows of artwork on the night before the exhibit opened. Each one of us had to pick a piece of artwork to write about. A month later, we would hold our own event, Visions in Verse, and would then reveal the poems we had written. It was both a challenging and rewarding experience.

Tonight was our selection night. I was preoccupied and not quite in the proper mood for the task. All week long, I had been doing research on Thoreau's "Mrs. Upham." I had already figured out who she was. I learned that she went to the Jersey Islands and wrote that chapter in her book about Henry's ancestry. I was still thinking and wondering about her and what might have happened between her and Mr. Thoreau on that ride down the river on the *War Eagle*.

I greeted my fellow writers as I walked into the display area. Soon each one of us was going her own way. I strolled down the first aisle, waiting for one of the colorful canvases to call out to me, so to speak. New England landscapes were among my favorites. I also liked illustrations that hinted at a story but didn't quite reveal all of it. I had yet to see any likely candidates.

I made the first turn and immediately saw a small painting called "Sunset on the Mississippi." Its hues were subtle. A pale yellow sun lowered toward a watery horizon. It was simple enough. But the scene was framed by the distinctive iron scroll work found on a classic old riverboat. "Whoa," I said softly to myself. Of course, my mind returned to Henry Thoreau and Margaret Upham and their trip along the mighty Mississippi in 1861. I stared at the painting and started considering its poetic possibilities. I imagined that the sun's rays were igniting the corn and wheat fields of Iowa, as the *War Eagle* steamed southward. I could come up with a fictional scenario, a reasonable explanation for why Mrs. Upham had been so impressed with Thoreau. Yes, I could probably do that.

But *should* I? I sighed. I wasn't sure I wanted to inflict my Thoreauvian obsession on my writing comrades and on our future audience. The writers had already heard me talk about Thoreau *ad infinitum*. I didn't want to bore anyone. So I kept weaving through the aisles, admiring all of the pieces and studying the options offered by some of them. But I always returned to "Sunset on the Mississippi." It was not as visually dramatic as the other scenes, but I already knew some of the details behind the tale I could tell with that one. My colleagues had been waiting for me to decide. I picked up the double-sided tape and put my emblem next to "Sunset on the Mississippi." Now I was committed to writing a poem about it.

The next night was the official opening of the exhibit. I got to meet Louise Stevens, the artist who painted the river scene. I asked her some basic questions about the piece, warning her that I didn't want to know *too* much. She told me that the painting was inspired by a trip she made in the late 1980s, when she boarded a sightseeing riverboat in Memphis for an excursion on the river. So in actuality, the view she had captured was of a portion of the Mississippi that Henry Thoreau and Margaret Upham did not see. Louise's real sunset had been over Arkansas, not Iowa. That was okay. I could wield some poetic license. I let Louise know that I intended to write about a different set of historical circumstances on another part of the river. But that was all I knew, and that was all I could tell her. I made sure she was available to attend our Visions in Verse poetry night on May 20.

Over the course of the next three weeks, I sketched out the details I wanted to include in the poem. While I arranged those puzzle pieces into a form that I liked, I remembered seeing an empty spot on a page in Thoreau's field notebook, just where a plant sample might have been pasted. The original leaf must have dropped out somewhere along the way. Or was its removal deliberate? I got a sudden urge to write about rocking chairs, and I threw that notion into the mix as a framing device. Finally, I put the words in the voice of an unknown third party narrator: perhaps a servant with a home-spun manner of speech. I practiced reading the poem aloud every day during that final week, and I tweaked a few word and punctuation choices for easier flow. Then it was time to release it into the world, or at least at this point, to a few dozen people in Gardner, Massachusetts.

Remembering Mrs. Upham
A fiction based on fact
Inspired by Louise Stevens' painting, *Sunset on the Mississippi*

She's gone now, she is;
And she had some kind of life, I'll tell you that.
Outlived two husbands and her daughter Marian.
Campaigned for suffrage
But just missed the chance to vote, herself.
Many's the day she'd sit in that rocker right there
And stare out the window, sway back and forth,
And tell us stories from her past.

She was always on the go, that woman.
Went to Italy, saw Paris.
She was never happier than when she
Had a carpetbag carrier in one hand
And a train or a boat ticket in the other.
And even though she got a few royalties from
That little brown book she wrote about England,
Her favorite tale
Was the one she said had started it all:
That time on the river
Coming down from St.Paul.

It was in the early days of the war.
The missus left Fort Snelling and her husband–
The first one, that is, the army doctor–
And took a steamboat back home
To have her baby.
It was on that ride that she met

Her first real writer:
That man Thoreau from Massachusetts.
And knowing her,
She must have bent his ear a fair amount
About writing and traveling,
Him having already done both.

She always said
The sun was just starting to set on the prairie
When she asked him if he'd ever gone abroad.
Imagine her surprise
When he told her in no uncertain terms, No.
He said that he believed
That the London and the Thames he'd seen
The month before in Canada
Were just as grand as
Their namesakes back in Britain.
And that the very river they were sailing on
Could be their own Ganges or Amazon or Nile;
And there was no need to go farther afield
To find such wonders.

The missus disagreed, of course.
And she stood up to make her point.
It was then that the steamboat hit a snag;
And to steady herself,
She grabbed the fancy iron railing–
Which by then
The summer sun had steamed to a near fire–
And she burnt her finger and palm
In just a few seconds.
Mr. Thoreau produced a leaf pressed in a book
And placed it in her hand to cool the wound.
(At this point she would always show us
What she called "the delightful scar;"
But I can admit to you now
That while *she* may have still seen it,
I never did.)

Him offering her first aid
In such a kind manner and all,
She decided not to argue with the man
Right then and there.
But she didn't know

But that she'd spent the rest of her life
Trying to prove him wrong.
She saw every inch of the world
That she was able to
And had a good old time doing it, she did,
And reported back to stateside magazines.
And sure enough,
When she finally got her chance,
She visited the land of his ancestors for him,
Since he never wanted to and never did.

And the way she told it,
It was as if we'd been there ourselves:
That we'd seen the blazing sun
Melting into the cornfields,
Felt the sudden pitch of the boat
And the heat of the railing
On what turned out to be
One of her favorite journeys, she said;
And the day that pointed her
In the direction of the rest of her life.

Yes, that wonderful old woman is gone now;
And when the house is as quiet as it can be,
That old rocker gets to swaying back and forth,
And I still hear her voice.

I gave Louise a framed copy of the poem, along with the paragraph of historical context I had read beforehand so that everyone would understand who and what I was talking about. She smiled and seemed to like it.

In general, our third Visions in Verse event was a mild success. We had a small but appreciative audience. Several people offered kind compliments afterward. I silently imagined that they had looked at Louise's painting and heard my lengthy poem and thought to themselves, "She got that whole story out of *that?*" Well, I had some help. When Henry David Thoreau is forever parked in the back room of your mind, it doesn't take much prodding for him to come forward. It is easy to see him in *anything.*

WHEN YOU GO: As with the section of this trip that follows the Mississippi River northbound, the easiest way to retrace this portion is to drive the designated Great River Road stretches in Minnesota and Wisconsin. In Minnesota, pick up U.S. 61 just south of St. Paul. Follow it to Red Wing, where you should stop to climb Barn Bluff. Then continue south along the western bank of the river. Cross any of the bridges at La Crosse, Wisconsin. Go to Riverside Park and tour the museum holding the *War Eagle* artifacts. Then take WI Route 35 and follow the river south to Prairie du Chien. Again, an additional consideration would be to take one of the riverboat cruises that are available on Lake Pepin or in La Crosse, Wisconsin.

FOR MORE INFORMATION

Barn Bluff, at the end of East Fifth Street, Red Wing, MN.
  Iowa Great River Road, www.iowagreatriverroad.com.

La Crosse Area Convention & Visitors Bureau, Riverside Park, 410 Veterans Memorial
  Drive, La Crosse, WI 54601. Phone (608) 782-2366.

La Crosse County Historical Society, Riverside Museum, Riverside Park, La Crosse, WI
  54601. Phone (608) 782-1980. www.lchsweb.org/riverside.html

Minnesota Great River Road, www.mnmississippiriver.com.

Red Wing Visitors & Convention Bureau, 420 Levee Street, Red Wing, MN 55066.
  Phone (651) 385-5934. www.redwing.org/

Upper Mississippi River National Wildlife and Fish Refuge, 51 East Fourth Street,
  Winona, MN 55987. Phone (507) 452-4232.
  www.fws.gov/midwest/UpperMississippiRiver.

Wisconsin Great River Road, www.wigreatriverroad.org.

RECOMMENDED READING

The "Uncle Peter" chapter of Mrs. Upham's *Hired Furnished*, if you can find a library that has it and/or will loan it to you. You can also read it online through Google Books. But in honor of her and other women writers who have been influenced by Henry David Thoreau, you can't go wrong with Annie Dillard's *Pilgrim at Tinker Creek* (New York: Bantam Books, 1974) or Anne LaBastille's *Woodswoman* (New York: E. P. Dutton, 1976).

NOTES ON THIS CHAPTER

The text of Thoreau's letter to Frank Sanborn, written from Red Wing, is reprinted on pages 618-622 of *The Correspondence of Henry David Thoreau* (ed. by Walter Harding and Carl Bode; New York: New York University Press, 1958).

The letters written by Horace Mann, Jr., that are here referenced are dated June 23, 24, 25, and 26, 1861.

Details about Red Wing came mostly from Christian A. Rasmussen's *A History of the City of Red Wing, Minnesota* (C.A. Rasmussen, 1933). The reference to the stagecoaches stopping at the Metropolitan Hotel appears on page 52; the paragraph about Thoreau and Mann's visit is on page 72; the new hose cart and hotel fire story appear on page 96; and the cessation of the quarry operation at Barn Bluff is on page 166. I was also given useful information by Diane Buganski, Library Services and Outreach, Goodhue County Historical Society, Red Wing.

The 2008 "Dozen Distinctive Destinations" of the National Trust for Historic Preservation can be seen online at http://www.preservationnation.org/travel-and-sites/sites/midwest-region/red-wing-mn-2008.html. A note about the "Top 25 Historic Destinations" article of the *National Geographic Traveler* can be accessed at http://www.redwing.org/index.php?page=Top_25_Historic_Destinations. The Archer Daniels Midland web site is found at http://www.adm.com.

John Pukite's *Hiking Minnesota* (Helena, Mont.: Falcon Publishing, 1998) was also helpful for describing Barn Bluff.

Information about Horace Brown Wilson was gleaned from a variety of sources, including William Henry Carman Folsom's *Fifty Years in the Northwest: With an Introduction and Appendix Containing Reminiscences, Incidents, and Notes* (with Elijah Evans Edwards; St. Paul: Pioneer Press Co., 1888) and *The American Educational Annual: A Cyclopaedia, or Reference Book for all Matters Pertaining to Education* (New York: J. W. Schermerhorn & Co., 1875, p. 88).

The description of the interior furnishings of the War Eagle appeared in *The Minnesotian* (St. Paul), April 15, 1854, as quoted in William J. Petersen's *Steamboating on the Upper Mississippi* (New York: Dover Publications, 1995). That book notes the existence of two separate steamboats called the *War Eagle* that were busy on the Mississippi during that time period. I am hopeful that I did not confuse the two. Additionally, a useful pamphlet compiled by Robert B. Taunt is *A Brief History of the Steamboat War Eagle, 1854-1870* (La Crosse, Wis.: La Crosse Packet Press, 2000). Copies may be purchased through The La Crosse County Historical Society.

The identity of "Mrs. Upham" was made with the help of the family trees found in Frank Kidder Upham's *Genealogy and family history of the Uphams, of Castine, Maine, and Dixon, Illinois: with genealogical notes of Brooks, Kidder, Perkins, Cutler, Ware, Avery, Curtis, Little, Warren, Southworth, and other families* (Frank Kidder Upham, 1887, pp. 29-30) as well as those posted on Ancestry.com. Helpful biographical sketches of Margaret and her family members are found in the online finding aid of the Wright Family Papers, a collection at the Massachusetts Historical Society, at http://www.masshist.org/findingaids/doc.cfm?fa=fa0136. I have included quotes from both the preface and the "Uncle Peter" chapters of *Hired Furnished*, Margaret's book.

Thoreau wrote about the three old letters from Peter Thoreau in the entry of his journal dated April 21, 1855: "Aunt Maria has put into my hands to-day for safe-keeping three letters from Peter Thoreau, dated Jersey (the first July 1st, 1801, the second April 22nd, 1804, and the third April 11th,1806) and directed to his niece 'Miss Elizabeth Thoreau, Concord, Near Boston,' etc.; also a 'Vue de la Ville de St. Helier,' etc., accompanying the first. She is not certain that any more were received from him. ... Aunt Maria thinks the correspondence ceased at Peter's death, because he was the one who wrote English."

At the time that Margaret wrote *Hired Furnished*, there were four biographies of Henry David Thoreau available for her perusal. I noted the two American ones in the text. But there were also two British-born books: *Thoreau: His Life and Aims*, by A. H. Japp / H. A. Page (1877), and *The Life of Henry David Thoreau*, by Henry S. Salt (1890, revised in 1896). Japp does not mention Thoreau's Jersey ancestry at all. Salt has a quick note about it. So Margaret B. Wright must have used Sanborn's information as a foundation.

I wonder if Margaret eventually read Sanborn's *First and Last Journeys of Thoreau, Lately Discovered Among His Unpublished Journals and Manuscripts* (1905) and came upon the sentence about "Mrs. Upham" meeting Henry Thoreau on the *War Eagle*.

Alas, months after writing "Remembering Mrs. Upham," I corresponded via e-mail with her great-grandson, Conrad E. Wright. He said that it was understood by family members that Margaret "did not like to look back to that portion of her life" in rural Illinois. So it turns out that the poem is even more fictional than I expected it would be. But perhaps meeting Mr. Thoreau was a bright spot in that otherwise dark time for her.

TRAVEL CHAPTER 14

Thursday, June 27, 1861
from Prairie du Chien to Milwaukee, Wisconsin
via the Milwaukee & Prairie du Chien Railroad

Expenses: Fare to Milwaukee, $9.75.
At Madison, .50.
In Milwaukee coach, .25.
At Lake House, .75.
Fare to Boston, $20.15.

1st 60 miles up the Valley of the Wisconsin—which looked broad & shallowbluffs 2 or 3 miles apart—Great abundance of tall spiderwort—alsored lilly—rudbeckia—blue flag white & yel. lilly & whitewater ranun-culus—Abundance of Mullein in Wisconsin.Madison—capital—& its 4 lakes–

—Thoreau's field notebook

We left Red Wing yesterday at about 2 p.m. on the Steamer *War Eagle* and arrived in Pra[i]rie du Chien at 8 a.m. to-day. The train for Milwaukee did not leave till 10 o'clock so we had to wait a while. It is rather cooler to-day than we have had for some time so it is very comfortable travelling. ... For the first 60 or 70 miles of travel to-day we kept in the valley of the Wisconsin River, which we crossed three times. It is a broad, very shallow river, with a sandy bottom; full of sand bars, many of which are bare at low water as is the case now. The pra[i]ries in the river bottom where they were not cultivated were cov-ered with flowers, among which were the Spiderwort, the wild tiger lily, the yellow Pucoon, &c. The marshy ponds are full of white lilies in bloom. We have not come through any large pra[i]ries today, it being mostly marshy meadows for the low ground and oak openings for the higher ground. The redwing blackbird is the most common bird there is all along the track in the marshes. You may think that I can write better, but I can-not, for this is one of the roughest roads I ever rode over.

—Horace Mann Jr.'s letter of June 27, 1861

It seemed as though the duo was always delayed at Prairie du Chien. When Henry Thoreau and Horace Mann, Jr., steamed up the Mississippi River more than a month earlier, the *Itasca* had made a prolonged stop here. Back then, the steamboat had arrived during the late afternoon hours. It had to wait for the train to arrive from Milwaukee so that passengers could make the rail-to-boat connection, if they needed to. Now the men had to wait several hours for the Milwaukee & Prairie du Chien Railroad to get ready to leave for its eastward trek across the state. And this time, Thoreau and Mann would be riding on it.

As both men noted, the first stretch of the day's journey followed the path of the Wisconsin River. Henry and Horace may have exchanged a few observations about this waterway, based on their new-found knowledge of both the Mississippi and the Minnesota rivers. After all, they had just spent the better part of the previous two weeks traveling by water. No wonder Horace was quick to point out the shallowness of the Wisconsin, and the presence of sand bars. Surely the *Frank Steele* would have been grounded here. Perhaps the two had a few laughs over that image, even while they simultaneously realized how close they had come to suffering that very predicament themselves.

From their written notes at least, it seemed that both men could still appreciate the appearance of this river. Former riverboat pilot Samuel Clemens might have commended them. He himself lamented the disturbing change in his own view of the Mississippi after he learned the intricacies of his work. Once he learned to read the signs, those clues of dangers that lay beneath the water's surface, his approach was different. He felt as though he had lost the ability to admire it merely as the handiwork of nature. Clemens wrote that "the romance and beauty were all gone from the river. All the value, any feature of it had for me now was the amount of usefulness it could furnish toward compassing the safe piloting of a steamboat." Fortunately for Thoreau and Mann, their time on steamboats had not jaded them to quite that extent.

Both men botanized from the train. Now they could catch glimpses of the taller plants of summer, the ones that could be most easily seen and identified from a passing window. The distinctive shapes and colors gave them away. The green kernel clusters of Spiderwort (*Tradescantia ohiensis*) had blossomed into threesomes with bluish and purplish petals. Stalks of Blue flag *(Iris virginica)* mirrored those hues, but with singular flowers poised atop them instead. Mullein (*Verbascum thaspus*) and Hoary puccoon (*Lithospermum canescens*) provided splashes of yellow to the landscape, and Turk's cap lily (*Lilium michiganense*) added orange. Prairieland coneflowers (*Rudbeckia*) raised their daisy-like faces to the sun. Pools of standing river water were littered with the white and yellow of Sweet-scented water lily (*Nymphaea odorata*) and the Small yellow pond lily (*Nuphar microphyllum*), while buttercups (*Ranunculus* sp.) rested low at the edges. Overseeing them all were the guardians of the marshes, the male red-winged blackbirds. They were hanging onto the tops of swaying grasses, loudly defining the boundaries of their tiny yet conquered territories. It's too bad that the train never paused at length at each town so that its passengers could explore the local terrain in person. Could anything be more beautiful than the American Midwest in the full bloom of summer?

Just before 1:30 p.m., the cars pulled into the capital city of Madison. Horace wrote:

> Madison is a very pretty place I should think and the lakes which surround it ... are very beautiful. The state house is a large building standing on a rise of ground near the track as we enter the city; it is built out of dark cream colored limestone, which can be quarried all over that section of the state.

Alas, Horace might *not* have been describing the state capitol building. He might have mistaken the facilities of the University of Wisconsin for the seat of government. The railroad tracks ran a bit closer to the school than they did to the capitol. What he saw might very well have been University Hall. Commencement ceremonies for the term had been held the previous evening, so the campus grounds would have been mostly empty by the time the train passed them. Perhaps a few undergraduates even came aboard in order to return home for the summer.

One who made that trip by foot instead of by rail was John Muir, age 23. Muir had just finished his first term at the university. Home for him was a farm near Portage, Wisconsin: a fifty-five mile trek due north of Madison and thus out of the path of the Milwaukee & Prairie du Chien Railroad. It is likely that Muir started walking homeward sometime that day. Did he stop to climb a favorite hill along the shore of Lake Mendota, in order to cast one last admiring glance at the university? And might he have seen the smoke of the locomotive as it first stopped in Madison, and then proceeded east, carrying with it the author of *Walden*? That's a possible scenario. Then again, the young man may very well have wanted to get an early start. If he began walking at dawn, he would have missed seeing the train.

John Muir was finishing his first semester at the University of Wisconsin when Thoreau and Mann passed through Madison. (*Courtesy of the Holt-Atherton Special Collections, University of the Pacific Library*)

John Muir had been born in Dunbar, Scotland. At the age of eleven, he immigrated to America with his father and two of his siblings. The rest of the family (making a total of eight children in all) arrived after farmland could be procured in central Wisconsin. John had a demanding father in Daniel Muir: one who not only expected his eldest son to perform a plethora of strenuous chores without complaint; but who also assumed that same boy should be able to quote any passage from the Bible upon request, from memory. John was a voracious reader and evidently found at least a little time of his own to experiment with inventions. His mechanical creations were exhibited and lauded at the Wisconsin State Fair in Madison in September 1860. Recognition of his talents earned him the right to enter the university during the next term.

But by that day in June 1861, John Muir had not yet read *Walden*; nor had he read any works written by Henry David Thoreau or even by Ralph Waldo

Emerson, the father of Transcendentalism. And Thoreau did not know anything about a young Scot who was studying at the University of Wisconsin.
Yet Muir would eventually follow in the Concord man's footsteps as one of
the most important figures in the field of American environmentalism.

Madison had about 12,000 residents when Thoreau and Mann's train
passed through it. And Wisconsin's real capitol building was in the midst of
undergoing a transformation. The first governmental edifice had become
too small for the burgeoning business of this state. Construction on a
replacement was in progress and was now in its fourth year. Eventually it
would even support a dome. Young Horace was correct in saying that the
structure was built with local stone.

The train spent the next four and a half hours crossing the eastern half
of Wisconsin.

When they pulled into the Milwaukee & Prairie du Chien station at
Fowler and Second Streets, the passengers learned that the city was operating under martial law. Men in various styles of uniform were armed and
patrolling the streets. The mayor had called in militia groups from all across
the state to keep the place in order. What was going on here?

By 1861, Milwaukee had about four times as many residents as
Wisconsin's state capital did. Many of them had German ancestry. More
than two dozen breweries were doing a brisk business here. So were a large
number of banks. According to one source, "almost anyone who could raise
$25,000 to buy Wisconsin bonds could establish himself as a banker and
start printing dollars as freely as his conscience allowed." And therein lay the
trouble. Just as Thoreau and Mann had witnessed in Chicago, the banks of
Milwaukee had been in crisis since the beginning of the war. Many of them
had been backed by bonds from Virginia, North Carolina, and Louisiana.
Since those funds were no longer accessible, money issued from those
sources was now worthless. But for members of the general public, it was
not an easy task to determine which banks were destined to be solvent and
which were not.

On Saturday, June 22, an announcement came that ten banks had folded
and that their currency could no longer be accepted as legal tender. Workers
throughout the city who had just gotten paychecks now learned "that a
week's wages wouldn't buy a single stein of beer." Disgruntled employees
held meetings over the weekend to develop a plan of action. By Monday
morning, June 24, their anger and frustrations had built to a fever pitch. A
group of 200 men assembled on a city street and marched to the financial
district with the steady beat of a brass band accompaniment. They picked

up additional supporters as they went. They raided and ransacked several banks, throwing papers and furniture out the front doors. Someone set fire to the litter. Bank clerks and owners fled their offices as best they could. The mob scene soon turned into a full-fledged riot. One source estimated that at its height, as many as one thousand people had been involved in the melee.

Milwaukee had a police force of twenty-three men: hardly enough to contain the crowd and to curtail its behavior. Mayor James Brown made an attempt to reason with his constituents, but someone lobbed an unidentified object at him and clunked him on the head. That's when he decided to call out the Montgomery Guards. Thirty-seven of the Guards had been scheduled to leave for Madison to receive war training at Camp Randall. Now they were instead fighting a battle on the home front. But when the residents somehow learned that the Guards' muskets were loaded with blanks instead of with live ammunition, they were encouraged to do even more damage. Only Hibbard's Zouaves, local soldiers wielding loaded rifles with bayonets, were ultimately able to disperse the crowd. About fifty individuals were arrested. Some individuals like the mayor, sustained minor injuries. Estimations of property loss were difficult to determine. But even some of the best and most legitimate banks had been completely gutted.

Henry Thoreau and Horace Mann, Jr., were visiting Red Wing, Minnesota, and were climbing to the top of Barn Bluff on that day. But the news from Milwaukee spread across the country, courtesy of the telegraph service. Young Horace even penned what he no doubt meant as an assurance to his mother as he and Mr. Thoreau rode the rails toward the troubled city: "There has been a riot in Milwaukee of which I suppose you have read long before this, but the Milwaukee paper says to-day that the city is quiet."

It had no choice to be otherwise. When the two men stepped down from the railroad car, Wisconsin's biggest city was being additionally patrolled by the Hudson City Light Guard, the Geneva Independents, the Sheboygan Rifles, and the Columbian Rifles. Perhaps it was the presence of so many military men that led Henry and Horace to hire a coach to travel the short distance from the station to the hotel. Soon they were safe and secure at the Lake House, a popular multi-story hostelry located at the corner of Lake and Ferry Streets. From there they could plan the rest of their journey home. A quick departure from Milwaukee probably looked like the best option.

The tracks of the former Milwaukee & Prairie du Chien Railroad still follow the path taken by Thoreau and Mann in 1861. The rails support mostly freight traffic now, though an occasional passenger excursion slips across them. And in season, the circus based in Baraboo uses the tracks to transport its animals and accoutrements to Milwaukee. Residents who are fortunate enough to live along that part of the line can get a closer view if the train makes a stop in their town.

Madison now boasts more than 233,000 residents. The Capitol building stands upon the same plot of ground as it did in 1861. But in the intervening years, the structure has experienced a wide variety of renovation and restoration projects. It now consists of four additional wings and a dome that rises more than 200 feet above the building. Topping the dome is a gilded bronze statue named "Wisconsin," which was crafted by noted sculptor Daniel Chester French of Concord, Massachusetts. Guided tours of the complex are available; and individuals are welcome to explore it themselves on almost any day of the year. Inside and out, it is a work of art, and one that is proudly shown off by native Badgers. A great time to see it is on Saturdays from mid-April to mid-November. That's when the Dane County Farmer's Market is held on the Square, along the grid of sidewalks surrounding the Capitol building. Good times and good buys are had by all who attend it.

The University of Wisconsin now serves more than 175,000 students. The system has thirteen four-year campuses, thirteen two-year campuses, and a commitment to educate anyone living in the state. The former University Hall, the building young Horace probably saw and noted, is now called Bascom Hall. It lost its dome to fire on October 10, 1916.

One twentieth-century scholar lamented the schedule that put Henry Thoreau and Horace Mann, Jr., in Milwaukee four days after the bank riots. Had their trip worked out differently, the two men could have spent more time in the city. They

> "could have found persons with similar botanical and natu-
> ral history interests, like the people they had met in
> Minneapolis: At the time Alexander Mitchell was head of the
> Milwaukee Horticultural Society and Increase Lapham was
> president of the Wisconsin Natural History Association. But
> Alexander Mitchell three days previously had been in the
> center of the bank rioting scene at his own bank on
> Michigan and Water Streets; and even on Thursday he was
> certainly still too preoccupied with bewildering financial
> problems to chat about botanical and horticultural matters."

According to another source, Mitchell had escaped to a steamboat chugging out onto Lake Michigan soon after the riots began. Just when he felt safe enough to return to the mainland remains unclear. But Mitchell would eventually be among the financiers who figured a way out of this particular dilemma. The banks bought more than a million dollars' worth of state bonds. Wisconsin could then afford to send troops to the south, and the local banks could redeem the currency issued by those ten wildcat banks. In theory, everybody won.

The State of Wisconsin is doing a bit better with its financial institutions these days. Only two banks from Wisconsin appear on the FDIC's Failed Bank List for the past decade (2000-2009). Neither one of them had been based in Milwaukee.

Milwaukee is now home to more than half a million people. Of the two dozen breweries operating in the city in 1861, only the Miller Brewery is still in business today. The presence of a number of micro-breweries still makes bar and brewery hopping a popular pastime for city visitors. And like all of the other hotels that Thoreau and Mann patronized, the Lake House is no longer in existence. A fire there on December 5, 1897, claimed the life of one of its guests. Five others were injured when they jumped from windows to escape the flames.

John Muir (1838-1914) spent two and a half years in Madison. He parted from the campus without a diploma in hand. "I was only leaving one University for another," he later explained: "The Wisconsin University for the University of the Wilderness." His professors had given him a foundation in chemistry, geology, and botany. Now he felt ready to explore the countryside on his own. Not only could he put that knowledge to practical use, but he could also discover what additional lessons nature had in store for him. Muir began making a series of long-distance "foot tours" throughout the American Midwest and into Canada. In 1867, he took several months to walk from Indiana to Florida. He kept a journal of his experiences along the way. He had hoped to travel even farther south, and to eventually follow the source of the Amazon River. Instead, he lay in bed for two months with a debilitating case of malaria. While he recuperated, however, he had a chance to decide what his next path should be.

Then he saw a newspaper ad that announced "cheap fares to California, where there were cooler forests and mountains and where his health and high spirits might revive." That must have sounded like a paradise to Muir, after he had endured the heat and disease of the American South. He sailed to Panama, crossed the isthmus by rail, and then sailed up the west coast. He landed in San Francisco on March 29, 1868. The story goes that he asked the first person he saw on the street to direct him to "any place that is wild." The trail he took led him to the Sierra and to Yosemite. There he found work as a ranch hand, a sawyer, a carpenter, and a summer sheep herder. He made enough money to live on, and he still had time to explore the mountains and the dynamic landscape that surrounded him.

In his third year of California living, John Muir was told by a friend that Ralph Waldo Emerson would soon be visiting the area. The friend, Jeanne Carr, was insightful enough to believe that Muir could someday be just as famous as Emerson, even though the younger man had yet to publish any of his nature observations. Carr made arrangements for the two men to meet. Muir played host for several days to Mr. Emerson and his Boston lawyer/bodyguard. He shared with them his plant collections and his pencil sketches. He took them on tours among the giant redwoods. And even though the encounter urged a certain kind of friendship between the two men, Muir was ultimately disappointed in this, their only face-to-face meeting. Emerson and his traveling companion rejected Muir's notion of sleeping under the stars, beneath the sylvan sentinels. They stayed at a hotel instead. They turned down his offer to spend a month of exploration and discovery together, among the peaks and lakes of this beautiful place. Instead, the Massachusetts men soon said their goodbyes and were headed back east. They were "full of indoor philosophy," Muir complained. They had "failed to see the natural beauty and fullness of promise of my wild plan," he said, and had allowed themselves to be relegated to "hotels and trails." This was indeed a "sad commentary on culture and the glorious transcendentalism." Perhaps it was best for them to leave.

Nevertheless, Muir was now prompted to read more of Emerson's essays and poetry than he had previously digested. And those pieces naturally led also to writings by Henry Thoreau. Muir had already read *The Maine Woods* and had sensed a kindred spirit in Thoreau. Here was a man who "would have been content with my log house," he wrote. After Emerson's visit, another friend sent Muir copies of *Walden* and *Excursions*. The books were soon marked with Muir's own notes and underlining. At the same time, he kept up a casual correspondence with Emerson, who was back in Concord. But the great man continued to disappoint. He urged Muir to "bring to an early close your absolute contracts with any yet unvisited glaciers or volcanoes, roll up your herbariums and poems, and come to the Atlantic Coast." After all, only by being ensconced at Harvard would he have an opportunity to work with Asa Gray and Louis Agassiz, the esteemed scientists who could best appreciate his theories and findings. Muir turned down the offer, of course. Emerson was treating the California naturalist the same way he had approached Henry Thoreau. He could write essays, pen letters, and give lectures that could inspire and encourage a protégé; but in some respects, it was only in do-as-I-say-not-as-I-do fashion. Thoreau wanted to go west; Muir wanted to stay there. Waldo Emerson did not fully understand that need in either man.

And neither did he understand how much work there was for John Muir to do in California. Over the course of the next twenty years, Muir wrote and published articles about the natural wonders he found and observed. He traveled to Alaska and made an extensive study of glaciers. He got married and bought his own ranch. Together with magazine editor Robert Underwood Johnson, he publicized the need to preserve unique habitats like the area around Yosemite. Their efforts were rewarded in 1890, when Congress approved the creation of Yosemite National Park, one of the first wilderness parks in the United States.

Land conservation was becoming a critical public issue, especially with the official closing of the American frontier. Not everyone expected the government to do as much as it should in this regard. Perhaps a group should be assembled of interested citizens who could serve as watchdogs over Yosemite and the mountains of California that so inspired its growing number of residents. The organization could resemble some of the great hiking clubs of Europe, but could do much more. And so was the Sierra Club formed in 1892. Two hundred and fifty people attended its first open meeting. John Muir was named the club's president. He held that position for the rest of his life.

In the summer of 1893, Muir finally had a chance to make his first trip to New England. He and Robert Underwood Johnson arrived in Boston late in the day on Wednesday, June 7. On Thursday, they took the train out to Concord. They rode past Walden Pond on their way into town. Once they left the depot, the two men spent most of the day walking. Johnson had been here for the American Revolution centennial celebration in 1875, so he could serve as an informal tour guide. They covered the same ground that most visitors do, beginning with the Revolutionary War sites and moving on to the transcendental ones. They strode through the town common and walked along Monument Street to reach the Old Manse, the rebuilt North Bridge, and the Minute Man Monument, crafted by Concordian Daniel Chester French. They passed the former homes of the Alcotts, the Hawthornes, and the Thoreaus. They called on Daniel Chester French but found his place empty, even though the sculptor and his wife were known to be in town. They were even given a tour inside the Emerson house. "It is just as he left it," wrote Muir. Alas, his correspondent had been gone from this residence for eleven years. But Muir knew where to find him.

The men walked up to Sleepy Hollow Cemetery and took the path that led to Author's Ridge. They put flowers on the graves of Henry David Thoreau and Ralph Waldo Emerson. "I think it is the most beautiful grave-yard I ever saw," remarked Muir.

> It is on a hill perhaps one hundred and fifty feet high in the woods of pine, oak, beech, maple, etc., and all the ground is flowery. Thoreau lies with his father, mother, and brother not far from Emerson and Hawthorne. Emerson lies between two white pine trees, one at his head, the other at [his] feet, and instead of a mere tombstone or monument there is a mass of white quartz rugged and angular, wholly uncut, just as it was blasted from the ledge. ... There is not a single letter or word on this grand natural monument. It seems to have been dropped there by a glacier, and the soil he sleeps in is glacial drift almost wholly unchanged since first this country saw the light at the close of the glacial period.

Leave it to John Muir to first analyze—and quite accurately, too—the geology of the landscape. Only after he got the lay of the land could he consider his reaction to the scene. "I did not imagine I would be so moved at sight of the resting-places of these grand men as I found I was," he wrote. He even thought he might like to make arrangements to join them, when his time came. But in that regard, his ties to his adopted home of California proved to be much stronger than his relationships with the Concord Transcendentalists.

Muir and Johnson used the path by Emerson's house to walk to Walden Pond: the one that Waldo and Henry must have followed themselves, years before. And once again, Muir's practiced eye immediately saw familiar terrain. Now he could confirm in person what he had suspected while reading the pages of *Walden* back in California: that this body of water was a kettle hole, left behind by a retreating glacier.

> It is a beautiful lake about half a mile long, fairly embosomed like a bright dark eye in wooded hills of smooth moraine gravel and sand, and with a rich leafy undergrowth of huckleberry, willow, and young oak bushes, etc., and grass and flowers in rich variety. No wonder Thoreau lived here two years. I could have enjoyed living here two hundred years or two thousand.

> It is only about one and a half or two miles from Concord, a
> mere saunter, and how people should regard Thoreau as a her-
> mit on account of his little delightful stay here I cannot guess.

Muir picked some wildflowers during this walk around Concord, so that he
could send them home to his seven-year-old daughter, Helen. By six o'clock,
he and Johnson had returned to Monument Street and the "Bullet Hole
House," which reportedly still carried evidence of that opening day of the
American Revolution. Here they had dinner with Emerson's son, Edward
Waldo Emerson, in the home of his in-laws, Judge John Shepard Keyes and
his wife, Martha (Prescott) Keyes. Muir might have been relieved to find that
whatever tensions he may have felt in his discourse with Waldo Emerson,
had not been transferred to the man's son. "Nothing could be more cordial
and loving than his reception of me," he said. After spending what must have
been a pleasant evening with good food and good company, the visitors were
asked by the Keyes to stay the night, but they demurred. Muir and Johnson
said their goodbyes, then rode back to their rooms in Boston "on a late
train," passing Walden Pond one last time.

John Muir would return to New England on four more occasions, but
never again to Concord. Yet, on many a printed page, the echo of Thoreau's
voice is found within Muir's own. "In Wildness is the preservation of the
World," Thoreau had written in the essay, "Walking." Muir saw that bid and
raised it. "The world needs the woods, and is beginning to come to them,"
he answered in "Flood-Storm in the Sierra." And Muir's *Travels in Alaska*
bears more than a few similarities to Thoreau's *The Maine Woods*. Both men
had journeyed north along their respective coasts to the wildest areas available to them. Both described in detail the harsh but beautiful environments
they found in those places. Who knows how their lives (and ours) might
have changed if young John Muir had stepped into Henry Thoreau's railroad car in Madison in 1861?

And who knows what America's national park system and its commitment to conservation would look like today if Muir had scurried to Boston
at Waldo Emerson's beckoning? Perhaps Thoreau himself had something to
do with Muir's decision. For by the time the Californian had received that
invitation from Concord, he had read *Excursions*, the first collection of
Thoreau writings to contain "Walking." There he found words that could
offer him friendly advice and confirm his chosen path.

> We go eastward to realize history and study the works of art
> and literature, retracing the steps of the race; we go westward

as into the future, with a spirit of enterprise and adventure.

We: Henry Thoreau and John Muir. One got as far as the Midwest. The other trekked the rest of the way to the Pacific. "Go confidently in the direction of your dreams," said Henry. Thank goodness both of these men did just that.

On Columbus Day weekend 1998, I was in the early stages of a personal Frank Lloyd Wright fascination. During this three-day holiday the previous year, I had been driving through western Pennsylvania. I had made a point of stopping to visit Fallingwater, the home that Wright designed to sit next to and over a rushing-water creek. I had loved the sheer nature-ness of the site. Accented as it was by the vibrant colors of autumn, the house was the perfect complement to that wild space. The forest seemed to need it to be there. The house could sit nowhere else. I immediately admired the architect's aim of building into the landscape. I decided to learn more about him and to see more of his work. I vowed to make Frank Lloyd Wright my Columbus Day tradition.

I did so, knowing that I would not have to go far from home to meet this obligation. At the time, I was living in northern Illinois. I knew that I had fairly easy access to Wright sites in the Midwest. You cannot live on the prairie and ignore him or the prevailing "Prairie Style" of architecture. I started collecting books and information. I bought William Allin Storrer's slim new pamphlet, *The Architecture of Frank Lloyd Wright: A Guide to Extant Structures* (Newark, N.J.: WAS Productions, 1997). I paged through it, studied the maps and imagined all of the road trips I could make. But I had already figured out where my tour should begin. I had seen and picked up brochures that advertised it; and during a few of my exploratory rambles, I had passed signs that pointed to it. So when Columbus Day came around again, I headed northwest to Spring Green, Wisconsin, and to Taliesin.

Frank Lloyd Wright (1867-1959) was another University of Wisconsin dropout. He had been born in Richland Center, a small settlement in the western part of the state, a few miles north of the Wisconsin River. He spent two unproductive semesters in Madison before he made his way to Chicago. There he found work as a draftsman, and he later became an apprentice to architect Louis Sullivan. By the age of 25, Wright had hung out his own shingle as an independent architect. The Prairie School and organic architecture were his signature statements. He designed and built his own home in Oak Park, Illinois; and soon his whole neighborhood was filled with Wright creations. The rest, as the saying goes, is history.

Wright was successful and famous by the time he returned to the Wisconsin River valley and to the land of his Welsh American ancestors. He began building Taliesin (pronounced taal-lee-ESS-in) as his own residence in 1911: fifty years after a train carrying Henry Thoreau and Horace Mann, Jr., passed less than two miles north of the site. Taliesin is said to mean "shining brow" in Welsh. The home is therefore nestled into the "brow" of a hill, not perched upon it. "No house should ever be *on* a hill or *on* anything," Wright wrote in his autobiography. "It should be *of* the hill. Belonging to it. Hill and house should live together each the happier for the other." His holdings here grew to include the Hillside Home School, which was a living space and working studio for his apprentices; the Tan-y-deri House, which was a home for his sister Jane; and the Midway Farm, which lay equidistant between Wright's house and the studio. A unique Romeo and Juliet Windmill was installed to pump water to the school. Today, visitors may see any and all of these features solely by guided tour.

When I got to the Spring Green area in 1998, I stopped first at the Frank Lloyd Wright Visitor Center. This building too was an illustration of the architect's work, and was originally constructed as a restaurant in 1956. It stood a few stories high; but at the same time, it somehow managed to lie low along the southern bank of the Wisconsin River. Its horizontal lines mirrored the surface of the water. Intermittent layers of local stone resembled the bluffs that lined the lower Wisconsin and upper Mississippi river valleys.

As a result, the structure blended into the surrounding landscape with very little effort: as Wright buildings often do.

I swooped through the gift shop while I waited for my tour to begin. I had chosen to join the shuttle tour of the grounds, as opposed to the one that led through the interior of the house itself. I had read enough about Wright's personal life to know that his home at Taliesin held within it a tragic history. I did not want to relive what was already a series of vivid events in my mind.

I had also paged through enough books and photographs to know that I was more intrigued by Wright's exteriors than by his interior design. Perhaps that was because I loved the outdoors. The concept of working *with* Nature rather than *against* her had a core appeal for me. I was also a bit intimidated by the overwhelming straight lines and 90-degree angles that were peppered throughout his rooms. I was a mess maker at heart. Ask anyone I've shared an office with, and they would be quick to agree. Even as I typed these words, I was surrounded by boxes, files, and piles of papers. My bookcases were filled to overflowing. The two-drawer cabinet was stuffed full. A stack of books about Frank Lloyd Wright teetered on top of the several inches of litter covering my desk. At least one volume was overdue for return to a nearby library. A master map of the route of the Journey West was taped onto the wall in front of me, along with other crucial pieces of information and inspirational postcards and messages. Every flat surface as far as my eye could see was serving as a paperwork repository, including the impromptu table made by the top edges of the twenty-volume encyclopedia I've had since childhood. Wright's philosophy of organic architecture mesmerized me. But the neatness and tidiness it hid inside made me uneasy. Those were not spaces I could live with. It would be sacrilege to put a folder bursting with photocopies and tourist brochures on a Frank Lloyd Wright desk. No, it was best for me to stay outside.

The slow ride with other visitors on the shuttle was both informative and picturesque. This was a quintessential example of Wisconsin farmland. It was beautiful and bucolic. To place pieces of Wright architecture at strategic points on this landscape just served to make a good thing better. We drove around the main residence, the Tan-y-deri house, and the Hillside School. Each one was interesting in its own way. Our on-board guide supplied the facts and details that added to what we could see for ourselves. But suddenly it was the Romeo and Juliet Windmill that most captured my attention.

Back where I came from, a windmill was a structure that was made of a maze of gray steel bands that met at a peak. It was crowned by a twirling, round propeller blade with a flat tail vane. It was not an unpleasant mechanism to gaze upon, but it could hardly be considered architectural. It generally faded into the background of any farm scene and usually stood beside a brick-red barn or a tiny rocky creek. I must have seen dozens, if not hundreds, of them during the first three and a half decades of my life in central and eastern Pennsylvania.

This Romeo and Juliet, this was something "out of the box." Perhaps a "paradigm shift" was a more accurate and more contemporary description. Two towers stood against one another. Their infrastructure was covered by tasteful wooden slats. The shorter tower had a hexagonal circumference, while the taller one had a footprint that was diamond shaped. Both wore hats. The traditional propeller blade with tail extended like a natural beanie on top of the second. Together they served as both windmill and water tower. And they had been doing so for more than 100 years, having survived at least one tornado that passed through this valley. This creation was a study in aesthetics, geometry, and physics. I wished I had always known about it. I would have come here sooner, just to stare at it.

I felt the same way about the Midway Barn. As we approached it, our guide explained that Wright had operated Taliesin as a working dairy farm. She said that his herd consisted only of tan Guernsey cows because he believed that black and white Holsteins would blemish his perfect, living canvas. "He thought they looked like crumpled up balls of newspaper thrown onto the grass," she said. I laughed out loud. I had seen my share of Holstein cows, and I had never thought of them in that fashion. But the image of Wright's philosophy made perfect sense. The guide continued talking about the sweeping contours of the fields on the other side of the road. I listened, but I was still admiring the barn. It was long and sleek and shared some of the colors and design choices of the visitor center. It definitely did not fit the pattern of a Pennsylvania Dutch bank barn, first and foremost because there was no earthen bank for a stone foundation to be built into. And it was nothing like my grandparents' English style barn, which had a sloping roof and wooden windbreaks sheltering the otherwise open doorway. In fact, this structure didn't look like a barn at all. And I was getting such a crick in my neck in studying it that I had to move my whole body around in my seat to keep it in view.

I was still deciding what to think about this building and how to describe it, when our shuttle took a turn. Suddenly the shape of the barn shifted. What originally looked like one large long building was actually broken into two, seemingly connected by some sort of second-floor bridge. I gasped, I was so surprised by the transformation. The guide was chattering away about something else on the property. I wondered why she wasn't pointing out the fact that the view of the barn had changed dramatically. I glanced back at her and the other tourists in the van. They were busy talking about some other aspect of Wright's architectural style. I guessed I was the only one who had noticed the mystique of the barn. Well, okay. I decided to keep the secret. I turned back and smiled to myself until the whole Midway farm complex disappeared from the window. I wished I could have walked through it and around it. Would it be filled with that wonderful hay and animal aroma that I remembered from playing in my grandparents' loft? Now, *this* would be an interior space I wouldn't have minded having time to explore. But onward we went, around the edges of the property, and ending up back at our starting point at the river.

It doesn't take much effort to think of Thoreau and Wright at the same time. Did Frank Lloyd Wright know that Henry Thoreau once passed through this valley on the train? Probably not. But he may have been beside himself with joy had he learned that fact. The man may not have earned a college degree, but he was exceedingly well read. He had studied and had been influenced by the writings of Thoreau, Emerson, and Walt Whitman, among many others. And while there is no evidence to suggest that Wright ever made the pilgrimage to Concord himself, he did bring its transcendental spirit to central Wisconsin by reading aloud passages of Thoreau and his colleagues to the students at Taliesin. When once asked by a scholar to describe what *Walden* and its author meant to him, Wright summed up his reply with just one line: "The history of American Architecture would be incomplete without Thoreau's wise observations on the subject." That was all that needed to be said.

Wait a minute. Henry David Thoreau, America's poster boy for the environmental movement and for all things nature, was also a student of architecture, and of those very man-made structures that insulated their inhabitants *from* nature? Well, of course he was. He had built his small house at Walden Pond. Just before he moved into it, he had helped his father build the family home near the train station in Concord. In his part-time work as a surveyor, he had an opportunity not only to analyze and measure individual properties, but also to convey their features into tangible and meticulously recorded forms on paper. He kept his eyes open during his daily walks. He was adept at reading the landscape and employing the tenets of place-based education, more than a century before those concepts became popular techniques for teaching elementary and secondary science. And fortunately for us, he wrote down his impressions of what he saw.

Thoreau and Frank Lloyd Wright led vastly divergent personal lives. And there are many issues upon which they probably would have disagreed and perhaps have even argued, if they had been permitted the chance to live in overlapping times. But some of the most famous Wright quotes sound downright Thoreauvian:

> Study nature, love nature, stay close to nature. It will never fail you. I believe in God, only I spell it "Nature."

Conversely, some of Thoreau's descriptions of New England architecture and the living conditions of his fellow residents might have been among the inspirational excerpts that Wright shared with his students. In the "Economy" chapter of *Walden*, he could have found these lines:

Most men appear never to have considered what a house is, and are actually though needlessly poor all their lives because they think that they must have such a one as their neighbors have. As if one were to wear any sort of coat which the tailor might cut out for him.

Would not both men thus look askance and aghast at the prevalence of the cookie-cutter developments of American suburbia?

Even Wright's rule of building a house into a hill instead of on top of it is a concept shared with an 1857 entry in Thoreau's *Journal*. There Henry commented on the appearance of a specific home he often passed in Concord.

A traveller of taste may go straight through the village without being detained a moment by any dwelling, either the form or surroundings being objectionable, but very few go by this house without being agreeably impressed, and many are therefore led to inquire who lives in it. Not that its form is so incomparable, nor even its weather-stained color, but chiefly, I think, because of its snug and picturesque position on the hillside, fairly lodged there, where all children like to be, and its perfect harmony with its surroundings and position. For if, preserving this form and color, it should be transplanted to the meadow below, nobody would notice it more than a schoolhouse which was lately of the same form. It is there because somebody was independent or bold enough to carry out the happy thought of placing it high on the hillside. It is the locality, not the architecture, that takes us captive.

Thoreau might have taken offense at Wright's compulsion to manipulate every last detail of the landscapes surrounding his buildings, however. "A tree out of place is a weed," said Wright. And he made sure that the views from each and every window of his Taliesin home were perfectly composed of aesthetically pleasing vistas, all the way to the horizon.

It seems unthinkable that Thoreau would agree with any philosophy that would make a tree, a grand woodland guard, such an object of disdain. Yet he did see the innate benefit for individuals to be able to see both the earth and the sky from their homes. He ruminated on this theory in his *Journal* in 1851. He thought then that too few houses were built to take advantage of the local views.

We love to see any part of the earth tinged with blue, cerulean, the color of the sky, the celestial color. I wonder that houses are not oftener located mainly that they may command particular rare prospects, every convenience yielding to this. The farmer would never suspect what it was you were buying, and such sites would be the cheapest of any. A site where you might avail yourself of the art of Nature for three thousand years, which could never be materially changed or taken from you, a noble inheritance for your children. The true sites for human dwellings are unimproved. They command no price in the market. Men will pay something to look into a travelling showman's box, but not to look upon the fairest prospects on the earth. A vista where you have the near green horizon contrasted with the distant blue one, terrestrial with celestial earth. The prospect of a vast horizon must be accessible in our neighborhood. Where men of enlarged views may be educated. An unchangeable kind of wealth, a *real* estate.

And what about the role of the cow in those landscapes? Our tour guide was evidently correct in conveying Mr. Wright's preference for Guernsey cows, based merely on how they looked while grazing in the fields. According to one account, the architect and the Taliesin dairy farm manager once held a quick debate about breeds. The cream production from the Guernseys was sagging; and Jack Sangster, the dairyman, noted that a switch to Holsteins might solve the problem.

Wright thought over the proposal for a moment and replied: "Jack, Holsteins are black and white. Black and white on green? No, black and white do not look good on green. Never bring anything black and white or red and white in the way of an animal in sight of my eyes—coffee and cream, which are the color of my Guernseys, on green, are the three most restful colors you can find. That is why I have Guernseys, and why I want nothing but Guernseys."

Oh, but Mr. Thoreau was of the opposite opinion. He did not mention breeds by names, but he did speak occasionally of their appearance when writing about the cows of Concord.

The color of the cows on Fair Haven Hill, how fair a contrast to the hillside! How striking and wholesome their clean brick-red! When were they painted? How carelessly the eye rests on them, or passes them by as things of course!

[The cows] occupy the most eligible lots in the town. I love to see some pure white about them; they suggest the more neatness.

No crumpled up balls of newspaper decorated his New England fields.

No, Henry Thoreau seems not to have cared what the cows looked like, as long as they were there. He encountered them as he walked around his hometown. Sometimes he interacted with them and wandered among them. And at other times, he just watched them.

> It is well to find your employment and amusement in simple and homely things. These wear best and yield most. I think I would rather watch the motions of these cows in their pasture for a day, which I now see all headed one way and slowly advancing,—watch them and project their course carefully on a chart, and report all their behavior faithfully,—than wander to Europe or Asia and watch other motions there; for it is only ourselves that we report in either case, and perchance we shall report a more restless and worthless self in the latter case than in the first.

It is also amazing now to see that when Thoreau wrote about local cows, he at times took them out of New England and placed them in the middle of a Midwestern landscape—an area he would not see himself, in some cases, for many years. In the Spring of 1850, he noted that a cow had escaped from her pasture and had to swim across the local waterway in order to get back home. "She was a buffalo crossing her Mississippi," he reported. Six years later, he studied the way that one particular animal spent her entire day grazing and chewing her cud. "The Mississippi is her drink," he wrote; "the prairie grass her food." With these notes, Thoreau might have been unconsciously doing what New England farmers were then doing in reality and in droves: moving their operations to the middle of the country. There the plowing was easier and the flatter land seemed to be the natural habitat for cattle. Thoreau and Mann saw that very trend as they rode the rails through Illinois and Wisconsin.

There is no need to embark here on an exhaustive comparison of the writings and the philosophies of Henry Thoreau and Frank Lloyd Wright. Perhaps at this point it is enough to say that it was certainly a uniquely American spirit that gave rise to both of these men and thus provided the impetus for their works.

My Columbus Day tradition with Frank Lloyd Wright's architecture lasted only a few more years. I visited his studio in Oak Park, and I toured his neighborhood. I drove past and studied random private homes in northern Illinois. I walked around one of his commercial commissions in southern

Wisconsin. But after I moved to Massachusetts in 2003, I found the trend harder to sustain. There were some properties in the Northeast that I could track down, but it wasn't the same. Besides, soon after my return to the East Coast, I concentrated following the path of Thoreau's Journey West. Frank Lloyd Wright was set aside for another day. Maybe I will get back to him eventually. In the meantime, I bought a brand-new guidebook to Wright sites. And every once in a while, I pick it up, flip through its pages, study the maps, and think of all the road trips that are possible.

But I had already been to Taliesin. I had fallen in love with Romeo and Juliet and with the Midway Barn from all of its angles. I could not imagine anything else ever coming close to them. It would not take much prompting at all for me to make a long-distance drive to see them and that beautiful Wisconsin landscape again. The fact that Frank Lloyd Wright's property lay close to the route of Thoreau and Mann's Journey West was a mere and happy accident. Two birds with one stone.

WHEN YOU GO: Following the old Milwaukee & Prairie du Chien rails is an easy task if you have a good road atlas. The tracks still play leapfrog with the Wisconsin River from Prairie du Chien to Spring Green. They even cross the river three times, exactly as Horace reported to his mother. You can drive along WI Route 60 on the north side of the waterway or along WI Route 133 on the south. Both provide great views of the water and the rails from time to time. Either way, this stretch makes for a leisurely and pastoral journey.

At Spring Green, migrate to U.S. 14 and head east. You will be going in the general direction of the tracks by continuing on U.S. 14 and then by turning onto WI Route 59 after passing the town of Oregon. That two-laner will lead you directly into Milwaukee, and you will see the tracks every now and then. To get closer to them, consult your trusty map. Or: if the quickest route appeals to you instead, catch I-94 in Madison and take it to Milwaukee. You won't see the rails at all by using the highway, but you'll make great time.

FOR MORE INFORMATION

Greater Madison Convention & Visitors Bureau, 615 East Washington Avenue, Madison, WI 53703. Phone (608) 255-2537. www.visitmadison.com

Kettle Moraine State Forest: Southern Unit Headquarters, S91 W39091 Highway 59, Eagle, Wisconsin 53119. Phone (262) 594-6200. dnr.wi.gov/org/land/parks/specific/kms

Lower Wisconsin State Riverway Board, 202 North Wisconsin Avenue, PO Box 187, Muscoda, WI 53573. Phone (608) 739-3188. lwr.state.wi.us

Milwaukee County Historical Society, 910 North Old World 3rd Street, Milwaukee, WI 53203. Phone (414) 273-8288. www.milwaukeehistory.net.

Old World Wisconsin, S103 W37890 Hwy 67, Eagle, WI 53119. Phone (262) 594-6300.

oldworldwisconsin.wisconsinhistory.org

Prairie du Chien Chamber of Commerce, 211 South Main Street, PO Box 326, Prairie du Chien, WI 53821. Phone (608) 326-8555. www.prairieduchien.org

Taliesin Preservation, Inc., 5607 County Road C, Spring Green, WI 53568. Phone (608) 588-7900. www.taliesinpreservation.org

Visit Milwaukee, 648 North Plankinton Avenue, Milwaukee, WI 53203. Phone (414) 273-3950. www.visitmilwaukee.com

RECOMMENDED READING

You can't go wrong with the early books of two Wisconsin naturalists: John Muir's *The Story of My Boyhood and Youth* and Aldo Leopold's *A Sand County Almanac*. Both are available in a variety of editions. Then bring yourself to the present day with Steven I. Apfelbaum and *Nature's Second Chance: Restoring the Ecology of Stone Prairie Farm* (Boston: Beacon Press, 2008).

NOTES ON THIS CHAPTER

The quote from Samuel Clemens about his changing views of the Mississippi River can be found in "Chapter IX: Continued Perplexities" in his book, *Life on the Mississippi*.

Some facts about Madison's Capitol building were found on the state's web site at http://www.wisconsin.gov/state/capfacts/history.html. Information about the Dane County Farmer's Market on the Square can be accessed at http://www.dcfm.org.

The basic facts of the Milwaukee bank riots can be found in Robert W. Wells' *This Is Milwaukee* (Garden City, N.Y.: Doubleday & Company, 1970). I supplemented his text with newspaper reports from the *Milwaukee Morning Sentinel* (June 27, 1861) and the *Massachusetts Weekly Spy* (issues from June 28, 1861 and July 3, 1861). Professor Harriet M. Sweetland of the University of Wisconsin-Milwaukee is the scholar who wondered what would have happened if Thoreau and Mann had visited Milwaukee in a more peaceful time. I quoted from her article, "Why Thoreau Spent One Night in Milwaukee" (*Historical Messenger of the Milwaukee County Historical Society* 18, December 1962: 3-9). According to the FDIC's "Failed Bank List" (http://www.fdic.gov/bank/individual/failed/banklist.html), two Wisconsin banks have gone under since 2000: the First National Bank of Blanchardville and the Bank of Elmwood.

Dr. Edmund A. Schofield, Jr., is the scholar who discovered the timing of John Muir's departure from Madison and the passing of the train carrying Thoreau and Mann through the capital city. His findings are included in his inspirational article, "John Muir's Yankee Friends and Mentors: The New England Connection" (*Pacific Historian* 29, 1985: 65-93). It was his research that led to my own. Many thanks again to David DePrez for pointing me in Ed's direction.

Additional Muir sources consulted include Michael P. Cohen's *The Pathless Way: John Muir and American Wilderness* (Madison: The University of Wisconsin Press, 1984), and Donald Worster's *A Passion for Nature: The Life of John Muir* (New York: Oxford University Press, 2008). The quote about California's "cooler forests and mountains" appears on page 147 of Worster's book. His account of Emerson's visit to the West Coast (pp. 209-215) was the best version I found about that event. The "University of the Wilderness" quote is from *Boyhood and Youth*, p. 268, as quoted in Roderick Nash's *Wilderness and the American Mind* (3rd ed. New Haven, Conn.: Yale University Press, 1982). The "sad commentary" quote was from *The Wilderness World of John Muir* (With an Introduction and Interpretive Comments by Edwin Way Teale. Boston: Houghton Mifflin, 1954, p. 164).

Muir's own description of his pilgrimage to Concord can be found in William Frederic Bade's *The Life and Letters of John Muir* (Boston: Houghton Mifflin, 1924, volume 2, pp.266-269). His visit is further detailed in J. Parker Huber's *A Wanderer All My Days: John Muir in New England* (Sheffield, Vermont: Green Frigate Books, 2006). Robert Underwood Johnson tells of his 1875 visit to Concord in *Remembered Yesterdays* (Boston: Little, Brown, 1923, pp.326-329), but doesn't provide any mention of his return there with Muir in 1893. By the way, just in case you are reading the chapter aloud: Concordians pronounce the surname "Keyes" to rhyme with "eyes," and not with "ease."

In 1897, the University of Wisconsin granted John Muir an honorary degree of Doctor of Laws (LL.D.).

One of my main sources of information about Frank Lloyd Wright was the beautiful coffee table book by Derek Fell called *The Gardens of Frank Lloyd Wright* (London: Frances Lincoln Limited, 2009). Its full-color photos took me back to Taliesin, to Romeo and Juliet, and to the Midway barn. From Fell's text did I glean the interchange between Wright and dairyman Jack Sangster (pp. 45-47), as well as the quote, "A tree out of place is a weed" (p. 41). Since the book was printed in London, I took the liberty of changing all of the instances of "colour" to "color" when I used the Guernsey cow story.

Wright's statement about the placement of a house in regard to a hill is found on page 168 of his book, *Frank Lloyd Wright: An Autobiography* (Petaluma, Calif.: Pomegranate Publishers, 2005). His assessment of Thoreau's contribution to "the history of American Architecture" comes from a letter written to Thoreau Society secretary Walter Harding, dated February 28, 1952, and held in a collection deposited with the Thoreau Institute at Walden Woods. Wright's letter actually contained a second line: "If I can find time, I'll go into it." Evidently, he didn't, so he didn't.

A new detailed guidebook of Wright sites is now available: Thomas A. Heinz's *Frank Lloyd Wright Field Guide* (Evanston, Ill.: Northwestern University Press, 2005). Its information and photographs will help anyone get a start on his or her own discovery trail. And if you want to learn more about the tragic events that took place behind the walls of Taliesin, I highly recommend reading Nancy Horan's *Loving Frank: A Novel* (New York: Ballantine Books, 2007). It may be fiction, but it reads like fact. And even though it was written and released well after my first visit to the property at Spring Green, it validated for me my reasons for admiring Wright's exteriors and for refusing to go inside the home. Your results may vary.

Henry Thoreau's quote about the house on the hillside in Concord is from his *Journal* entry dated November 26, 1857. His notion of combining earth and sky in every view is found in the entry dated May 25, 1851. His cow observations are written in entries of July 16, 1851; July 1, 1852; and October 5, 1856. The ones that mention the Mississippi River are dated Spring 1850 (found in volume two of the Dover edition of the *Journal*, on pp. 18-19), and May 17, 1856.

Travel Chapter 15

Friday, June 28, 1861 to Wednesday, July 3, 1861
Milwaukee to Mackinac Island
via the steamship Edith

28 By propeller Edith to Mackinaw—Milwaukee best harbor on lake (of settled places)—& shore rocky at S end of Lake—good harbors behind islands & at traverse bay in NE, 9 miles wide & cannot see across—but see land loom **some times** on each side from mid. 28' at eve leave Sheboygan & steam NE to Carp River.

29 10 am at Carp River & Carp Lake Pass Manitou Islands on left in fore noon & op. Fox islands run into Carp River & leave there at noon & steam N x W to Beaver (or mormon islands) with the first hut & mormon houses—Leave there at eve **& reach** Mackinaw 2 am

—Thoreau's field notebook

While they were steaming down the Mississippi River, Henry Thoreau and Horace Mann, Jr., learned about a special service provided by the Buffalo and Lake Huron Railway Company. They either heard about it from fellow travelers or saw the advertisement in a local newspaper. Three times a week, steamboats ran between Chicago and Goderich in Canada West, "touching at all intermediate ports." Milwaukee was one of those ports, and so was Mackinac Island. Sailing across both Lake Michigan and Lake Huron was involved. The service was aimed at "Shippers of Produce and Merchandise," because the four steamboats involved generally handled freight loads. From Goderich, the Buffalo and Lake Huron Railway Company could take either people or materials to Toronto. Connections to other eastern cities could be made from there.

Why would our travelers choose to take a different route home? At least four reasons come to mind.

1. They had concerns about the war activity. Though May and June had brought about only a few battles south of the Mason-Dixon line, there was no telling what might happen in the weeks to come. This route was about as far north as they could travel. Hopefully, it was out of reach of the fighting.

2. They wanted to continue the adventure and see new places. Perhaps this was also a chance to avoid the Rev. Robert Collyer, who had asked them to look him up on their return trip. They needn't have worried. Collyer had volunteered for the U.S. Sanitary Commission, a group that ministered to fallen soldiers. He had left Chicago and was already in Washington, D.C.

3. They wanted specifically to stop on Mackinac Island. Perhaps young Horace had a say in their itinerary at this point. He had been to the island four years earlier with his parents and his two brothers. He might have convinced Henry that it was an interesting place to visit and would provide an opportunity for them to spend a few days botanizing. Horace could also reminisce about his father and relive the good times the family had had there.

4. They wanted to save money. Horace wrote to his mother that these tickets cost at least five dollars less than those for the trip west. The deal included an indefinite layover at Mackinac Island.

In any event, Henry and Horace boarded the eleven-year-old propeller steamboat *Edith* in Milwaukee on June 28th. In addition to the two Massachusetts men, the *Edith* carried as cargo 100 barrels of flour and three safes. They sailed north along the coast of Wisconsin to Sheboygan. After dark, they headed northeast and began their trip across Lake Michigan. This was a new experience for Henry Thoreau. He had never been on one of the Great Lakes, or on any lake that was big enough to resemble an ocean. What was his reaction? Unfortunately, he didn't record his impressions on paper.

Jerry Dennis, Michigan native and author of *The Living Great Lakes*, can provide a twenty-first century view of a trip across Lake Michigan at that point:

> [Y]ou're out of sight of land much longer than you are within sight of it. About the time the Wisconsin shore disappears, and the rest of the way across, the overwhelming impression is of an immense and powerful body of water that could

indeed be ocean. If waves are 2-3 feet near shore, they'll be 4-6 in the open lake. If there was wind—and there probably was—then undoubtedly some of the passengers and perhaps Thoreau and Mann themselves suffered sea-sickness. The wind would have likely been from the southwest, so the Wisconsin shore would have been protected, but by the time the vessel reached mid-lake the long southern fetch would have funneled up the lake for about 200 miles, creating white-caps and steep wind waves. And the waves would have been coming from abeam, making the vessel roll and pitch. Waves on the Great Lakes are shorter in duration and more erratic than in saltwater—they only rarely become rollers—resulting in seas so choppy that even the most seasoned ocean sailors can find a crossing difficult to stomach.

Young Horace wrote home that they "had a very pleasant day on the lake." It had been "a beautiful day" with a few clouds in the afternoon, "& a little cool on the lake." But would he have admitted to his mother if he and Mr. Thoreau had gotten seasick?

At 10 a.m. on June 29th, the *Edith* docked at a settlement called Carp River. If the travelers were looking at a map, they no doubt could see that they were basically at the "little finger" of the Michigan "mitten." This was a place of very few people, where a fish-laden waterway flowed from an interior lake into the much bigger Lake Michigan. Chippewa Indians still lived in the area and were preached to by Presbyterian missionaries from the East Coast. The lumbering industry was already a key business. The *Edith* probably made this stop for either wood or fish. Carp River had both. And in the two hours they spent here, Thoreau and Mann did a bit of botaniz-ing along the shorelines. Clasping hound's tongue was one of the plants they found here.

At noon, they were off again. The Manitou and Fox Islands passed on their port side, and the entrances to Grand Traverse Bay and Little Traverse Bay showed up at starboard. The *Edith* docked at Beaver Island for a few hours. From 1847-1856, this island had supported a Mormon settlement. Thoreau noted that some of the houses were still standing, although the inhabitants were long gone.

The *Edith* left Beaver Island in the evening and steamed into the Straits of Mackinac, toward Mackinac Island. It is possible that her guide, Captain Hunt, chose to approach the trickiest part of this voyage at night in order to be guided by the lighthouses that were strategically located along the Michigan coastline. Dangerous reefs lay in wait for inexperienced sailors.

According to Jerry Dennis,

> they likely passed Gray's Reef around 10 p.m, not quite fully dark that close to the summer solstice, but surely dark enough to have been a cause of anxiety for the crew. The Waugoshance Lighthouse had been built in 1851, which was a big help. And no doubt the captain knew the water well. But still, those dolomite reefs reach far into the lake and are unforgiving. If the night was clear, Thoreau would have been treated to an astonishingly bright night sky, with a clear view in 360 degrees, and no lights anywhere to mask the stars.

The *Edith* docked at Mackinac Island at 2 a.m. on June 30, 1861. Henry Thoreau and Horace Mann found lodging at the Mackinac House on nearby Main Street.

Throughout Thoreau's notes, he consistently spelled the name "Mackinaw." To that end, he wrote the word as he heard it spoken. No matter whether it appears today as "Mackinac" or "Mackinaw," the name is accurately pronounced exactly the way Henry wrote it.

They spent four days here. Mackinac Island was not yet a haven for tourists, but it certainly provided a valuable harbor that lay conveniently between Lakes Michigan and Huron. At three miles long and two miles wide, Mackinac may have been a bit bigger than Thoreau would have liked.

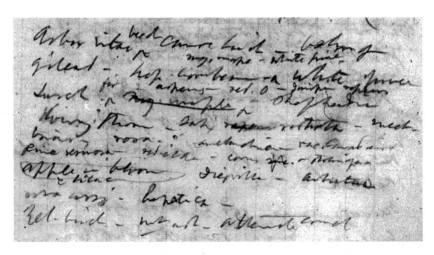

A portion of page 76 of Thoreau's notebook, which lists plants found on Mackinac Island. The phrase "apple in bloom" is circled, with a later note "& lilac" added beneath. (*Reproduced from the original manuscript in The Huntington Library, San Marino, California*)

"An island always pleases my imagination," he once wrote, "even the smallest, as a small continent and integral portion of the globe. I have a fancy for building my hut on one." Well, here he was, on a unique and intriguing outcropping of limestone. It was time to explore.

The largest and most immediate feature seen from their hotel was Fort Mackinac, perched on the bluff right above the tiny town. The fort began as a British post during the American Revolutionary War. At the war's conclusion, the island and the fort became part of the United States. The British occupied it again after an invasion during the War of 1812. A peace treaty two years later restored ownership to the Americans. John Jacob Astor promptly built an American Fur Company office on the island. Thus began the lucrative fur trade in the area. Military hostilities ceased.

But the fort had not been unaffected by the outbreak of the Civil War. In April 1861, all of the soldiers and their families left Mackinac and headed to Washington, D.C., to help protect the Union capital. Only Ordnance Sergeant William Marshall remained behind to take care of Fort Mackinac. It is not known if he may have opened the door for visitors to explore the grounds. Thoreau mentioned the fort in his plant inventory; but he may have found his samples on the hillsides that surrounded the stone walls, and not inside of them.

Four days on the island offered even more opportunities to botanize than Henry and Horace had when they stopped at Niagara Falls. Thoreau's "Plants at Mackinaw" inventory took up four pages of his notebook. Here he saw arborvitae, sugar maples, red oaks, beeches, larches, white spruce, and junipers; gooseberries, strawberries, and ground cherries; buttercups, yarrow, and hemlock parsley, along with dozens of other flowers and plants. But just as at Carp River, the clasping hound's tongue was the "most conspic. & prevailing" specimen he saw on Mackinac.

"Spring disappears in stones of shore," he wrote. While many natural springs occur on the island, only one is described in the published histories as "water gushing out of the solid rock." This was a feature located on the eastern edge of the island, not far from Arch Rock, another natural site. Thoreau and Mann botanized around both areas. Future residents would name the water Dwightwood Springs.

From the sheer amount of plants listed in Thoreau's notebook, we can assume that the two men did quite a lot of exploring around the island. Both might have been invigorated by the place itself. When young Horace and his family visited Mackinac during the summer of 1857, his father wrote to a friend:

I never breathed such air before and this must be some that was clear out of Eden and did not get cursed. I sleep every night under sheet, blanket and coverlit, and no day is too warm for smart walking or vigorous bowling. The children are crazy with animal spirits and eat in such a way as to demonstrate the epigastric paradox that quantity contained may be greater than the container.

Could young Horace have remembered the food? Maybe that was a viable reason for this detour.

Future readers and scholars would wonder about the state of Henry's health while he was on Mackinac Island. He never remarked about such things in his notebook. But he did write "Sat by fire July 2nd." Some interpreted that note to mean that he was so sick that he had to sit by a fire to comfort himself, possibly even by being bundled up in blankets. But if we remember that Thoreau most often used his notebook to keep track of unusual phenomena, we can look at that line a bit differently. The Spring of 1861 had been a cool one throughout the northern part of the country. Chances are that the air was still chilly on Mackinac Island, even though it was summertime. For residents to build fires, especially in the evening, would not have been out of the ordinary—at least, not for them. Thoreau obviously found the situation interesting enough to make a note of it.

But while Thoreau and Mann were warming themselves by the fire, perhaps they turned their heads away occasionally from the flames and focused their eyes instead on the night sky. A comet with a huge tail was lighting up the Northern hemisphere that week. Newspapers all over the world were reporting on it, because scientists had not expected it.

The Comet.—This mysterious stranger which has recently surprised our astronomers is rapidly moving out of the range of vision, and in the course of a few days will probably not be visible to the naked eye. Its career has been short and brilliant. On the 2d and 3d of July it exceeded in size and brilliancy any comet which has made its appearance in several centuries. There have been some attempts to identify the stranger as the comet of Charles V., but as we have had the reappearance of that one regularly for several years, we conclude that Charles' comet is played out. The new comet is undoubtedly among the largest and most magnificent, whose visits have been recorded.

—*St. Lawrence Republican and Ogdensburgh Weekly Journal*

[W]hen the weather has been favorable, a bright and well defined comet has been visible in the heavens, its train extending over an arc of more than one hundred degrees from the head of the Great Bear. The appearance of this strange visitor confounds, for the time, the theories of astronomers, who had not prophesied its coming, and have no accurate record of its flight. Its nucleus is very bright, and, with its imposing train, seen under favorable auspices, is a spectacle very rarely to be witnessed. From what depths of space it comes, or on what mission it is bound is not yet known. Prof. Bond, who made his observations from the observatory of Harvard College, says it is not the comet of 1264, commonly known as the Charles V. comet, which has been many times expected and promised, and for which Donati's comet in 1858 was for some time mistaken.

—Massachusetts Weekly Spy

Sitting as they were, on a rather remote and dark island in the middle of the Great Lakes, Henry Thoreau and Horace Mann, Jr., and everyone else on Mackinac should have been treated to a natural light show beyond compare.

Perhaps they weren't the only two people sitting around that fire. In Thoreau's Mackinac notebook entries, he mentioned a man he called "Johnson" on one page and "Wilm Johnson" on another. He further identified him as "county clerk born by half breeds & French." And then Thoreau related some of the native lore of the island, which this "Johnson" must have told him. It's possible he overheard this man talk but didn't quite pay complete attention to him. Maybe the sight of the comet distracted him.

Visitors to Mackinac Island can still climb up to view the shoreline through Arch Rock, just like Thoreau and Mann did.

At the time of Thoreau and Mann's visit, Mackinac Island served as the county seat of Mackinac County. William Miengun Johnston (1811-1863) served as the Mackinac County Clerk from 1853-1854 and from 1859-1863. He indeed had mixed ancestry: his father was Irish (John Johnston) and his mother was Ojibwe (Ozhauscadaywayquay, known as "Susan"). William's oldest sister, Jane, was the first wife of explorer and ethnologist Henry Rowe Schoolcraft, whose books Thoreau had read. Schoolcraft had at one time been the Indian agent for this part of the Midwest. Though William Johnston was considered to be the black sheep of the family, his knowledge of local history and native culture was considered accurate enough to be included in the book *Old Mackinaw: Or, the Fortress of the Lakes and Its Surroundings* by William Peter Strickland (Philadelphia: James Challen & Son, 1860). The volume had just been released the year before Thoreau's visit, so he may have caught a glimpse of it somewhere. But Johnston is not referred to as the county clerk in the book, and Thoreau was almost always accurate in his citations of published sources. So it is quite likely the two men instead met in person. An avid storyteller suddenly found new ears for his tales.

What is not likely would have been for William Johnston to acknowledge himself as Henry Rowe Schoolcraft's brother-in-law. William's sister had died almost twenty years earlier. Schoolcraft had remarried and was living in Washington, D.C. Henry Thoreau probably did not know of Johnston's connection with Schoolcraft. This is unfortunate. Thoreau had read the man's six-volume *Historical and Statistical Information Respecting the History, Condition, and Prospects of the Indian Tribes of the United States* (Philadelphia: Lippincott, 1851-1857). He had copied passages from the books into his own "Indian books," a series of journals in which he collected information about the natives of America. To meet someone who had a personal link to Schoolcraft might have been an interesting realization for Thoreau. Then again: he had here in front of him a man with native blood and knowledge of both the native lifestyle and mythology. Perhaps Henry merely put down his pen and listened.

Today fewer ships sail across the Great Lakes than they did in 1861. Freighters and carriers can sometimes be seen in the distance, from the shores. No regularly scheduled passenger line leaves Milwaukee with Mackinac Island as a destination. The only auto ferry that crosses Lake

Michigan leaves from Manitowoc, Wisconsin, and heads for Ludington, Michigan. In Michigan, auto ferries also run from Charlevoix to Beaver Island and from Cheboygan to Bois Blanc Island. Passenger ferries run from Leland to the Manitou Islands. And Mackinac Island can be accessed by passenger ferries from both Mackinaw City and St. Ignace—unless it is wintertime, when the latter port is used, until thick ice interferes with travel.

Each July, the Chicago Yacht Club holds a race on Lake Michigan, from Chicago to Mackinac Island. The first such race was held in 1898. It has been done on a consistent basis since the early 1900s.

The port that Henry Thoreau wrote about as "Carp River" is the current town of Leland, Michigan. Its waterfront boasts an historic harbor known as Fishtown. Here excursions for the Manitou Islands are launched. Local craftsmen have studios and shops. It may very well be that the *Edith* docked right here for two hours on June 29, 1861. Efforts are underway to preserve this piece of traditional Americana.

The steamboat *Edith* was dismantled and made into a barge in 1872.

Mackinac Island is no longer the county seat of Mackinac County, as it was when Henry and Horace visited and when William Johnston served as county clerk. Those offices were moved to St. Ignace on the Upper Peninsula in 1882. They remain there today. The Henry Rowe Schoolcraft Indian Agency Office and part of the Johnston family home have been preserved and are both located in Sault Ste. Marie, also on the Upper Peninsula.

Mackinac Island is home to a little more than 500 year-round residents. But during the summertime, it plays host to thousands of visitors. In at least one respect, it may resemble the time when Henry Thoreau and Horace Mann, Jr., were here: no motorized vehicles are permitted on its streets. On a bright summer day, the main thoroughfares can become a busy mix of pedestrians, bicyclists, and horse-drawn carriages and wagons. Walking along its sidewalks is an aromatic experience, with waves of warm fudge wafting out of select storefronts, and the scent of straw and manure rising from the roadway. The combination is not necessarily as nasty as it may sound.

Fort Mackinac was an active military outpost throughout the nineteenth century. In 1875, Mackinac National Park was created. It was only the second such protected property in the country. The post commander was named the park superintendent, and the soldiers soon found themselves taking care of the fort and incoming tourists instead of artillery fire. After the government shut down the fort in 1895, the new Mackinac Island State Park Commission took over its management. Michigan had its first state park.

In 2009, an interesting donation was made to The Thoreau Society collections at the Thoreau Institute at Walden Woods in Lincoln, Massachusetts. Included with other pieces of Thoreauviana was a framed botanical specimen marked with this handwritten description: "*Cornus canadensis*, L., Northern shore of Michigan, opposite Mackinaw. coll. H. Mann." The bunchberry leaf must have been plucked by young Horace or even by Henry sometime during their journey through the area. Since no settlements yet existed directly "opposite" Mackinac Island at the time, it's even possible that the leaf came from Carp River (Leland) or Beaver Island. Horace's sense of geography might not have been as keen as that of Mr. Thoreau.

The original Mackinac House on Main Street burned down in February 1887. It was rebuilt and reopened as The New Mackinac. During the Depression of the 1930s, the tourist trade lapsed and the hotel deteriorated. It was purchased by the city in 1938 and torn down. Today that lot is a small park with information kiosks and plenty of benches for tired walkers to rest upon.

A variety of events and festivals are held on the island. Featured among these is the Lilac Festival, which lasts for ten days each June. Some of the largest lilacs in the world grow on Mackinac Island.

After more than a century of discussion and speculation, a suspension bridge was finally constructed between "the mitten" of Michigan and its Upper Peninsula in the 1950s. When it opened on November 1, 1957, the Mackinac Bridge was the longest suspension bridge in the world. Now it's merely in third place. The five-mile-long span carries traffic over the Straits of Mackinac, from Mackinaw City to St. Ignace. You can get a decent view of it from the water when you take one of the ferries to Mackinac Island.

"Did he mention the lilacs? You know we're famous for our lilacs."

The question took me by surprise. I mentally kicked myself for being unprepared for it. I scanned my brain for a decent answer. Maybe even a correct one.

I was at the tail end of a presentation at the Mackinac Island Public Library in August 2009. I had just gone through the whole route of Thoreau and Mann's "Journey West" for an audience of two dozen people. They have been attentive and receptive and quite kind for the better part of an hour. I projected photos from my version of the trip onto a small screen. I showed them actual pages of Thoreau's notebook that referred to Mackinac Island. Now it was time for questions, and an islander named Jean started us off with a stumper.

"I don't think he did," I said. I knew I had a puzzled look on my face. A general gasp of disbelief seemed to rise up from the crowd.

"Well, when did the Lilac Festival start?" Suddenly everyone was talking at once. Somehow we established that the official event began in the 1940s. From that point on, it was a matter of creative problem solving. "How long were the bushes here before that? Remember, Henry and Horace came here in 1861." Again, I heard murmured possibilities.

One voice rose above the rest. "Father Marquette brought them." The buzz in the room got a little louder.

"*Father Marquette?*" I couldn't stop myself from expressing shock at the name. A few blocks away from us, a more than life-sized statue of Jacques Marquette (1637-1675) stood atop a tall pedestal in the middle of the park in front of Fort Mackinac. He wore full ankle length raiment with an equally long cape. I wondered: How would he have transported lilac cuttings from Belgium to the middle of North America: tucked in his pockets, or within the folds of his skirt? (A scene from the movie *French Kiss* flipped through my mind: the one when Kevin Kline's character smuggled American grapevines to France on a plane, and Meg Ryan's character thought he was up to no good.) And why would Marquette, or any of the other missionaries, specifically bring *lilacs*, and not vegetables or other edible plants? I could not understand the logic behind the premise.

One man shook his head at me. I pointed to him and tried to get the others to pay attention and to let him speak. He continued to shake his head. When the room quieted down, he expressed his opinion. "Is *said* to. Is said to. Father Marquette *is said to* have brought the lilacs." Ah. So maybe he didn't. That was a different story.

I directed the chatter back to the subject of the talk. "Well, if the lilacs were here in 1861, and if Thoreau didn't mention them in his notes, maybe it was because he knew they were planted by man and not by nature. He might have been more intrigued by the native plants and not by the ones introduced by the settlers." I hoped that statement would save face. I had already told them that "arborvitae" topped Thoreau's Mackinac plant inventory. I understood his hierarchy, now that I had visited the island myself. I saw the distinctive evergreens *everywhere*. The ones I passed on the hike to

Arch Rock were so big and gnarly that I expected a hobbit or maybe even Yoda himself to pop out from behind them. They looked otherworldly.

More members of the audience had questions, and then the session was over. It was fun. As I packed everything up into one suitcase for my return ferry trip, I exchanged stories and contact information and shook hands with a few individuals. I hoped to someday return to Mackinac Island. It was a wonderful place to visit.

But of course, that question about the lilacs haunted me all the way back across the water. If I had had my laptop with me, I could have given the audience a more accurate answer. The transcript of Thoreau's notebook was stored on my computer. As it was, I had to wait until I got to my hotel room in Petoskey to check.

Within minutes, I found the lilacs. Thoreau listed them just once, which was unusual for him. His notebook contained several versions of the trip plant inventory. The same names appeared over and over, multiple times. But on his page 76, along with other species seen on the island, he wrote "apple in bloom" and just beneath those words in tinier letters, "& lilac." Henry's handwriting could be difficult to read, but both of those lines were clear and concise. He *did* see lilacs. But he didn't make a big deal out of them. We could interpret that note in at least four ways. One: maybe Thoreau didn't see *a lot* of lilacs. Two: maybe he considered them only in afterthought. Three: maybe Horace saw them and told Henry about them later. Or four: maybe I was accidentally correct when I told the audience that Thoreau was more interested in documenting native species than in counting cultivated ones.

I spent more than a month doing research on lilacs. I started with Thoreau's journal, not the notebook he kept on this trip, but the one he wrote in for most of his adult life. He regularly recorded when flowers in the Concord area began to bloom. Though he tended to concentrate on the native flora, the lilacs in his own neighborhood did not escape his notice. Throughout the 1850s, Thoreau mentioned them in various stages of advancement. On select days in March or April, he noted that the buds were beginning to "look swollen" or to "show a little green." But it was generally during the third week of May when the blossoms unfolded. "The lilac is scented at every house," he wrote on May 22, 1853. Through those words, I could almost inhale the perfumed, heavy air of spring.

Henry Thoreau obviously recognized that the bushes were propagated by humans, not by animals or by wind-blown seeds. And when the people were gone, the presence of lilacs was a sure indicator that someone had once lived there. He wrote about this very phenomenon in the "Former Inhabitants; and Winter Visitors" chapter of *Walden*. He spent several pages describing the local properties that former slaves and emancipated black freemen had once occupied:

> Still grows the vivacious lilac a generation after the door and lintel and the sill are gone, unfolding its sweet-scented flowers each spring, to be plucked by the musing traveller; planted and tended once by children's hands, in front-yard plots,—now standing by wall-sides in retired pastures, and giving place to new-rising forests;—the last of that stirp, sole survivor of that family. Little did the dusky children think that the puny slip with its two eyes only, which they stuck in the ground in the shadow of the house and daily watered, would root itself so, and outlive them, and the house itself in the rear that shaded it, and grown man's garden and orchard, and tell their story faintly to the lone wanderer a half-century after they had grown up and died,—blossoming as fair, and smelling as sweet, as in that first spring. I mark its still tender, civil, cheerful, lilac colors.

His hints at the plant's resilience are echoed more than a century later by John L. Fiala in his book *Lilacs: A Gardener's Encyclopedia:*

> The lilac has always been an ideal traveler, ever ready to be off on a new journey, needing little care and only remote concern. Once planted it could fend for itself and readily withstand severe cold. Lilacs became perfect settlers in the new homeland of temperate North America.

Their origins lay in the mountains of Asia: more than likely, in the Balkans. People had taken them from that native habitat so that they could add flavor to the gardens of France and England. From Fiala's work and other books on the subject, I learned that lilacs indeed migrated to this country during pre-colonial and colonial times. Thomas Jefferson had them at Monticello. George Washington wrote about cutting some bushes down at Mount Vernon. (Instead of cherry trees, perhaps?) They were with the first settlers at Williamsburg, Virginia. And the lilacs at the Wentworth-Coolidge Mansion in Portsmouth, New Hampshire, are said to date to 1750.

But what about the ones on Mackinac Island? I found a number of older, popular sources that cited the French missionaries as responsible for their introduction. That must have been where the "Father Marquette" reference originated. At first it was difficult for me to dismiss such tales. Frances

Margaret Fox may not have been a botanist, but she sure did spin a convincing word picture for young people in her book, *Flowers and Their Travels*, back in 1936:

> No one knows who brought the first lilac to our shores. Old letters, old diaries, and ancient records of every sort have been searched in the vain hope of finding when and where the first lilac traveler landed here. Jesuit Fathers brought lilacs or lilac seeds with them from their old home across the sea, and planted them where Indians were their only neighbors. Lilacs love cold winters and to this day, at Mackinac Island in the Straits of Mackinac, great lilacs grow and blossom that were planted by those Mission Fathers. The Indians are gone, the fur-traders have vanished, the canoes are seen no more on the sparkling blue waters, but every year the faithful lilacs bloom and fill the air with fragrance in memory of the long ago.

What a beautiful, romantic image! But the more I read, the more I realized that Fox and the others who perpetuated this kind of scene were wrong. I returned to the expert, John L. Fiala:

> That the Mackinac (pronounced MAC-i-naw) lilacs were planted by French Jesuit missionaries working in the area in the late 1600s, or by the early permanent settlement in the 1700s, appears to be a myth. That the lilacs on the island are among the largest in North America is due to favorable growing conditions, but they are not as old as local lore would have it.

And Henry Thoreau and/or Horace Mann, Jr., saw them there in 1861. So the bushes must at least pre-date their visit.

I searched the Internet. The city of Rochester, New York, holds a lilac festival that has been celebrated annually since 1898. According to its web site, Rochester's Highland Park claims to be the "Lilac Capital of the World." I had seen those hillsides, covered with hundreds of bushes. I wasn't there during their flowering season, though. I should go back. Rochester's festival is held for ten days in the middle of May. That time period corresponds with Thoreau's documentation of seeing lilacs blossom in Massachusetts during the third week of May. Rochester and Concord lie at similar latitudes. Global warming between his time and ours might account for a slightly earlier appearance of the flowers now.

In contrast, Mackinac Island's lilac festival is held for ten days in the middle of June. The island lies above the 45th parallel, which is the midpoint between the North Pole and the Equator. Naturally, the growing season is shorter. Considering that fact, I came up with another possibility behind Henry Thoreau's notes, "apple in bloom" and "& lilac." He might have made those specific remarks because of the *timing*. He and Horace were on the island from June 30 to July 4, 1861. Thoreau wasn't used to seeing lilacs blooming so late in the year. The scientist in him may have demanded that he document the sighting. Maybe his note wasn't designed merely to indicate the presence of the species. Maybe the emphasis instead was with the implied phrase "in bloom."

Books and web sites are fine and dandy; but sometimes you need to consult some living, breathing experts. Brian Leigh Dunnigan, curator of maps for the William L. Clements Library of the University of Michigan, had already provided me with some crucial details for my research. He identified Thoreau's reference to "Carp River" as being the present-day town of Leland, Michigan. Brian was also the author of *A Picturesque Situation: Mackinac before Photography, 1615-1860* (Detroit: Wayne State University Press, 2008). He owned a place on the island and was a meticulous historian. I sent him an e-mail and asked for his opinions on the lilacs of Mackinac. He was quick to reply:

> [T]hat is a whole project in itself. I will tell you that, while attempting to read every possible description of Mackinac up to 1860, I did not find a single reference to lilacs. If Thoreau mentioned them in 1861, that might be the earliest reference. My theory at this point is that they were not brought to Mackinac by the French missionaries. They either came with the New England Protestant missionaries of the 1820s or the early cottagers of the 1860s-70s. Gurdon Hubbard built the first cottage in the Annex (post 1860) and named it "The Lilacs." … The oldest known lilac tree on the island probably dates to the 1870s-80s.

This was terrific news: that Thoreau's documentation might be the first! And like other islanders, Brian used the term "tree," not "shrub" or "bush." On Mackinac the specimens are so big, that the residents call them "trees."

When I talked with botanist and year-round islander Patricia "Trish" Martin over the phone, she confirmed what Brian had written. She was familiar with his research and agreed that Thoreau's note might now be the first written documentation of the Mackinac lilacs. "We have the largest lilacs," she said, "but not necessarily the oldest." Because the island was basically a big stack of limestone, "We have everything you need to grow them.

They don't take any work, and they look gorgeous. They're showy one part of the year and provide great background during the rest. And," she added, "having lilacs that are more than 100 years old is kind of cool."

What about that theory about the French missionaries? "No, no, no," she said. She could not be more adamant. Trish believed that notion came about when someone made an error of association. Horticulturists outside of Paris did some work with lilac cultivars in the 1700s. The varieties that resulted were generally called "French hybrids." Once upon a time, some-one heard that term in reference to some of the lilacs on Mackinac Island and mistakenly linked it to the people also known to have historically been in the area. But the current trees were not 300 years old. The missionaries did not bring them. Like Brian, Trish thought it was more likely that the lilacs were introduced by New Englanders who relocated to the island in the mid-1800s. Gurdon Hubbard, builder of the cottage named "The Lilacs," for example, had been originally from Vermont.

During the lilac festival of June 2007, Trish Martin had the opportunity to work with three members of the International Lilac Society, in an effort to determine the age of some of the trees. She got permission from local prop-erty owners who appeared to own the largest lilacs. Then Zelimir Borzan, Charles D. Holetich, and Freek Vrugtman took small bore samples from the trunks. (The wounds would grow over and heal within a year.) By counting the rings and doing a bit of calculation, they could determine the age (with a 2% margin of error) of that particular trunk. The challenge was that lilacs grow in such bunches that the oldest stems or branches may die and wither away while the rest of the plant is still growing and sending out blooms. There was no way to know by sight if the oldest parts were being tested.

The scientists' results generally confirmed what Trish had predicted: that the oldest Mackinac lilacs were no older than 130-140 years old. That placed them in the range of being planted between 1870 and 1880. Maybe the specific trees and branches that Thoreau and Mann saw were no longer sprouting.

Amazingly enough, Henry Thoreau conducted a similar lilac test just nine months before visiting Mackinac Island. Taking a core sample wasn't his method, however. He just went to one of those abandoned properties and chopped off a branch. According to his journal, one October day he:

> Cut one of the largest of the lilacs at the Nutting wall, eight-een inches from the ground. It there measures one and five sixteenths inches and has twenty distinct rings from centre, then about twelve very fine, not thicker than previous three; equals thirty-two in all. It evidently dies down many times, and

yet lives and sends up fresh shoots from the root.

It's too bad he didn't try the same experiment on those trees on Mackinac. Then he could have provided more information than just their appearance.

So: Did Henry Thoreau see and mention the lilacs? Yes, Jean, he did. They were still in bloom when he visited Mackinac. And as far as we know today, that little line in Thoreau's field notebook appears to be the earliest written documentation of the existence of the lilacs on Mackinac Island. Thanks for asking such an intriguing question! Next?

WHEN YOU GO: This portion of Thoreau and Mann's trip can be difficult to retrace in its entirety, especially if you don't want to cross Lake Michigan by boat. But you *must* take the ferry to Mackinac Island. The few miles between the island and the mainland are covered in less than twenty minutes. And any time spent on the island is well worth that effort.

If you want to stop at the places that Thoreau and Mann did, then Fort Mackinac itself must be on your list. You might even get there in time for the cannon firing. Buildings that our travelers would have seen (if they had been permitted inside) include the Post Headquarters, the Soldiers' Barracks, the Post Guardhouse, and all of the Blockhouses. The fort also provides a great view of the town and harbor below.

Additional sites they saw include Arch Rock and Dwightwood Springs. These examples of the island's natural phenomena can be seen during a bicycle trip around the outside of the island. The round trip is 8.2 miles long and can be accomplished in under three hours, no matter what your two-wheeled expertise might be.

Another wonderful place to visit is the site of the old "Carp River" and the Fishtown harbor of Leland. A drive from there and through Traverse City, Petoskey, and Charlevoix along U.S. 31 makes for a terrific tour of northwestern Michigan.

FOR MORE INFORMATION:

Chicago Yacht Club, 400 East Monroe Street Chicago, IL 60603-6403. Phone (312) 861-7777. www.cycracetomackinac.com.

Fishtown Preservation Society, PO Box 721, Leland, MI 49643. Phone (231) 256-8878. www.FishtownPreservationSociety.org.

Leelanau Historical Society & Museum, 203 East Cedar Street, PO Box 246, Leland, MI 49654. Phone (231) 256-7475. www.leelanauhistory.org.

Leland Michigan Chamber of Commerce. Phone (231) 256-0097. www.LelandMI.com.

Little Traverse History Museum, 100 Depot Court, Petoskey, MI 49770. Phone (231) 347-2620. www.petoskeymuseum.org.

Mackinac Island Lilac Festival, Mackinac Island Tourism Bureau, PO Box 451. Mackinac Island, MI 40757. Phone 800-454-5227. www.mackinacislandlilacfestival.org/

Mackinac Island Tourism Bureau, Phone (800) 454-5227.
www.mackinacisland.org

Mackinac State Historic Parks, PO Box 873, Mackinaw City, MI 49701. Phone (231) 436-4100. www.mackinacparks.com.

RECOMMENDED READING:

Thoreau's essay "Walking," since you might do a lot of that on Mackinac Island. The text is available online and in most Thoreau anthologies.

NOTES ON THIS CHAPTER

I am indebted to writer Jerry Dennis for offering his insights about sailing over Lake Huron. I quoted from his e-mail correspondence of November 18, 2009. His book *The Living Great Lakes* (New York: Thomas Dunne Books, 2003) provided terrific background information about the entire Great Lakes region.

Brian Leigh Dunnigan, curator of maps at the William L. Clements Library of the University of Michigan, identified the old "Carp River" as the present-day town of Leland, Michigan. Additional sources of historical information about that area include Joseph Littell's *Leland: An Historical Sketch* (1920) and Edmund M. Littell's *100 Years in Leelanau* (Leelanau County Prospector's Club, 2007).

The *Edith*'s cargo of "100 barrels of flour and three safes" was evidently listed in that day's issue of the *Milwaukee Sentinel*. It was referred to by Harriet M. Sweetland in her article, "Why Thoreau Spent One Night in Milwaukee," in the *Historical Messenger of the Milwaukee County Historical Society* 18 (December 1962): pages 3-9.

Thoreau's island quote comes from the "Wednesday" chapter of *A Week on the Concord and Merrimack Rivers*.

The quote by Horace Mann the elder was taken from page 294 of Louise Hall Tharp's *Until Victory: Horace Mann and Mary Peabody* (Boston: Little, Brown and Company, 1953).

Newspaper accounts of the Comet of 1861 appeared in the July 16, 1861, issue of the *St. Lawrence Republican* and *Ogdensburgh Weekly Journal*, as well as the July 10, 1861, issue of the *Massachusetts Weekly Spy*.

Printed sources of information about Mackinac Island include: *Historic Mackinac Island Visitor's Guide* (Phil Porter, ed. Mackinac Island: Mackinac State Historic Parks, 2004); Eugene T. Petersen's *Mackinac Island: Its History in Pictures* (Mackinac Island: Mackinac State Historic Parks, 1973); Edwin O. Wood's *Historic Mackinac: The Historical, Picturesque and Legendary Features of the Mackinac Country* (New York: Macmillan, 1918); and Phil Porter's *Mackinac: An Island Famous in These Regions* (Mackinac Island: Mackinac State Historic Parks, 1998). Steven C. Brisson, chief curator for the Mackinac State Historic Parks, also provided assistance.

The staff of the Mackinac County Clerk's office confirmed for me that William Johnston was the county clerk in 1861. Further information about Johnston was gleaned from William Peter Strickland's *Old Mackinaw: Or, the Fortress of the Lakes and Its Surroundings* (Philadelphia: James Challen & Son, 1860) and Dwight H. Kelton's *Annals of Fort Mackinac* (Chicago: Fergus, 1882).

Sources about lilacs include: Jennifer Bennett's *Lilacs for the Garden* (Willowdale, Ont.: Firefly Books, 2002); John Fiala's *Lilacs: A Gardener's Encyclopedia* (rev. & updated by Freek Vrugtman. Portland: Timber Press, 2008); Frances Margaret Fox's *Flowers and Their Travels* (Indianapolis: The Bobbs-Merrill Company, 1936); and Susan Delano McKelvey's *The Lilac*

A Monograph (New York: Macmillan, 1928).

Ray Angelo's *Botanical Index to the Journal of Henry David Thoreau* (Salt Lake City: Peregrine Smith Books, 1984) was invaluable in tracking every instance of Thoreau's notations about lilacs.

I quoted from an e-mail from Brian Leigh Dunnigan dated October 13, 2009, and from a phone conversation with Patricia Martin on November 21, 2009. Trish referred me to an article that she wrote and was available online: "Could Popular Legend of 300-Year-Old Lilacs on Mackinac Be True?" *Mackinac Island Town Crier*, June 16, 2007, found at http://www.mackinacislandnews.com/news/2007-06-16/Columnists/Nature_Notes.html.

TRAVEL CHAPTER 16

Thursday July 4 to Sunday July 7, 1861
Mackinac Island to Toronto
via the steamship Sun
and the Buffalo & Lake Huron Railway and Grand Trunk Railway

Expenses: At Goderich, .22
On road, .05
Rosin House, Toronto, $3.50

July 4—9 ? p.m., take propeller Sun for Goderich, which we
reach at 10 p.m., July 5th.

July 6th, Goodrich to Toronto. Towns often pretty large in
the midst of stumps & no trees set out.

July 7, Sunday in Toronto. *Veronica Americana*, park by
Toronto College.

—Thoreau's field notebook

After spending about four days on Mackinac Island, Henry Thoreau and
Horace Mann once again used the shipping service offered in cooperation
with the Buffalo and Lake Huron Railway Company. They boarded the *Sun*,
an 1854 wooden package freight propeller piloted by Captain Jones, on the
evening of the Fourth of July. It took a full day to sail southeast along the
northern coast of Michigan and then to cross Lake Huron and to land at
Goderich, Canada West.

This was Thoreau's first encounter with Lake Huron, of course. Yet he
used this body of water as a metaphor in the first chapter of his first book,
A Week on the Concord and Merrimack Rivers. There he described, for his readers, the origins of the Concord River, and how the Assabet and Sudbury
Rivers flowed together to form one waterway. The Sudbury River in particular could become a wider wetland when winter melted into spring:

In Concord it is, in summer, from four to fifteen feet deep, and from one hundred to three hundred feet wide, but in the spring freshets, when it overflows its banks, it is in some places nearly a mile wide. Between [the towns of] Sudbury and Wayland the meadows acquire their greatest breadth, and when covered with water, they form a handsome chain of shallow vernal lakes, resorted to by numerous gulls and ducks. Just above Sherman's Bridge, between these towns, is the largest expanse, and when the wind blows freshly in a raw March day, heaving up the surface into dark and sober billows or regular swells, skirted as it is in the distance with alder-swamps and smoke-like maples, it looks like a smaller Lake Huron, and is very pleasant and exciting for a landsman to row or sail over.

The naturalist writer was exaggerating for effect when he penned these words. He had read travel narratives and knew the Great Lakes from the accounts of those who had gone before. But it wasn't until this trip that he had a chance to see them in person and to sail across two of them. Perhaps he remembered that passage as he and young Horace steamed over the surface of Huron, the second largest of the Great Lakes. As the *Sun* made its way to the middle in the full light of day, without any view of any shoreline in any direction; and as the captain dealt with whatever wave action the weather might have provided, did Thoreau look around and sigh a gigantic "Oops"? In no way could a marsh in Massachusetts reasonably compare with such an environment, on any scale. He must have realized this fact. But had Henry Thoreau been unconsciously yearning for a Journey West all along, as indicated by that casual reference in the first paragraph of the first book he had ever written?

Again, Thoreau and Mann steamed across one of the Great Lakes. Without knowing what the weather was like during that 24-hour period, it's difficult to know how their trip actually proceeded. But twenty-first century author and Michigan native Jerry Dennis can offer a possible scenario:

[T]he shores of Michigan as [they] left Mackinac Island and headed down Huron would have been so dark that they formed a kind of black void beneath the stars. ... If the wind had gone down in the evening—as it often does in summer—the lakes might have calmed. When they're mirror calm you can get the sensation that you're soaring through a sphere of darkness, with equally vast numbers of stars above and below. It's as if you're passing through the center of the Milky Way.

Add to that vision, the chance of seeing the Comet of 1861 igniting the sky, and our travelers and the crew of the *Sun* might have witnessed quite the astronomical spectacle.

Like the *Edith* that the men had sailed with across Lake Michigan, the *Sun* was a freight-hauling propeller boat. A typical load for her consisted of 1,489 barrels of flour; 16,003 bushels of wheat; two casks of ashes; and five bales of wool. How had Henry and Horace managed to talk their way on board a ship not meant to carry passengers? Did the captain take pity on those travelers who were trying to avoid running into any war activities rising from the South? And how did the duo make the day-long trip: perched atop a huge bale of wool for the duration?

It's not as if the harbor at Goderich accommodated only commodity carriers. A passenger steamboat called *Kaloolah* made trips along Lake Huron's eastern shore that summer. It sailed from Sarnia, located at the St. Clair River outlet, to the Canadian coastline towns of Goderich, Kincardine, Inverhuron, Port Elgin, and Saugeen. The boat made connections with other steamboats headed for the Detroit River and with the major railways of the day. Unfortunately, its route did not lead in a homeward direction for Thoreau and Mann.

In any event, the *Sun* arrived at Goderich on the evening of July 5. Henry and Horace had to wait until the real sun showed up the following morning in order to catch the first train to Toronto.

Goderich had been founded in 1827; and it was the first town created in the Canada Company's million-acre Huron Tract. Being first meant that all of the district (and later, county) offices were established here as well. Thoreau and Mann had landed in the most important settlement in this part of Canada West.

It was only natural for a town to develop where the Maitland River flowed into Lake Huron. And once the railroad arrived, so did small manufacturers and community services. In 1861, Goderich supported a population of 3,227 residents. It had nine hotels, seven churches, a school, two weekly newspapers, three doctors, and at least a dozen lawyers. Shipbuilding and foundry work were among the industries that employed substantial numbers of workers. But there were also cigar makers, shoemakers, and tanners conducting cottage businesses in the town.

What distinguished Goderich from other communities of its size and era was its unique Square. It was large and octagonal. Leading from a huge center plot were eight streets: North, South, East, and West, with Hamilton,

Kingston, Montreal and Colborne set between. The building that acted as the hub of this wheel was the grand two-story Huron County Courthouse, erected in 1856. The proceedings behind those stone walls guaranteed work for all of the lawyers in town.

By 1861, the railroad had reached just one edge of this town. The northern half of Goderich had been laid out to fit into the natural semi-circular curve of the Maitland River. The railway company would eventually build tracks between the river and the town, all of the way to the harbor. But the original depot lay on the southeastern tip, along the Huron Road. Thoreau and Mann could have walked to it from the dock by following West Street, passing through the Square and in front of the Courthouse, and continuing on Kingston Street to the Huron Road. Along the way they would have seen hotels that offered meals. Perhaps breakfast cost twenty-two cents in Goderich that morning. Or perhaps they rented a carriage for the ride across town instead.

Henry Thoreau and Horace Mann, Jr., probably boarded a train of the Buffalo and Lake Huron Railway Company at 9 a.m. on July 6, 1861. The first leg of their journey that day was a straight shot covering the 45 miles between Goderich and Stratford. It took almost two hours. Along the way, the travelers could survey the surrounding landscape. Farmers were evidently still in the process of clearing the land.

If their view landed upon more stumps than trees, it wasn't for the lack of publicity of a local businessman. N.T. Custead bought seven-inch long ads in the *Huron Signal* to tout the virtues of his Goderich Nursery. He had available for purchase seven varieties of fruit trees, six kinds of berry bushes, and "a general assortment of the more hardy Deciduous and Evergreen Trees & Shrubs."

> [W]e beg to remind the Public that our Stock is complete in all its branches and that we are prepared to furnish Trees of every description at prices that will compare favorably with any other establishment in the Province.
>
> We would invite inspection by all interested to Trees planted by ourselves in the Nursery grounds last Fall and Spring on soil exactly similar, and which have since then received the same cultivation and attention.

The habitat was suitable. All that was necessary was the money and the labor.

As the train pulled into Stratford, it crossed over the eastern end of the Mill Pond. This was a wider portion of the Avon River that flowed through the town. Yes, here was another Stratford on Avon, located thousands of miles west of the original place where Shakespeare once wrote and performed. At 2,809 residents, it was similar in size to Concord, Massachusetts. Henry and Horace might have felt comfortable here. They had a two-hour layover in Stratford before they needed to catch their next rail connection. Thoreau might have spent five cents on a purchase during the wait.

Then the two men took an eastbound train along the Grand Trunk Railway. The names of the towns they passed through represented some of the original homelands of the settlers: Hamburg, Baden, Berlin, Breslau, Guelph, Acton, Georgetown, Brampton, Weston, Carlton. Massachusetts had an Acton and a Weston too, and neither one was very far from Concord. Sometimes shadows of that shared mother country passed before their eyes.

Toronto was half the size of Chicago then, with 50,000 residents, but it was still the largest city in Canada West. The Grand Trunk depot was within sight of the harbor and Lake Ontario. Stretching into the water were wharves for various businesses. Wooden planks covered the streets of the city. But just two months later, there would be streetcars operating on rails on some of them. It must have been a bustling place, aiming toward further advancements.

The Rossin House sat at the southeast corner of the intersection of King and York Streets. From the GTR station, it was about a seven-block walk: four blocks east and three blocks north. The hotel had been constructed four years earlier by the Rossin brothers, two local jewelers, at a cost of $275,000 (55,000 pounds). A wheat field had formerly occupied that spot. Now standing at five stories tall and with 252 rooms for guests, the Rossin House quickly ranked among the most elegant of Toronto's accommodations.

Official gatherings of various kinds were held at the hotel. Visiting dignitaries often stayed there. Prince Albert himself had visited Toronto just two weeks before Thoreau and Mann did; and of course, he stayed at the Rossin House. The Queen's husband had been on an extensive North American tour early that summer. He had seen Niagara Falls and had been squired around the city of Hamilton before boarding a steamboat that could transport him across that western corner of Lake Ontario. When he reached Toronto,

> About 5,000 or 6,000 people had assembled to pay him an enthusiastic welcome. Arrived at the Rossin House, he presented himself at one of the windows, and was most loudly cheered. The royal party expressed themselves as highly pleased with the arrangements for their comfort. Had it not

been for the express commands of the Queen that no public demonstration should take place, a very different reception would have been accorded the Prince. He was, however, deeply gratified with the quiet enthusiasm manifested.

Were Henry Thoreau and young Horace Mann as "highly pleased with the arrangements" during their two-night stay? Neither one offered a written opinion of the Rossin House. But it hardly seems like the kind of place one could have groused about. At $1.75 a night, it wasn't even as expensive as the Delavan House in Albany (assuming international exchange rates were comparable).

The campus of the University of Toronto was located about a mile directly north of the Rossin House, and was thus within walking distance. The school was first established as King's College in 1827, and was then controlled by the Church of England. In 1850, it severed its ties with the church and changed its name to the University of Toronto. Its acreage and park-like atmosphere must have been what attracted Thoreau and Mann to walk there and do a bit of botanizing. It would have offered the closest "wild area" to the hotel. The *Veronica americana* that Henry saw was American brooklime, a member of the snapdragon family. One assumes that the trees and the other plants found on the campus were deemed somehow too common for him to mention.

Thoreau and Mann had been traveling for almost two months. The northern and southern regions of their country had been officially at war with each other while the two men were away from home. The travelers had seen volunteer units leaving from many of the towns along their route. And during that same time period, the people of Canada wondered and worried about what this American strife might mean to them. The possibility existed that the fighting could make its way north to their own territory. At least one newspaper editor in Canada West thought that appropriate measures should be taken to protect their own residents.

It would be well, indeed, if a few regiments of the line were at once sent to garrison different parts of Canada while the rebellion lasts. There is no knowing what the undisciplined and uncontrollable levies of United States' militia may take it in their heads to do, and possibly a quarrel with Great Britain might be made the pretext for an assault on Canada. It is just as well to be prepared for a next-door neighbor who smells so very strongly of gunpowder, and who is rather erratic in his movements.

Early on, the Canadians understood too what an American blockade and the loss of access to Southern cotton would mean to the British textile mills. "England shall be cut off from the supply of an article which forms, next to the iron trade, the staple of her manufactures," wrote the same journalist. "[T]he daily bread of four or five millions of the working classes of England depends upon the supply of that article." Strained relations between Great Britain and the United States, such as they were, might even result in associated repercussions for Canada that it surely did not need or want. How could Canadian officials prepare themselves for any contingency?

They decided to hold an election.

The Provincial Parliament had met from March 16 to May 18, 1861. In those sixty-four days, the representatives had proposed, passed laws and conducted all of their necessary business. Then they adjourned. An election would normally have taken place much later in the year. The members' terms were not slated to expire until the end of December; and their positions were secure until February 1862, when the winning candidates would take over the seats. That was the established legal protocol.

But the American war cast a different light on the Provincial political process. What if the Parliament had to be re-assembled hastily, as a reaction to an action taken on the other side of the invisible border? The authorities felt that they needed to be ready for such an emergency, complete with fresh or re-elected representatives. As a result, special two-day elections were scheduled in the middle of the summer, throughout the various districts of the provinces. Toronto's elections were held on July 5th and 6th.

The large city was divided into two jurisdictions. Running for the seat to represent West Toronto were current Mayor Adam Wilson (Reformer) and former Mayor John Beverley Robinson (Conservative). Robinson was a lawyer who had so wanted to establish a first-class hotel in Toronto that he had single-handedly raised $134,000 to help build the Rossin House, years earlier. With such personal ties to the hotel, he may have used it as a campaign headquarters.

The battle for East Toronto was between John Willoughby Crawford (Conservative), president of the Royal Canadian Bank, and George Brown (Reformer), owner and editor of the Toronto *Globe*. Brown had been a very vocal member of Parliament since 1852, and he was seen as a party leader. He published impassioned letters to the voters each day on the front page of *Globe*, hoping to garner public support. He obviously expected to win.

The results were tallied and immediately publicized after the polls closed on the second day of the voting. Adam Wilson won over John Beverley Robinson in West Toronto. And John Willoughby Crawford beat incumbent George Brown in East Toronto. According to one succinct newspaper report: "There was considerable excitement." One suspects that a "frenzy" might be closer to the truth. And it may have lasted several days, if not longer.

Into this political maelstrom ventured our two unsuspecting American travelers. Their train had pulled into the Toronto station a little after 5 p.m. on July 6, the second and final day of the election. The younger of the two men was not even old enough to vote back in his homeland. The older man, by conscious choice, had never voted in any election in his life. Indeed, he had spent one night in jail for non-payment of a state tax he believed to be both frivolous and unjust. And now these two found themselves in another country and in the frenetic aftermath of a special election that had been held specifically because of the turmoil caused by their own nation. It must have been a scene brimming with politicians and politicking, with grand celebrations and with expressed disappointments. Perhaps a saunter across a wooded and serene college campus provided a welcome retreat from the post-election hoopla and hullabaloo that no doubt swirled around downtown Toronto and the Rossin House.

After his visit to Lower Canada and Montreal in 1850, Henry Thoreau wrote:

> What makes the United States government, on the whole, more tolerable,—I mean for us lucky white men,—is the fact that there is so much less of government with us. Here it is only once in a month or a year that a man *needs* remember that institution ... but in Canada you are reminded of the government every day. It parades itself before you. It is not content to be the servant, but will be the master.

This election was a prime example. He had seen a proliferation of British soldiers back then, too. "On every prominent ledge you could see England's hands holding the Canadas, and I judged by the redness of her knuckles that she would soon have to let go." Well, even eleven years later, that still wasn't the case.

Two days in Toronto might have been enough of an international experience for Henry and Horace. What a mess to find oneself in, eh?

Freighters and carriers still transport goods over the surface of the Great Lakes, including that of Lake Huron. Some even dock at Goderich. Today no public touring ships or ferries sail from Mackinac Island or from eastern Michigan to the Canadian coastline.

But each July, the Bayview Yacht Club of Detroit sponsors a sailing race from Port Huron to Mackinac Island. The tradition began in 1925, and is held in any kind of weather. It takes place one week after the Chicago Yacht Club runs its sister race from Chicago to Mackinac.

The rails of the former Buffalo and Lake Huron Railway line still follow a northern arc around Goderich then beat a straight path for Stratford. But these days they convey merely materials, not people. In Stratford, both options are possible along the old Grand Trunk Railway, which is served by a freight line and by VIA Rail. In the city of Toronto, GO Transit makes more frequent stops for commuter traffic.

In 1866, Goderich flour mill owner Sam Platt paid mechanic Peter MacEwan to run a drilling rig in the harbor, in order to prospect for oil. Instead they struck rock salt. They had tapped into a previously unknown geological deposit called the Michigan Salt Basin. The salt was so white and so pure that it won first prize at the Paris Exhibition in 1867. Mass production and distribution of the commodity soon began, and it continues today. The Goderich mine of Sifto Canada, Inc., is the largest such operation in the world. It can retrieve six million tons of salt per year. Sifto is the second-largest employer in the town.

Goderich is now home to more than 7,500 residents and is known as the Prettiest Town in Canada. Its octagonal Square still creates an impressive center for a variety of businesses and activities. The stone Victorian courthouse in the middle of it all was unfortunately lost to fire in 1954. In its place stands a sturdy structure that reflects the municipal art deco design favored by North Americans in the late 1950s. It is nonetheless impressive, but not in the same way that the original had been.

At the harbor and by the water's edge, you can still look over Lake Huron from the Main Beach. You may see freighters on their way to Chicago or Detroit. You can hike up the trail to the top of the bluff to visit the 1847 lighthouse or to witness a stunning sunset. The nearby 1907 Canadian Pacific Railway station is being restored and is a photo opportunity, even though it is not the one that Thoreau and Mann used. Another distinctive but abandoned depot of the Canadian National Railway can be found at the end of East Street. It was built in 1902, and it too post-dates our travelers' time here. Buildings that date to Henry and Horace's visit include the Huron Historic Gaol (now a museum) on Victoria Street and the Livery (formerly a livery stable, now a theater) on South Street. Both were built in the 1840s.

The original wooden frame structure that served as the station for the Buffalo and Lake Huron Railway Company was dismantled long ago. First, it was divided into two halves. Then both sections were moved to Essex Street, on the western edge of town. The old floor joists, rafters, and wallboards today can be found in the houses located at 126 Wilson Street and 127 Essex Street. Both are private dwellings and have undergone significant alterations. But parts of the old railway station that Thoreau and Mann visited still exist, albeit in a different form.

In Stratford, the former Mill Pond is now called Lake Victoria. And that city is now best known for its Stratford Festival of Canada, which began in 1953. Theatrical performances run from April through November and attract thousands of visitors from around the world to this part of Ontario.

Back in 1861, this section of the Grand Trunk Railway included a stop in Berlin. But you won't find that name on a contemporary map. During the First World War, a movement arose to change the name of the city so that it would not have any kind of connection with Berlin, Germany. A local referendum was held in 1916. As a result, the name of the city was officially changed to Kitchener, in honor of Lord Herbert Horatio Kitchener (1850-1916), Britain's Secretary of State for War. He had recently died at sea.

As they had done in Hamilton without knowing it, Henry Thoreau and Horace Mann once again crossed the Niagara Escarpment during this portion of their train ride. Today you can find that intersection and the Bruce Trail in the area of Limestone, between Acton and Georgetown. The trail crosses Ontario Provincial Highway 7 at around Silver Creek.

With more than two million residents, Toronto has grown to become Canada's largest city. The campus of the University of Toronto and its Queen Park still make a nice natural respite from the streets around it, on foot or by car. Many more parks and green areas are located around the metropolis.

The elegant old Rossin House was destroyed by fire in 1862. It was rebuilt the following year. In 1909, its name was changed to the Prince George Hotel. The building was torn down in the 1960s to make way for more contemporary structures to serve the surrounding financial district. Today rising up from that corner looms the 25-story Standard Life Centre, a tower of granite and glass that opened in 1984. Its address is 121 King Street West. The Toronto Stock Exchange is located just across the street.

Prince Albert (1819-1861) returned to Great Britain after his Canadian visit and was soon reported to be in ill health. He died of typhoid fever at the end of the year.

In spite of its contentious outcome, all four candidates in the 1861 Toronto elections continued to lead lives in the political arena. Sir Adam Wilson (1814-1891) served as a representative in the Legislative Assembly through 1863. He went on to become a judge in the court system, and eventually gained the status of chief justice of the Court of the Queen's Bench. He was knighted in 1887.

John Willoughby Crawford (1817-1875) finished his term of representation in the Legislative Assembly and moved to the House of Commons in the 1870s. He was appointed Lieutenant-Governor of Ontario in 1873, and was in that office when he died two years later. John Beverley Robinson (1821-1896) served in the House of Commons for several decades. He was Ontario's Lieutenant-Governor in the 1880s.

Though he dipped in and out of politics over the course of his life, George Brown (1818-1880) ultimately played a major role in the process of Canadian Confederation. He helped to negotiate with the British government, and he actively promoted the confederation initiative in speeches and in the pages of the *Globe*. (Canada became a Dominion in 1867.) He refused the offer of the Lieutenant-Governor's position when John Willoughby Crawford died in 1875. Four years later, he refused knighthood. In 1880, George Brown was shot in the leg by a former and disgruntled *Globe* employee. A month and a half later, Brown died of gangrene.

Back in Massachusetts, the Sudbury River marshes that Thoreau claimed looked like a "smaller Lake Huron," are now protected as part of the Great Meadows National Wildlife Refuge.

In early October 2009, I was in an art gallery, standing before a portrait of a man named Thoreau. The painting was a study in the color brown. The subject was a tidy person, neatly dressed. His brown hair was meticulously combed. His brown eyes focused on something to the left of the painter. His jacket, shirt and tie—all in shades of brown—were perfectly smoothed into place. The hint of high cheekbones gave depth to an otherwise thin face. And the man's demeanor leaned toward the serious side. He was not smiling; but neither was he frowning, exactly. With this image, he was forever 25 years old. Who knew what developments awaited him?

I was visiting the McMichael Canadian Art Collection in Kleinburg, north of Toronto. Its expansive acreage of lawns and woodlands more closely resembled that of a public park or of a posh but rustic estate, which was indeed what it once was. The main building was crafted of logs and field-stones that blended naturally into the surrounding landscape. Inside, the exhibits ranged from examples of First Nations and Inuit craftsmanship to the Group of Seven and contemporary artists. The museum boasted 100% Canadian content.

So it was not a painting of Henry David Thoreau that I scrutinized. It was instead a portrayal of Canadian illustrator and designer Thoreau MacDonald (1901-1989), as depicted by Lawren S. Harris in 1926. How did someone born in Toronto get the name Thoreau? For that explanation we must turn to his father, who was also an artist and was one of the founders of the Group of Seven: James Edward Hervey MacDonald (1873-1932).

Born in England, J. E. H. MacDonald was a teenager when his family relocated to Canada. Here he attended art school and apprenticed with the Toronto Lithographing Company. In 1895, he joined a commercial art firm called Grip Limited, where he learned how to do calligraphy and design illustrations for ads, posters, bookplates, and books. He spent almost twenty years with the company and eventually rose to the position of head designer. In 1899, he married Harriet Joan Lavis, whom he had been courting for several years and considered to be a "perfect friend." It is said that the couple shared "an almost religious dedication to the American author and naturalist, Henry David Thoreau." That explained why they named their first and only child after the Transcendentalist. And the MacDonalds must have been true devotees, for Henry Thoreau's popularity was still in a relative infancy at the turn of the century, forty years after his death.

He may have given his son the name; but it could be argued that J. E. H. MacDonald himself embraced the Thoreauvian spirit. He was adept with pen and ink and applied them with practicality for pieces due at his place of employment. But he began to explore the possibilities of landscape paint-ing during his walks along the Humber River and in nearby High Park, both on the western edge of Toronto. Here he found his own personal Walden. The spaces inspired his creativity. "There are dozens of pictures in High Park now coming home," he wrote. "Wherever I look the landscape took the most beautiful composition and color." For more than a dozen years, he sketched and painted scenes from those places. One biographer said that the park and the river "pleased his love of nature and renewed his poetic soul."

As I wove around groups of visiting school children in the rooms of the McMichael, I saw stunning examples of J. E. H. MacDonald's paintings: *Woodland Brook, Forest Wilderness,* all were vibrant. Some of the canvasses were immense. Some represented the scenery of Algoma, the district that lay north of Lake Huron and north of Sault Ste. Marie. MacDonald made several "sketching trips" there by train with friends, seemingly in search of wilderness. Henry Thoreau had found a similar ruggedness and rawness of nature when he traveled to Mount Katahdin in Maine. Algoma and northern Maine lie at about the same latitude.

During the 1910s, MacDonald crossed paths and associated with other artists who traveled around the country and painted such vivid landscapes. They saw Canada through Canadian eyes and set down their interpretations on colorful canvasses. In 1920, these men became known as the Group of Seven. Along with J. E. H. MacDonald, its members were Franklin Carmichael, Lawren S. Harris, A.Y. Jackson, Frank H. Johnson, Arthur Lismer, and F. H. Varley. According to an exhibit sign,

> The painters believed that the Canadian environment created a distinct national experience. They felt that, through their exploration, study and depiction of the landscape, a unique artistic expression of Canada's own character would emerge. For many Canadians, the Group's wilderness travels and artistic experiments have come to symbolize a central theme in the nation's cultural heritage.

The McMichael was considered to be the "spiritual home" of the Group of Seven. Examples of their work were on display along these walls. Some of the members and their wives were even buried in a small cemetery on the property. The MacDonalds were not to be found here, however. The couple was instead interred in Toronto.

The gallery itself was a work of art. Wide windows appeared at intervals so that visitors could look outside and see examples of the nature that inspired the creativity housed within. On this overcast and foggy early fall morning, though, the just-turning trees did not hold much glamour. More color could be found inside the building than out. But I had been given a lot to think about. I was encouraged to do more research on both J. E. H. MacDonald and his son Thoreau when I got back home.

J. E. H. MacDonald's most famous painting was also initially his most controversial. He called it *The Tangled Garden.* It showed up in every book I could find about him and the Group of Seven. The title described it well. It was an Impressionistic view of a lush, overgrown plot that was sliding from summer into autumn. Sunflowers were so heavy with seed that their heads were weighted downward. Other full-bloom flowers blazed in the background. It was an actual piece of the MacDonald property in Thornhill forever captured in oil. Plantings there had included hollyhocks, delphiniums, phlox, and chrysanthemums. Son Thoreau once said, "The original Garden was and is on the west side of our house and shows the old horse stable in the background. It seemed true and realistic enough to me."

Alas, the critics did not agree. When the painting was put on exhibit with the Ontario Society of Artists in 1916, both it and its creator were attacked in the press. "It is what one might call an incoherent mass of colour," said the *Daily Star* reviewer. The *Toronto Star* went a step further. "It is what one might call 'an incoherent mass of colour', for at first glance, it seems a purposeless medley of crude colours which gradually explain themselves as standing for blooms in a flower bed in full sunshine." But it was Hector Charlesworth in *Saturday Night* who really let loose in an article called "Pictures That Can Be Heard:"

> The chief offender seems to be J. E. H. MacDonald who certainly does throw his paint pots in the face of the public. That Mr. MacDonald is a gifted man who can do something worthwhile when he sets his mind to it, is shown in his *Laurentian Village, October*, which is well composed and rich and subdued in colour. Across the gallery from it, however, is *The Tangled Garden* which a discriminating spectator attempted to praise by saying it was not half as bad as it looked. In the first place the size of the canvas is much too large for the relative importance of the subject, and the crudity of the colours, rather than delicate tracery of the vegetation seems to have appealed to the painter; but it is a masterpiece as compared with *The Elements* or *Rock and Maple* [two other pieces by MacDonald] which for all they convey might just as well have been called *Hungarian Goulash* and *Drunkard's Stomach*.

Obviously, Mr. Charlesworth neither understood nor appreciated the spirit of Impressionism.

MacDonald was stirred to write a letter to the *Globe* editor in response. "It would seem to be a fact that in a new country like ours, which is practically unexplored artistically, courageous experiment is not only legitimate but vital to the development of a living Canadian art," he wrote. Hence the need for the formation of the Group of Seven, which soon followed. MacDonald had placed a $500 price tag on *The Tangled Garden*. It was the highest figure he had ever given one of his pieces. In his lifetime, no one came forth with the money. The artist's family finally donated it to the National Gallery of Canada in Ottawa in 1939. It is proudly displayed there today.

Knowing that J. E. H. MacDonald was a fan of Henry Thoreau, it is easy enough today to consider *The Tangled Garden* as an embodiment of that Transcendental influence. Finding beauty in what others might see as mundane or messy was something Henry did and wrote about on a regular basis. "Nature loves variety in all things," he said, a century and a half before the concept of biodiversity was brought forth. "She offers us too many good things at once." She "abhors a straight line;" and "Out of foulness Nature thus extracts beauty." He knew that only too well, as a lover of swamp-walking. "We love to see Nature fruitful in whatever kind. It assures us of her vigor and that she may equally bring forth the fruits which we prize." "I was inclined to think that the truest beauty was that which surrounded us but which we failed to discern, that the forms and colors which adorn our daily

The Tangled Garden (1916) by James Edward Hervey MacDonald, a member of the Canadian Group of Seven and a Thoreau devotee. (*Courtesy The National Gallery of Canada*)

life, not seen afar in the horizon, are our fairest jewelry." Take *that*, Mr. Charlesworth. MacDonald could have even used one of Thoreau's most quoted lines as a subtitle for *The Tangled Garden*: "In Wildness is the preservation of the World." And quite frankly, the fact that the critics of the day didn't like the painting gives it even more Thoreauvian appeal.

Like his hero, J. E. H. MacDonald also took the time to "Go West." During the last decade of his life, he made a number of sketching trips to the Canadian Rockies. He and the other Group of Seven artists and their successors continued to travel around the country, jot down what they saw, then recreate those impressions with paint on canvas. They left a legacy body of work that defined both Canadian art and the Canadian identity.

And what of Thoreau MacDonald, the young man I saw in that portrait at the McMichael? He too became an artist and was practiced in a variety of media. He was best known as "a master of lettering and layout." His boldness in pen and ink and brush drawing can still be admired on magazine covers, bookplates, and books. He illustrated a posthumous book of his father's poetry, *West by East and Other Poems*. He once even did a promotional piece for The Thoreau Society, based in the United States.

Thoreau MacDonald's approach to depicting the natural world is eerily reminiscent of that other Thoreau who lived in another country and in the century before him.

> Thoreau mentioned in an interview that he never drew his pen and ink drawings of the rural landscape while actually out in the field. Instead he would go for a walk and look about and then, when he came home later, he would sit down and draw the scenes from memory. Thoreau understood that he couldn't capture the reality of the natural world in black and white ink drawings but he could replicate *the memory* of being there.

That passage described Thoreau MacDonald's method. But those who have studied Henry Thoreau's writing technique could tell you a similar story. And that's what had brought me to Toronto on a day in autumn, picking up where he left off. Henry gave us just the field notebook for the Journey West: just the snippets and jottings he made while on the road and out in nature. He didn't have the chance to "sit down and draw the scenes from memory." I have had to drive along his route and see them for myself and fill in the blanks accordingly. And hopefully, with at least a bit of accuracy.

J. E. H. MacDonald was probably unaware that his hero Henry David Thoreau had traveled with Horace Mann, Jr., through the Toronto area in

1861. The biographies that were available at the time barely mention the trip. What might he have thought, had he realized that their paths had crossed over the same terrain? And what might Henry Thoreau have thought of having a visible impact on a Canadian artist, his son and his friends? The scenarios make for interesting contemplation.

On Henry Thoreau's first trip over the northern border in 1850, he wrote: "I fear that I have not got much to say about Canada, not having seen much; what I got by going to Canada was a cold." Evidently a few Canadians caught much more than that from *him*.

WHEN YOU GO: Henry Thoreau and Horace Mann's rail travels on that July day are fairly easy to follow today. Take Highway 8 from Goderich to Stratford. The tracks will be about a quarter of a mile to the south, paralleling the road for the duration. You will pass through farmland with some woods and through a number of smallish towns along the way. Perhaps some of the trees you see are descendents of those from Mr. Custead's Goderich Nursery, way back when.

You could take a passenger train from Stratford to Toronto. If you prefer to go by car, Highway 7 will lead you most of the way, at least through Georgetown. The railroad tracks play leap-frog with the two-lane road on occasion on that trip. From that point, you'll have to rely on a good map to get you through Brampton and into Toronto. You'll have your choice of the 400 series of highways at that point, if you wish to take the fast approach.

But sometime during your visit to Toronto, you should drive the length of Lake Shore Boulevard from west to east. This shoreline path offers views of the harbor and the downtown skyline and also provides a turn-off for York Street. About three blocks north is the site of the old Rossin House at the corner of York and King Streets. Be prepared for Toronto to bustle much more than it ever did in 1861, with or without election fever.

FOR MORE INFORMATION

Bayview Yacht Club, 100 Clairpointe, Detroit, MI 48215. Phone (313) 822-1853. www.byc.com/mack/

The Bruce Trail Conservancy, PO Box 857, Hamilton, ON Canada L8N 3N9. Phone (905) 529-6821. www.brucetrail.org.

GO Transit, 20 Bay Street, Suite 600, Toronto, ON Canada M5J 2W3. Phone (888) 438-6646. www.gotransit.com

High Park, 1873 Bloor Street West, Toronto, ON Canada. Phone (416) 392-1748. www.highpark.org.

Huron County Museum, 110 North Street, Goderich, ON Canada N7A 2T8. Phone (519) 524-2686. www.huroncounty.ca/museum/hcm.php

Huron Historic Gaol and Governor's House, 181 Victoria Street North, Goderich, ON Canada N7A 2T8. Phone (519) 524-6971. www.huroncounty.ca/museum/hhg.php

McMichael Canadian Art Collection, 10365 Islington Avenue, Kleinburg, ON Canada L0J 1C0. Phone (905) 893-1121. www.mcmichael.com.

Ontario Ministry of Natural Resources, Ontario Parks, 300 Water Street, 6th Floor, PO Box 7000, Peterborough, ON Canada K91 8M5. Phone 800-667-1940. www.mnr.gov.on.ca

Ontario Travel, 1000-201 City Centre Drive, Mississauga, ON Canada L58 4E4. phone 905-804-5480. www.ontariotravel.net/

Stratford City Centre Committee, 47 Downie Street, Stratford, ON Canada N5A 1W7. Phone (519) 273-2461. www.stratfordcitycentre.ca/

Stratford Festival of Canada, Box 520, 55 Queen Street, Stratford, ON Canada N5A 6V2. Phone (519) 271-4040. www.stratfordfestival.ca.

Tourism Goderich, 91 Hamilton Street, Goderich, ON Canada N7A 2K5. Phone (519) 524-6600. www.goderich.ca

Tourism Toronto, 207 Queen's Quay West, PO Box 126, Toronto, ON Canada M5J 1A7. Phone (416) 203-2600. www.seetorontonow.com/

VIA Rail Canada, www.viarail.ca.

RECOMMENDED READING:

Thoreau's essay "Civil Disobedience," as a tribute to the Toronto elections of 1861. For the Group of Seven, "The American Scholar" by Ralph Waldo Emerson seems appropriate. Its first paragraph asserts: "Our day of dependence, our long apprenticeship to the learning of other lands, draws to a close. The millions that around us are rushing into life, cannot always be fed on the sere remains of foreign harvests. Events, actions arise, that must be sung, that will sing themselves." Both essays can be found online and in various anthologies.

NOTES ON THIS CHAPTER

I am once again indebted to writer Jerry Dennis for offering his insights about sailing over Lake Huron. I quoted from his e-mail correspondence of November 18, 2009. His book *The Living Great Lakes* (New York: Thomas Dunne Books, 2003) provided terrific background information.

The town of Goderich is pronounced "GOD-rich," which could be why Thoreau wrote it as "Goodrich" in his notes. The list of goods carried by the *Sun*, the schedule of the *Kaloolah*, and Mr. Custead's nursery ad were all seen in the October 16, 1861, issue of the *Huron Signal*. Descriptions of nineteenth-century Goderich were found in James Scott's *The Settlement of Huron County* (Toronto: The Ryerson Press, 1966) and Thelma Coleman's *The Canada Company* (Stratford: Cumming Publishers, 1978). Reg Thompson and the staff of the Goderich branch of the Huron County Library System provided valuable research assistance during my visit and in the months afterward. So did the staff of the Stratford Public Library and the Toronto Reference Library. Barry Page, Chair of Heritage Goderich, provided the details of the fate of the original Buffalo and Lake Huron Railway station.

On Sunday, August 21, 2011, an F3 tornado passed through Goderich, mirroring the walk taken by Thoreau and Mann. Although the buildings mentioned in this chapter survived, many century-old trees around the courthouse did not. Your visit to Goderich will look different than mine.

Prince Albert's arrival in Toronto was reported in the June 26, 1861, issue of the *London Free Press* of Canada West. Resources about Toronto and the Rossin House include Bruce West's *Toronto* (Toronto: Doubleday Canada Limited, 1979) and G. Mercer Adam's *Toronto, Old and New* (Toronto: The Mail Printing Company, 1891).

Much Civil War news was reported in the Canadian papers. The quotes about arming the border and the effects of a blockade were found in the May 18, 1861, issue of the *London Free Press*. That publication was also a source for events leading up to the special election, in various issues released in May and June 1861. Election results and the ensuing "considerable excitement" was the press release sent to North American newspapers. I saw it in the July 10, 1861, issue of the *Massachusetts Weekly Spy*.

Biographical information for the four candidates from Toronto was gotten from a variety of sources that included entries found in the *Encyclopedia Canadiana* (Toronto: Grolier of Canada Limited, 1968). Adam Wilson had actually been running in two jurisdictions in that 1861 election: hoping to either represent York North or Toronto West. Many thanks to Reg Thompson for pointing out this unique situation, and also for unraveling for this clueless American the finer details of Canadian politics.

Thoreau's quote about Canada's in-your-face government comes from "The Walls of Quebec" chapter of *A Yankee in Canada*. The "England's hands" passage and the "catching a cold" passage are both in the "Concord to Montreal" chapter.

Information about J. E. H. MacDonald was found in a variety of sources. *The Tangled Garden* (text by Paul Duval. Scarborough, Ont.: Cerebrus / Prentice-Hall, 1978) included the critics' reviews. Robert Stacey's *J. E. H. MacDonald, Designer: An Anthology of Graphic Design, Illustration and Lettering* (Toronto: Archives of Canadian Art, 1996) includes the quote from Thoreau MacDonald about *The Tangled Garden*. Also helpful were Paul Duval's *Canadian Impressionism* (Toronto: McClelland & Stewart, Inc., 1990) and Bruce Whiteman's *J. E. H. MacDonald* (Kingston, Ont.: Quarry Press, 1995). But none of the articles and books I consulted could offer a definitive explanation of how J. E. H. and Joan MacDonald came to be so influenced by Thoreau. I'd like to know more.

Henry Thoreau's *Journal* was the source for all but one of the quotes I used to support the Transcendental nature of *The Tangled Garden*. "Nature loves variety in all things..." is dated June 25, 1852. "She offers us too many good things at once" is from October 21, 1855. "Nature ... abhors a straight line ..." is from February 27, 1857. "Out of foulness Nature thus extracts beauty" is from July 14, 1860. "We love to see Nature fruitful ..." is from August 30, 1851. "I was inclined to think that the truest beauty was that which surrounded us ..." is from September 18, 1858. "In Wildness is the preservation of the World" appears in the essay "Walking."

Thoreau MacDonald is described by Ray Nash in *Thoreau MacDonald's Notebooks* (Moonbeam, Ont.: Penumbra Press, 1980). MacDonald's method is outlined in "Q&A: Seth" by Sean Rogers, *The Walrus*, August 21, 2008, found online at

http://www.walrusmagazine.com/blogs/2008/08/21/an-interview-with-seth-part-one.

Travel Chapter 17

Monday, July 8, 1861 to Tuesday, July 9, 1861
Toronto to Ogdensburg
via the Grand Trunk Railway

Expenses: on road	.11
at Ogdensburg	.75
Paper	.05
Lunch	.11
Supper	.10

July 8, To Ogdensburg.

—Thoreau's field notebook

Horace's last known letter home was sent from Mackinac Island. Henry's last dated notebook entry of any substance includes the brief direction: "July 8. To Ogdensburg." But with the help of the items listed on Thoreau's expense account and a few primary sources of the day, the rest of their trip home can be pieced together as a likely series of circumstances and decisions.

Thoreau and Mann left Toronto's Rossin House and boarded a train of the Grand Trunk Railway of Canada heading east at 8:30 p.m. on July 8, 1861. They spent the next thirteen hours settled within the confines of a railroad car, on their only overnight rail journey. Since most of the trip was done in the dark, they could not see much of the surrounding landscape, nor could they botanize from the car windows. Perhaps they could still see the comet enflaming the nighttime sky.

The Grand Trunk followed the northern coastline of Lake Ontario and eventually rolled past the Thousand Islands along the St. Lawrence River. It stopped at the largest towns along the route: fifteen minutes in Cobourg (just after midnight); five minutes in Belleville; 45 minutes in Kingston (at 5 a.m.); and five minutes in Brockville. The two travelers finally left the train at Prescott Junction at 9:25 a.m. on July 9, 1861. They were able to cross the St. Lawrence to reach Ogdensburgh (as it was officially spelled then), New

York, on the ferry that made the trip every half hour.

What were they thinking as they steamed across the water? They had just witnessed a rather wild election in Toronto. Now they were leaving a land that was heading toward Confederation and were returning to one that was in the process of coming apart (due to the formation of a Southern *Confederacy*) after spending three quarters of a century in relative unity. Those who thought the war would take just three months to settle were now being proven short-sighted, if not altogether wrong. There was no way for Henry and Horace to know what the future might hold, for themselves or for their country.

Once they reached American soil, they may have had to check in at the nearby stone Custom House, which was already fifty years old. They could admire the tower of the rather squat harbor lighthouse. Then they had to find the right railroad connections to take them back to Concord, Massachusetts. They had already bought their through-tickets in Milwaukee, so they were assured of having reserved seats. But unfortunately, their scheduling wasn't quite on target this time. The fact that they ate both lunch and supper there indicates that they were hanging out in Ogdensburgh for some reason. And it was a good enough one. They had missed the most convenient express train service to Boston for that day. They had to wait until it was offered again: at 4 a.m. the next morning.

How might Henry and Horace have spent the intervening hours? Why, in botanizing, of course. Thoreau's plant inventories include several species seen or collected in Ogdensburgh: Hounds tongue (*Cynoglossum officinale*), Stickseed (*Echinospermum lappula*), and a form of Spurge (*Euphorbia* sp.). He continued to be confounded by an "unknown Borraginaceous plant" that he had seen all over the upper Great Lakes area, from northern Michigan and Mackinac Island, to Toronto and in Ogdensburgh. Evidently the specimen had hairy leaves and was similar in appearance to the herbs known as borages. He never more fully identified it in his notes.

Located as it was along the St. Lawrence and at the mouth of the Oswegatchie River, Ogdensburgh was an important transportation center of the day. Many of its eight thousand residents were involved in managing the distribution of lumber and grain to other parts of the continent. They were poised to handle commodities and cargo as well as living, breathing travelers. Several hotels operated within a few blocks of the harbor.

It's possible that one of them charged 75 cents a night, without meals; and that perhaps Henry and Horace actually had a place to sleep while they waited for the morning train. The station for the Northern Railroad was a good ten-block walk east from the ferry dock. Just a casual saunter from one to the other would have led the men past a variety of businesses and along the St. Lawrence shoreline, where the plant life could be scrutinized as well.

They might have been intrigued if they had had a chance to hear stories from the North Country history. This international borderland had a bit of conflict in its past. Over in Prescott sat Fort Wellington, clearly visible from this side of the river. When Henry and Horace saw it, the post lay vacant. It had been first constructed around the time of the War of 1812. Though Prescott had not been attacked by the Americans back then, the British did cross the icy river and capture Ogdensburgh in February, 1813. Serving seemingly no purpose over the next few decades, the first Fort Wellington was left to deteriorate. It was rebuilt in the late 1830s but had been abandoned again by 1854.

Ogdensburgh's combat history dated back much further. The settlement began as an Indian mission called Fort La Presentation in the mid-1700s. The last naval battle of the French and Indian War was fought here in 1760. The British renamed the place Fort Oswegatchie and occupied its grounds even after the end of the American Revolution. Jay's Treaty forced them finally to leave the post in 1796. The structure itself was dismantled after the War of 1812. Perhaps someone pointed out to our travelers the site of the old fort, which had stood on the same spit of land that the lighthouse had been built upon.

When Thoreau and Mann walked through the village, Ogdensburgh was still riding a patriotic high from its huge Fourth of July celebration. Five days earlier, the townspeople had greeted the rising sun with a thirteen-gun salute and the ringing of every bell from every tower. At least one hundred flags were unfurled throughout the community; including one special Stars and Stripes made of two hundred yards of material. It hung from a pole at the corner of Ford and Patterson Streets and was said to be the largest flag in the country. Henry and Horace probably had a chance to see it, days later.

After the flags were raised, Ogdensburgh residents held a parade that led from the Seymour House hotel to the Presbyterian Church. Two local bands and various fire company vehicles and officials joined veterans of the War of 1812, members of the clergy and village authorities as they proceeded down the street. Even "Citizens and Strangers" were invited to participate. From newspaper reports, it is unclear how many people, if any, were left to serve as bystanders.

The church was the scene of the formal "exercises," as was the case in the nineteenth century. One man read aloud the entire Declaration of

Independence. A local minister delivered an inspirational oration. Then the entire audience sang "The Army Hymn" by Oliver Wendell Holmes. At the conclusion of the program, the group marched to the Town House to enjoy "a splendid collation" that had been "prepared by the ladies." In other words: lunch. In the afternoon, a regatta was held on the St. Lawrence River. The prospect of sailing in five races "had drawn out some of the finest and fleetest sporting craft on our Northern waters." The evening brought a torchlight procession that was led by the Ogdensburgh Zoaves. "Nearly three hundred torches were borne in the procession, while twelve hundred Roman Candles filled the air with a blaze of dazzling beauty." What a party!

Yes, it was the war that had brought such patriotism to this village on the northern edge of the Union. Some folks thought that the day might be "the last Fourth of July this country would ever see." There was no telling what would happen now, thanks to "our deluded Southern brethren." The editor of *The Advance* rebutted the opinion and reassured his public:

> The annual return of the glorious day is as certain as the seasons in their time. Our country has not yet accomplished the mission for which she was destined, nor filled her appointed sphere amid the powers of the earth. The blackest clouds are overpast, and ere long the morning light will stream forth in bright effulgence.

He was wrong, of course. Things would get worse before they could get better.

Henry Thoreau and Horace Mann, Jr., no doubt saw tri-color bunting still hanging from downtown buildings. Surely tiny bits of colored paper and remnants of burnt torches and fireworks still littered the corners and crevasses of Ogdensburgh's streets. Perhaps a few youngsters were still lighting fires and setting off random firecrackers, as their kind would continue to do on national holidays a century and a half later. Or maybe the skies were clear that night, and everyone could instead look up and admire nature's counterpart, the comet. In any event, no matter what was happening in the Fourth of July afterglow, Henry and Horace had a singular goal in Ogdensburgh: they needed to catch the early morning train.

Naturally, all of the towns along Canada's original Grand Trunk Railway route have grown since 1861. Orchards and farmland still separate many of them. With more than 117,000 residents, Kingston is now the largest shore-line city between Toronto and Montreal. VIA Rail passenger trains run between those three cities, as do freight loads. Alas, the trains no longer stop at each and every town, as the old GTR used to. However, the GO Transit's Lakeshore East line runs between Toronto and Oshawa and makes local community stops. And hikers and bicyclists can skirt the entire Lake Ontario coastline in Canada via the Waterfront Trail, which leads from Niagara-on-the-Lake to the Quebec border.

Prescott's Fort Wellington served as a military outpost again in the late 1860s; but it was soon generally abandoned as an active fort. On occasion it served as a training ground or as a storehouse. In 1925, it became a national historic site. A decommissioned cannon sits poised upon one of its ramparts, aimed at New York.

Ogdensburg dropped the "h" in its name when it was chartered as a city in 1868. Its Custom House still guards the mouth of the Oswegatchie River and still acts as offices for current customs officials. The structure itself is now known to be the oldest federal government building in the country. On the western shore of the Oswegatchie is the 1834 harbor lighthouse, now a private residence. The nearby Riverside Avenue park offers a panoramic view of the St. Lawrence and the opposite shoreline. An ornamental cannon is perched in the yard and is, of course, aimed at Ontario.

A movement is afoot to rebuild historic Fort La Presentation in Ogdensburg. The reconstruction will not sit in the exact same spot as the original fort, but the city has already become involved in historic reenactments of events that were part of the French and Indian War.

Passenger rail service is no longer available in Ogdensburg. The old Northern Railroad station is gone. The property where it once stood now houses the Port of Ogdensburg Marine Terminal complex. Some freight loads still leave this facility by rail.

But don't be surprised if you still hear train whistles as you walk around and visit Ogdensburg. The distinctive sound comes from over the water, from the Canadian side of the St. Lawrence, where regular passenger and freight service still use the rails of the old Grand Trunk. Coincidentally enough, one set of those whistles always seems to blow at 4 a.m. Timed as they are to Henry and Horace's departure, the tones translate an additional eerie feeling across that broad, liquid mile.

The biggest transformation to the area came in 1959-1960. That's when the St. Lawrence Seaway officially opened and the Ogdensburg-Prescott

International Bridge was built over the river, connecting Ontario with New York a few miles north of Ogdensburg. The need for an hourly ferry between the two cities was eliminated—as was the direct line of business leading into downtown Ogdensburg. According to native and historian Dr. Paul Russell, the bridge "became a symbol of the decline of Ogdensburg." "When the ferry was replaced by a bridge outside the city, the entire city … became subject to urban renewal initiatives that resulted in urban destruction. They tore down the downtown." Some empty storefronts and barren lots still linger.

Yet the city of Ogdensburg has survived; and it remains home to almost 13,000 residents. Promoters talk about its industrial and transportation facilities. They focus additionally on the "breathtaking scenery and natural beauty, a rich cultural history, and abundant recreational opportunities" that can be found during all four seasons in St. Lawrence County, New York. I can attest that it is a beautiful area to visit.

I had successfully navigated around Toronto and was now hours away from the city, heading east on Highway 2. The rain was gone, and the day had turned into a beautiful blue sky day of autumn. I enjoyed the leisurely drive through the towns and the farmland, with occasional glimpses of Lake Ontario and the railroad tracks. From the driver's side window, I yelled hellos to all of the domesticated four-foots: the cows, the horses, the sheep, and the occasional donkey. It was a fun ride.

Suddenly it occurred to me that I had neglected to figure out a Thoreauvian adventure for this leg of the journey. At least a dozen apple orchards were already behind me. One farm even had a corn maze. I mentally chastised myself for not having stopped earlier. Thoreau loved apples, of course. That was why the crab apple trees of the Midwest had caught his attention. I could have spun a tale about that. But by the time I thought of it, I had advanced beyond the natural orchard habitat of southeastern Ontario. There were none in sight, and there was no time to turn back.

I consulted my maps and guidebooks while on the move. Time sitting at a red light became a useful moment for quick research. In the pages of my books, I saw a variety of historical sites coming up; but none of them seemed relevant to my purpose. I decided to just keep on going, in the hopes that something interesting and good would surface.

When I reached the town of Napanee, I noticed a grouping of colorful tents and street vendors down the block. There were lots of pumpkins and harvest-oriented displays, perfect for this first Saturday in October 2009. A sign told me that this was the "Scarecrow Festival." While I looked for a place to park, a pair of horses pulled a hay wagon along the other side of the street. Both children and adults were packed on top of it. Maybe this was what I was looking for.

Minutes later, I walked among the vendors as a local rock band was playing a John Mellencamp song. I had to remind myself that I was in Canada. The crafts and homemade products on the tables were similar to those of every fall festival I had ever attended in the States. They were nice enough, even beautiful, but I didn't see anything unduly inspirational. I bought a box of Girl Guides cookies, both as a good deed and also to amuse my co-workers on the following Monday. I could see their startled faces and hear their confused queries. "Girl Scout cookies, at this time of the year? Oh, wait. Girl *Guides*? Where did these come from?" That would be fun.

But I made no other purchases. And I wondered if Napanee had been the right stop after all.

As I pulled back on to the main street, I noticed that this town had painted murals on the sides of a few of its buildings. The artwork probably represented important facts in local history or events with local connections. And one in particular made me catch my breath. It was of a locomotive, an old-fashioned one, pulling several passenger cars across a large stone arch bridge. It was from the right era. I snapped a few photos of it until the light changed and traffic forced me to move on.

Minutes later, I understood why the mural was there. I saw the railroad bridge itself. It was huge. It wasn't as tall as the Whistler bridges in the Berksires, but it was impressive nevertheless. I drove through it and turned

The distinctive stone arch bridge still carries the railroad line through Napanee, Ontario.

into the lot of Springside Park. I spent some time looking up and walking through the four oldest stone archways, marveling at the masonry work of the nineteenth century. Across the lawn lay a series of waterfalls of the Napanee River. They powered the first saw mill and grist mill in this area, and they provided a reason for a settlement to grow here. The roaring river dropped in steps and ledges: some man-made, some natural. Two people, presumably a mother and a young son, stood on the opposite shore, fishing. They each made a few casts while I took in the whole scene.

With sudden clarity, I saw in this spot the symbolic essence of this Journey West made by Henry Thoreau and young Horace Mann. Rivers and rails, side by side. The power of nature versus the power of industrialization. The two men used both over the course of their two-month adventure. They traveled over tracks owned by seventeen different railroad companies. But they also sailed up the Mississippi and the Minnesota Rivers and across Lake Michigan and Lake Huron. They took advantage of both methods of transportation.

Indeed, you could say that throughout Thoreau's life, it was almost always about the water. His first book was *A Week on the Concord and Merrimack Rivers*. His second was *Walden*. He made trips to Cape Cod and had a chance to study the Bay and the beach of the Atlantic Ocean. He lived in a town where the Assabet and the Sudbury Rivers flowed into each other to form the Concord. And he had experience paddling all of them. Fishing in them, too. And when the railroad came to town and intruded on that western edge of Walden Pond, he was initially judgmental. But he soon grew to depend on the railroad as the quickest way to get to Boston and Worcester and other cities where he was due to lecture. The majority of this last excursion of Thoreau's life was made mostly by rail. What a Transcendental turnaround.

Because their Grand Trunk Railway train passed through Napanee in the wee hours of the morning, Thoreau and Mann did not see this river and its falls and the mills standing next to them. That's a shame, because it offered the kind of habitat they may have wanted to explore a bit further. Their last encounter with water on this trip would be with a steamboat ferry across the St. Lawrence River. Lucky them.

Hours after leaving Napanee, I white-knuckled it across the two-lane bridge just beyond Prescott, focusing on the metallic song it sang to me from beneath my tires. I could lower its pitch by slowing down, which I chose to do in the extreme because no cars were behind me. I tried not to peek at the surface of the St. Lawrence, which seemed to be *way* too far below me. I popped in a favorite music CD to help boost my confidence to make it across. Truly, I am not really afraid of heights. I can stand on the crest of a mountain. I am simply uncomfortable taking a ski lift to reach the top of it. I'm a land animal at heart. I need something stable underneath my feet, connecting me to dear Mother Earth. And a mere two-lane suspension bridge with just a few pillars holding it up didn't quite fit the bill for my peace of mind and my sinking stomach. I was petrified.

But along with that feeling were others that I couldn't quite identify, as I crawled across that bridge. I was leaving Canada to return to the United States. I was relieved to be coming home, I guess. At the same time, I had gotten used to being in a slightly different environment for the past four days. I was somewhat sad to be saying goodbye to Ontario. As I coasted ever so slowly toward the New York shoreline, I also remembered that this was the final leg of the Journey West for me. I had divided the trip into sections and had approached them at various times to fit my own schedule. As soon as my tires hit the ground—and it couldn't be soon enough for me—I would have done it all. I would have tucked the final piece into the jigsaw puzzle. I would have come full circle. It was almost as if I was bringing Henry and Horace along with me on this stretch.

After I paid the bridge toll and explained myself to the customs agent, I drove into downtown Ogdensburg with one destination in mind. I proceeded down State Street to its end at the river and the park. Along the way I saw signs announcing gas prices measured by the gallon, not the liter. From now on I wouldn't have to do a mathematical calculation every time I saw a speed limit or a destination sign. No more metric conversions for me. Tonight I would reluctantly put my colorful Canadian bills back into my suitcase and get out the mossy green ones with the Presidential faces. Queen Elizabeth would no longer be guarding my wallet.

I pulled into a spot that faced the river that I just crossed. This was not my first time in this space, but it was the first time I had approached it from "over there." This park was always the epitome of peacefulness and thoughtfulness for me. The air here was silent today, broken only by some declarations of imagined offenses among a few seagulls. It was a perfect time for speculation and dreaming.

I stood at the mouth of the Oswegatchie River, a natural harbor site for Ogdensburg. The stone customs house was not far away. Some of the willows and maples here were old enough to have been saplings in 1861. I looked across the wider water and could envision a steam ferry proceeding slowly in this direction, chugging its way across the St. Lawrence. What was it like for Henry and Horace on that day? Did they have the same kinds of feelings I just had? Were they tired, exhausted? On that morning of July 9, 1861, the sun might have been shining on their faces and into their eyes. They had been on the road for almost two months, and they were facing two more days' worth of travel. But surely they must have seen this shoreline as being one step closer to home. I felt as though I could stand there and stare at their ghosts forever.

Later, when I got into my hotel room, I opened the windows. All night long, I heard the train whistles from the Ontarian side of the river. One set happened at exactly 4 a.m. Someone or something was going somewhere else. Soon I would be too.

WHEN YOU GO: Today the fastest and most direct drive from Toronto to Prescott is via the MacDonald-Cartier Freeway, the 401. Exit 721B leads you directly onto the Prescott-Ogdensburg International Bridge and across the St. Lawrence River. Upon landing in New York State, follow NY Route 37 south to Ogdensburg.

But where's the excitement and adventure in taking a multi-lane, impersonal artery?

I recommend heading east on the 401 only from Toronto to Oshawa. You'll still be able to see the railroad tracks because they lie just south of the roadway for much of that section. Exit in or near Oshawa and take Ontario Provincial Highway 2 the rest of the way to Prescott. You'll pass through every town that Thoreau and Mann's train did. You'll be able to find the tracks fairly easily, if you wish. And you'll get to see a lot of interesting sights, including snippets of Lake Ontario and the Thousand Islands. The trip won't take quite as long as it took our two travelers, but it might last as much as nine hours, especially if you make stops along the way.

The Ogdensburg-Prescott International Bridge is more than a mile long and is just two lanes wide. If even the thought of driving over a high and narrow bridge makes you shake in your shoes, you might consider making a diversion. You can try instead the Thousand Islands Bridge, which lies well west of Prescott, at Selton, Ontario, and connects Ontario's Highway 137 with U.S. I-81. It even traverses some of the islands. And the Seaway International Bridge in Cornwall lies well east of Prescott and provides a link with NY Route 37 in Massena, New York. I cannot speak for the stress level or the drivability that either span may offer.

In Ogdensburg, you should be able to find the Riverside Park rather easily. To reach the site of the old Northern railroad station from the park, drive or walk east on Riverside Avenue to Patterson Street. Turn left, and the property will soon be on your right.

To get an even better view of the tracks, travel east on Ford Street. Park at the convenience store where Ford and Greene Streets come together. Look to the north and walk to the bridge that spans the railroad tracks. Be aware of traffic patterns as you cross. From that vantage point, you can look down on the rails and see their progress in both directions. Odds are good that you won't see a contemporary working train while you're standing there, though. You'll have to imagine the old Northern Railroad locomotive and the cars that carried Henry Thoreau and Horace Mann ever closer to home.

FOR MORE INFORMATION

Custom House, 127 Water Street, Ogdensburg, NY

Fort La Presentation Association, PO Box 1749, Ogdensburg, NY 13669. Phone (315) 394-1749. www.fortlapresentation.net

Fort Wellington National Historic Site of Canada, PO Box 479, Prescott, ON Canada K0E 1T0. Phone (613) 925-2896. www.pc.gc.ca/lhn-nhs/on/wellington/index.aspx

Go Transit, 20 Bay Street, Suite 600, Toronto, ON Canada M5J 2W3. Phone (888) 438-6646. www.gotransit.com

Greater Ogdensburg Chamber of Commerce, 1020 Park Street, Ogdensburg, NY 13669. Phone (315) 393-3620. www.webiety.com/chamber/chamber.aspx

Napanee & District Chamber of Commerce and Tourism Information Centre, 47 Dundas Street East, PO Box 431, Napanee, ON Canada K7R 3P5. Phone (613) 354-6601. napaneechamber.ca

Ontario Ministry of Natural Resources, Ontario Parks, 300 Water Street, 6th Floor, PO Box 7000, Peterborough, ON Canada K91 8M5. Phone (800) 667-1940. www.mnr.gov.on.ca

Ontario Travel, 1000-201 City Center Drive, Mississauga ON Canada L58 4E4. Phone (905) 804-5480. www.ontariotravel.net/

St. Lawrence Islands National Park of Canada, 2 County Road 5, RR 3, Mallorytown, ON Canada K0E 1R0. Phone (613) 923-5261. www.pc.gc.ca/eng/pn-np/on/lawren/index.aspx

VIA Rail Canada, www.viarail.ca.

Waterfront Trail, 372 Richmond Street West, Suite 308, Toronto, ON Canada M5V 1X6. Phone (416) 943-8080 ext. 321. www.waterfronttrail.org.

RECOMMENDED READING

Thoreau's essay "Life Without Principle." "Let us consider the way in which we spend our lives," he wrote. "This world is a place of business." He then railed against that foundation. The essay can be found in a variety of anthologies and online sites.

NOTES ON THIS CHAPTER

The last letter Horace sent to his mother was from Mackinac Island and was written on July 1, 1861. The last dated entry that Thoreau wrote in his notebook read "July 8. To Ogdensburg." Without any additional clues left by the two men, the rest of their journey has to be deciphered with the use of other sources. These include Henry's expense account plus period railroad schedules, newspapers, and published histories.

The first question that arises is: *How* did Henry and Horace travel from Toronto to Ogdensburgh: by steamboat or by train? In Thoreau's list of expenses, he uses the term "on road" for a purchase made between Toronto and Ogdensburgh. I believe he truly meant they were on a road: a railroad. He used the same terminology for a purchase made between Goderich and Toronto, when they were definitely traveling by train. I do not believe he would have written "on road" if he and Horace had been sailing across Lake Ontario on a steamboat.

The only train line available in that direction at that time was the Grand Trunk Railway of Canada. From Toronto they would have had to ride to Prescott Junction, and then take a ferry across the St. Lawrence River to Ogdensburgh. No bridge spanned the river at that point.

The next question is: *When* did they leave Toronto on the 8th? According to a railroad schedule published during the summer of 1861, there were two options: a train that left Toronto at 8:30 p.m. and landed in Prescott Junction at 9:25 a.m. the next morning; and one that left Toronto at 6:30 a.m. and got to Prescott Junction at 4:45 p.m. the same day.

Looking at Henry's expense account provides the next clue. In his field notebook, he indented the costs for the paper, lunch, and dinner underneath the item marked "At Ogdensburg." That indicates to me that he incurred all three of those costs in Ogdensburgh. If that's true, then only the time of the first train departure makes sense. Ending up on the New York side in mid-morning would mean that the travelers would have somehow had to eat lunch and dinner. And maybe the subsequent train that left the next morning had such an early departure time that breakfast was out of the question.

An additional hint exists to indicate that Henry and Horace took the evening train out of Toronto. Or rather, it *doesn't* exist. Thoreau wrote down the names of plants he saw in Toronto and in Ogdensburgh, but none along the route between the two communities. And he made no references to what the landscape looked like between the two of them. That says to me that he didn't see it. He didn't botanize from the train windows. Considering this fact along with the more likely of the two train departures results in the scenario I have posed in this chapter.

The last question for this section is: When did they leave Ogdensburgh? The printed railroad schedule booklet did not mention a 4 a.m. express train to Boston. But ads for such a service appeared in both the Burlington (Vt.) *Free Press* and the *St. Lawrence Republican and Ogdensburgh Weekly Journal*. Again, the timing makes sense, given the other factors mentioned above. However, I will admit to being only 90% sure of my theory.

Details about Prescott's Fort Wellington were gleaned from the park's web site. The promotional lines about Ogdensburg came from its town web site.

Anna Maria College colleague Dr. Paul Russell was only too happy to provide personal knowledge and experiences about his hometown of Ogdensburg and that part of New York State. I quoted from his e-mail message of October 5, 2009. Paul earned my infinite admiration when he revealed to me that he has walked the length of the Ogdensburg-Prescott International Bridge. I could barely drive across it.

Both *The Advance* and the *St. Lawrence Republican and Ogdensburgh Weekly Journal* announced and reported on the 1861 Fourth of July celebration. The passages I quoted were from the July 12, 1861, edition of *The Advance*. I accessed it from the Northern New York Library System web site at http://news.nnyln.net.

Travel Chapter 18

Wednesday, July 10, 1861
Ogdensburg to Boston
via the Northern Railroad, Vermont Central Railroad,
Northern NH Railroad, Concord Railroad of NH,
and Boston & Lowell Railroad

Expenses: Berth, .50

It must have been a relief to finally leave Ogdensburg at 4 a.m., even though it meant that the travelers had 400 miles and sixteen and a half hours of steady riding in store that day. At 50 cents, a berth in a railroad car should have seemed like a true bargain; it provided a place to nap along the way. They left Ogdensburg about an hour before sunrise and crossed northern New York on the Northern Railroad line. The express train followed the tracks of five different railroad companies that day, but it's a fairly safe assumption that Henry and Horace didn't have to leave their car to make any connection changes. Stops were nevertheless still made at most of the stations.

New York—which can appear deceptively small on state maps—is much wider when witnessed in person. It took four and a half hours to cross that broad expanse of St. Lawrence lowland located just north of the Adirondacks. Because of the lay of the land, travelers heading east could catch only a glimpse of those mountains to the south, depending on the weather. Perhaps both Henry and Horace were sleeping that morning and were not looking out a south-facing window as the day dawned. They would not have missed much.

But over those mountains and about fifty miles to the south lay North Elba, the site of John Brown's farm and, by now, his grave. A public celebration of the abolitionist's life had been held there a year earlier. Henry Thoreau had not attended the event. Instead he sent his text of "The Last Days of John Brown" to the organizers. It was read aloud and was later published in William Lloyd Garrison's newspaper, *The Liberator*. Henry's ride on this day was the closest he would ever come to setting foot on Brown's property.

At Rouse's Point, they entered Vermont by crossing the Alburgh Tongue peninsula and launching onto the rails of the Vermont Central. Thoreau had been in Rouse's Point back in the fall of 1850, during his trip to Canada with Ellery Channing. The two had taken a steamer up Lake Champlain and then sailed up the Richelieu River to St. John's, with Montreal as their destination. A little more than a week later and after venturing as far as Quebec City, they retraced their steps to get home. But back then, on the way north, Henry wasn't sure what to expect at the border on his first international excursion:

> The number of French-Canadian gentlemen and ladies among the passengers, and the sound of the French language, advertised us by this time that we were being whirled towards some foreign vortex. And now we have left Rouse's Point, and entered the Sorel River, and passed the invisible barrier between the United States and Canada. The shores of the Sorel, Richelieu, or St. John's River are flat and reedy, where I had expected something more rough and mountainous for a natural boundary between two nations.

That same "invisible barrier" sat less than a mile away as the cars now passed over the Richelieu River and headed for the Green Mountains. If Thoreau was awake at the time (8:30 a.m.), he might have caught one last quick peek at Canada before the tracks turned south.

The express train followed the eastern edge of Lake Champlain and arrived in Burlington, Vermont, at eleven o'clock. Coming into the downtown station and passing so close to the water, the riders should have had a clear, breathtaking view of the lake and the hazy blue silhouettes of New York's Adirondacks standing beyond the opposite shore. On Thoreau's previous ride to Burlington in 1850, he and Channing had taken a different set of tracks to approach the town from the south. Their route then used the Fitchburg Railroad, the Cheshire Railroad, and the Rutland & Burlington Railroad, allowing them to first see Lake Champlain at the town of Vergennes. At that time, they steamed across it to reach Plattsburgh, New York.

> It lies there so small ... but beautifully quiet... It does not say, "Here I am, Lake Champlain," as the conductor might for it. ... We got our first fair view of the lake at dawn, just before reaching Plattsburgh, and saw blue ranges of mountains on either hand, in New York and in Vermont, the former especially grand. A few white schooners, like gulls, were seen in the distance ... but it was such a view as leaves not much to be said; indeed, I have postponed Lake Champlain to another day.

Well, it was another day; but there was no time to disembark and take in or explore the beauty of Samuel de Champlain's discovery. The express continued on its way south, crossing the state of Vermont through the Green Mountains, which by July would have been brimming with that summer hue as they towered four thousand feet above the cars, made miniature by comparison. After stopping in the capital city of Montpelier, the train followed the branches of the White River as it hurried on to the Connecticut River at the settlement of White River Junction. There the cars passed into the realm of the Northern New Hampshire Railroad as soon as they crossed the bridge.

When the train stopped in Enfield, N.H., it was directly across Mascoma Lake from the Enfield Shaker village. That expansive settlement with dozens of buildings included the five-story Great Stone Dwelling. Built in 1841, it was the largest Shaker building ever constructed. In 1861, about 263 Believers lived in this community, which they called the "Chosen Vale." Twenty years earlier, more than 300 individuals were part of the village. Just like their brethren in Hancock and Harvard, Massachusetts, the membership at Enfield reflected the religion's declining membership.

Within the boundaries of the town of Franklin, the train passed close to the birthplace of Daniel Webster (1782-1852). If any single politician could have been considered the bane of Henry Thoreau's existence, it might very well have been Daniel Webster. The man had reportedly courted Thoreau's maiden aunt, Louisa Dunbar, when they were both young and living in New Hampshire. He continued to visit her in Concord after she moved in with the Thoreaus in the early 1830s. But even though he successfully represented Massachusetts and Northern interests during his terms in both the U.S. House and the Senate, the once-popular Daniel Webster plummeted out of favor with his Northern constituents as soon as he supported the despised Fugitive Slave Law and the Compromise of 1850. To know that a presumed friend of such a dedicated anti-slavery family as the Thoreaus had backed that travesty, must have confounded Henry and wounded each one of the women in his household.

Four years later, and two years after Webster himself was gone, Henry Thoreau was still invoking the senator's name in speech and in print—and not necessarily in a flattering manner. When he took the platform at the rally in Framingham, Massachusetts, on July 4, 1854, Thoreau pounced on the law that required Northerners to return runaway slaves to their owners in the South. There was no need to make a conscious effort to throw such a document down and crush it under one's heels, he said, for its "natural habitat is in the dirt. It was born and bred, and has its life only in the dust and mire, on a level with the feet, and he who walks in freedom ... will inevitably tread on it, and so trample it under foot,—and Webster, its maker, with it, like the dirt-bug and its ball." Five weeks later, when the book *Walden; or Life in the Woods* was released, readers learned of the author's propensity for finding spirituality while communing alone with nature, not in the ceremonial setting of organized religion:

> I delight to come to my bearings,—not walk in procession with pomp and parade, in a conspicuous place, but to walk even with the Builder of the universe, if I may,—not to live in this restless, nervous, bustling, trivial Nineteenth Century, but stand or sit thoughtfully while it goes by. What are men celebrating? They are all on a committee of arrangements, and hourly expect a speech from somebody. God is only the president of the day, and Webster is his orator.

Even death could not silence the senator's tongue. But at least Thoreau envisioned Daniel Webster doing heavenly work and not on a commission to speak elsewhere.

Continuing south toward New Hampshire's state capital, the train skirted the edge of the town of Canterbury. Seven miles west lay another Shaker community, home to 240 Believers at the time. Population had decreased by 20 since 1840, but overall, the Canterbury Shakers were still doing well.

Concord, New Hampshire, was for many years the home of the 14th U.S. President, Franklin Pierce (1804-1869). He and his family had lived there in the 1840s. And after he served in Washington in the 1850s, Pierce bought 60 acres of farmland just west of the downtown area. His intention was to build a permanent home on the property. In the meantime, he and his wife lived in a rental on South Main Street. Just as the residents of Kinderhook, N.Y., sought out local landowner Martin Van Buren for war-time advice, so the people of Concord contacted Franklin Pierce for comfort and counsel. Pierce had recently written to Van Buren to suggest having a joint meeting of the former chiefs of state, but nothing ever came of that idea. He was probably in the Concord area when Henry and Horace's train passed through the capital city. But as they would not have stopped to see Van Buren in Kinderhook, neither would they give a minute to Pierce in this other Concord. No matter that the former President had been a college classmate and a close friend to Nathaniel Hawthorne, who was in turn a colleague of Henry Thoreau and an uncle to Horace Mann, Jr.

Onward rattled the express train, now following the rails of the Concord, Manchester & Lawrence Railway to Nashua, New Hampshire. Ironically this portion of the journey mirrored the path of Henry Thoreau's very first excursion: the one with his brother John in 1839. Back then the two men paddled their boat first up the Concord River, and then up the Merrimack to that "other" Concord in New Hampshire. No railroad followed the waterway back then. But the intervening years had seen advancements in the industrialization of the Merrimack River valley. More than two decades later, the region may have been unrecognizable to Henry's eyes.

Manchester was the quintessential example of that growth. When the Thoreau brothers sailed past it, only two thousand people lived there. By the time Henry and Horace's train led them past the settlement it was more than 20,000 bodies strong. Back in 1839, the Thoreaus had been impressed by the sight of the Merrimack River's Amoskeag Falls, the reason for the creation of the community of Manchester and its mill. "But we did not tarry to examine them minutely," Henry wrote, "making haste to get past the village here collected, and out of hearing of the hammer which was laying the foundation of another Lowell on the banks." He predicted correctly. Manchester would someday be just as big a mill town as was Lowell, Massachusetts.

In Nashua, the express train switched to the tracks of the Boston & Lowell. Speak of the devil. It was now an 80-minute ride between Manchester and Lowell. When Thoreau wrote of the latter in *A Week on the Concord and Merrimack*, he condemned the damming of the river and the businesses that were powered by the project.

> Perchance, after a few thousands of years, if the fishes will be patient, and pass their summers elsewhere, meanwhile, nature will have leveled the Billerica dam, and the Lowell factories, and the Grass-ground River [will] run clear again, to be explored by new migratory shoals...

Henry Thoreau still straddled the line between an agricultural age and an industrial one. He was fascinated enough with the machinery of the mills to get personal tours of the facilities in West Concord, in Clinton, and in Worcester, Massachusetts. Simultaneously in *Walden*, he expressed his doubts about the operations.

> I cannot believe that our factory system is the best mode by which men may get clothing. The condition of the operatives is becoming every day more like that of the English; and it

cannot be wondered at, since, as far as I have heard or observed, the principal object is, not that mankind may be well and honestly clad, but, unquestionably, that the corporations may be enriched.

And as he passed by those mills in 1861, some of them had already landed government contracts. They were sewing uniforms to outfit Union soldiers.

We assume that our weary travelers arrived in Boston at 8:30 p.m. But the Fitchburg Railroad was done for the day. No friends or relatives greeted the two men in a carriage to take them home, and no trains ran out to Concord until morning. They must have overnighted in either the Boston & Lowell station or the Fitchburg station, which were separated by just three blocks along Causeway Street. Thus they joined the ranks of those stranded travelers who find themselves waiting, one more time, for the next ride out of town.

But maybe that wait wasn't such a bad deal after all. If Thoreau and Mann made their way to the Fitchburg station, they could have spent those hours in one of Thoreau's favorite places in the city. He once wrote to H.G. O. Blake on the state of accommodations in Boston:

> As for the Parker House, I went there once, when the Club was away, but I found it hard to see through the cigar smoke, and men were deposited about in chairs over the marble floor, as thick as legs of bacon in a smoke-house. It was all smoke, and no salt, Attic or other. The only room in Boston which I visit with alacrity is the Gentlemen's Room at the Fitchburg Depot, where I wait for the cars, sometimes for two hours, in order to get out of town. It is a paradise to the Parker House, for no smoking is allowed, and there is far more retirement.

Once again Henry Thoreau disdained the accommodations of the fanciest hotels and instead found comfort in the kinds of places where others did not. The Fitchburg station must have been at least architecturally grand, though. It has been described as "a granite Norman castle." It even featured a performance hall on its second floor, where Swedish singer Jenny Lind gave several standing-room-only concerts in 1850. One could spend time in far worse places, it seems.

If a copy of that day's *Boston Journal* was lying around, either man might have picked it up to learn what was happening close to home, since they had been gone for so long. Skimming past the requisite war news, they would have come across the details of a shocking accident that had happened the previous day in Cambridge. Frances Appleton Longfellow had been heating sealing wax when her dress caught fire, quickly enveloping her in flames. Her husband Henry Wadsworth tried to extinguish the blazing material himself and sustained burns on his hands and wrists. The newspaper reported that the woman, though "terribly burned," had "rallied a little, and her physicians entertained some hopes of her ultimate recovery." The prediction had been printed too soon. Mrs. Longfellow died at about the same time that Henry and Horace were pulling into the station in Burlington, Vermont. The mother of six would be heralded in the papers the following day as "a universal favorite with all classes" and "one of the most noble and accomplished women in the country, of great personal beauty and of dignified presence." Unaware of the full story, Thoreau might still have felt a pang of sympathy for the poet and professor who had taught him a bit of German at Harvard, and who on more than one occasion shared dinner with him around a Transcendental table.

Henry David Thoreau and Horace Mann, Jr., were close to home, but they weren't quite there yet. They had one more day and one more short train ride to go.

This portion of Henry Thoreau and Horace Mann's trip has been the most disturbed, as far as the railroad lines are concerned. Several of them are missing. The former Northern (New York) Railroad line handles freight trains only for the few miles from Ogdensburg to Norwood. The rest of that route has been abandoned; and for much of it, the rails and the sleepers are gone. The Vermont Central line is still active for both freight and for passengers. But at White River Junction, the tracks turn southward and follow the Connecticut River into Massachusetts. Rail service does not cross east into New Hampshire at that point today. The Northern (New Hampshire) Railroad has been abandoned; and part of its route is now a rail-trail for hikers and bicyclists. The line that runs from Concord to Nashua is currently devoted solely to freight cars. The old Boston & Lowell is now part of the MBTA, however; and as such, it supports both freight and commuter traffic.

But movements are afoot in New Hampshire to restore passenger service on the path represented by Thoreau and Mann's journey across that state. Folks can envision the benefit of linking Concord, N.H., with a metro

Boston line, so that automobile traffic on Route 3 and I-93 can be avoided. Some would like the rails restored to the old Northern (New Hampshire) Railroad beds, consequently displacing the hikers and the bikers. Such a move would re-establish a Boston connection with Vermont and thus, even with Montreal. Improving the local rail system is a current transportation priority for residents of the Granite State.

Visitors can make a side trip to the preserved John Brown Farm, located on the outskirts of Lake Placid, N.Y. The Daniel Webster Birthplace too is now a state historic site. The house where he was born had previously been moved to another part of the property, and a large farmhouse had been built in its place. The land was acquired by the Webster Birthplace Association in 1910, and the birth house was restored to its original location. The Pierce Manse, where the former president lived in the 1840s, has been restored and can be toured in Concord, N.H. The Pierces never got around to building a home on that expansive acreage outside of town. And in Lowell, it's possible to see the James Abbot McNeill Whistler (1834-1903) house, now a Museum of Art. Whistler's father helped design the railroads of New England. His mother posed for his most famous painting, *Arrangement in Grey and Black*.

The Shaker villages in Enfield and Canterbury, New Hampshire, are additional historical properties and tourist destinations. Enfield's last ten Believers moved to the Canterbury site in 1923. That community survived until its last Shaker sister in residence died in 1992. Today the only active Shaker settlement is located in Sabbathday Lake, Maine.

Manchester is now the largest city in New Hampshire, with a 2010 census population tally of 109, 565. The Amoskeag Manufacturing Company, the major clothing mill in the city, went bankrupt in 1935. But the distinctive brick buildings in Manchester's downtown area are a joy to behold, for they have been restored and repurposed. Down the river in Lowell (population 105,167), some of the old mill buildings have been preserved as an historic site dedicated to the textile industry. Lowell also celebrates the life of native son Jack Kerouac.

A union railroad station was built in Boston in the early 1890s. It was called North Station, and it eliminated the need for multiple depots on Causeway Street. That building was torn down in 1928 to make way for the Boston Garden, an indoor arena which embraced the station as part of its design. Today's renovated North Station shares its footprint with the TD Garden, as the facility is now named. Anyone attending a concert or witnessing a Celtics or Bruins game can afterward ride right down an escalator and grab the next train home. If you miss the last departure just after midnight, you might find yourself in the same predicament as Henry Thoreau and Horace Mann, Jr., did. You'll have to wait for hours for the early morning train.

I felt as though I was perched upon a wrinkle in time, embracing two eras at once. I found a small concrete rise to rest on for the moment. Its position was at the eastern end of the platform of the present-day train station in White River Junction, Vermont. Here tracks led in all four cardinal directions. I sat with my back to the Connecticut River and I watched. There was much to see.

To my left, people were waiting with quiet expectation. They stared at the westbound tracks, which glistened in the fall morning sunlight. Expensive cameras were poised at the ready. Some folks walked to the far side of the rails, studying possible photographic angles. Except for a few whispered comments, no one spoke. Yet the very air was weighed down by the fact that something important was about to happen here.

To my right, families were gleefully and noisily boarding the cars of the Green Mountain Railroad. The excursion train was scheduled to take them on a short ride north along the Connecticut River and then to return the same way. It was a bustling, merry scene. The green and gold GMR engine tooted its high-pitched horn. Last-minute tourists scampered up the steps. As a nearby clock struck 11 a.m., the engine began to roar, and it slowly pulled them all away. A few folks took pictures. Some waved to the riders. They knew they would all be back in an hour.

Simultaneously at the far intersection, the automatic warning bells began to ding. The red lights flashed. One-armed guard gates dropped on either side of the tracks. A different roar came from the west. Then we heard the standard two-tone call: two long whistles, one short, another long. Around the curve came a sleek Amtrak silver bullet. Shutters clicked as the rail fans around me took action shots of a real-life train doing real-time work. The engine eased up; and with steel wheels a-squeaking, it came to its stop at the station.

Suddenly surfacing were a few travelers with bags and suitcases, hugging friends and relatives before they embarked for places unknown. Springfield, Hartford, New York City. They had business or personal commitments elsewhere. White River Junction was just their starting point today. They made their goodbyes in English or in French, and they climbed into the cars. A glimpse of movement behind the tinted windows was all we could catch of them inside. The blue-suited conductor looked around for stragglers, and then pulled himself up as well. Without much fanfare at all, the gray machine inched away: a metallic caterpillar of five passenger cars with an engine at each end, the better to climb those New England mountains. The train turned south, following the natural valley of the Connecticut River. Everyone watched until it disappeared from view. Then the show was over. The rail fans walked away with satisfaction on their faces. The luckiest ones had gotten a few good photographs from the encounter.

It was September 12, 2009, and I was in White River Junction to attend The Glory Days of the Railroad Festival. This event is held on the second Saturday in September. It was my third time here in the past six years; and it was one of my favorite places to visit. Here the White River flows into the Connecticut River. Streets and parking lots were filled with just as many vehicles from New Hampshire as from Vermont. The village itself had an atmosphere that alternated between trendy and traditional, with New Age kinds of businesses renting spaces in historic brick buildings. But today the railroads were the focus.

The downtown area was cordoned off to accommodate vendors and displays. A large tent acted as an impromptu amphitheater with stage and seating. A variety of local musical groups performed there throughout the day. Old-fashioned engineer hats were the fashion norm, for anyone of any age. The train station itself was packed full, as people bought tickets for the Green Mountain excursions or examined the memorabilia in the building. Some explored the 1892 Boston & Maine Locomotive 494 that loomed nearby. There were kid-friendly activities and a variety of food choices. The festival gets bigger every year. I always learn something from a railroader or happen upon new information just by walking around White River Junction.

This day I chatted with Kenneth Cushing, who was writing a history of the Northern Railroad in New Hampshire. We soon realized that our research covered some of the same ground, literally. Kenneth's display included a map with vintage photos of all of the original stations along the Northern route. I asked him if any of those buildings survived from the year 1861; and after some thought, his reply was a sad "No." I guess there was no need for me to go looking for them myself, then. Not only had the track been pulled up; but the stations where Henry and Horace's express train stopped were gone as well. For that reason, it was wonderful that Kenneth was assembling the historical details and relevant images. I anticipated reading his finished book someday.

Stephen Flanders stepped up to join in our conversation. "Those tracks should never have been removed," he told us. Steve was the treasurer of the New Hampshire Railroad Revitalization Association. From him I found out about the initiatives to restore passenger rail service across the river: from Concord to Lowell and thus on to Boston; and also from where we were standing to New Hampshire's state capital. The latter would mean reconstructing the old Northern line and finding a way for rail-trail users and locomotives to share adjacent lanes. That sounded like a real challenge to me. I was glad I didn't have to be the one to figure out that compromise. But I was heartened to learn that rail travel was not considered to be ancient history to the people of New Hampshire.

During my first Glory Days visit back in 2004, I participated in as many of the activities as I could. I was searching for some Thoreauvian (and Mannly) connection, as usual. I took the Green Mountain Railroad excursion that rattled along the Connecticut River. It was a leisurely ride through a beautiful landscape. It was enjoyable and reminiscent of older days. But it hadn't been quite what I was looking for.

I also rode in an odd contraption—a 1930 Reo Rail Bus—across the otherwise abandoned railroad bridge to West Lebanon, N.H., the town right across the water. The hybrid vehicle ran quietly and looked like something that belonged on a highway: but with steel-rimmed wheels instead of tires and a cow catcher instead of a front grill. On the other side, we wound through old rail yards and headed under a bridge that carried NH Route 12A over us. The driver pointed out the numbers painted vertically on one of the metal bridge supports: 148 / 76. "148 rail miles to Boston," he said. (And probably 76 miles to Concord, N.H.) That's when I got a little shiver. Henry and Horace had 148 miles to go on that day when their express train came through here. They traveled on this very rail bed and over the timbers of the same Connecticut River bridge that we just did. *This* was it. What might look like random numbers painted on a post became my personal link to the past, to 1861, and to the two Concord men who rode through here, on their way back home.

Any time I return to the area of White River Junction and West Lebanon, I find a way to revisit the bridge support with the numbers painted on it. The festival line-up usually includes an unusual rail conveyance that will take you for a ride over the river to the New Hampshire side. That is a good way to see "148.76." I always smile, take additional photos, and think of Henry Thoreau and young Horace Mann, with still many miles ahead of them.

In each season, there are interesting experiences to be had in White River Junction. But if you need a specific reason to visit, The Glory Days of the Railroad Festival in September is a good one.

WHEN YOU GO: Today a drive from Ogdensburg to Boston is tedious at best. Contemporary riders who take a stab at the journey will no doubt end up just as weary as Henry and Horace must have grown. But the scenery is always well worth the trip.

Take NY Route 68 East from Ogdensburg to Canton; then follow U.S. Route 11 across the breadth of northernmost New York. The trip will take between two and a half and three hours. You can listen to French radio stations from Quebec the whole length of the roadway if you wish. The old Northern Railroad grade lies on the north side of the road at first. Even if you don't seek it out, you'll see a perfect example of a remnant on the western edge of the village of Brushton. There a homeowner has made the most of the old Northern infrastructure, as an invisible rail bridge spans Farrington Brook. The original stonework of the bridge abutments has been woven into some elaborate landscaping. Thoreau and Mann passed over that creek before any of those houses were built. A starch factory sat in their place, as noted by a metal historical marker.

If you want to make a side trip to the John Brown farm near Lake Placid, you can turn south onto NY Route 30 at Malone. Hook up with NY Route 86 to drive through Saranac Lake and then Lake Placid. Remember that you'll be driving through the Adirondack Mountains for 56 miles each way. Pay attention to the weather conditions.

At Rouse's Point, use U.S. Route 2 and VT Route 78 to enter Vermont and hitch up with I-89, which leads all the way to Concord, N.H. The two bridges heading east are very road-like and easy to drive across. The Vermont Central tracks parallel the roadway in several sections and then leave it to trace the courses of the Winooski and White Rivers. Sure, you could take some smaller routes through the valleys in order to find the rails more often. But if you choose to do that, you truly won't be able to see the forest for the trees. I recommend sticking with I-89 to drive south and east across Vermont. Only then will you be able to appreciate the grandeur of the Green Mountains. A brief diversion to the Ben & Jerry's Ice Cream Factory in Collegeville, just north of Waterbury, may be in order, however. Also note that a few miles northwest of White River Junction, the Appalachian Trail crosses the interstate, the river, and the railroad line.

In New Hampshire, the abandoned line of the old Northern Railroad lies well north of I-89. U.S. Route 4 follows it more intimately than the interstate does. At Boscawen, switch to U.S. Route 3. Take U.S. Route 3A or I-93 from Concord to Manchester. Then return to U.S. Route 3 at least as far as Lowell. From there to Boston? Well, it's a complicated and congested drive, even if you're not trying to follow a set of railroad tracks. Thoreau and Mann's express train passed through North Billerica, Haverhill, Woburn, and West Medford before arriving in Boston. You might be able to figure out a mirror route with various roads if you have a good road atlas with you. But by car the easier plan is to take Route 3 to I-95 north and I-93 south and into the city.

Only two portions of Henry and Horace's ride can be duplicated on the rails themselves. The first is across Vermont via Amtrak, from St. Albans to White River Junction. The other is from Lowell to Boston via the MBTA's Lowell line.

⁀≋

FOR MORE INFORMATION

Amtrak, www.amtrak.com

Canterbury Shaker Village, Canterbury, NH 03224. Phone (603) 783-9511. www.shakers.org.

Daniel Webster Birthplace, Franklin, NH www.nhstateparks.org/state-parks/alphabetical-order/daniel-webster-birthplace.

Enfield Shaker Museum, 24 Caleb Dyer Lane, Enfield, NH 03748. Phone (603) 632-4346. www.shakermuseum.org

Glory Days of the Railroad Festival, Hartford Parks & Recreation Department, 171 Bridge Street, White River Junction, VT 05001. www.glorydaysoftherailroad.org

Greater Boston Convention & Visitors Bureau, 2 Copley Place, Suite 105, Boston, MA 02116. Phone (800) 888-5515. www.bostonusa.com

Greater Merrimack Valley Convention and Visitors Bureau, 9 Central Street, Suite 201, Lowell, MA 01852. Phone (978) 459-6150. www.merrimackvalley.org

Green Mountain National Forest, 231 North Main Street, Rutland, VT 05701. Phone (802) 747-6700.

John Brown Farm, 115 John Brown Road, Lake Placid,, NY 12946-3248. Phone (518) 523-3900. www.nps.gov/history/nR/travel/underground/ny4.htm

Lake Champlain Regional Chamber of Commerce, 60 Main Street, Suite 100, Burlington, VT 05401. Phone (802) 863-3489. www.vermont.org

Lowell National Historical Park, 67 Kirk Street, Lowell, MA 01852-1029. Phone (978) 970-5000. www.nps.gov/LOWE/index.htm

Manchester Historic Association, 129 Amherst Street, Manchester, NH. Phone (603) 622-7531. www.manchesterhistoric.org.

Massachusetts Bay Transportation Authority, 10 Park Plaza, Suite 3910, Boston, MA 02116. www.mbta.com.

New Hampshire Office of Travel and Tourism, PO Box 1856, Concord, NH 03302. Phone (800) 386-4664. www.visitnh.gov

Pierce Manse, 14 Horse Shoe Pond Road, Concord, NH. www.politicallibrary.org/Pierce-Manse/Visit.aspx

St. Lawrence Chamber of Commerce, 101 Main Street, Canton, NY 13617-1248. Phone (877) 228-7810. northcountryguide.com/

Vermont Department of Tourism and Marketing, 134 State Street, Montpelier, VT 05602. Phone (800) 828-5980. www.vermontvacation.com

Whistler House Museum of Art, 243 Worthen Street, Lowell, MA 01852-1822. Phone (978) 452-7641. www.whistlerhouse.org

RECOMMENDED READING

In the "Wednesday" chapter of *A Week on the Concord and Merrimack Rivers*, Thoreau describes the mills of Manchester, New Hampshire, circa 1839. He describes his 1850 trip north through Vermont and over Lake Champlain in the "Concord to Montreal" chapter of *A Yankee in Canada*. Both texts can be found online and in various print editions.

NOTES ON THIS CHAPTER

As with the travel section covered in the previous chapter, a total reconstruction of this day's journey had to be devised from a variety of sources. My theory is that Henry and Horace left Ogdensburgh on the 4 a.m. express train to Boston on July 10, 1861. That summer's railroad schedule booklet did not mention such a service. But ads for it appeared in both the Burlington (Vt.) *Free Press* and the *St. Lawrence Republican and Ogdensburgh Weekly Journal.* The timing makes sense, given the other factors mentioned in the previous chapter. And the fact that the men bought a berth says to me they knew the trip would be seamless and long.

But what railroad lines did that express train follow? This time the printed schedules helped define them as: the Northern Railroad; the Vermont Central; the Northern (N.H.) Railroad; the Concord, Manchester & Lawrence Railway; and the Boston & Lowell Railroad. If the travelers had had an opportunity to leave the express, they might have been able to land in Concord a day earlier. They might have been able to take a line like the Worcester & Nashua from the town of Nashua to Groton Junction (now known as Ayer), and then ride the Fitchburg Railroad to Concord. But this time one of Horace's letters provides a clue. While the two men were steaming across Lake Michigan on the *Edith*, Horace wrote to his mother that the tickets they had just bought to Boston included stops in "Goderich, Stratford, Ogdensburg, Rouse's Point, Vermont Central R.R. and Lowell." The mention of Lowell seals the deal. They evidently had to use the Boston & Lowell Railroad, which led them directly to Boston without a chance of diversion to Concord on that same day.

Additional railroad history for this section was found in Alvin F. Harlow's *Steelways of New England* (New York: Creative Age Press, Inc., 1946) as well as Robert M. Lindsell's *The Rail Lines of Northern New England: A Handbook of Railroad History* (Pepperell, Mass.: Branch Line Press, 2000). Harlow described the Fitchburg station in Boston as "a granite Norman castle." He also reported on the Jenny Lind concerts held there. *Mapping Boston* (ed. by Alex Krieger and David Cobb with Amy Turner. Cambridge, Mass.: MIT Press, 1999) helped to pinpoint the exact locations of the railroad lines and stations over the course of many decades.

Statistics and details about the Enfield and Canterbury Shaker settlements again come from Priscilla J. Brewer's *Shaker Communities, Shaker Lives* (Hanover, N.H.: University Press of New England, 1986). Additional information about Enfield was found on the museum's web page, "Enfield Shaker Village History," at http://www.shakermuseum.org/history.htm. The Canterbury Shaker Village web site, http://www.shakers.org, was helpful as well.

Thoreau's quote about the French Canadians and the "invisible barrier" between the countries is found in the "Concord to Montreal" chapter of *A Yankee in Canada*, as is his description of Lake Champlain.

The courting of Thoreau's Aunt Louisa by Daniel Webster is found on pages 21 and 22 of Walter Harding's *The Days of Henry Thoreau* (New York: Dover Publications, 1982). Thoreau's quote about Webster being the maker of the Fugitive Slave Law is found in his essay "Slavery in Massachusetts." His Webster quote from *Walden; or, Life in the Woods* is in the "Conclusion" chapter.

Information about Franklin Pierce's activities in the early days of the Civil War came from

Peter A. Wallner's biography *Franklin Pierce: Martyr for the Union* (Concord, N.H.: Plaidswede Publishing, 2007).

The librarians at the Manchester City Library let me know that the 1860 census figure for Manchester's population was 20,107. Thoreau's comment about nature someday reclaiming the Billerica dam comes from the "Saturday" chapter of *A Week on the Concord and Merrimack Rivers*. The disparagement about how mills are run appears in the "Economy" chapter of *Walden*.

It was in a letter to Harrison Gray Otis Blake, dated January 1, 1859, that Henry Thoreau extolled the virtues of the Fitchburg station in Boston. The text appears as Letter Forty-one in *Letters to a Spiritual Seeker* (ed. by Bradley P. Dean, New York: W. W. Norton, 2004).

Notices about the accidental burning of Frances Appleton Longfellow appeared in the July 10, 1861, issues of the *Boston Journal* and the *Boston Transcript*. The stories were reprinted in the *Worcester Daily Spy* on July 11, 1861.

Travel Chapter 19

Thursday, July 11, 1861
Boston to Concord
via the Fitchburg Railroad

Expenses: Fare to Concord, $1.10.

After spending the night in a Boston train station, Henry Thoreau and Horace Mann, Jr., were finally able to cover the last twenty miles of their two-month Journey West today. They probably took the first train the Fitchburg Railroad had to offer. It left Boston at 7:30 a.m.

This was a familiar trip for Thoreau. He had ridden over these tracks a number of times since the railroad had first reached Concord in June 1844. That was the summer before he moved to the pond. He knew the stops along the way: Charlestown, Somerville, Waverly, Waltham (the only station they would stop at that morning), Weston, and Lincoln. He knew what to look for, once the cars coasted past the Lincoln platform. He could watch the next two miles of rolling landscape slip past the window, and then—there, through the trees! A glimpse of water, glistening with the morning sunlight.

> Why, here is Walden, the same woodland lake that I discovered so many years ago; where a forest was cut down last winter another is springing up by its shore as lustily as ever; the same thought is welling up to its surface that was then; it is the same liquid joy and happiness to itself and its Maker, ay, and it may be to me. It is the work of a brave man surely, in whom there was no guile! He rounded this water with his hand, deepened and clarified it in his thought, and in his will bequeathed it to Concord. I see by its face that it is visited by the same reflection; and I can almost say, Walden, is it you?

> It is no dream of mine,
> To ornament a line;
> I cannot come nearer to God and Heaven
> Than I live to Walden even.

I am its stony shore,
And the breeze that passes o'er;
In the hollow of my hand
Are its water and its sand,
And its deepest resort
Lies high in my thought.

The cars never pause to look at it; yet I fancy that the engineers and firemen and brakemen, and those passengers who have a season ticket and see it often, are better men for the sight. The engineer does not forget at night, or his nature does not, that he has beheld this vision of serenity and purity once at least during the day. Though seen but once, it helps to wash out [Boston's] State Street and the engine's soot. One proposes that it be called "God's Drop."

The trees around the pond were in full leaf. Thoreau had missed his favorite places pass through the noticeable growth and greening that came with late spring and early summer. Nature was almost at her height for the year, and he had not witnessed her climb. At least, not here, at home.

While he sometimes found fault with his hometown and with its residents, it must have been heartening for Thoreau to see Concord come into view once again. With a population of just over twenty-two hundred, the town was tiny in comparison to some of the communities he had seen in his

The old Fitchburg Railroad line is now used by the Massachusetts Bay Transit Authority. Many times a day, commuters can get a glimpse of Walden Pond from their train seats.

travels. That number was dwindling a bit. Some of the young men had left town wearing the colors of the Union army. The four Melvin brothers were among them. And before the month was over, Concordians would learn that a few of their native sons had been engaged in a battle at a little stream in Virginia called Bull Run. Some of them would not return.

The adults were keeping busy in the meantime. Ralph Waldo Emerson gave a lecture the previous evening at Tufts College on Walnut Hill in Medford. His topic was "Celebration of the Intellect," in which he advised school officials and students to stay true to their tasks in the midst of war. "The brute noise of cannon has, I know, a most poetic echo in these days when it is an instrument of freedom and the primal sentiments of humanity," he said. But work on the campus was just as valuable as that on the battlefield, if not more, he insisted. "Against the heroism of soldiers I set the heroism of scholars, which consists in ignoring the other. You shall not put up in your Academy the statue of Caesar or Pompey, of Nelson or Wellington, of Washington or Napoleon, of Garibaldi, but of Archimedes, of Milton, of Newton." His words could have been taken as quite controversial. The boys in his audience could just as easily have found themselves fighting and dying in skirmishes south of the Mason-Dixon line; and not in reading and writing and listening to professors ramble on for hours in the halls of an academy safely situated on a hill within sight of Boston harbor.

But perhaps Mr. Emerson was not addressing that group at all. He may have instead been speaking directly to his own seventeen-year-old son Edward, who might even have been in attendance. Back in May, "Eddy" eagerly worked out with the Concord "drill club," a handful of men and boys that met every morning at the armory to practice at soldiering. In June, they had to reluctantly relinquish all of their guns to genuine enlistees. The club dissolved, even though some of the participants were so consumed with their duty that they wanted to keep practicing without real-life weapons. But something else happened in the intervening months, while Henry and Horace were on the road. Someone talked to Eddy, or some change came about that made him consider his life in a different light. On the day of Thoreau and Mann's return, Edward Waldo Emerson was very likely hitting the books instead of shouldering a rifle. He was due to take his examinations for entrance into Harvard College in just a few days.

Down the road at Orchard House, Bronson Alcott was tending his garden. Earlier in the summer he had planted a variety of goodies there, including potatoes, sweet corn, beans, and cucumbers. As was his wont, Bronson explained his task in philosophic terms in his journal. "The mind needs to come into tender relations with the earth and treat that most intimate of all spots with something akin to piety, since a personal presence is diffused through every part of it, and divinity there awaits to meet us always." Put more simply: the Transcendentalist was finding God in his vegetables.

From time to time, Alcott would run into Nathaniel Hawthorne, his reclusive next-door neighbor:

> Find him walking on his hill-top. He says he can think of nothing but the state of the country. He wishes to go to the seaside and recruit for a month or more; says he likes Concord as well as any place to live in, but remembers London with pride and could spend his life there delightfully. Wonders if some means cannot be devised to bring us oftener together, and seems to feel the want of more society than he has here.

But if Hawthorne longed for personal interaction, he did so only on his own terms. He had just outfitted the Wayside with additional rooms—some with the express purpose of offering various escape routes if unwanted visitors should stop by the house. Now he could retreat to his "sky parlor," the tower that rose as a single third-story room above the original roofline. There he could write without interruption. And though its windows offered an inspirational view of the meadows across the street, Hawthorne deliberately turned his back to them. He had developed this technique years earlier when he and his bride Sophia Peabody moved into the Old Manse, close to where the North Bridge once spanned the Concord River. Hawthorne found it best to stand at a slanted desktop, facing a wall, to pen his stories.

That spring the women of Concord had been "sewing violently on patriotic blue shirts," as twenty-eight-year-old Louisa May Alcott wrote to a distant correspondent. She herself would rather be writing. "I lay down my needle & take up my pen with great inward contentment, the first article being my abomination & the last my delight." She had watched her neighbors practicing for war.

> Edward Emerson has a company of "Concord Cadets" who poke each others eyes out, bang their heads & blow themselves up with gunpowder most valiantly & will do good service by & by I've no doubt if there is anything left of them when ordered to the field.

Even as she made fun of the boys at their game, she longed to join it. She understood too what options she was limited to, simply by gender. "Are you going to have a dab at the saucy Southerners?" she asked a male friend. "I long to fly at some body & free my mind on several points, but there is no opening for me at present so I study Dr Home on 'Gun shot wounds,' & get my highly connected self ready to go as a nurse when the slow coaches at Washington begin to lay about them & get their fellow men into a comfortably smashed condition." Like Edward, Louisa was studying for her future.

None of their friends or relatives knew exactly when Henry David Thoreau and Horace Mann, Jr., would be returning. So in all likelihood, no one greeted them at the station when their train arrived at 8:23 a.m. The two men gathered up their belongings one last time and stepped down from their railroad car. Perhaps a few personal words were exchanged, as well as a clap or two about the shoulders, and then they parted. Constant companions, no more.

Young Horace may have scampered that last block down Sudbury Road, eager to share the stories of his adventures with his brothers and his mother. Henry may have watched him go. Then the older man had to turn and walk in the opposite direction. He had been to The West. He had traveled thousands of miles and had seen many wonders. Now he was back home. And he no doubt realized how much work he had left to do.

Today the Fitchburg Railroad line belongs to the MBTA, the Massachusetts Bay Transit Authority. Both commuters and long-distance travelers use it to get from one place to another. Trains pass the western edge of Walden Pond several times each day.

The population of Concord is now about eight times greater than it was in Thoreau's day: with 17,668 residents counted in the 2010 census. Five Concordians were killed in the first battle at Bull Run, near Manassas, Virginia. Perhaps no other family in town suffered more loss during the Civil War than the Melvins. Asa, John, and Samuel Melvin were members of Company K of the First Massachusetts Heavy Artillery. All gave their lives in service to the Union cause. James C. Melvin, their surviving brother, commissioned Concord sculptor Daniel Chester French to craft a memorial to honor them. French's "Mourning Victory" still stands watch over their graves at a curve in the lane in Sleepy Hollow Cemetery.

On July 14 and 15, Edward Waldo Emerson (1844-1930) took his examinations for Harvard College. The next day brought the news that he was formally accepted into the school. He graduated from the college in 1866, and then went on to study at Harvard Medical School. He got his medical degree in 1874. He married Concordian Annie Shepard Keyes, and they had six children. Edward was one of the first people to edit his father's journals for posthumous publication.

Ralph Waldo Emerson (1803-1882) continued to lecture steadily for several years. He wrote a book of poetry and two other volumes over the course of the next two decades. In 1867, he received a Doctor of Letters degree from Harvard. "Bush," the stately Emerson home, caught fire on July 24, 1872. The people of Concord worked together to drag many possessions outside to safety, but portions of the structure were gutted. The Emersons were forced to move temporarily to the Old Manse. Waldo and his daughter Ellen made an extensive tour of Europe and Egypt soon afterward. When they returned in May 1873, they were astonished to learn that friends had restored "Bush" in their absence. They had come home to a warm, town-wide welcome. But by then the man whose words had inspired many of the Transcendentalists was beginning to show the symptoms of what we now recognize as Alzheimer's disease. His public appearances gradually diminished.

Louisa May Alcott (1832-1888) was persistent in her intention to serve as a nurse during the Civil War. In December 1862, she was finally accepted by the Union Hotel Hospital in Georgetown, near Washington, D.C. Her tenure there was unfortunately brief. By January 1863, Louisa had fallen ill with typhoid pneumonia. She was treated in the manner of the day: with regular doses of mercurous chloride, then known as calomel. She suffered from the poisonous aftereffects for the rest of her life. But she wrote *Hospital Sketches* about her experience; and the book helped her make her mark as a writer. In 1868-1869, she released the two parts of a novel for girls called *Little Women*. With its success and that of subsequent episodes, she helped support the entire Alcott family.

Bronson Alcott (1799-1888) served as the superintendent of the schools in Concord through the year 1865. He was known for submitting exceedingly lengthy and preachy school reports. His other publications included *Concord Days*, a memoir. What he is most remembered for is the creation of the Concord School of Philosophy, which ran from 1879-1888. During its second year, he had a wooden chapel-like school built on the Orchard House property. Educators, authors, and philosophers came from all over the country to attend its sessions. The structure remains standing and is still used for special programs today.

Nathaniel Hawthorne (1804-1864) worked on and published several additional short stories. His book *Our Old Home* came out in 1863. The following year he was already in poor health when he embarked on an extensive carriage ride throughout New Hampshire with his old college friend, Franklin Pierce. Hawthorne died during the trip, leaving his beloved Sophia to take care of their three children: Una, Julian, and Rose, all young adults.

During Thoreau's lifetime, no bridge spanned the Concord River at the point where the first battle of the American Revolution was fought. The Old North Bridge had been removed in 1793, and it was not replaced until 1875. In the first line of his "Concord Hymn," Ralph Waldo Emerson referred to the original structure as "rude." That one adjective reflected the simple construction of a series of wooden planks with no permanent stonework in place for support, except at each shoreline. The bridge that stands there today is a recent replacement and was installed just a few years ago.

In spite of the reputation Thoreau unduly gave it, Walden Pond and its surrounding acreage are far more wooded today than they ever were when he lived there. The place that he made famous has an even more intricate and busy history than he might have imagined. An amusement park was built adjacent to the railroad line in the mid-1860s. Excursion trains brought visitors from Boston and other cities, and dropped them off right by the water's edge. After that site burned down and was abandoned in 1902, the evolution of the automobile led even more people to the pond. Ownership of the property eventually transferred from individual families to the state. Intrusions from encroaching development have been fought on a regular basis by conservationists and followers of Henry Thoreau. Today Walden Pond State Reservation is managed by Massachusetts' Department of Conservation and Recreation. Hikers, fishermen, long-distance swimmers, and sun bathers can be found there almost every day of the year.

Henry Thoreau may have been writing to just H.G.O. Blake when he extended his famous invitation in 1857: "Come & be Concord, as I have been Worcestered." But each year during the second week of July, a hundred or more people from around the world answer that old summons. They converge on Concord.

The Annual Gathering of The Thoreau Society takes place on the weekend closest to Henry's birthday, July 12. The four-day conference attracts a wide range of followers: academics, fans, practitioners, students, teachers, even curious walk-ins. Some admire Thoreau for his writing, some for his philosophies, and some for his approach to nature. Some are here to speak; others are here to listen. There are lectures, panel discussions, and tours around the town. You can take a guided walk to Sleepy Hollow Cemetery or go on a nature hike with some of the most knowledgeable people in the area. The event truly has something for everybody.

I remember the first time I attended an "A.G.," as we call it, back in July 2001. I was immediately impressed when I walked into the Masonic Lodge, where many of the sessions are held. A large blue and gold banner hanging on the wall of the main meeting room announced the fact that the lodge was formed by Paul Revere. You can't escape history in Concord. It's everywhere you look and wander. Sites can easily date back to before the beginning of the American Revolution and the "shot heard 'round the world," as Mr. Emerson called it. And close by will be places where the Transcendentalists formed their own quiet revolution, half a century later.

The Masonic lodge in Concord owns the building where Henry Thoreau once taught school. The Thoreau Society meets here every July, on the weekend closest to Thoreau's birthday.

The Masonic Lodge itself has Thoreauvian connections. No, Henry was not a Mason. He was not into secret societies. (He would probably be chagrined and appalled to learn of the existence of an organization based upon *him*.) But he had been inside that building. Just after he graduated from Harvard, he took on a teaching job for the town of Concord. The Center School shared the brick structure with the Masons. Thoreau taught classes in what is now the reception area, just inside the front door. He lasted only two weeks in the position before the interference of a school official appeared to constrain him in the performance of his duties. He resigned. Even so, it's a special opportunity to be able to walk where one's hero has walked. Emotions can run high here.

The conference resembles any other gathering of people who share the same interests. You meet new people, and you discover that you speak the same language. You don't have to explain who Emerson and Thoreau were or what Transcendentalism might mean to you. You can throw into casual conversation phrases like "living deliberately," "different drummer," or even "transparent eyeball," and know that your companion will probably understand the reference without question. You don't have to explain why you are here. Your presence is explanation enough.

But if you want to vocalize your reasons, you can. One question that is frequently heard is: "How did you come to Thoreau?" That's the opener for which everyone has a story. Like me, many people were impressed after reading "Civil Disobedience" or passages from *Walden* in high school English classes. Some came upon him in college; others, in adulthood. Some read Emerson first and were led from The Great Man to his protégé and immediately found the kindred spirit they were searching for all along. The tales vary in origin and in substance, but they all share a common ending. Somehow in the aftermath, Thoreau's words and deeds changed their own lives. Hence, the need to be in Concord and in the company of others who feel the same way. In that manner, we follow in the historic and esteemed footsteps of Calvin H. Greene and Dr. Samuel Arthur Jones of Michigan, of the Rev. Robert Collyer and B. B. Wiley of Chicago, of Mary Newbury Adams of Dubuque, and of John Muir of California.

The 2009 Annual Gathering was a great time to reconnect with old friends. Ed Schofield was conducting a session about the ecology of Walden Pond and Walden Woods. Dale Schwie was busy with society board duties: helping with registration and the introductions of speakers. Historical interpreter Richard Smith was in attendance and at some point would be donning the garb and persona of Henry Thoreau. I got the chance to chat privately with each one of them and with other Thoreauvian friends over the course of the weekend. The e-mails we exchanged throughout the rest of the year just could not compare with real-life, face to face talk.

That A.G. marked the fifth year that I led the Memorial Walk around Walden Pond on the Saturday morning of the conference. This tradition was begun by J. Parker Huber in 1996, as a way to pay tribute to Walter Harding (1917-1996). Harding had been one of the founders of The Thoreau Society and had served as its secretary and newsletter editor for fifty years. His *The Days of Henry Thoreau: A Biography* remained one of the foundation sources of information about the man. Every Thoreau researcher who followed Walter Harding owed him a debt of gratitude for the sheer volume and the meticulous details that characterized his body of work. The members of the organization wanted a symbolic activity to remember their valued colleague.

Parker originally framed the walk in the spirit of the Eastern practice of *Pradakshina*, which was a way of honoring someone or something by walking around it, clockwise. By making a left turn at the beach house and by keeping the water to our right for the duration of the hike, we paid our respects to Walden Pond and whatever it represented to us. The act was specifically dedicated to the memories of Walter Harding and Henry Thoreau. Individual participants were able to additionally walk for anyone else they had in mind. Coincidentally, this circling mirrored the old New England town government requirement of "circumambulating the bounds." Every few years, officials from each town had to physically walk around their town borders, confirming that the lines were still somehow intact. Surveyor Henry Thoreau had accompanied area selectmen on some of those saunters.

This time, about a dozen people showed up at the Thoreau house replica near the parking lot just after a park employee unlocked the gate at 7 a.m. The early hour limited the number of walkers who arrived, as did the fact that the entire trip would be performed in thoughtful silence. But before we started, we fanned out into a circle. We went around and introduced ourselves, noted what watershed we lived in, and named the person(s) we were dedicating our walk to. Since we had a slightly larger group this time, it took a while for everyone to share their information. And then we were off, with me leading the single file line. To the long-distance swimmers and the joggers that we passed and nodded to along the way, we must have resembled a human embodiment of Robert McCloskey's *Make Way for Ducklings*.

Around the pond we went, surefooted and without speaking.

Each year the walk is different. Oh, the path is the same; but the experience itself can vary greatly. I try to watch for animal life as I go. Being quiet and at the head of the pack often gives me an undue advantage to come upon unsuspecting creatures. Sometimes little birds dart through the brush next to us. Sometimes chipmunks chase one another nearly underneath our feet. One year, the pond's resident red-tailed hawk landed in a tree right above us and screeched at us. It was a spine-chilling sound, on that warm summer morning. And even though we are really marching only a few feet away from one another on that trail, each participant has a unique experience. I am amazed by what some of them tell me they saw or felt, after we return to the parking lot, an hour later.

I also steal deliberate glances at Walden Pond, always to the right. I am reminded of two quotes from Thoreau's *Walden*. I can see exactly what he meant when he wrote: "Walden is blue at one time and green at another, even from the same point of view. Lying between the earth and the heavens, it partakes of the color of both." What Thoreau put in more poetic terms was that the water reflects whatever it can: either the surrounding trees or the sky. And he was absolutely right. And if I see clouds "in" the water, I think of another passage from the book: "Heaven is under our feet as well as over our heads." He was looking at a frozen surface when he wrote those words. But that sentence and its sentiment can apply to almost anything we see while we are walking in the woods.

As I approached the western edge of the pond, I began to wonder about trains. I never check the MBTA schedule before the walk, and I don't wear a watch. But I always hope that for the sake of the other walkers behind me, we somehow end up near the tracks when a commuter goes rattling past. I began to listen intently, hoping to hear a distant rumble. I smiled and was nearly giddy with joy when my ears caught a faint, low roar. Was I imagining it? No. It was getting louder and closer. I slowed down my pace. Our entire line happened to be standing on the glacial ridge between the pond and the railroad tracks. I came to a halt and held up my hand to tell everyone else to stop as well. And then it came, with its silver double-decker cars shining in the sun, speeding past us, carrying folks from the outland into the big city of Boston. Each section boldly proclaimed in purple and gold letters that the train offered free WIFI to its riders. Once again I felt as though I was standing on a wrinkle in time. To be perched between Walden Pond and wireless Internet service! Surely, Life couldn't get much weirder than that.

When we got to the site where Thoreau's small house once stood, we each found a personal place for contemplation. I had warned the group that we would do this. Each walker could spend as much time as he or she wished on what we considered to be sacred ground. The trail back to the parking lot was easy enough for even a newcomer to find and follow.

We spread out. Still, no one spoke. We could hear the blue jays and crows and other birds in the trees high above us. The sound of rustling leaves led my eyes to the gray flurry of a squirrel, busy in its search for treasures, ignoring us. In the ever-present background was the white noise of traffic on nearby MA Route 2. Someone walked over to stand in the invisible door-way of the cabin, to look toward the water and see the view that greeted Henry every morning. Others placed stones from home on the large memorial cairn. A few people took the time to read the informational signs posted by the park service. The wooden placard next to the cairn had been recently refurbished. In bold white letters it proclaimed: "I went to the woods because I wished to live deliberately." The words seemed to pose a silent challenge to us in return. "Why are *you* here? What are *you* doing with *your* lives, anyway?"

I paid my respects and saw all I needed to see, so I began to saunter back to the beach and parking lot. Along the way I reached out and squeezed a leaf of sweet-fern as I passed a patch of it. I held my fingers to my nose and inhaled the delicious, heady aroma. I learned to do that while walking behind Parker Huber during my first years at the Gathering. I have made a point of imitating him ever since. I silently showed the leaves to the walker behind me, and he smiled and nodded in return. He was familiar with the plant and knew what it smelled like, too.

Back at the parking lot, I finally had a chance to chat with my fellow walkers. Everyone had had a different experience, and it was all good. They all thought I had planned ahead and had deliberately timed the walk to meet the train. I explained that it was merely a happy accident and that it had never happened before during my tenure as Memorial Walk leader. All agreed that it was a remarkable sensation.

We drove back to town to attend the society business meeting, to hear the keynote speaker, and then to have lunch. While we ate, friend Richard Smith—or, more correctly, Henry David Thoreau himself—delivered his famous speech, "A Plea for Captain John Brown" to the crowd. 2009 was the 150th anniversary of Brown's raid on Harpers Ferry, Virginia. Accordingly, our conference theme was "Social Awareness: Thoreau and the Reform Movement." Outfitted in his usual wool suit on this hot July day, "Henry" gave his fiery message to a welcoming audience. They cheered and applauded loudly at his conclusion.

Richard was one of the people I met during my first Annual Gathering, and he has been a friend ever since. Some folks look at our nametags and our surnames and mistakenly assume that we're somehow related. Other than in our devotion to Thoreau, we're not. But we're from the same age group and we share a lot of the same ideas. We laugh at the same jokes and listen to the same classic rock music.

Richard Smith first started portraying Thoreau more than ten years ago, when he was still living in his native Ohio. He had earned a degree in history from the University of Akron. He had participated in Civil War reenactments and had also been a member of the Society of Longhunters, a group who portrayed Ohio frontiersmen at the time of the American Revolution. Then in 1994, Richard took a job at Hale Farm and Village in Bath, Ohio. Introducing the interpretive technique of "living history," he became the schoolmaster for the 1840s community. He immersed himself in the literature of the day in order to more accurately depict his character. That's when he landed upon Emerson's essay "Nature" and the writings of the Transcendentalists. Reading Emerson led him to Thoreau and to *Walden*. "That was the beginning of the end for me," he admitted. "I was doomed."

He portrayed Thoreau in Ohio, and then moved to the Concord area in the late 1990s. He has been "Henry" ever since. He speaks to school groups and travels all over the country as Thoreau. On select weekends, he sits in the house replica by the Walden Pond parking lot. Unsuspecting visitors are surprised to see Henry there, writing at his desk, dressed in period clothes. He introduces himself, welcomes them into his house, and engages them in conversation. The exchange is fun and enlightening for all of the participants, on both sides of the table.

A precocious eighth grader once asked him: "Mr. Thoreau, if you knew that 150 years from now there would be a guy in Concord pretending to be you, what would you do?"

Without a second's hesitation, Richard (as Henry) answered, "I would tell him to get his own life and leave mine alone."

It's funny. Neither Richard nor I seem to have any immediate plans to heed that advice.

During the Annual Gathering, I often take a few newbies for a walk up the hill to Sleepy Hollow Cemetery. There, on Authors Ridge, lie the plots of the Thoreaus, the Hawthornes, the Alcotts, and the Emersons. Visitors will have left gifts on the graves: pine cones, rocks, acorns, letters, even coins. Henry's small stone is often piled high with such stuff this weekend.

I usually pick up a sprig of pine needles to lay before the marker. My companions follow suit.

But introducing that place to others isn't the same as being there alone, thinking and listening. This time I climbed the hill of the ridge by myself. And when the Thoreau stones came into view and my eyes caught the sight of the small one carved with the name HENRY, tears started to fall, without warning. I could barely see through them to approach the plot.

Day in and day out for many years, I had been researching and writing every move that Henry David Thoreau and Horace Mann, Jr. made during the course of their Journey West. They were thus continually alive for me. They had been my friends and my companions along the many miles of my reenactment of their adventure. I tried to see all of those places through their eyes, based upon their written words and presumed attitudes. To suddenly see the gravestone with the name HENRY on it was almost too much to bear. It brought home the fact that I knew but was not willing to remember. It turned out that he had not been with me on the trip at all. He rested here, on Authors Ridge, the entire time. Reality could be a tough concept to handle.

I did then what I had done a few months earlier, when I visited a similar stone merely marked HORACE at a cemetery sixty miles south of this site. I leaned over and put my hand on the top edge of the stone. Even in the heat of summer, the granite was cold and smooth beneath my fingers. Crying made my voice waver as I said, "I'm writing about the Journey West. Everyone will learn what happened." I waited for and received an imagined response of silent thanks. I nodded, let go, and stood up. I walked a few steps to return to the paved path, sniffling.

I quickly looked around the cemetery. Nobody else was here. I was overwhelmed and overcome. I grabbed the front of my t-shirt and sobbed into it.

WHEN YOU GO: If you study a map intently, you might be able to unravel a knot of roads that can lead you along the old Fitchburg Railroad tracks. But there's really only one authentic way to recreate this section of the Journey West. Start at Boston's North Station and board a train on the MBTA's Fitchburg line. Ride the rails from Boston to Concord. Make sure you have a seat on the right-hand (northern) side of the car. When the train leaves the Lincoln station, you should focus your complete attention to the landscape passing by your window. For a while you will see just banks of brush and trees. Without any warning at all, you'll come to a place that opens up a little, with pine trees beside the tracks and water lying beyond them. That's Walden Pond. You might even see hikers and other park visitors standing near the tracks. Then the train will duck under MA Route 2 and will soon be pulling into the Concord station.

If the weather is nice and you have the time and are wearing durable shoes, you should consider walking back to the Walden Pond State Reservation from town. Follow Thoreau Street east to Walden Street and then to the intersection of MA Route 2 and MA Route 126. Be careful crossing the lanes of traffic. Walk south along MA Route 126, and the pond will eventually be seen to your right. A trail leads around the water and to the site where Henry Thoreau once lived deliberately, in a house he built on Emerson land.

FOR MORE INFORMATION:

Concord Chamber of Commerce, 100 Main Street, Suite 310-2, Concord, MA 01742. Phone (978) 369-3120. www.concordchamberofcommerce.org

Concord Museum, 200 Lexington Road, Concord, MA 01742. Phone (978) 369-9609. www.concordmuseum.org.

Freedom's Way Heritage Area, 94 Jackson Road, Devens, MA 01434. Phone (978) 772-3654. www.freedomsway.org.

Great Meadows National Wildlife Refuge, 73 Weir Hill Road, Sudbury, MA 01776. Phone (978) 443-4661. greatmeadows.fws.gov.

Greater Merrimack Valley Convention and Visitors Bureau, 9 Central Street, Suite 201, Lowell, MA 01852. Phone (800) 443-3332. www.merrimackvalley.org.

North Bridge Visitor Center, Minute Man National Historical Park, 174 Liberty Street, Concord, MA 01742. Phone (978) 369-6993. www.nps.gov/mima.

The Old Manse, 269 Monument Street, Concord, MA 01742. Phone (978) 369-3909. www.trustees.org/pages/346_old_manse.cfm.

Orchard House, 399 Lexington Road, Concord, MA 01742. Phone (978) 369-4118. www.louisamayalcott.org.

Ralph Waldo Emerson Memorial House, 28 Cambridge Turnpike, Concord, MA 01742. Phone (978) 369-2236. rwe.org/emersonhouse/index.php.

Sleepy Hollow Cemetery, Bedford Street, Concord, MA 01742. Phone (978) 318-3233.

Walden Pond State Reservation, Route 126, Concord, MA 01742. Phone (978) 369-3254. www.mass.gov/dcr/parks/walden/index.htm

The Wayside, Minute Man National Historical Park, Lexington Road, Concord, MA 01742. Phone (978) 369-6975. www.nps.gov/mima.

RECOMMENDED READING:

The rest of *Walden*, especially the chapters "Economy," "Where I Lived, and What I Lived For," "The Village," "The Ponds," and the "Conclusion." In addition, I highly recommend learning "the rest of the story" by reading W. Barksdale Maynard's *Walden Pond: A History* (New York: Oxford University Press, 2004). Thoreau's fascination with, and immersion in, water, including Walden Pond, is detailed in Robert Lawrence France's *Thoreau on Water: Reflecting Heaven* (Boston: Houghton Mifflin, 2001), *Profitably Soaked: Thoreau's Engagement with Water* (Sheffield, Vermont: Green Frigate Books, 2003) and *Deep Immersion: The Experience of Water* (Sheffield, Vermont: Green Frigate Books, 2003).

Notes on this Chapter

As with the portions detailed in the previous two chapters, this final section of the journey has to be reconstructed from a variety of sources.

By taking the express train, Henry and Horace had ended up on the Boston & Lowell line. That means that the two men had to ride first to Boston, and then ride back out to Concord. However, no trains went back out to Concord after 8:30 p.m. The expense account lists the "Fare to Concord," which confirms the fact that no friend or relative was on hand to pick them up in Boston. The earliest train to Concord would have been at 7:30 the next morning.

Only one reliable source appears on the surface to refute my theory about Henry and Horace's schedule for the last four days of their journey. In his memoir *Henry Thoreau As Remembered By a Young Friend* (1917), Edward Waldo Emerson includes the following note on page 147:

On my birthday, in the early summer, just before I went to take my examination for Harvard, my father and mother invited Thoreau and Channing, both, but especially Thoreau, friends from my babyhood, to dine with us. When we left the table and were passing into the parlour, Thoreau asked me to come with him to our East door—our more homelike door, facing the orchard. It was an act of affectionate courtesy, for he had divined my suppressed state of mind and remembered that first crisis in his own life, and the wrench that it seemed in advance, as a gate leading out into an untried world. With serious face, but with a very quiet, friendly tone of voice, he reassured me, told me that I should be really close to home; very likely should pass my life in Concord. It was a great relief.

This is a touching and visual memory. We can see Henry Thoreau taking young Edward aside—one Harvard grad talking to a future one—and giving the boy some promise that he would survive the college experience and would someday return to his hometown. But if we take Edward at his word, we have a problem. Edward Emerson's birthday fell on July 10. If this encounter really did take place during a dinner party that day, then Thoreau would have had to have gotten back home from Minnesota by then. How is this possible?

The notion requires a bit more investigation. And we first have to consider that Edward—Dr. Emerson, by the time he wrote that book—was recalling an event that had happened more than fifty years earlier. Thoreau's words obviously made an impact on him; enough that he remembered them, many decades later. What he might not have gotten quite correct was the timing of the advice.

Primary sources like personal letters and journals unveil a different scenario. Edward's father was definitely giving a commencement speech at Tufts College on July 10, though that event may have taken place in the afternoon. Mr. Emerson might have had time to return to Concord later that same day. Edward's mother Lidian was definitely in Plymouth, visiting friends and family. She wrote her son a birthday letter from the coast and wished she could be with him on his special day. (*The Selected Letters of Lidian Jackson Emerson*, ed. by Delores Bird Carpenter. Columbia, Mo.: University of Missouri Press, 1987, p. 211.) It seems unlikely that Edward would have had a birthday party on his exact date of birth that year, without one or both of his parents present.

What could have happened instead was a celebration of his acceptance to Harvard or a bon voyage send-off before he was due to appear in Cambridge in August. Henry Thoreau would have attended such an event. And that would have been the perfect occasion for dispensing advice. In the course of my research, I thought I had uncovered an indisputable source that lent credence to such a scenario. Alas, now that I return to the topic, I cannot locate that confirmation.

But even the primary sources distort some of the facts of this time. Ralph Waldo Emerson wrote to a correspondent that "Edward is to be examined for College on Monday & Tuesday, 12 & 13 July." (*The Letters of Ralph Waldo Emerson in Six Volumes*, ed. by Ralph L. Rusk. New York: Columbia University Press, volume five, p. 250.) The trouble is that those days of the week don't correspond with those dates. Contemporary scholars figure more accurately that Edward indeed took the exams on Monday and Tuesday, which the calendar says were July 14th and 15th. He was accepted by Harvard on July 16th.

The fact that Emerson lectured at Tufts on the tenth of July is noted in Albert J. von Frank's *An Emerson Chronology* (New York: G.K. Hall & Co., 1993). The text of his speech "Celebration of the Intellect" can be found online.

Concord's "drill club" of potential soldiers who held early morning practices is mentioned in correspondence by three young women in town. Louisa May Alcott describes them in a letter dated May 19, 1861, to Alfred Whitman (in *The Selected Letters of Louisa May Alcott*, edited by Joel Myerson and Daniel Shealy. Athens, Ga.: The University of Georgia Press, 1995). Una Hawthorne writes about them in a letter to her aunt, Elizabeth Palmer Peabody, dated June 5, 1861 (*In The Wayside: Home of Authors* by Margaret M. Lothrop. New York: American Book Company, 1968.) Ellen Tucker Emerson mentions her brother's activities in a letter to Edith, dated May 10, 1861 (*In The Letters of Ellen Tucker Emerson*, edited by Edith E. W. Gregg. Kent, Ohio: The Kent State University Press, 1982).

The contents of Bronson Alcott's garden and his encounters with Nathaniel Hawthorne are found in entries in his journal for that summer. (*The Journals of Bronson Alcott*, selected and edited by Odell Shepard. Boston: Little, Brown and Company, 1938).

Louisa May Alcott's comments about the sewing and her intention to turn to war-time nursing are found in the same letter mentioned above.

Thoreau's "Walden, is it you?" quote comes from "The Ponds" chapter of *Walden*, as does the statement about the water being simultaneously blue and green. "Heaven is under our feet as well as over our heads" is found in the chapter called "The Pond in Winter."

Great Circle Sailing

To the sick the doctors wisely recommend a change of air and scenery. Thank Heaven, here is not all the world. The buckeye does not grow in New England, and the mockingbird is rarely heard here. The wild goose is more of a cosmopolite than we; he breaks his fast in Canada, takes a luncheon in the Ohio, and plumes himself for the night in a southern bayou. Even the bison, to some extent, keeps pace with the seasons, cropping the pastures of the Colorado only till a greener and sweeter grass awaits him by the Yellowstone. ... The universe is wider than our views of it.

Yet we should oftener look over the tafferel of our craft, like curious passengers, and not make the voyage like stupid sailors picking oakum. The other side of the globe is but the home of our correspondent. Our voyaging is only great-circle sailing.

—Henry David Thoreau, "Conclusion," Walden

Here we should stop Thoreau before he encourages us to become more introspective and to travel within ourselves. For while that might be a worthy trip, so too is the physical act of "great circle sailing." The phrase refers to guiding a ship across the rounded surface of our great blue marble, and carving the shortest arc between two points. Henry Thoreau and Horace Mann, Jr., did just that on their Journey West. It took steel rails, the course of the Mississippi, and several bodies of Great Lakes waters to form a safe and circuitous route between Massachusetts and Minnesota. The path was so practical that present-day highways still follow portions of it.

Regarded more than a century later, this 1861 excursion can be approached as a study in similarities and contrasts. Here were two single New England men who were interested in documenting their discoveries of nature. Both had lost their fathers two years earlier. Both had strong mothers leading supportive families. During his lifetime, each man would briefly court one woman; and after being turned down once, neither would attempt another courtship. While each was described at times as a serious individual, he was also known to have a good sense of humor and to enjoy music. And in the end, both men lost their lives to the most common disease of the nineteenth century.

On the other hand, Henry David Thoreau and Horace Mann, Jr., represent two sides of the story: a combination of the experienced man and the young disciple, of both beginnings and endings. One was a Harvard grad, who didn't much care about being one, while the other was a prospective Harvard student who would wind up working in academia. One was destined to become one of the most quoted authors in American literature, while the other would always be shadowed by his father's fame. This trip was a mere prelude for Horace, who would embark on a longer and more important journey three years later. For Henry, it was his final lengthy excursion. How prophetic it was that the last leg of it traced the path of his first important one: the trip on the Concord and Merrimack Rivers with his brother John. That adventure began it all, for it prompted his residency at Walden Pond, the writing of his two major books, and the rest of his literary career.

On the way home, Horace mailed his last letter from Mackinac Island on June 30, 1861. Henry's last note is dated July 8th in Toronto. If either man scribbled jottings after those dates, the scraps have been lost. Were they tired? Were they both ill? Were they still talking to each other by then? Had the rumblings of war forced them to take that longer, more northern route home? Were they beginning to realize, as were other Northerners, that the country's conflict would last much longer than originally expected? Was it obvious to both of them that their own journey had lasted long enough? After they stepped down from the railroad car in Concord, how often did they see one another?

Perhaps after an obligatory farewell handshake at the station, Henry and Horace followed their own roads, knowing that they were headed in very different directions.

It was immediately apparent that the journey was not as therapeutic as Thoreau's family members, friends, and doctor had hoped. Henry realized it himself. To his friend Daniel Ricketson, he wrote a few sentences about the trip, adding the comments, "I have been sick so long that I have almost forgotten what it is to be well. ... If I do not mend very quickly I shall be obliged to go to another climate again very soon." Nevertheless, he soon made a short jaunt to visit Ricketson in New Bedford, Massachusetts. There he sat for a local photographer one last time. Looking very much as he must have appeared during the excursion, Henry bore a full, grizzled beard and stared solemnly into the camera lens. His sister Sophia later described the image as "very lifelike and one of the most successful likenesses we ever saw," and one that showed "scarcely at all Henry's loss of health."

In the battle with consumption, it was the invalid's responsibility to make every attempt to get well. Failing that: the point would come when the invalid's duty was to tie up loose ends and to make appropriate preparations. Henry Thoreau clearly understood the truth of his own situation. He spent the next nine months working with his sister Sophia to firm up various essays and to assemble a few books that had been left hitherto unfinished. Bronson Alcott spent an evening with Henry in January 1862. Later he wrote that it was "sad to find him failing and feeble. ... The most he may hope for is to prepare his manuscripts for others' editing, and take his leave of them and us. I fear he has not many months to abide here." Word spread; and a number of other friends paid visits to Thoreau in his last days. Ralph Waldo Emerson and Ellery Channing stopped by on a regular basis. H.G.O. Blake and Theo Brown came from Worcester. Even his one-time jailer, Sam Staples, dropped in and later reported that he had "never spent an hour with more satisfaction. Never saw a man dying with so much pleasure and peace." After months of continuous decline, Henry David Thoreau died at home on the morning of May 6, 1862. He was forty-four years old.

Concord mourned the loss. Children were excused early from school to attend his funeral. Emerson read the eulogy. Bronson Alcott recited excerpts from Henry's writings. The choir sang a special hymn written by Channing, which began:

> Hearest thou the sobbing breeze complain
> How faint the sunbeams light the shore,—
> His heart more fixed than earth or main,
> Henry! That faithful heart is o'er.

The Hawthornes attended the services, as did Blake and Brown. Ricketson was too distraught to make the trip from New Bedford. A procession accompanied Thoreau's casket to the New Burying Ground at the foot of Bedford Street. There he was placed beside his father, his brother and his sister in the Dunbar family lot. "No truer American existed than Thoreau," Emerson lamented. "The country knows not yet, or in the least part, how great a son it has lost."

A promising botanical career and a second excursion awaited Horace Mann, Jr., as he enrolled in the Lawrence Scientific School at Harvard. He was in the right place at the right time to work closely with two of the most important scientists of his day. He first took zoology with Louis Agassiz, and then read botany with Asa Gray. Horace continued to do his best when left to his own course of study and when not forced to participate in the structure of formal classes. During his leisure time, he found rewarding work in preparing anatomical displays for Agassiz's new Museum of Comparative Zoology, and even donated specimens that he collected around his Concord home. Mary Mann recalled that at one point, the "reign of snakes was a reign of terror to the uninitiated, especially when on one occasion six or seven goodly sized ones escaped from the place of their confinement in the house and were not to be found for many days." Such occurrences were not uncommon among true nature collectors. Thoreau once wrote in his *Journal*: "That large hornets' nest which I saw on the 4th is now deserted, and I bring it home. But in the evening, warmed by my fire, two or three come forth, and crawl over it, and I make haste to throw it out the window." Sometimes it was possible to get a tad too close to nature.

In early 1864, Dr. Gray encouraged Horace to accompany another Harvard man on a scientific mission to the Sandwich (Hawaiian) Islands. William Tufts Brigham was three years older than Horace, had already earned a master's degree, and had been a museum curator of mineralogy before resigning that position in order to make the excursion. This journey was more exotic than Horace's trip to Minnesota with Thoreau. In February, Horace took a steamer from New York to Panama. He rode a train across the isthmus, and then steamed north to meet William Brigham in San Francisco. The two spent time botanizing in California and Nevada before sailing for Hawai'i, which they reached on May 5. William and Horace rented a house and spent nearly a year exploring, collecting, and documenting the natural life they found in Honolulu and on the islands. Their research added many new species of flowering plants to existing records. By all accounts, both men were in their element. Years later, William remembered that he had often seen Horace "in perfect ecstasy over the discovery of some new plant after a hard climb up some island precipice." The young man's health seemed to improve as well, which was assumed to be a result of the bracing climate and the additional time spent outdoors.

But scientific work alone did not fill their days. During their travels they met Sanford Ballard Dole, who would later become president of the Republic of Hawai'i (1894) and the first territorial governor (1900-1903). (Sanford's younger cousin, James Drummond Dole, would eventually establish Hawai'i's canned pineapple industry.) The men also dealt with banker Charles Reed Bishop, who helped them manage their expenses and often entertained them at his home. Bishop was a native of Glen Falls, New York, who had toured and then had decided to stay in the islands in 1846. In 1850, he had married Princess Bernice Pauahi, the last descendant of the royal Kamehameha family. The Harvard men kept good company while they were far away from home.

Horace sailed back to Massachusetts by himself in the spring of 1865, while William stayed behind to teach for a term at O'ahu College. The younger man brought back 25 boxes "of plants, minerals, corals, shells, and other marine creatures" that the two had gathered in the islands. Upon his return to Harvard, he discovered that a major change had taken place while he was exploring the other side of the globe. Dr. Gray had offered his private herbarium to the college. His only stipulation was that a separate fireproof brick building be erected to house the 200,000 specimens and 2,200 books previously held in his home. Funds were raised, and the new facility opened in early 1865. Now that Gray's preserved plant collection was protected, he needed a curator to oversee it. He chose Horace. This was indeed an honor, coming from the preeminent scientist who had become the young man's mentor. Only six years earlier, Horace had published a small plant catalog based on Gray's famous *Manual of the Botany of the Northern United States.* Now he was working with and for the man! His star was certainly rising.

Like his father, Horace was a tireless worker and was passionate about his career. Only once did he consider romance, and then he was uncertain how to go about courting Miss Hattie E. Folsom of Concord. Based on his brother George's advice, Horace had decided to write several letters to her while he was in Hawai'i. He saw her a few times after he returned to Massachusetts, but she rebuffed his tentative advances and declined any gifts he offered to her. Hattie's father was the Reverend Nathaniel Smith Folsom, a Congregationalist minister, and Horace's "Unitarianism and Darwinism" might have been "something of a hardship in the mind of a rather religious young lady." In 1877, Miss Folsom married Edwin Pascal Davis, an iron foundry operator from Lawrence. Just as Thoreau's Transcendentalism had come between him and Ellen Sewall, Horace's religious and scientific beliefs appear to have done the same with Hattie Folsom. And after failing once, Horace—like Henry—did not try again.

Though much of his time was spent at Harvard, Horace did not forget Concord. Beginning in 1866, he corresponded with Mr. Emerson about the possibility of creating a herbarium for the Concord town library. Waldo obviously enjoyed encouraging young protégés. And if funds were needed for such a project, he could either supply them himself or find additional donors. Henry Thoreau hadn't had enough time to put together a "plant library" for Concord. Horace could take his place in that regard. In due time, Emerson gathered supportive financing from twelve local subscribers and raised enough money to have a cabinet built to house the specimens. All that was needed was for Horace to fill it.

That year, the Mann family relocated to Cambridge. Mary Mann sold the house in Concord in order to be closer to her sons, for by now George and Benjamin were also attending Harvard. She could then keep a closer eye on her eldest, who was still not in the best of health. Horace's condition seemed to improve after the Hawaiian expedition; but now that he was home, he spent many hours working at the college. Widespread belief remained that consumption struck individuals who spent too much time inside buildings and away from the sun. One visitor to the Mann house at this time remembered seeing "a window of blue glass, which had been installed in the hope that the sunlight passing through this glass would have a therapeutic value." This technique was considered a reasonable enough cure in the 1860s.

When Horace applied for his bachelor's degree, he offered as proof of his worthiness the completed and detailed "Enumeration of Hawaiian Plants," which was published in the *Proceedings of the American Academy of Arts and Sciences* on September 11, 1866. His degree was conferred upon him in 1867, and a bound copy of his work was printed in July of that year. He authored several related papers that were accepted by scientific periodicals. He corresponded with other botanists around the country and exchanged plant specimens with them. In order to make such trading easier, he compiled a *Catalogue of the Phaenogamous Plants of the United States, East of the Mississippi and of the Vascular Cryptogamous Plants of North America North of Mexico*. His connections and publishing diligence led to an invitation to give lectures in the rooms of the Boston Society of Natural History. The boy who had once had difficulties with formal education was now a man being acknowledged by the scientific community he had long wanted to join.

His work with the Harvard herbarium continued, even though his professor at first had some misgivings about the arrangement. While corresponding with a colleague, Asa Gray described Horace as "slow-minded, not over well prepared." In the garden, Gray said, "he hardly knows beans from peas, a sage from a Foxglove." Yet he saw that the young man was "bent on being a botanist, and will succeed, I think." Over time, the scientist grew to have confidence in his young assistant. When Dr. and Mrs. Gray left for an extended European tour in September 1868, Horace Mann was left in charge not only of the herbarium, but also of the botanic garden and of the classes of the botanical department. Again it seemed as if he was well on his way to carving out his own brilliant career in botany.

But he was a victim of his time, and he could not escape consumption. Surely he must have felt himself growing weaker as the months passed. And he must have deliberately concealed his condition so that Dr. Gray would have no qualms about traveling overseas. On November 7, four days before his death, Horace wrote to Dr. Gray and described the "slight cold, or probably a couple of them" that he had suffered and that had "laid me on my back ... with a recurrence of many of my former symptoms and the addition of new ones." He apologized for not being able to continue his work, and he speculated on the possibility of taking a short leave of absence from Harvard in order to heal. His words clearly show his feeling of helplessness:

> You see I am completely "demoralized." You cannot imagine the grief with which I thus find all our plans broken in upon & completely unturned. The only direction in which I can look for any consolation is in regaining my normal condition as soon as possible. I feel that however little I am at present doing for you, that I may be of use to you after your return from abroad, & perhaps even more so than now, and if I am too presumptuous in this belief, I hope I may be of use to Botany in our country, & when I think of giving up Botany and turning to anything else, all seems a blank.

Mary Mann sent a follow-up letter to Gray on November 10.

> Horace has come within an inch of his life by eating a tumbler full of whipped cream & wine which a friend brought him, & which neither he nor I knew to be indigestible but he was in a very delicate state. He has suffered unutterable tortures from it, and it has reduced him fearfully. ... It will be long, long before he can do any thing again, & I do not know that he will ever be the man he was.

After enduring that painful ordeal, Horace Mann, Jr., died at home on November 11, 1868. He was just 24 years old. According to his autopsy, "only one half of one lung remained." His condition had been advancing for quite some time. Did he catch tuberculosis from Thoreau during their Minnesota trip seven years earlier? Or was he susceptible to such a disease all along, since he wrestled with bouts of sickness throughout his childhood? Though we'll never know for sure, it seems likely that Horace's death was caused by a combination of factors which included those two circumstances. Sole blame should not be placed on Thoreau's shoulders or on the trip to Minnesota.

Asa Gray was in France when he received yet another letter from Mary Mann, this time announcing Horace's death. Devastated, he wrote to a friend: "My heart bleeds for poor Mrs. Mann, who was wrapped up in Horace, and who feels it as the greatest of disappointments. To me, also, it is a very great disappointment of long-cherished hopes." Gray assumed he had found a worthy successor, and now that person was gone. A month later he wrote at the end of a long letter: "I have left no room to speak of the most sad loss of Mann, very sad. How it will affect me I cannot tell now, but suppose it will bring us home next fall." When the Grays returned to Harvard in 1869, the reality of the situation hit home. "The loss of Mann has frustrated all my hopes and expectations," he wrote. "I had intended my absence to establish him in the work, so that the laborious detail at least might be hereafter taken by him. Now I see no one to replace him."

Hours before Horace took his last breath, members of the American Academy of Arts and Sciences unanimously voted him into their fold. This accolade is remarkable not only for its gift to someone so young, but also for the contrast it shows between Mann and Thoreau. Horace would have been delighted and overjoyed to be considered a true scientist at last. Henry refused such conformity. When Thoreau was offered a membership in the Association for the Advancement of Science in 1853, he respectfully declined. His official reply cited an inability to attend long-distance meetings. In the pages of his journal he confided that he doubted that his idea of science agreed with that of the organization. Regarding the request to specify a branch of science as an interest, he reflected, "The fact is I am a mystic, a transcendentalist, and a natural philosopher to boot. Now I think of it, I should have told them at once that I was a transcendentalist. That would have been the shortest way of telling them that they would not understand my explanations."

Horace Mann, Jr., was laid to rest in a family plot in the North Burial Ground in Providence, Rhode Island. A two-story granite obelisk, placed first for his father, marks the spot. Inscribed on the monument are lines from Ralph Waldo Emerson's poem "Threnody," which was written after the death of his own five-year-old son Waldo in 1842: "What is excellent, / As God lives is permanent, / Hearts are dust, hearts' loves remain; / Heart's love will meet thee again." Another promising young person was gone too soon.

Left behind were many Hawaiian notes that Horace had not yet organized. His fellow traveler William T. Brigham set about going through them, and he issued a few papers. He also stepped in and taught Horace's botany classes for a year. But many notes remain unpublished and are still on file at

Harvard. Brigham himself returned to Hawai'i twice: for a visit in 1880, and to stay in 1889. William Tufts Brigham became the first curator and director of Honolulu's Bernice Pauahi Bishop Museum, a cultural and natural history facility that his old friend Charles Reed Bishop set up as a memorial to his wife. Brigham is credited with the good work of that museum. He devoted so much interest to his subject that he made two around-the-world trips "in order to view other museums' Polynesian collections and see the latest display techniques." He held the top post until 1918, when he stepped down to become the curator of anthropology. He died in 1926. He lived the kind of life that his friend Horace could have lived, if only he had been given the chance.

Another project that was left unfinished was the Concord herbarium. A special six-foot-high cabinet that Emerson referred to as a "Plant-Case" had been installed in the Concord library the previous year. Emerson assured Horace that he need provide only the collection, for other men in the community would gladly learn how to "defend it from bugs and other insects." Horace must have put this task aside in his last year, working diligently at Harvard while at the same time hiding his failing health. He never met his personal obligation to the Concord subscribers. But he left notes for his mother; and it was she who sorted through the plants and chose the most appropriate ones. Just how many of the promised 1200 samples of the "Flora of Massachusetts" were sent, is difficult to ascertain. It was hoped "that when any farmer or citizen of Concord found a plant unknown to them,—by carrying it to the Library, they could identify it, & learn its name." Emerson expressed his gratitude to Mary Mann by writing to her that "heaven, I hope, will some day send us another lover of Nature & of men as earnest & perfect in his intention & power,—though we must wait long for much excellence as Horace had." The plant collection remained in Concord until 1958, when library officials donated it to Harvard University. Samples are still on file there.

In 1869, Mary Mann sold the rest of Horace's personal herbarium to Andrew Dickson White, the president of Cornell University. Consisting of more than 7,500 mounted species—many of them from Hawai'i—the acquisition became a foundation for the science department's collection. A number of botanists benefited from Horace's generosity while he was alive, whenever he traded plant samples with them. Some of those specimens can still be found in collections at Harvard and at other sites in Massachusetts. But not all of his gatherings found an academic home. Someone once paging through his father's diaries came upon a forgotten flower labeled with its

Latin name and the notation "Redwing Bluff, Redwing, Minn., June 24, 1861 (Journey with Mr. Thoreau)." The son had used his father's book as an impromptu plant press. And although he and Henry had been traveling for more than a month when he wrote that note, the polite young man still referred to his companion as "Mr. Thoreau."

Horace Mann, Jr.'s slight mark upon the earth also lives on in several botanical works housed in the depths of university libraries. During his two excursions, he always took notes, and he always wrote home. Letters and portions of a diary are scattered in a variety of academic archives. His name and his extensive observations were included posthumously in William Hillebrand's book, *Flora of the Hawaiian Islands: A Description of the Phanerogams and Vascular Cryptogams* (New York: B. Westermann, 1888). And while it is now officially listed as an endangered species, Mann's Bluegrass (*Poa mannii*), named after its discoverer, still lends a few intricate stems to the natural habitat of Hawai'i.

What had the Journey West meant for young Horace? Well, it probably sealed his fate as a botanist. Yes, he had taken his shotgun along on the trip. Yes, he had sent a keg full of critters home to his mother. And yes, he had assured her in a letter that his "hunting fibres" would "not get tired ... nor come any where near it." But by the time the two men were steaming back down the Mississippi River, Horace was mentioning plants more often than animals in his notes. Perhaps by that time, Henry had convinced him of the inhumanity and the needlessness of collecting lifeless bodies. Or perhaps Henry quietly showed him by example that plants were equally as fascinating, required no chase, and were easier to study, either while still growing in their natural habitats or while meticulously filed as samples in a collection. Just two years after Thoreau and Mann's return, Michigan resident Calvin H. Greene visited Concord and met young Horace. Without having any previous knowledge of Mann's background, Greene noticed that the young man had an intense interest in botany. The Journey West had served as a training ground for Horace Mann, Jr. It was an introduction to his greater adventures and experiences in Hawai'i and at Harvard.

Henry Thoreau's legacy is of course much greater than that of his one-time traveling companion. His sister and closest friends put the wheels in motion to make it so. With Sophia's help, Henry had finished a number of manuscripts. After his death, *Atlantic Monthly* ran seven of his essays, including "Walking," "Wild Apples," and "Life Without Principle." Though he saw only two books published during his lifetime, four posthumous ones were released before the decade ended: *Excursions* (1863), *The Maine Woods*

(1864), *Cape Cod* (1864), and *A Yankee in Canada, with Anti-Slavery and Reform Papers* (1866). A volume of Thoreau's letters, edited by Emerson, was printed in 1865; another one was assembled by Frank Sanborn and released almost 30 years later. H.G.O. Blake inherited Henry's *Journal* from Sophia Thoreau in 1876. He eventually culled appropriate passages from those notebooks and made them public in four seasonal volumes: *Early Spring in Massachusetts* (1881), *Summer* (1884), *Winter* (1888), and *Autumn* (1892). The *Journal* was printed in its near entirety in 1906, when Houghton Mifflin published it as part of a twenty-volume set of his writings. Ellery Channing wrote the first Thoreau biography in 1873. It was followed by several biographical books written by Frank Sanborn. Additional publications of biography and literary criticism escalated during the twentieth century, when more admirers picked up the cause on both sides of the Atlantic. To this day, primary documents continue to be found, read, printed, and discussed. *Walden* itself has been reprinted hundreds of times since its first release in 1854.

What had the Journey West meant for Henry Thoreau? Well, it was both the pinnacle of all of his excursions, and the culmination of all of his natural history projects. Those other journeys—along the Concord and Merrimack Rivers, to Montreal, to Cape Cod, to Walden Pond, and to the depths of the Maine woods—were mere stepping stones to this longer, more intricate undertaking. From those others, he had learned how to be open to the act of observation and to the wider view of whatever universe he found himself in. Back then, it was by foot and by paddle that he explored new territories. This time, it was by rail and by steam that Thoreau scrutinized a larger landscape of North America. He witnessed its passage from forests to farmland, and from prairies to plains. Yes, he had read various accounts of these changes, as told by previous explorers. But the printed page paled in comparison to the first-person experience. Now he knew the truths himself. He had seen them. And he had finally made the western excursion he had longed for.

Standing in such singular ecosystems as those found on Goat Island, Mackinac Island, and Barn Bluff, Henry Thoreau was also able to apply his home-grown theories on unfamiliar properties, away from the comfort and convenience of Concord. Here he saw his own discoveries about seed dispersion and tree succession confirmed, again and again: this time, with species he had never even seen before. With the downy fluff dropped by the cottonwoods. With the distinctive grasses that skirted each one of the Great Lakes. And then there was the joy of tracking down the elusive crab apple tree! His knowledge of natural science and his self-taught methodology had never been as tested as they were during these two months. No wonder he was exhausted.

That's not to say that people didn't enter the picture. Thoreau could neither ignore nor avoid the residents and fellow travelers he encountered along the way. Given the chance, he would surely have written once again about that strangest creature of all, *Homo sapiens*. And his ruminations would have plunged into delicious political commentary. On that front, there were almost too many topics to tackle: the war, the soldiers in training, the bankers of Chicago and Milwaukee, the candidates in Canada. Add to those the Dakota, the kinds of individuals who swirled around them, and the conditions that existed at the Lower Sioux Agency. Surely Thoreau had opinions about all of it, about everything he had seen. Unfortunately this time, he kept them to himself.

Had Henry Thoreau been able to leave us a definitive travel narrative called *The Journey West; Or, America's Nature in the Face of War*, it would have been much more than *Mr. Thoreau Goes to Minnesota*. It would have been his *magnum opus*: the final and complete representation of everything he had worked toward in his lifetime. It would have pulled all of his interests together into one volume. The book would have proudly cradled *Walden* on our bookshelves. Both scientists and English majors would have studied its pages for verification and for inspiration. Even casual readers would have found intriguing details in each chapter. Cities and towns along the Journey West route would be celebrating the fact that Thoreau had once passed through their neighborhoods. Such a publication would have served to increase his popularity and to heighten his reputation much sooner. Who knows what pithy statements from its text would still be quoted today?

And yet, for someone who hasn't traveled in Concord in more than 140 years, Henry Thoreau's works are still to be found in just about every corner of the earth. Posters and t-shirts carry his familiar words of wisdom. "Civil Disobedience" and excerpts from *Walden* appear in high school American literature textbooks. Coffee table books featuring nature photography are augmented with selections from his journals. A man who rejected fame during his lifetime has gained it emphatically afterwards. Because he had the courage of his convictions to write down what he saw and what he thought about it, his words have inspired millions. During his final days, Henry said, "You know it's respectable to leave an estate to one's friends." In that case, each one of us has inherited a fortune, and Thoreau's friends are countless.

The country may not have known how great a son it had lost back in 1862; but thanks to the efforts of Thoreau's friends, family, and disciples, his fame continues to grow. In the early 1870s, someone arranged for the graves of the immediate family members to be moved up the hill to a plot in Sleepy Hollow Cemetery adjacent to that of the Nathaniel Hawthorne family. Sophia may have quietly assumed that her relatives were of a similar social standing, and that her brother's writing prowess was on equal footing with that of the famous short story teller. The move was prophetic. Now granite markers lead the casual visitor directly to the Thoreaus on Authors Ridge, just steps away from the Hawthornes, the Alcotts, and the Emersons. Grateful visitors place mementos on selected graves, and Henry's plot is often covered with the most pine cones, pebbles, and pennies. Walden Pond has become such a place of pilgrimage that when the surrounding woods was threatened with development, supporters and celebrities formed organizations to thwart the travesty. It is now a state-run recreation area that appeals to local swimmers and fishermen. Visitors still come from around the world to pay homage to the site. They bring stones to add to the cairn. They come to see and to stand at the spot that still rings with Thoreau's words:

> I went to the woods because I wished to live deliberately, to front only the essential facts of life, and see if I could not learn what it had to teach, and not, when I came to die, discover that I had not lived.

When the elder Horace Mann passed away in 1859, his friend Dr. Samuel Gridley Howe led a campaign to raise a statue to his honor in downtown Boston. Henry Thoreau was asked to sign a petition and to donate money for that project. He dismissed the request. He later remarked in his journal that he turned it down because he "thought a man ought not any more to take up room in the world after he was dead. We shall lose one advantage of a man's dying if we are to have a statue of him forthwith." Nevertheless, a statue of Mann was erected and now stands before the Massachusetts State House in the Commonwealth's capital city.

Ironically enough, at the Walden Pond State Reservation twenty miles northwest, another statue stands in front of a small house. A bronze figure of Henry David Thoreau perpetually reaches an outstretched hand due south. The individuals who permanently placed that figure should have rotated it a few degrees clockwise. Then its fingers would be more appropriately pointing to the pond across the street. And to the spot farther along the shoreline that marked Thoreau's two-year hiatus from Concord town life.

And to the West.

NOTES

Thoreau's letter to Daniel Ricketson was dated August 15, 1861, and appears on page 625 of *The Correspondence of Henry David Thoreau* (Walter Harding and Carl Bode, eds. New York: New York University Press, 1958). His remarks about his invitation to membership in the Association for the Advancement of Science are found in the same source, in a letter dated December 19, 1853, as well as in his *Journal* entry dated March 5, 1853. Thoreau's hornets' nest story is in his *Journal* entry dated October 24, 1858. His quote about leaving an estate to friends is from Edward Waldo Emerson's *Henry Thoreau, as Remembered by a Young Friend, Edward Waldo Emerson* (Boston: Houghton Mifflin Company, 1917, p. 117). The living deliberately quote is from the "Where I Lived, and What I Lived For" chapter of *Walden*. Thoreau wrote of his disdain for statues in his *Journal* entry of September 18, 1859.

Sophia Thoreau's reaction to his last photograph appears on page 318 of *Daniel Ricketson and His Friends: Letters, Poems, Sketches, Etc.* (Boston: Houghton Mifflin and Company, 1902).

Bronson Alcott's January 1862 visit to Thoreau is noted on pages 342-343 of *The Journals of Bronson Alcott* (Boston: Little, Brown and Company, 1938). Sam Staples' deathbed visit is quoted from Walter Harding's *The Days of Henry Thoreau* (New York: Dover Publications, 1982, p. 460). Channing's hymn is found in *A Thoreau Profile* (Milton Meltzer and Walter Harding, compilers. Concord, Mass.: Thoreau Foundation, Inc., 1972, p. 282). Emerson's eulogy, "Thoreau," is contained in *The Portable Emerson* (New ed. Edited by Carl Bode. New York: Penguin Books, 1981).

Mary Mann's statement about the snakes is from page 43 of "A Sketch of the Life of the Late Horace Mann, by a Friend and Associate" (*Bulletin of the Essex Institute*, February 1869, vol. 1, no. 2). William Brigham's memory of Horace is reported on page 45 of the "Sketch." The description of Horace's boxes comes from Roger G. Rose's *A Museum to Instruct and Delight: William T. Brigham and the Founding of Bernice Pauahi Bishop Museum* (Honolulu: Bishop Museum Press, 1980, p. 22).

A main source for information about Horace Mann, Jr., is Robert L. Straker's typed manuscript, *Horace Mann, 1844-1868* (Cornell University, 1956), held at the Concord Free Public Library. His work includes impressions about Hattie Folsom and her father; Horace's letter of November 7, 1868, to Dr. Gray; Mary Mann's letter to Gray; Horace's autopsy results; Emerson's letter of May 17, 1866, to Horace; and Emerson's letter of June 24, 1869, to Mary Mann.

A digital copy of the "Subscription for Herbarium, 1866" appears on the library web site at http://www.concordlibrary.org/scollect/Emerson_Celebration/Em_Con_60.html. The note about the blue glass window appears in Louise Hall Tharp's *Until Victory: Horace Mann and Mary Peabody Mann* (Boston: Little, Brown and Company, 1953, p. 317). The incident of finding a plant in the elder Horace's diary is from this Tharp book as well, on page 336. Horace told his mother about his "hunting fibres" in a letter dated June 23, 1861.

Asa Gray wrote to Joseph D. Hooker about Horace on March 19, 1866, and on May 20, 1867. He wrote to Joseph Henry about Horace on December 18, 1869. Those excerpts can be found in A. Hunter Dupree's *Asa Gray, 1810-1888* (New York: Atheneum, 1968, p. 337). Gray's letters to Charles Wright (November 29, 1868) and to John Torrey (December 5, 1868) are included in *Letters of Asa Gray* (Edited by Jane Loring Gray. Boston: Houghton, Mifflin and Company, 1893).

William Brigham's museum work is detailed in Marjorie Kelly's article, "Scholarship versus Showmanship at Hawaii's Bishop Museum: Reflections of Cultural Hegemony." (*Museum Anthropology* vol. 18, no. 2, 1994, p. 39).

I once found documentation about Mary Mann's sale of the collection to Andrew Dickson White in an online "History of Cornell," at http://www.rootsweb.com/~nytompki/Landmarks/cornell_ch15.htm. At the time of this writing, that page is no longer available. I also received information about Horace's personal herbarium in an e-mail dated August 29, 2005, from Ray Angelo of Harvard University.

Acknowledgements

If it takes a village to raise a child, then it seems to take an entire world to write a book. I have many people to thank for their support of this project. I hope I remember them all. In addition to the people and facilities acknowledged previously in these pages:

Thanks to my father, Lewis K. Hosfeld, for deciding at age 80 to read *Walden* for the first time, just to see what I was talking about.

Thanks to those friends who lent moral support over the years by regularly asking questions, and who even appeared to be at least a little bit interested in the answers. This group includes John D. Andrews, Michael Boover, Mary Lynn Brannon, George Cheatle, Michael Donnelly, Laryssa Duncan, Susan Eliason, Kevin Gallery, Nicholas Gorgoglione, Christine Holmes, and Deb Perryman. Thanks to the Women of Words (WOW) writing group, including Kathy Bennett, Dorothy Hayden, and Marie MacDonald, for tolerating and listening to my progress reports. Thanks to Alice Baron of Anna Maria College's Mondor-Eagen Library and Marie Lehmann of the Athol Public Library, two angels of the world of interlibrary loan. They helped me borrow the resources I needed to establish background information.

Thanks to all of the public and academic libraries I visited for research purposes, across ten states and in Ontario, even if it was only for a few minutes. If I named you all, the list would be extensive.

Thanks to publisher Robert Lawrence France for taking a chance. Thanks to leading Thoreau Scholar Laura Dassow Walls for honoring my work with her own insightful foreword.

Many thanks to authors Jerry Dennis, J. Parker Huber, and David K. Leff for their kind words and valuable feedback. Jerry additionally supplied first-hand knowledge of Great Lakes navigation. Parker stepped in at the eleventh hour when I needed personal advice. David participated in the 2009 Memorial Walk around Walden Pond.

Thanks to the manuscript readers who live along the Journey West route, and who duly proofread the chapters dedicated to their familiar stomping grounds. This group includes George Cheatle (Rochester, N.Y.); James W. Bond & Greg Smith (Grimsby, Ontario); Maureen Fennie Corulla (Niagara Falls Public Library, Niagara Falls, N.Y.); Brian Leigh Dunnigan (University of Michigan, Ann Arbor, Mich.); Stacy Iwanicki (Volo Bog State Natural Area, Ingleside, Ill.); Valerie Blaine (Tekakwitha Forest Preserve, St. Charles, Ill.); Rich & Fern Hosfeld (Stoughton, Wis.); Patricia Martin (Mackinac Island,

Mich.); Reg Thompson (Huron County Library System, Goderich Branch, Goderich, Ontario); Paul Russell (Anna Maria College, Paxton, Mass., and formerly of Ogdensburg, N.Y.); and Paul & Virginia Carr (Bedford, N.H.).

Five individuals were my First Readers. Paula Botch and Jan VanVaerenewyck didn't know much about Henry David Thoreau when this project began. They are both accomplished poets and writers, however, and are fellow members of WOW. Each one approached the manuscript in her own way, for which I am grateful. And I got to show them Concord in person, in return.

Richard E. Smith not only knows Thoreau inside and out, but he plays him in real life, at Walden Pond and at many other venues. Thanks, friend, for questioning vital statements and for correcting others. I always value your opinions.

Dale Schwie, an independent scholar from Minneapolis, has been promoting Thoreau's Journey West for longer than I have been connected to the topic. I thank him for being my western correspondent and for reading the manuscript with a critical eye. He and his wife Kay also squired me around the Twin Cities area and provided me with local insights. Their unflagging support has been one of my sources of motivation.

This book never would have been possible without the inspiration and initial research supplied by Edmund A. Schofield, Jr. Ed's physical presence can be found in several instances here. But in reality, he was the force behind it all. Ed read the chapters as they were spit from the printer, and he was quick to raise points and ideas that I would never have thought of. Unfortunately, he missed reading the last two chapters I wrote. Ed Schofield left us on April 17, 2010. He passed quietly that morning as he sat in Worcester's Union Station, waiting for the train to Boston. Indeed, he was a Transcendentalist to the end. If only my fingers had flown faster over the keyboard! I can only hope that the release of *Westward I Go Free* serves as a partial repayment for his six years of friendship, mentorship, walks around Walden Pond and Worcester, and multi-hour pep talks. I would give anything to be able to place the finished volume into his hands.

Just as these pages were sent to the publisher, the official 2010 U.S. census records were released and publicized. The Worcester *Telegram & Gazette* proudly announced the results on its front page: Worcester's population stood at 181,045. Providence's came in at 178,042. The Heart of the Commonwealth was once again the second largest city in New England. Somewhere, Ed is smiling.

INDEX

GREEN FRIGATE BOOKS SPECIAL SERIES:

—Flâneur/Peripatetic Productions—

A Wanderer All My Days: John Muir in New England—J. Parker Huber

Ultreia! Onward Progress of the Pilgrim—Robert L. France

Westward I Go Free: Tracing Thoreau's Last Journey—Corinne Hosfeld Smith

Seeing The Songs: A Poet's Journey to the Shamans in Ecuador—Gary F. Margolis

A Flâneur/Peripatetic Production

Deep travel engages the mind as much as it does the body, contributing toward what might be referred to as an "active intellect". Whether strolling about a city or engaging in discussions while venturing into the countryside, Flâneur/Peripatetic Productions are devoted to exploring those roads, within and without, that are truly less travelled.

GREEN FRIGATE BOOKS

"THERE IS NO FRIGATE LIKE A BOOK"

Words on the page have the power to transport us, and in the process, transform us. Such journeys can be far reaching, traversing the landscapes of the external world and that within, as well as the timescapes of the past, present and future.

Green Frigate Books is a small publishing house offering a vehicle—a ship—for those seeking to conceptually sail and explore the horizons of the natural and built environments, and the relations of humans within them. Our goal is to reach an educated lay readership by producing works that fall in the cracks between those offered by traditional academic and popular presses.